I0083934

The
1850 CENSUS
of
GEORGIA
SLAVE OWNERS

Compiled by
Jack F. Cox

CLEARFIELD

Copyright © 1999 by Jack F. Cox
All Rights Reserved.

Printed for
Clearfield Company, Inc. by
Genealogical Publishing Co., Inc.
Baltimore, Maryland
1999

Reprinted for
Clearfield Company, Inc. by
Genealogical Publishing Co., Inc.
Baltimore, Maryland
2000, 2001

International Standard Book Number: 0-8063-4837-2
Made in the United States of America

Introduction

In 1850 and 1860 a census of slave owners was taken by the U.S. government. Compiled for each of the 93 counties in Georgia at the time, this record showed the number of slaves by sex and color under the name of the owner or the overseer. Unfortunately, no names were given for the slaves. The handwritten originals of the census records can be found in the U.S. archives in Washington, D.C. This book was taken from microfilm copies located at Lake Blackshear Regional Library in Americus, Georgia, and the Washington Memorial Library in Macon, Georgia.

As is common in old documents, some of the handwriting is very readable, some very difficult to decipher, and some impossible to read. Muscogee and Richmond counties, two of the largest counties in the state in terms of population at the time, are in the most difficult to read category. Also, since spelling seemed to be at the discretion of the census taker, always be sure to check every possible spelling; e.g., "Hickson, Hixon, Hixxon."

When you take the number of slave owners and divide by the population, you find that less than ten percent of the population of Georgia owned slaves in 1850. By far, the largest number of slave owners were in Glynn County, a coastal county famed for rice production.

This work could not have been completed without the valuable assistance of my wife, Earline Buchanan Cox, and my son, Carey Buchanan Cox.

As in all works of this type, some errors might be found in spite of the most diligent efforts to find and correct them.

Name	Number	County
? , James	2	Taliaferro
(?) ,Kate	13	Columbia
? , William H.	1	Taliaferro
? , Rebbica	2	Talbot
? , John W.	4	Stewart
(?)	1	Columbia
? , G. W.	2	Stewart
? , Wm. B.	11	Taliaferro
? , George	4	Taliaferro
?, Jesse	3	DeKalb
(?)	5	Columbia
(?)	1	Dade
(?)	1	Dade
(?)	19	Decatur
(?)	16	Decatur
(?)	14	Decatur
(?)	10	Decatur
(?)	10	Decatur
(?)	8	Decatur
(?)	7	Decatur
(?)	4	Decatur
(?)	3	Decatur
(?)	3	Decatur
(?)	2	Decatur
(?)	2	Decatur
(?)	1	Decatur
(?)	1	Decatur
(?)	1	Decatur
(?)	1	Decatur
(?)	1	Decatur
(?)	1	Decatur
(?)	1	Decatur
(?)	1	Decatur
(?)	1	Decatur
(?)	8	Decatur
(?), Charles	42	Columbia
(?), Elias	31	Decatur
(?), Richard	2	Columbia
(?), G. G.	13	Decatur
(?), G. R.	1	Coweta
(?), M.	1	Decatur
(?), N.	3	Decatur
(?), S. R.	2	Decatur
?	1	DeKalb
?	1	DeKalb
? , James B.	2	DeKalb
? , Anderson	7	Dooly
? , Charles	1	Dooly
? , John L.	5	Dooly
?,	5	Dooly
?, A. M.	1	DeKalb
?, P. P.	2	DeKalb
?, William	10	DeKalb
(?)	2	Columbia

Name	Number	County
(?)	1	Columbia
(?), Frances	2	Columbia
(?), Jos.	1	Coweta
AVERY, John	5	Putnam
BARNARD, Jesse	12	Putnam
BARNETTE, John	11	Putnam
EVANS, John A.	15	Sumter
FOLDS, Geo.	22	Putnam
LEE, A. P.	16	Randolph
MITCHELL, William	8	Talbot
PERIFOY, ?	7	Putnam
TURK, Avington	25	Putnam
UNREADABLE, Francis	2	Richmond
WILLIS, Robt.	15	Putnam
WINSLIT, D. C.	5	Putnam
(?)	29	Columbia
(?) , Purval H.	9	Coweta
(?) , Gilbert	1	Columbia
(?) , Martha	23	Columbia
(?), Franklyn	13	Columbia
(?), John	5	Decatur
(?), Mike	3	Columbia
(?), William	10	Columbia
(?), H.	1	Coweta
(?), John	4	Coweta
(?), M. A.	1	Coweta
(?), Mary	7	Columbia
(?), William A.	6	Columbia
;PETTIGRU, J. E.	9	Butts
?	1	Putnam
AARON, James C.	4	Jasper
AARON, Michel	2	Jasper
ABBETT, Henry	2	Stewart
ABBETT, James	2	Stewart
ABBOT, James	1	Thomas
ABBOT, Mrs. S.	2	Bibb
ABBOTT, Alex	2	Cherokee
ABBOTT, Cato R.	4	Warren
ABBOTT, Jacob	6	Cherokee
ABBOTT, John	1	Cherokee
ABBOTT, William	5	Warren
ABERCROMBIE, Abner	5	Upson
ABERCROMBIE, Hugh	10	Walton
ABERCROMBIE, James	9	Campbell
ABERCROMBIE, John	1	Campbell
ABERCROMBIE, Joseph	1	Campbell
ABERCROMBIE, Thomas M.	3	Walton
ABNERY, Martin	4	Heard
ABNEY, James	1	Meriwether
ABOTT, A. G.	2	Muscogee

1

Name	Number	County	Name	Number	County
ABRAHAM, Rachael	10	Chatham	ADAMS, George W.	3	Jasper
ABRAHAM, Bernard	7	Richmond	ADAMS, H. G.	5	Elbert
ABRAHAMS, Dorothea	3	Chatham	ADAMS, Hopewell	1	Washington
ABRAHAMS, J. estate	9	Chatham	ADAMS, Hopewell	5	Washington
ABRAMS, J. L.	1	Coweta	ADAMS, J.	1	Muscogee
ACHISON, James A.	15	Troup	ADAMS, J.	1	Troup
ACHORD ?, John F	1	Washington	ADAMS, J. B.	2	Elbert
ACHORD, John	8	Washington	ADAMS, J. G. B.	4	Gordon
ACOCK, Jesse	1	Monroe	ADAMS, J. M.	2	Elbert
ACOCK, Richard M.	2	Walker	ADAMS, James	8	Elbert
ACOCK, Sebron R.	6	Oglethorpe	ADAMS, James	16	Jasper
ACOCK, W.	2	Pike	ADAMS, James	17	Upson
ACOLS, J. W.	2	Morgan	ADAMS, James D.	1	Clarke
ACOSTA, E. J.	4	Camden	ADAMS, Jesse	1	Franklin
ACOSTA, D. C.	8	Camden	ADAMS, John	1	Franklin
ACRE, Alfred L.	10	Talbot	ADAMS, John W.	7	Pike
ACREE, L. S.	6	Baker	ADAMS, Jordan	3	Washington
ACREE, Seaborn	1	Taliaferro	ADAMS, Joseph	3	Laurens
ACREE, Seaborn	1	Taliaferro	ADAMS, Lasa	8	Lowndes
ACREE, Wilie	13	Taliaferro	ADAMS, Levi M.	4	Merriwether
ACREY, Absalem	1	Meriwether	ADAMS, Manassa	1	Laurens
ADAIR, Bozeman	1	Paulding	ADAMS, Mary	4	Pike
ADAIR, Edward	9	Murray	ADAMS, Mary S.	19	Butts
ADAIR, J. F.	1	Henry	ADAMS, Matthias	1	Montgomery
ADAIR, James	1	Paulding	ADAMS, Mrs. M. M.	16	Clarke
ADAIR, Jones	1	Morgan	ADAMS, N. M.	2	Elbert
ADAIR, Robert S.	2	Gwinnett	ADAMS, Patrick	18	Muscogee
ADAIR, Wm.	2	Henry	ADAMS, Peter	9	Lee
ADAIR, Wm. H. P.	2	Merriwether	ADAMS, R. C.	28	Elbert
ADAM, James	5	Clinch	ADAMS, Sarah	5	Lowndes
ADAM, Albert	1	Richmond	ADAMS, Sarah L.	4	Muscogee
ADAM, James	3	Richmond	ADAMS, T. B.	2	Elbert
ADAMS, ?	2	Talbot	ADAMS, Thomas	5	Chatham
ADAMS, ? H.	4	Wilkes	ADAMS, W.	2	Elbert
ADAMS, Albert T.	3	Thomas	ADAMS, Wiley	24	Montgomery
ADAMS, Arnold L.	22	Washington	ADAMS, Wiley	9	Muscogee
ADAMS, Eleaza	31	Monroe	ADAMS, William	2	Jasper
ADAMS, Jefferson	2	Pike	ADAMS, Wm.	5	Laurens
ADAMS, A.	1	Elbert	ADAMS, Wm. H.	6	Elbert
ADAMS, Absalom	1	Carroll	ADAMS, Wm. L.	1	Monroe
ADAMS, Ann	8	Jasper	ADAMS, Zeban	5	Taliaferro
ADAMS, Augustus	1	Newton	ADAMS, ? R.	1	Putnam
ADAMS, Benjamin	14	Upson	ADAMS, B. W.	10	Putnam
ADAMS, Carter	9	Upson	ADAMS, B. F.	53	Putnam
ADAMS, Caswell	12	Lowndes	ADAMS, Ben	4	Columbia
ADAMS, Cathrin	3	Upson	ADAMS, Benjamin	2	Talbot
ADAMS, Daniel	25	Houston	ADAMS, Bennett	6	Baker
ADAMS, David	3	Houston	ADAMS, Cam	10	Chattooga
ADAMS, Dennis	4	Thomas	ADAMS, Charles	8	Talbot
ADAMS, Ed B.	3	Clarke	ADAMS, D. R.	47	Putnam
ADAMS, Edward H.	11	Jasper	ADAMS, D. R.	14	Putnam
ADAMS, Elizabeth	14	Jones	ADAMS, Daniel	3	DeKalb
ADAMS, Ezekiel H.	42	Macon	ADAMS, David E.	33	Chatham
ADAMS, George	11	Muscogee	ADAMS, E. A.	3	Talbot

Name	Number	County	Name	Number	County
ADAMS, E. C.	12	Chattooga	ADCOCK, James	1	Walton
ADAMS, Edward	22	Talbot	ADCOCK, John C.	13	Meriwether
ADAMS, Edwin	8	Talbot	ADCOCK, Simon	2	Walton
ADAMS, George W.	5	Chatham	ADCOCK, Wyatt A.	2	Walton
ADAMS, J.	10	Putnam	ADDAMS, Jesse	2	Cherokee
ADAMS, J.	4	Putnam	ADDERHOLD, Lewis	5	Franklin
ADAMS, J. J.	1	Chatham	ADDERHOLD, Michl.	1	Carroll
ADAMS, J.F.	33	Putnam	ADDERHOLT, Abraham	7	Franklin
ADAMS, James	4	Richmond	ADDERHOLTZ, J.	3	Bibb
ADAMS, James	7	Stewart	ADDINGTON, John Sr.	5	Gilmer
ADAMS, Jas.	2	Henry	ADDINGTON, March	3	Union
ADAMS, John	9	Baker	ADDISON, Christopher	5	Franklin
ADAMS, John	40	Henry	ADDY, Jesse	5	Merriwether
ADAMS, John	20	Talbot	ADDY, Jacob	12	Coweta
ADAMS, John	15	Talbot	ADERHOLD, A. F.	3	Franklin
ADAMS, John	1	Talbot	ADERHOLD, J. H.	2	Franklin
ADAMS, John M.	21	Richmond	ADKERSON, N. L.	10	Troup
ADAMS, John Q.	8	Dooly	ADKINS, Aaron	44	Warren
ADAMS, Jonathan	2	Baker	ADKINS, Booker	8	Oglethorpe
ADAMS, Jonathan	8	Putnam	ADKINS, Isaac F.	5	Warren
ADAMS, Jos.	7	Coweta	ADKINS, J.	6	Wilkinson
ADAMS, Levin	4	Sumter	ADKINS, Jobe	1	Houston
ADAMS, Martha	6	Talbot	ADKINS, Jobe	1	Jasper
ADAMS, Mary	2	Columbia	ADKINS, John	2	Houston
ADAMS, Mary L.	2	Chatham	ADKINS, John	23	Warren
ADAMS, Philip	18	Talbot	ADKINS, Joseph	19	Henry
ADAMS, Robert	14	Putman	ADKINS, Joseph	9	Warren
ADAMS, Robert	10	Talbot	ADKINS, Joseph C.	11	Pike
ADAMS, Saml.	14	Stewart	ADKINS, L. C. C.	2	Henry
ADAMS, Samuel	19	Talbot	ADKINS, P. P.	9	Henry
ADAMS, Sarah	18	Chatham	ADKINS, Eli S.	2	Talbot
ADAMS, Sarah	8	Richmond	ADKINS, Henry	3	Talbot
ADAMS, Sarah	7	Talbot	ADKINS, Joel	1	DeKalb
ADAMS, Sarah A.	35	Putnam	ADKINS, John W.		
ADAMS, Simeon	1	Chatham	agt for HARRIS, J.P.		Houston
ADAMS, S.S.	1	Thomas	ADKINSON, A.	1	Henry
ADAMS, Sumer	4	Dooly	ADKINSON, A.	1	Morgan
ADAMS, T.	14	Chattooga	ADKINSON, A. A.	2	Morgan
ADAMS, Thomas	29	Thomas	ADKINSON, George H.	1	Franklin
ADAMS, Thomas	6	Walker	ADKINSON, Thomas	15	Morgan
ADAMS, Thomas Sen.	46	Thomas	ADKINSON, Thos. J.	1	Morgan
ADAMS, Thos.	1	Coweta	ADKINSON, Wm. D.	3	Monroe
ADAMS, W.	3	Talbot	ADKINSON, R. A. L.	10	Bibb
ADAMS, W. E.	46	Putnam	ADKINSON, Sara S.	42	Taliaferro
ADAMS, William	14	Columbia	ADKINSON, T.S.	5	Walker
ADAMS, William	5	Dooly	ADKINSON, Zachariah	3	Richmond
ADAMS, Winiford	11	Dooly	AERIDGE, E.	3	Crawford
ADAMS, Wm. F.	2	DeKalb	AERP, Danl.	3	Henry
ADAMS, Eldridge	4	Talbot	AERWOOD?, Edward H.	6	Harris
ADAMSON, J. W.	1	Henry	AGEE, Christopher	1	Wilkes
ADAMSON, N. C.	5	Henry	AGER, E. K.	87	Floyd
ADAMSON, W. C.	1	Henry	AIKEN, John	18	Newton
ADAMSON, H. W.	2	Tatnall	AIKEN, Rhoda	11	Clarke
ADCOCK, Barnett	1	Walton	AIKEN, Samuel	9	Newton

3

Name	Number	County	Name	Number	County
AIKEN, William	3	Newton	ALDERMAN, Elija	11	Thomas
AIKEN, Jos.	1	Coweta	ALDERMAN, Enoch	2	Marion
AIKEN, Wm.	2	Butts	ALDERMAN, George	1	Lowndes
AIKENS, William	11	Hancock	ALDERMAN, Mathew	2	Emanual
AIKERS, John	10	Troup	ALDERMAN, Timothy	3	Thomas
AINSWORTH, James	3	Washington	ALDERMAN, Timothy	8	Lowndes
AINSWORTH, James	1	Washington	ALDERMAN, D.	1	Bullock
AKERS(?), John R.	3	Bibb	ALDERMAN, Thomas	3	Bullock
AKERS, Samuel	22	Troup	ALDRED, James	3	Warren
AKIN, Charles P.	8	Jasper	ALDRED, Thomas	9	Warren
AKIN, M.	1	Henry	ALDRED, William	13	Warren
AKIN, Sarah	6	Monroe	ALDRICH, Whipple	8	Camden
AKIN, Thomas	11	Jasper	ALDRIDGE, Jas.	5	Carroll
AKIN, Wm. S. B.	2	Clarke	ALDRIDGE, Wm.	2	Clarke
AKIN, Warren	14	Cass	ALDRIDGE?,		
AKINS, George	1	Franklin	Mrs. Hudley	4	Houston
AKINS, Jacob C.	24	Greene	ALEN, Frances M.	22	Burke
AKINS, James	36	Jasper	ALEXANDER, A. L.	55	Wilkes
AKINS, John H.	3	Pike	ALEXANDER, ?	4	Elbert
AKINS, Job S.	2	Thomas	ALEXANDER, C. C.	13	Greene
AKINS, Penelopy	1	Washington	ALEXANDER, David H.	8	Gwinnett
AKINS, Samuel S.	15	Jasper	ALEXANDER, Emily	6	Monroe
AKINS, Sherrod	4	Wayne	ALEXANDER, F. J.	1	Elbert
AKINS, William	1	Franklin	ALEXANDER, J.	10	Henry
AKINS, Wm.	6	DeKalb	ALEXANDER, J. L.	2	Henry
AKRIDGE, M. M.	33	Clarke	ALEXANDER, J. W.	14	Elbert
AKRIDGE, N.	1	Chattooga	ALEXANDER, James	1	Gwinnett
ALAN, Egbert	2	Sumter	ALEXANDER, James L.	4	Pike
ALAWAY, Wm.	1	Coweta	ALEXANDER, Jas. H.	5	Liberty
ALBERSON, Edward	3	Cherokee	ALEXANDER, John	2	Jackson
ALBERT, J.	10	Henry	ALEXANDER, John M.	3	Floyd
ALBERT, J. F.	1	Henry	ALEXANDER, John M.	2	Franklin
ALBERT, J. T.	3	Henry	ALEXANDER, John P.	26	Gilmer
ALBERT, R. T.	3	Henry	ALEXANDER, John R.	8	Floyd
ALBERT, T.	2	Henry	ALEXANDER, John W.	17	Jefferson
ALBERTSON, J. H.	8	Pulaski	ALEXANDER, Joseph	8	Jackson
ALBEY, William	13	Lincoln	ALEXANDER, L. B.	9	Monroe
ALBIA, Tilmon	5	Lincoln	ALEXANDER, L. P.	1	Pike
ALBRIGHT, A. P.	4	Muscogee	ALEXANDER, M.	1	Henry
ALBRIGHT, Henry	3	Walker	ALEXANDER, Martha	13	Gwinnett
ALBRITIAN,			ALEXANDER, Martha	1	Gwinnett
McGilbra F.	26	Sumter	ALEXANDER,		
ALBRITON, Allen	17	Houston	Martin T.	22	Early
ALBRITTON, Herman	1	Muscogee	ALEXANDER, P.	43	Elbert
ALBRITTON, Jesse J.	1	Lowndes	ALEXANDER, R.	4	Oglethorpe
ALBRITTON, Littleton	3	Houston	ALEXANDER, R. B.	5	Muscogee
ALBRITTON, Matthew	1	Lowndes	ALEXANDER, Robert	2	Muscogee
ALBRITTON, Peko?	4	Muscogee	ALEXANDER, Robert B.	12	Muscogee
ALBRITTON, Thomas	2	Ware	ALEXANDER, S.	10	Elbert
ALBRITTON, William	2	Muscogee	ALEXANDER,		
ALBRITTON, A.M.	8	Randolph	Samuel F.	31	Gwinnett
ALCOM, Simon B.	22	'Twiggs	ALEXANDER, Smith	2	Clarke
ALDEN, Augustus	4	Cobb	ALEXANDER, T. N.	3	Hall
ALDEMAN, Samuel	2	Thomas			

4

Name	Number	County	Name	Number	County
ALEXANDER,			ALFRIEND, S. H.	5	Hancock
Thomas W.	4	Gwinnett	ALFRIEND, Wm.	5	Greene
ALEXANDER, U.	2	Henry	ALFRIEND, Edward W.	7	Taliaferro
ALEXANDER, W.	9	Elbert	ALGIERS, Elizabeth	1	Macon
ALEXANDER, W.	1	Henry	ALGOOD, A. P.	7	Chattooga
ALEXANDER, W. B.	2	Elbert	ALIN, A.	1	Pike
ALEXANDER, W. D.	49	Merriwether	ALIN, G. N.	1	Pike
ALEXANDER, William	7	Franklin	ALISAN, Jesse	2	Taliaferro
ALEXANDER, William	14	Hall	ALISON, M.	2	Troup
ALEXANDER, William	7	Jones	ALISTON, Elias	30	Morgan
ALEXANDER, Willis	21	Monroe	ALKINSON,		
ALEXANDER, Wm.	2	Heard	Daniel R.	22	Thomas
ALEXANDER, Wm. E.	3	Floyd	ALKINSON, Mary	25	Thomas
ALEXANDER, A.	2	DeKalb	ALKINSON, Mary E.	3	Thomas
ALEXANDER, Benjamin	2	Tatnall	ALLAN, Ch.	7	Talbot
ALEXANDER, Cullin	40	Randolph	ALLBRITTON, Y. G.	1	Stewart
ALEXANDER, E.	13	Bibb	ALLDAY, Green	4	Stewart
ALEXANDER, H. C.	1	Coweta	ALLDAY, J. F.	1	Stewart
ALEXANDER, Jefferson	2	Gordon	ALLDAY, Will	2	Stewart
ALEXANDER, John	6	Baker	ALLEN, (?)	15	Decatur
ALEXANDER, Jos. Y.	4	Coweta	ALLEN, A. H.	1	Troup
ALEXANDER, M. H.	59	Randolph	ALLEN, A.S.	5	Pike
ALEXANDER, P. W.	2	Chatham	ALLEN, Abraham	29	Jones
ALEXANDER, Patience	2	Taliaferro	ALLEN, Albin	1	Lincoln
ALEXANDER, Sarah	2	Dade	ALLEN, Alfred	1	Jasper
ALEXANDER, T. R.	18	Elbert	ALLEN, B. C.	4	Laurens
ALEXANDER, Wm.	28	Putnam	ALLEN, B. D.	1	Jefferson
ALEXANDER, Wm.	1	Taliaferro	ALLEN, Benjamin W.	20	Liberty
ALEXANDER, Wm.	1	Taliaferro	ALLEN, Beverly	5	Forsyth
ALEXANDER, Zekiel	1	Stewart	ALLEN, Bryan	20	Floyd
ALFORD, Batsheba	6	Pike	ALLEN, Bryant S.	7	Jasper
ALFORD, Isham	7	Merriwether	ALLEN, C.	7	Troup
ALFORD, J.	8	Troup	ALLEN, C. J.	24	Morgan
ALFORD, J. V. A.	6	Henry	ALLEN, C. W.	3	Upson
ALFORD, James	2	Fayette	ALLEN, Charles	1	Clarke
ALFORD, James A.	8	Troup	ALLEN, Charles	21	Morgan
ALFORD, M. E.	62	Troup	ALLEN, Charles	29	Upson
ALFORD, Obadiah	2	Hancock	ALLEN, Coleman A.	3	Fayette
ALFORD, S.	30	Troup	ALLEN, Daniel A.	24	Pike
ALFORD, S. H.	5	Hancock	ALLEN, David	2	McIntosh
ALFORD, S. W.	3	Troup	ALLEN, David P.	4	Walker
ALFORD, William H.	1	Harris	ALLEN, Drewey N.	1	Merriwether
ALFORD, Ben	6	Columbia	ALLEN, E. W.	8	Lee
ALFORD, Guilford	40	Columbia	ALLEN, E. W.	5	Murray
ALFORD, James	7	Columbia	ALLEN, Eason	81	Laurens
ALFORD, Wiley	4	Troup	ALLEN, Eliale M.	5	Cobb
ALFORD, Wm.	7	Putnam	ALLEN, Elijah	1	Henry
ALFRED, James	4	Houston	ALLEN, F.	7	Troup
ALFRED, William W.	5	Houston	ALLEN, F. M.	6	Walton
ALFRED, H. Estate of	24	Putnam	ALLEN, Frances	2	Jones
ALFRED, John	5	Putnam	ALLEN, G. S.	2	Henry
ALFRIEND,			ALLEN, George	16	Cobb
Benjamin C.	7	Greene	ALLEN, George H.	3	Walton
ALFRIEND, Edward D.	39	Greene	ALLEN, George S.	14	Warren

Name	Number	County	Name	Number	County
ALLEN, Gideon H.	1	Walton	ALLEN, Sherod	8	Jefferson
ALLEN, Harris	15	Jasper	ALLEN, Stephen W.	2	Pike
ALLEN, Henry	5	Habersham	ALLEN, T.	10	Henry
ALLEN, Henry	10	Madison	ALLEN, Thomas	10	Houston
ALLEN, Henry	3	Thomas	ALLEN, Thomas J.	13	Pike
ALLEN, Hugh	25	Houston	ALLEN, Thomas O.	1	Morgan
ALLEN, Isaac	12	Thomas	ALLEN, Thompson	3	Habersham
ALLEN, J. W.	27	Hancock	ALLEN, Thos. M. L.	1	Forsyth
ALLEN, J. W. B.	3	Walton	ALLEN, Thos. J.	9	Greene
ALLEN, James	2	Elbert	ALLEN, W. F.	1	Troup
ALLEN, James	19	Franklin	ALLEN, W. G.	10	Elbert
ALLEN, James	3	Jasper	ALLEN, W. P.	13	Fayette
ALLEN, James	5	Merriwether	ALLEN, W. R.	1	Morgan
ALLEN, James M.	9	Pike	ALLEN, Washington	4	Gwinnett
ALLEN, James P.	35	Houston	ALLEN, William	24	Houston
ALLEN, James W.	23	Jefferson	ALLEN, William	18	Jasper
ALLEN, Jno. B.	2	Fayette	ALLEN, William	1	Lowndes
ALLEN, John	15	Early	ALLEN, William G.	1	Hall
ALLEN, John	6	Greene	ALLEN, William J.	1	Harris
ALLEN, John	7	Jasper	ALLEN, Wm.	14	Pulaski
ALLEN, John	1	Marion	ALLEN, Wm. C.	8	Hall
ALLEN, John	4	Putnam	ALLEN, Alexander M.	5	Richmond
ALLEN, John	2	Warren	ALLEN, David	1	Bibb
ALLEN, John A.	5	Jasper	ALLEN, Elisha A.	38	Burke
ALLEN, John P.	17	Burke	ALLEN, Frank	11	Columbia
ALLEN, John P.	21	Walton	ALLEN, Ira	2	Stewart
ALLEN, John S.	7	Muscogee	ALLEN, J. W.	7	Crawford
ALLEN, John W.	34	Twiggs	ALLEN, John W.	1	Richmond
ALLEN, Josiah	18	Merriwether	ALLEN, Joseph	3	Stewart
ALLEN, Josiah Z.	21	Monroe	ALLEN, Josiah	2	Talbot
ALLEN, L. A.	5	Floyd	ALLEN, Mrs. Frances	14	Burke
ALLEN, Lark B.	6	Thomas	ALLEN, Nancy	2	Burke
ALLEN, Mary	6	Fayette	ALLEN, Nicholas	7	Talbot
ALLEN, Mary G.	4	Upson	ALLEN, P.	2	Crawford
ALLEN, Mary M.	6	Jefferson	ALLEN, P. R.A.by		
ALLEN, Minerua J.	5	Troup	Agt.A.W. Whitehead	36	Richmond
ALLEN, Nancy	1	Gwinnett	ALLEN, Richd.	5	Richmond
ALLEN, Nancy	7	Merriwether	ALLEN, Robert	23	Pike
ALLEN, Nathaniel	28	Morgan	ALLEN, Robert A.	8	Chatham
ALLEN, Parham	17	Hancock	ALLEN, Robert A. & Co.	13	Chatham
ALLEN, Patrick H.	11	Fayette	ALLEN, Samuel A.	4	Burke
ALLEN, Pleasant J.	6	Pike	ALLEN, Stephen	4	Talbot
ALLEN, Polly	1	Madison	ALLEN, Susan	4	Richmond
ALLEN, Robert	10	Chattooga	ALLEN, Thos.	1	Chattooga
ALLEN, Robert	5	Hall	ALLEN, William	1	Richmond
ALLEN, Robert	5	Hall	ALLEN, William A.	3	Walton
ALLEN, Robert	19	Twiggs	ALLEN, William M.	4	Warren
ALLEN, Robert H.	5	Pike	ALLEN, William Y.	1	Walton
ALLEN, Robt.	10	Habersham	ALLEN, Willis	20	Wilkinson
ALLEN, S.	5	Elbert	ALLEN, Wm.	7	Bibb
ALLEN, S. H. J.	1	Habersham	ALLEN, Wyley	1	Warren
ALLEN, S. W.	188	Elbert	ALLEN, Young	2	Upson
ALLEN, Samuel	5	Jasper	ALLEOND, Mark	3	Richmond
ALLEN, Sarah	5	Troup	ALLEY, William	8	Muscogee

Name	Number	County	Name	Number	County
ALLEY, Wm. C.	2	Habersham	ALSTAN, Henry	8	Lumpkin
ALLEY, Wm. W.	10	Habersham	ALSTON, Henry	27	Union
ALLEY, Francis H.	1	Chatham	ALSTON, James	13	Monroe
ALLEY, John	2	Randolph	ALSTON, Matthew	12	Monroe
ALLGOOD, Hillery	1	Laurens	ALSTON, T. M.	11	Union
ALLGOOD, John Y.	3	Paulding	ALSTON, T. P.	21	Habersham
ALLISON, Alexander	22	Troup	ALSTON, W. H.	3	Muscogee
ALLISON, Charity	8	Gwinnett	ALSTON, N. C.	9	Stewart
ALLISON, Green A.	5	Harris	ALSTON, Sarah	2	Bibb
ALLISON, Gwynn	4	Greene	ALTMAN, James	1	Houston
ALLISON, John	1	Clarke	ALTMAN, Frederick C.	1	Richmond
ALLISON, John	4	Morgan	ALUM, Hobson	6	Fayette
ALLISON, Margaret	3	Gwinnet	ALVIS, Ashley	1	Muscogee
ALLISON, R. Estate	3	Wilkes	AMBROS, Jacob M.	1	Walton
ALLISON, Robt.	16	Greene	AMBROS, Warren	17	Jasper
ALLISON, S. P.	2	Randolph	AMBROS, W. S.	3	Wilkes
ALLISON, W. R.	3	Butts	AMBROS, Hartwell	3	Taliaferro
ALLISON, William	22	Butts	AMERSON, Warren	4	Bibb
ALLMAN, Hezekiah	6	Heard	AMES, Lewis	7	Oglethorpe
ALLMAN, J. M.	1	Morgan	AMES, Thos.	30	Oglethorpe
ALLMAN, Jacob	9	Harris	AMES, Jos.	14	Coweta
ALLMAN, James	1	Morgan	AMES, Wm.	31	Coweta
ALLMAN, James R.	10	Upson	AMMONDS, W. B.	9	Henry
ALLMAN, Jas. M.	1	Morgan	AMMONS, John	1	Wayne
ALLMAN, Jesse F.	1	Harris	AMMONS, W. D.	3	Harris
ALLMAN, Solomon	1	Heard	AMMONS, Richard	1	Talbot
ALLMAN, Wm. M.	6	Elbert	AMOS, George	2	Harris
ALLMAN, John R.	6	Clarke	AMOS, William M.	7	Merriwether
ALLMAN, N.	12	Chattooga	AMOS, Wortham	10	Muscogee
ALLMON, Holston	14	Heard	AMOS, A. T.	7	Randolph
ALLOY, Peter	5	Stewart	AMOS, E. M.	7	Crawford
ALLSTON, W.	1	Morgan	AMOS, George W.	14	Talbot
ALLUMS, Edward	7	Troup	AMOSS, Benjamin B.	9	Troup
ALMAN, Isaac	3	Harris	AMOSS, Beverly	8	Hancock
ALMAN, J. W.	4	Elbert	AMOSS, Caroline J.	4	Hancock
ALMAN, John A.	7	Houston	AMOSS, James	5	Troup
ALMAN, Moses	4	Meriwether	AMOSS, James	9	Troup
ALMAN, Simeon	6	Harris	AMOSS, James	21	Troup
ALMAN, Asmon	1	DeKalb	AMOSS, John	15	Hancock
ALMAND, J. W.	8	Elbert	AMOSS, Talbot R.	6	Troup
ALMAND, M. T.	3	Elbert	AMOSS, Wm.	7	Hancock
ALMON, W. D.	1	Newton	AMOURUS, Moses	4	Chatham
ALMON, W. W.	1	Newton	ANARCUS?, B.	1	Elbert
ALMOND, Jesse	24	Merriwether	ANDARSON, J.	1	Elbert
ALMOND, Edw. L.	13	Richmond	ANDARSON, A. P.	1	Elbert
ALMONDS, A. J.	9	Henry	ANDERSON, Daniel S.	32	Walker
ALMONDS, Wiley	1	Stewart	ANDERSON, E. R.	45	Wilkes
ALMZ, N. C. estate	20	Chatham	ANDERSON, E. W.	12	Wilkes
ALSABROOKS, Asa	2	Talbot	ANDERSON, Elijah	6	Troup
ALSOBROOKS, Anderson, Agt.	23	Upson	ANDERSON, George W. H.	2	Walker
ALSOBROOK, John	1	Talbot	ANDERSON, Henry	11	Thomas
ALSOBROOK, William	1	Talbot	ANDERSON, Isaac L.	5	Warren
ALSOBROOKS, Lewis	7	Talbot	ANDERSON, James	17	Upson

7

Name	Number	County
ANDERSON, James Agt.	62	Upson
ANDERSEN, John	2	Lumpkin
ANDERSON, (?)	4	Decatur
ANDERSON, A.	2	Muscogee
ANDERSON, A. H.	5	Floyd
ANDERSON, Augustus H.	92	Burke
ANDERSON, David	11	Gwinnett
ANDERSON, Derrell	3	Franklin
ANDERSON, Enoch	8	Franklin
ANDERSON, Francis	9	Pike
ANDERSON, George H.	6	Newton
ANDERSON, George W.	92	Chatham
ANDERSON, H. R.	5	Franklin
ANDERSON, Henry	5	Pulaski
ANDERSON, Henry Jun.	6	Newton
ANDERSON, Henry Sen.	7	Newton
ANDERSON, Isaac	6	Floyd
ANDERSON, Jacob	13	Pike
ANDERSON, James	76	Burke
ANDERSON, James	2	Jefferson
ANDERSON, James	9	Murray
ANDERSON, John	5	Cobb
ANDERSON, John	1	Forsyth
ANDERSON, John	1	Macon
ANDERSON, John	14	Monroe
ANDERSON, John	1	Monroe
ANDERSON, John	1	Murray
ANDERSON, John	32	Pulaski
ANDERSON, John L.	5	Cobb
ANDERSON, Jos. A.	35	Liberty
ANDERSON, Joseph P.	1	Cobb
ANDERSON, Joseph S.	33	Newton
ANDERSON, L. B.	2	Harris
ANDERSON, Lane	1	Early
ANDERSON, Michall	7	Cass
ANDERSON, Miss Sarah A.	12	Liberty
ANDERSON, Moses	10	Thomas
ANDERSON, Mrs.	1	Liberty
ANDERSON, Nancy	6	Clarke
ANDERSON, Nathan	1	Walker
ANDERSON, Newton	10	Newton
ANDERSON, Rachael	23	Laurens
ANDERSON, Robt.	14	Pulaski
ANDERSON, S. J.	9	Morgan
ANDERSON, Stewart	38	Greene
ANDERSON, Thomas	5	Cobb
ANDERSON, Thomas	27	Pike
ANDERSON, Thomas F.	1	Franklin
ANDERSON, Thomas F.	15	Jackson
ANDERSON, Thos.	78	Wilkes
ANDERSON, W. estate	5	DeKalb
ANDERSON, W. C.	6	Upson
ANDERSON, William	1	Jefferson
ANDERSON, William	5	Lumpkin
ANDERSON, William	7	Pike
ANDERSON, William J.	16	Houston
ANDERSON, William P.	11	Cobb
ANDERSON, William W.	2	Jasper
ANDERSON, William W.	28	Warren
ANDERSON, Wm. Q.	30	Wilkes
ANDERSON, A. G.	8	Coweta
ANDERSON, David	1	DeKalb
ANDERSON, Edward C.	65	Chatham
ANDERSON, Fathe	15	Taliaferro
ANDERSON, George W.	15	Baldwin
ANDERSON, Henry	1	Stewart
ANDERSON, J. S.	1	Butts
ANDERSON, James	14	Burke
ANDERSON, James Junr.	1	Burke
ANDERSON, John	1	Bullock
ANDERSON, John S.	2	Butts
ANDERSON, John W.	122	Chatham
ANDERSON, Jonathan	5	Tatnall
ANDERSON, L. T.	2	Bibb
ANDERSON, Martin	15	Stewart
ANDERSON, Mrs. M. E.	20	Liberty
ANDERSON, Nelson	1	DeKalb
ANDERSON, S.	8	Chattooga
ANDERSON, Saml. J.	1	DeKalb
ANDERSON, T. M.	2	Chattooga
ANDERSON, Vinson	5	Telfair
ANDERSON, William	1	Bullock
ANDERSON, William	4	Screven
ANDERSON, Wm.	1	Burke
ANDERSON, Wm. for MATTHEWS,J.H.	28	Habersham
ANDERSON, Wm. T.	1	Bibb
ANDERSON, Wm. U.	7	Coweta
ANDRE, William	1	Chatham
ANDREW, James O.	24	Newton
ANDREW, Michael	4	Lincoln
ANDREWS, Abesha	23	Twiggs
ANDREWS, Celia	2	Wilkes
ANDREWS, Elizabeth	3	Twiggs
ANDREWS, G.	11	Wilkes
ANDREWS, Green	5	Washington
ANDREWS, Hansford	2	Liberty
ANDREWS, Edward Q.	11	Liberty
ANDREWS, H. G.	8	Henry
ANDREWS, H. H.	5	Newton
ANDREWS, Hannah	4	Glynn
ANDREWS, Isham G.	14	Twiggs
ANDREWS, James	7	Upson

Name	Number	County	Name	Number	County
ANDREWS, James G.	2	Jasper	ANSLEY, Thomas	7	Newton
ANDREWS, James W.	3	Twiggs	ANSLEY, Allen	3	Talbot
ANDREWS, Jas. L.	1	Troup	ANSLEY, F. W.	7	Randolph
ANDREWS, Jno.	11	Wilkes	ANSLEY, Frances A.	1	Dooly
ANDREWS, Johana	5	Fayette	ANSLEY, Jesse	17	Richmond
ANDREWS, John	4	Butts	ANSLEY, Jesse L.	1	Richmond
ANDREWS, John A.	1	Twiggs	ANSLEY, Martin	13	Crawford
ANDREWS, John F.	3	Liberty	ANSLEY, Thomas	3	Sumter
ANDREWS, John J.	8	Harris	ANSLEY, Wm.	19	DeKalb
ANDREWS, John S.	20	Liberty	ANSLY, James	6	Upson
ANDREWS, John w.	7	Hancock	ANSLY, Josephus	1	Upson
ANDREWS, L. D.	12	Hancock	ANTHONY, A. L.	18	Merriwether
ANDREWS, L. R.	11	Muscogee	ANTHONY, Anderson	8	Gwinnett
ANDREWS, Martha	11	Merriwether	ANTHONY, Elizabeth	6	Franklin
ANDREWS, Mary A.	3	Clarke	ANTHONY, J. G.	4	Hancock
ANDREWS, Matthew	1	Greene	ANTHONY, J. W.	14	Merriwether
ANDREWS, R. B.	5	Henry	ANTHONY, James	1	Monroe
ANDREWS, Richard	4	Troup	ANTHONY, Mary R.	56	Wilkes
ANDREWS, Rokow?	1	Greene	ANTHONY, Martin	3	Jackson
ANDREWS, Samuel	3	Muscogee	ANTHONY, Mathew J.	8	Madison
ANDREWS, Warren	2	Greene	ANTHONY, Milton	4	Burke
ANDREWS, Warren E.	1	Greene	ANTHONY, Milton	1	Monroe
ANDREWS, Wm.	1	Greene	ANTHONY, M.S.	15	Wilkes
ANDREWS, A.	15	Decatur	ANTHONY, Nancy	26	Wilkes
ANDREWS, Edward	1	Crawford	ANTHONY, Polly	5	Fayette
ANDREWS, G.	7	Crawford	ANTHONY, Thomas B.	9	Madison
ANDREWS, Garrett	36	Baker	ANTHONY, Whitfield	1	Floyd
ANDREWS, James	3	Bibb	ANTHONY, Dr. E. L.	16	Burke
ANDREWS, Jno.	5	Crawford	ANTHONY, William	6	Columbia
ANDREWS, John	5	Dooly	ANTIGNOE, Wm. M. D.	21	Richmond
ANDREWS, Joseph	22	Bibb	ANTIGONE & EVANS	3	Richmond
ANDREWS, L.	3	Screven	ANTONY, Lavoesin ? L.	4	Richmond
ANDREWS, L. F. W.	2	Bibb	APPLEBY, Cynthia	3	Jackson
ANDREWS, L.R.	11	Putnam	APPLEBY, H. C.	3	Jackson
ANDREWS, N.	1	Crawford	APPLEBY, James	13	Jackson
ANDREWS, Robert	1	Butts	APPLEBY, Wm.	8	Jackson
ANDREWS, Saml.	54	Stewart	APPLEBY, Wm. D.	5	Jackson
ANDREWS, Saml.	1	Stewart	APPLEWHITE, Charles	1	Stewart
ANDREWS,			APPLEWHITE, John	13	Burke
Temperance H.	1	Richmond	APPLEWHITE, Samuel	2	Stewart
ANDREWS, Thos.	3	Crawford	APPLEWHITE, Thomas	5	Stewart
ANDREWS, William G.	42	Upson	APPLING, James	11	Oglethorpe
ANDREWS, W. S.	5	Butts	APPLING, Walter A.	12	Clarke
ANDREWS, Wm.	5	Richmond	APPLING, W. A. Sr.	50	Clarke
ANDREWS, Wm.	31	Wilkes	APPLING, W. A. Jr.	42	Clarke
ANES, Mary	2	Monroe	ARCHARD, John S.	6	Chatham
ANGELY, A.W.	1	Twiggs	ARCHER, James	4	Effingham
ANGLAND, Henry	2	Cobb	ARCHER, James T.	4	Heard
ANGLIN, Henry	4	Twiggs	ARCHER, Martha	1	Harris
ANSELON & EVANS	1	Richmond	ARCHER, Wm. Jr.	12	Hancock
ANSLEY, Benjamin	2	Newton	ARCHER, Wm. J.	2	Clarke
ANSLEY, James	1	Warren	ARCHER, Artemas	13	Burke
ANSLEY, Jesse	1	Newton	ARCHER, David	1	Screven
ANSLEY, Mary	7	Pike	ARCHER, H. A.	1	Jackson

9

Name	Number	County
ARCHY, William	6	Washington
ARD, A. W.	18	Wilkinson
ARENDALL, John	5	Franklin
ARENDALL, N. L.	1	Franklin
ARENDELE, Laughlin	4	DeKalb
ARGO, Bernardo J.	5	Clarke
ARGO, Nimrod	1	DeKalb
ARGROVES, Allen	1	Merriwether
ARICHARDSON, Robert	2	Upson
ARINGTON, Henry	9	Twiggs
ARKWRIGHT, Thomas	4	Chatham
ARLIM, Jesse	8	Decatur
ARLINE, Jethro	11	Laurens
ARLINE, H.	13	Decatur
ARLINE, H.	12	Decatur
ARLINE, James	11	Baker
ARLINE, Thomas P.	2	Baker
ARMER, Robert	2	Hall
ARMOR, James N.	28	Greene
ARMOR, N. D.	2	Wilkes
ARMOR, Reuben B.	16	Greene
ARMOR, Richard W.	5	Harris
ARMOR, William	5	Greene
ARMOR, Wm. Sen.	36	Greene
ARMOUR, R. W.	2	Lincoln
ARMSTEAD, Jesse M.	2	Greene
ARMSTEAD, John	11	Walton
ARMSTEAD, A.	8	Elbert
ARMSTED, James W.	1	Walton
ARMSTRONG, A.	6	Oglethorpe
ARMSTRONG, A.	6	Oglethorpe
ARMSTRONG, Alexander	13	Washington
ARMSTRONG, Caroline	13	Glynn
ARMSTRONG, Edward	7	Washington
ARMSTRONG, F. C.	15	Wilkes
ARMSTRONG, Hugh	13	Warren
ARMSTRONG, James G.	7	Washington
ARMSTRONG, John	6	Forsyth
ARMSTRONG, John	5	Gordon
ARMSTRONG, John	15	Greene
ARMSTRONG, Lucinda	11	Oglethorpe
ARMSTRONG, Margaret	8	Greene
ARMSTRONG, Martin W.	3	Gwinnett
ARMSTRONG, Sarah	7	Glynn
ARMSTRONG, Thomas	2	Warren
ARMSTRONG, Thomas	2	Warren
ARMSTRONG, J. W.	11	Bibb

Name	Number	County
ARMSTRONG, John	1	DeKalb
ARMSTRONG, M.	7	Crawford
ARMSTRONG, William C.	13	Stewart
ARMSTRONG, William H.	7	Washington
ARMSTUPH, William	5	Effingham
ARNETT, Albert W.	9	Wilkes
ARNETT, Berry A.	26	Wilkes
ARNETT, F. G.	40	Decatur
ARNETT, F. G.	26	Decatur
ARNETT, Oliver C.	58	Wilkes
ARNETT, Wm. G.	7	Wilkes
ARNOLD(?), Mrs.	11	Decatur
ARNOLD, Allen J.	25	Wilkes
ARNOLD, C. S.	38	Washington
ARNOLD, C. S.	21	Washington
ARNOLD, H. J.	9	Walton
ARNOLD, James	3	Ware
ARNOLD, James J.	4	Twiggs
ARNOLD, Jas.	27	Wilkes
ARNOLD, Jas. Est.	14	Wilkes
ARNOLD, Jesse H.	19	Walton
ARNOLD, John	3	Hancock
ARNOLD, Joshua P.	3	Walton
ARNOLD, Moses	50	Wilkes
ARNOLD, S. C.	4	Oglethorpe
ARNOLD, Thomas M.	1	Walton
ARNOLD, Washington	7	Oglethorpe
ARNOLD, William	7	Upson
ARNOLD, Anderson	1	Gwinnett
ARNOLD, Austin A.	7	Campbell
ARNOLD, Camma	7	Jackson
ARNOLD, Chesley	23	Oglethorpe
ARNOLD, D.	2	Elbert
ARNOLD, E. B.	25	Henry
ARNOLD, Eliza	1	Burke
ARNOLD, Elizabeth F.	6	Gordon
ARNOLD, F. W.	6	Morgan
ARNOLD, Henry	20	Hancock
ARNOLD, J. B.	5	Morgan
ARNOLD, J. Y.	2	Elbert
ARNOLD, John	4	Oglethorpe
ARNOLD, John B.	7	Macon
ARNOLD, John F.	28	Cobb
ARNOLD, John S.	1	Jackson
ARNOLD, Mahala	6	Floyd
ARNOLD, Obadiah	11	Hancock
ARNOLD, Owen	13	Pike
ARNOLD, Park E.	70	Oglethorpe
ARNOLD, Richard	3	Oglethorpe
ARNOLD, Solomon P.	8	Greene
ARNOLD, Susan	4	Oglethorpe
ARNOLD, Thomas	1	Hancock

Name	Number	County	Name	Number	County
ARNOLD, W. B.	1	Morgan	ASH, Charles B.	7	Chatham
ARNOLD, Washington	7	Oglethorpe	ASH, George A.	20	Chatham
ARNOLD, Wiley	21	Hancock	ASHBURN, John C.		
ARNOLD, William	22	Cobb	agt for AVERETT,J.	122	Houston
ARNOLD, William C.	5	Jefferson	ASHBY, John	6	Twiggs
ARNOLD, William H.	5	Pike	ASHCROFT, E. S.	8	Coweta
ARNOLD, Willis	25	Madison	ASHER, Thomas J.	2	Dade
ARNOLD, A. C.	8	Putnam	ASHFIELD, Jas.	31	Putnam
ARNOLD, Chas. W.	37	Coweta	ASHFORD, Charlotte	16	Troup
ARNOLD, Geo. W.	33	Coweta	ASHFORD, Thomas	43	Troup
ARNOLD, Hugh P.	20	Coweta	ASHFORD, Wm. H.	2	Clarke
ARNOLD, J. agent	27	Crawford	ASHHURST, Joseph M.	7	Union
ARNOLD, J. G.	3	Coweta	ASHLEY, Allen	17	Laurens
ARNOLD, Jas.	67	Coweta	ASHLEY, Charles	2	Lincoln
ARNOLD, Peter	3	Bibb	ASHLEY, Charles E.	5	Greene
ARNOLD, R. D., exec.	9	Chatham	ASHLEY, Wm.	5	Greene
ARNOLD, Rich. J.	186	Bryan	ASHLEY, Cornelius	74	Telfair
ARNOLD, Richard D.	18	Chatham	ASHLEY, Natt	76	Telfair
ARNOLD, W.W.	3	Putnam	ASHLEY, Wm. P.	19	Camden
ARNOLD, Wm.	2	Bibb	ASHMORE, Jeremiah	7	Lincoln
ARNOLD, Wm.	9	Coweta	ASHMORE, Joseph	5	Liberty
ARNOLD, Wm.	13	Putnam	ASHMORE,		
ARNOLD, Wm. G.	65	Coweta	Mrs. Caroline	1	Liberty
ARNOLD, Wm. P.	3	Putnam	ASHMORE, William	6	Lincoln
ARNOW, C. J.	1	Glynn	ASHURST, John M.	7	Putnam
ARNOWS, Jos.	2	Camden	ASHURST, M.F.	13	Putnam
ARNOWS, Peter	5	Camden	ASHWORTH, Jasper	2	Gilmer
ARRINGTON, Abner	5	Jefferson	ASKEW, A. G.	3	Harris
ARRINGTON, Chas.	1	Carroll	ASKEW, Abriah	24	Pike
ARRINGTON, Henry	17	Jefferson	ASKEW, Ann	8	Harris
ARRINGTON, Jane	1	Jefferson	ASKEW, Augustus	11	Marion
ARRINGTON, P. G.	2	Macon	ASKEW, B. S.	5	Heard
ARRINGTON, Sherod	27	Jefferson	ASKEW, Benjamin	18	Jones
ARRINGTON, Thomas	17	Twiggs	ASKEW, David R.	7	Fayette
ARRINGTON, Willis	1	Jefferson	ASKEW, Elizabeth	4	Hancock
ARRINGTON, Francis	2	Richmond	ASKEW, J.	1	Henry
ARRINGTON, John	1	Talbot	ASKEW, J. A.	21	Morgan
ARRINGTON, Wm. D.	2	Coweta	ASKEW, James	17	Heard
ARTHUR, Thos.	2	Oglethorpe	ASKEW, Jas. B.	5	Greene
ARTHUR, Tobbert	2	Oglethorpe	ASKEW, John M.	1	Harris
ARTHUR, A. W .	6	Crawford	ASKEW, Nancy	7	Greene
ARTHUR, Basil K.	2	Burke	ASKEW, Wm.	14	Hancock
ARTIPIC?, J. B.	3	Bibb	ASKEW, E. G.	1	Bibb
ASBELL, Bryant	4	Twiggs	ASKEW, Henry J.	3	Dooly
ASBELL, Chiba?	7	Twiggs	ASKEW, Jas.	9	Randolph
ASBELL, John	29	Twiggs	ASKEW, Jas. P.	1	Coweta
ASBERRY, Richard T.	3	Taliaferro	ASKIN, William	9	Monroe
ASBURY, John	6	Houston	ASPENNALL, Elijah	8	Bullock
ASBURY, Redmon T.	3	Greene	ASTON, Sarah	4	Coweta
ASBURY, Richard	7	Oglethorpe	ATCHERSON,		
ASBURY, Sarah	4	Greene	James R.	20	Walton
ASH, Robert R.	4	Franklin	ATCHERSON, John	10	Walton
ASH, William	8	Franklin	ATCHERSON, N. G.	3	Walton
ASH, William	1	Franklin	ATCHINSON, David	1	Warren

11

Name	Number	County	Name	Number	County
ATCHINSON, John A.	1	Warren	AUSTIN, Charles	23	Fayette
ATCHINSON, Mary	12	Coweta	AUSTIN, Clisbe	1	Murray
ATHAN, Nathaniel	6	Talbot	AUSTIN, Davis W.	2	Houston
ATKINS, Abram	4	Jackson	AUSTIN, Harrison	11	Troup
ATKINS, Benjamin	15	Jackson	AUSTIN, John M.	7	Walton
ATKINS, John C.	2	Walker	AUSTIN, John P.	8	Newton
ATKINS, William	10	Dooly	AUSTIN, L. T.	44	Muscogee
ATKINSON,	9	Camden	AUSTIN, Mary	11	Walton
ATKINSON, Elizabeth	2	Gwinnett	AUSTIN, Nathaniel	27	Gwinnett
ATKINSON, James	7	Greene	AUSTIN, J. B.	1	Carroll
ATKINSON, John	3	Burke	AUSTIN, John C.	2	DeKalb
ATKINSON, Lewis	8	Butts	AUSTIN, N.	16	Carroll
ATKINSON, Thos. J. P.	4	Greene	AUSTIN, Samuel	3	Thomas
ATKINSON, William	5	Gwinnett	AUSTIN, Stewart	3	Chatham
ATKINSON, Wyley F.	1	Gwinnett	AUSTIN, Thos.	5	DeKalb
ATKINSON, Abner	9	Butts	AUSTIN, Wm.	19	Campbell
ATKINSON, Alexr.	38	Camden	AUTREY, Jacob	2	Clarke
ATKINSON, Cornelius	14	Butts	AUTREY, M. C.	1	Carroll
ATKINSON, Edmund	84	Camden	AUTREY, Wm.	4	Carroll
ATKINSON, Irvin	17	Chattooga	AUTRY, Alexander	14	Lumpkin
ATKINSON, S. C.	1	Bibb	AUTRY, Jacob	3	Carroll
ATKINSON, Shade	6	Baker	AUTRY, R. M.	1	Forsyth
ATKINSON, T. P.	10	Butts	AVAN, F. C.	7	Twiggs
ATTAWAY, (?)	6	Coweta	AVANT, Henry	7	Jasper
ATTAWAY, A. F.	3	Franklin	AVANT, L. S.	7	Bibb
ATTAWAY, Goodwin	7	Burke	AVARA, B.	1	Crawford
ATTAWAY, James	2	Franklin	AVARIT ?, ?H.	2	Washington
ATTAWAY, Mary J.	1	Muscogee	AVARY, Charles	1	Floyd
ATTAWAY, Wm.	1	Burke	AVEN, James	3	Talbot
ATTAWAY, C.	6	Floyd	AVEN, John	8	Talbot
ATTAWAY, David	24	Burke	AVEREL, William	1	Richmond
ATTAWAY, Harley	5	Burke	AVERET, Drery	7	Talbot
ATTAWAY, Shubel	1	Burke	AVERETT, Alexander	3	Jefferson
ATWATER, E. B.	47	Upson	AVERETT,		
ATWELL, Reubin	8	Jefferson	Alexander Jr.	2	Jefferson
ATWELL, James	15	Richmond	AVERETT, Archd.	12	Lowndes
ATWELL, Jeremiah	4	Richmond	AVERETT, David	2	Muscogee
ATWOOD, Henry	123	McIntosh	AVERRETT, James	24	Twiggs
ATWOOD, Thomas	1	Cass	AVERETT, Joseph	2	Jefferson
AUCHERS, Samuel M.	7	Walton	AVERETT, Thomas	2	Lincoln
AUDAS, Tuttle H.	16	Hancock	AVERETT, Allen	4	Stewart
AUDERSERE?, William	3	Newton	AVERETT,		
AUDOINE, A. L.	1	Bibb	Charles C. P.	1	Richmond
AUGUSTA CANAL			AVERETT, Epply	1	Early
COMP.	15	Richmond	AVERETT, James estate	122	Houston
AUGUSTA MANU-			AVERETT, John	1	Putnam
FACTURING Co.	4	Richmond	AVERETT, John	1	Talbot
AUKENLECK, Jno. B.	3	Muscogee	AVERFELT,		
AULDERMAN, Sarah	7	Baker	Frederick W.	2	Chatham
AULT, Henry	2	Murray	AVERIT (EVERETT?),		
AUREA, Mrs,	1	Taliaferro	Abner	30	Early
AUST, Sarah A.	1	Glynn	AVERIT, Mary	6	Monroe
AUSTIN, Allen J.	15	Muscogee	AVERITT, Albright	8	Muscogee
AUSTIN, Augustus B.	10	Muscogee	AVERITT, Solomon	2	Muscogee

12

Name	Number	County	Name	Number	County
AVERRY, Geo. W.	2	DeKalb	AYERS, Obideah	8	Franklin
AVERRY, Wm.	1	DeKalb	AYERS, Asher	5	Bibb
AVERY, Absolem C.	4	Cherokee	AYERS, J. B.	17	Bibb
AVERY, Francis E.	3	Merriwether	AYERS, Wm.	1	Cass
AVERY, Isaac B.	1	Fayette	BABB, K.	3	Henry
AVERY, Jacob	5	Cherokee	BABB, Mercer	4	Harris
AVERY, Needham	4	Newton	BABB, Brinkley	4	Baldwin
AVERY, Samuel	9	Newton	BABCOCK, J. W.	16	Bibb
AVERY, William	2	Houston	BABER, M.	10	Bibb
AVERY, William	1	Newton	BACCUS, John	4	Walton
AVERY, Ambrose J.	17	Columbia	BACCUS, Joseph	1	Walton
AVERY, H. W.	1	DeKalb	BACHALOR, Blakey	1	Putnam
AVERY, Isaac	2	Putnam	BACHELOAR, Cordy	2	Putnam
AVERY, Madison	20	Columbia	BACHELOR, Nathaniel	7	Harris
AVERY, Margaret	3	Putnam	BACHELOR, Blakey	5	Putnam
AVERY, Martha	1	Putnam	BACHELOR, L.	7	Putnam
AVERY, Richard	14	Columbia	BACHLOTT, John	18	Camden
AVERY, Sarah	32	Columbia	BACHLOTT, A.	10	Camden
AVERY, Wm.	17	Carroll	BACKER, A.	2	Muscogee
AVIRY, James	14	Columbia	BACKLEY, Louisa	5	Chatham
AWBRY, Thomas	3	Heard	BACKWELL, J. W.	7	Pulaski
AWBRY, John P.	3	Heard	BACON, Alexander E.	1	Jackson
AWBRY, Munroe	1	Heard	BACON, Edwin H.	93	Liberty
AWBRY, Philip A.	5	Heard	BACON, Elizabeth	1	Laurens
AWBRY, Thos. M.	2	Heard	BACON, Henry	9	Camden
AWBRY, Wm. G.	11	Heard	BACON, Henry W.	8	Liberty
AWBRY, Wm. J. T.	6	Heard	BACON, John E.	15	Muscogee
AWTRY, ?	5	Morgan	BACON, John E.	4	Muscogee
AWTRY, ?	3	Morgan	BACON, Joseph R.	31	Liberty
AWTRY, ?	1	Morgan	BACON, Langston	8	Marion
AWTRY, E. A.	1	Morgan	BACON, Lyddal l	3	Houston
AWTRY, Hiram H.	1	Morgan	BACON, Mrs. Martha	32	Liberty
AXON, Mrs. Ann	40	Liberty	BACON, Mrs. Mary	10	Liberty
AYCOCK, Benj.	1	Marion	BACON, Mrs. Mary J.	24	Liberty
AYCOCK, Houston	11	Floyd	BACON, Milton E.	18	Troup
AYCOCK, Isaac	5	Marion	BACON, Wm. H.	1	Jackson
AYCOCK, Joel	11	Newton	BACON, Alfred	4	Tatnall
AYCOCK, John	2	Cass	BACON, Edmund	18	Columbia
AYCOCK, John	2	Newton	BACON, Elbert	6	Tatnall
AYCOCK, John B.	1	Cobb	BACON, John	9	Tatnall
AYCOCK, Joshua	22	Marion	BACON, John B.	8	Chatham
AYCOCK, P.	10	Oglethorpe	BACON, Mary	2	Richmond
AYCOCK, Rebekuh	5	Newton	BACON, Nathaniel	1	Bryan
AYCOCK, Richard	3	Newton	BACON, Nicholas C.	9	Warren
AYCOCK, Emanuel C.	1	Bullock	BACON, Thomas J.	18	Troup
AYCOCK, Jas. M.	2	Cass	BACON, William	2	Talbot
AYCOCK, REDICK	7	Walton	BADGER, A. B.	5	Randolph
AYCOCK, Robert	2	Walton	BADGER, J. B.	16	DeKalb
AYER, A. K.	16	Muscogee	BADGER, Levin	10	Putnam
AYERS, A.	10	Troup	BAGBY, Benjamin M.	1	Gwinnett
AYERS, Jeddiah	2	Franklin	BAGBY, James	2	Newton
AYERS, Jno. B.	9	Carroll	BAGBY, James H.	2	Greene
AYERS, Moses	5	Habersham	BAGBY, Jefferson	1	Newton
AYERS, Moses	2	Habersham	BAGBY, William K.	7	Newton

Name	Number	County	Name	Number	County
BAGELY, Thomas M.	5	Floyd	BAILEY, Samuel S.	5	Murray
BAGG, Preston?	3	Muscogee	BAILEY, Wiley	1	Walker
BAGGERS, A. J.	1	Carroll	BAILEY, William	3	Murray
BAGGET, Susan	13	Monroe	BAILEY, William	5	Washington
BAGGET, Stephen	3	Campbell	BAILEY, William E.	12	Wayne
BAGGETT, Bennett	2	Walker	BAILEY, Wm.	10	Troup
BAGGS, Archabal	40	McIntosh	BAILEY, Ann	37	Butts
BAGGS, Archibald	8	Liberty	BAILEY, D. J.	57	Butts
BAGGS, David S.	46	Liberty	BAILEY, D. J.	7	Butts
BAGGS, James	18	McIntosh	BAILEY, David	20	Camden
BAGGS, John	1	Troup	BAILEY, David C.	8	Burke
BAGGS, Wm. A.	10	Liberty	BAILEY, E. J.	3	DeKalb
BAGGS, Zenas L.	17	Liberty	BAILEY, Ezekiel	8	Coweta
BAGGS, David	7	Tatnall	BAILEY, Henry	8	Camden
BAGLAY, David	3	Sumter	BAILEY, Isaiah	1	Richmond
BAGLEY, Henry	3	Forsyth	BAILEY, Jas.	11	Coweta
BAGLEY, Wiley	4	Forsyth	BAILEY, Jno.	10	Randolph
BAGLEY, Wm.	9	Muscogee	BAILEY, John	38	Bibb
BAGLEY, James	13	Putnam	BAILEY, John	8	Bryan
BAGLEY, James D.	1	Baldwin	BAILEY, John	7	Coweta
BAGLEY, Lewis	5	Baldwin	BAILEY, Mary	3	Randolph
BAGLEY, Thomas	8	Bibb	BAILEY, R. J.	10	Coweta
BAGLEY, William S.	1	Baldwin	BAILEY, S. T.	20	Bibb
BAGLLY, Wm.	2	Randolph	BAILEY, Stephen	25	Butts
BAGLY, Polly H.	1	Cherokee	BAILEY, W. S.	1	Chattooga
BAGNON, Watkins	2	Clarke	BAILEY, W. T.	2	Coweta
BAGSHAW, Catherine	1	Chatham	BAILEY, William	1	Coweta
BAGWELL, J. G. M.	10	Franklin	BAILEY, William E.	2	Baker
BAGWELL, John A.	1	Cass	BAILEY, Wm.	10	Butts
BAGWELL, Larkin	2	Gwinnett	BAILEY, Wm.	8	Camden
BAGWELL, Robert	1	Gwinnett	BAILEY, Wm.	5	Carroll
BAGWILL, John J.	1	Cherokee	BAILY, Benj. H.	4	Gordon
BAILELY, Nancy	5	Chatham	BAILY, Daniel	1	Jefferson
BAILEY, C. B.	4	Walker	BAILY, E.	2	Elbert
BAILEY, C. C.	29	Troup	BAILY, Elizabeth	3	Pulaski
BAILEY, Charles	3	Fayette	BAILY, Jas.	7	Pulaski
BAILEY, Charles	3	Fayette	BAILY, Mary	9	Monroe
BAILEY, D.	2	Henry	BAILY, Saml. M.	10	Forsyth
BAILEY, Elijah	26	Henry	BAILY, Thos.	5	Meriwether
BAILEY, Elisha	1	Jackson	BAILY, W. F.	24	Newton
BAILEY, Ephraim	12	Wilkes	BAILY, William S.	1	Montgomery
BAILEY, F. C.	9	Cass	BAILY, Alston	1	Coweta
BAILEY, Francis	3	Murray	BAILY, Ben	2	Columbia
BAILEY, Geo.	8	Wilkes	BAILY, Elizabeth	1	Walker
BAILEY, James	4	Jackson	BAILY, Harrison	1	Baker
BAILEY, Jane	6	Jasper	BAILY, John L.	7	Baker
BAILEY, John	6	Washington	BAILY, M.	17	Randolph
BAILEY, John estate	186	Camden	BAILY, O.H.P.	4	Talbot
BAILEY, Pierce	80	Warren	BAILY, Robert	1	Baker
BAILEY, Ralph	11	Jackson	BAILY, William	13	Baker
BAILEY, Russell	8	Wilkes	BAILY, Wm.	1	Walker
BAILEY, Sam A.	14	Muscogee	BAINS, James Y.	4	Merriwether
BAILEY, Samuel	33	Clarke	BAINS, Jane	9	Heard
BAILEY, Samuel	27	Jackson	BAIRD, J. B.	3	Muscogee

14

Name	Number	County	Name	Number	County
BAIRD, John	1	Franklin	BAKER, W. F. E.	17	Liberty
BAIRD, John	2	Heard	BAKER, William T.	4	Chatham
BAIRD?, W. B.	6	Pike	BAKER, Wm. J.	2	Laurens
BAIRD, W. W.	9	Wilkes	BAKER, Wm. Q.	51	Liberty
BAISDEN, Thomas	17	Sumter	BAKER, Wm. S.	56	Liberty
BAITY, A. D.	6	Pulaski	BAKER, A.	5	Stewart
BAITY, Francis	6	Jackson	BAKER, Alfred	14	Richmond
BAITY, L.	1	Meriwether	BAKER, Green	1	DeKalb
BAITY, Wm. A.	3	Jackson	BAKER, Henry	8	Richmond
BAJERON, Elisha	5	Burke	BAKER, Jethro	8	DeKalb
BAJERON, John	1	Burke	BAKER, Joel	15	Cass
BAKER, A. B.	3	Troup	BAKER, John	28	Columbia
BAKER, John	10	Floyd	BAKER, John W.	7	Baldwin
BAKER, Absalom	11	Cobb	BAKER, Lark	1	DeKalb
BAKER, Benj.	15	Floyd	BAKER, S.	7	Decatur
BAKER, C. B.	13	McIntosh	BAKER, Sarah	18	Chatham
BAKER, Celia	1	Warren	BAKER, Thomas B.	27	Bryan
BAKER, E. F.	1	Clarke	BAKER, Thomas K.	3	Richmond
BAKER, Early	4	Troup	BAKER, Willis P.	23	Talbot
BAKER, Easter	8	Jones	BAKER, Wm.	3	DeKalb
BAKER, Edwin	3	Warren	BAKER?, Jonathan	15	Pike
BAKER, Greene	5	Warren	BALDING, Wm.	1	Walker
BAKER, Henry H.	45	Warren	BALDWELL, O. H. P.	2	Walker
BAKER, Hugh	1	Cobb	BALDWIN, Benjamin	18	Merriwether
BAKER, James	2	Fayette	BALDWIN, C. J.	30	Morgan
BAKER, James L.	2	Marion	BALDWIN, Hartwell	1	Paulding
BAKER, Jefferson	1	Walton	BALDWIN, James	1	Muscogee
BAKER, Jesse	12	Cass	BALDWIN, John R.	17	Morgan
BAKER, Jesse L.	20	Newton	BALDWIN, Joseph	5	Chatham
BAKER, Jesse T.	2	DeKalb	BALDWIN, Mrs. Mary	10	Burke
BAKER, John	1	Heard	BALDWIN, Robert F.	28	Macon
BAKER, John	9	Liberty	BALDWIN, T. B.	30	Morgan
BAKER, John	2	Pike	BALDWIN, Andrew J.	9	Randolph
BAKER, Jonathan	2	Washington	BALDWIN, G. H.	5	Stewart
BAKER, Joshua	2	Walker	BALDWIN, H. F.	29	Putnam
BAKER, Laurence	15	Newton	BALDWIN, Mary	6	Richmond
BAKER, Littleton	1	Chattooga	BALDWIN, Moses	3	Randolph
BAKER, M.	61	Elbert	BALDWIN, Samuel	65	Stewart
BAKER, Mary	2	Chatham	BALDWIN, Samuel	24	Talbot
BAKER, Morell	16	Harris	BALDWIN, Samuel	6	Talbot
BAKER, Mrs. Ann S.	11	Liberty	BALDWIN, Thomas	4	Talbot
BAKER, Nancy	8	Walton	BALDWIN, W. L.	1	Walton
BAKER, Nancy	10	Warren	BALDY, William H.	51	Burke
BAKER, Newnan	4	Newton	BALES ?, Bryan	22	Taliaferro
BAKER, Richard F.	16	Liberty	BALES, Henry P.	2	Taliaferro
BAKER, Ruthy	3	Jones	BALEY, Sarah	6	Fayette
BAKER, S.	1	Irwin	BALEY, William H.	10	Jasper
BAKER, Sealy			BALEY, Williamson	8	Jasper
(widow of Jordan Baker)	12	Laurens	BALEY, Elijah	4	Campbell
BAKER, Silas	4	Troup	BALIS, Eliza	4	Columbia
BAKER, T. G. W.	13	Liberty	BALKCOM, Bryant	8	Jones
BAKER, Thomas	6	Newton	BALKCOM, Ichabod	6	Jones
BAKER, Thos. estate	30	Liberty	BALL, James	4	Stewart
BAKER, Thomas H.	10	Washington	BALL, John F.	10	Stewart

15

Name	Number	County	Name	Number	County
BALL, Milton C.	41	Baker	BANKS, Ralph	19	Pike
BALL, Mrs.	3	Tatnall	BANKS, Richard	11	Hall
BALL, Sopah	18	Stewart	BANKS, Richard O.	22	Pike
BALL, Susan H.	12	Coweta	BANKS, Sally	4	Walton
BALLARD, Daniel	2	Fayette	BANKS, Sarah B.	9	Pike
BALLARD, E.	1	Wilkinson	BANKS, Thomas	9	Murray
BALLARD, Elijah	13	Fayette	BANKS, William	15	Monroe
BALLARD, James	1	Upson	BANKS, William	6	Upson
BALLARD, M.	7	Henry	BANKS, Wm. R.	1	Monroe
BALLARD, Mary	4	Wilkinson	BANKS, Andrew J.	2	Baldwin
BALLARD, Thomas W.	5	Pike	BANKS, Johanna	1	Chatham
BALLARD, W. G.	34	Morgan	BANKS, John H.	5	Sumter
BALLARD, William	9	Morgan	BANKS, Leonard	5	Bryan
BALLARD, Wm. B.	2	Fayette	BANKS, Reason	21	Baldwin
BALLARD, Wm. R.	1	Coweta	BANKS?, John	24	Muscogee
BALLARD, Edward	33	Columbia	BANKSTON,		
BALLARD, Jesse	2	Coweta	Willoby S.	2	Pike
BALLARD, W. L.	4	Randolph	BANKSTON, Barnwell	3	Harris
BALLARD, Westley	3	Coweta	BANKSTON, John	9	Gwinnett
BALLARD, Wm.	2	Coweta	BANKSTON, L.	12	Henry
BALLARD, Wm. Sen.	2	Coweta	BANKSTON, Wm. H.	15	Monroe
BALLENGER, Joseph	3	Madison	BANKSTON, Henry	3	DeKalb
BALLENGER, William	2	Madison	BANKSTON, Sarah	4	Butts
BALLERD, Jesse	6	Morgan	BANNINGS, J. L.	4	Merriwether
BALLEW, Joshua M.	2	Gordon	BANOUS?, Jeremiah	5	Cherokee
BALLEW, Robert	3	Walker	BANUS, Moses	1	Houston
BALLEW, Robert	2	Walker	BAPTIST, Polly	2	Chatham
BALLEW, Thomas L.	1	Walker	BARATTE, Augustus	2	Camden
BALLEW, William	2	Walker	BARBEE, Sarah	2	Jasper
BALLOU, John	2	Chatham	BARBER, Darius	1	Thomas
BALLOW, Samuel F.	4	Chatham	BARBER, D. J.	3	Muscogee
BALWEN, Thos. B.	15	Oglethorpe	BARBER, George T.	2	Heard
BALY, Pierce	3	Taliaferro	BARBER, J. F.	1	Pulaski
BANCROFT, Dyer C.	15	Jasper	BARBER, John W.	2	Washington
BANCROFT, Joseph			BARBER, M.	1	Pulaski
trustee	18	Chatham	BARBER, Rachael	3	Wilkes
BANDY, George	2	Murray	BARBER, Robert	29	Clarke
BANDY, Mary	1	Bryan	BARBER, Samuel	18	Jones
BANKMAN, George	1	Chatham	BARBER, Thos.	16	Pulaski
BANKS, Benjamin W.	19	Jasper	BARBER, Thomas	19	Washington
BANKS, Elbert J.	15	Monroe	BARBER, William	23	Cobb
BANKS, Elizabeth	1	Newton	BARBER, William	1	Merriwether
BANKS, Ely	1	Pike	BARBER, Asa	6	Baker
BANKS, F. A.	19	Morgan	BARBER, George W.	16	Butts
BANKS, H.	5	Pike	BARBER, Isaac	1	Bryan
BANKS, John	1	Pike	BARBER, J. W.	19	Butts
BANKS, John C.	4	Jasper	BARBER, Jemmima	6	Screven
BANKS, John H.	14	Monroe	BARBER, M. C.	1	Butts
BANKS, Josiah	1	Newton	BARBER, Mathew	17	Butts
BANKS, Josiah C.	25	Jasper	BARBER, S.	1	Decatur
BANKS, Nancy	10	Jasper	BARBER, Samuel	1	Sumter
BANKS, Pleasant E.	8	Jasper	BARBER, Spencer	2	Sumter
BANKS, Priscilla	24	Jasper	BARBER, Thomas S.	7	Screven
BANKS, Ralph	13	Habersham	BARBOUR, Samuel	77	Jasper

Name	Number	County
BARBOUR, Samuel	10	Jasper
BARBOUR?, William	1	Muscogee
BARBRE, Allen	2	Randolph
BARBREE, Thomas	2	Stewart
BARCLAY, E. S.	11	Union
BARCLAY, William	4	Jasper
BARCLAY, E. E.	1	Stewart
BARCLEY, Ann W.	84	Chatham
BARCLEY, Ann W.	72	Chatham
BARDWELL, R. N. R.	5	Muscogee
BAREFEET, Richard	3	Bibb
BAREFIELD, John	9	Jones
BAREFIELD, John J.	9	Jones
BAREFIELD, Solomon	3	Houston
BAREFIELD, Chapman	2	Talbot
BAREFIELD, F.	3	Randolph
BAREFIELD, J. S.	26	Bibb
BAREFIELD, J. S. agt.	20	Bibb
BAREMORE ?, Hardam	2	Talbot
BAREN, A. L.	4	Butts
BARENTINE, H.	1	Crawford
BARETT, William	5	Pike
BARFIELD, Benj.	10	Henry
BARFIELD, J. H.	2	Henry
BARFIELD, J. M.	5	Henry
BARFIELD, Jesse	1	Macon
BARFIELD, John	1	Campbell
BARFIELD, Rachel	4	Wilkinson
BARFIELD, Samuel	29	Pike
BARFIELD, Carswell	2	Burke
BARGAINIER, John	8	Jefferson
BARGAINIER, William	16	Jefferson
BARGE, Hannah	1	Washington
BARGE, John	1	Fayette
BARGE, Thomas	27	Marion
BARGE, Richmond	17	Campbell
BARGER, Chas. D.	14	Cass
BARGES, B. F.	12	Stewart
BARHAM, T. T .	20	Henry
BARIE, Louis	1	Chatman
BARIE, Charles E.	3	Chatman
BARKER, Alsey	9	Lumpkin
BARKER, Eldridge	1	Walton
BARKER, Gray	5	Lumpkin
BARKER, James	1	Lumpkin
BARKER, John	1	Early
BARKER, John	1	Lumpkin
BARKER, John R.	4	Gwinnett
BARKER, Joseph	5	Thomas
BARKER, Lewis	7	Heard
BARKER, Nancy	1	Troup
BARKER, Rillis	5	Walton
BARKER, Rufus	9	Floyd
BARKER, Sterling F.	2	Marion
BARKER, Thomas	9	Pike
BARKER?, John	3	Pike
BARKLEY, R. J.	9	Morgan
BARKLEY, J. M.	6	Butts
BARKLY, Andrew	13	Monroe
BARKLY, John A.	11	Twiggs
BARKSDALE, Alfred	20	Hancock
BARKSDALE, Alfred	13	Hancock
BARKSDALE, Green B.	1	Warren
BARKSDALE, John	13	Twiggs
BARKSDALE, N. G.	108	Lincoln
BARKSDALE, John	9	Hancock
BARKSDALE, Elizabeth	2	Greene
BARKSDALE, John E.	9	Talbot
BARKSDALE, John M.	15	Warren
BARKSDALE, Mary	14	Baldwin
BARKSDALE, Nat	5	Putnam
BARKSDALE, Samuel	15	Warren
BARKSDALE, Terrill	19	Talbot
BARKSDALE, Thomas T.	12	Warren
BARKSDALE, William B.	15	Warren
BARKSDALE, William C.	1	Troup
BARLON, Albert	2	Walton
BARLOW, H.	2	Wilkinson
BARLOW, James	29	Laurens
BARLOW, James	22	Sumter
BARLOW, Rich.	26	Butts
BARLOW, Thomas	8	Sumter
BARLOW, Tillman	1	Baker
BARLOW, W. W.	37	Sumter
BARLOW, Wade	2	Sumter
BARMORE, Lucy	5	Merriwether
BARNARD, Jane S.	10	Chatham
BARNARD, John B.	125	Liberty
BARNARD, Jonathan	20	Marion
BARNARD, Mary A.	11	Chatham
BARNARD, Solomon S.	28	Liberty
BARNARD, C. E.	9	Chatman
BARNARD, Daniel	7	Tatnall
BARNARD, Jas.	74	Camden
BARNARD, Wm.	1	Camden
BARNES, Benjamin	1	Hancock
BARNES, Benjamin	4	Houston
BARNES, E. S.	28	Hancock
BARNES, Enos	1	Lumpkin
BARNES, Ephraim	6	Hancock
BARNES, Franklin	5	Newton
BARNES, Gideon	13	Pike
BARNES, Gilla	25	Heard
BARNES, James	27	Jones
BARNES, James G.	4	Jones

17

Name	Number	County	Name	Number	County
BARNES, Jethro H.	2	Fayette	BARNETT, Robert	3	Baker
BARNES, John	14	Butts	BARNETT, William	10	DeKalb
BARNES, Jordan	26	Merriwether	BARNETTE, John	32	Heard
BARNES, Joshua	15	Hancock	BARNETTE, Wm.	12	Putnam
BARNES, Lucy	3	Harris	BARNEY, Margaret	19	Richmond
BARNES, Michael	2	Jasper	BARNHAM, Abner	41	Houston
BARNES, Nathan	3	Hancock	BARNHAM, Elijah	21	Houston
BARNES, Oscar	2	Harris	BARNHAM, James	5	Houston
BARNES, Robert C.	10	Jasper	BARNHAM, Mrs. Cely	7	Houston
BARNES, Samuel M.	1	Walker	BARNHAM, Solomon	7	Houston
BARNES, Thomas	29	Merriwether	BARNHAM, William	36	Houston
BARNES, William	1	Twiggs	BARNHART, Howard	4	Hancock
BARNES, William M.	2	Merriwether	BARNHEART, J.	17	Henry
BARNES, William P.	1	Jones	BARNHORT, John	32	Greene
BARNES, A.	2	Coweta	BARNS, J. H.	29	Merriwether
BARNES, B.	19	Crawford	BARNS, James V.	2	Meriwether
BARNES, Bethenia	10	Jones	BARNS, John S.	3	Merriwether
BARNES, Eliza	16	Putnam	BARNS, Jesse	6	Sumter
BARNES, Elizabeth	4	Richmond	BARNSLEY, Godfry	8	Cass
BARNES, H.	14	Decatur	BARNWELL, E. W.	2	Effingham
BARNES, Henry	16	Butts	BARNWELL, Eliza	8	Chatham
BARNES, J.	2	Bibb	BARNWELL, Elizabeth	8	Chatham
BARNES, James	6	Talbot	BARNWELL, James	5	Cobb
BARNES, Jas.	2	Crawford	BARNWELL, John B.	1	Chaham
BARNES, John A.	9	Richmond	BARNWELL, Robert	10	Gordon
BARNES, L. H.	2	Bibb	BARNWELL, Thos. B.	1	Gordon
BARNES, Marick	5	Baker	BARNWELL, William	4	Cobb
BARNES, Nathaniel	5	Putnam	BARNWELL, William	1	Hall
BARNES, Virgil	5	Columbia	BARNWELL, William	1	Hall
BARNES, William	22	Burke	BARON, David	6	Pulaski
BARNES, William	18	Talbot	BARON, Thos. G.	17	Cass
BARNET, J. W.	2	Troup	BARON, Wiley W.	5	Richmond
BARNET, Nathan	5	Butts	BARR, James	1	Jasper
BARNET, Larkin	20	Floyd	BARR, John H.	2	Cobb
BARNET, Saml.	15	Crawford	BARR, John W.	1	Jasper
BARNETT, A. G.	4	Henry	BARR, R. W.	10	Elbert
BARNETT, B. H.	16	Oglethorpe	BARR, James	4	Talbot
BARNETT, Benjamin K.	7	Oglethorpe	BARR, Lewis	1	Stewart
BARNETT, David	11	Oglethorpe	BARR, Thomas	1	Stewart
BARNETT, Frederick	4	Walton	BARRENTON, Elza	4	Thomas
BARNETT, J. H.	1	Murray	BARRET, Thomas	1	Thomas
BARNETT, John D.	14	Oglethorpe	BARRET, Wm.	5	Heard
BARNETT, John L.	3	Jasper	BARRETT, David	8	Gordon
BARNETT, John P.	16	Wilkes	BARRETT, Jacob	190	McIntosh
BARNETT, John W.	5	Muscogee	BARRETT, James	1	Walton
BARNETT, Joseph	1	Oglethorpe	BARRETT, James E.	13	Houston
BARNETT, Miles	5	Gwinnett	BARRETT, Jas. W.	9	Clarke
BARNETT, P. J.	44	Wilkes	BARRETT, Joel	1	Murray
BARNETT, Saml.	13	Wilkes	BARRETT, John	4	Hall
BARNETT, Saml. G.	3	Jackson	BARRETT, Joseph	3	Gordon
BARNETT, T. G.	6	Henry	BARRETT, R. J.	1	Wilkes
BARNETT, William H.	44	Madison	BARRETT, Richard	3	Walton
BARNETT, Wm.	25	Wilkes	BARRETT, Robert T.	9	Wilkes
BARNETT, James	15	Morgan	BARRETT, S. C.	1	Oglethorpe

Name	Number	County	Name	Number	County
BARRETT, W. D.	12	Elbert	BARTHELMESS, John	4	Chatham
BARRETT, William	2	Forsyth	BARTIN, Allen	1	Dooly
BARRETT, William	19	Pike	BARTLET, William M.	9	Campbell
BARRINGER, John	17	Muscogee	BARTLETT ?, Thomas	15	Richmond
BARRINGTON, John	19	Baldwin	BARTLETT, Blake	4	Newton
BARRON, Ann			BARTLETT, George T.	14	Jasper
& Elizabeth	11	Chatham	BARTLETT, James C.	5	Jasper
BARRON, Arlington	24	Jones	BARTLETT, John		
BARRON, B.	22	Elbert	estate of	34	Baker
BARRON, Benjamin	106	Jones	BARTLETT, John E.	8	Houston
BARRON, Henry	4	Butts	BARTLETT, Mary	11	Jasper
BARRON, Henry	3	Jefferson	BARTLETT, Mrs.	8	Muscogee
BARRON, James F.	6	Jones	BARTLETT, Wm. A.	12	Lee
BARRON, James M.	6	Upson	BARTLETT, Alpaus	1	Stewart
BARRON, Ridley	2	Monroe	BARTLETT, Daniel	2	Stewart
BARRON, William	4	Houston	BARTLETT, James	25	Baker
BARRON, William	6	Upson	BARTLETT, Rachel	1	Stewart
BARRON, William E.	7	Jefferson	BARTLETT, Thomas	1	Richmond
BARRON, Wm. estate	55	Burke	BARTLETTE, Walker	1	Merriwether
BARRON, Moses L.	2	Sumter	BARTLEY, James	4	Harris
BARRON, Samuel estate	28	Burke	BARTON, Dr. W.	2	Burke
BARRON, Sarah	28	Burke	BARTON, Elizabeth	12	Early
BARRON, Thomas	12	Talbot	BARTON, German	14	Thomas
BARRON, Thomas	4	Talbot	BARTON, Jane	10	Newton
BARROT, Nineon	5	Upson	BARTON, Jefferson	6	Cherokee
BARROTT, M. L.	5	Greene	BARTON, John	8	Houston
BARROW, Aaron	16	Burke	BARTON, John W.	8	Paulding
BARROW, Barnabas	1	Monroe	BARTON, Sarah	2	Walton
BARROW, David C.	17	Oglethorpe	BARTON, Theodosius	3	Chatham
BARROW, Edward D.	13	Pike	BARTON, W.	5	Henry
BARROW, George S.	1	Pike	BARTON, William G.	2	Merriwether
BARROW, Harmon H.	1	Muscogee	BARTON, Wm. T.	1	Cass
BARROW, Jacob	13	Muscogee	BARTON, William C.	2	Chatham
BARROW, John G.	1	Thomas	BARTON, Wm. H.	1	Randolph
BARROW, Moses	8	Morgan	BARTOW, Francis S.	7	Chatham
BARROW, Philip	10	Carroll	BARTS?, T.	19	Floyd
BARROW, Sterling T.	6	Houston	BARWICK, Nathan	1	Washington
BARROW, Thomas	4	Marion	BASDEN, William G.	3	Muscogee
BARROW, Warren	25	Monroe	BASHLER, J. H.	3	Chatham
BARROW, Wiley	33	Macon	BASHURS, Sarah	2	Putnam
BARROW, Wm. M.	3	Marion	BASKEN, James G.	20	Houston
BARROW, Robert	1	Burke	BASKEN, Robert W.	27	Houston
BARRY, C. M.	3	Chattooga	BASKERVILLE, Robert	4	Newton
BARRY, Patrick	14	Clarke	BASKIN, Jas.	8	Carroll
BARRY, Walton	8	Paulding	BASKIN, William O.	10	Houston
BARRY, William	2	Newton	BASLER, Anthony	2	Chatham
BARRY, John	2	Richmond	BASON, Jacob W.	19	Houston
BARRY, N. M.	1	Chattooga	BASS, ? H.	1	Putnam
BARSHALL, M.	1	Muscogee	BASS, Benj. J.	3	Hancock
BARSTOW, E. B.	54	Chatham	BASS, Cullen	1	Harris
BARTAN, Henry	2	Hall	BASS, Edmond S.	9	Houston
BARTEE, James	7	Marion	BASS, Elizabeth	26	Hancock
BARTEE, Thomas P.	10	Stewart	BASS, Francis M.	5	Newton
BARTEN, Winny	1	Franklin	BASS, G. W.	12	Hancock

Name	Number	County	Name	Number	County
BASS, Ingram	19	Hancock	BATEY, Nat.	56	Columbia
BASS, James	22	Hancock	BATEY, William W.	9	Thomas
BASS, John	9	Newton	BATHRON?, Genett	1	Pike
BASS, John J.	5	Hancock	BATIE, Henrie	3	Houston
BASS, Lewis	19	Troup	BATLER?, John R.	11	Lee
BASS, Mary R.	10	Hancock	BATOR?, Randolph	4	Merriwether
BASS, Milton	15	Hancock	BATTEA, Bryant	4	Houston
BASS, N.	84	Floyd	BATTERSBY, William	3	Chatham
BASS, Nancy	9	Troup	BATTEY, Robt.	7	Floyd
BASS, Obedience	6	Warren	BATTLE, Bethia	14	Hancock
BASS, Persons	10	Chattooga	BATTLE, Calvin	60	Monroe
BASS, Robert L.	33	Muscogee	BATTLE, Caroline M.	16	Troup
BASS, Wm. F.	2	Clarke	BATTLE, Caroline M.	10	Troup
BASS, ;H.	41	Putnam	BATTLE, Cullen R.	1	Marion
BASS, A. C.	2	Talbot	BATTLE, Currren	56	Warren
BASS, P.	1	Chattooga	BATTLE, Henry L.	11	Monroe
BASS, Puritha	1	Putnam	BATTLE, J. B.	39	Hancock
BASS, U.	26	Putnam	BATTLE, James	16	Monroe
BASS, William	27	Putnam	BATTLE, Joel C.	6	Troup
BASSENGER, Jane	5	Chatham	BATTLE, John	9	Monroe
BASSET, Eliza	1	Macon	BATTLE, Joseph J.	41	Marion
BASSET, J. N.	3	Troup	BATTLE, Lazarus W.	48	Troup
BASSET, John	9	Troup	BATTLE, Thomas	73	Monroe
BASSETT, John W.	2	Houston	BATTLE, Warren L.	14	Marion
BASSETT, Stephen	5	Houston	BATTLE, Wm. R.	10	Lee
BASSETT, Eliza	1	Talbot	BATTLE, Oliver L.	61	Taliaferro
BASSETT, Ezekiel	3	Clarke	BATTLE, T. W.	5	Stewart
BASSETT, R.	4	Bibb	BATTLE, Wm. R.	24	Taliaferro
BASSY, William W.	11	Stewart	BATTS, Henry	15	Lee
BASTIN, Charles	9	Columbia	BATTS, Jackson	9	Lee
BASTIN, Mary	12	Columbia	BATTS, John	12	Lee
BASTIN, Nancy	2	Columbia	BATTS, George	41	Washington
BATEMAN, Claburn	3	Houston	BATTS, Sarah	12	Burke
BATEMAN, Jemima	8	Marion	BATTY, ? H.	10	Richmond
BATEMAN,			BATTY, G. M.	10	Floyd
Mrs. Charity	14	Houston	BATTY, Thomas W.	12	Jefferson
BATEMAN, W. B.	2	Lee	BATTY, W. H.	44	Jefferson
BATEMAN, William	42	Early	BATY, Robert	21	Stewart
BATEMAN, William M.	6	Houston	BATY, Thos.	5	Chattooga
BATEMAN, Anthony	6	Richmond	BAUGH, James	2	Muscogee
BATEMAN, C.	8	Crawford	BAUGH, John	1	Newton
BATEMAN, Green W.			BAUGH, Peter	14	Hancock
Agt for TARVER	97	Houston	BAUGH, Peter agent	5	Muscogee
BATEMUN, Seaborn M.	9	Houston	BAUGH, T. J.	2	Hall
BATES, Anthony	1	Harris	BAUGH, William	4	Gwinnett
BATES, Anthony N.	7	Gwinnett	BAUGH, Wm.	20	Putnam
BATES, Horace J.	39	Newton	BAUGHAM, John	2	Coweta
BATES, James M.	44	Chatham	BAUGHAN, J. A.	3	Butts
BATES, John	12	Murray	BAUGHAN, Jas.	3	Butts
BATES, Julius	3	Murray	BAULCOM, James	7	Twiggs
BATES, Wm. T.	1	Fayette	BAUM, J. P.	3	Chatham
BATES, Anderson	27	Talbot	BAXLEY, Jeremiah	1	Fayette
BATES, Mathias	11	Cherokee	BAXLEY, A. H.	6	Screven
BATES, William C.	6	Burke	BAXLEY, Eliza	1	Richmond

Name	Number	County	Name	Number	County
BAXLY, Aaron	2	Walton	BEALL, Elias	9	Talbot
BAXTER, Eli H.	71	Hancock	BEALL, Erasmus	86	Stewart
BAXTER, Joseph W.	1	Gwinnett	BEALL, James E.	1	Troup
BAXTER, Mary	11	Clarke	BEALL, James M.	20	Troup
BAXTER, N. N.	4	Murray	BEALL, Jesse N.	20	Warren
BAXTER, R.	3	Henry	BEALL, Jeremiah	41	Baker
BAXTER, Reuben	1	Burke	BEALL, Jeremiah	6	Baldwin
BAXTER, Andrew	5	Cass	BEALL, Littleberry	11	Richmond
BAXTER, Eliza	15	Carroll	BEALL, Mary C.	9	Upson
BAXTER, Maary	1	Burke	BEALL, Mary H.	13	Wilkes
BAXTER, Nathaniel	4	Cass	BEALL, Nancy	14	Troup
BAXTER, Samuel	8	Burke	BEALL, O.P.	3	Randolph
BAXTER, William	5	Talbot	BEALL, Robert A.	11	Warren
BAXTER, William L.	4	Burke	BEALL, Saml.	9	Wilkinson
BAYARD, Nicholas	14	Cobb	BEALL, Saml.	5	Wilkinson
BAYE, Mishae ?	13	Walton	BEALL, Samuel	2	Upson
BAYLEY, William	5	Floyd	BEALL, Samuel	32	Warren
BAYNE, John	3	Baldwin	BEALL, Sarah	10	Warren
BAYNES, Elbert	32	Jasper	BEALL, T.R.	3	Wilkinson
BAYNES, John	20	Jasper	BEALL, Thomas, Agt.	4	Upson
BAYNES, Judith	6	Jasper	BEALL, Thomas G.	9	Talbot
BAYS, Nathaniel	2	Troup	BEALL, Thomas N.	29	Talbot
BAZEMORE,			BEALL, William A.	4	Richmond
Madison T.	9	Jones	BEALL, William H.	6	Warren
BAZEMORE, T. J.	8	Bibb	BEALL, Wm. O.	6	Wilkinson
BAZEMORE, Wash	2	Crawford	BEALL, William P.	31	Richmond
BAZMORE, James A.	2	Screven	BEALL, Wm.	3	Carroll
BEACH, William	3	Muscogee	BEALLE, Thomas E.	57	Columbia
BEACHAM, Lewis	7	Laurens	BEALLE, Thomas W. E.	5	Chatham
BEADDLES, Jos.	32	Coweta	BEALLE, William T.	16	Dooly
BEADDLES, Wm.	21	Coweta	BEALLS, Ann	1	Chatham
BEAL, Jeremiah	12	Harris	BEALS?, O. B.	3	Effingham
BEAL, N. H.	40	Houston	BEAM, Sol	1	Walton
BEAL, Salina	1	Jefferson	BEAMEN, J. C.	6	Houston
BEAL, Alexander R.	14	Columbia	BEAN, Adison	1	Monroe
BEAL, James L.	14	Twiggs	BEAN, A.	2	Coweta
BEAL, N. W.	6	Bibb	BEAN, Edmond C.	1	Stewart
BEALE, G. F.	3	Jefferson	BEARD, Johnathan	5	Hall
BEALE, Charles T.	4	Burke	BEARD, R. E.	1	Franklin
BEALE, J. D.	5	Crawford	BEARDEN, Edward	3	Fayette
BEALE, T. E. W.	50	Columbia	BEARDEN, Elizabeth	1	Fayette
BEALE, Thomas C.	7	Richmond	BEARDEN, Francis	1	Fayette
BEALE, William P.	30	Burke	BEARDEN, Milton P. G.	8	Clarke
BEALL, Augustus	8	Warren	BEARDEN, P. B.	8	Clarke
BEALL, C. C.	1	Wilkinson	BEARDEN, Richard	2	Lumpkin
BEALL, Daniel	17	Upson	BEARDEN, Wm.	3	Marion
BEALL, Elias	32	Harris	BEARDIN, Erasmus	10	Floyd
BEALL, Elias	15	Walton	BEARDIN, W. W.	3	Fayette
BEALL, Erastus	25	Warren	BEARDIN, David H.	1	Putnam
BEALL, Henry H.	1	Cobb	BEARDLING, Richd.	4	Carroll
BEALL, James S.	47	Dooly	BEARS, Betsy,	2	Chatham
BEALL, Jeptha	20	Morgan	BEARTH ?, Richard P.	2	Walton
BEALL, Patrick H.	25	Montgomery	BEASLELY, Robt.	5	Bibb
BEALL, Doughty	2	Richmond	BEASLEY, Abraham	1	Jefferson

Name	Number	County	Name	Number	County
BEASLEY, Abram	8	Jefferson	BECK, James W.	4	Warren
BEASLEY, Buckner	8	Muscogee	BECK, John W.	5	Murray
BEASLEY, Hiram	4	Clarke	BECK, Jourdan	2	Muscogee
BEASLEY, James	1	Chattooga	BECK, Massineah	8	Henry
BEASLEY, James	1	Emanual	BECK, Thomas P.	4	Warren
BEASLEY, James	2	Jefferson	BECK, W.	15	Henry
BEASLEY, James	5	Thomas	BECK, William A.	19	Murray
BEASLEY, Jarrell	32	Troup	BECK, William H.	11	Troup
BEASLEY, Jas.	6	Henry	BECK, Samuel	8	Rabun
BEASLEY, John	3	Gwinnett	BECKHAM, Absolam P.	1	Pike
BEASLEY, John J.	10	Jones	BECKHAM, Andrew G.	4	Pike
BEASLEY, Mary	2	Jones	BECKHAM, James	41	Pike
BEASLEY, Moms	2	Cherokee	BECKHAM, James D.	5	Pike
BEASLEY, Mrs. Susan	11	Liberty	BECKHAM, James M.	6	Pike
BEASLEY, R.	3	Wilkes	BECKHAM, Joseph C.	5	Pike
BEASLEY, Stephen W.	24	Troup	BECKHAM, Labon	13	Pike
BEASLEY, William A.	1	Fayette	BECKHAM, Solomon G.	8	Pike
BEASLEY, Wm. A.	12	Greene	BECKHAM, William C.	22	Pike
BEASLEY, William P.	31	Troup	BECKLER, Peter	1	Muscogee
BEASLEY, Charles	1	Bibb	BECKS, J. A.	4	Pike
BEASLEY, David	11	Bullock	BECKWITH, Jeremiah	3	Merriwether
BEASLEY, Enoch	2	Bullock	BECKWITH, T.	1	Randolph
BEASLEY, John	1	Richmond	BECKWORTH, Hansell	3	Sumter
BEASLEY, Robert	7	Bibb	BEDDELL, Charles	15	Harris
BEASLEY, Robert	3	Bibb	BEDDINGFIELD, Willis	8	Macon
BEASLEY, William	9	Baker	BEDDINGFIELD, Allen	1	Bibb
BEASLY, Thos. H.	3	Effingham	BEDDINGFIELD, Gick?	2	Twiggs
BEASLY, Berry W.	1	Stewart	BEDDINGFIELD, L.	3	Bibb
BEASLY, Martha	3	Bullock	BEDELL, Charles E.	7	Talbot
BEASON, J. L.	6	Putnam	BEDELL, Martha	8	Talbot
BEASON, Peggy A.	14	Walker	BEDENBAUGH, L.	1	Coweta
BEATTEE, Wm. J.	2	Lowndes	BEDFORD, Ann	7	Lumpkin
BEAUCHAMP, Mrs. L.	9	Meriwether	BEDFORD, George	1	Lumpkin
BEAUCHAMP, William	1	Meriwether	BEDGOOD, John	5	Washington
BEAUCHAMP, John	1	Butts	BEDGOOD, Mary	1	Burke
BEAUFORD, S.	27	Bibb	BEDINGFIELD,		
BEAVDERS, Paartha	8	Clarke	Hampton	2	Twiggs
BEAVERS, John	1	Pike	BEDINGFIELD, Hardy	2	Twiggs
BEAVERS, John M.	3	Jasper	BEDINGFIELD, Mrs.	1	Stewart
BEAVERS, C. B.	11	Chattooga	BEDLE ?, James	2	Walton
BEAVERS, J. F.	17	Chattooga	BEECHAM, John	2	Lee
BEAVERS, Robert O.	28	Campbell	BEELAND, James M.	5	Jasper
BEAVERS, Ruben C.	10	Campbell	BEELAND, Thomas	2	Jones
BEAVERS, Sarah	5	Campbell	BEFORE, Alen	1	Pike
BEAVERS, Wm. J.	22	Campbell	BEGGARLY,		
BEAVIS, J.	4	Henry	Francis W.	5	Merriwether
BEATY, Hugh	9	Walton	BEHU, George W.	2	Thomas
BEATY, Hugh Gar.	2	Walton	BELAH, Samuel	2	Butts
BEAZLEY, H. J.	1	Elbert	BELAMY, A.	4	Pike
BECHLOR, George	2	Lumpkin	BELCHER, Arch	23	Newton
BECK, Allen B.	35	Twiggs	BELCHER, G. W.	1	Jefferson
BECK, Alexander	15	Hancock	BELCHER, Mary	5	Jasper
BECK, Charles	1	Muscogee	BELCHER, Mrs.	4	Early
BECK, Elias	3	Henry	BELCHER, Obadiah R.	12	Jasper

Name	Number	County	Name	Number	County
BELCHER, Adam	6	Bulloch	BELL, Railey	19	Jones
BELCHER, D.	7	Dade	BELL, Richard	3	Hall
BELCHER, Eliza	7	Randolph	BELL, Richard	9	Oglethrope
BELCHER, Sarah	16	Screven	BELL, Roger	1	Walton
BELINGER, Jno. N.	12	DeKalb	BELL, Sanford L.	1	Murray
BELK, Amadus	1	Marion	BELL, Sarah	1	Merriwether
BELK, Denson	9	Marion	BELL, Simeon	15	Burke
BELK, Joseph	25	Marion	BELL, Thomas	33	Elbert
BELK, Wm. A.	8	Marion	BELL, Thos.	4	Oglethorpe
BELL, Allen S.	12	Walton	BELL, Thos. A.	10	Oglethorpe
BELL, Benajah	3	Wilkes	BELL, W. H.	1	Forsyth
BELL, Benjamin	5	Washington	BELL, W. J.	7	Oglethorpe
BELL ? , Joseph S.	4	Richmond	BELL, William	3	Monroe
BELL, Josiah B.	5	Pike	BELL, William M.	10	Cherokee
BELL, A. B.	1	Elbert	BELL, William M.	2	Hall
BELL, A. S.	3	Forsyth	BELL, William O.	3	Cherokee
BELL, A. S.	1	Jefferson	BELL, Wm.	7	Jackson
BELL, Ann	8	Oglethorpe	BELL, A.	27	Putnam
BELL, Archibald S.	1	Jasper	BELL, A. J.	13	Dade
BELL, C. C.	33	Wilkinson	BELL, Arthur	15	Burke
BELL, David	20	Elbert	BELL, Benjamin	6	Burke
BELL, David	2	Emanual	BELL, C. A.	3	Stewart
BELL, E.	14	Elbert	BELL, Catherine	2	Chatham
BELL, Elizabeth	13	Walton	BELL, Charles H.	2	Chatham
BELL, Green	4	Oglethorpe	BELL, David	15	Chatham
BELL, Henry S.	3	Chatham	BELL, Elias	3	Stewart
BELL, Hiram	3	Burke	BELL, Fredick	20	Stewart
BELL, J.	3	Elbert	BELL, Green	3	Burke
BELL, J. C.	41	Merriwether	BELL, Henry D.	12	Richmond
BELL, Jackson	3	Jackson	BELL, Hugh	6	Early
BELL, James	14	Hancock	BELL, J. H.	3	Stewart
BELL, James H.	8	Cherokee	BELL, James	8	Burke
BELL, James H.	6	Cherokee	BELL, Jas.	14	Coweta
BELL, James M.	1	Cobb	BELL, John G.	15	Columbia
BELL, James M.	1	Hall	BELL, John T.	6	Coweta
BELL, John	4	Wilkes	BELL, Joseph	42	Tatnall
BELL, John A.	13	Oglethorpe	BELL, Joseph D.	11	Burke
BELL, John H.	1	Walton	BELL, Patsy	10	Columbia
BELL, John L.	2	Hall	BELL, S.	7	Decatur
BELL, John S.	1	Clarke	BELL, Sampson	23	Stewart
BELL, John S.	3	Murray	BELL, Samuel P.	3	Chatham
BELL, Jonathan	23	Oglethorpe	BELL, Sarah L.	9	Campbell
BELL, Jonathan	1	Oglethorpe	BELL, Savannah	7	Richmond
BELL, Joseph	35	Oglethorpe	BELL, Tom	11	Columbia
BELL, Joseph S.	1	Forsyth	BELL, Wm.	2	Decatur
BELL, M.	10	Elbert	BELL, Wm.	5	Taliaferro
BELL, Malinder	20	Monroe	BELL, Wm. L.	4	Coweta
BELL, Martha F.	6	Warren	BELLAH, Mary	10	Newton
BELL, Mary	4	Cherokee	BELLAH, Thomas	2	Newton
BELL, Mrs. E. E.	43	Hancock	BELLAK, Samuel	2	Newton
BELL, Nareysa	9	Hall	BELLAMY, Lucy	7	Franklin
BELL, Noble J.	1	McIntosh	BELLAMY, Pleasant	1	Franklin
BELL, R. D. S.	15	Muscogee	BELLAMY, William	26	Franklin
BELL, R. D. S.	7	Muscogee	BELLAR, James	6	Meriwether

23

Name	Number	County	Name	Number	County
BELLERY ?, J. R.	9	Wilkinson	BENNETT, Richard	2	Monroe
BELLINGER, John F.	8	DeKalb	BENNETT, Richard	1	Troup
BELLUNE, James C.	5	Glynn	BENNETT, Sallie	5	Clinch
BELLWARE?, Joseph	1	Taliaferro	BENNETT, Thomas	4	Jackson
BELSHER, Abraham	10	Burke	BENNETT, Thos.	2	Butts
BELSHUR, Mourning	10	Burke	BENNETT, William	3	Franklin
BELT, Dr. R. B.	11	Burke	BENNETT, William B.	1	Walton
BELT, Lloyd C.	19	Columbia	BENNETT, William H.	85	McIntosh
BELVIN?, James W.	44	Houston	BENNETT, Wm.	16	Lincoln
BELYEW, Berry	8	Talbot	BENNETT, Alexander	4	Chatham
BEMAN, C. P.	39	Hancock	BENNETT, William	21	Burke
BEMAN, David	13	Meriwether	BENNING, Henry L.	60	Muscogee
BEMAN, H. S.	2	Hancock	BENNING, Malinda	13	Harris
BEMAN, Susan	13	Warren	BENNING,		
BEMBRY, Miles	9	Pulaski	Miss Augusta	23	Harris
BEMBRY?, Marina	33	Pulaski	BENNING, Richd.	22	Harris
BENCE, M. J.	2	Henry	BENNING, Richd. E.	6	Harris
BENDER, W. J.	5	Laurens	BENNING, Thomas C.	5	Chatham
BENEFIELD, Cader	2	Muscogee	BENNING, Tom	12	Columbia
BENEFIELD, Henry	1	Heard	BENNINGFILD, Hardy	4	Walton
BENEFIELD, John	13	Talbot	BENNS, Charles	1	Cobb
BENEFIELD ?,			BENOIST, James	1	Chatham
Solomon	2	Walton	BENOIST, John	1	Chatham
BENETT, James A.	2	Walton	BENSON, Franklin		
BENFORD, Betsy A.	10	Morgan	Agt for WESTBROOK	40	Houston
BENFORD, Joseph	12	Jasper	BENSON, Jas.	1	Wilkes
BENINGFIELD,			BENSON, Jas. C.	2	Carroll
Mrs. Ednay	12	Stewart	BENSON, John	4	Lincoln
BENNEFIELD, Hardy	2	Gwinnett	BENSON, Joseph	1	Troup
BENNEFIELD, Bradford	1	Bibb	BENSON, Joseph	3	Wilkes
BENNEFIELD, T. L.	3	Bibb	BENSON, Perrin	4	Clarke
BENNET, Nevel	6	Hall	BENSON, Thos.	20	Meriwether
BENNET, Sarah	1	Pulaski	BENSON, Elizabeth	2	Butts
BENNET, Sarah	4	Thomas	BENSON, J. W.	1	Bibb
BENNET, B. J.	4	Butts	BENSON, Levi	9	Carroll
BENNET, Lewis	1	Baker	BENSON, R. A.	7	Bibb
BENNET, L. H.	2	Troup	BENSON, William	3	Columbia
BENNETT, Abby A.	1	Chatham	BENSON, Wm.	20	Wilkes
BENNETT, Andrew F.	3	Chatham	BENTLEY, John	29	Lincoln
BENNETT, Aron	4	Emanual	BENTLEY, B. B.	33	Lincoln
BENNETT, Asa	3	Jackson	BENTLEY, W. P.	3	Lincoln
BENNETT, Benjamin	7	Emanual	BENTLEY, D.	2	Crawford
BENNETT, Cornelius B.	9	Fayette	BENTLEY, Moses	5	Troup
BENNETT, E.	1	Henry	BENTLEY, Saml.	3	Crawford
BENNETT, Eli	1	Newton	BENTLY, D. W.	1	Henry
BENNETT, J. P.	1	Lee	BENTLY, J. T.	15	Henry
BENNETT, James	2	Franklin	BENTLY, M. M.	2	Henry
BENNETT, Jane	2	Cass	BENTLY, Margaret	7	Newton
BENNETT, John	11	Emanual	BENTON, Abba	16	Jasper
BENNETT, Mary	3	Upson	BENTON, Eujenius	17	Harris
BENNETT, Mary	1	Walton	BENTON, George	5	Monroe
BENNETT, Nancy	6	Newton	BENTON, Henry	5	Monroe
BENNETT, Peter	1	Forsyth	BENTON, James	14	Jasper
BENNETT, Reuben	17	Greene	BENTON, John	25	Jasper

Name	Number	County	Name	Number	County
BENTON, John	4	Monroe	BERRY, William	1	Newton
BENTON, John	3	Pike	BERRY, A. J.	1	Randolph
BENTON, Loyd	4	Clarke	BERRY, Andrew J.	72	Coweta
BENTON, Mordica	6	Monroe	BERRY, Ben	33	Columbia
BENTON, Nelson M.	14	Cobb	BERRY, David	10	Butts
BENTON, Sarah	7	Monroe	BERRY, Samuel	2	Randolph
BENTON, William	6	Monroe	BERRYHILL, Alexander	11	Jefferson
BENTON, Amos	8	Bibb	BERRYHILL, John	4	Floyd
BENTON, Frances	1	Richmond	BERRYHILL,		
BENTON, Francis	2	Stewart	William R.	5	Floyd
BENTON, George	7	Stewart	BERRYMAN, Charles T.	3	Madison
BENTON, George W.	1	Chatham	BERRYMAN, Robert W.	2	Madison
BENTON, Hexy Ann	1	Richmond	BERRYMAN, Wilson P.	3	Madison
BENTON, J.	1	Decatur	BERSON, Joseph	1	Campbell
BENTON, Jacob	2	Coweta	BERTRAM, A. D.	3	Carroll
BENTON, Nelson	44	Columbia	BESSANT, Abram	7	Camden
BERANS, Thos. J.	2	Columbia	BESSANT, John	5	Camden
BERG, Seigmund	1	Chatham	BESSANT, Mary J.	9	Camden
BERGES, P. F.	5	Lincoln	BESSENT, P. G.	6	Newton
BERK, James G.	14	Harris	BEST, George	3	Effingham
BERK, Patrick	1	Taliaferro	BEST, John	4	Early
BERK, Wm.	3	Taliaferro	BEST, L. H.	4	Screven
BERLIN, Campbell	24	Harris	BESTON ?, Moses	16	Walton
BERNARD, Ed	9	Muscogee	BETHA, Jesse	137	Early
BERNARDY, M.	18	Camden	BETHEA, Philip P.	2	Hancock
BERNER, William	1	Murray	BETHEA, William P.	7	Merriwether
BERNSIDE, William	19	Bullock	BETHEL, Benjamin	9	Upson
BERRIAN, J. M.	26	Floyd	BETHEL, Thomas H.	14	Upson
BERRIE, Elizabeth	54	Glynn	BETHUNE, Elizabeth	5	Pike
BERRIE, William A.	13	Glynn	BETHUNE, James M.	9	Muscogee
BERRIE, C. A.	63	Camden	BETHUNE, Benjamin	71	Baldwin
BERRIE, R. J.	23	Camden	BETHUNE, John G.	5	Stewart
BERRIEN, John M.	142	Chatham	BETHUNE, Marion	2	Talbot
BERRIEN, Thos.	22	Cass	BETTERTON, Levi	8	DeKalb
BERRY, Andrew L.	11	Walker	BETTON, S. D.	3	Randolph
BERRY, Edmund	9	Paulding	BETTS, F. G.	1	Henry
BERRY, A. M.	28	Hancock	BETTS, Jonathan M.	4	Walton
BERRY, A. M.	28	Hancock	BETTS, W. O.	5	Henry
BERRY, Benj.	1	Muscogee	BETTS, Wm.	4	DeKalb
BERRY, C. M.	15	Newton	BEVEL, Claborn	21	Effingham
BERRY, Elias	4	Murray	BEVEL, Stephen	9	Effingham
BERRY, James	14	Floyd	BEVEL, William D.	1	Monroe
BERRY, James	4	Newton	BEVERAGE, John L.	6	Baker
BERRY, James E.	25	Hancock	BEVERLY, James	3	Talbot
BERRY, Jesse	3	Harris	BEVERLY, Jas. C.	1	Carroll
BERRY, John B.	27	Effingham	BEVERLY, John F.	1	Baker
BERRY, John G.	1	Muscogee	BEVERLY, William M.	8	Dooly
BERRY, John J.	23	Hancock	BEVILL, Granville	28	Lowndes
BERRY, John T.	18	Hancock	BEVILL, Jas. F.	16	Lowndes
BERRY, Mary	4	Warren	BEVILL, John W.	1	Muscogee
BERRY, Robert	1	Jones	BEXLEY, Jas.	9	Coweta
BERRY, Ruben O.	2	McIntosh	BICKERS, John	14	Greene
BERRY, Sarah	1	Jones	BICKLY, Simeon	2	Talbot
BERRY, W.	6	Henry	BICKLY, Simeon	1	Talbot

Name	Number	County	Name	Number	County
BICKLY, Solomon	2	Talbot	BIRCH, Pendleton	1	Talbot
BIDDENBACK, Joshua	6	Effingham	BIRD, Adam	3	Emanual
BIDFORD, Jonas M.	2	Cherokee	BIRD, Bary	3	Morgan
BIGBY, Benj. M.	1	Randolph	BIRD, Braxton	40	Monroe
BIGBY, J. W.	7	Coweta	BIRD, David L.	4	Warren
BIGBY, John	2	Coweta	BIRD, D. H.	5	Cherokee
BIGBY, John	26	Coweta	BIRD, Edward	15	Effingham
BIGGERS, David	2	Oglethorpe	BIRD, Edward	10	Effingham
BIGGERS, Elizabeth	12	Muscogee	BIRD, George	2	Jones
BIGGERS, James J. W.	2	Muscogee	BIRD, Gustavis H.	15	Madison
BIGGERS, Lorenzo M.	15	Muscogee	BIRD, James	1	Franklin
BIGGERS, Marion	11	Muscogee	BIRD, James L.	1	Madison
BIGGERS, Mrs.	7	Clarke	BIRD, James R.	21	Liberty
BIGGERS, P. Jefferson	27	Muscogee	BIRD, John	6	Jones
BIGGERS, William	44	Greene	BIRD, John	26	Troup
BIGGERS, Stephen	1	DeKalb	BIRD, John C.	11	Warren
BIGGS, Joseph E.	7	Talbot	BIRD, John G.	12	Cherokee
BIGGS, Willis J.	6	Clarke	BIRD, Joseph	26	Troup
BIGHAM, James A.	7	Jefferson	BIRD, Juda	4	Cherokee
BIGHAM, John V.	1	Stewart	BIRD, Margreet	5	Warren
BIGNON, John	6	Columbia	BIRD, Mary	2	Morgan
BILBO, John	46	Chatham	BIRD, Mrs. Sarah	18	Liberty
BILBO, Wm. G.	2	Coweta	BIRD, P. M.	10	Hall
BILLIEU, D. L.	4	Hall	BIRD, Phebe	57	Morgan
BILLING, Sam A.	13	Muscogee	BIRD, Philemon	7	Walker
BILLINGSLEA, J. F.	15	Greene	BIRD, Richard A.	5	McIntosh
BILLINGSLEA,			BIRD, Robert	4	Hancock
James A.	72	Jones	BIRD, Robert	1	Walton
BILLINGSLIE, John	40	Harris	BIRD, Tamlin J.	7	Heard
BILLINGSLIE, Winson	34	Harris	BIRD, Thomas	14	Gordon
BILLINGSLY, Alexander	9	Taliaferro	BIRD, Thomas J.	5	Emanaul
BILLINGSLLEY, James	4	Rabun	BIRD, William	1	Emanual
BILLINGSLY, Frances	62	Taliaferro	BIRD, William	8	Hall
BILLINGSLY,			BIRD, Wm.	7	Troup
James W.	13	Taliaferro	BIRD, Wilson	23	Hancock
BILLUPS, J. H.	6	Oglethorpe	BIRD, Wilson J.	9	Madison
BILLUPS, John	94	Clarke	BIRD, Andrew	1	Bullock
BILLUPS, Mrs. E. A.	2	Muscogee	BIRD, Benton	2	Sumter
BILLUPS, Edward S.	3	Clarke	BIRD, Buford	21	Taliaferro
BINFORD, John	1	Twiggs	BIRD, Cyrus	9	Bryan
BING, Wm.	2	Bibb	BIRD, Edy	5	Bullock
BINGHAM, Elijah	5	Coweta	BIRD, Eleanor	22	Bryan
BINION, John R.	7	Hancock	BIRD, Eliza	20	DeKalb
BINION, Sidney	11	Hancock	BIRD, Eliza M.	3	Chatham
BINKEL, Thompson	6	Carroll	BIRD, George L.	16	Taliaferro
BINNINGTON, Edward	3	Thomas	BIRD, J. J.	7	Decatur
BINNS, David	10	Harris	BIRD, J. Jun	12	Decatur
BINNS, B.	19	Talbot	BIRD, J. Sen.	15	Decatur
BINNS, C.	22	Wilkes	BIRD, Jackson	7	Bryan
BINNS, Sarah	13	Wilkes	BIRD, Jackson	1	Bullock
BINS, Christopher	3	Talbot	BIRD, John	43	DeKalb
BINS, John	1	Talbot	BIRD, John L.	9	Taliaferro
BINT, John T.	1	Emanual	BIRD, Parker	5	Bullock
BIRCH, Robt. S.	19	Coweta	BIRDINE, Samuel	1	Cobb

Name	Number	County	Name	Number	County
BIRDSONG, Edw.	2	Muscogee	BIVINS, W.	4	Bibb
BIRDSONG, Edwin F.	9	Warren	BIVINS, William	1	Chatham
BIRDSONG, G. W.	27	Oglethorpe	BIVINS?, Sidney	3	Habersham
BIRDSONG,			BLACK, A. H.	5	Jackson
George L. D.	20	Paulding	BLACK, C. B.	18	Harris
BIRDSONG, J. L.	19	Hancock	BLACK, C. D.	4	Chattooga
BIRDSONG, J. W.	2	Troup	BLACK, Edward	38	Meriwether
BIRDSONG, Jas.	9	Troup	BLACK, J. A.	21	Murray
BIRDSONG, Rebecca	14	Hancock	BLACK, J. R.	1	Forsyth
BIRDSONG, Robert	16	Oglethorpe	BLACK, J. S.	2	Henry
BIRDSONG, Robert B.	32	Early	BLACK, J. W.	13	Elbert
BIRDSONG, Charles	6	Talbot	BLACK, James H.	12	Macon
BIRE, Elisha	2	Cobb	BLACK, John W.	4	Troup
BIRGE, Dr. L. N. Jr.	1	Gwinnett	BLACK, Joseph	2	Forsyth
BIRT, Henry	1	Chatham	BLACK, Joseph	1	Pike
BISHOFF, John J.	1	Clarke	BLACK, Joseph F.	6	Cobb
BISHOP, Bryce H.	19	Clarke	BLACK, Joshua	1	Jefferson
BISHOP, Cary	1	Houston	BLACK, Lawson	1	Walker
BISHOP, Henry	6	Clarke	BLACK, Mary A.	1	Oglethorpe
BISHOP, John	1	Monroe	BLACK, Nathaniel	17	Harris
BISHOP, John A.	2	Lee	BLACK, Nathaniel	5	Harris
BISHOP, Mathew	2	Houston	BLACK, Robt. C.	13	Marion
BISHOP, Nancy J.	20	Pulaski	BLACK, Thomas	12	Elbert
BISHOP, P. J.	5	Henry	BLACK, Thomas	2	Upson
BISHOP, Thomas	1	Clarke	BLACK, W. S.	5	Meriwether
BISHOP, William N.	3	Murray	BLACK, Wm. A.	52	Marion
BISHOP, Wilson	29	Greene	BLACK, Wm. L.	1	Marion
BISHOP, Dempsey	5	Cass	BLACK, A. G.	15	Screven
BISHOP, Graham	1	Randolph	BLACK, Cyrus	11	Coweta
BISHOP, J. H.	3	Bibb	BLACK, George S.	29	Cass
BISHOP, James B.	6	Richmond	BLACK, James	1	Campbell
BISHOP, Reuben	1	DeKalb	BLACK, Sheming?	23	Putnam
BISHOP, Sophia	3	Richmond	BLACK, Thomas	3	Campbell
BIVEN, David	2	Houston	BLACK, William A.	3	Chatham
BIVENS, W. L.	13	Butts	BLACKBORN, John	18	Lincoln
BIVIN, George	29	Thomas	BLACKBUM, B. R.	2	Harris
BIVIN, Mary	1	Muscogee	BLACKBURN, Augustus	5	Carroll
BIVINS, Franklin N.	10	Houston	BLACKBURN, Drayton	27	Early
BIVINS, George W.	31	Houston	BLACKBURN, Henry	1	Harris
BIVINS, James	6	Monroe	BLACKBURN, Jno. L.	63	Harris
BIVINS, John T.	10	Jones	BLACKBURN, Jno. L.	10	Harris
BIVINS, Joseph W.	2	Chatham	BLACKBURN, Lewis	25	Cherokee
BIVINS, Martin L.	27	Marion	BLACKBURN, Jas. r.	5	Screven
BIVINS, Shadrach	3	Marion	BLACKBURN, Stephen	2	Screven
BIVINS, Stephen	36	Jones	BLACKHAM, March?	1	Richmond
BIVINS, Thomas	35	Marion	BLACKMAN, A. O.	4	Muscogee
BIVINS, Wm.	9	Marion	BLACKMAN, Charles	1	Macon
BIVINS, Appleton	14	Baldwin	BLACKMAN,		
BIVINS, Daniel	5	Henry	Col. James	17	Gwinnett
BIVINS, Elbert	7	Cass	BLACKMAN, Elijah	4	Harris
BIVINS, James	73	Sumter	BLACKMAN, Ellison	2	Harris
BIVINS, R.	8	Bibb	BLACKMAN, Hollis	12	Harris
BIVINS, Rowland	34	Bibb	BLACKMAN, James	42	Harris
BIVINS, Saml.	2	Carroll	BLACKMAN, James J.	8	Harris

Name	Number	County
BLACKMAN,		
William R	12	Harris
BLACKMAN, Wm.	1	Macon
BLACKMAN, James	5	DeKalb
BLACKMAN, John	9	DeKalb
BLACKMAN?, Martha	3	Harris
BLACKMON, Waitmon	6	Monroe
BLACKMON, William	6	Paulding
BLACKMON, Thomas	3	Talbot
BLACKSHAW?,		
E. H. & J. J.	31	Pulaski
BLACKSHEAR, E. F.	38	Laurens
BLACKSHEAR, E. H.	39	Laurens
BLACKSHEAR, Ed. J.	37	Laurens
BLACKSHEAR,		
Emily G.	55	Thomas
BLACKSHEAR,		
Harriet B.	113	Thomas
BLACKSHEAR, J. J. F.	23	Laurens
BLACKSHEAR, Josiah	3	Twiggs
BLACKSHEAR, Mrs. Y.	54	Laurens
BLACKSHEAR,		
Thomas E.	81	Thomas
BLACKSHER, Jno.	6	Randolph
BLACKSTOCK,		
Daniel K.	3	Pike
BLACKSTOCK, R. W.	3	Forsyth
BLACKSTOCK, Wm.	5	Forsyth
BLACKSTON, Wade	2	Columbia
BLACKSTONE, James	3	Richmond
BLACKWELL, ?	3	Walton
BLACKWELL, Ambrose	5	Fayette
BLACKWELL, E.	19	Elbert
BLACKWELL, J. W.	36	Elbert
BLACKWELL, James B.	6	Cobb
BLACKWELL, Jeddiah	16	Lumpkin
BLACKWELL, Jerroyal	5	Lumpkin
BLACKWELL, Jesse	1	Hall
BLACKWELL, Joseph	80	Elbert
BLACKWELL, Josiah	1	Hall
BLACKWELL, R.	13	Elbert
BLACKWELL, Rebessa	4	Walker
BLACKWELL, S. D.	15	Elbert
BLACKWELL, Samuel	21	Jasper
BLACKWELL, Thomas	2	Walker
BLACKWELL, A. K.	8	Murray
BLAIN, James T.	5	Greene
BLAIR, Alison T.	1	Murray
BLAIR, Joseph	1	Campbell
BLAIR, Francis	4	Chatham
BLAKE, Allen	21	Hall
BLAKE, Amy	7	Effingham
BLAKE, H. W.	7	Hall
BLAKE, Isabella	4	Newton

Name	Number	County
BLAKE, Moses	4	Monroe
BLAKE, Mrs. Hannah	6	Liberty
BLAKE, Ellenor	6	Bibb
BLAKE, G. J.	7	Bibb
BLAKE, James	17	DeKalb
BLAKELY, D. E.	4	Clarke
BLAKELY, Robert	4	Monroe
BLAKELY, Saml.	14	Clarke
BLAKEY, B. A.	6	Wilkes
BLAKEY, J.	30	Randolph
BLAKEY, John	13	Stewart
BLAKEY, Judith	10	Wilkes
BLALOCK, Cade J.	11	Lowndes
BLALOCK, Ida	37	Upson
BLALOCK, J. L.	7	Merriwether
BLALOCK, John S.	14	Meriwether
BLALOCK, Reuben	7	Upson
BLALOCK, Sarah	3	Gordon
BLALOCK, Thomas	10	Merriwether
BLALOCK, Zadoc	3	Fayette
BLALOCK, R.	1	Crawford
BLALOCK, Thos.	2	Columbia
BLALOCK, Wm.	6	Cass
BLANCE, John C.	1	Chatham
BLANCE, Joseph G.	8	Paulding
BLANCHARD, (?)	22	Columbia
BLANCHARD,		
Billington S.	11	Warren
BLANCHARD, Thomas	19	Harris
BLANCHARD, Ben	26	Columbia
BLANCHARD, James	9	Columbia
BLANCHARD, Jefferson	19	Columbia
BLAND, Agnes	4	Washington
BLAND, Henry	6	Washington
BLAND, John	4	Washington
BLAND, Micajah	12	Washington
BLAND, Simeon	9	Washington
BLANDENBUG, Lewis	7	Meriwether
BLANDENBURG, A.	17	Merriwether
BLANDFORD, Frances	30	Jones
BLANE, C.	5	Muscogee
BLANKENSHIP, Felix	3	Muscogee
BLANTON, A. G.	1	Harris
BLANTON, Benjamin	34	Pike
BLANTON, Jno. J.	4	Forsyth
BLANTON, Wyatt	1	Harris
BLANTON, William	6	Talbot
BLANTON?,William M.	20	Pike
BLASENGAME, J. G.	18	Crawford
BLASENGAME, John	27	Walton
BLAYLOCK, David	1	Jefferson
BLEAKLLY, Arthur	1	Richmond
BLEATWRIGHT, Wm.	2	Greene
BLEDSO, L.	1	Randolph

Name	Number	County
BLEDSOE, J. H.	4	Henry
BLEDSOE, John N.	2	Hancock
BLEDSOE, Miller	1	Oglethorpe
BLEDSOE, A. W.	2	Coweta
BLEDSOE, B.	6	Carroll
BLEDSOE, Caleb	1	Butts
BLEDSOE, J. M.	20	Butts
BLEDSOE, John	2	Coweta
BLEDSOE, L. M.	14	Chattooga
BLEDSOE, Robert	67	Putnam
BLEDSOW, Robt.	52	Putnam
BLEDSUER, John	12	Newton
BLEW, John	4	Houston
BLEWET(?), (?)	6	Decatur
BLISS, Mary M.	3	Chatham
BLISS, W. W.	2	Pike
BLISSITT, Reason	8	Henry
BLITCH, Hannah	10	Effingham
BLITCH, Benj.	1	Effingham
BLITCH, Henry	3	Effingham
BLITCH, Keelana	5	Effingham
BLITCH, Simeon	1	Effingham
BLITCH, Thomas	2	Effingham
BLITCH, Thos.	2	Effingham
BLITCH, William	6	Bryan
BLITHE, Leroy	6	Troup
BLIZZARD, Daniel	20	Jasper
BLOCKER, Stephen	22	Early
BLODGET, Foster Sr.	20	Richmond
BLODGET, H. M.	98	Chatham
BLOIS, James F.	2	Chatham
BLOIS, P. estate	5	Chatham
BLOOD, George	1	Monroe
BLOODWITH, Pressley	1	Baldwin
BLOODWORTH, David M.	20	Pike
BLOODWORTH, Henry	6	Wilkinson
BLOODWORTH, Hiram	6	Monroe
BLOODWORTH, J. L. M	20	Pike
BLOODWORTH, Miles	2	Wilkinson
BLOODWORTH, Thomas W.	1	Pike
BLOODWORTH, W.	3	Pike
BLOSSOMGIN, Wyatt	6	Monroe
BLOUNT, C. M.	14	McIntosh
BLOUNT, David E.	33	Jones
BLOUNT, G. W.	7	Hancock
BLOUNT, Isaac	2	Hancock
BLOUNT, J. W.	16	Meriwether
BLOUNT, Joseph	5	Houston
BLOUNT, Joseph agt for STILES, B.	56	Houston

Name	Number	County
BLOUNT, Thomas Estate	77	Jones
BLOUNT, Augustus W.	4	Burke
BLOUNT, Edward H.	20	Burke
BLOUNT, Emily	1	Richmond
BLOUNT, H. J.	17	Burke
BLOUNT, Jacob	7	Decatur
BLOUNT, John	1	Richmond
BLOUNT, John T.	31	Talbot
BLOUNT, Lucy	5	Talbot
BLOUNT, M. F.	10	Decatur
BLOUNT, M. R.	31	Washington
BLOUNT, Richard	5	Decatur
BLOUNT, Stephen W.	20	Burke
BLOUNT, William H.	29	Warren
BLOUT, Mary L.	9	Baldwin
BLOW, Benjamin M.	3	Jones
BLOW, James	2	Wilkinson
BLOW, Richard	23	Jones
BLOW, Samuel	10	Jones
BLOW, William	3	Jones
BLOW, Micajah	10	Talbot
BLOW, Wesley	1	Talbot
BLUE, James	17	McIntosh
BLUE, Simion	5	Marion
BLUE, Samuel	1	Dooly
BLUNT, A. E.	1	Murray
BLUNT, Jacob	7	Pulaski
BLUNT, Marshall	13	Monroe
BLUNT, John	4	Decatur
BLUNT, S. A.	13	Randolph
BLUNT, William L.	9	Columbia
BLY, James	4	Union
BLYTHE, Wm. R.	9	Greene
BOAD, G. R. by agt. RIGHT, Wm.	5	Morgan
BOAG, Samuel W.	12	Floyd
BOATRIGHT, John	2	Washington
BOATRIGHT, Zelphah	5	Washington
BOATWRIGHT, Clayton	12	Pulaski
BOATWRIGHT, George E.	8	Washington
BOATWRIGHT, Raleigh	6	Pulaski
BOATWRIGHT, Wm.	2	Fayette
BOAWDNO?, P. C.	4	Bibb
BOAZ, Meshack	18	Gordon
BOBO, B.	1	Elbert
BOBO, Benjamin	9	Floyd
BOBO, Willis	4	Floyd
BOCHERT, A.	3	Chatham
BODDIE, B. V. R.	34	Harris
BODDIE, Nathan V.	94	Troup
BODIE, B. V. R.	1	Harris
BOGAN, Caswell	3	Jasper

Name	Number	County	Name	Number	County
BOGAN, John	28	Jasper	BOMAN, Robert	20	Monroe
BOGARDIS, Henry A.	1	Chatham	BOMAN, Daniel	8	Stewart
BOGER, Peter C.	18	Cherokee	BOMAN, J.	10	Bibb
BOGGERS, Robert	1	Heard	BOMAN, B.H.C.	1	Cass
BOGGINS, Elisha	2	Heard	BOMAR, Jno.	2	Carroll
BOGGINS, Robert	5	Heard	BOMAR, Adam R.	2	Campbell
BOGGS, A.	11	Clarke	BOMAR, B. F.	2	DeKalb
BOGGS, Ezekiel	2	Jackson	BOMAR, Barbary	10	Campbell
BOGGS, James	1	Oglethorpe	BOMAR, E. P.	4	Campbell
BOGGS, John R.	4	Habersham	BONA, E.	7	Elbert
BOGGS, Richard	3	Clarke	BONA, Eppy W.	8	Elbert
BOGGS, Wm. M.	10	Jackson	BONA, Joel	1	Elbert
BOGGS, Archibald	6	Richmond	BONA, R. W.	2	Elbert
BOGGS, James	2	Talbot	BONA, T. J.	2	Elbert
BOGGS, William	2	Talbot	BONA, Willis	7	Elbert
BOHANNEN, Jas.	15	Pulaski	BOND ? , James Rill ?	5	Taliaferro
BOHANNON, Henry	7	Dooly	BOND, A. E.	1	Forsyth
BOHANNON, L.	1	Troup	BOND, Elizabeth	3	Merriwether
BOHANNON, Philomon	8	Dooly	BOND, Hilliard	2	Merriwether
BOHANNON, Jos.	68	Coweta	BOND, Hilsman	1	Merriwether
BOHLAN, Mary	1	Richmond	BOND, J.	40	Lee
BOHLER, William	4	Lincoln	BOND, John P.	11	Twiggs
BOHLIN, Job A.	2	Richmond	BOND, Malinda	4	Pike
BOIFEUILLET, George	2	Chatham	BOND, Mary	1	Madison
BOIFFEIULLET,			BOND, William P.	4	Merriwether
John T.	2	Chatham	BOND, Augustus	6	Richmond
BOIL, E.	1	Bibb	BOND, Charles	15	Columbia
BOISCLAIR, Peter	25	Richmond	BOND, E.	5	Bibb
BOLAND, James	2	Marion	BOND, Isaac	1	Richmond
BOLD, Frank	1	Union	BOND, J. M.	1	Campbell
BOLD, James	8	Union	BOND, James	106	Baker
BOLD, Johannon	1	Union	BOND, Jno.	2	Randolph
BOLD, Robert	2	Union	BOND, John	2	DeKalb
BOLE, John	15	Campbell	BOND, Jos.	8	Bibb
BOLGAS, John	2	Merriwether	BOND, Joseph	66	Baker
BOLGER, Henry	9	Merriwether	BOND, Joseph	17	Baker
BOLGER, John H.	1	Merriwether	BOND, Lucy	4	Butts
BOLIN, D.	2	Troup	BOND, Pembrake P.	4	Richmond
BOLIN, William	29	Pike	BOND, William	2	Talbot
BOLIN, Thomas	5	Columbia	BOND?, J.		
BOLING, John	4	Pulaski	by W. H. OWENS	150	Lee
BOLING, William J.	8	Jefferson	BONDS, Angan	5	Jackson
BOLLINEAU, Augustus	2	Chatham	BONDS, Archibald	5	Walker
BOLLING, T. T.	19	Chattooga	BONDS, Dudly	26	Gwinnett
BOLLOUGH, James K.	1	Chatham	BONDS, James M.	4	Walker
BOLT, M.	7	Chattooga	BONDS, John	2	Elbert
BOLTON, C. L.	60	Wilkes	BONDS?, M.	2	Elbert
BOLTON, George W.	28	Oglethorpe	BONDS?, W.	1	Elbert
BOLTON, Manoah	60	Oglethorpe	BONE, F. K.	1	Elbert
BOLTON, (?)	16	Columbia	BONE, George	2	Floyd
BOLTON, Robert	1	Dooly	BONE, Leonard	1	Franklin
BOLTON, Samuel	6	Putnam	BONE, William	1	Madison
BOLTON, Thos. W.	12	Coweta	BONE, John	6	Richmond
BOMAN ?, H.	1	Walton	BONE, W. H.	2	Coweta

Name	Number	County	Name	Number	County
BONE, Wm.	1	Bibb	BOON, Ratliffe	21	Stewart
BONER, T. E.	18	Baker	BOON, Zeke	6	Carroll
BONES, Ransom	8	Hall	BOONE, Robt.	2	Muscogee
BONES?, John	1	Habersham	BOONE, J. R.	3	Bibb
BONEY, Stephen	3	Telfair	BOONE, William	1	DeKalb
BONFORD, Henry W.	9	Jasper	BOONE, Willis	22	Crawford
BONNELL, John M.	2	Newton	BOOTH, Irving R.	1	Ware
BONNELL, Wm.	4	Bullock	BOOTH, Robert	4	Morgan
BONNER, Allen	1	Morgan	BOOTH, Robt.	2	Clarke
BONNER, G. H.	1	Troup	BOOTH, Robt.	14	Troup
BONNER, Bonnett W.	1	Cobb	BOOTH, Robt. L.	5	Troup
BONNER,			BOOTH, Tho.	57	Pulaski
Bonnett W. Sen.	1	Cobb	BOOTH, Wm.	9	Oglethorpe
BONNER, Henry	1	Baldwin	BOOTH, Wm.	4	Oglethorpe
BONNER, John	60	Hancock	BOOTH, James A.	2	Talbot
BONNER, Thomas S.	29	Morgan	BOOTH, Milton S.	3	Stewart
BONNER, Thos.	5	Morgan	BOOTH, Thos.	4	Randolph
BONNER, Thos. Jr.	1	Morgan	BOOTH, William	4	Talbot
BONNER, B. F.	2	Bibb	BOOTHE, George	7	Clarke
BONNER, Bedford B.	38	Talbot	BOOTHE, William S.	11	Harris
BONNER, Bedford B.	4	Talbot	BOOTHE, Zachariah	34	Muscogee
BONNER, Frances	31	Baldwin	BOOTHE, John	2	Tatnall
BONNER, Jas. M	3	Putnam	BOOTY, John L.	26	Monroe
BONNER, John	11	Talbot	BOOZIER, Daniel	13	Meriwether
BONNER, Oliver H.	18	Baldwin	BOOZIER, Henry	8	Meriwether
BONNER, Thos.	1	Putnam	BOOZIER, Langdon	2	Meriwether
BONNER, William	7	Troup	BORDEN, Andrew	1	Gordon
BONNER, William G.	1	Baldwin	BORDEN, Thomas L.	1	Jones
BONNOR, Zadoc	24	Carroll	BORDERS, A. H.	7	Harris
BONNOR, Thos.	26	Carroll	BORDERS, A. L.	4	Walker
BONNOR, W. F.	1	Carroll	BORDERS, Abner H.	16	Troup
BONSON?, Thos.	5	Carroll	BORDERS, Abram	4	Pike
BOOK ?, Lucinda	2	Twiggs	BORDERS, Abram	4	Pike
BOOKER, Efford M.	20	Wilkes	BORDERS, Ewell	6	Harris
BOOKER, James	4	Meriwether	BORDERS, Isaac	32	Jackson
BOOKER, John W.	27	Wilkes	BORDERS, Mrs. Emma	4	Harris
BOOKER, Leroy	10	Troup	BORDERS, Richard A.	1	Jackson
BOOKER, R. Agt.	10	Wilkes	BORDERS, Stephen	17	Harris
BOOKER, Richerson,	103	Wilkes	BORDERS, Stephen	14	Harris
BOOKER, T. J.	7	Lincoln	BORDERS, William	2	Pike
BOOKER, William M.	2	Wilkes	BOREN, John	9	Wilkes
BOOKING?, Mildridge	9	Heard	BORING, Sarah	2	Cherokee
BOOKS, John	2	Monroe	BORING, Thomas	4	Cherokee
BOOKS, J. A.	7	Stewart	BORING, Isaac	8	Putnam
BOOLES, S. W.	11	Henry	BORN, John A.	12	Gwinnett
BOON, A. C.	5	Greene	BORN, Jacob	1	DeKalb
BOON, Allen	1	Heard	BORN, James H.	4	DeKalb
BOON, B.	1	Troup	BORN, John M.	11	DeKalb
BOON, Bolling	2	Wayne	BORNERS, Enoch H.	3	Jackson
BOON, Ratliff	1	Forsyth	BOROUM, William	5	Lincoln
BOON, Rebecca	7	Greene	BORUM, John N.	6	Campbell
BOON, Wm.	3	Carroll	BORUM, Sarah	6	Madison
BOON, Elsey	3	Baldwin	BOSHELL, H. G.	2	Greene
BOON, Jesse	1	Stewart	BOSMON, Wm.	9	Putman

Name	Number	County	Name	Number	County
BOSS, Henry W.	2	Walker	BOUGH, William	4	Troup
BOSTICK, Louisa	1	Jefferson	BOUGHN?, John	17	Oglethorpe
BOSTICK, Bethenia P.	2	Jones	BOUGHTON, Seth N.	1	Baker
BOSTICK, Charles D.	16	Jasper	BOULET, Peter D.	9	Richmond
BOSTICK, Hillory	4	Muscogee	BOULINEAU, Joseph	4	Richmond
BOSTICK, James H.	15	Jefferson	BOULTER, James	1	Muscogee
BOSTICK, L. B.	11	Jefferson	BOULTON, Leonard	3	Madison
BOSTICK, N. L.	1	Jefferson	BOUMAND, B. M.	3	Elbert
BOSTICK, R.	2	Twiggs	BOUNER, Ann	1	Jones
BOSTICK, Rhesa	41	Jefferson	BOUNER, Joseph G.	1	Jones
BOSTICK, Thornton P.	6	Jones	BOUNT, Elizabeth	11	Decatur
BOSTICK, William	5	Newton	BOUNT, Thomas H.	37	Burke
BOSTICK, H. H.	1	Dooly	BOUREFIELD (?), (?)	3	Columbia
BOSTON, George	9	Effingham	BOURGUIN, Edward	13	Chatham
BOSTON, George W.	40	Effingham	BOURGUIN, Roselle	14	Effingham
BOSTON, Ira	13	Screven	BOURGUIN, Benedict	21	Chatham
BOSTON, John	8	Chatham	BOURK, Ann M.	20	Chatham
BOSTON, Thomas	4	Thomas	BOURKE, Joseph	4	Chatham
BOSTWICK, A. B.	16	Morgan	BOURKE, Thomas	3	Chatham
BOSTWICK, A. G.	1	Clarke	BOUSON, Henry	5	Troup
BOSTWICK, Charles C.	1	Cobb	BOUTH, A. W.	2	Elbert
BOSTWICK, Dr. J.	5	Wilkinson	BOUTH, E.	8	Elbert
BOSTWICK, J. R.	5	Jefferson	BOUTH, R.	8	Elbert
BOSTWICK, Littleberry	12	Morgan	BOUTH, V. E.	1	Elbert
BOSTWICK, Robert B.	15	Cobb	BOUTWELL, Stephen	1	Baker
BOSTWICKE, Thos.			BOWAN, M. M.	4	Irwin
estate	33	Burke	BOWDEN, C. W.	2	Jackson
BOSTWITH,			BOWDEN, Elias	2	Marion
Little Berry	38	Burke	BOWDEN, Elizabeth	2	Merriwether
BOSWEL, J. C.	6	Dade	BOWDEN, Elliot C.	12	Greene
BOSWELL, Elijah	18	Morgan	BOWDEN, Joshua	8	Gordon
BOSWELL, Elkanah	5	Wilkes	BOWDEN, M. A.	2	Pike
BOSWELL, John J.	14	Muscogee	BOWDEN, Rachael	1	Marion
BOSWELL, Johnson	17	Greene	BOWDEN, Robt. C.	6	Greene
BOSWELL, Josiah	26	Putnam	BOWDEN, William	1	Greene
BOSWELL, Josiah	6	Putnam	BOWDEN, William	11	Monroe
BOSWELL, Sarah	6	Putnam	BOWDEN, D. W.	16	Putnam
BOSWICK, Lott	1	Emanual	BOWDEN, Simeon	2	Stewart
BOSWICK, Nathan	5	Emanual	BOWDEN, Turner	3	Stewart .
BOSWICK, Nathan Sr.	4	Emanual	BOWDIN, Alford	5	Monroe
BOSWORTH, Richard	3	Marion	BOWDOIN, J. W.	3	Henry
BOSWORTH, William	1	Muscogee	BOWDOIN, Nancy	1	Jasper
BOTHWELL, Ebbin	23	Jefferson	BOWDRE , Pharby	95	Columbia
BOTHWELL, James	4	Jefferson	BOWDRIE, A.	72	Wilkes
BOTHWELL, John W.	24	Jefferson	BOWDRIE, Benj. T.	61	Wilkes
BOTHWELL, David J.	21	Dooly	BOWDRIE, E.	7	Wilkes
BOTHWELL, James T.	10	Richmond	BOWDRIE, Joseph	7	Upson
BOTHWELL, Samuel	1	DeKalb	BOWEL, Geo.	2	Coweta
BOTHWILL, W. C.	8	Dooly	BOWEN, C. C.	10	Fayette
BOTTOM, Martha	1	Richmond	BOWEN, D.	4	Henry
BOTTOMS, James	5	Pike	BOWEN, Durham	8	Houston
BOTTON, E. P.	2	Henry	BOWEN, Elisha	2	Muscogee
BOUCLAIR ?,			BOWEN, Horatio	48	Jones
Valentine W.	4	Richmond	BOWEN, Jno.	5	Carroll

32

Name	Number	County	Name	Number	County
BOWEN, M. D.	1	Henry	BOYD, Benjamin	1	Gilmer
BOWEN, Mary	2	Washington	BOYD, Elizabeth	3	Pike
BOWEN, Perry	14	Jackson	BOYD, Gicovia	1	Pike
BOWEN, S.	5	Lee	BOYD, Hugh	2	Merriwether
BOWEN, Thomas J.	13	Jackson	BOYD, James	1	Murray
BOWEN, Thomas O.	26	Jones	BOYD, James	4	Pike
BOWEN, Wm.	8	Carroll	BOYD, John	2	Lowndes
BOWEN, William H.	1	Warren	BOYD, John	4	Meriwether
BOWEN, Caleb P.	1	Jackson	BOYD, John F.	7	Muscogee
BOWEN, D. C.	1	Dooly	BOYD, Joseph N.	10	Troup
BOWEN, F. D.	9	Carroll	BOYD, Josiah F.	5	Pike
BOWEN, Hezekial	2	Bullock	BOYD, Nancy	6	Newton
BOWEN, Horatio C.	42	Coweta	BOYD, R. C.	4	Troup
BOWEN, James	3	Bullock	BOYD, R. H.	16	Merriwether
BOWEN, John	2	Bullock	BOYD, Robt.	9	Jefferson
BOWEN, John	1	Putnam	BOYD, Stephen estate	6	Burke
BOWEN, Nathan	1	Dooly	BOYD, Susan	11	Troup
BOWEN, Saml. H.	5	Coweta	BOYD, T.	4	Troup
BOWEN, Silas	3	Bullock	BOYD, W.	9	Troup
BOWEN, Thos. M.	6	Coweta	BOYD, William	1	Merriwether
BOWEN, William	3	Dooly	BOYD, Allen	10	Burke
BOWEN, William P.	41	Chatham	BOYD, Benjamin	16	Burke
BOWER, George M. T.	2	Newton	BOYD, Hez	43	Columbia
BOWER, David	9	Crawford	BOYD, J. C.	2	Butts
BOWER, Isaac	1	Baldwin	BOYD, Jack	1	Columbia
BOWERS, Coleman	1	Cobb	BOYD, James	1	Burke
BOWERS, Edy	4	Franklin	BOYD, John	58	Columbia
BOWERS, Thomas W.	1	Franklin	BOYD, John	15	DeKalb
BOWERS, David	4	Stewart	BOYD, Kizziah	5	DeKalb
BOWERS, James M.	4	Richmond	BOYD, Mary	3	Richmond
BOWERS, Levi	7	Coweta	BOYD, Milton	8	Merriwether
BOWERS, Philomen	11	Stewart	BOYD, Wiley	5	Talbot
BOWIN, H.	29	Elbert	BOYER, Ann	1	Hancock
BOWIN, N.	1	Lee	BOYER, C. W.	9	Walton
BOWIN, W. M.	40	Elbert	BOYER, George	3	Hancock
BOWLES, Jackson	22	Greene	BOYER, John	12	Hancock
BOWLES, H. H.	5	Harris	BOYER, Wm. M.	17	Hancock
BOWLES, L. B.	1	Harris	BOYER, James	2	Stewart
BOWLES, Levi	8	Thomas	BOYETT. Leroy	1	Randolph
BOWLES, Nelson	8	Merriwether	BOYETTE, Josiah	3	Randolph
BOWLING, John S.	4	Oglethorpe	BOYINGTON, E.	6	Henry
BOWLING, Mary A.	16	Oglethorpe	BOYKEN, Elizabeth	13	Richmond
BOWLING, William	7	Cherokee	BOYKIN, F. A.	32	Merriwether
BOWMAN, Francis	5	Greene	BOYKIN, John T.	34	Troup
BOWMAN, George B.	1	Heard	BOYKIN, Mrs. N.	8	Muscogee
BOWMAN, Henry	1	Murray	BOYKIN, B. L.	7	Screven
BOWMAN, John	4	Hall	BOYKIN, D.	1	Screven
BOWMAN, John Jr.	10	Bibb	BOYKIN, John B.	5	Screven
BOWN?, Daniel D.	3	Gwinnett	BOYLE, Joseph	5	Cass
BOX, L. A.	1	Randolph	BOYLE, Peter	8	Forsyth
BOX, Thomas N.	4	Chatham	BOYLE, Rebecca	2	Jones
BOYCE, Brookley ?	17	Walton	BOYLE, Robert	18	Chattooga
BOYCE, Mary	8	Troup	BOYLE, Thomas	1	Chatham
BOYD, Banai	18	Lowndes	BOYLE, William H.	1	Troup

Name	Number	County	Name	Number	County
BOYNTON, C. A.	3	Talbot	BRADLEY, John	1	Newton
BOYNTON, J.J.	5	Twiggs	BRADLEY, John	4	Randolph
BOYNTON, J. J.	55	Twiggs	BRADLEY, John S.	8	Liberty
BOYNTON, Augustus	7	Talbot	BRADLEY, Mary	4	Jones
BOYNTON, Jordan	14	Talbot	BRADLEY, Newman	13	Liberty
BOYNTON, Moses	45	Talbot	BRADLEY, Richard T.	9	Lee
BOYNTON, Moses	12	Talbot	BRADLEY, W. D.	29	Lincoln
BOYNTON, Rebecca	8	Talbot	BRADLEY, Bryant	2	Bibb
BOYNTON, Snow	13	Talbot	BRADLEY, Charles A.	2	Baker
BOYNTON, Willaard	25	Stewart	BRADLEY, Mary A.	10	Chatham
BOYNTON, Willard	26	Stewart	BRADLEY, Richard	13	Chatham
BOYNTON, Willard	7	Stewart	BRADLEY, Wm.	1	DeKalb
BOYNTON, Williard	32	Stewart	BRADLY, Marion	1	Morgan
BOYT, James	7	Upson	BRADLY, Asa	1	Union
BOZEMAN, C. M.	6	Pulaski	BRADLY, N.	1	Coweta
BOZEMAN, Reddick	9	Houston	BRADSHAW, H. C.	1	Elbert
BOZEMAN, T. F	18	Muscogee	BRADSHAW, James	12	Dooly
BOZEMAN, Wm. W.	1	Twiggs	BRADSHAW, John	21	Pulaski
BOZEWELL, Nathaniel	15	Monroe	BRADSHAW, Jonas	1	Harris
BRACE, John	2	Cobb	BRADSHAW, Mary W.	13	Wilkes
BRACEY, India	1	Carroll	BRADSHAW, Olif	2	Dooly
BRACH?, ?	4	Oglethorpe	BRADSHAW, Francis A.	9	Burke
BRACK, Miles F.	25	Burke	BRADSHAW, John	2	Richmond
BRACK, John	2	Tatnall	BRADSHAW, Sarah E.	6	Wilkes
BRACKET, Bradford	1	Lumpkin	BRADSHAW, Shadrack	16	Warren
BRACKETT, ?, W.	2	Habersham	BRADSHAW, William	1	Talbot
BRADBERRY, Ann	4	Chatham	BRADSHAW, Woodson	20	Warren
BRADBERRY, John	11	Talbot	BRADWELL, Jas. S.	9	Liberty
BRADBERY, James	1	Randolph	BRADY, Thomas	5	Macon
BRADBURY, William	7	Pike	BRADY, A. J.	2	DeKalb
BRADDY, John	6	Greene	BRADY, Jas.	8	Butts
BRADFIELD, James	10	Troup	BRADY, Jas.	1	Coweta
BRADFIELD, Lewis	3	Troup	BRADY, R. H.	12	Troup
BRADFIELD, William	8	Troup	BRADY, William	1	Sumter
BRADFORD			BRADY, Wright	21	Sumter
& PITMAN	29	Burke	BRAGG, Enoch	6	Upson
BRADFORD, Archibald	3	Cherokee	BRAGG, George	6	Madison
BRADFORD, Jas. A.	4	Muscogee	BRAGG, Humphrey A.	2	Madison
BRADFORD, Jefferson	6	Oglethorpe	BRAGG, Joseph	8	Madison
BRADFORD, John	1	Lowndes	BRAGG, Russel J.	1	Madison
BRADFORD, Rease	8	Oglethorpe	BRAGG, Saml.	23	Wilkinson
BRADFORD, Richd.	13	Wilkes	BRAILSFORD,		
BRADFORD, Robert	4	Troup	William	50	McIntosh
BRADFORD, Wm.	1	Lowndes	BRAK, H.	1	Randolph
BRADFORD, Henry	12	Crawford	BRAKE ?, Frederick H.	3	Richmond
BRADFORD, J. J.	10	Crawford	BRAKEFIELD, Elisha	8	Harris
BRADFORD, John	1	Cass	BRAKEFIELD, Elisha	5	Harris
BRADLEY & GILES	65	Chatham	BRAMBLET, Joel	1	Forsyth
BRADLEY, Alvis	1	Heard	BRAMBLET, N.	3	Hall
BRADLEY, Amy	14	Wilkes	BRAMBLITT, Newton	2	Gwinnett
BRADLEY, Eli	1	Liberty	BRAMLETT, L. W.	29	Wilkes
BRADLEY, J. F.	1	Floyd	BRANAN, C.	1	Wilkinson
BRADLEY, J. M.	8	Elbert	BRANAN, W.	6	Henry
BRADLEY, James	1	Madison	BRANAN, Alexander	9	Sumter

Name	Number	County	Name	Number	County
BRANAN, James	2	Wilkinson	BRANSFORD, William	5	Talbot
BRANCH, D.	3	Irwin	BRANTLEY, Aaron	9	Washington
BRANCH, John	54	Greene	BRANTLEY, Celia	13	Washington
BRANCH, John W.	5	Cherokee	BRANTLEY, Dolley	14	Jones
BRAND?, Thomas D.	1	Macon	BRANTLEY, Green	52	Washington
BRANDEN, Thos.	5	Cass	BRANTLEY, Harris	43	Washington
BRANDON, F. L.	5	Chattooga	BRANTLEY, Harris	17	Washington
BRANDON, James	2	Jasper	BRANTLEY, James	4	Washington
BRANDON, Joseph P.	4	Gwinnett	BRANTLEY, James	1	Chatham
BRANDON, Mary	5	Gwinnett	BRANTLEY, James	16	Marion
BRANDON, Mary	1	Gwinnett	BRANTLEY, James M.	16	Monroe
BRANDON, James	12	Richmond	BRANTLEY, Jeptha	8	Washington
BRANDON, James	4	Richmond	BRANTLEY, John	1	Warren
BRANDON, John	19	Richmond	BRANTLEY, John W.	8	Jones
BRANEN, William	1	Floyd	BRANTLEY, W. H.	25	Hancock
BRANHAM, Henry R.	16	Newton	BRANTLEY, Wm. F.	8	Hancock
BRANHAM, Henry	29	Putnam	BRANTLEY, Edward	22	Baldwin
BRANHAM, Jas.	5	Talbot	BRANTLEY, J. W.	4	Bibb
BRANHAM, Joel	12	Putnam	BRANTLEY, James M.	9	DeKalb
BRANHAM, W. R.	5	Bibb	BRANTLEY, Spencer	2	Washington
BRANNAN, Alexander	1	Bullock	BRANTLEY, William	3	Washington
BRANNAN, C. H.	1	Wilkinson	BRANTLEY, William	1	Washington
BRANNAN, Edmund	20	Bullock	BRANTLEY, William	14	Dooly
BRANNAN, H.	5	Stewart	BRANTLEY, Wm.	8	DeKalb
BRANNAN, H.	18	Wilkinson	BRANTLEY, W. T.	1	Walton
BRANNAN, Ishmail	1	Talbot	BRANTLY, Benjamin	7	Greene
BRANNAN, Tyra	1	Talbot	BRANTLY, Elizabeth	1	Montgomery
BRANNAN, William	7	Bullock	BRANTLY, F. M.	8	Meriwether
BRANNAN, William	2	Bullock	BRANTLY, Frances	2	Hancock
BRANNAN, William	2	Bullock	BRANTLY, Harris	9	Marion
BRANNEN, John	9	Bullock	BRANTLY, Joshua	20	Walton
BRANNEN, Nancy	5	Bullock	BRANTLY, L . F.	1	Hancock
BRANNER, Benj.	2	Chattooga	BRANTLY, Livy G.	3	Walton
BRANNER, John W.	5	Oglethorpe	BRANTLY, Lucy	27	Monroe
BRANNER?, W.			BRANTLY, Mark	7	Monroe
by agt. JOHNSTON,R.	35	Morgan	BRANTLY, T. J.	2	Hancock
BRANNON, A. F.	13	Muscogee	BRANTLY, W. T.	5	Clarke
BRANNON, B. O.	2	Henry	BRANTLY, William	3	Washington
BRANNON, Calvin	11	Harris	BRANTLY, James	1	Taliaferro
BRANNON, Cephus	1	Harris	BRANTLY, Zechariah	5	Washington
BRANNON, James	3	Cobb	BRANTON, D. J.	10	Decatur
BRANNON, Jno. F.	1	Harris	BRAPILL, John	1	Muscogee
BRANNON, Lettice	1	Madison	BRASELTON, Green C.	1	Jackson
BRANNON, Thomas	3	Pike	BRASELTON, Mary	24	Jackson
BRANNON, Barney	16	Screven	BRASIEL, Timothy	6	Washington
BRANNON, Henry	1	Talbot	BRASIER, A.	1	Coweta
BRANNON, Hope H.	18	Screven	BRASSEL, James T.	31	Sumter
BRANNON, Hugh	1	Talbot	BRASSELL, James	5	Fayette
BRANNON, James W.	1	Baldwin	BRASSWILL, Uriah	7	Thomas
BRANNON, Thomas H.	1	Screven	BRASWELL, Caswell	2	Thomas
BRANSBY, Mary	1	Chatham	BRASWELL, George	1	Gwinnett
BRANSBY, Thomas	1	Chatham	BRASWELL, Isaac F.	8	Meriwether
BRANSFORD, James	3	Talbot	BRASWELL, Kinard	50	Thomas
BRANSFORD, John	23	Talbot	BRASWELL, Samuel G.	4	Thomas

Name	Number	County	Name	Number	County
BRASWELL, Sarahan	2	Houston	BREWER, D.	4	Wilkinson
BRASWELL, Jacob S.	1	Harris	BREWER, Elishu	14	Morgan
BRASWELL, S.	10	Decatur	BREWER, English	2	Muscogee
BRASWELL, T.	1	Crawford	BREWER, Ettrula?	8	Newton
BRASWELL, W. B.	1	Decatur	BREWER, James	3	Marion
BRAWNER, Asa	13	Pike	BREWER, Jamesa	1	Liberty
BRAWNER, Pliney	13	Morgan	BREWER, J. C.	3	Wilkinson
BRAY, John	2	Oglethorpe	BREWER, John	7	Morgan
BRAY, Thos. H.	4	Pike	BREWER, John	15	Muscogee
BRAY, G.	1	Crawford	BREWER, L. R.	4	Pike
BRAY, Lucy	21	Warren	BREWER, Martha	7	Troup
BRAY, Richard L.	14	Warren	BREWER, Mary	1	Hancock
BRAY, William	31	Talbot	BREWER, Q. C.	19	Walton
BRAZELL, G. H.	29	Twiggs	BREWER, Sarah	1	Walton
BRAZELL, Hez.	3	Randolph	BREWER, Susan	1	Marion
BRAZELL, James	6	Talbot	BREWER, Thos. A.	8	Bibb
BRAZELL, John	1	Tatnall	BREWER, Wm.	6	Forsyth
BRAZELLE, Mansfield	1	Stewart	BREWER, Wm.	2	Marion
BRAZELTON, Augustus	2	Floyd	BREWER, Green H.	2	Telfair
BRAZELTON, Elizabeth	6	Hall	BREWER, Sarah	5	Telfair
BRAZIER, E. W.	11	Monroe	BREWER, Wm.	1	Cass
BRAZIER, John C.	1	Monroe	BREWINGTON, Wm. J.	17	Putnam
BRAZIER, Wesly	3	Monroe	BREWNER, A. C.	4	Randolph
BRAZIL, James	7	Jefferson	BREWNER, Mary	2	Randolph
BRAZIL, John	2	Pulaski	BREWSTER, Hugh	2	Paulding
BRAZIL, William	11	Fayette	BREWSTER, Louisa	3	Cherokee
BRAZIL, D. W.	9	Bibb	BREWSTER, Sheriff	20	Paulding
BRAZIL, S.	1	Decatur	BREWSTER, Blake D.	5	Talbot
BRAZLETON, William	18	Morgan	BREWSTER, Hugh	16	Coweta
BREADLOVE, R. F.	3	Walton	BREWTON, Benjamin	15	Tatnall
BREAZEAL, Willis	47	Burke	BREWTON, Jonathan	7	Tatnall
BREED ?, Catherine	1	Warren	BREWTON, Nathan J.	4	Tatnall
BREED, Nathan	5	Henry	BREWTON, Samuel	12	Tatnall
BREED, Jno.	4	Henry	BRIAN, John R.	2	Walker
BREEDLOVE, James	1	Merriwether	BRIANT, J. R.	2	Irwin
BREEDLOVE, John	2	Wilkinson	BRIANT, Mrs. Oatham	46	Houston
BREEDLOVE, Joseph	2	Merriwether	BRICE, Wm. T.	6	Floyd
BREEDLOVE,			BRICE, Frances	5	Thomas
Nathl. G.	7	Hancock	BRICE, J. E.	4	Crawford
BREEDLOVE, John A.	10	Baldwin	BRICKWELL, N.	1	Coweta
BREEDLOVE, Lennard	8	Talbot	BRIDGEMAN, Isaac	1	Walker
BREEDLOW, Nathan	1	Monroe	BRIDGEMAN, S.D.	2	Walker
BREHAM, E.	6	Randoph	BRIDGEMAN, S. D.	2	Walker
BRENAN, Edward	1	Muscogee	BRIDGEMAN,		
BRENAN, Thomas	1	Richmond	Temperance	8	Walker
BRENNAN, Patrick	2	Richmond	BRIDGER, George	2	Effingham
BRENSON, Lucy	9	Burke	BRIDGERS, E. J.	3	Greene
BRENT?, Willoughby	2	Pike	BRIDGES, Allen	8	Houston
BREON?, Benjamin	1	Burke	BRIDGES, Bennett	13	Jones
BRESTAW ?, Abner N.	4	Taliaferro	BRIDGES, C. L.	2	Henry
BRETT, Henry	1	Washington	BRIDGES, Hardy	14	Greene
BREWAR, S.	16	Elbert	BRIDGES, James	1	Greene
BREWER, A.	13	Henry	BRIDGES, James	10	Oglethorpe
BREWER, Catherine	4	Monroe	BRIDGES, Jas.	1	Coweta

36

Name	Number	County	Name	Number	County
BRIDGES, Jno. agent	11	Laurens	BRINKLEY, William F.	6	Warren
BRIDGES, Jonathan	1	Muscogee	BRINSEN, Adam	6	Baker
BRIDGES, Jorden agent	19	Monroe	BRINSON, Benjamin E.	3	Emanual
BRIDGES, Levi	2	Upson	BRINSON, Cyprian	5	Lowndes
BRIDGES, Louisa	2	Fayette	BRINSON, Jane W.	12	Thomas
BRIDGES, Mary	1	Madison	BRINSON, Isaac J.	5	Jefferson
BRIDGES, Mary	9	Stewart	BRINSON, Mills M.	24	Lowndes
BRIDGES, Nathaniel	21	Greene	BRINSON, Moses	27	Jefferson
BRIDGES, R. C.	4	Fayette	BRINSON, Mrs. Nancy	13	Burke
BRIDGES, Rebecca	3	Merriwether	BRINSON, Nancy	2	Lowndes
BRIDGES, Sarah	5	Monroe	BRINSON, Adam	16	Screven
BRIDGES, Sarah	1	Muscogee	BRINSON, Adam C.	23	Screven
BRIDGES, William	6	Oglethorpe	BRINSON, Dadiel	7	Burke
BRIDGES, Ansel	5	Coweta	BRINSON, James	6	Burke
BRIDGES, B. L.	1	Randolph	BRINSON, John	5	Screven
BRIDGES, Daniel	1	Dooly	BRINSON, Mathew	12	Baker
BRIDGES, Dicy	2	Stewart	BRINSON, Reuben B.	2	Baker
BRIDGES, G. B.	6	Butts	BRINSON, Samuel	2	Randolph
BRIDGES, Hered	17	Putnam	BRINSON, Shepherd	7	Burke
BRIDGES, Jacob	10	Randolph	BRINSON, Simeon	20	Burke
BRIDGES, James	14	Stewart	BRINSON, Thos.	2	Decatur
BRIDGES, Jas.	6	Coweta	BRISCO, John	30	Oglethorpe
BRIDGES, John	4	Richmond	BRISCO, Lucian	2	Oglethorpe
BRIDGES, Jonathan ?	1	Stewart	BRISCOE, J. P. H.	1	Jackson
BRIDGES, Mrs. Francis	1	Stewart	BRISCOE, Augustus	12	Marion
BRIDGES, Mrs. Mary	7	Stewart	BRISCOE, Ralph	24	Walton
BRIDGES, R. B.	14	Coweta	BRISCOE, Smith	16	Columbia
BRIDGES, S.	16	Randolph	BRISCOE, Waters	28	Walton
BRIDGES, Simeon A.	1	DeKalb	BRISTOW ?, Martha	1	Taliaferro
BRIDGES, Sol. T.	49	Coweta	BRISTOW, John T.	2	Taliaferro
BRIDGES, Thos. W.	6	Coweta	BRIT, Benjamin	5	Baldwin
BRIDWELL, J. W.	3	DeKalb	BRIT, William	2	Laurens
BRIGES, Robert	2	Stewart	BRITAIN, H. S.	24	Clarke
BRIGGES, John F.	10	Oglethorpe	BRITIAN, William E.	8	Meriwether
BRIGGS, Henry	2	Lowndes	BRITON, Thos. J.	11	Oglethorpe
BRIGHAM, Henry	1	Chatham	BRITT, James	1	Baker
BRIGHAM, John	3	Muscogee	BRITT, S.	2	Decatur
BRIGHAM, John	1	Burke	BRITTAIN, Henry	21	Oglethorpe
BRIGHAM, William	8	Burke	BRITTON, E.	4	Troup
BRIGHT, B. C.	3	Henry	BROACH, John M.	14	Jones
BRIGHT, William A.	1	Houston	BROACH, Rachael	17	Jones
BRIGHTWELL, John M.	2	Oglethorpe	BROACH, Thos. A.	3	Heard
BRIGHTWELL, William B.	12	Oglethorpe	BROACH, Mrs. Sarah	4	Stewart
BRIGHTWELL, J.	1	Stewart	BROADMAN, Jas. W.	5	Bibb
BRIM, Rebecca	2	Bibb	BROADNAX, Mrs. E.	8	Muscogee
BRIM?, E.	4	Bibb	BROADWAY, James	3	Dooly
BRIMBERG, Wm. H.	12	Walton	BROADWELL, John	1	Forsyth
BRIMM, J.	2	Lee	BROADWELL, J. M.	4	Elbert
BRINER ?, James	12	Walton	BROCK, Benjamin	8	Walker
BRINES, J.C. Extr.	4	Walton	BROCK, Charles	5	Jackson
BRINKLEY, Abraham	23	Warren	BROCK, George	2	Gilmer
BRINKLEY, Samuel L.	4	Warren	BROCK, J. P.	1	Jackson
BRINKLEY, Wiley	3	Tatnall	BROCK, James L.	9	Henry
			BROCK, Nancy W.	14	Henry

Name	Number	County	Name	Number	County
BROCK, C. W.	8	Baker	BROOKS, Isaac	6	Marion
BROCK, Henry	1	Campbell	BROOKS, Isaac	12	Troup
BROCK, Jas. agent	65	Bibb	BROOKS, Isham	6	Talbot
BROCKINTON,			BROOKS, Iverson L.	32	Jones
Saml. A.	3	Camden	BROOKS, Ivey	58	Houston
BROCKMAN, ---	2	DeKalb	BROOKS, J.	3	Meriwether
BROCKMAN, W. H.	6	Clarke	BROOKS, J. B.	1	Muscogee
BRODDUS, Edward A.	12	Jasper	BROOKS, J. T.	1	Meriwether
BRODDUS, Thomas C.	36	Jasper	BROOKS, Jacob	16	Jackson
BRODENAX, Samuel	12	Newton	BROOKS, James	1	Greene
BRODIE ?, Alexr.	1	Richmond	BROOKS, James	3	Hall
BRODNAX, William E.	3	Richmond	BROOKS, James	3	Hall
BROGDEN, Georgia	1	Gordon	BROOKS, John	1	Camden
BROGDEN, Harrison R.	3	Gwinnett	BROOKS, John	16	Harris
BROGDEN, Wiley E.	1	Gordon	BROOKS, John	14	Paulding
BROGDON, George	20	Gwinnett	BROOKS, John S.	25	Macon
BROGDON, Hope J.	8	Gwinnett	BROOKS, Jordan P.	2	Chatham
BRONNER, A.	1	Muscogee	BROOKS, Larkin	2	Morgan
BRONNER, Elizabeth	14	Harris	BROOKS, Levinia	8	Twiggs
BRONNER, H. T.	14	Butts	BROOKS, Magnus A.	5	Jackson
BRONSON, Joseph	3	Muscogee	BROOKS, Middleton	11	Jackson
BRONSON, Thomas	23	Muscogee	BROOKS, Miss Nancy	5	Muscogee
BRONSON, D. L.	17	Randolph	BROOKS, Moses	2	Franklin
BROOK, David	1	Merriwether	BROOKS, Mrs.	1	Muscogee
BROOK, Jesse	8	Heard	BROOKS, P. R.	4	Greene
BROOK, Maxey	5	Troup	BROOKS, Richard E.	5	Oglethorpe
BROOK, Robert	2	Heard	BROOKS, Sarah	1	Jones
BROOK, John	4	Decatur	BROOKS, Susan	7	Paulding
BROOK, Wm. M.	18	Decatur	BROOKS, Thomas P.	7	Oglethorpe
BROOKE, Wm. T.	3	Taliaferro	BROOKS, Thos.	10	Henry
BROOKIN, William	21	Burke	BROOKS, William	1	Cobb
BROOKING, Fred E.	24	Hancock	BROOKS, William	14	Greene
BROOKING, Rebecca A.	11	Hancock	BROOKS, William	10	Jones
BROOKING, Rebecca A.	3	Hancock	BROOKS, William	9	Merriwether
BROOKING, L. B.	37	Baker	BROOKS, William	6	Morgan
BROOKINS, Benj.	7	Washington	BROOKS, William	13	Muscogee
BROOKINS, Haywood	6	Washington	BROOKS, William W.	3	Greene
BROOKINS, Isaac	4	Randolph	BROOKS, Balam	2	Stewart
BROOKNER, Charles T.	1	Walker	BROOKS, Berry	1	Coweta
BROOKS, Alexander R.	1	Paulding	BROOKS, Butha	1	Taliaferro
BROOKS, Alfred	27	Jackson	BROOKS, E. G.	3	Oglethorpe
BROOKS, Allen T.	5	Harris	BROOKS, Edward	5	Sumter
BROOKS, Augustus J.	3	Greene	BROOKS, J. S.	14	Crawford
BROOKS, C. C.	2	Jackson	BROOKS, Jno.	1	Henry
BROOKS,			BROOKS, John	4	Coweta
Christopher C.	13	Muscogee	BROOKS, John	1	Stewart
BROOKS, Daniel	1	Marion	BROOKS, Joseph	6	Talbot
BROOKS, E.	6	Oglethorpe	BROOKS, M. A.	2	Bibb
BROOKS, Edward	34	Macon	BROOKS, Mary	9	Crawford
BROOKS, Edward	1	Macon	BROOKS, Paskel	1	Campbell
BROOKS, F. M.	4	Muscogee	BROOKS, Robert	4	Talbot
BROOKS, Felix	12	Jones	BROOKS, S. W.	9	Randolph
BROOKS, Henry	5	Troup	BROOKS, Saml.	3	Randolph
BROOKS, Hiram	10	Jasper	BROOKS, Turner	2	Talbot

Name	Number	County	Name	Number	County
BROOKS, W. H.	12	Crawford	BROWN, John	4	Wayne
BROOKS, W. W.	12	Coweta	BROWN, John A.	11	Walton
BROOKS, Wm.	4	Decatur	BROWN, John Ann	4	Washington
BROOKS, Wm. H.	3	Randolph	BROWN, Lewis	4	Upson
BROOKS, Wyatt	6	Stewart	BROWN, Lewis S.	1	Wilkes
BROOM, Adam	2	Warren	BROWN, M.	7	Washington
BROOM, James M.	1	Warren	BROWN, Martha	4	Washington
BROOM, Leroy	11	Greene	BROWN, Mary	45	Washington
BROOM, Miles G.	7	Greene	BROWN, Mary L.	10	Troup
BROOME, Rufus	27	Troup	BROWN, Nancy	1	Washington
BROOME, Rufus	5	Troup	BROWN, Richard S.	10	Washington
BROSON, Lewis	8	Gwinnett	BROWN, Robert W.	16	Troup
BROTEN, John	12	Newton	BROWN, Samual	2	Emanual
BROUGHTON, Cornelius	1	Glynn	BROWN, Samuel A.	6	Walton
BROUGHTON, Edward	9	Troup	BROWN, Sarah	4	Washington
BROUGHTON, Edward	57	Troup	BROWN, Sarah W.	6	Washington
BROUGHTON, John A. by agt.	28	Morgan	BROWN, S. Willard	30	Thomas
BROUGHTON, John A.	7	Jasper	BROWN, Thomas T.	5	Walker
BROUGHTON, John H.	70	Greene	BROWN, ?	2	Irwin
BROUGHTON, John T.	16	Greene	BROWN, ?	5	Muscogee
BROUGHTON, Mary	16	Morgan	BROWN, A. E.W.	25	Hancock
BROUGHTON, Cecilia	1	Chatham	BROWN, A. M.	12	Henry
BROUGHTON, Elijah	8	Chatham	BROWN, A. M.	1	Morgan
BROUGHTON,John A. by CONNELL, W.	19	Morgan	BROWN, A. R.	4	Henry
BROUGTON, Jacob S.	10	Clarke	BROWN, A. S.	12	Hancock
BROUN, A. J.	1	Elbert	BROWN, Alexander	7	Monroe
BROUN, E.	22	Elbert	BROWN, Alexander D.	1	Jones
BROUN, E. J.	2	Elbert	BROWN, Amos	24	Morgan
BROUN, H.	1	Elbert	BROWN, B. A.	23	Camden
BROUN, M. G.	4	Elbert	BROWN, Balus	1	Henry
BROUN, R. J.	8	Elbert	BROWN, Benjamin	13	Madison
BROUN, W. .B	2	Elbert	BROWN, Catherine	2	Heard
BROUN, B.	3	Elbert	BROWN, D.	1	Pike
BROUNAR, H. P.	28	Elbert	BROWN, David M.	18	Houston
BROUNAR, J. F.	12	Elbert	BROWN, David M.	10	Houston
BROUNAR, J. M.	12	Elbert	BROWN, Dempsey	4	Fayette
BROUNER, S. J.	20	Elbert	BROWN, Dempsey	55	Houston
BROUNOR, James	5	Elbert	BROWN, E. H.	1	Elbert
BROWN, A.	30	Wilkinson	BROWN, Ebeneezer	4	Jefferson
BROWN, A. A.	3	Wilkinson	BROWN, Elijah	27	Clarke
BROWN, E.	27	Washington	BROWN, Elizabeth	5	Jackson
BROWN, Franklin	1	Upson	BROWN, Elizabeth	18	Jefferson
BROWN, George W.	27	Thomas	BROWN, Elizabeth E.	43	Hancock
BROWN, Georgia Ann	5	Washington	BROWN, Enoch	35	Marion
BROWN, Handy	3	Thomas	BROWN, Enoch C.	9	Dooly
BROWN, Henry T.	4	Upson	BROWN, Ezekiel	3	Clarke
BROWN, James G.	3	Washington	BROWN, Ezekiel	19	Harris
BROWN, Jesse	5	Emanual	BROWN, Ezekiel	21	Pike
BROWN, John	11	Troup	BROWN, G. W.	1	Elbert
			BROWN, Geo. A.	14	Marion
			BROWN, George	3	Monroe
			BROWN, George L.	1	Gordon
			BROWN, H. W.	2	Pike
			BROWN, Hampton	5	Muscogee

39

Name	Number	County
BROWN, Henry	1	Emanual
BROWN, Henry	37	Jones
BROWN, Henry	32	Marion
BROWN, Henry T.	1	Dooly
BROWN, Hezekiah	27	Lowndes
BROWN, Isaac M.	3	Pike
BROWN, Isham	1	Houston
BROWN, J. A.	1	Elbert
BROWN, J. F.	6	Muscogee
BROWN, J. R.	1	Henry
BROWN, J. S.	2	Merriwether
BROWN, J. W.	1	Houston
BROWN, James	10	Emanual
BROWN, James	1	Franklin
BROWN, James	1	Habersham
BROWN, James	4	Marion
BROWN, James	3	Merriwether
BROWN, James	3	Merriwether
BROWN, James B.	8	Early
BROWN, James F.	5	Burke
BROWN, James H.	16	Habersham
BROWN, James J.	13	Jefferson
BROWN, James L.	7	Greene
BROWN, James L.	6	Greene
BROWN, James M.	3	Harris
BROWN, James N.	12	Houston
BROWN, James N.	11	Morgan
BROWN, Jas.	1	Irwin
BROWN, Jas. C .	1	Carroll
BROWN, Jno. K.	1	Pulaski
BROWN, John	4	Butts
BROWN, John	11	Greene
BROWN, John	9	Marion
BROWN, John	35	Monroe
BROWN, John	12	Monroe
BROWN, John	1	Morgan
BROWN, John E.	21	Hall
BROWN, John F.	2	Cass
BROWN, John F.	6	Harris
BROWN, John M.	7	Gordon
BROWN, John S.	3	Hancock
BROWN, John T.	17	Macon
BROWN, Joseph	1	Marion
BROWN, Joseph	1	Monroe
BROWN, Joseph E.	5	Cherokee
BROWN, Joseph T.	3	Muscogee
BROWN, Joshua	3	Camden
BROWN, Josiah	4	Newton
BROWN, Josiah S.	5	Baldwin
BROWN, Kisiah	13	Morgan
BROWN, L. Q. C. D.	17	Jefferson
BROWN, Larkin M.	1	Cobb
BROWN, Lennon?	5	Newton
BROWN, Leroy	9	Heard
BROWN, Luisa	1	Oglethorpe
BROWN, Luke	2	Pike
BROWN, M.	17	Henry
BROWN, M. W.	38	Hall
BROWN, Marcus	2	Meriwether
BROWN, Martin	1	Henry
BROWN, Mary	7	Gwinnett
BROWN, Mary	3	Gwinnett
BROWN, Mary	13	Monroe
BROWN, Mary continued	1	Gwinnett
BROWN, Middleton	1	Fayette
BROWN, Milton A.	18	Houston
BROWN, Mrs. C.	8	Meriwether
BROWN, Nichols	1	Franklin
BROWN, Oliver	1	Campbell
BROWN, Oscar A.	12	Harris
BROWN, Oscar V.	3	Harris
BROWN, P.	10	Henry
BROWN, P. F.	5	Harris
BROWN, R.	7	Elbert
BROWN, R.	1	Henry
BROWN, R.	2	Merriwether
BROWN, R. W.	7	Hall
BROWN, Richard J.	16	Jefferson
BROWN, Robert	18	Harris
BROWN, Robert	16	Jasper
BROWN, Robert	41	Jones
BROWN, Robert G.	3	Madison
BROWN, Robt.	2	Forsyth
BROWN, Ruben	81	Monroe
BROWN, Russel J.	8	Jasper
BROWN, S.	8	Irwin
BROWN, Samuel	7	Newton
BROWN, Sarah M.	12	Campbell
BROWN, Silas	2	Cobb
BROWN, Stephen	45	Houston
BROWN, Stephen A.	10	Newton
BROWN, Stephen J.	23	Pike
BROWN, Sterling E.	1	Gwinnett
BROWN, Thomas	2	Lee
BROWN, Thomas J.	10	Marion
BROWN, Thomas P.	10	Jefferson
BROWN, Thos.	10	Oglethorpe
BROWN, Thos. M.	1	Oglethorpe
BROWN, Tolliver	13	Jefferson
BROWN, Turner	5	Bibb
BROWN, U. F.	1	Wilkes
BROWN, Valentine	26	Greene
BROWN, William	32	Houston
BROWN, William	4	Merriwether
BROWN, William	1	Morgan
BROWN, William	1	Muscogee
BROWN, William	1	Muscogee

Name	Number	County	Name	Number	County
BROWN, William	7	Newton	BROWN, Nancy	13	Talbot
BROWN, William	6	Newton	BROWN, Rachael	1	Bibb
BROWN, William Jun.	2	Newton	BROWN, Robert M.	3	DeKalb
BROWN, William R.	27	Houston	BROWN, Robt. Y.	13	Coweta
BROWN, William T.	1	Houston	BROWN, Samuel B.	3	Baldwin
BROWN, W. L.	1	Walton	BROWN, Samuel G.	1	Burke
BROWN, Wm.	17	Heard	BROWN, Seaborn	8	Richmond
BROWN, Wm.	2	Macon	BROWN, T. A.	10	Bibb
BROWN, Wm. B.	8	Coweta	BROWN, Thomas	16	Talbot
BROWN, Wm. M.	49	Marion	BROWN, Vincent	4	Cass
BROWN, W. T.	14	Walton	BROWN, W. B.	1	Dooly
BROWN, Zachues	2	Emanual	BROWN, William	41	Richmond
BROWN, A. B.	4	Coweta	BROWN, William G.	7	Washington
BROWN, Absolom	1	Richmond	BROWN, William M.	44	Bullock
BROWN, Alford	3	Talbot	BROWN, William R.	2	Dooly
BROWN, Benjamin	24	Stewart	BROWN, Wm. F.	28	Dooly
BROWN, Catherine	3	Baker	BROWN, Jas. E.	27	Randolph
BROWN, Daniel M.	8	Richmond	BROWN?, Simson	30	Morgan
BROWN, David	45	Camden	BROWNAR, J.	2	Elbert
BROWN, David P.	20	Baldwin	BROWNER, John	10	Franklin
BROWN, E. D.	44	Baldwin	BROWNING, E. C.	4	Monroe
BROWN, E. J.	6	Sumter	BROWNING, J. A.	1	Clarke
BROWN, E.R.	5	Sumter	BROWNING, Jeptha	23	Clarke
BROWN, Elijah	5	Stewart	BROWNING, John	9	Newton
BROWN, Elizabeth	6	Burke	BROWNING, John C.	20	Thomas
BROWN, Elizabeth	3	Burke	BROWNING, Joshua R.	35	Walton
BROWN, Ervin	1	Dooly	BROWNING, William	1	Montgomery
BROWN, G. W.	5	Stewart	BROWNING, William	8	Thomas
BROWN, Henry	4	Randolph	BROWNING, Andrew	2	DeKalb
BROWN, Hollinger	26	Stewart	BROWNLEE, Jas.	9	Butts
BROWN, Hugh	20	Camden	BROWNSON, H. W.	5	Bibb
BROWN, Isaac	9	Pike	BROXTON, James R.	1	Burke
BROWN, James	2	DeKalb	BROYLES, Charles E.	5	Murray
BROWN, James F.	8	Baldwin	BRUCE, A. D.	6	Harris
BROWN, James J.	2	Dade	BRUCE, A. J.	4	Greene
BROWN, James L.	32	Burke	BRUCE, Archibald	2	Merriwether
BROWN, Jas.	9	Coweta	BRUCE, D. M.	2	Pulaski
BROWN, Jas.	6	Coweta	BRUCE, John A.	5	Greene
BROWN, Jesse	3	Randolph	BRUCE, Robert	11	Franklin
BROWN, John	1	Columbia	BRUCE, J. A.	1	Coweta
BROWN, John B.	2	Dooly	BRUCE, James	2	Richmond
BROWN, John H.	1	Burke	BRUCE, John M.	25	Talbot
BROWN, John T.	11	Burke	BRUCE, Wilson	3	Troup
BROWN, Jos. T.	22	Coweta	BRUCE, W. W.	6	Chattooga
BROWN, Joseph	39	Talbot	BRUCK, Richard	1	Houston
BROWN, Joseph	8	Talbot	BRUCKMAN, Henry	3	DeKalb
BROWN, Joseph	1	Talbot	BRUCKNER, Martin E.	1	Lincoln
BROWN, Killis	3	DeKalb	BRUEN, Matilda	2	Chatham
BROWN, L. H.	10	Sumter	BRUER, George	1	Troup
BROWN, M.H.	21	Randolph	BRUER, Septamus	1	Monroe
BROWN, Madison	2	Coweta	BRUICE, David	2	Franklin
BROWN, Meredith	10	DeKalb	BRUINAG?, Thomas A.	26	Bibb
BROWN, Morgan S.	1	Baker	BRUNAR, James	25	Elbert
BROWN, Mrs. Lidea	7	Stewart	BRUNDAGE, A. R.	19	Twiggs

Name	Number	County	Name	Number	County
BRUNDAGE, Jesse	13	Hancock	BRYANT, A. N.	3	Chattooga
BRUNDAGE, Jesse	100	Stewart	BRYANT, A. R.	1	Chattooga
BRUNER, D.	2	Wilkinson	BRYANT, A. T. Estate	39	Twiggs
BRUNETT, S. P.	22	Randolph	BRYANT, Alender	3	Pike
BRUNNER, Isaac	5	Chatham	BRYANT, Asbury	3	Muscogee
BRUNSON, John F.	4	Baker	BRYANT, B. B.	7	Lee
BRUNT, James	1	Pike	BRYANT, Benjamin	72	Houston
BRUNT, John	9	Pike	BRYANT, Bird	3	Jasper
BRUNTLEY, J. H.	3	Bibb	BRYANT, Bohn	3	Meriwether
BRUSTER, James	9	Campbell	BRYANT, Braxton	6	Oglethorpe
BRUTON, Abraham	2	Franklin	BRYANT, Frederick B.	9	Houston
BRUTON, D. L.	18	Decatur	BRYANT, George A.	34	Harris
BRUTON, Nathan	41	Bullock	BRYANT, Goode	43	Jefferson
BRUWER, Joseph	1	Paulding	BRYANT, Hiram	1	Jones
BRYAN, Alford	14	Thomas	BRYANT, Hugh	11	Hall
BRYAN, Edward	29	Thomas	BRYANT, James S.	1	Murray
BRYAN, Erastus J.	13	Macon	BRYANT, James T.	3	Walker
BRYAN, Est.	15	Screven	BRYANT, Jasper	1	Morgan
BRYAN, Hardy	40	Thomas	BRYANT, Jno.	4	Henry
BRYAN, Hardy H.	11	Thomas	BRYANT, John	14	Jones
BRYAN, James M.	21	Twiggs	BRYANT, John	1	Murray
BRYAN, James S.	5	Washington	BRYANT, John D.	7	Liberty
BRYAN, Jesse	14	Greene	BRYANT, John W.	2	Lee
BRYAN, John	21	Houston	BRYANT, Joseph M.	35	Twiggs
BRYAN, John	17	Lowndes	BRYANT, L. O.	11	Pulaski
BRYAN, John L.	7	Macon	BRYANT, Mary	40	Twiggs
BRYAN, Joseph	39	Hancock	BRYANT, Nancy	1	Gordon
BRYAN, Martha	16	Macon	BRYANT, Needham	20	Lee
BRYAN, Nathan	42	Macon	BRYANT, Robert	3	Harris
BRYAN, Nathan Jr.	1	Macon	BRYANT, Rolin	25	Floyd
BRYAN, Needham	1	Houston	BRYANT, R. M.	3	Walker
BRYAN, Norman	5	Monroe	BRYANT, Richd.	3	Wilkes
BRYAN, Penelope	19	Washington	BRYANT, Samuel	2	Jackson
BRYAN, Richard	1	Greene	BRYANT, Sylvanus S.	30	Houston
BRYAN, Samuel O.	23	Wayne	BRYANT, W.	4	Morgan
BRYAN, Seaborn C.	29	Houston	BRYANT, William	1	Hall
BRYAN, Thomas	20	Walker	BRYANT, William	35	Twiggs
BRYAN, William	15	Greene	BRYANT, Wm.	7	Henry
BRYAN, William	33	Houston	BRYANT, Wm. agt.	31	Bibb
BRYAN, William	9	Monroe	BRYANT, A.	10	Chattooga
BRYAN, William G.	4	Washington	BRYANT, D.	2	Decatur
BRYAN, Wm. H.	1	Gordon	BRYANT, David C.	30	Stewart
BRYAN, William M.	2	Walker	BRYANT, E.	1	Chattooga
BRYAN, Augustus	1	Columbia	BRYANT, Elijah L.	4	Campbell
BRYAN, B. M.	3	Butts	BRYANT, F. W.	1	Putnam
BRYAN, Catharine	4	Chatham	BRYANT, George	1	Campbell
BRYAN, David	78	Talbot	BRYANT, J.	8	Decatur
BRYAN, Martin L.	16	Screven	BRYANT, James M.	11	Telfair
BRYAN, Richard	3	Tatnall	BRYANT, Jas.	24	Putnam
BRYAN, Thos.	12	Randolph	BRYANT, John H.	15	Talbot
BRYAN, Wilford	19	Randolph	BRYANT, Loverd	58	Stewart
BRYANS, J.	35	Henry	BRYANT, Thomas W.	1	Chatham
BRYANS, Lewis W.	12	Wayne	BRYANT, W. H.	3	Putnam
BRYANS, T. H.	5	Henry	BRYANT, William	1	Richmond

Name	Number	County
BRYANT, William	11	Stewart
BRYANT?, Charles	2	Franklin
BRYAS, Anna	14	Butts
BRYAS, R. G.	7	Butts
BRYCE, Jas.	1	Carroll
BRYDIE, Archibald	2	Clarke
BRYSON, Eliza.	5	Richmond
BRYSON, Harper C.	3	Richmond
BRYSON, R.	2	Chattooga
BUCHAN, Jno.	16	Pulaski
BUCHAN, Peter	1	Troup
BUCHANAN, Amariah	2	Heard
BUCHANAN, Duncan	3	Montgomery
BUCHANAN, James	12	Early
BUCHANAN, John	11	Early
BUCHANAN, W. H.	1	Clarke
BUCHANAN, G. B. estate of Maryann	6	Baldwin
BUCHANAN, J.	4	Irwin
BUCHANAN, Thomas	8	Baldwin
BUCHANNAN, James C.	4	Jasper
BUCHANNAN, Jesse	14	Harris
BUCHANNON, Elizabeth	11	Jackson
BUCHANNON, Wm. T. M.	8	Heard
BUCHANNON, John W.	1	DeKalb
BUCK, A.	7	Troup
BUCK, L. B.	7	Jefferson
BUCK, William	21	Washington
BUCK, Wright W.	1	Washington
BUCKAN, Jas.	1	Pulaski
BUCKAN, John	1	Pulaski
BUCKANNON, Alexander	10	Talbot
BUCKANNON, Joseph	1	Talbot
BUCKELEW, J. P.	1	Henry
BUCKELEW, James F.	1	Pike
BUCKEN, Tavener	1	Franklin
BUCKHANAN, Isaac	5	Paulding
BUCKHANNAN?, Nicodemus	2	Pike
BUCKHANNON, H.	4	Coweta
BUCKHANNON, T. J.	2	Chattooga
BUCKHANON, Chas. W.	16	Walton
BUCKNER, A.	8	Henry
BUCKNER, Alfred	7	Pike
BUCKNER, Ardm? S.	4	Pike
BUCKNER, Claborn	6	Baldwin
BUCKNER, Eli	7	Henry
BUCKNER, Param	1	Monroe
BUCKNER, Reason	11	Jones
BUCKNER, Daniel	5	Baldwin

Name	Number	County
BUCKNER, L. D.	6	Baldwin
BUCKNER, Pleasant	1	Sumter
BUCKNER, Richmond	9	Putnam
BUCKNER, Solomon	3	Putnam
BUCKNER, Wm. T.	1	Putnam
BUD, Zachariah	3	Heard
BUELL, James M.	8	Troup
BUFF, Daniel W.	9	Houston
BUFFINGTON, Ellis	11	Hall
BUFFINGTON, Henderson	5	Fayette
BUFFINGTON, Mazza?	5	Hall
BUFFINGTON, W.	4	Elbert
BUFFINGTON, W. C.	4	Pike
BUFFINGTON, W. J.	5	Hall
BUFFORD, Wm. D.	6	Wilkes
BUFFORD, Wm. P.	9	Troup
BUFORD, Alfred	16	Cass
BUFORD, William H.	3	Richmond
BUFORT, Sarah	2	Oglethorpe
BUGAMY, John	10	Pike
BUGG, H. C.	14	Oglethorpe
BUGG, Ben	40	Columbia
BUGG, G.	1	Columbia
BUGG, James	38	Stewart
BUGG, Obedience	12	Richmond
BUGG, Robert W.	9	Richmond
BUICE, A. D.	2	Harris
BUIE, James	33	Screven
BUILFORD, Wm.	3	Randolph
BUKER, E. W.	1	Chatham
BULAND, Benjamin	16	Crawford
BULARD, Middleton	2	Cobb
BULINGTON, Elizabeth	12	Dooly
BULKLEY, Justice R.	3	Richmond
BULL, Jesse J.	24	Twiggs
BULL, Orvelle A.	4	Troup
BULL, W. H.	3	Twiggs
BULLARD, Allen B.	10	Twiggs
BULLARD, B. N.	5	Elbert
BULLARD, Daniel	16	Twiggs
BULLARD, James	13	Putnam
BULLARD, Kenneda ?	3	Twiggs
BULLARD, Lewis	17	Washington
BULLARD, Nancy A.	2	Jasper
BULLARD, Robert	30	Macon
BULLARD, W. G.	10	Elbert
BULLARD, Calvin	1	Stewart
BULLARD, Jannany	3	Campbell
BULLARD, Needham	27	Burke
BULLARD, Thomas	15	Campbell
BULLARD, Wiley	25	Stewart
BULLEK, William B.	2	Walton
BULLER, Daniel C.	9	Dooly

Name	Number	County
BULLER, Elizabeth	1	DeKalb
BULLINGER, John	6	Cobb
BULLINGTON, Joseph R.	1	Jones
BULLOCH, Doctor L.	2	Marion
BULLOCH, James	4	Marion
BULLOCK, Alexander	1	Paulding
BULLOCK, Alexander G.	5	Madison
BULLOCK, Cordy	3	Marion
BULLOCK, Eliza	1	Chatham
BULLOCK, estate	1	Muscogee
BULLOCK, Jeffrian	1	Merriwether
BULLOCK, Martha	19	Cobb
BULLOCK, Martha	12	Cobb
BULLOCK, N.	3	Cass
BULLOCK, Nathanial H	4	Paulding
BULLOCK, Richard H.	8	Madison
BULLOCK, William B.	38	Chatham
BULLOCK, Archibald	3	Chatham
BULLOCK, Irvin	10	Dooly
BULLOCK, J. A.	2	Wilkinson
BULLOCK, J. T.	2	Troup
BULLOCK, James	1	Wilkinson
BULLOCK, William G.	1	Chatham
BULLOCK, William G.	14	Walton
BULLOCK, William H.	5	Chaham
BULLOCK, Willis	2	Wilkinson
BULLOCK, Wyatt	6	Walton
BULLS, Willis	1	Forsyth
BULOCK estate	1	Muscogee
BUMLEY, Stephen G.	2	Hancock
BUNCH, Doctime Estate of	13	Richmond
BUNCH, G.	2	Wilkes
BUNCH, Joseph E.	6	Richmond
BUNCK, Charles	1	Richmond
BUNCKLEY, Mary	2	Camden
BUNCKLEY, Thos.	7	Camden
BUNDRICK, Zac	2	Crawford
BUNDRIDGE, David	12	Sumter
BUNDRIDGE, Elijah	11	Sumter
BUNDY, Lewis	2	Heard
BUNER ?, William	4	Wilkinson
BUNKLEY, Elizabeth	9	Greene
BUNKLEY, George W.	5	Pike
BUNKLEY, Howel F.	12	Greene
BUNKLEY, James	42	Talbot
BUNKLEY, Jesse	18	Troup
BUNKLEY, William H.	15	Troup
BUNN, Jeremiah W.	29	Houston
BUNN, Marcus H.	23	Houston
BUNN, Civility	3	Burke

Name	Number	County
BUNN, Moses L.	6	Burke
BUNS ?, William P.	4	Richmond
BUNT, Abingdon	1	DeKalb
BUNTING, G. A.	4	Houston
BUNTON, Wm. W.	1	Lee
BUNTS, Lucretia	4	Chatham
BURCH, Benjamin	25	Laurens
BURCH, E.	89	Elbert
BURCH, Edward	1	Pulaski
BURCH, Jas. A.	6	Pulaski
BURCH, Mary A.	8	Campbell
BURCH, William	13	Floyd
BURCH, Wm. W.	11	Floyd
BURCH, Ann	5	Talbot
BURCH, M. N.	5	Bibb
BURCH, Thos.	1	Crawford
BURCH, Wm.	11	Taliaferro
BURCKHALTER, John L.	24	Warren
BURDELL, Dr. F. V.	9	Burke
BURDETT, Jno. G.	8	Wilkes
BURDETT, Jos. T.	5	Wilkes
BURDETT, Joseph T.	4	Wilkes
BURDETT, Thos. P.	40	Wilkes
BURDETT, Wm. H.	3	Wilkes
BURDETTE, J. W.	2	Wilkes
BURDIT?, James O.	3	Harris
BURFORD, Henry	3	Butts
BURFORD, Thos. M.	29	Harris
BURFORD, Philip H.	10	DeKalb
BURFORD, T. B.	15	Butts
BURFORD, Thos. B.	24	Butts
BURFORD, V. B.	23	Butts
BURFORD, W. H.	3	Butts
BURGA, John	11	Monroe
BURGA, Levin	6	Monroe
BURGAMY, John	1	Laurens
BURGE, Dalton	11	Floyd
BURGE, John	2	Jasper
BURGE, Lorenza	7	Cobb
BURGE, Nancy	49	Cass
BURGE, Thomas	24	Newton
BURGE, Wm.	4	Cass
BURGER, Wm.	4	Crawford
BURGESS, Abner	2	Franklin
BURGESS, Benjamin	3	Gilmer
BURGESS, Jonathan	16	Greene
BURGEY, J. M.	1	Putnam
BURGNOR, John	3	Bibb
BURGS?, J. S.	14	Bibb
BURISS, John	14	Forsyth
BURK, Charles J.	16	Greene
BURK, Charles Senr.	9	Greene
BURK, Elsathine	10	Macon

44

Name	Number	County	Name	Number	County
BURK, James	5	Greene	BURNES, M. S.	5	Chattooga
BURK, L.	2	Twiggs	BURNES, James C.	79	Twiggs
BURk, Littleton L.	12	Troup	BURNES, Nancy	4	Twiggs
BURK, Ricd.	1	Muscogee	BURNET, Isma	9	Emanual
BURK, Robert	9	Monroe	BURNET, James H.	7	Hancock
BURK, Thomas	38	Franklin	BURNET, James H.	1	Thomas
BURK, W. B.	2	Meriwether	BURNET, John H.	1	Macon
BURK, A.	3	Coweta	BURNET, Jas.	5	Bibb
BURK, Charles	2	Chatham	BURNET, Martin	1	Crawford
BURK, Eliza	3	Stewart	BURNETT, Hosea A.	1	Jackson
BURK, John	8	Talbot	BURNETT, Jas.	14	Elbert
BURK, Jourden M.	2	Sumter	BURNETT, John	25	Lincoln
BURKE, Henry	1	Burke	BURNETT, John	13	Lincoln
BURKE, Hugh L.	1	Jefferson	BURNETT, John	5	Muscogee
BURKE, John	24	Wilkinson	BURNETT, John H.	3	Chattooga
BURKE, Mary	1	Jefferson	BURNETT, John S.	2	Floyd
BURKE, N.	11	Wilkinson	BURNETT, Margaret	17	Glynn
BURKE, Richard E.	7	Clarke	BURNETT, Martin C.	10	Monroe
BURKE, David	10	Screven	BURNETT, Saml. M.	11	Glynn
BURKE, James	5	Screven	BURNETT, Willey	5	Jackson
BURKE, Martha	7	Screven	BURNETT, William	4	Morgan
BURKE, N. B.	2	Telfair	BURNETT, Geo.	1	Chattooga
BURKE, Rodney, H.	2	Burke	BURNETT, Valentine	7	Campbell
BURKE, Simeon	13	Screven	BURNETTE, A. T.	1	Jackson
BURKE, William	4	Stewart	BURNEY, G. B.	30	Wilkinson
BURKES, John	2	Troup	BURNEY, J. F.	7	Wilkinson
BURKES, John	2	Upson	BURNEY, J. H.	3	Forsyth
BURKET, Mathew	1	Appling	BURNEY, John w.	44	Jasper
BURKETT, Andrew A.	1	Twiggs	BURNEY, M.A.	4	Forsyth
BURKETT, C.	4	Twiggs	BURNEY, Milton	3	Wilkinson
BURKETT, Chanaty	5	Twiggs	BURNEY, T. J.	34	Morgan
BURKETT, Thos. W.	3	Twiggs	BURNEY, T. W.	23	Monroe
BURKHALTER, ?	2	Clinch	BURNEY, W. W.	28	Morgan
BURKHALTER,			BURNEY, William	32	Glynn
David N.	19	Marion	BURNEY, L. M..	3	Coweta
BURKHALTER, Jas. A.	10	Pulaski	BURNEY, M. W.	8	Coweta
BURKHALTER, John	21	Marion	BURNHAM, Bryan	1	Lowndes
BURKHALTER,			BURNHAM, Alfred	4	Telfair
Michael	6	Jones	BURNLEY, Perry J.	9	Warren
BURKHALTER,			BURNLEY, Richmond	35	Hancock
Polly C.	36	Pulaski	BURNS, Brewer	9	Camden
BURKHALTER, Elam	4	Cass	BURNS, David M.	28	Jackson
BURKHALTER,			BURNS, E. R.	4	Henry
Vaughters	1	Tatnall	BURNS, Henry	35	Twiggs
BURKHOLTS, Peter	12	Dooly	BURNS, James H.	3	Jackson
BURKS, George	1	Troup	BURNS, John	1	Cherokee
BURKS, John H.	1	Wilkes	BURNS, John	5	Floyd
BURKS, Wiley P.	28	Merriwether	BURNS, Jos.	5	Floyd
BURKS, William	2	Newton	BURNS, Samuel T.	33	Wilkes
BURKS, William G.	1	Newton	BURNS, Susannah	1	Cherokee
BURKS, Abell F.	6	Sumter	BURNS, T. P.	3	Newton
BURKS, Absalom	1	Sumter	BURNS, Thos. J.	10	Twiggs
BURKS, Henry	2	Sumter	BURNS, William B.	1	Franklin
BURN, Thomas	9	DeKalb	BURNS, Benj. C.	7	Carroll

Name	Number	County	Name	Number	County
BURNS, O. S.	5	Stewart	BURTON, N.	12	Elbert
BURNS, Thomas H.	61	Screven	BURTON, Robt .	26	Marion
BURNSIDE, Thomas	3	Fayette	BURTON, Thomas	29	Hancock
BURNSIDE, John	2	Bullock	BURTON, William	1	Burke
BURNSIDE, Thos.	1	Columbia	BURTON, William F.	2	Walton
BURNSIDE, William	3	Bryan	BURTON, A.	3	Dooly
BURNSTEIN, Edward C.	2	Fayette	BURTON, A. J.	3	Bibb
BURR, J.	4	Pike	BURTON, E. M.	7	Randolph
BURR, Augustus P.	1	Cobb	BURTON, G. W .	2	Decatur
BURR, H.	14	Talbot	BURTON, Mrs. Susan	45	Burke
BURR, Zach	16	Talbot	BURTON, Robt. P.	28	Camden
BURR, Zach	5	Talbot	BURTON, Simeon L.	2	Burke
BURRIS, A.	3	Cass	BURTON, Thomas	13	Elbert
BURRNET, Susanna	3	Bibb	BURTON, Thomas B.	2	Baker
BURROUGHS, Henry K.	17	Cobb	BURTY, Joshua	1	Cherokee
BURROUGHS, James	11	Madison	BURZA, Thomas	6	Monroe
BURROUGHS, William	4	Franklin	BUS, T. H.	7	Heard
BURROUGHS,			BUS ?, Thomas	4	Walton
William F.	1	Madison	BUSBAY, Wm.	1	DeKalb
BURROUGHS, Benjamin	22	Chatham	BUSBIN, John	4	Oglethorpe
BURROUGHS, Betsy	7	Columbia	BUSBY, B. A.	47	Liberty
BURROUGHS, Catherine	8	Chatham	BUSBY, Mary	1	Houston
BURROUGHS, Davis	21	Cass	BUSBY, E.	2	Bibb
BURROUGHS, James	7	Columbia	BUSBY, Joshua	2	Richmond
BURROUGHS, Joseph H.	10	Chatham	BUSDEN, Ray	1	Coweta
BURROUGHS, O. L.	1	Chatham	BUSEY, Lucy	4	Muscogee
BURROWS, Jacob G.	3	Muscogee	BUSEY, Nathaniel	20	Muscogee
BURROWS, Wm.	2	Carroll	BUSH, Daniel T.	2	Franklin
BURROWS, G.	2	Carroll	BUSH, Fer ?	1	Wilkinson
BURSON, Hazael G.	2	Warren	BUSH, Jackson	19	Monroe
BURSON, Isaac	4	Walton	BUSH, James	26	Early
BURSON, Mary	1	Marion	BUSH, James	5	Upson
BURSON, Seaborn C.	3	Walton	BUSH, S. J.	5	Wilkinson
BURSON, Thomas H.	3	Upson	BUSH, Thomas	2	Houston
BURSTINER?, Mathew	7	Effingham	BUSH, Thomas J.	7	Muscogee
BURT, E. B.	1	Oglethorpe	BUSH, W. M.	21	Oglethorpe
BURT, H. L.	7	Hancock	BUSH, William H.	7	Wilkinson
BURT, J. J.	8	Chattooga	BUSH, William J.	2	Muscogee
BURT, John	7	Monroe	BUSH, Daniel S.	1	Richmond
BURT, Mildred	15	Talbot	BUSH, David B.	15	Talbot
BURT, Moody	90	Columbia	BUSH, David B.	10	Talbot
BURT, Wm. M.	3	Troup	BUSH, Elijah	1	Dooly
BURTON ? , James T.	4	Richmond	BUSH, Elizabeth	13	Stewart
BURTON, A. T .	4	Elbert	BUSH, Joseph	6	Burke
BURTON, Benj.	42	Marion	BUSH, Margaret	10	Chatham
BURTON, Benjamin H.	12	Franklin	BUSKET, Robert	1	Newton
BURTON, E. M.	13	Wilkes	BUSSEY, Charles	8	Jasper
BURTON, F.	13	Elbert	BUSSEY, C. H.	16	Wilkes
BURTON, Isaish	18	Merriwether	BUSSEY, H. T.	6	Wilkes
BURTON, John	2	Walton	BUSSEY, Malikiah	20	Pike
BURTON, John N.	5	Jackson	BUSSEY, Thomas J.	1	Pike
BURTON, Joseph	1	Oglethorpe	BUSSEY, Thos.	4	Gordon
BURTON, L.	7	Elbert	BUSSEY, Wade	7	Gordon
BURTON, Mary	2	Merriwether	BUSSEY, David	9	Talbot

Name	Number	County	Name	Number	County
BUSSEY, Mary	2	Richmond	BUTLER, William C.	1	Jones
BUSSEY, Nathan	25	Talbot	BUTLER, A.	2	Decatur
BUSSEY, T. Z.	2	Stewart	BUTLER, Ann G.	3	Bryan
BUSSY, Benjamin P.	34	Merriwether	BUTLER, B.	1	Bryan
BUSSY, Charles	8	Lincoln	BUTLER, C.	7	Decatur
BUSSY, N. J.	14	Lincoln	BUTLER, David	10	Putnam
BUSSY, Nathan	19	Lincoln	BUTLER, Elizabeth	15	Randolph
BUSSY, William D.	8	Effingham	BUTLER, Emma	16	Putnam
BUSSY, William R.	2	Merriwether	BUTLER, Felix R.	1	Dooly
BUSSY, James	5	Stewart	BUTLER, Gabriel	2	Dooly
BUSSY, H. H.	6	Meriwether	BUTLER, Gilbert	13	Chatham
BUSTER ? . Edw.	13	Richmond	BUTLER, H.	2	Randolph
BUSTIAN, C.	10	Putnam	BUTLER, Henry S.	12	Randolph
BUSTIAN, John	21	Talbot	BUTLER, Isaac	6	Dooly
BUSTIAN, Thomas	22	Troup	BUTLER, Isaiah	2	Richmond
BUSTLE, Daniel	1	Lee	BUTLER, J.	13	Decatur
BUTCHER, Elisha	1	Gordon	BUTLER, J. R.	3	Decatur
BUTLER, Wm. C.	1	Floyd	BUTLER, James	1	Bryan
BUTLER, Ann	6	Oglethorpe	BUTLER, Jeremiah R.	8	Richmond
BUTLER, Dempsey	20	Pike	BUTLER, Jno. G. est.	2	Bryan
BUTLER, Edmand M.	15	Monroe	BUTLER, John R.	7	Putnam
BUTLER, Eliza	2	Chatham	BUTLER, John W.	36	Columbia
BUTLER, General	7	Jackson	BUTLER, N. K.	16	Richmond
BUTLER, George	1	Cobb	BUTLER, Robert M.	1	Baker
BUTLER, George	1	Madison	BUTLER, Tarleton	9	Burke
BUTLER, Henry	16	Walton	BUTLER, Wm.	18	Randolph
BUTLER, Henry Agent	8	Upson	BUTLER,		
BUTLER, Hosea	2	Gordon	Worthington C.	2	Chatham
BUTLER, Isaac	6	Troup	BUTLOR, ?	14	Elbert
BUTLER, Isaac H.	3	Monroe	BUTT, Alfred	2	Union
BUTLER, J. P. estate	523	McIntosh	BUTT, Elijah	25	Dooly
BUTLER, James M.	18	Chatham	BUTT, John	8	Union
BUTLER, James M.	2	Monroe	BUTT, John	6	Warren
BUTLER, James P.	11	Harris	BUTT, Lavinea	7	Warren
BUTLER, Jas.	16	Henry	BUTT, Priscilla	52	Muscogee
BUTLER, Jesse	2	Clarke	BUTT, Priscilla	11	Muscogee
BUTLER, Jesse	5	Liberty	BUTT, Sarah	5	Union
BUTLER, Joel	20	Wilkinson	BUTT, Wm. B.	29	Marion
BUTLER, John	5	Wilkes	BUTT, Wm. B.	4	Marion
BUTLER, John A.	13	Liberty	BUTT, E. C.	3	Talbot
BUTLER, Larkin	1	Jackson	BUTT, E. C.	1	Talbot
BUTLER, Larkin	4	Meriwether	BUTT, Eldridge	42	Talbot
BUTLER, Martha	4	Dooly	BUTT, Richard L	5	Talbot
BUTLER, Martha P.	3	Floyd	BUTT, William M.	23	Campbell
BUTLER, Mary	8	Monroe	BUTTERWORTH,		
BUTLER, Mrs. C.	7	Bibb	T. E.	1	Hall
BUTLER, Nancy M.	14	Jackson	BUTTLER, James J.	7	Dooly
BUTLER, Ophelia L.	3	Chatham	BUTTLER, R. S.	8	Pike
BUTLER, Patrick R.	1	Madison	BUTTRILL, Burwell	4	Heard
BUTLER, T. J.	1	Jackson	BUTTRILL, Thomas	20	Heard
BUTLER ?, Thomas	12	Walton	BUTTRILL, Thomas	2	Heard
BUTLER, Toliver	1	Walker	BUTTRILL, Thomas T.	41	Warren
BUTLER, William	9	Bryan	BUTTRILL, Asa	19	Butts
BUTLER, William	15	Harris	BUTTRILL, Button	26	Butts

Name	Number	County	Name	Number	County
BUTTS, Benjamine K.	29	Hancock	BYRD, Mary Ann	10	Richmond
BUTTS, Catherine	2	Oglethorpe	BYRN, Richard	1	Newton
BUTTS, Edward A.	4	Hancock	BYROM, Nancy	13	Murray
BUTTS, Henry	3	Upson	BYROM, William H.	20	Houston
BUTTS, Henry T.	8	Upson	BYRON, (?). W.	1	Coweta
BUTTS, J. C.	13	Morgan	BYRON, James W.	1	Pike
BUTTS, Jas. J.	23	Hancock	BYRON, Jas.	6	Coweta
BUTTS, Jesse G.	21	Hancock	BYRON, Jas. A.	1	Coweta
BUTTS, Jesse G.	2	Upson	BYRUM, John G.	6	Pike
BUTTS, Martha	17	Merriwether	BYUS, Elizabeth	3	Harris
BUTTS, Mary A.	2	Monroe	CABANIS, H.K.	5	Campbell
BUTTS, Peter P.	8	Upson	CABANISS, E. G.	9	Monroe
BUTTS, Wm. R.	7	Hancock	CABAS, Emily	12	Chatham
BUTTS, A. G.	6	Bibb	CABBADGE, John B.	5	Chatham
BUTTS, Arthur J.	9	Baldwin	CABBADGE, Martha E.	4	Chatham
BUTTS, E. J.	5	Baldwin	CABEAN, Alexander	9	Talbot
BUTTS, George W.	14	Baldwin	CABENESS, Amanda	1	Stewart
BUTTS, Jefferson	1	Bryan	CABINESS, Henry B.	3	Floyd
BUTTS, L. P.	12	Cass	CABINESS, Sarah		
BUTTS, Lewis	23	Baldwin	estate	25	Jones
BUTTS, R. J.	8	Troup	CADE, D. B.	25	Elbert
BUTTS, S.	20	Randolph	CADE, G.	36	Elbert
BUTTS, William R.	19	Baldwin	CADE, Bedford	20	Wilkes
BUYMAN, R.	3	Randolph	CADE, James	10	Wilkes
BUYNAM ? R.	1	Randolph	CADE, Joseph H.	3	Wilkes
BUYS, Caswell	16	Monroe	CADE, Wiley P.	5	Stewart
BUYS, Henry	2	Monroe	CADE, Wm.	14	Wilkes
BUYS, John	5	Monroe	CADLE, Archibald	1	Richmond
BYARD, John	2	Muscogee	CADLE, George S.	1	Richmond
BYER, Bluford	1	Jackson	CADLE, Silas M.	1	Richmond
BYERS, Jno.	1	Carroll	CADWELLER, Curtes	1	Gwinnett
BYERS, Robert	1	Butts	CAFFER?, John	10	Pulaski
BYERS, Joel	11	Butts	CAFFER?, Peter	8	Pulaski
BYERS, Wm.	7	Butts	CAGLE, G. B. Manager	10	Henry
BYINGTON, James L.	2	Baker	CAHOUSE?, Ezekiel N.	6	DeKalb
BYNE, Oliver P.	2	Burke	CAIN, Valentine	5	Gordon
BYNE, William	41	Burke	CAIN, Elisha	57	Jefferson
BYNE, Edmund	20	Burke	CAIN, James	42	Jefferson
BYNE, Henry	24	Burke	CAIN, James F.	5	Jones
BYNE, John S.	7	Burke	CAIN, John	1	Forsyth
BYNE, Thomas	14	Burke	CAIN, John	10	Gwinnett
BYNGTON, Miss Julia	2	Muscogee	CAIN, John W.	1	Walker
BYNTON, Clara	2	Stewart	CAIN, William A.	3	Gwinnett
BYNUM, Hesse An	13	Washingoton	CAIN, John	7	Stewart
BYNUM, John	9	Columbia	CAIN, John R.	14	Baker
BYNUM, Thomas	10	Talbot	CAIRNS, Thos.	3	Carroll
BYRD, Daniel M.	14	Gwinnett	CALAHAN, Andrew	4	Oglethorpe
BYRD, Hiniant?	15	Houston	CALAHAN, John	1	Jackson
BYRD, Nathan	3	Houston	CALAWAY, E. H.	20	Oglethorpe
BYRD, William D.	14	Gwinnett	CALAWAY, G. W.	21	Oglethorpe
BYRD, Edwood	20	Screven	CALAWAY, Sarah	5	Monroe
BYRD, Henry	5	Richmond	CALAWAY, William	35	Monroe
BYRD, J. T.	1	Coweta	CALBARD?, T.	12	Elbert
BYRD, John J.	1	Richmond	CALDEA, George W.	14	McIntosh

Name	Number	County	Name	Number	County
CALDER, George	1	Bryan	CALHOUN, S.	15	Chattooga
CALDERLARK, Nathan	13	Gordon	CALHOUN, Stringer	1	Dooly
CALDWELL, Andrew H.	6	Walker	CALHOUN,		
CALDWELL, Early	1	Hancock	William H. Jr.	6	Richmond
CALDWELL, Eliza M.	12	Pike	CALIF, Ebenezer	1	Jones
CALDWELL, Henry A.	4	Pike	CALIWAY, Jesse	1	Monroe
CALDWELL, J. M.	1	Henry	CALLAHAN, Henry	4	Greene
CALDWELL, James	12	Jones	CALLAHAN, Jacob	4	Walton
CALDWELL, John	2	Walker	CALLAHAN, W.	5	Greene
CALDWELL, John J.	7	Pike	CALLAN, Thos.	1	Wilkes
CALDWELL, Josiah	2	Greene	CALLAWAY, James	5	Merriwether
CALDWELL, Mrs. M.	14	Meriwether	CALLAWAY, James	4	Merriwether
CALDWELL,			CALLAWAY, Joshua S.	7	Fayette
Oliver H. P.	2	Pike	CALLAWAY,		
CALDWELL, Rebecca	1	Gwinnett	Abraham B.	19	Stewart
CALDWELL, Robert	19	Jones	CALLAWAY,		
CALDWELL, Robert L.	4	Gwinnett	Aristedes	4	Wilkes
CALDWELL, Robert N.	6	Walker	CALLAWAY, C.	27	Wilkes
CALDWELL, Sarah	3	Greene	CALLAWAY, Carlton	14	Wilkes
CALDWELL, William	1	Jones	CALLAWAY, Elmore	36	Putnam
CALDWELL, William H.	3	Gwinnett	CALLAWAY, Enoch	35	Wilkes
CALDWELL, Wm. H.	10	Carroll	CALLAWAY, Henry T.	2	Wilkes
CALDWELL, C. M.	2	Camden	CALLAWAY, Jesse	105	Wilkes
CALDWELL, H.	2	Camden	CALLAWAY, J. H.	12	Randoph
CALDWELL, Wm. A.	1	Coweta	CALLAWAY, John	1	Baldwin
CALDWELL, Yelverton	11	Talbot	CALLAWAY, Levi	5	Wilkes
CALE, Edmand	1	Screven	CALLAWAY, Paarker	115	Wilkes
CALELOUGH, Alex	22	Carroll	CALLAWAY, M. P.	53	Wilkes
CALENA?, Elizabeth	1	Lee	CALLAWAY, Miles	6	Wilkes
CALEWAY, Edward	33	Monroe	CALLAWAY,		
CALHOUN, (NO NAME)	13	Talbot	Seaborn, Jr.	20	Wilkes
CALHOUN, A.	5	Muscogee	CALLAWAY,		
CALHOUN, Alexander	11	Walker	Seaborn Sr.	30	Wilkes
CALHOUN, Burril R.	3	Montgomery	CALLAWAY, Thos. W.	17	Wilkes
CALHOUN, David W.	2	Floyd	CALLAWAY,		
CALHOUN, F. A.	24	Elbert	William A.	6	Troup
CALHOUN, Hansel	9	Jefferson	CALLAWAY,		
CALHOUN, James	1	Harris	William A.	23	Troup
CALHOUN, James H.	3	Dooly	CALLAWAY,		
CALHOUN, James J.	6	Montgomery	William W.	7	Troup
CALHOUN, John C.	3	Troup	CALLAWAY, Wm. R.	16	Wilkes
CALHOUN, Josiah	2	Harris	CALLAWAY, Woodson	31	Wilkes
CALHOUN, Thomas B.	12	Montgomery	CALLAWAY, W. R.	58	Stewart
CALHOUN, Vincent	5	Houston	CALLEN, A.	3	Stewart
CALHOUN, Washington	1	Jefferson	CALLEN, Martha	1	Stewart
CALHOUN, William	13	Jefferson	CALLIER, Henry	9	Talbot
CALHOUN, William H.	31	Houston	CALLIER, James	18	Talbot
CALHOUN, Wm. B.	4	Hancock	CALLIN, Chas.	5	Richmond
CALHOUN, A. B.	12	Coweta	CALLOWAY, Catherine	10	Hancock
CALHOUN, Duncan	17	Talbot	CALLOWAY, J.	15	Henry
CALHOUN, James M.	11	DeKalb	CALLOWAY, John L.	4	Walton
CALHOUN, John C.	3	Baker	CALLOWAY, L. J.	11	Greene
CALHOUN, Jos.	31	Coweta	CALLOWAY, M.	11	Henry
CALHOUN, P. M.	2	Crawford	CALLOWAY, R. S.	11	Greene

Name	Number	County	Name	Number	County
CALLY, Elizabeth	27	Washington	CAMP, J. Jun.	2	Henry
CALLY, John	1	Stewart	CAMP, J. W.	5	Forsyth
CALMPBELL, Mary	1	DeKalb	CAMP, Jane	8	Campbell
CALON ?, James P.	1	Richmond	CAMP, Jerard	7	Newton
CALOWAY, E. R.	4	Henry	CAMP, John	6	Warren
CALOWAY, H. W.	2	Henry	CAMP, Joseph	6	Campbell
CALOWAY, J. H.	5	Henry	CAMP, Joseph L.	1	Cobb
CALOWAY, John	4	Pike	CAMP, Mark	1	Gwinnett
CALOWAY, Wm. A.	6	Henry	CAMP, Martin	1	Walker
CALVIN, James P.	12	Richmond	CAMP, Merrit	7	Gwinnett
CALWELL, Creed	1	Merriwether	CAMP, Nathan	2	Fayette
CALWELL, E.	4	Troup	CAMP, Robert B.	15	Gwinnett
CALWELL, John F.	3	Troup	CAMP, Sterling	3	Warren
CAMAK, H. S.	10	Clarke	CAMP, T. Y.	1	Morgan
CAMBELL, C.	8	Bibb	CAMP, W. W.	1	Fayette
CAMBELL, Virginia	9	Putnam	CAMP, Walton	1	Gwinnett
CAMDEN, M. J.	2	Cherokee	CAMP, A.	5	Coweta
CAMEL, Jasper	6	Jasper	CAMP, Benjamin	14	Campbell
CAMEON, S.	4	Merriwether	CAMP, George	7	Coweta
CAMERON, Allen	3	Montgomery	CAMP, Hiram	21	Coweta
CAMERON,			CAMP, Mary	6	Coweta
Benjamin H.	64	Troup	CAMP, N. F.	13	Butts
CAMERON, Jacob C.	1	Gordon	CAMP, Thomas	5	Campbell
CAMERON, James H.	38	Troup	CAMPBELL, ?	35	Richmond
CAMERON, Duncan	1	Telfair	CAMPBELL, A. J.	2	Houston
CAMERON, John	31	Screven	CAMPBELL, Andrew	16	Oglethorpe
CAMERON, John	12	Talbot	CAMPBELL, Archibald	6	Marion
CAMERON, Mary	7	Troup	CAMPBELL, B. A.	3	Oglethorpe
CAMERON, R.	12	Chattooga	CAMPBELL,		
CAMERON, Sarah	18	Troup	Caroline M.	2	Chatham
CAMERON, Thomas	3	Troup	CAMPBELL, Catte M.	70	Merriwether
CAMERON, Thomas	16	Troup	CAMPBELL, Cooley	42	Jasper
CAMERON, Thomas	8	Walton	CAMPBELL, Cooley	1	Jasper
CAMEY?, William	1	Hall	CAMPBELL, Darcus	1	Jasper
CAMFIELD, Rebecca	7	Richmond	CAMPBELL, David	8	Wilkes
CAMMEL, William M.	2	Monroe	CAMPBELL, David C.	45	Houston
CAMMING, William	5	Richmond	CAMPBELL, Duncan	1	Paulding
CAMP, A.	18	Henry	CAMPBELL, E. F. W.	11	Houston
CAMP, A. L.	3	Morgan	CAMPBELL, F. C.	11	Oglethorpe
CAMP, Aaron	5	Walker	CAMPBELL, F. W.	11	Jasper
CAMP, Abern	7	Walton	CAMPBELL, J. G.	1	Elbert
CAMP, Andy	6	Walker	CAMPBELL, J. H.	8	Henry
CAMP, Arthur T.	12	Cobb	CAMPBELL, James	5	Cass
CAMP, B. S.	17	Jackson	CAMPBELL, James T.	1	Twiggs
CAMP, Burk	9	Jackson	CAMPBELL, John	26	Jasper
CAMP, David A.	1	Jackson	CAMPBELL, John	1	Muscogee
CAMP, E. J.	1	Forsyth	CAMPBELL, John B.	1	Warren
CAMP, E. M.	2	Franklin	CAMPBELL, Joseph	9	Gordon
CAMP, Edonton	12	Habersham	CAMPBELL, M.	8	Harris
CAMP, Henry	1	Marion	CAMPBELL, M. H.	1	Henry
CAMP, Hope H.	6	Walton	CAMPBELL, Mary An	4	Pike
CAMP, Hosea	19	Paulding	CAMPBELL, Mrs. L.	41	Morgan
CAMP, J.	13	Henry	CAMPBELL, N. H.	1	Forsyth
CAMP, J.	2	Henry	CAMPBELL, Nicholas	1	Marion

Name	Number	County	Name	Number	County
CAMPBELL, Richard	1	Jasper	CANNON, James	1	Wilkinson
CAMPBELL, Richard B.	4	Walker	CANNON, John R.	12	Thomas
CAMPBELL, S. P.	16	Henry	CANNON, Joshua	2	Merriwether
CAMPBELL, Thomas	1	Pike	CANNON, Miles	5	Wilkinson
CAMPBELL, W. B.	11	Elbert	CANNON, Wiley	6	Muscogee
CAMPBELL, W. D.	2	Elbert	CANNON, William H.	1	McIntosh
CAMPBELL, W. L.	2	Henry	CANNON, William J.	3	McIntosh
CAMPBELL, W. W.	2	Newton	CANNON, Elizabeth	6	Carroll
CAMPBELL,			CANNON, G. W.	1	Randolph
William C.	12	Merriwether	CANNON, H. W.	2	Rabun
CAMPBELL, C. W.	2	Screven	CANNON, James W.	10	Sumter
CAMPBELL, D. C.	18	Baldwin	CANNON, John M.	3	Sumter
CAMPBELL, Edwd. F.	19	Richmond	CANNON, Mary	3	DeKalb
CAMPBELL, Henry F.	4	Richmond	CANON, R. H.	7	Cass
CAMPBELL, Henry J.	10	Telfair	CANOR ?, Discon	1	Thomas
CAMPBELL, J. H.	9	Stewart	CANT, Susan	8	Chatham
CAMPBELL, James	1	Campbell	CANTELAU, W. B.	36	Lincoln
CAMPBELL, James R.	2	Taliaferro	CANTRELL, B. L.	2	Lumpkin
CAMPBELL, Joseph	3	Butts	CANTRELL, Harris	2	Lumpkin
CAMPBELL, MARY	6	Richmond	CANTRELL, James	5	Lumpkin
CAMPBELL, Norman			CANTRELL, Martha	9	Lumpkin
agt for SHARPE	17	Lowndes	CANTRELL, Stephen	2	Lumpkin
CAMPBELL, Robert	8	DeKalb	CANTRELL,		
CAMPBELL, Robert	8	Richmond	Elizabeth A.	3	Cherokee
CAMPBELL, Robt. Jr.	2	Richmond	CANTRELL, James M.	9	Campbell
CAMPBELL, T. J.	1	Butts	CAONER, Isaac	2	Richmond
CAMPBELL, Thomas	6	DeKalb	CAPEL, Elizabeth	5	Merriwether
CAMPBELL, W. B.	1	Coweta	CAPPEL, R.	4	Henry
CAMPBELL, William	3	Campbell	CAPPS, M. D.	6	Bibb
CAMPFIELD, Charles H.	4	Chatham	CARACTER, Jacob	44	Talbot
CAMUTH, Robert	4	Cobb	CARAKER, James	2	Talbot
CANADA, Andrew	1	Greene	CARAKER, James L.	3	Talbot
CANADY, Thomas	3	Bryan	CARAKERS, Elizabeth	2	Muscogee
CANADY, W. C.	1	Bibb	CARATHERS, Louisa	3	Chatham
CANDLER, Henry	17	Macon	CARAWAY, John	4	Upson
CANDLER, Henry F.	11	Franklin	CARAWAY, John	4	Upson
CANDLER, W. H.	2	Columbia	CARAWAY, Samuel	1	Upson
CANDLER?, George	11	Muscogee	CARD, Abraham	27	Jones
CANDLERS, S. C.	12	Carroll	CARDELL, Peter	1	Jasper
CANE ?, Whitfield	2	Stewart	CARDEN, Andrew J.	1	Pike
CANE, J. T.	13	Harris	CARDEN, Charles	14	Monroe
CANEDY, Edward	6	Bryan	CARDIN, Moses	9	Elbert
CANIAN?, H.	2	Bibb	CARDIN, C.T.	7	Randolph
CANIDAY, J. W.	3	Lee	CARDIN, T. M.	13	Randolph
CANIDAY, Thomas	2	Lee	CARDWELL, John M.	40	Greene
CANIDAY, W.	4	Lee	CAREKER, Daniel	3	Talbot
CANIDAY, W.	4	Lee	CAREY, Ebenezer	2	Richmond
CANIDY, John	5	Monroe	CAREY, Patrick	1	Richmond
CANIFAX ?, Isburn	2	Upson	CARGIL, Augustus	5	Butts
CANN, William	4	Bibb	CARGILE, Mary	20	Butts
CANNON, Ann C.	7	Chatham	CARGILE, Charles	6	Butts
CANNON, Elias	1	Gwinnett	CARGILE, J. M.	2	Butts
CANNON, George W.	1	Pike	CARHART, J. D.	4	Bibb
CANNON, Henry estate	10	McIntosh	CARIKER, Jacob	4	Pike

51

Name	Number	County	Name	Number	County
CARIKER, John	2	Pike	CARMICHAEL, Arthur	3	Coweta
CARISTARPHEN, W.	3	Crawford	CARMICHAEL, H. W.	4	Butts
CARITHER, John J.	4	Oglethorpe	CARMICHAEL, Jas. Y.	3	Coweta
CARITHERS, Amos	8	Madison	CARMICHAEL, John C.	10	Richmond
CARITHERS, Berry T.	2	Madison	CARMICHAEL, Mary E.	8	Richmond
CARITHERS, James W.	4	Madison	CARMICHAEL, N. H.	1	Chattooga
CARITHERS, John J.	1	Madison	CARMICHAEL, R.	1	Coweta
CARITHERS, Nathan W.	3	Oglethorpe	CARMICHAEL, Robert D.	4	Richmond
CARITHERS, Penelope	3	Madison	CARMICHAEL, Wm. T.	6	Coweta
CARITHERS, Robert	3	Oglethorpe	CARMICHAEL, Wm. W.	2	Coweta
CARITHERS, Russel J.	1	Madison	CARMIKAEL, William	4	Cherokee
CARITHERS, Samuel W.	2	Madison	CARMODY, Ellen	2	Chatham
CARITHERS, William C.	14	Madison	CARNENE?, Margaret	1	Gwinnett
CARLAN, James	1	Chatham	CARNES ESTATE	1	Richmond
CARLEY, Frances	1	Chatham	CARNES, E.	2	Henry
CARLEY, Jno. G.	1	Wilkes	CARNES, James	4	Paulding
CARLILE, M.	3	Talbot	CARNES, John	1	Muscogee
CARLISLE, Allen	4	Talbot	CARNES, John	4	Paulding
CARLISLE, Sarah	11	Cass	CARNES, Joseph H.	1	Cherokee
CARLISLE, Susan	1	Talbot	CARNES, Robt. W. guard	7	Muscogee
CARLISLE, William W.	2	Troup	CARNES, E. S.	2	Bibb
CARLISLLE, Matthew	1	Talbot	CAROL, Sarah	21	Monroe
CARLOS, Wm.	5	Bibb	CARPENTER, Bailey	21	Burke
CARLTON, D. M.	2	Elbert	CARPENTER, J.	44	Elbert
CARLTON, James	5	Greene	CARPENTER, John T.	1	Cass
CARLTON, Archibald	32	Greene	CARPENTER, Thomas	1	Cass
CARLTON, Frances	1	Cobb	CARPENTER, Calvin	11	Burke
CARLTON, Isaac	8	Thomas	CARPENTER, Craven	2	Burke
CARLTON, Isac R.	1	Clinch	CARPENTER, Duane	1	Burke
CARLTON, James Senr.	39	Greene	CARPENTER, George W.	4	Upson
CARLTON, John	7	Thomas	CARPENTER, Thos.	3	Coweta
CARLTON, Joseph B.	17	Clarke	CARPERS?, Wiley O.	5	Morgan
CARLTON, L. D.	31	Greene	CARR, Aaron	3	Wilkinson
CARLTON, Peter	1	Thomas	CARR, B.	14	Newton
CARLTON, R. J.	18	Greene	CARR, Charles	11	Gwinnett
CARLTON, Samuel R.	22	Clarke	CARR, E.	4	Floyd
CARLTON, Travis	15	Greene	CARR, Eli	5	Hancock
CARLTON, E.	3	Coweta	CARR, Green B.	3	Hancock
CARLTON, T. W.	4	Coweta	CARR, Jas. W.	3	Hancock
CARLYLE, Willis	2	DeKalb	CARR, Jesse	24	Hancock
CARMICHAEL, Gilbert	21	Macon	CARR, Jesse C.	5	Floyd
CARMICHAEL, J. M.	10	Henry	CARR, John P.	29	Newton
CARMICHAEL, John	7	Butts	CARR, John P.	51	Newton
CARMICHAEL, John Sr.	2	Paulding	CARR, Joseph N.	1	Houston
CARMICHAEL, Joseph	12	Butts	CARR, Joseph N. agt for FELDER, S.	48	Houston
CARMICHAEL, Reuben	1	Greene	CARR, N. J.	1	Hancock
CARMICHAEL, A.	5	Coweta	CARR, Samuel	1	Jasper
CARMICHAEL, Andrew W.	6	Richmond	CARR, Thaddeus	1	Hancock
			CARR, Thos. A.	6	Jackson

Name	Number	County	Name	Number	County
CARR, William	10	Floyd	CARSON, Wm. E.	11	Greene
CARR, William A.	31	Clarke	CARSON, Andrew	20	Burke
CARR, George W.	2	Crawford	CARSON, J. W.	2	Carroll
CARR, J. R.	7	Chattooga	CARSON, Joseph	2	Putnam
CARR, Lewis	3	Richmond	CARSON, Seth agt.	28	Bibb
CARR, M. G.	5	Carroll	CARSON, T. E.	2	Coweta
CARR, Perry C.	7	Crawford	CARSON, T. J.	30	Butts
CARR, Smith D.	1	Baker	CARSTARPHEN, J. J.	5	Dooly
CARR, W. S.	2	Butts	CARSTARPHEN, T. C.	6	Stewart
CARR, William M.	2	Screven	CARSWELL, B. S.	23	Jefferson
CARRALL, S. J.	3	Morgan	CARSWELL, E. R.	47	Jefferson
CARRAWAY, John T.	1	Talbot	CARSWELL, Elizabeth	7	Twiggs
CARRIE, G. T.	1	Greene	CARSWELL, James W.	13	Jefferson
CARRIE, John	4	Richmond	CARSWELL, Matthew J.	22	Burke
CARRIER, Henry	1	Chatham	CARSWELL, Dr. E. R.	7	Burke
CARRINGTON,			CARSWELL, Enoch	7	Burke
Daniel	7	Wilkes	CARSWELL, John F.	34	Burke
CARROL, Caleb	1	Thomas	CARSWELL, John W.	30	Burke
CARROL, Calvin	2	Thomas	CARSWELL,		
CARROL, Curtis	2	Thomas	Mathew estate	23	Burke
CARROL, James	1	Thomas	CARSWELL, Thos.	1	DeKalb
CARROL, John	22	Gwinnett	CARSWELL, W. A.	8	Chatham
CARROL, John O.	8	Thomas	CARSWELL, Wm. S.	26	Screven
CARROL, John M.	1	Floyd	CARTEN, Martha	1	Bibb
CARROL, John W.	4	Campbell	CARTER, Anderson C.	4	Macon
CARROL, Joshua	2	Thomas	CARTER, B. F.	2	Troup
CARROL, Manson	8	Thomas	CARTER, C. N .	15	Murray
CARROL, Manson	1	Thomas	CARTER, Calvin	2	Marion
CARROL, Rhoda	13	Gwinnet	CARTER, Christopher	32	Newton
CARROL, William T.	2	Thomas	CARTER, David J.	6	Macon
CARROLL, Aladin	2	Greene	CARTER, Edward	29	Walton
CARROLL, D.	6	Henry	CARTER, Elijah	2	Lowndes
CARROLL, H. H.	3	Pike	CARTER, Farrish	255	Murray
CARROLL, J. J.	3	Henry	CARTER, George	6	Lowndes
CARROLL, James	16	Lowndes	CARTER, George	9	McIntosh
CARROLL, Jesse	9	Lowndes	CARTER, George	1	Oglethorpe
CARROLL, John	2	Newton	CARTER, H.	8	Twiggs
CARROLL, John F.	11	Lowndes	CARTER, Hamden C.	14	Jackson
CARROLL, Marcus L.	6	Fayette	CARTER, Harriet	1	Wilkes
CARROLL, N.	5	Henry	CARTER, Hezekiah	1	Pike
CARROLL, Thomas M.	2	Marion	CARTER, I. J.	3	Randolph
CARROLL, James	2	DeKalb	CARTER, Isaac	15	Appling
CARRUTH, W. F.	1	Cobb	CARTER, Isaac Sen.	2	Lowndes
CARRUTHERS, J. W.	7	Pulaski	CARTER, James	9	Elbert
CARRUTHERS, Jas. L.	6	Lowndes	CARTER, James	2	Lowndes
CARRY, Alexander	2	DeKalb	CARTER, James H.	9	Marion
CARRY, Thomas C.	8	Stewart	CARTER, James M.	1	Franklin
CARSON, Walter	1	Clarke	CARTER, Jane	3	Wilkes
CARSON, David	2	Franklin	CARTER, Jas.	1	Camden
CARSON, David P.	22	Jones	CARTER, Jesse	1	Appling
CARSON, John	11	Monroe	CARTER, Jesse	1	Jackson
CARSON, John T.	6	Macon	CARTER, Jesse	4	Lowndes
CARSON, Joseph J.	23	Macon	CARTER, Jesse	69	Talbot
CARSON, Merideth	9	Jefferson	CARTER, Jesse W.	4	Clinch

Name	Number	County	Name	Number	County
CARTER, John	4	Lowndes	CARTER, James W.	1	Rabun
CARTER, John	36	Walton	CARTER, Jason	9	Stewart
CARTER, John D.	5	Muscogee	CARTER, Jno	4	Randolph
CARTER, John L.	17	Meriwether	CARTER, Jno.	13	Crawford
CARTER, John R. J.	12	Wilkes	CARTER, Joel	8	Crawford
CARTER, John W.	12	Thomas	CARTER, John	6	Richmond
CARTER, Joseph	3	Monroe	CARTER, John	2	Richmond
CARTER, Joseph W.	12	Wilkes	CARTER, John	1	Talbot
CARTER, L.	36	Elbert	CARTER, John K. M.	2	DeKalb
CARTER, Lesley G.	11	Oglethorpe	CARTER, Milton	19	Newton
CARTER, Lucinda	1	Walker	CARTER, Robt.	2	Putnam
CARTER, M. M.	5	Merriwether	CARTER, Roda	20	DeKalb
CARTER, Madison	3	Marion	CARTER, Sarah	8	Richmond
CARTER, Magnus	4	Oglethorpe	CARTER, Thomas W.	1	DeKalb
CARTER, Martha	32	Harris	CARTER, Thos.	3	DeKalb
CARTER, Melley	5	Appling	CARTER, Thos. O.	6	Coweta
CARTER, Micajah	9	Franklin	CARTER, W.	1	DeKalb
CARTER, Paul	11	Appling	CARTER, W. B.	20	Putnam
CARTER, Paul	3	Appling	CARTER, Walter	11	Talbot
CARTER, Richard	3	Appling	CARTER, Weniford	7	Talbot
CARTER, Robert G.	16	Oglethorpe	CARTER, Wiley	15	Sumter
CARTER, Robert G.	2	Oglethorpe	CARTER, Wiley	19	Warren
CARTER, Robert M.	6	Walton	CARTER, William	25	Stewart
CARTER, Robt.	8	Muscogee	CARTER, William P.	24	Stewart
CARTER, Rolly W.	14	Paulding	CARTER, Wm.		
CARTER, Tempy	13	Jasper	adm for LUMDEN, J. G.	25	Floyd
CARTER, Thomas	4	Laurens	CARTER, Wm.T.	3	Taliaferro
CARTER, Thomas	5	Newton	CARTLEDGE, James	50	Lincoln
CARTER, W. W.	2	Meriwether	CARTLEDGE, Jeremiah	6	Muscogee
CARTER, William	6	Floyd	CARTLEDGE, Ben	7	Columbia
CARTER, William	12	Harris	CARTLEDGE, James	15	Columbia
CARTER, William	3	Lowndes	CARTLEDGE, John	55	Columbia
CARTER, William	14	Oglethorpe	CARTLEDGE, John	1	Richmond
CARTER, William	12	Oglethorpe	CARTLIDGE, A.	7	Decatur
CARTER, William E.	1	Gordon	CARTWRIGHT, J. D.	1	Carroll
CARTER, William V.	6	Walton	CARTWRIGHT, James	2	Greene
CARTER, Willis M.	2	Walton	CARTWRIGHT, John	39	Greene
CARTER, Blake	4	Talbot	CARTWRIGHT,		
CARTER, C. B.	1	Chatham	John A.	3	Greene
CARTER, Daniel	9	Coweta	CARTWRIGHT, Martha	7	Greene
CARTER, David	19	Screven	CARTWRIGHT,		
CARTER, Dr. E. J.	52	Burke	Margaret	18	Talbot
CARTER, Edward P.	10	Merriwether	CARUTH, James	1	Madison
CARTER, Elizabeth	1	Chatham	CARUTH, L. .D.	1	Forsyth
CARTER, Ezekel	1	Stewart	CARUTHERS, Jane	5	Jones
CARTER, Farish	55	Baldwin	CARUTHERS, Jane A.	12	Chatham
CARTER, Francis	3	Coweta	CARUTHERS, John	10	Chatham
CARTER, George	7	Putnam	CARUTHERS, Joseph	30	Pulaski
CARTER, H.	1	Crawford	CARUTHERS, William	4	Walker
CARTER, Isaac	46	Burke	CARVER, Caty	1	Telfair
CARTER, Jacob	5	Stewart	CARVER, Mary	4	Bibb
CARTER, James	21	Butts	CARVER, Robert	4	Bibb
CARTER, James	8	Talbot	CARVILLA ?,		
CARTER, James H.	4	Richmond	Constantine	5	Washington

Name	Number	County	Name	Number	County
CARY, Edward	5	Muscogee	CASTELLOW, William	8	Jasper
CARY, John	12	Upson	CASTENS, James	7	Talbot
CARY, Thomas J.	5	Muscogee	CASTLEBERRY, C.	1	Forsyth
CARY, Mrs.	10	Bibb	CASTLEBERRY, Davis	3	Marion
CASAWAY, William	5	Talbot	CASTLEBERRY, Ezra	6	Warren
CASDY?, John M.	3	Gwinnett	CASTLEBERRY,		
CASELBURY, Jeptha	3	Monroe	Thomas	2	Jasper
CASEN, B.	1	Merriwether	CASTLEBERRY, Wm.	1	Forsyth
CASEY, D. P.	1	Hall	CASTLEBERRY, J.	8	Crawford
CASEY, Michael	3	Chatham	CASTLEBERRY, James	1	Sumter
CASEY, William	2	Franklin	CASTLEBERRY,		
CASEY, Abraham	1	Camden	Simeon	11	Talbot
CASEY, Henry	9	Columbia	CASTLEBERY, G. W.	50	Randolph
CASEY, Wm.	1	Randolph	CASTLEBURY, Arena	1	Hall
CASH, ?	5	Elbert	CASTLEBURY, Edwin	1	Lumpkin
CASH, Benj. W.	12	Jackson	CASTLEBURY, Jane	15	Lumpkin
CASH, Elizabeth	1	Jackson	CASTLEBURY,		
CASH, Joel	2	Walton	Samuel	1	Lumpkin
CASH, N.	4	Habersham	CASTLEBURY,		
CASH, Reuben	2	Habersham	Sarah F.	12	Troup
CASH, C.	2	Chattooga	CASTLEBURY, W.	6	Early
CASH, E.	1	Bibb	CASTLEN, William	44	Monroe
CASH, James	1	Campbell	CASTLES, John	2	Clarke
CASH, Oswald E.	4	Richmond	CASWELL, George L.	14	Wilkinson
CASH, Stephen	15	DeKalb	CASWELL, S. M.	39	Wilsinson
CASH, Thos.	1	Wilkes	CASWELL ?, Saml.	1	Richmond
CASH, William	14	DeKalb	CASWELL, Isham	3	Heard
CASHAM, John B.	1	Lowndes	CASWELL, Elizabeth	17	Putnam
CASHIN, James E.	6	Richmond	CASWELL, James	6	Richmond
CASHLAN, Stephen	18	Houston	CASWELL, John	6	Putnam
CASLIN, John B.	27	Upson	CASWELL, Joseph	8	Talbot
CASON, Adam	22	Warren	CASWELL?, R. C.	5	DeKalb
CASON, Dennis	18	Washington	CASWELL, William E.	101	Wilkinson
CASON, James M.	14	Warren	CATCHING, J. W. T.	8	Greene
CASON, John F.	4	Warren	CATCHING, Joseph	51	Greene
CASON, John W.	2	Paulding	CATCHING, Rufus R.	5	Greene
CASON, Mariott	3	Jefferson	CATCHING, Seymour	5	Stewart
CASPER, David	1	Putnam	CATCHINGS, R. G.	19	Stewart
CASPER, Henry	2	Walker	CATCHINGS, Seymour	35	Stewart
CASS, Jesse	16	Habersham	CATE, J. N.	3	Murray
CASS, John	7	Chatham	CATER, M. M. K.	83	Glynn
CASS, Moses A.	2	Murray	CATER, Asa	1	Coweta
CASS?, Jacob J.	2	DeKalb	CATER, T.	1	Crawford
CASSEDY, Henry	9	Effingham	CATER, T. J.	6	Bibb
CASSELL, Absalom	1	Troup	CATES, Eleanor	8	Gwinnett
CASSELL, Arthur B.	5	Macon	CATES, James	2	Gwinnett
CASSELL, John	14	Decatur	CATES, John	1	Monroe
CASSELLS, Samuel	8	Chatham	CATES, L. M.	17	Gwinnett
CASSELS ?, Mark	1	Troup	CATES, Hosea B.	8	Burke
CASSELS, Thos. Q.	34	Liberty	CATES, J.	1	Bullock
CASSIDY, Hugh	14	Effingham	CATES, John L.	3	Burke
CASSON, H.	1	Chatham	CATES, Mrs. Aramintha	24	Burke
CASTELLAW, H. estate	22	Chatham	CATES, Thomas	16	Burke
CASTELLOW, John	2	Jasper	CATHEY, Sarah	9	Floyd

Name	Number	County	Name	Number	County
CATHON, Larkin	5	Franklin	CENTRAL RAILROAD	123	Chatham
CATHY, John B.	3	Stewart	CERRETHAS, John	1	Walton
CATHY?, J. Y.	2	Pike	CHADWICK, Harrison	1	DeKalb
CATLETT, Ezekiel	2	Habersham	CHAFFEN, David	2	Richmond
CATLIN, Lyman S.	12	Richmond	CHAFFEN, Edward B.	1	Walton
CATO, Amanda L.	6	Sumter	CHAFFIN, James J.	3	Muscogee
CATO, Bioh	2	Stewart	CHAFFIN, John	4	Jasper
CATO, Christopher	3	Wilkes	CHAFFIN, Moses	6	Jasper
CATO, James	6	Washington	CHAFFIN, Thomas	3	Muscogee
CATO, William W.	14	Troup	CHALKER,		
CATO, Wm.	3	Wilkes	Benjamin G.	1	Warren
CAUDLE, Benj.	4	Franklin	CHALKER, Hodges	7	Warren
CAUDLE, Green B.	5	Troup	CHALKER, James	2	Houston
CAUDLE, James H.	3	Jones	CHALKER, Samuel	1	Warren
CAUGHMAN, James	12	Heard	CHAMBER, Allen	1	Wilkinson
CAULEY, Elihu	19	Marion	CHALMERS, H. J. agt.	9	Chatham
CAULSLEY, ?	1	Putnam	CHAMBERLAIN,		
CAUSEY, John	6	Macon	Remberence	27	Jasper
CAUSEY, Sarah	8	Cobb	CHAMBERLAN, W. S.	4	Stewart
CAUSEY, A.	1	Crawford	CHAMBERS, Alex	1	Cass
CAUSEY, L. M.	9	Crawford	CHAMBERS, Appling T.	3	Houston
CAUSEY, L.B.	5	Sumter	CHAMBERS, Bricy	4	Hancock
CAUSEY, Saml.	4	Crawford	CHAMBERS, Edwin	2	Pike
CAUSEY, W. J.	2	Crawford	CHAMBERS, James M.	16	Muscogee
CAUSY, Jno. R.	4	Randolph	CHAMBERS, Jas. R.	3	Fayette
CAUTHEN, Thomas H.	5	Pike	CHAMBERS, Jesse	16	Forsyth
CAUTHORN, Thomas	3	Upson	CHAMBERS, John	3	Fayette
CAVEN, Amanda	4	Richmond	CHAMBERS, Joseph	2	Habersham
CAVENAH, Sarah	3	Burke	CHAMBERS, Joseph	1	Hancock
CAVENDER, George W.	4	Walker	CHAMBERS,		
CAVENDER, John H.	1	Walker	Joseph W.	1	Gwinnett
CAVENDER, Robert	6	Hall	CHAMBERS, M. C.	1	Habersham
CAVENDER, O. C.	6	Coweta	CHAMBERS, Martha	8	Wilkinson
CAVER, James	9	Lincoln	CHAMBERS, N. F.	5	Carroll
CAVER, Vastine	7	Merriwether	CHAMBERS, Robert	1	Jones
CAWLEY, Austin W.	9	Merriwether	CHAMBERS, Saml. M.	1	Habersham
CAWLEY, Chany	2	Monroe	CHAMBERS, William	1	Wilkinson
CAWLEY, Vincent	1	Merriwether	CHAMBERS, Wm.	11	Forsyth
CAWLEY, William	1	Stewart	CHAMBERS, Wm.	5	Habersham
CAWLY, Valentine	1	Merriwether	CHAMBERS, Wm. H.	10	Muscogee
CAWTHON, Chestly	3	Franklin	CHAMBERS, D. A.	4	Randolph
CAWTHON, William	5	Franklin	CHAMBERS, J. T.	5	Carroll
CAWTHORNE, J. H.	2	Henry	CHAMBERS, John	4	Baldwin
CAWTHRON, John	50	Morgan	CHAMBERS, P. H.	13	Butts
CAY, Richmond	52	Liberty	CHAMBLEE, Geo. W.	16	Jackson
CAYTO, Thomas	3	Taliaferro	CHAMBLES, Thos.	1	Troup
CAYTON, E. B.	3	Oglethorpe	CHAMBLES, Wm.	13	Troup
CEAD?, James J.	4	DeKalb	CHAMBLES,		
CEALEY, J. A. D.	43	Pulaski	William H.	1	Franklin
CELEY?, Mary	4	Chatham	CHAMBLESS, John	13	Marion
CENTER, C. A.	9	DeKalb	CHAMBLESS, Littleton	3	Marion
CENTERS, Martha	1	Chatham	CHAMBLESS, Sarah	15	Monroe
CENTRAL R. ROAD			CHAMBLESS,		
& CO.	6	Jones	Zachariah	8	Marion

Name	Number	County	Name	Number	County
CHAMBLESS, Andrew	8	Talbot	CHANDLER, J. N.	7	Franklin
CHAMBLESS, Andrew	7	Talbot	CHANDLER, Joseph	13	Franklin
CHAMBLESS, Lewis	5	Talbot	CHANDLER, Mary	5	Franklin
CHAMBLESS, Susan	16	Talbot	CHANDLER, Mary	11	Gordon
CHAMBLESS, Wm.	6	Randolph	CHANDLER, Mary	2	Jackson
CHAMBLIN, Prucence	22	Columbia	CHANDLER, Permal	1	Chattooga
CHAMBLIS, Martin	1	Cherokee	CHANDLER, Perry	3	Fayette
CHAMBLISS,			CHANDLER, Robert	6	Murray
William H.	10	Monroe	CHANDLER, Solomon	24	Jackson
CHAMBLISS, Jesse	9	Sumter	CHANDLER, W. A.	3	Merriwether
CHAMLESS, Green	3	Monroe	CHANDLER, W. A.	3	Oglethorpe
CHAMLESS, John	50	Monroe	CHANDLER, A.	1	Coweta
CHAMLESS, John	3	Monroe	CHANDLER, H.	2	Coweta
CHAMLESS, Monroe	7	Monroe	CHANDLER, John	2	Columbia
CHAMLESS, Thomas	4	Monroe	CHANDLER, Sarah	4	Bibb
CHAMLESS, Timothy	10	Monroe	CHANDLER, Thos.	11	Carroll
CHAMLESS, Zacharus	9	Monroe	CHANDLER, William	8	Burke
CHAMLESS, Jackson	2	Bibb	CHANDLOR, A.	7	Elbert
CHAMLESS, Saml.	7	Bibb	CHANEY, James	20	Montgomery
CHAMLESS, Wm.	18	Bibb	CHANEY, Linton	3	Morgan
CHAMLISS, Edmond	8	Monroe	CHANEY, R. M.	7	Monroe
CHAMPION, Aaron	3	Chatham	CHANEY, Richard	6	Montgomery
CHAMPION, Abel	3	Marion	CHANEY, S. A.	3	Morgan
CHAMPION, Elias	16	Muscogee	CHANEY, W. W.	15	Laurens
CHAMPION, Frances	8	Fayette	CHANLER, Benj. C.	1	Gordon
CHAMPION, George H.	23	Marion	CHANLON, Minard	7	Taliaferro
CHAMPION, Jesse W.	62	Greene	CHANY, Lucy L.	2	Morgan
CHAMPION, Phileman	1	Muscogee	CHAPBELL, John B.	1	Oglethorpe
CHAMPION, Willis	1	Fayette	CHAPBELL?, John B.	26	Oglethorpe
CHAMPION, Wm. C.	1	Fayette	CHAPIN, Thomas P.	5	Jasper
CHAMPION, Alpha	10	Sumter	CHAPLER, Robert	5	Columbia
CHAMPION, Henry	6	Bibb	CHAPLIN, William F.	11	Chatham
CHAMPION, M.	1	Stewart	CHAPMAN, Abner	5	Warren
CHAMPION, Thos.	1	Crawford	CHAPMAN, Ambrose	43	Monroe
CHANCE, Henry	11	Burke	CHAPMAN, Amos?	1	Pike
CHANCE, James estate	12	Burke	CHAPMAN, Asa W. F.	2	Jasper
CHANCE, C.	1	Henry	CHAPMAN, B. T.	7	Pike
CHANCE, J.	2	Crawford	CHAPMAN, E.	4	Elbert
CHANCE, James	6	Baker	CHAPMAN, E. M.	1	Murray
CHANCEY, Amos	10	Houston	CHAPMAN, Elijah	12	Liberty
CHANCEY, Jackson	2	Morgan	CHAPMAN, Elizabeth	2	Hancock
CHANCEY, Wm.	1	Crawford	CHAPMAN, Frances J.	16	Liberty
CHANCY, Christopher	1	Appling	CHAPMAN, Jacob	1	Meriwether
CHANCY, Henry	1	Houston	CHAPMAN, James L.	5	Monroe
CHANCY, John	5	Houston	CHAPMAN, John	11	Chatham
CHANDLER, Asa	11	Fayette	CHAPMAN, John	13	Liberty
CHANDLER, B. G. N.	4	Jackson	CHAPMAN, John	1	Merriwether
CHANDLER, Bailey	15	Jackson	CHAPMAN, John F.	2	Muscogee
CHANDLER, Charles J.	1	Walton	CHAPMAN, John H.	3	Walker
CHANDLER, D. T. B.	2	Jackson	CHAPMAN, John H.	10	Jackson
CHANDLER, Dudley J.	1	Madison	CHAPMAN, Joseph	2	Cass
CHANDLER,			CHAPMAN, Lucy	3	Jasper
Fresvan M.	1	Jackson	CHAPMAN, Margaret A.	12	Chatham
CHANDLER, J. C.	8	Oglethorpe	CHAPMAN, Marion	6	Hall

Name	Number	County	Name	Number	County
CHAPMAN, Micajah	2	Warren	CHATHAM, Wm.	2	Forsyth
CHAPMAN, Nancy	2	Warren	CHATIN, Robert	11	Lumpkin
CHAPMAN, Phebo	4	DeKalb	CHATMAN, J.	16	Twiggs
CHAPMAN, Robt.	1	Muscogee	CHATMAN, John	49	Twiggs
CHAPMAN, Sarah	4	Pike	CHATMON, Margaret	14	Twiggs
CHAPMAN, Syntha	13	Monroe	CHAVIOUS ?, George	11	Richmond
CHAPMAN, W. W.	15	Pike	CHAVIOUS ?, Wm. B.	1	Richmond
CHAPMAN, Charles F.	6	Chatham	CHEACK?, D. W.	1	Elbert
CHAPMAN, Chas. W.	2	Richmond	CHEATHAM, A. R.	11	Jefferson
CHAPMAN, D. S.	15	Carroll	CHEATHAM, Isham	6	Madison
CHAPMAN, G. M.	3	Crawford	CHEATHAM, James L.	3	Jefferson
CHAPMAN, John	14	Taliaferro	CHEATHAM, John J.	5	Jackson
CHAPMAN, Nathan	9	Taliaferro	CHEATHAM, John L.	3	Harris
CHAPMAN, S. T.	6	Bibb	CHEATHAM, Semual	1	Franklin
CHAPMAN, Saml. W.	11	Taliaferro	CHEATHAM, C. A.	5	Stewart
CHAPMAN, Stephen	44	Bibb	CHEAVES, Thos.	6	Carroll
CHAPMAN, Thomas	11	Taliaferro	CHECK, S. P.	1	Franklin
CHAPMAN, Wm. H.	11	Taliaferro	CHEEK, James	3	Murray
CHAPMON, ?	2	Elbert	CHEEK, John	1	Heard
CHAPMOND, Edmond	13	Stewart	CHEEK, Rolling	2	Franklin
CHAPPEL, G. W.	4	Meriwether	CHEEK, Wm.	1	Heard
CHAPPEL, Margaret	1	Merriwether	CHEEK, P.	1	DeKalb
CHAPPELEAR,			CHEELEY, John	44	Warren
James H.	3	Franklin	CHEELEY, Mary	6	Jackson
CHAPPELL, Alexander	7	Twiggs	CHEELY, Henry L.	6	Washington
CHAPPELL, Elija	1	Emanual	CHEELY, L. W.	9	Hancock
CHAPPELL, George	6	Murray	CHEELY, Thos. J.	22	Hancock
CHAPPELL, A. H.	37	Bibb	CHEELY, Thomas	1	Washington
CHAPPELL, Joseph J.	6	Sumter	CHEEN ?, Benj. T.	14	Richmond
CHAPPELL, Levin C.	2	Twiggs	CHEEVES, Isaac G.	22	Macon
CHAPPELL, Thomas	7	Twiggs	CHENAULT, A. D.	9	Lincoln
CHARIER, A.	1	Chatham	CHENAULT, J. M.	17	Lincoln
CHARLES, John	5	Chatham	CHENEY,		
CHARLES, P. L.	1	McIntosh	Dr. Franklin W.	63	Greene
CHARLTON, Elizabeth	10	Effingham	CHENEY, Wm. O.	30	Greene
CHARLTON, Elizabeth	4	Effingham	CHENY, Isaac	46	Talbot
CHARLTON, Robert M.	13	Chatham	CHENY, John S.	2	Upson
CHARLTON, Sarah	28	Chatham	CHERRY, Howel	34	Monroe
CHASE, Albon	3	Clarke	CHERRY, Poindexter	12	Marion
CHASE, Rhoda	1	Chatham	CHERRY, William	1	Houston
CHASION ?, John	12	Richmond	CHERRY, Wm. A.	4	Bibb
CHASTAIN ?, Amelia	9	Richmond	CHERRY, F.	1	Randolph
CHASTAIN, A.	1	Hall	CHERRY, H. J.	3	Bibb
CHASTAIN, J. B.	1	Union	CHERRY, J. H.	8	Bibb
CHASTAIN, James	6	Lee	CHERRY, J. T.	2	Bibb
CHASTAIN, John	1	Hall	CHERRY, T.	4	Bibb
CHASTAIN, Wm.	14	Lee	CHERRY, Wm.	1	Decatur
CHASTAIN, James M.	1	Baker	CHERY?, S. S.	2	Pike
CHASTAIN, Renney	3	Thomas	CHESHIN, W. J.	1	Muscogee
CHASTANE, John M.	23	Houston	CHESHIRE, Colon	5	Marion
CHATFIELD, Isaac	3	Upson	CHESHIRE, J. T.	2	Randolph
CHATFIELD, Isaac	123	Upson	CHESSER, William T.	3	Liberty
CHATFIELD, John	11	Merriwether	CHESSIN, John		
CHATHAM, Syloania	4	Forsyth	agt for LAMAR, H.	29	Houston

Name	Number	County	Name	Number	County
CHESTER, Norman S.	3	Cobb	CHRISLER, Absalom	13	Jackson
CHESTER, Wm. P.	7	Murray	CHRISLER, Jeptha S.	1	Jackson
CHESTER, S.	6	Decatur	CHRISTAN, C. W.	19	Elbert
CHESTER, Wm.	9	Decatur	CHRISTAN, J. M.	25	Elbert
CHESTNUT, Jane	5	Newton	CHRISTAN, J. R. A.	19	Elbert
CHESTNUT, Samuel	1	Newton	CHRISTAN, W.	1	Elbert
CHEVERS, J. M.	53	Troup	CHRISTEN?, Robert	1	Effingham
CHEVERS, John R.	125	Chatham	CHRISTIAN, Cephus	1	Newton
CHEVES, John R.,			CHRISTIAN, Charles	2	Chatham
plantation no. 2	166	Chatham	CHRISTIAN, D. W.	10	Monroe
CHEVES, Langdon	121	Chatham	CHRISTIAN, E. T.	8	Troup
CHEWINGS, Wm. F.	22	DeKalb	CHRISTIAN, Edmond	1	Muscogee
CHILDERS, ?	4	Elbert	CHRISTIAN, G. W.	1	Newton
CHILDERS, Darling J.	11	Floyd	CHRISTIAN, Harriett	1	Fayette
CHILDERS, John	46	Houston	CHRISTIAN, Henry P.	2	Monroe
CHILDERS, John	27	Pulaski	CHRISTIAN, Isaac	14	Newton
CHILDERS, Masler	2	Oglethorpe	CHRISTIAN, Isaac	3	Newton
CHILDERS, Doctor	3	Stewart	CHRISTIAN, James	1	Newton
CHILDERS, Isaac	1	Crawford	CHRISTIAN, Presley	3	Newton
CHILDERS, John	2	Talbot	CHRISTIAN, Rufus	2	Newton
CHILDERS, N.	6	Crawford	CHRISTIAN, Thomas	1	Muscogee
CHILDERS, Richard	6	Troup	CHRISTIAN, Thomas C.	3	Murray
CHILDERS, Virgil A.	24	Baker	CHRISTIAN, Thomas O.	6	Murray
CHILDS, Henry	9	Jones	CHRISTIAN, William C.	1	Madison
CHILDS, Jas.	15	Henry	CHRISTIAN, Addison	14	Columbia
CHILDS, Jeremiah	1	Upson	CHRISTIAN, Ann	6	Richmond
CHILDS, John S.	20	Heard	CHRISTIAN, E.C.B.	1	Cass
CHILDS, Mathew	8	Houston	CHRISTIAN, James	12	Stewart
CHILDS, Michael S.	31	Jones	CHRISTIE, Geo.	5	Randolph
CHILDS, N. S.	1	Hancock	CHRISTIE, J. A.	1	Troup
CHILDS, Sarah	28	Jones	CHRISTIE, Luke	5	Chatham
CHILDS, William	7	Jones	CHRISTIE, Nathan	10	Randolph
CHILDS, Willis S.	9	Jones	CHRISTIE, Sarah	4	Chatham
CHILDS, Otis	1	Baldwin	CHRISTMAS, Jeremiah	1	Houston
CHILES, Joseph	42	Jones	CHRISTMAS, Absalom	3	Dooly
CHILES, Lewis G.	1	Franklin	CHRISTMAS, Henry M.	1	Dooly
CHILES, William	27	Talbot	CHRISTOPHER,		
CHISHOLM, J. F.	5	Muscogee	Elizabeth	18	Walton
CHISHOLM, Wm. A.	6	Muscogee	CHRISTOPHER, Lucy	11	Clarke
CHISHOLM, T. J.	21	Decatur	CHRISTOPHER,		
CHISOLM, E. D.	14	Paulding	Richard	17	Oglethorpe
CHISOLM, Thomas A.	8	Paulding	CHRISTOPHER, Lazina	14	Bibb
CHITWOOD, G. G.	1	Habersham	CHRISTOPHER, Thos.	1	Troup
CHIVERS, Lydia	1	Muscogee	CHRISTOPHER,		
CHIVES, F.	5	Crawford	Wm. H.	9	Bibb
CHIVES, Grief	31	Crawford	CHRISTY, John H.	3	Clarke
CHIVERS, C. F.	6	Washington	CHUB, Isaac	1	Morgan
CHIVERS, Jas. A.	17	Wilkes	CHUBBEDGE, John	4	Chatham
CHIVERS, Joel R.	16	Wilkes	CHUNN, Amos	15	Merriwether
CHIVERS, Thomas	6	Twiggs	CHUNN, Amos Srn.	26	Merriwether
CHIVERS, Thos. H.	11	Wilkes	CHUNN, Jonathan	8	Merriwether
CHOATE, Thomas W.	51	Jones	CHUNN, Samuel L.	10	Cass
CHOCKLY, Guer?, E.	2	Pike	CHUPP, Jacob	7	DeKalb
CHOICE, Tully	7	Hancock	CHURCH, Alonzo	9	Clarke

Name	Number	County
CHURCH, Rachel	4	Camden
CHURCH, Sylvanus	1	Camden
CHURCHILL, W. W.	19	McIntosh
CHURCHILL, Calvin B.	50	Burke
CILGO, Abner	1	Putnam
CIMBROUGH (KIMBROUGH) W. G.	7	Putnam
CINARD, Martin	1	Floyd
CISSON, J. B.	5	Crawford
CISTRUNK, Thomas W.	1	Merriwether
CITY COUNCIL OF AUGUSTA	2	Richmond
CIVELES, Jas.	9	Troup
CLAGHORN, Joseph S.	7	Chatham
CLAIBORN, Henry	2	Talbot
CLAKELY, Elijah	15	Fayette
CLANCY, M. J.	7	Clarke
CLAND, A.	1	Pike
CLANTON (?), (?)	109	Columbia
CLANTON, Turner	137	Columbia
CLAP, Julius R.	17	Muscogee
CLAPP, H. H.	2	Walton
CLAPP, W. C.	1	Muscogee
CLAR, B. W.	26	Putnam
CLARD, Gilbert	16	Monroe
CLARDY, Bennett	6	Cass
CLARK, Ann C.	12	Glynn
CLARK, Armiel	1	Murray
CLARK, Benj. T.	3	Greene
CLARK, Benjamin	34	Muscogee
CLARK, C. C.	3	Monroe
CLARK, Calfrey	5	Montgomery
CLARK, Corge	1	Burke
CLARK, David	28	Houston
CLARK, Edmond	8	Jefferson
CLARK, Edward	15	Monroe
CLARK, Elbert O.	8	Gordon
CLARK, Elenor	1	Montgomery
CLARK, Eli K.	9	Clarke
CLARK, Flournoy	4	Lowndes
CLARK, Francis	9	Laurens
CLARK, G. W.	1	Pike
CLARK, George	30	Jasper
CLARK, Harlow	2	Montgomery
CLARK, Henry G.	1	Meriwether
CLARK, Henry G.	1	Meriwether
CLARK, J.	4	Lumpkin
CLARK, J. A.	19	Elbert
CLARK, J. A.	8	Walton
CLARK, J. C. F.	7	Lee
CLARK, J. Q. N. F.	3	Laurens
CLARK, J.C.	10	Henry
CLARK, Jacob	2	Muscogee
CLARK, James	7	Burke
CLARK, James	4	Liberty
CLARK, James	12	Merriwether
CLARK, James	24	Thomas
CLARK, James L.	17	Laurens
CLARK, James W.	3	Jefferson
CLARK, Jefferson	9	Lumpkin
CLARK, Jno. R.	16	Henry
CLARK, John	1	Cherokee
CLARK, John	20	Jasper
CLARK, John	1	Jefferson
CLARK, John	13	Liberty
CLARK, John	1	Muscogee
CLARK, John	3	Pike
CLARK, John D.	1	Houston
CLARK, John J.	7	Richmond
CLARK, John M.	5	Newton
CLARK, John W.	1	Dooly
CLARK, Joseph	5	Chatham
CLARK, Joshua	2	Lee
CLARK, Josiah	6	Morgan
CLARK, L.	3	Elbert
CLARK, L. H.	26	Troup
CLARK, Lucretia	9	Jones
CLARK, Lucy	39	Morgan
CLARK, Matthew	12	Laurens
CLARK, Nathan	2	Gwinnett
CLARK, Nicholas P.	14	Liberty
CLARK, Nimrod	10	Montgomery
CLARK, Noah	1	Jones
CLARK, Peter	3	Greene
CLARK, Philip	10	Jefferson
CLARK, Reuben	6	Habersham
CLARK, Reuben guardin for free person	1	Habersham
CLARK, Robert	1	DeKalb
CLARK, Samuel	5	Montgomery
CLARK, Seaborn J.	2	Morgan
CLARK, Seaton	3	Muscogee
CLARK, Semus H.	11	Macon
CLARK, T. F.	1	Henry
CLARK, V. H.	4	Troup
CLARK, W. W.	6	Newton
CLARK, Wiley	8	Houston
CLARK, William	3	Jefferson
CLARK, William	13	Liberty
CLARK, William	1	Merriwether
CLARK, William	3	Montgomery
CLARK, William	7	Muscogee
CLARK, William B.	7	Harris
CLARK, William F.	10	Chatham
CLARK, William F.	23	Houston
CLARK, William J.	5	Houston
CLARK, Wilson	1	Monroe

Name	Number	County
CLARK, Wm. D.	28	Elbert
CLARK, Wm. L.	10	Muscogee
CLARK, Wm. M.	2	Marion
CLARK, Y. H.	2	Oglethorpe
CLARK, Z. H.	40	Oglethorpe
CLARK, Z. H.	5	Oglethorpe
CLARK, Adeline E.	5	Richmond
CLARK, Ann	5	Bryan
CLARK, Charles E.	9	Richmond
CLARK, Council	1	Dooly
CLARK, D. F.	5	Bibb
CLARK, Dr. Samuel E.	22	Burke
CLARK, F. J.	1	Camden
CLARK, George	1	Chatham
CLARK, Henry E.	6	Richmond
CLARK, Hiram	3	Butts
CLARK, Horace	1	Richmond
CLARK, J.	9	Crawford
CLARK, J. H.	26	Putnam
CLARK, James	47	Stewart
CLARK, James	14	Stewart
CLARK, James	5	Stewart
CLARK, James	1	Stewart
CLARK, James	2	Sumter
CLARK, James S.	102	Sumter
CLARK, John	1	DeKalb
CLARK, John	3	Screven
CLARK, Joseph L.	3	Richmond
CLARK, N. C.	2	Bibb
CLARK, Richard	13	Bryan
CLARK, Robert	32	Columbia
CLARK, Samuel	3	Butts
CLARK, Samuel B.	13	Richmond
CLARK, Sarah	1	Burke
CLARK, Thomas	1	Chatham
CLARK, W. D.	10	Bibb
CLARK, W. F.	2	Butts
CLARK, William G.	1	Sumter
CLARK, William S.	6	Stewart
CLARK, William Sr.	4	Sumter
CLARK, Wm.	1	Decatur
CLARK, Wm.	11	DeKalb
CLARK, Wm. H .	49	DeKalb
CLARKE, A. S.	3	Jefferson
CLARKE, Elizabeth	36	Hall
CLARKE, Henry	3	Hall
CLARKE, John	12	Hall
CLARKE, Charles	14	Burke
CLARKE, Charlotte	6	Stewart
CLARKE, Dr. John W.	17	Burke
CLARKE, James	7	Stewart
CLARKE, Jesse	20	Columbia
CLARKE, Richard H.	9	Warren
CLARKE, William T.	12	Warren

Name	Number	County
CLARKE, Wm. H.	5	Camden
CLARY, Daniel	4	Lincoln
CLARY, James	27	Screven
CLATON, Samuel	36	Baker
CLAXTON, Robert E.	2	Harris
CLAY, Adam	5	Camden
CLAY, Augustus	20	Walton
CLAY, James J.	1	Jasper
CLAY, John	2	Morgan
CLAY, John H.	1	Cobb
CLAY, Nicholas H.	2	Hancock
CLAY, Paten	20	Wilsinson
CLAY, Sarah	9	Lee
CLAY, Eliza C.	155	Bryan
CLAY, M.	1	Crawford
CLAY, William	8	Washington
CLAYTON, Edward P.	8	Clarke
CLAYTON, Geo. R.	2	Houston
CLAYTON, Isham H.	7	Lowndes
CLAYTON, John	26	Cass
CLAYTON, John W.	1	Cass
CLAYTON, Julia	12	Clarke
CLAYTON, P. A.	7	Muscogee
CLAYTON, Phillip	9	Early
CLAYTON, Edw. T.	1	Richmond
CLAYTON, M.	16	Meriwether
CLAYTON, Saml.	9	Randolph
CLAYTON, W. W.	48	Clarke
CLAYTON, William	1	Burke
CLEATEON ?, Middleton	1	Walton
CLEAVELAND, Absalom	17	Marion
CLEAVELAND, B.	11	Troup
CLEAVELAND, George C.	8	Murray
CLEAVELAND, William E.	6	Murray
CLEAVELAND, Thomas	5	Murray
CLEAVLAND, R.	4	Troup
CLECKLER, Elijah A.	1	Campbell
CLECKLER, Henry	1	Campbell
CLEGG, Archibald	1	Richmond
CLEGG, Thomas	5	Walton
CLEGG, William O.	2	Walton
CLEGG, Wm. T.	1	Walton
CLEGHOM, C. C.	7	Chattooga
CLEGHORN, James	1	Chatham
CLELAND, William estate	15	Jones
CLELAND, Williamina	9	Chatham
CLEM, Henry agent	1	Muscogee
CLEMENS, Mary	7	Walker
CLEMENT, Hugh	8	Murray

Name	Number	County
CLEMENT, Jacob A.	12	Marion
CLEMENT, John	2	Chattooga
CLEMENT, John A.	2	Twiggs
CLEMENTS, Adam	1	Walker
CLEMENTS, Merriwether	20	Franklin
CLEMENTS, Bishop	77	Merriwether
CLEMENTS, Charles	19	Fayette
CLEMENTS, D.	34	Henry
CLEMENTS, George W.	1	Walker
CLEMENTS, Jacob	14	Montgomery
CLEMENTS, Jacob C.	1	Montgomery
CLEMENTS, James	2	Jefferson
CLEMENTS, James	12	Monroe
CLEMENTS, John	3	Lowndes
CLEMENTS, Mary	2	Monroe
CLEMENTS, P. R.	11	Harris
CLEMENTS, Philip	5	Morgan
CLEMENTS, R. H.	5	Morgan
CLEMENTS, T. H.	2	Henry
CLEMENTS, T. H.	6	Henry
CLEMENTS, Thomas	5	Marion
CLEMENTS, Thomas	12	Monroe
CLEMENTS, William	23	Jefferson
CLEMENTS, Isham	10	Stewart
CLEMENTS, John	7	Telfair
CLEMENTS, William A.	4	Stewart
CLEMMONS, Wm.	1	Chattooga
CLEMMONS, J. B.	1	Chattooga
CLEMMONS, Thomas	17	Talbot
CLEMONS, Henry A.	1	Cass
CLEMONTS, Nelson	18	Stewart
CLENDENEN, A. W. T.	5	Wallker
CLERK, Littleton	7	Fayette
CLERKLER, Jacob	1	Walker
CLERMENT, Aaron	2	Hall
CLEVAND, Jeremiah	5	Franklin
CLEVDAN?, Wm.	1	Merriwether
CLEVELAND, A.	15	Henry
CLEVELAND, A. A.	31	Wilkes
CLEVELAND, Benj.	8	Habersham
CLEVELAND, Benjamin	17	Harris
CLEVELAND, D.	8	Elbert
CLEVELAND, Early	20	Monroe
CLEVELAND, J. H.	2	Elbert
CLEVELAND, J. M.	12	Elbert
CLEVELAND, J. M.	5	Elbert
CLEVELAND, Martha	1	Habersham
CLEVELAND, P.	15	Elbert
CLEVELAND, R.	22	Elbert
CLEVELAND, R.	2	Henry
CLEVELAND, Rhoda	4	Henry
CLEVELAND, Robert M.	13	Gwinnett
CLEVELAND, Wm. M.	2	Henry
CLEVELAND, R.	8	Crawford
CLEVELAND, W. C.	44	Crawford
CLEVEN, (CLEVELAND?) James	3	Stewart
CLEVY ?, Charles M.	8	Richmond
CLEWIS, C. agent	22	Crawford
CLEWIS, John	2	Thomas
CLIATT, Isaac	2	Stewart
CLIATT, Jesse	11	Stewart
CLICK, Wm. S.	1	Bibb
CLIETT, (?)	16	Columbia
CLIETT, James	4	Lincoln
CLIETT, George	11	Columbia
CLIETT, Jeremiah L. Z.	12	Richmond
CLIETT, John	24	Columbia
CLIETT, Minor	14	Columbia
CLIETT, Sarah	4	Columbia
CLIETT, W. J.	5	Columbia
CLIFTON, Alanson	1	Greene
CLIFTON, Daniel	2	Jones
CLIFTON, George W.	2	Emanual
CLIFTON, Unice	1	Emanual
CLIFTON, Ezekiel	5	Screven
CLIFTON, Ezekiel	15	Tatnall
CLIFTON, Leven C.	4	Screven
CLIFTON, Mrs.	5	Tatnall
CLIFTON, Thomas	2	Tatnall
CLIFTON, Versvany?	1	Stewart
CLIFTON, William	2	Baker
CLIFTON, William	5	Tatnall
CLIGG, C. D.	1	Walton
CLINCH, D. L. estate	237	Camden
CLINE, W. M.	1	Pike
CLINE ?, William	6	Walton
CLINTON, Jas. C.	1	Henry
CLINKSCALES, B.	1	Walker
CLOPTON, David	19	Paulding
CLOPTON, P. P.	27	Meriwether
CLOPTON, Thomas	10	Putnam
CLORE, Wm. M.	5	Cass
CLOUD, A. J.	3	Henry
CLOUD, Burton	4	Gwinnett
CLOUD, Carroll A.	34	Chatham
CLOUD, E.	8	Henry
CLOUD, Elijah	2	Macon
CLOUD, Elisha	6	Macon
CLOUD, D.	1	Decatur
CLOUD, Jas.	8	Crawford
CLOUD, Joel	18	Warren
CLOUD, L.	14	Henry
CLOUD, M.	7	Decatur
CLOUGH, John S.	7	Ware
CLOUTS, Jacob	12	Cobb

Name	Number	County	Name	Number	County
CLOWDIS, R.R.	1	Chattooga	COBB, N. F.	2	Paulding
CLOWER, C. J.	2	Meriwether	COBB, Nathaniel	1	Muscogee
CLOWER, D. M.	3	Clarke	COBB, P. S. Q.	37	Houston
CLOWER, Green A.	58	Jones	COBB, Rowland	5	Gordon
CLOWER, Green A.			COBB, Saml.	3	Cherokee
& Peter L.	48	Jones	COBB, Samuel B.	6	Troup
CLOWER, James M.	16	Monroe	COBB, Seth	6	Muscogee
CLOWER, Margaret	5	Merriwether	COBB, Thomas R. R.	15	Clarke
CLOWER, Peter	27	Jones	COBB, William	7	Muscogee
CLOWER, Peter L.	74	Jones	COBB, William A.	21	Upson
CLOWER, Thos.	2	Harris	COBB, Col. by overseer	206	Baldwin
CLOWERS, John T.	13	Monroe	COBB, H. W.	4	Cass
CLOWERS, Monroe	12	Monroe	COBB, Horatio	6	Tatnall
CLOWN?, James	1	Muscogee	COBB, Isaac E.	12	Carroll
CLUBB, Jas. A.	11	Camden	COBB, James T.	3	DeKalb
CLUBBS, Sarah	1	Camden	COBB, Lewis	1	Tatnall
CLYATT, Alfred M.	12	Houston	COBB, Mary	1	Decatur
CLYATT, James M.	1	Lowndes	COBB, Nancy	3	DeKalb
COACHMAN, Claudia	17	Chatham	COBB, Peter	3	Camden
COACHMAN, J.	83	Decatur	COBB, Robert W.	6	DeKalb
COALEY, A. R.	35	Pulaski	COBB, Thomas	21	Dooly
COALEY, Donalson	20	Pulaski	COBB, Wiley	35	Dooly
COALEY, Turner	11	Pulaski	COBB, William	5	Cherokee
COALMAN, John	1	Monroe	COBB, William	1	Talbot
COALS, H. H.	1	Pike	COBB, Wm. T.	2	DeKalb
COALSON, A. J.	82	Pulaski	COBURN, Moses	3	Chatham
COALSON, John	8	Pulaski	COCHRAINE?, ?	10	Lumpkin
COALSON, William L.	4	Houston	COCHRAN, A. C.	1	Wilkinson
COALSON, William S.	38	Houston	COCHRAN, Allen	73	Monroe
COALSON, Wm.	2	Carroll	COCHRAN, Banister	5	Morgan
COANS, Sarah	6	Early	COCHRAN, D. A.	13	Harris
COATES, William	1	Clarke	COCHRAN, D. A.	1	Harris
COATNEY, Stephen	5	Merriwether	COCHRAN, James	1	Morgan
COATS, Abner G.	1	Harris	COCHRAN, John	1	Laurens
COATS, John	13	Harris	COCHRAN, Jubil	18	Jasper
COATS, John J.	8	Chatham	COCHRAN, Neal F.	4	Oglethorpe
COATS, Mary	10	Wilkes	COCHRAN, Robert	1	Hall
COATS, Wm.	12	Wilkes	COCHRAN, Samuel H.	1	Pike
COBB, (?)	5	Columbia	COCHRAN, Sarah	35	Morgan
COBB, Alexander	5	Troup	COCHRAN, Sarah	30	Oglethorpe
COBB, Ammon	7	Warren	COCHRAN, Sol	15	Forsyth
COBB, Aquella	7	Muscogee	COCHRAN, T. G.	9	Morgan
COBB, Charles H.	2	Upson	COCHRAN, W. W.	2	Henry
COBB, Enoch	11	Forsyth	COCHRAN, Cheadle	32	Campbell
COBB, George W.	15	Harris	COCHRAN, J. M.	15	Cass
COBB, H. B.	7	Hall	COCHRAN, John	9	Baker
COBB, Henry	1	Lincoln	COCHRAN, John	1	DeKalb
COBB, Howell	11	Clarke	COCHRAN, John M.	13	Baker
COBB, Howell	20	Houston	COCHRAN, Levi	14	Bibb
COBB, Jacob L.	12	Murray	COCHRAN, Littleton	6	Campbell
COBB, Joseph	10	Marion	COCHRAN, Mary	9	Columbia
COBB, L. M.	1	Henry	COCHRAN, Saml. W.	9	Cass
COBB, Levi	5	Monroe	COCHRAN, Seaborn	1	DeKalb
COBB, Mrs.	3	Hancock	COCHRAN, Thomas	2	Chattooga

Name	Number	County	Name	Number	County
COCHRAN, W.W.	6	Campbell	COHEN, David	1	Chatham
COCHRAN, Wm. B.	2	Richmond	COHEN, Isaac	3	Chatham
COCK, Isaac P.	46	Lee	COHEN, Moses S.	4	Chatham
COCK, Augustus	5	Richmond	COHEN, Octavus	10	Chatham
COCK, Frances H.	1	Richmond	COHEN, C. E.	3	Chatham
COCKRAN, Neal F.	11	Oglethorpe	COHEN, D. Lopez	10	Chatham
COCKRELL, Thomas	4	Marion	COHEN, G. P.	17	Camden
COCKRON, Martin C.	23	Pike	COHEN, J. P.	3	Chatham
COCKRON?, James	1	Baker	COHEN, John J.	2	Richmond
COCKS, J.	1	Elbert	COHEN, Moses A.	6	Chatham
COCROFT, James	10	Greene	COHEN, Solomon	23	Chatham
CODE, John	1	Muscogee	COHRAN, H. T.	1	Pike
CODEN?, Ephrem M.	1	Habersham	COIN, Tyra	4	Marion
CODY, Benjamin	4	Warren	COKER, Abner	1	Fayette
CODY, Columbus C.	5	Warren	COKER, David	1	Merriwether
CODY, Edmund	10	Warren	COKER, Robert G.	2	Jones
CODY, Elias	1	Talbot	COKER, John	4	Sumter
CODY, James	1	Warren	COKER, William	7	Sumter
CODY, Jeptha M.	23	Warren	COLBERT, Ann	4	Monroe
CODY, Lawson	24	Talbot	COLBERT, Francis	4	Monroe
CODY, Micheal M.	20	Warren	COLBERT, Jackson	11	Talbot
CODY, Patric	2	Bryan	COLBERT, John G.	15	Hancock
CODY, Peter	4	Baker	COLBERT, John G.	15	Hancock
CODY?, Jesse	13	Habersham	COLBERT, Lindsey G.	38	Madison
CODY, Rebecca	37	Warren	COLBERT, M. L.	1	Floyd
CODY, Robert D.	14	Warren	COLBERT, Peyton H.	20	Madison
COE, Mary A.	14	Chatham	COLBERT, Sanders W.	40	Madison
COE, Hayden	7	DeKalb	COLBERT, Sarah	18	Madison
COE, Perry	2	Crawford	COLBERT, A.	9	Crawford
COFER, Eli M.	1	Clarke	COLBERT, David A.	8	Talbot
COFER, Henry J.	11	Lincoln	COLBERT, J.	31	Crawford
COFER, Jos. B.	12	Wilkes	COLBERT, J. G.	12	Crawford
COFER, L. C.	4	Morgan	COLBERT, Nancy	16	Talbot
COFER, Mary	2	Wilkes	COLBERT, Thomas	47	Coweta
COFER, Mather	7	Putnam	COLBERT, Thompson	15	Cass
COFER, Thos. L.	6	Wilkes	COLBERT, William B.	16	Stewart
COFFEE, Edward	5	Clarke	COLBURT, F.	42	Bibb
COFFEE, Elisha	2	Murray	COLBY, John Estate	106	Greene
COFFEE, Edward	4	Rabun	COLBY, Nelson	2	Meriwether
COFFEE, Martha	2	Union	COLBY, William	3	Richmond
COFFEY, R.	1	Chattooga	COLCLOUGH, John	26	Greene
COFIEL, Green	10	Troup	COLDER, Nathaniel M.	11	Cobb
COFIEL, Willis	25	Troup	COLDING, Mary A.	4	Chatham
COFIELD, Warren	8	Troup	COLDING, John M.	4	Screven
COFIELD, Willis Jr.	13	Troup	COLDWELL, John M.	5	Floyd
COFFIN, Edmund	1	Cherokee	COLDWELL, Thomas	6	Lee
COFFIN?, Lewis	1	Gwinnett	COLE, A. W.	1	Gwinnett
COFIL, Uriah	15	Troup	COLE, Giles	3	Houston
COGBORN, Eliz.	1	Clarke	COLE, Joseph T.	2	Pike
COGBURN, J. A.	39	Putnam	COLE, Robert	4	Merriwether
COGDELL, Richard	15	McIntosh	COLE, L. D.	9	Walton
COGGIN, John	1	Pike	COLE, Sarah	19	Clarke
COGGIN, John Sr.	32	Pike	COLE, Sarah	2	Heard
COGGIN, Mathew	5	Pike	COLE, Sarah	4	Paulding

Name	Number	County	Name	Number	County
COLE, Wm.	13	Monroe	COLLENS, Mary	7	Wilkinson
COLE, Wm. L.	1	Merriwether	COLLENS, William	4	Wilkinson
COLE, William	4	Union	COLLEY, Frances	53	Wilkes
COLE, Benjamin L.	25	Chatham	COLLEY, Frances S.	17	Walton
COLE, C. B.	5	Bibb	COLLEY, James	1	Habersham
COLE, Chas. J.	24	Camden	COLLEY, Joel	22	Newton
COLE, Hetty	2	Chatham	COLLEY, Z.	1	Early
COLE, John B.	8	Stewart	COLLEY, Abner P.	4	Baker
COLE, John D.	1	Chatham	COLLEY, George	12	Baker
COLE, John E.	2	Randolph	COLLEY, Jasper	1	Talbot
COLE, Robt.	1	Coweta	COLLEY, John	24	Baker
COLE, Robt. D.	3	Coweta	COLLEY, Spain	23	Wilkes
COLE, Samul	1	Campbell	COLLEY, William	57	Baker
COLE, Wm.	20	Camden	COLLIER, Benjamin	20	Early
COLEBY, John M.	3	Houston	COLLIER, Benjamin T.	9	Houston
COLEMAN, Alfred	2	Macon	COLLIER, D. W.	9	Monroe
COLEMAN, Allen	3	Jackson	COLLIER, E. C.	9	Upson
COLEMAN, B. F.	12	Muscogee	COLLIER, E. C. Agt.	40	Upson
COLEMAN, Charlotte	1	Jefferson	COLLIER, E. V.	2	Oglethorpe
COLEMAN, Elisha	4	Emanuel	COLLIER, Edward V.	21	Oglethorpe
COLEMAN, Elisha	1	Emanual	COLLIER, Henry	1	Early
COLEMAN, Emilia	8	Emanual	COLLIER, Jesse C.	11	Early
COLEMAN, G. S.	3	Floyd	COLLIER, John F.	7	Monroe
COLEMAN, H. W.	19	Hancock	COLLIER, John V.	37	Oglethorpe
COLEMAN, J. G.	22	Hancock	COLLIER, Joseph	2	Early
COLEMAN, James	5	Muscogee	COLLIER, Joseph A.	30	Harris
COLEMAN, John	2	Laurens	COLLIER, M. W.	5	Gordon
COLEMAN, John	6	Liberty	COLLIER, P.	5	Cobb
COLEMAN, John T.	1	Muscogee	COLLIER, Pleasant C.	5	Monroe
COLEMAN, Lindsey	7	Jefferson	COLLIER, Randolph	3	Pike
COLEMAN, Lucy	2	Emanual	COLLIER, Rebecca	13	Monroe
COLEMAN, Mathew	3	Emanual	COLLIER, Robert M.	15	Upson
COLEMAN, Milby?	6	Muscogee	COLLIER, Thomas G.	8	Early
COLEMAN, W.	16	Hancock	COLLIER, Thos. S.	1	Coweta
COLEMAN, W. R.	1	Laurens	COLLIER, Wm. E.	12	Lee
COLEMAN, W. T.	1	Laurens	COLLIER, William	8	Upson
COLEMAN, Watson, R.	4	Gilmer	COLLIER, B. W.	11	Butts
COLEMAN, Wilcomb	18	Emanual	COLLIER, George W.	25	Baker
COLEMAN, William P.	5	Muscogee	COLLIER, J. H.	29	Crawford
COLEMAN, Wm. T.	5	Liberty	COLLIER, J. J.	5	Coweta
COLEMAN, Alfred	2	Cass	COLLIER, James	3	DeKalb
COLEMAN, J. G.	4	Bibb	COLLIER, John	5	DeKalb
COLEMAN, James L.	92	Richmond	COLLIER, Merrill	14	DeKalb
COLEMAN, Mary	3	Bibb	COLLIER, Mrs.	4	DeKalb
COLEMAN, Thomas C.	3	Dooly	COLLIER, Needham W.	17	Baker
COLEMAN, Thos.	3	Randolph	COLLIER, Thomas	6	Clarke
COLEMAN, Wm.	24	Randolph	COLLIER, Wesley	3	DeKalb
COLEN, W. R.	9	Stewart	COLLIER, William V.	14	Talbot
COLEY ?, Dobson	35	Twiggs	COLLINS, ? S.	8	Richmond
COLEY, Helen	3	Clarke	COLLINS, Seven	7	Troup
COLEY, Mary	1	Jefferson	COLLINS, (?)	14	Columbia
COLEY, Wm.	2	Twiggs	COLLINS, Alex. W.	2	Macon
COLIN, James	5	Stewart	COLLINS, Danil	3	Cobb
COLLARS, Richard	3	Merriwether	COLLINS, Ellea	2	Madison

Name	Number	County	Name	Number	County
COLLINS, Emaline	11	Fayette	COLLINS, John	13	Columbia
COLLIINS, Emeline	6	Washington	COLLINS, John M.	9	Richmond
COLLINS, Emeline	4	Washington	COLLINS, John Y.	1	Baker
COLLINS, Gibson	8	Wilkes	COLLINS, Joseph	7	Tatnall
COLLINS, H.	1	Lee	COLLINS, Julia	2	Bibb
COLLINS, Isham	3	Marion	COLLINS, M. H.	2	Campbell
COLLINS, James A.	9	Cobb	COLLINS, Mrs.	8	Tatnall
COLLINS, James A.	4	Cobb	COLLINS, Niel	4	Tatnall
COLLINS, James M.	1	Washington	COLLINS, Perry	11	Tatnall
COLLINS, James P.	4	Oglethorpe	COLLINS, R. & C.	71	Burke
COLLINS, John	9	Madison	COLLINS, Robert r.	6	Tatnall
COLLINS, Josiah	3	Hancock	COLLINS, Robt.	41	Bibb
COLLINS, Major L	5	Washington	COLLINS, Samuel	8	Butts
COLLINS, Nancy	2	Warren	COLLINS, Samuel	3	Butts
COLLINS, Pernell	5	Harris	COLLINS, Stephen	28	Bibb
COLLINS, Rebecca	3	Twiggs	COLLINS, Willis	4	Talbot
COLLINS, Stephen	25	Marion	COLLINS, Wm.	3	Dooly
COLLINS, Stephen Z.	15	McIntosh	COLLINSWORTH,		
COLLINS, Thomas	6	Monroe	M. L.	16	Putnam
COLLINS, Thomas B.	9	Oglethorpe	COLLS, P. M. agent	4	Habersham
COLLINS, Thompson	5	Union	COLLUM, Alfred	1	Murray
COLLINS, Timothy	1	Walton	COLLY, John O.	7	Wilkes
COLLINS, W. G.	5	Oglethorpe	COLQUIT, Johnathan	6	Upson
COLLINS, W. G.	3	Oglethorpe	COLQUITT, F. M.	12	Upson
COLLINS, W. M.	4	Greene	COLQUITT, N. G.	21	Upson
COLLINS, William	14	Oglethorpe	COLLYER, Cordelia	10	Habersham
COLLINS, William	11	Oglethorpe	COLQUET, Joseph E.	6	Oglethorpe
COLLINS,			COLQUETT, W. H.	25	Oglethorpe
William A. S.	53	Columbia	COLQUITT, A. B.	6	Meriwether
COLLINS, Wm.	25	Bibb	COLQUITT, Mildred	11	Oglethorpe
COLLINS, A. M.	5	Talbot	COLQUITT, W. J.	15	Oglethorpe
COLLINS, A. W.	1	Coweta	COLQUITT, W. T.	32	Muscogee
COLLINS, Andrew J.	1	Tatnall	COLQUITT, Walter L.	2	Muscogee
COLLINS, Berryan	9	Tatnall	COLQUITT, A. H.	10	Bibb
COLLINS, Bryant	3	Stewart	COLS, William J.	3	Dade
COLLINS, Bryant	7	Talbot	COLSON, Charles H.	5	Warren
COLLINS, C.	1	Bibb	COLSON, Edward	9	Thomas
COLLINS, Cornelius	19	Columbia	COLSON, Isaac	3	Early
COLLINS, David	18	Baldwin	COLSON, John W.	10	Burke
COLLINS, Dennes J.	5	Richmond	COLSON, Armisted F.	2	Burke
COLLINS, Eliza O.	2	Richmond	COLSON, Susan R.	3	Burke
COLLINS, George W.	11	Sumter	COLSON, William	8	Burke
COLLINS, George W.	9	Tatnall	COLSTON, James	2	Elbert
COLLINS, Irben	5	Butts	COLT, Mary	31	Greene
COLLINS, J.	2	Bibb	COLT, Wm.	51	Hancock
COLLINS, J. A.	2	Butts	COLTER, Alfred B.	7	Floyd
COLLINS, J. J.	49	Dooly	COLTER, Travis	1	Cass
COLLINS, Jackson	3	Tatnall	COLUMBUS FACTORY	4	Muscogee
COLLINS, Jacob	3	Cherokee	COLVARD, Alpheus	1	Columbia
COLLINS, James	3	Stewart	COLVIN, Jesse	5	Harris
COLLINS, James	7	Talbot	COLVIN, Mary	2	Henry
COLLINS, James M.	3	Richmond	COLVIN, Price	2	Henry
COLLINS, Jesse	13	Decatur	COLVIN, Tarlton	1	Henry
COLLINS, John	13	Columbia	COLVIN, Danl.	7	Columbia

Name	Number	County	Name	Number	County
COLWELL, Charles T.	11	Houston	CONE, Jno. F.	17	Harris
COLWELL, Glenn	1	Pike	CONE, John M.	6	Greene
COLWELL, Green	1	Jasper	CONE, Jonathan B.	1	Washington
COLWELL, Lidda	6	Morgan	CONE, Joseph	21	Merriwether
COLWELL, Samuel A.	8	Houston	CONE, William B.	1	Murray
COLYER, Edwin	1	DeKalb	CONE, Joseph	8	Thomas
COLYER, Meridith	13	DeKalb	CONE, Aaron	9	Bullock
COMBERLY, M. N.	3	Carroll	CONE, Barbara	3	Bullock
COMBS, A. G.	5	Henry	CONE, J. S.	4	Bibb
COMBS, S. T.	9	Floyd	CONE, James	15	Bullock
COMBS, Elizabeth	2	Wilkes	CONE, James	5	DeKalb
COMBS, Emeline	1	Bibb	CONE, Joseph	2	Bullock
COMBS, Frances	18	Taliaferro	CONE, Peter	2	Bullock
COMBS, Hiram	2	DeKalb	CONE, Rebecca	10	Columbia
COMBS, Nathan	2	Walker	CONE, Reuben	8	DeKalb
COMBS, P. F.	1	Wilkes	CONE, Thomas	4	Dooly
COMBS, William	1	Chatham	CONE, Thomas S.	1	Walker
COMBS?, Noah	1	Floyd	CONE, William	1	Bullock
COMER, ?	2	Muscogee	CONE, William B.	7	Dooly
COMER, Andrew J.	1	Jones	CONELL, Geo.	4	Laurens
COMER, Frederick	15	Muscogee	CONELLY, J. H.	1	Walker
COMER, George W.	11	Jasper	CONELLY, John	1	Walker
COMER, Reuben S.	1	Clarke	CONELLY, Leander A.	1	Walker
COMER, Thomas J.	6	Jasper	CONER, Thomas	5	Twiggs
COMER, W. J.	1	Floyd	CONERAY, Ellen	7	Chatham
COMER, A.	81	Houston	CONEY, A.	1	Chattooga
COMER, Anderson	11	Bibb	CONEY, Amanda	3	Dooly
COMER, James	2	Talbot	CONEY, C. C.	6	Lee
COMMANDER,			CONEY, James E.	3	Lee
John W.	1	Macon	CONEY, Joel	63	Laurens
COMPTON, Doctor F.	2	Pike	CONEY, Sarah	12	Pulaski
COMPTON, Geo. W.	1	Houston	CONGER, D.	1	Clarke
COMPTON, John	1	Campbell	CONGER, E. M.	3	Henry
COMPTON, Jordan	16	Jasper	CONGER, Mary	7	Cobb
COMPTON, Pleasant M.	8	Jasper	CONGER, R. E.	1	Henry
COMPTON, Aaron	3	Sumter	CONGER?, Bird	1	Cobb
COMPTON, C.	2	Decatur	CONGLETON, B. A.	16	Monroe
COMPTON, Pleasant	7	Baldwin	CONIOR?, Nancy	1	Campbell
COMRARD, Alex.	3	Gordon	CONLEY, Henry H.	6	Habersham
COMWELL, George agt.	1	Chatham	CONLEY, Benj.	2	Richmond
CONALY, C. M.	11	DeKalb	CONLEY, Benj.	1	Richmond
CONAWAY, Henry	1	Warren	CONLEY, Chas.	3	DeKalb
CONAWAY, Turner	3	Warren	CONLEY, Christopher	7	DeKalb
CONCLE, H.	1	Henry	CONLEY, Patrick	2	DeKalb
CONCLE, H. Sen.	6	Henry	CONLEY, Thos. W.	6	DeKalb
CONDEY, Caleb W.	1	Gilmer	CONLY, Abram.	1	DeKalb
CONE, ?. C.	10	Dooly	CONLY, Gatsy	3	Wilkinson
CONE, F. H.	14	Greene	CONLY, T.	1	Wilkinson
CONE, J. B.	1	Hancock	CONN, George M.	4	Chatham
CONE, Jackson	4	Merriwether	CONNALLY, Nathaniel	1	Murray
CONE, James	8	Thomas	CONNALLY, Samuel F.	10	Murray
CONE, James	9	Washington	CONNALLY, Thomas	7	Murray
CONE, Jesse B.	3	Washington	CONNALLY, William	13	Murray
CONE, John	14	Thomas	CONNALY, William	1	Murray

Name	Number	County
CONNEL, James	18	Thomas
CONNEL, John	6	Butts
CONNELL, Clarissa	2	Montgomery
CONNELL, Daniel	15	Greene
CONNELL, J. A.	1	Elbert
CONNELL, Jessee	4	Jefferson
CONNELL, T.	1	Henry
CONNELL, Thomas	1	Jefferson
CONNELL, Lawrence	2	Chatham
CONNELL, Thos. H.	4	Butts
CONNELL,, Daniel J.	2	Jefferson
CONNELLY, C.	26	Merriwether
CONNELLY, P. B.	95	Jefferson
CONNELLY, Patrick B.	82	Jefferson
CONNELLY, B. J.	13	Campbell
CONNELLY, Joseph	1	Bibb
CONNELY, Patrick	12	Burke
CONNELY, Patrick B.	20	Burke
CONNELY, Robert F.	51	Burke
CONNER, Abel	1	Greene
CONNER, Briern	1	Chatham
CONNER, Elijah	7	Warren
CONNER, James G.	1	Montgomery
CONNER, John	3	Cherokee
CONNER, John	3	Newton
CONNER, Thomas B.	4	Montgomery
CONNER, Z. C.	1	Floyd
CONNER, Ann	4	Screven
CONNER, Isaac	25	Screven
CONNER, Lucretia	2	Screven
CONNER, Martin	1	Burke
CONNER, T.	5	Merriwether
CONNER, Wilson	6	Screven
CONNER, Z. T.	10	Bibb
CONNERS, C. W.	2	Oglethorpe
CONNOR, W. L.	1	Screven
CONRAD, Joseph V.	3	Chatham
CONSTANTINE, Barnard	9	Chatham
CONVERSE, Albert	4	Lowndes
CONWAY, Charles	1	Effingham
CONYERS, Henry	33	Houston
CONYERS, W. D.	60	Newton
CONYERS, Daniel	4	Cass
CONYERS, J. F.	12	Randolph
CONYERS, John E.	9	Coweta
COODY, Lewis T.	1	Lowndes
COODY, C. M.	6	Butts
COOFER?, A. D.	1	Floyd
COOGLE, John	4	Macon
COOK, ?. C.	24	Muscogee
COOK, A. A.	25	Hancock
COOK, B. T.	22	Lee
COOK, David	7	Clarke
COOK, E. B.	6	Jefferson
COOK, E. M.	1	Henry
COOK, Elijah	71	Harris
COOK, Elijah	53	Harris
COOK, Elijah	1	Muscogee
COOK, Elizabeth	18	Harris
COOK, Francis	19	Monroe
COOK, G. W.	1	Cherokee
COOK, Hope H.	15	Heard
COOK, Isaac N.	2	Thomas
COOK, J. H.	2	Henry
COOK, James	25	Clarke
COOK, James	25	Muscogee
COOK, James	4	Newton
COOK, James C.	13	Muscogee
COOK, James E.	2	Floyd
COOK, James J.	3	Monroe
COOK, James R.	4	Troup
COOK, James S.	2	Washington
COOK, Jno.	21	Henry
COOK, John	1	Butts
COOK, John	5	Cherokee
COOK, John R.	1	Houston
COOK, John R.	1	Jefferson
COOK, John R.	34	Macon
COOK, John W.	3	Clarke
COOK, Joshua	1	Greene
COOK, L. P.	3	Morgan
COOK, Martha	13	Troup
COOK, Mary	9	Newton
COOK, Nathan	4	Clarke
COOK, Nevison	5	Hall
COOK, Philip	7	Macon
COOK, Reuben	13	Newton
COOK, S. T.	6	Henry
COOK, T.	2	Henry
COOK, Thomas B.	1	Cobb
COOK, Tilman agt for COBB, P.S.Q.	37	Houston
COOK, W.T.O.	13	Elbert
COOK, William	87	McIntosh
COOK, William	1	Talbot
COOK, William C.	10	Early
COOK, Wm. M.	1	Clarke
COOK, Zilpha	2	Twiggs
COOK, Andrew J.	2	Burke
COOK, B. L.	8	Randolph
COOK, C. L.	17	Screven
COOK, Clark J. estate	2	Richmond
COOK, Cobb	38	Coweta
COOK, E. B.	14	Bibb
COOK, Elizabeth W.	1	Baldwin
COOK, G.W.	1	DeKalb
COOK, George	5	Campbell

Name	Number	County	Name	Number	County
COOK, H. S.	4	Chatham	COOPER, John C.	2	Gwinnett
COOK, H.M.	22	Crawford	COOPER, John M.	9	Chatham
COOK, Hamlin J.	23	Baker	COOPER, John T.	8	Houston
COOK, Henry	3	Randolph	COOPER, Jonathan	5	Madison
COOK, Henry K.	2	Chatham	COOPER, Joseph W.	17	Wilkes
COOK, J. H.	22	Coweta	COOPER, Lemuel H.	4	Walton
COOK, James R.	2	Campbell	COOPER, Levy M.	15	Gwinnett
COOK, John	11	Coweta	COOPER, Mark A.	22	Cass
COOK, John	1	Talbot	COOPER, Martha P.	1	Gwinnett
COOK, John D.	9	Burke	COOPER, Mary	10	Chatham
COOK, John J.	13	Talbot	COOPER, Mrs.	5	Camden
COOK, Jourden	1	Sumter	COOPER, Mrs. Nancy	26	Houston
COOK, Kalin?	8	Bibb	COOPER, Nancy	1	Troup
COOK, Martha	4	Talbot	COOPER, Temple F.	12	Franklin
COOK, Mary	2	Sumter	COOPER, Vina	5	Upson
COOK, McKEEN	13	Randolph	COOPER, William	37	Effingham
COOK, Richard M.	1	Burke	COOPER, William B.	8	Lowndes
COOK, Shem	4	Carroll	COOPER, William C.	3	Muscogee
COOK, Susan G.	4	Bibb	COOPER, William H.	3	Troup
COOK, Thos.	20	Butts	COOPER, Willis	4	Walton
COOK, Willis	22	Baker	COOPER, Willis	6	Walton
COOK, Zadoc	31	Clarke	COOPER, Wm.	38	Houston
COOKE, George W.	8	Harris	COOPER, Wyley	42	Cass
COOKE, W. A.	19	Hancock	COOPER, Abner	1	Stewart
COOKE, Hamlin J. agent	6	Baker	COOPER, Benjamin	3	Campbell
COOKSEY, William H.	25	Walton	COOPER, Elbert	2	Randolph
COOKSY, Robert	33	Walton	COOPER, Eli	2	Randolph
COOLEY, Bryant	3	Jasper	COOPER, Eliz.	5	Richmond
COOLEY, E. D.	6	Troup	COOPER, G. W.	1	Lee
COOLY, Brinkley	6	Heard	COOPER, George W.	6	Screven
COOLY, Benjamin	2	DeKalb	COOPER, H.	1	Chatham
COOMBS, D. H.	17	Twiggs	COOPER, J. F.	2	Stewart
COOMBS, James	16	Laurens	COOPER, J. P.	7	Bibb
COON, George	3	Merriwether	COOPER, James M. V.	4	Richmond
COON, John A.	2	Chattooga	COOPER, Jas	4	Randolph
COOPEDGE, Charles	8	Pike	COOPER, Jas.	3	Randolph
COOPEDGE, Thomas	2	Pike	COOPER, John E.	2	Richmond
COOPEDGE, Wm. N.	4	Pike	COOPER, Newton	1	Taliaferro
COOPER & GILLILANE	3	Chatham	COOPER, Robert	'1	Stewart
COOPER, Adam	3	Pike	COOPER, S.	3	Decatur
COOPER, Alexander H.	1	Muscogee	COOPER, Stephen H.	1	Chatham
COOPER, Bennett	2	Paulding	COOPER, Thomas W.	1	Chatham
COOPER, Bleke J.	8	Walton	COOPER, Virginia	1	Richmond
COOPER, Davis	2	Hancock	COOPER, Wilson W.	28	Screven
COOPER, Geo. F.	8	Houston	COPE, John B.	6	Chaham
COOPER, Henry	1	Laurens	COPE, George L. Jr.	13	Chatham
COOPER, Henry	8	Newton	COPE, George L. Sen.	11	Chatham
COOPER, J. W.	2	Pike	COPE, John H.	4	Chatham
COOPER, James	6	Cherokee	COPELAN, Jasper N.	10	Greene
COOPER, James	6	Muscogee	COPELAN, John	19	Greene
COOPER, James	2	Wilkes	COPELAN, John D.	6	Greene
COOPER, James F.	8	Cobb	COPELAN, Obediah	14	Greene
COOPER, Jesse	4	Houston	COPELAN, Richard	13	Newton
COOPER, John	2	Chatham	COPELAN, Scott	1	Lowndes

Name	Number	County	Name	Number	County
COPELAN, John	20	Greene	CORNET, Henry	1	Harris
COPELAND, B.	39	Morgan	CORNETT, Unah D.	7	Paulding
COPELAND, D. T.	1	Henry	CORNETT, Uriah D.	7	Gordon
COPELAND, E.	1	Henry	CORNWELL, George W.	14	Jasper
COPELAND, Henry	2	Marion	CORNWELL, George	2	Chatham
COPELAND, John T.	12	Harris	CORRELLOAN, Edw.	7	Richmond
COPELAND, Josiah C.	6	Heard	CORRETHUS, Hugh	6	Walton
COPELAND, Peter	25	Harris	CORRIELL, Abram S.	2	Richmond
COPELAND, S.	2	Henry	CORRY, J. S.	36	Elbert
COPELAND, S.	1	Muscogee	CORRY, William A.	35	Greene
COPELAND, W.	3	Henry	CORSEY, Right F.	5	Heard
COPELAND, W.	1	Henry	CORSEY, L.	19	Bibb
COPELAND, William	26	Harris	CORUM?, Thos	2	Randolph
COPELAND, William	10	Harris	CORVOISIE, James A.	3	Chatham
COPELAND,			CORYELL, Joseph	23	Campbell
William Sen.	6	Harris	CORYELL, Martha A.	4	Campbell
COPELAND, William	8	Walker	COSBAY, L.	3	Elbert
COPELAND, A.	30	Talbot	COSBY, David	7	Wilkes
COPELAND, Isaac	10	Talbot	COSBY, Lucy	6	Wilkes
COPELAND, Massey M.	1	Richmond	COSBY, Oliver	6	Walton
COPELIN, J. N.	3	Murray	COSBY, Overton	2	Richmond
COPELIN, William	28	Merriwether	COSBY, Tom	1	Columbia
COPLAND, Robert	3	Thomas	COSGROVE, Teacne ?	2	Richmond
COPLAND, William	6	Stewart	COSKERY, John	9	Richmond
COPLIN, Robertus	6	Stewart	COSNAHAM, Thos.	35	Burke
COPP, Daniel D.	9	Chatham	COSTELL, James	2	Richmond
CORBAN, Sampson	3	Wilkes	COSTEN, Francis	1	Walker
CORBEN, N. B.	8	Crawford	COSTON, James	10	Washington
CORBET, John C.	13	Washington	COSTON, John	2	Forsyth
CORBETT, Michael	1	Cobb	COSY, James A.	2	DeKalb
CORBETT, Thomas	8	Decatur	COTHRAN, John	5	Pike
CORBIN, Henry L.	27	Macon	COTHRAN, Wade	45	Cass
CORBIN, James W.	3	Pike	COTHRAN, Wade S.	17	Floyd
CORBIN, Samuel P.	115	Crawford	COTHRAN?, Francis M.	5	Pike
CORBIT, George	2	Stewart	COTHREN, James	18	Pike
CORBIT, Jas.	9	Stewart	COTHRON, Ashley	37	Decatur
CORBITT, Edwin C.	10	Early	COTON?, Walton	40	Meriwether
CORBITT, Wm. W.	2	Macon	COTTEN, James G.	18	Harris
CORDEN, John	1	Chatham	COTTEN, Pleasant G.	4	Harris
CORDER, Emanual	6	Harris	COTTER, Alexander	5	Walker
CORDRY, Daniel	2	Muscogee	COTTILL, Robert T.	2	Paulding
CORKER, Almirian	5	Burke	COTTING, D. G.	11	Wilkes
CORKER, Ann J.	18	McIntosh	COTTING, D. G.	2	Wilkes
CORKER, Drury	43	Burke	COTTINGHAM,		
CORKER, James A.	7	Burke	James D.	16	Talbot
CORKER, Minerva	4	Burke	COTTLE, Cullen	7	Talbot
CORLEW, Elias B.	2	Greene	COTTLE, James	2	Troup
CORLEY, N. L.	2	Gwinnett	COTTLE, Nancy	43	Sumter
CORLEY, Elizabeth	2	Talbot	COTTON, Charles	10	Upson
CORLEY, Higden	1	Talbot	COTTON, James K.	6	Cobb
CORLEY, J. W.	1	Coweta	COTTON, John	33	Monroe
CORMELL?, R. D.	3	Habersham	COTTON, Smith	14	Harris
CORMICK, Lewis	2	Richmond	COTTON, Smith	8	Harris
CORNELISON, Sarah	5	Wilkes	COTTON, Stephen G.	7	Macon

Name	Number	County
COTTON, William	14	Monroe
COTTON, Wm.	12	Troup
COTTON, Cary	6	Coweta
COTTON, Chas.	5	Bibb
COTTON, Edwin	5	Randolph
COTTON, Eli	10	Coweta
COTTON, John	11	Campbell
COUCH, Grenett	2	Upson
COUCH, Irvin	5	Upson
COUCH, J. M.	2	Henry
COUCH, John	1	Pike
COUCH, Mary	1	Jasper
COUCH, T.	9	Hall
COUCH, George	12	Talbot
COUCH, James	10	Talbot
COUCH, Josiah	1	Coweta
COUCH, Kinon	26	Talbot
COUCH, Matthew	11	Coweta
COUCH, Wm.	20	Upson
COUGHTON, Austin	9	Sumter
COULTER, Matilda	2	Cherokee
COULTER, William	5	Jones
COULTER, William M.	1	Walker
COULTER, William Q.	2	Jones
COUNCIL, Lovey	6	Wilkinson
COUNNRY(?), B. H.	44	Coweta
COUNTRYMAN, John	5	Sumter
COUNTRYMAN, M.H.	3	Sumter
COUNTS, John	1	Chatham
COUPER, J. Hamilton	112	Glynn
COUPER,		
William Audley	130	Glynn
COURRIE, Malcom	3	Montgomery
COURSEY, Alfred	1	Washington
COURSEY, Mrs.	2	Tatnall
COURTER, Susan	1	Chatham
COURTNEY, Nancy	18	Lumpkin
COURTNEY, Thomas	1	Richmond
COUSINS, John	2	Clarke
COUSINS, R. H.	20	Merriwether
COUSINS, William	31	Morgan
COUTER, Samuel	6	Effingham
COVAN, David	6	Troup
COVEY, John	11	Muscogee
COVIN, Lazrus S.	4	Troup
COVINGTON, Anderson	1	Pike
COVINGTON, Edward	6	Muscogee
COVINGTON, Elias	1	Gordon
COVINGTON, J.	2	Meriwether
COVINGTON, John	4	Hall
COVINGTON, Noah B.	4	Jefferson
COVINGTON, Seabron	11	Pike
COVITON?, J. T.	10	Habersham
COWAN, A. S.	13	Walton

Name	Number	County
COWAN, Stephen	15	Jackson
COWAN, William	8	Jackson
COWAN, Wm. A	13	Twiggs
COWAN, William M.	2	Murray
COWAN, Franlin	9	Stewart
COWARD, Abe	14	Camden
COWARD, William	8	Monroe
COWARD, John	3	Tatnall
COWARD, Reuben	3	Tatnall
COWART, Amariah	7	Early
COWART, Augustus M.	4	Emanual
COWART, Cullin	1	Early
COWART, Eleazar	6	Emanual
COWART, Geo. F.	3	Bibb
COWART, Maliciah	1	Early
COWART, William	2	Effingham
COWART, Zachariah	13	Early
COWART, Edna	32	Sumter
COWART, J. H.	2	Bibb
COWART, Perry	2	Putnam
COWDEN, Jonathan	2	Carroll
COWDERY, L. L.	5	Muscogee
COWEN, E. A.	4	Hall
COWEN, G. V.	9	Pulaski
COWEN, J.	4	Hall
COWEN, John	3	Pulaski
COWEN, S. D.	9	Jackson
COWEY, William	28	Floyd
COWL, Ausberry	3	Stewart
COWLES, E. M.	1	Baldwin
COWLES, F.	6	Putnam
COWLES, Mary	1	Baldwin
COWLS, Jos.	2	Putnam
COX, Absalom	8	Upson
COX, Agnes	1	Morgan
COX, Albert E.	9	Troup
COX, Albert E.	23	Troup
COX, Andrew	10	Meriwether
COX, Aris	10	Franklin
COX, Asa	12	Harris
COX, Benjamin F.	5	Troup
COX, Carey	3	Cobb
COX, Cary	4	Monroe
COX, Chapman	6	Jones
COX, Charles	12	Troup
COX, Charnick L.	3	Murray
COX, Cullen	4	Macon
COX, Cullen	3	Macon
COX, David	3	Heard
COX, Dennis?	24	Muscogee
COX, Duncan?	1	Harris
COX, E. J.	1	Merriwether
COX, Elizabeth	22	Clarke
COX, Elizabeth	17	Greene

71

Name	Number	County	Name	Number	County
COX, Franklin	2	Effingham	COX, Ichabod	13	Stewart
COX, H.	1	Oglethorpe	COX, Ichabod	8	Stewart
COX, Jacob R.	1	Murray	COX, James R.	12	Stewart
COX, James	7	Dooly	COX, John H.	1	Burke
COX, James	14	Harris	COX, John M.	1	Stewart
COX, James	3	Jefferson	COX, Joseph	10	Putnam
COX, James	9	Lee	COX, Seaborn J.	22	Burke
COX, James	5	Marion	COX, Simeon	2	Putnam
COX, James	2	Pike	COX, William	29	Burke
COX, Jessie	6	Muscogee	COX, William B.	1	Stewart
COX, John	3	Chatham	COX, Wlm. T.	13	Putnam
COX, John	1	Dooly	COX, Wm.	1	Decatur
COX, John	6	Washington	COYERT?, Hubbard	16	Hall
COX, John	9	Washington	COYLE, T. C.	5	Baldwin
COX, John H.	30	Burke	COZART, Anthony	32	Monroe
COX, John M.	7	Cherokee	COZART, G. P.	11	Wilkes
COX, John M.	5	Dooly	COZART, W. M.	3	Houston
COX, John W.	3	Dooly	COZART, W. R.	4	Lee
COX, L.	1	Irwin	CRABB, B.	3	Henry
COX, Lemual	11	Muscogee	CRABB, J. B.	2	Henry
COX, Leuisa	1	Jefferson	CRAFT, A.	19	Elbert
COX, Lewis	8	Troup	CRAFT, J.	4	Elbert
COX, Mary A.	5	Chatham	CRAFT, Mary	2	Jackson
COX, Mary D.	23	Oglethorpe	CRAFT, W. J.	4	Elbert
COX, Mary D.	1	Oglethorpe	CRAFT, W.	1	DeKalb
COX, Matthew	2	Franklin	CRAFT, W.	9	Elbert
COX, Nancy M.	7	Houston	CRAFT, Wm.	2	Bibb
COX, P. B.	10	Pike	CRAFTON, J. H.	3	Putnam
COX, Paton L.	9	Monroe	CRAFTON, Normon	1	Stewart
COX, Robert	10	Cobb	CRAFTON, S. B.	5	Washington
COX, Robert M.	9	Houston	CRAIG, Franklin A.	2	Troup
COX, Samuel	1	Fayette	CRAIG, George W. F.	19	Gwinnett
COX, Snepson? H.	67	Oglethorpe	CRAIG, James M.	2	Troup
COX, Thomas	4	Gwinnett	CRAIG, John E.	20	Gwinnett
COX, Wade C.	5	Putnam	CRAIG, John E.	4	Troup
COX, William	107	Morgan	CRAIG, Robert	47	Gwinnett
COX, William	5	Pike	CRAIG, Wm.	13	Clarke
COX, William C.	2	Troup	CRAIG, B. M.	28	Crawford
COX, William J.	28	Madison	CRAIG, John	4	Richmond
COX, William P.	14	Walton	CRAIGMILES, James M.	3	Murray
COX, Wm.	8	Marion	CRAIGMILES, P. M.	12	Murray
COX, Wm. R.	13	Wilkes	CRAME, Wm. G.	6	Heard
COX, A. B.	1	Camden	CRAMER, Joseph	17	Oglethorpe
COX, B. C.	11	Bryan	CRAMER?, Samuel H.	2	Oglethorpe
COX, B. M.			CRAMER, Washington	1	Walker
(Bartley Martin)	42	Baker	CRAMLY, Elender	3	Murray
COX, B. M.			CRANDALL, Edwin A.	3	Warren
(Bartley Martin)	9	Baker	CRANDER, L. P. A.	1	Pike
COX, Benjamin	11	Burke	CRANE, Jos. R.	3	Wilkes
COX, C. T.	4	Sumter	CRANE, Ross	22	Clarke
COX, Cary	35	Putnam	CRANE, Spencer	47	Jasper
COX, Chappel	22	Stewart	CRANE, Spencer C.	13	Heard
COX, Elmanual R.	13	Bryan	CRANE, Susan	11	Heard
COX, I.M.	8	Stewart	CRANE, Herman A.	10	Chatham

Name	Number	County
CRANE, William H.	5	Richmond
CRANE?, Andrew	8	Harris
CRANFORD, Benjamin	1	Twiggs
CRANFORD, John	1	Twiggs
CRANFORD, Seaborn	31	Pike
CRANFORD, William	10	Twiggs
CRANSTON, Uriah	1	Chatham
CRAPP, Geo.	12	Randolph
CRAPP, J.J.	13	Randolph
CRAPP, Jno.	28	Randolph
CRAPP, M.E.	5	Randolph
CRAVEN, Thos. W.	11	Floyd
CRAVEN, D.	2	Chattooga
CRAVER. A. D.	1	Troup
CRAVER, Daniel	2	Troup
CRAVER, Lewis T.	23	Harris
CRAVER, Philip	3	Harris
CRAVEY, Joshua	3	Telfair
CRAVEY, William	3	Stewart
CRAVON, D. B.	3	Troup
CRAW, Casey	2	Butts
CRAWFORD, Anderson	41	Early
CRAWFORD, Andrew	13	Pike
CRAWFORD, Andrew	10	Pike
CRAWFORD, B.	1	Elbert
CRAWFORD, B. E.	3	Elbert
CRAWFORD, Charles Y.	9	Newton
CRAWFORD, David	1	Monroe
CRAWFORD, David	22	Newton
CRAWFORD, Eliza E.	5	Forsyth
CRAWFORD, Emanuel	4	Effingham
CRAWFORD, Ezekiel	3	Thomas
CRAWFORD, Geo. W.	23	Jefferson
CRAWFORD, George	10	Monroe
CRAWFORD, Hinton	18	Greene
CRAWFORD, Hugh	32	Franklin
CRAWFORD, James	9	Pike
CRAWFORD, Joel	136	Early
CRAWFORD, Joel	5	Newton
CRAWFORD, John	13	Cass
CRAWFORD, John	9	Clarke
CRAWFORD, John A.	2	Merriwether
CRAWFORD, John H.	6	Chatham
CRAWFORD, John L.	2	Warren
CRAWFORD, Levi M.	13	Clarke
CRAWFORD, M. A.	1	Henry
CRAWFORD, Martin J.	45	Muscogee
CRAWFORD, Mary C.	3	Madison
CRAWFORD, Mathew	3	Gwinnett
CRAWFORD, Matthew	10	Franklin
CRAWFORD, Nancy	1	Monroe
CRAWFORD, Nell	9	Greene
CRAWFORD, Noel	10	Greene
CRAWFORD, Robert	32	Pike
CRAWFORD, S.	14	Henry
CRAWFORD, T. S.	38	Henry
CRAWFORD, Thomas	19	Greene
CRAWFORE, Thomas	10	Walton
CRAWFORD, Vincent	4	Pike
CRAWFORD, W. B.	2	Elbert
CRAWFORD, W. H. B.	3	Morgan
CRAWFORD, Watson A.	3	Upson
CRAWFORD, William	25	Upson
CRAWFORD, William Agt.	11	Upson
CRAWFORD, William J.	4	Harris
CRAWFORD, William L.	7	Jasper
CRAWFORD, William T.	10	Harris
CRAWFORD, Winn	17	Lincoln
CRAWFORD, A .	3	Coweta
CRAWFORD, A. L.	2	Burke
CRAWFORD, Anderson	53	Columbia
CRAWFORD, Betsy	4	Columbia
CRAWFORD, C.	21	Crawford
CRAWFORD, Charles	18	Columbia
CRAWFORD, Cynthia	6	Baker
CRAWFORD, George W.	13	Richmond
CRAWFORD, H. S.	3	Cass
CRAWFORD, Jackson	8	Bibb
CRAWFORD, Martha	10	Decatur
CRAWFORD, Mary Ann	50	Columbia
CRAWFORD, N. A.	15	Columbia
CRAWFORD, Nathan	56	Columbia
CRAWFORD, Uriah	11	Talbot
CRAWFORD, W. B.	10	Baker
CRAWFORD, William H.	13	Sumter
CRAWFORD, Wm. L.	15	Randolph
CRAWLY, Ginather?	2	Pike
CRAWLY, Zachariah	6	Pike
CREACH, Hiram	3	Screven
CREAMER, Christopher G.	11	Chatham
CREAMER, Simeon	5	Campbell
CREAMER, William	6	Chatham
CREAR, William H.	1	Pike
CREAR, Daniel	1	Pike
CREAR, William Sr.	1	Pike
CREDILLE, Polly	23	Greene
CREDILLE, Henry R.	4	Greene
CREDILLE, J. G.	2	Henry
CREDILLE, Sarah	6	Greene
CREDILLE, Wm.	26	Greene
CREDILLE, Wm. S.	7	Greene

Name	Number	County	Name	Number	County
CREDILLE, Wm.G.	5	Greene	CROCKETT, Floyd	36	Richmond
CREECH, David B.	2	Telfair	CROFFORD, R. G.	4	Campbell
CREIGHTON, John	5	Jackson	CROFT, David	3	Cherokee
CRENSHAW, David	6	Jackson	CROKER, Robt. H.	1	Richmond
CRENSHAW, G. S.	1	Pike	CROLEY, Benj.	5	Oglethorpe
CRENSHAW, Mary	24	Warren	CROLL, Samuel K.	22	Talbot
CRENSHAW,			CROLY, Briant H.	6	Walton
Temperence	3	Gwinnett	CROMMON, Mary	1	Jasper
CRENSHAW, Wm. L.	13	Greene	CROMWELL, Nancy	16	Monroe
CRENSHAW, Henry	5	Taliaferro	CROMWELL, W.	4	Muscogee
CRENSHAW, Sidney R.	1	Taliaferro	CROMWELL, Nahom	4	Baldwin
CRESS, Lewis	3	Richmond	CROOK, Elizabeth	6	Harris
CREW, John	2	Muscogee	CROOK, James	20	Harris
CREWS, Archibald	1	Wayne	CROOK, James	15	Harris
CREWS, R. J.	15	Harris	CROOK, Jane	6	Chattooga
CRIBB, Sarah	1	Jones	CROOK, John G.	1	Chatham
CRICHTON, Eleanor	1	Camden	CROOK, Osborn	9	Harris
CRICHTON, Louisa	2	Camden	CROOK, L. W.	5	Chattooga
CRIDDLE, C.	5	Henry	CROOK, Williams	6	Chattooga
CRIDER?, Martha	3	Heard	CROOKS, Osborn	83	Harris
CRIM, John B.	19	Walton	CROOM, Richard	11	Washington
CRIMER, R. D.	1	Franklin	CROPP, H. D.	1	Muscogee
CRIMES, William	5	Stewart	CROSBEY, Jas. A.	1	Troup
CRISTIAN, J. G.	3	Stewart	CROSBY, Asa	1	Twiggs
CRISTIAN, N. T.	2	Randolph	CROSBY, B. R.	20	Heard
CRISTOPHER, Wm.	5	Coweta	CROSBY, J.	1	Heard
CRISWELL, Lawson	3	Wilkinson	CROSBY, John	15	Heard
CRISWELL, S.	3	Wilkinson	CROSBY, Silas	4	Appling
CRISWOLD, William	1	Muscogee	CROSBY, Susan	3	Heard
CRITENDON, Wm.	15	Henry	CROSHAW, J.	9	Muscogee
CRITINGTON, R. M.	2	Elbert	CROSLY, Harris	2	DeKalb
CRITINGTON, W. M.	1	Elbert	CROSLY, Gardner	10	DeKalb
CRITTENDEN, James	3	Marion	CROSLY, George W.	1	DeKalb
CRITTENDEN,			CROSS, ?	5	Dooly
Cincinnatus	25	Sumter	CROSS, George	2	Early
CRITTENDEN, Oliver	3	Sumter	CROSS, John W.	1	Houston
CRITTENDON, Carter	2	Richmond	CROSS, Littleton	8	Emanual
CRITTTENDEN, George	3	Morgan	CROSS, Young	2	Lee
CROCKER, Dawson	1	Richmond	CROSS, Augustus	9	Burke
CROCKER, D. E.	4	Twiggs	CROSS, D. T.	1	Dooly
CROCKER, E. E.	13	Twiggs	CROSS, Enon	20	Burke
CROCKER, John	8	Stewart	CROSS, James	16	Burke
CROCKER, John R.	4	Richmond	CROSS, James	5	Dooly
CROCKER, Mary	36	Twiggs	CROSS, John R.	2	Coweta
CROCKER, William	1	Stewart	CROSS, L. J.	3	Dooly
CROCKER,			CROSS, Mrs. Rebecca	5	Burke
William N. L.	58	Macon	CROSS, Z.	1	Cherokee
CROCKET, D. A.	1	Morgan	CROSS, Zachariah	1	Cheokee
CROCKET, Wm. F.	1	Heard	CROSS?, Joseph L.	14	Lee
CROCKETT, J.	40	Henry	CROSSEN, Charnes?	1	Merriwether
CROCKETT, J.	1	Henry	CROSSLY, Clayton M.	1	Taliaferro
CROCKETT, J.			CROUCH, James	2	Meriwether
manager	4	Henry	CROUCH, Thomas	11	Merriwether
CROCKETT, Floyd	37	Burke	CROUCH, George	11	Muscogee

74

Name	Number	County	Name	Number	County
CROUCH, Wm.	9	Crawford	CRUMP, George H.	48	Richmond
CROUD?, Shadrach	4	Heard	CRUMP, Samuel	34	Columbia
CROW, Abel	3	Walker	CRUMPLER, James H.	1	Dooly
CROW, Carlisle	2	Hall	CRUMPLER, John B.	3	Dooly
CROW, Casey	2	Walton	CRUSE, John	1	Merriwether
CROW, Elisha	1	Jasper	CRUTCHFIELD, George	12	Greene
CROW, Mary	4	Muscogee	CRUTCHFIELD, John	1	Greene
CROW, Moore H.	10	Franklin	CRUTCHFIELD, Martin	1	Pulaski
CROW, Mrs. R.	1	Meriwether	CRUTCHFIELD,		
CROW, Nancy	7	Clarke	Parsons	2	Jones
CROW, Randolph C..	6	Franklin	CRUTCHFIELD,		
CROW, T. W.	4	Henry	Stapleton	22	Jones
CROW, W. F.	1	Henry	CRUTCHFIELD, U.	6	Pulaski
CROW, William	17	Jasper	CRUTCHFIELD, F.	8	Crawford
CROW, William T.	1	Franklin	CRUTCHFIELD, H.	14	Crawford
CROWDER, Fedric	26	Monroe	CRUTCHFIELD, J.	2	Crawford
CROWDER, Geroge W.	9	Pike	CRUTCHFIELD, T. P.	17	Wilkinson
CROWDER, Mark	22	Merriwether	CRUTCHFIELD, Thos.	4	Crawford
CROWDER, R. P.	11	Merriwether	CRY, David	6	Talbot
CROWDER, Wade L.	5	Monroe	CUBBEDGE,		
CROWDER, A.	7	Coweta	Stephen J. M.	2	Chatham
CROWDER, William	2	Chatham	CUISON, C.	1	Elbert
CROWDES, W. B.	12	Oglethorpe	CULBERSON,		
CROWELL, M. J.	1	Henry	Augustus	3	Walker
CROWELL, Churchwell	19	Cass	CULBERSON, James	39	Troup
CROWELL, E. L.	3	DeKalb	CULBERSON, James H.	2	Walker
CROWELL, Jesse	16	Decatur	CULBERSON, Jeremiah	1	Walker
CROWLEY, Charles	9	Morgan	CULBERSON, John P.	6	Troup
CROWLEY, Robert	14	Morgan	CULBERSON,		
CROWLEY, Simon	5	Morgan	Sherwood F.	6	Troup
CROWLEY, Stephen K.	11	Pike	CULBERSON,		
CROWLEY, Wilham	4	Morgan	Sherwood F.	6	Troup
CROWNAN, Michael	7	Jefferson	CULBERSON,		
CROWVELLIER, Dorice	1	Chatham	William P.	5	Troup
CROXTON, Elihu	3	Sumter	CULBERTSON, J. H.	10	Floyd
CROXVILLE, Benjamin	3	Jefferson	CULBERTSON, Jeff	1	Wilkes
CROZIER, Elizabeth	1	Lincoln	CULBERTSON, John	1	Coweta
CROZIER, John	1	Randolph	CULBRATH, John	13	Greene
CRUCE?, Stephen	1	Gwinnett	CULBRET, William	2	Oglethorpe
CRUD ?, Darlin	1	Thomas	CULBRETH, William	27	Columbia
CRUGER, Nicholas	4	Chatham	CULBRETH, William	25	Walton
CRUGER, N.	72	Baker	CULLARS, Allen	5	Lincoln
CRUIT, Saml.	8	Crawford	CULLARS, Elizabeth	5	Lincoln
CRUMB, Jas.	10	Camden	CULLARS, George	6	Lincoln
CRUMB, Mary	11	Camden	CULLARS, Josiah	10	Lincoln
CRUMBIE, W.	6	Henry	CULLARS, Josiah	2	Lincoln
CRUMBLY, Alex	5	Randolph	CULLEN, Hugh	2	Chatham
CRUMBY, G.	2	Henry	CULLEN, P. B. D.	5	Houston
CRUMBY, William	3	Stewart	CULLENS, Augustus A.	1	Washington
CRUMLEY, Anthony	11	Stewart	CULLENS, Miles I.	12	Baldwin
CRUMP, R.	7	Elbert	CULLENS, Wiley	20	Baldwin
CRUMP, Richard L.	2	Franklin	CULLINS, Augusta A.	14	Washington
CRUMP, Robert	12	Franklin	CULLINS, F. B.	4	Washington
CRUMP, Elizabeth	10	Richmond	CULPEPPER, Charles	4	Houston

Name	Number	County	Name	Number	County
CULPEPPER, David S.	11	Dooly	CUMMINGS ? ,		
CULPEPPER, G.W.	2	Meriwether	Ann Estate	11	Richmond
CULPEPPER, Gardner	28	Lee	CUMMINGS ?, Henry H.	8	Richmond
CULPEPPER, Joel	17	Harris	CUMMINGS ?, Sarah M.	3	Richmond
CULPEPPER, Lewis B.	8	Pike	CUMMINGS, Jesse	1	Appling
CULPEPPER, Marina	2	Harris	CUMMINS, D.	8	Pike
CULPEPPER, Mrs. Jane	40	Houston	CUMMINS, John	2	Heard
CULPEPPER,			CUMMINS, Sarah	3	Greene
Sampson R.	17	Warren	CUMMINS?, Harmon	1	Heard
CULPEPPER,			CUNARD, Jemima	1	Jasper
Temperence	10	Dooly	CUNARD, John	1	Jasper
CULPEPPER, A .	7	Stewart	CUNINGHAM, James	1	Oglethorpe
CULPEPPER, Benjamin	5	Dooly	CUNINGHAM, Philip	16	Upson
CULPEPPER, Chadwell	5	Dooly	CUNINGHAM, Jane	4	Bibb
CULPEPPER, David	11	Baker	CUNNINGHAM, Alexr.	1	Richmond
CULPEPPER, Elisha	2	Talbot	CUNNINGHAM, C. T.	9	Murray
CULPEPPER, John	2	Sumter	CUNNINGHAM, Charles	109	Jefferson
CULPEPPER, Mary	3	Dooly	CUNNINGHAM, George	18	Newton
CULPEPPER, Pelilatha?	5	Baker	CUNNINGHAM, J. C.	14	Lincoln
CULPEPPER, Stephen M.	3	Jones	CUNNINGHAM, J. W.	5	Merriwether
CULPEPPER, Wash.	1	Columbia	CUNNINGHAM,		
CULPH, Benjamin A.	5	Houston	James W.	1	Macon
CULREHOUSE?,			CUNNINGHAM, John	4	Chatham
G. A. agt.	35	Bibb	CUNNINGHAM, John	22	Greene
CULVER, Augustus	6	Hancock	CUNNINGHAM,		
CULVER, Elizabeth	6	Hancock	John Sen.	5	Chatham
CULVER, Erasmus V.	22	Greene	CUNNINGHAM, Moses	8	Newton
CULVER, G. W.	14	Hancock	CUNNINGHAM, P. H.	33	Jackson
CULVER, H. C.	51	Hancock	CUNNINGHAM, Robt.	4	Cherokee
CULVER, H. H.	13	Hancock	CUNNINGHAM,		
CULVER, I. F.	8	Hancock	Thomas	15	Greene
CULVER, Isaac	20	Hancock	CUNNINGHAM,		
CULVER, J. G.	10	Hancock	Thomas W.	7	Gwinnett
CULVER, Joel N.	2	Gwinnett	CUNNINGHAM, Thos.	3	Clarke
CULVER, Joshua B.	10	Hancock	CUNNINGHAM, W.	3	Oglethorpe
CULVER, Joshua J.	5	Hancock	CUNNINGHAM, W. J.	17	Forsyth
CULVER, Leroy C.	12	Hancock	CUNNINGHAM, Wm.	7	Merriwether
CULVER, Levin D.	11	Hancock	CUNNINGHAM, Wm. B.	3	Pike
CULVER, Levin E.	7	Hancock	CUNNINGHAM,		
CULVER, Wm. H.	21	Hancock	Wm. T.	3	Macon
CULVER, William	1	Stewart	CUNNINGHAM,		
CULVERHOUSE, G. P.	1	Crawford	William M.	2	Troup
CULVERSON, D. H.	4	Coweta	CUNNINGHAM, A. W.	8	Decatur
CUMINS, Charles	27	Harris	CUNNINGHAM, Charles	35	Richmond
CUMMING, David	21	Washington	CUNNINGHAM,		
CUMMING, Eli	12	Washington	Henry T.	7	Talbot
CUMMING, John	12	Muscogee	CUNNINGHAM, P.	3	Bibb
CUMMING, Mrs. S. M.	25	Liberty	CUNNINGHAM, Robt.	1	Randolph
CUMMING, Penelope	2	Macon	CUNNINGHAM, Wm. A.	3	Coweta
CUMMING, George B.	4	Chatham	CURETON, A. M.	3	Newton
CUMMING, Green E.	6	Washington	CURETON, Huldah	3	Jones
CUMMING, Robert	20	Washington	CURETON, Jas.	9	Coweta
CUMMING, Susan M.	8	Chatham	CURRELL, Spencer	10	Chatham
			CURREY, Willis	3	Monroe

Name	Number	County	Name	Number	County
CURREY, Wily	13	Monroe	DAGGERS, John R.	3	Muscogee
CURRINGTON, Wm. P.	2	Coweta	DAGGETT, Eyra	6	Baldwin
CURRY, (?)	11	Decatur	DAGNELL, Ambrose	7	Columbia
CURRY, Elaner	2	Lincoln	DAILEY, D.	21	Henry
CURRY, James W.	12	Walker	DAILEY, J.	8	Henry
CURRY, John	12	Washington	DAILEY, J. manager	5	Henry
CURRY, Mary E.	15	Washington	DALELY, Amelia	1	Chatham
CURRY, Pleasant W.	7	Walker	DALEY, Amelia	1	Chatham
CURRY, Robert F.	21	Walker	DALLAS, Edwin	9	Upson
CURRY, Silvanus T.	2	Emanual	DALLAS, George W.	24	Meriwether
CURRY, Thomas J.	1	Jones	DALLAS, H. W.	13	Troup
CURRY, Thompson	16	Jasper	DALLAS, Wm.	3	Troup
CURRY, William	1	Butts	DALLES, Rebecca	19	Lincoln
CURRY, William W.	41	Washington	DALLES, Wm.	48	Lincoln
CURRY, A. S.	17	Decatur	DALLIS, D. B.	9	Lincoln
CURRY, C.	16	Decatur	DAME, John	3	Chatham
CURRY, D.	12	Decatur	DAMERALL, William S.	5	Baker
CURRY, James G.	11	Sumter	DAMERON, Polly	10	Jackson
CURRY, Lassiter	1	Sumter	DAMERON, Uriah	1	Jackson
CURRY, M.	15	Decatur	DAMICIN?, Lucinda	3	Bibb
CURRY, Whitmill	1	Sumter	DAMIEL, Robert C.	42	Oglethorpe
CURTIS, Calab	12	Pike	DAMON, J. H.	7	Bibb
CURTIS, Mary	1	Hancock	DAMPIER, Keziah	1	Lowndes
CURTIS, Nancy E.	3	Carroll	DAMPIER, Samuel	2	Lowndes
CURTIS, T. C.	1	Newton	DANA, Francis J.	3	Chatham
CURTIS, William	8	Gordon	DANAL, E.	9	Chattooga
CURTIS, Alfred	2	Chattooga	DANCER,		
CURTIS, David D.	27	Columbia	Madison agent	18	Muscogee
CURTIS, David L.	9	Richmond	DANELLY, Wade	28	Crawford
CURTIS, Francis	5	Camden	DANFORTH, John C.	1	Campbell
CURTIS, J. T.	5	Crawford	DANFORTH, James M.	4	Richmond
CURTIS, L.	2	Crawford	DANFORTH, Saml.	8	Wilkes
CURY, William L.	2	Baldwin	DANIEL, Aaron	3	Thomas
CURTWRIGHT,			DANIEL, Alexander	6	Heard
Samuel	41	Troup	DANIEL, Alferd	4	Newton
CURTWRIGHT,			DANIEL, Allen	7	Marion
Samuel	17	Troup	DANIEL, Allen C.	3	Madison
CUTHBERT, Alfred	119	Jasper	DANIEL, Andrew J.	7	Houston
CUTLIFF, John	38	Lincoln	DANIEL, Andrew J.	10	Troup
CUTTER, Anna	5	Bibb	DANIEL, Beaten	7	Newton
CUTTS, William S.	1	Dooly	DANIEL, Benton	3	Heard
CUYLER, Jane	4	Effingham	DANIEL, C. N.	16	Greene
CUYLER, Tell	7	Floyd	DANIEL, Cathrin	11	Upson
CUYLER, R.R.	10	Chatham	DANIEL, Curtis	1	Houston
CUYLER, William H.	42	Chatham	DANIEL, D.	8	Elbert
DABBS, Jesse	4	DeKalb	DANIEL, D. O.	8	Twiggs
DABBS, John	6	DeKalb	DANIEL, E.	1	Hall
DABNEY, Henry	2	Muscogee	DANIEL, E.	3	Lee
DABNEY, James	3	Newton	DANIEL, Edmund	10	Heard
DABNEY, John	2	Newton	DANIEL, Edmund	1	Heard
DABNEY, Garland	7	DeKalb	DANIEL, Egbert P.	38	Pike
DACUS, Penelope A.	8	Walton	DANIEL, Elisha H.	3	Cobb
DADD, Robt.	1	Laurens	DANIEL, Elizabeth	2	Morgan
DAGG, J. L.	6	Greene	DANIEL, Ezekiel	10	Washington

Name	Number	County	Name	Number	County
DANIEL, George	4	Newton	DANIEL, E. P.	13	Butts
DANIEL, H. K.	7	Laurens	DANIEL, Enoch	37	Liberty
DANIEL, Hannah	2	Dooly	DANIEL, Henry	2	Sumter
DANIEL, Hopkins	5	Upson	DANIEL, James H.	9	Sumter
DANIEL, Isaac	1	Jasper	DANIEL, James K.	51	Baker
DANIEL, Isham	9	Heard	DANIEL, Jesse	20	Baldwin
DANIEL, J. G.	3	Merriwether	DANIEL, John	2	Talbot
DANIEL, James	34	Madison	DANIEL, John	7	Talbot
DANIEL, James	6	Pike	DANIEL, John A.	1	Sumter
DANIEL, James H.	2	Floyd	DANIEL, John W.	11	Baldwin
DANIEL, James L.	29	Jefferson	DANIEL, Julius	1	Sumter
DANIEL, Jas. S.	23	Pulaski	DANIEL, Major	1	Burke
DANIEL, Jasper N.	6	Washington	DANIEL, Moss	1	Richmond
DANIEL, Jefferson	4	Harris	DANIEL, Nathaniel	1	Baker
DANIEL, Jeptha	8	Heard	DANIEL, O.	3	Talbot
DANIEL, Jesse	9	Newton	DANIEL, P. (Priscilla)	20	Talbot
DANIEL, John	1	Cass	DANIEL, R. M.	1	Decatur
DANIEL, John	3	Laurens	DANIEL, Rachael	2	Bibb
DANIEL, John	16	Pulaski	DANIEL, Thomas	11	Sumter
DANIEL, John A.	2	Madison	DANIEL, William	7	Sumter
DANIEL, Joseph	4	Marion	DANIEL, William C.	129	Chatham
DANIEL, Lemuel	6	Heard	DANIEL, Wm. B.	1	Randolph
DANIEL, Mrs. Jane	5	Liberty	DANIEL, Wm. H.	16	Coweta
DANIEL, Martin B.	11	Upson	DANIEL, Young	40	Talbot
DANIEL, Moses	12	Thomas	DANIEL, Young	27	Talbot
DANIEL, N. P.	5	Pike	DANIEL, Zachariah	1	Sumter
DANIEL, O. P.	67	Greene	DANIELL, Jereh. M.	14	Clarke
DANIEL, R. F.	1	Cherokee	DANIELL, Josiah	6	Clarke
DANIEL, R. W.	20	Jefferson	DANIELL, William B.	6	Clarke
DANIEL, Robert H.	50	Jasper	DANIELL, Robert	10	Clarke
DANIEL, Russel J.	36	Jackson	DANIELL, William C.	13	Chatham
DANIEL, Saml. B.	47	Greene	DANIELLLY, Thomas F.	10	Jasper
DANIEL, Saml. E.	32	Wilkes	DANIELS, Isham	6	Houston
DANIEL, Sampson	8	Washington	DANIELS, Noah	1	Houston
DANIEL, Samson	5	Washington	DANIELS, Peter	6	Houston
DANIEL, Sarah	2	Jones	DANIELS,		
DANIEL, Silas	10	Washington	Ransome Y. B.	2	Houston
DANIEL, T. J.	6	Elbert	DANIELS, Stephen	4	Houston
DANIEL, Thos.	2	Harris	DANIELS, Stephen	1	Houston
DANIEL, W.	1	Henry	DANIELS, Wm.	5	Decatur
DANIEL, W.	1	Pulaski	DANILL, Nathaniel	27	Newton
DANIEL, Wesley A.	11	Dooly	DANILL, Stephen	5	Newton
DANIEL, William	21	Greene	DANILLY, Sarah	1	Bibb
DANIEL, William	9	Muscogee	DANILY, Francis	13	Monroe
DANIEL, Williford A.	1	Muscogee	DANILY, John	1	Monroe
DANIEL, Wm.	15	Laurens	DANNER, Geo.	3	Wilkes
DANIEL, Woodson	9	Oglethorpe	DANNER, Mary	2	Wilkes
DANIEL, Abel	1	Stewart	DANSBY, Daniel T.	23	Heard
DANIEL, Alexander	8	Sumter	DANSBY, Daniel T.	1	Heard
DANIEL, Asa	5	Talbot	DANSBY, Joshua D.	18	Heard
DANIEL, Bryan	27	Richmond	DANSBY, Wm.	21	Heard
DANIEL, C.	1	Bibb	DANSBY, Wm.	3	Heard
DANIEL, Chesley C.	5	Burke	DANSBY, William F.	22	Troup
DANIEL, Cordy	5	Clarke	DANSLER, Jacob B.	1	Murray

Name	Number	County	Name	Number	County
DARACOTT, F.W. Est.	16	Wilkes	DART, Urbanus	11	Glynn
DARBY, John	9	Monroe	DASHER, Andrew J.	5	Lowndes
DARBY, Isaac	2	Stewart	DASHER, Benj.	2	Effingham
DARDEN, Abner	14	Floyd	DASHER, Benjamin	1	Effingham
DARDEN, Edmond B.	20	Jasper	DASHER, Christian H.	20	Lowndes
DARDEN, George W.	16	Heard	DASHER, George	11	Effingham
DARDEN, Henry W.	4	Marion	DASHER, Godliph	42	Effingham
DARDEN, James	2	Murray	DASHER, Hannah	5	Effingham
DARDEN, James M.	42	Jasper	DASHER, Israel	2	Chatham
DARDEN, Jethro	33	Warren	DASHER, James A.	9	Lowndes
DARDEN, John	6	Monroe	DASHER, John	2	Effingham
DARDEN, Lucy	9	Monroe	DASHER, Joshua	8	Effingham
DARDEN, Robert S.	8	Heard	DASHER, Rebecca	4	Effingham
DARDEN, Samuel	22	Merriwether	DASHER, Samuel	3	Effingham
DARDEN, Willis	37	Troup	DASHER, Susan C.	7	Lowndes
DARDEN, Wilson	24	Monroe	DASHER, William B.	11	Effingham
DARDEN, Wm. F.	3	Monroe	DASHER, B. W.	1	Chatham
DARDEN, B. H.	11	Butts	DASHER, John	1	Tatnall
DARDEN, David E.	9	Taliaferro	DASHER, Joshua	25	Tatnall
DARDEN, Elbert	5	Sumter	DASHER, Thomas	1	Bullock
DARDEN, Jesse	2	Taliaferro	DASHUR?, John A.	4	Floyd
DARDEN, John	26	Talbot	DASSY, Willis	8	Pulaski
DARDEN, Mary	2	Talbot	DAUGHERTY, John	20	Coweta
DARDEN, Micajah	19	Sumter	DAUGHERTY, William	31	Walker
DARDEN, Warren	7	Sumter	DAUGHTRY, Lamb	22	Screven
DARDEN, Washington	21	Bibb	DAUGHTRY, Thomas	7	Screven
DARDEN, Wm. F.	1	Floyd	DAUGHTRY, Will T.	4	Butts
DARDEN, Zachariah	2	Taliaferro	DAUKINS, Thomas	1	Houston
DARDIN, Henry	1	Twiggs	DAVENPORT, Clark W.	9	Oglethorpe
DAREY, Sarah	1	Randolph	DAVENPORT, E.	7	Clarke
DARK, Leroy	2	Merriwether	DAVENPORT, H. S.	5	Forsyth
DARK, O. P.	2	Merriwether	DAVENPORT, Hugh M.	9	Chatham
DARK, R. B.	13	Meriwether	DAVENPORT, James A.	3	Houston
DARLEY, James	1	Emanual	DAVENPORT, Jesse	1	Clarke
DARLEY, Sarah	1	Harris	DAVENPORT, John	13	Pike
DARLEY, Tarlton	4	Jefferson	DAVENPORT, Joiett	6	Clarke
DARLEY, Thomas	2	Montgomery	DAVENPORT, Lucy	5	Newton
DARLEY, William J.	2	Walton	DAVENPORT, P.	1	Henry
DARLING, Joseph	4	Richmond	DAVENPORT, Smith	14	Marion
DARLINGTON, Martha			DAVENPORT, Susan	22	Oglethorpe
estate	10	Burke	DAVENPORT, W. W.	37	Oglethorpe
DARMING?, J. B.	11	Irwin	DAVENPORT, William	53	Morgan
DARNELL, Benjamin	1	Newton	DAVENPORT, Henry	17	Sumter
DARNELL, James M.	1	Campbell	DAVENPORT, M. N.	4	Clarke
DARNELL, David	13	Campbell	DAVENPORT, Sarah R.	12	Chatham
DARRACOTT, John F.	22	Lowndes	DAVENPORT, Walter T.	6	Sumter
DARSEY, Benj.	18	Liberty	DAVENPORT, William	4	Campbell
DARSEY, James	18	Liberty	DAVEY, Wilborn	18	Talbot
DARSEY, James	3	Lowndes	DAVID, John	11	Heard
DARSEY, Jno.	6	Henry	DAVID, Berry M.	2	Madison
DARSEY, Jesse	3	Decatur	DAVID, F. M.	7	Jackson
DARSEY, Wm. A.	4	Decatur	DAVID, Haden J.	6	Jackson
DARSY, John	6	Decatur	DAVID, Henry F.	9	Franklin
DART, Ann	10	Glynn	DAVID, Isaac	1	Madison

Name	Number	County	Name	Number	County
DAVID, Jacob W.	13	Harris	DAVIS, Auspin G.	14	Lincoln
DAVID, James H.	10	Jackson	DAVIS, Baldwin	45	Monroe
DAVID, James J.	4	Madison	DAVIS, Benj.	24	Twiggs
DAVID, James M.	1	Madison	DAVIS, Benj. H.	1	Harris
DAVID, John T.	3	Harris	DAVIS, Benjamin	3	Bibb
DAVID, Morasett	8	Madison	DAVIS, Benjamin	1	Effingham
DAVID, Peter	17	Madison	DAVIS, C.	1	Floyd
DAVID, Russel C.	6	Jackson	DAVIS, Charles	2	McIntosh
DAVID, William	13	Stewart	DAVIS, Charles A.	3	Greene
DAVID, William A.	1	DeKalb	DAVIS, Charles D.	7	Walton
DAVIDSON, A.	2	Troup	DAVIS, Christian	11	Houston
DAVIDSON, Albert	3	Harris	DAVIS, Cidney C.	2	Morgan
DAVIDSON, Allen	3	Wilkinson	DAVIS, D. J.	3	Early
DAVIDSON, Carey	12	Jones	DAVIS, Daniel	40	Lumpkin
DAVIDSON, D.	7	Troup	DAVIS, Daniel	15	Troup
DAVIDSON, David W.	5	Monroe	DAVIS, Daniel D.	2	Appling
DAVIDSON, Delila	1	Monroe	DAVIS, David	4	Newton
DAVIDSON, Druery M.	6	Monroe	DAVIS, Delila	6	Lumpkin
DAVIDSON, Eli S.	14	Troup	DAVIS, E. C.	1	Muscogee
DAVIDSON, Elizabeth	3	Jasper	DAVIS, E. H.	6	Newton
DAVIDSON, Isiah	6	Harris	DAVIS, E. W.	1	Thomas
DAVIDSON, James	2	Monroe	DAVIS, Ebenezer	1	Pike
DAVIDSON, James M.	14	Greene	DAVIS, Eli	18	Merriwether
DAVIDSON, John	53	Harris	DAVIS, Epsey	1	Muscogee
DAVIDSON, John	17	Troup	DAVIS, Francis	1	Marion
DAVIDSON, John Jr.	2	Jasper	DAVIS, G. C.	17	Morgan
DAVIDSON, John Sen.	2	Jasper	DAVIS, G. W.	14	Hancock
DAVIDSON, John H.	1	Wilkinson	DAVIS, G. W.	14	Hancock
DAVIDSON, Joseph	4	Heard	DAVIS, G. W.	1	Upson
DAVIDSON, Joseph	8	Twiggs	DAVIS, George F.	2	Harris
DAVIDSON, Larkin	22	Muscogee	DAVIS, Goodrum	6	Washington
DAVIDSON, Mary	1	Hancock	DAVIS, H.	6	Wilkinson
DAVIDSON, Talbot	25	Upson	DAVIS, Henry	1	Bullock
DAVIDSON, Wm.	4	Troup	DAVIS, Henry	9	Habersham
DAVIDSON, Wm. D.	1	Floyd	DAVIS, Ichabod	9	Macon
DAVIDSON, Paul	11	Taliaferro	DAVIS, Isaac	1	Floyd
DAVIE, R. W.	12	Lincoln	DAVIS, Isaac M.	7	Franklin
DAVIE, R. W.	2	Lincoln	DAVIS, Isiah	7	Murray
DAVIE, Randolph	45	Lincoln	DAVIS, Israil P.	3	Paulding
DAVIES, James W.	17	Richmond	DAVIS, J.	3	Henry
DAVINPORT, John	29	Harris	DAVIS, J. B.	12	Jefferson
DAVINPORT,			DAVIS, J. J.	2	Henry
William H.	10	Harris	DAVIS, J. L.	2	Pulaski
DAVIS (?), Mary	39	Columbia	DAVIS, James	9	Harris
DAVIS, James C.	1	Harris	DAVIS, James	4	Pike
DAVIS, John	6	Greene	DAVIS, James	10	Putnam
DAVIS, (?)	6	Columbia	DAVIS, James	5	Ware
DAVIS, A. J.	18	Jefferson	DAVIS, James A.	1	Harris
DAVIS, Abner	1	Marion	DAVIS, James G.	4	Houston
DAVIS, Albert	1	Gordon	DAVIS, James W.	3	Hall
DAVIS, Alice	1	Thomas	DAVIS, Jesse	16	Effingham
DAVIS, Archibald	34	Monroe	DAVIS, Jesse M.	51	Lee
DAVIS, Arthur	1	Montgomery	DAVIS, Joel A.	3	Washington
DAVIS, Arthur	7	Morgan	DAVIS, Joel E.	13	Troup

Name	Number	County	Name	Number	County
DAVIS, John	36	Early	DAVIS, Oren	34	Wilkinson
DAVIS, John	1	Oglethorpe	DAVIS, Osburn	13	Muscogee
DAVIS, John	2	Pike	DAVIS, P. B. J. ?	35	Macon
DAVIS, John	6	Twiggs	DAVIS, P. L.	9	Oglethorpe
DAVIS, John	10	Walker	DAVIS, Pleasant	6	Upson
DAVIS, John	10	Washington	DAVIS, Rchael	1	Randolph
DAVIS, John Jr.	6	Early	DAVIS, Richard R.	26	Early
DAVIS, John E.	6	Chatham	DAVIS, Richman	1	Monroe
DAVIS, John J.	3	Gwinnett	DAVIS, Robert	2	Effingham
DAVIS, John M.	4	Morgan	DAVIS, Samuel	35	Greene
DAVIS, John M.	5	Thomas	DAVIS, Sebron	11	Oglethorpe
DAVIS, John M.	1	Warren	DAVIS, Sheppaard	1	Effingham
DAVIS, John M. F.	1	Walton	DAVIS, Silas N.	14	Troup
DAVIS, John T.	9	Jackson	DAVIS, Sterling G.	1	Jackson
DAVIS, John W.	1	Chatham	DAVIS, Stibbs F.	2	Chatham
DAVIS, Jonathan	5	Pike	DAVIS, T.	11	Elbert
DAVIS, Jonathan	3	Walker	DAVIS, T. A.	2	Elbert
DAVIS, Jonathan G.	9	Troup	DAVIS, T. S.	2	Elbert
DAVIS, Jonathan P.	3	Wilkes	DAVIS, Theodesius	3	Thomas
DAVIS, Jordan	1	Marion	DAVIS, Thomas	2	Meriwether
DAVIS, Jos.	9	Jackson	DAVIS, Thomas	12	Muscogee
DAVIS, Joseph	7	Harris	DAVIS, Thomas	1	Muscogee
DAVIS, Joseph E.	1	Houston	DAVIS, Thomas	1	Troup
DAVIS, Joseph E.			DAVIS, Thomas	5	Washington
agt for EVERETT,J.A	132	Houston	DAVIS, Thomas C.	5	Jasper
DAVIS, Joseph J.	5	Monroe	DAVIS, Thomas C.	3	Murray
DAVIS, Joshua	18	Jones	DAVIS, Thos.	16	Morgan
DAVIS, Joshua	1	Marion	DAVIS, Thos.	21	Troup
DAVIS, Josiah	3	Greene	DAVIS, Thos. J.	14	Floyd
DAVIS, L.	5	Gordon	DAVIS, Vincent	21	Warren
DAVIS, L. D.	11	Lumpkin	DAVIS, W. M.	1	Cherokee
DAVIS, Levi	1	Gwinnett	DAVIS, W. T.	4	Elbert
DAVIS, Lewis	5	Jefferson	DAVIS, W.? T.	11	Morgan
DAVIS, Lewis F.	5	Heard	DAVIS, William	1	Cherokee
DAVIS, M. G.	29	Morgan	DAVIS, William	3	Meriwether
DAVIS, M. J.	18	Oglethorpe	DAVIS, William	1	Murray
DAVIS, Major	3	Harris	DAVIS, William B.	18	Monroe
DAVIS, Majr. Joel	1	Gwinnett	DAVIS, William C.	15	Newton
DAVIS, Maneal	1	McIntosh	DAVIS, William M.	60	Houston
DAVIS, Mary	3	Morgan	DAVIS, William P.	8	Jefferson
DAVIS. Mary	3	Thomas	DAVIS, William T.	1	Meriwether
DAVIS, Mary H.	38	Monroe	DAVIS, Wilson L.	12	Newton
DAVIS, May A.	13	Harris	DAVIS, Wm.	3	Clarke
DAVIS, Milton	5	Gilmer	DAVIS, Wm.	2	Heard
DAVIS, Mitchell	9	Jefferson	DAVIS, Wm.	8	Marion
DAVIS, Morgan N.	8	Macon	DAVIS, Wm. H.	1	Early
DAVIS, Mrs.	1	Muscogee	DAVIS, Wm. M.	2	Union
DAVIS, Mrs. H. A.	7	Muscogee	DAVIS, Wm. S.	1	Heard
DAVIS, Mrs. M.	1	Meriwether	DAVIS, Young	7	Habersham
DAVIS, Mrs.?	1	Muscogee	DAVIS, A.	7	Crawford
DAVIS, Moses	7	Warren	DAVIS, Andrea S.	5	DeKalb
DAVIS, Nancy	6	Gwinnett	DAVIS, Benj.	19	Randolph
DAVIS, Nancy	42	Jefferson	DAVIS, Cross R.	4	Talbot
DAVIS, Nathaniel	1	Marion	DAVIS, D.	17	Crawford

Name	Number	County
DAVIS, D. J.	4	Bibb
DAVIS, Doctor	4	Putnam
DAVIS, E.	24	Bibb
DAVIS, Edward	10	Stewart
DAVIS, Eli A.	2	DeKalb
DAVIS, Elisha	6	Stewart
DAVIS, Ethan	8	DeKalb
DAVIS, Evan	12	Columbia
DAVIS, Francis W.	7	Sumter
DAVIS, G. B.	1	Coweta
DAVIS, G. W.	1	Crawford
DAVIS, H.	7	Crawford
DAVIS, H. J.	12	Crawford
DAVIS, H. W.	8	Carroll
DAVIS, Henry	1	Stewart
DAVIS, Isaac	1	Stewart
DAVIS, J. H.	4	Bibb
DAVIS, J. M.	14	Crawford
DAVIS, J. V.	21	Coweta
DAVIS, James	4	Sumter
DAVIS, James M.	13	Talbot
DAVIS, Jas.	22	Putnam
DAVIS, Jesse	1	Bryan
DAVIS, Jno. H.	1	Carroll
DAVIS, John	2	Campbell
DAVIS, John	7	Crawford
DAVIS, John V.	4	Putnam
DAVIS, Josiah	9	McIntosh
DAVIS, L.	29	Crawford
DAVIS, L. H.	8	Carroll
DAVIS, Lavonia	8	Crawford
DAVIS, Lewis	8	Baker
DAVIS, Margaret	5	DeKalb
DAVIS, Moses	6	DeKalb
DAVIS, Moses	12	Talbot
DAVIS, O. H.	5	Randolph
DAVIS, Richard	7	Putnam
DAVIS, Richard	14	Randolph
DAVIS, Robert B.	2	Dooly
DAVIS, Roblin	9	Burke
DAVIS, Sam L.	4	Bryan
DAVIS, Samuel	17	Burke
DAVIS, Samuel	2	Richmond
DAVIS, Samuel	3	Tatnall
DAVIS, Samuel P.	53	Burke
DAVIS, Sarah	17	Baldwin
DAVIS, Sarah A.	19	Baldwin
DAVIS, Thomas	3	Burke
DAVIS, Thomas W.	29	Burke
DAVIS, Thos. J.	37	Putnam
DAVIS, W. J.	12	Randolph
DAVIS, Wiley	1	Randolph
DAVIS, William A.	33	Baldwin
DAVIS, William H.	7	Chatham
DAVIS, William L.	4	Baker
DAVIS, William W.	60	Burke
DAVIS, William W.	8	Richmond
DAVIS, Wm. C.	11	Putnam
DAVIS, Wm. N.	1	Carroll
DAVIS, Wm. R.	3	DeKalb
DAVIS. Soln.	2	Crawford
DAVISON, Harry Ann	6	Harris
DAVISON, Heard	1	Richmond
DAVISON, John	8	Richmond
DAVISON, Thos.	3	Troup
DAVITTE, John C.	10	Paulding
DAWASON, Henry	4	Burke
DAWS, Joel	13	Jasper
DAWSON, Davis	47	Upson
DAWSON, G. M.	1	Clarke
DAWSON, George O.	15	Greene
DAWSON, H. C.	2	Muscogee
DAWSON, John E.	7	Muscogee
DAWSON, John R.	7	Muscogee
DAWSON, Johnathan	7	Upson
DAWSON, Malachi	9	Upson
DAWSON, Reuben J.	27	Greene
DAWSON, Richard S.	1	Effingham
DAWSON, Robert T.	10	Heard
DAWSON, Susan	45	Greene
DAWSON, Thomas H.	6	Dooly
DAWSON, William J. in town	12	Greene
DAWSON, Wm. C.	51	Greene
DAWSON, Christopher	6	Chatham
DAWSON, James C.	1	Richmond
DAWSON, M. E.	3	Bibb
DAWSON, P. H.	11	Putnam
DAWSON, Richard	2	Chatham
DAY, A. C.	1	Cass
DAY, Allenson A.	1	Jones
DAY, Alonzo	12	Chatham
DAY, Alonzo Jr.	1	Chatham
DAY, Benson	4	Walton
DAY, Berry	3	Newton
DAY, John J.	4	Muscogee
DAY, Jonathan Joiner	1	Troup
DAY, Joseph	53	Jones
DAY, Mrs. M. A.	2	Muscogee
DAY, Robert	5	McIntosh
DAY, William	6	Morgan
DAY, C.	4	Bibb
DAY, Joseph	10	Randolph
DAY, Moses	5	Troup
DAY, N. C.	8	Walton
DAY, Richard B.	3	Richmond
DAY, S. B.	3	Bibb

Name	Number	County
DEADWILDER, William	1	Jasper
DEADWYLAR, J. P.	9	Elbert
DEADWYLAR, J.G.	9	Elbert
DEADWYLAR, V. H.	6	Elbert
DEADWYLER, Asa	18	Madison
DEADWYLER, H. R.	24	Elbert
DEADWYLER, Martin	23	Madison
DEAL, Furney	8	Burke
DEAL, John	4	Stewart
DEAN, Abram	13	Floyd
DEAN, Calvin	4	Wilkinson
DEAN, Charles	1	Gwinnett
DEAN, Charles P.	8	Muscogee
DEAN, David	15	Muscogee
DEAN, Elijah	14	Muscogee
DEAN, Elizabeth	2	Washington
DEAN, Gideon B.	36	Liberty
DEAN, Henry	21	Harris
DEAN, James	138	Houston
DEAN, James	1	Houston
DEAN, James	4	Wilkinson
DEAN, James M.	4	Franklin
DEAN, Jno.	1	Carroll
DEAN, John	1	Wilkinson
DEAN, Joel	13	Floyd
DEAN, John	39	Clarke
DEAN, Lewis	4	Wilkinson
DEAN, Matthew	18	Greene
DEAN, Obediah	6	Franklin
DEAN, Rebecca	1	Upson
DEAN, Simion	1	Muscogee
DEAN, Stephen	1	Muscogee
DEAN, Wm. A.	31	Bibb
DEAN, Edward	8	Campbell
DEAN, Gibson	1	Talbot
DEAN, Henry	11	DeKalb
DEAN, James	63	Bibb
DEAN, Jas.	22	Bibb
DEAN, Jefferson	6	DeKalb
DEAN, John	12	Talbot
DEAN, John	3	Talbot
DEAN, Lemuel	10	DeKalb
DEAN, Penelopy	3	Randolph
DEANE, Henry L.	1	Pike
DEANWRIGHT, C. W.	5	Chattooga
DEARING, A. P.	6	Clarke
DEARING, Elijah	18	Wilkes
DEARING, Lemual A.	3	Newton
DEARING, Wm.	17	Lee
DEARING, William	32	DeKalb
DEARING, William E.	10	Richmond
DEARSON, H. G.	1	Pike
DEARSON, Joseph C.	3	Pike
DEARSON, Julia	4	Pike
DEAS ?, Alex.	3	Richmond
DEAS, Mary	17	Heard
DEAS, Stephen	1	Richmond
DEASON, John M.	40	Early
DEASON, Thomas	1	Marion
DEASON, Wm.	4	Marion
DEATON, Thomas	1	Paulding
DEATON, Kedar	36	Baker
DEAVERS, John	10	Hall
DEAVORS, Abraham	2	Cherokee
DEAVORS, Isaac B.	6	Dooly
DEBBY?, Mrs. Mary	2	Houston
DEBLOIS, John A.	4	Muscogee
DEBOOROUGH, Jas.	1	Randolph
DEBOSE, T. D.	24	Lee
DECK, J. T.	32	Chattooga
DECK, Walron	1	Walker
DECKINS, Hansil	2	Dooly
DECKLE, Nancy	7	Emanual
DECKSON, Julian	4	Cherokee
DEDDRICK, John	4	Lee
DEEKE, ?	2	Richmond
DEES, John M.	9	Lowndes
DEESE, Joel	2	Wilkinson
DEFINAL?, D. J.	1	Pulaski
DEFNIL, William	8	Houston
DEFOR, Jas.	3	Carroll
DEFORE, Elizabeth	7	Monroe
DEFOUR, David B.	1	Jones
DEGERNETT, R. R.	21	Putnam
DEGINPERT, Martha	5	Burke
DEGRAFFENREID, E. L.	1	Muscogee
DeGRAFFENREID, Wm.	4	Bibb
DeGRAFFENREID, John	41	Decatur
DEIHL, Nicholas	1	Jefferson
DEIL, Kimian	1	Lee
DEISER?, Joshua	1	Effingham
DEKEL, John W.	4	Thomas
DEKLE, John	2	Emanual
DEKLE, Littleton	4	Emanual
DeLACY, John	4	Merriwether
DeLAMATAR ?, Ira	18	Walton
DELAMON, Jno. C.	7	Pulaski
DELAMON, Richard F.	15	Pulaski
DeLANEY, John B.	9	Troup
DeLANNEY, Gustavus	60	Stewart
DELANNOY, John J.	7	Chatham
DeLANNY, Mariah	29	Baldwin
DELANY, Wm. F.	8	Dooly
DELAROUCHE, Aime	90	Camden
DELEGAL, C. W.	65	McIntosh

Name	Number	County	Name	Number	County
DELEGAL, Edward J.	69	Liberty	DENMARK, Thos. J.	9	Lowndes
DELEGAL, Henry H.	33	Liberty	DENMARK, James	3	Bullock
DELEMAR, Charles	10	Butts	DENMARK, Jane	2	Bullock
DELK, David	10	Liberty	DENMARK, Thomas M.	1	DeKalb
DELK, David	1	Murray	DENMEAD?, Edward	41	Cobb
DELK, John	10	Thomas	DENMON, U. L.	11	Gordon
DELK, Thomas r.	1	Wilkinson	DENNARD, Ezekiel	9	Lowndes
DELOACH, A. W.	1	Harris	DENNARD, John	3	Houston
DELOACH, Augustus	1	Harris	DENNARD, Jacob	7	Stewart
DELOACH, David J.	3	Wayne	DENNARD, John		
DELOACH, Marshal	1	Harris	agt for DURHAM, H.	42	Houston
DELOACH, Simeon	8	Talbot	DENNARD, Thomas		Stewart
DeLOATCH, James H.	3	Bullock	DENNEY, Washington	1	Troup
DeLOATCH, John	15	Bullock	DENNICE, John R.	3	Clarke
DeLOATCH, William	8	Bullock	DENNIS, Alford	3	Monroe
DELONEY, William G.	14	Early	DENNIS, Daniel	24	Lee
DELONEY, Gustavus	4	Stewart	DENNIS, Hiram	9	Troup
DELORD, Feliny	16	Oglethorpe	DENNIS, Jacob	7	Paulding
DELPH, J. P.	1	Randolph	DENNIS, Jesse M.	4	Upson
DEM?, Jeptha	5	Muscogee	DENNIS, Joel	1	Harris
DEMAREST, David	7	Clarke	DENNIS, John	4	Chatham
DEMERE, Ann	17	Chatham	DENNIS, Simion	14	Monroe
DEMERE, Lewis	43	Camden	DENNIS, Wm. Jr.	99	Putnam
DEMERE, Raymon P.	31	Bryan	DENNIS, Wm. T.	3	Macon
DEMERE, Paul	35	Camden	DENNIS, Elizabeth	4	Talbot
DEMEREST?, David	6	Greene	DENNIS, G. K.	5	Coweta
DeMERUSO, S. F.	4	Bibb	DENNIS, Isaac	11	Crawford
DEMING, George L.	8	Baldwin	DENNIS, John	1	Sumter
DEMLER, Augustus G.	13	Chatham	DENNIS, M.	123	Putnam
DEMMERA, John	24	McIntosh	DENNIS, Peter E.	6	Talbot
DEMOTT, A.	1	Camden	DENNIS, Saml.	3	Crawford
DEMPSEY, D.	2	Bibb	DENNY, Bicroft	29	Bryan
DEMSEY?, Eli	14	Floyd	DENNY, John D.	5	Meriwether
DENARD, Hugh L.	63	Houston	DENNY, John W.	12	Jefferson
DENARD, Isaac	2	Stewart	DENNY, Samuel	27	Jefferson
DENARD, John	17	Baker	DENNY, William D.	1	Harris
DENARD, William	26	Baker	DENSON, Eli	13	Floyd
DENARD, William	7	Sumter	DENSON, James M.	4	Jasper
DENDRICK, Merida	10	Putnam	DENSON, John D.	1	Glynn
DENDT, J. G.	21	Coweta	DENSON, John H.	30	Twiggs
DENDY, Charles L.	15	Harris	DENSON, Joseph	58	Harris
DENEWAY, John B.	2	Stewart	DENT, Mary A.	4	Chatham
DENGAS ?, Leon P.	7	Richmond	DENT, Alexander	1	Muscogee
DENHAM, D. D.	6	Fayette	DENT, George	53	Clarke
DENHAM, T. J.	2	Butts	DENT, George C.	145	McIntosh
DENIS, H. J.	3	Putnam	DENT, J. C.	8	Heard
DENIS, M.	19	Putnam	DENT, Joseph	3	Muscogee
DENKINS, P. S.	10	Bibb	DENT, Richard	2	Muscogee
DENKINS, Saml.	7	Bibb	DENT, Rich H.	1	Wilkes
DENKINS?, Horace	7	Marion	DENT, Sarah	1	Muscogee
DENMAN, Chapleigh	2	Murray	DENT, Thos.	2	Heard
DENMAN, Monroe	3	Gordon	DENT, William	1	Muscogee
DENMAN, J. W. A.	5	Carroll	DENT, Wm. B. W.	10	Heard
DENMARK, Reding	6	Bullock	DENT, Wm. B. W.	1	Heard

Name	Number	County	Name	Number	County
DENT, J. W.	10	Crawford	DICKEN, H. T.	7	Butts
DENT, Roderick	1	Richmond	DICKENS, Isaac A.	3	Wilkes
DENT, Wm. B. W.	7	Coweta	DICKENS, Marion	1	Monroe
DENTON, Drusilla	1	Warren	DICKENSON, W. A.	1	McIntosh
DENTON, John	17	Effingham	DICKENSON, Samuel	4	Upson
DENTON, James	7	Baldwin	DICKENSON, Robert B.	6	Walker
DENTON, Jas.	6	Bibb	DICKERSON, Calvin	18	Morgan
DERBY, James	11	Hancock	DICKERSON, Henry A.	2	Jasper
DERDEN, David	8	Meriwether	DICKERSON, H. J.	18	Chatham
DERICOTT, James	2	Taliaferro	DICKERSON, James	12	Cass
DERICOTT, Jonas B.	14	Taliaferro	DICKERSON, Roger Q.	3	Baker
DERKS, J.	1	Henry	DICKEY, James	16	Early
DERNONEY?, Samuel	2	Campbell	DICKEY, John	4	Habersham
DERRICK, Lucy	3	Rabun	DICKEY, John	4	Pike
DERRY, Wm. C.	1	Putnam	DICKEY, John B.	1	Gilmer
DESSAU, A.	2	Bibb	DICKEY, Mrs. Hannah	8	Gilmer
DESSEAU, M. H.	1	Muscogee	DICKEY, William	4	Dooly
DEUDY, William H.	13	Harris	DICKEY, William J.	67	Thomas
DEUDY, Charles L.	6	Harris	DICKINSON, A.	9	Hancock
DEUNK, Jacob	2	Pulaski	DICKINSON, Clark M.	25	Pike
DEVANE, Frances	8	Lowndes	DICKINSON, Isaac	28	Upson
DEVANPORT, J. M.	5	Hancock	DICKINSON, Isaac	28	Upson
DEVAUGHN, E.	7	Henry	DICKINSON, John D.	5	Floyd
DEVAUGHN, John	6	Fayette	DICKENSON, Levi	15	Upson
DEVAUGHN, Katherine	3	Fayette	DICKINSON, N.	4	Cherokee
DEVAUGHN, M. B.	6	Henry	DICKINSON, R. P.	2	Elbert
DEVEAUX, Isaac	2	Chatham	DICKINSON, T. T.	1	Elbert
DEVENPORT, B.	6	Troup	DICKINSON, D. J.	3	Decatur
DEVENPORT, D. S.	1	Troup	DICKINSON, D. P.	25	Decatur
DEVEREAUX, Ann	26	Hancock	DICKINSON, David F.	61	Richmond
DEVEREAUX, W. W.	19	Hancock	DICKINSON, David W.	6	Cobb
DEVEREAUX, Albert C.	32	Baldwin	DICKINSON, Roger O.	64	Baker
DEVERGEA, John L.	9	McIntosh	DICKINSON, S.	12	Decatur
DEVILLE, Charles	3	Richmond	DICKINSON, W. C.	2	Decatur
DeVILLERS, Georgia	1	Chatham	DICKINSON, Wm.	2	Decatur
DEW, Jonathan	22	Floyd	DICKSON, Curry	10	Hancock
DEWBERRY, H. G.	13	Harris	DICKSON, D. M.	5	Troup
DEWBERRY, Madison	8	Monroe	DICKSON, David	86	Hancock
DEWBERRY,			DICKSON, David	3	Newton
Thomas M.	53	Monroe	DICKSON, G. M.	1	Muscogee
DEWBERRY, William	1	Monroe	DICKSON, George W.	2	Warren
DEWBERRY,			DICKSON, James M.	5	Hancock
William G.	8	Pike	DICKSON, John	28	Hancock
DEWBERRY, Irby	26	Talbot	DICKSON, M.	5	Troup
DEWS, John J.	21	Baker	DICKSON, Mark S.	5	Upson
DIAL, Joseph S.	13	Cherokee	DICKSON, Michael	22	Lincoln
DIAL, D. W.	3	Coweta	DICKSON, Michael	8	Walker
DIAMOND, James J.	2	DeKalb	DICKSON, N.	1	Elbert
DIBBIE, Wm.	8	Bibb	DICKSON, Robert	10	Fayette
DIBBLE, Oscar J. H.	7	Chatham	DICKSON, Thos. J.	49	Hancock
DICKEN, M. G.	4	Clarke	DICKSON, Thomas	3	Wilkinson
DICKEN, R.R.	3	Clarke	DICKSON, William	6	Hancock
DICKEN, Richd.	2	Clarke	DICKSON, William	6	Wilkinson
DICKEN, Wm.	7	Clarke	DICKSON, William E.	2	Clarke

Name	Number	County	Name	Number	County
DICKSON, Wm.	19	Hancock	DINKLER, Fannie	3	Richmond
DICKSON, Anna	12	Bibb	DISEROONE, Sarah	3	Bibb
DICKSON, B.	2	Crawford	DISHAZE, R.	8	Twiggs
DICKSON, C. B.	2	Crawford	DISHAZO. R.	1	Twiggs
DICKSON, J. A.	1	Crawford	DISHEROON, Ervin	1	Murray
DICKSON, James	18	Baldwin	DISHEROON, Isaac	9	Murray
DICKSON, John	21	Bibb	DISHONGN, Jesse T.	3	Gwinnett
DICKSON, John	4	Talbot	DISMUK, Jesse	5	Butts
DICKSON, Josiah	16	Bibb	DISMUKE, John F.	4	Jasper
DICKSON, Salatha	17	Talbot	DISMUKE, William	11	Stewart
DICKSON, Wm.	14	Crawford	DISMUKES, Jas.	4	Putnam
DICKSON, Wm.	4	Crawford	DISMUKES, John	2	Meriwether
DIGBY, Berry	9	Jasper	DISMUKES, William	7	Pike
DIGBY, John B.	11	Jasper	DISMUKES, James Z.	18	Talbot
DIKES, Benny	47	Early	DISMUKES, James Z.	18	Talbot
DIKLE, Ansel	10	Thomas	DISMUKES, William H.	16	Baldwin
DIKLE, Bithania	1	Thomas	DISON, Epsy	6	Early
DIKLE, George A.	1	Thomas	DIVERS, John	2	Murray
DIKLE, John G.	10	Thomas	DIVINE, William F.	7	Campbell
DIKLE, Thomas E.	2	Thomas	DIX, Gabriel (overseer?)	13	McIntosh
DIKLE, Welttey	10	Thomas	DIX, James T.	59	Troup
DILL, Ann	17	Lincoln	DIXON, Allen	1	Camden
DILL, Mrs.	1	Early	DIXON, B.	6	Troup
DILL, Peter C.	3	Lincoln	DIXON, John B. F.	15	Thomas
DILL, Ann	8	Richmond	DIXON, John L.	40	Merriwether
DILL, James B.	12	Screven	DIXON, R. K.	14	Jefferson
DILLARD, Bryant	1	Pulaski	DIXON, Saml.	3	Wilkinson
DILLARD, Edmond	7	Muscogee	DIXON, Thomas	1	Macon
DILLARD, Isaac	17	Oglethorpe	DIXON, A.	3	Chattooga
DILLARD, John	21	Monroe	DIXON, Bryant	12	Sumter
DILLARD, John	2	Muscogee	DIXON, E.	1	Chattooga
DILLARD, Joseph B.	27	Oglethorpe	DIXON, Elizt.	6	Coweta
DILLARD, Kerk	11	Monroe	DIXON, F.	2	Bibb
DILLARD, Lemuel	28	Cass	DIXON, Hansel H.	5	Sumter
DILLARD, Marietta	5	Washington	DIXON, John	1	Bullock
DILLARD, Richard	13	Oglethorpe	DIXON, Martha R.	2	Sumter
DILLARD, Richard	1	Oglethorpe	DIXON, Robert	3	Stewart
DILLARD, Thomas	3	Walton	DIXON, Robert H.	69	Talbot
DILLARD, Almina	8	Stewart	DIXON, Robert J.	24	Burke
DILLARD, Colin	3	Bibb	DIXON, Thomas	9	Stewart
DILLARD, James	9	Rabun	DIXON, Thomas J.	8	Burke
DILLARD, James	19	Stewart	DIXON, Turner B.	2	Sumter
DILLARD, N. P.	6	Dooly	DIXON, Warren	24	Sumter
DILLARD, Tolivar	23	Burke	DIXON, Wiley P.	15	Coweta
DILLIARD?, David	1	Houston	DIXON, William C.	10	Baldwin
DILLON, John	10	Chatham	DIXON, Wm. H.	18	Coweta
DILLON, M. A.	2	Muscogee	DLAMAX, James	1	Newton
DILLON, David R.	4	Chatham	D'LAMOTTA, Jacob	7	Chatham
DILLON, John T.	4	Butts	D'LYON, Isaac	8	Chatham
DILLON, M. A.	2	Chatham	D'LYON, Levi	14	Chatham
DILLON, Margaret	16	Chatham	D'LYON, Levi S.	17	Effingham
DILLWORTH, Junius	1	Greene	D'LYON, Mordecai S.	5	Chatham
DILWORTH, Jno. H.	22	Camden	D'LYON, James W.	6	Chatham
DIMONAL, F. C.	3	Carroll	D'LYON, Rebecca	2	Chatham

Name	Number	County	Name	Number	County
D'MARTIN, James	1	Chatham	DOLES, Francis	8	Muscogee
DO, William	4	Decatur	DOLES, Jesse	1	Houston
DOBB, Jessey	4	Cobb	DOLES, Mrs.	4	Muscogee
DOBBINS, James L.	1	Heard	DOLES, Vicy	3	Houston
DOBBINS, John S.	14	Habersham	DOLTON, Jesse	45	Oglethorpe
DOBBINS, M. G.	6	Henry	DOLVIN, James	15	Greene
DOBBINS, Moses W.	7	Jackson	DOMINEY, D.	2	Wilkinson
DOBBINS, Wm. E.	1	Heard	DOMINICK, James	1	Pike
DOBBINS, Samuel	4	Columbia	DOMINICK, Andrew	44	Coweta
DOBBINS?, William	4	Paulding	DOMINICK, Benj. C.	3	Richmond
DOBBS, Asa	26	Cobb	DOMINY?, Joseph	1	Laurens
DOBBS, David	39	Cobb	DONAHOO, Cornelius	7	Cobb
DOBBS, Elisha	26	Merriwether	DONAHOO, James	1	DeKalb
DOBBS, Jenkins	9	Houston	DONALDSON, Joseph	26	Cherokee
DOBBS, Jesse	20	Elbert	DONALDSON, Robert	1	Thomas
DOBBS, John	3	Madison	DONALDSON, Thomas	7	Murray
DOBBS, Joseph	12	Cobb	DONALDSON, Mathew	3	Bullock
DOBBS, Saml.	1	Harris	DONALDSON, Robert	2	Bullock
DOBBS, Silas	12	Merriwether	DONALSON, (?)	1	Decatur
DOBBS, Elizabeth	3	Cherokee	DONALSON, Reuben	1	Gwinnett
DOBBS, John	17	Cass	DONALSON, James	3	Decatur
DOBS, L.	2	Cobb	DONALSON, John	38	Decatur
DOBSON, H. H.	2	Floyd	DONALSON, Jonathan	21	Decatur
DOBSON, S. W.	2	Walker	DONALSON, N.	18	Decatur
DOBSON, Rufus	1	Gordon	DONALSON, Reubin	23	Decatur
DODD, J. W.	8	Floyd	DONALSON, Silas H.	1	DeKalb
DODD, James E.	1	Fayette	DONALSON, Wm	57	Decatur
DODD, John	5	Forsyth	DONALSON, Wm. Sen.	13	Decatur
DODD, John S.	1	Fayette	DONAN, James R.	2	Marion
DODD, John W.	8	Floyd	DONAN, Lucy	3	Marion
DODD, Christopher	2	Cass	DONNAN, T.	1	DeKalb
DODD, Thomas	5	Cass	DONNELLY, P.	2	Wilkes
DODDS, Jas. M	5	Coweta	DONOVAN, Owin	2	Burke
DODDS, John F.	6	Coweta	DOODY, William	5	Chatham
DODDS, Wm. H.	1	Coweta	DOOLEY, Bennett	9	Franklin
DODGE, E. T.	1	Richmond	DOOLEY, Hamilton	5	Franklin
DODGE, Plumun ?	13	Richmond	DOOLEY, Jesse	1	Franklin
DODGER?, J. L.	5	Pike	DOOLIN, A. B.	26	Macon
DODGIN, John L.	4	Walton	DOOLY, B. J.	8	Elbert
DODSON, Green	5	Newton	DOOLY, M. N.	5	Elbert
DODSON, Henretta	3	Muscogee	DOOLY, Wm.	53	Elbert
DODSON, J. N.	2	Henry	DOOLY, Thos.	22	Columbia
DODSON, Joel	7	Jasper	DOOMAS, C.	5	Randolph
DODSON, John J.	3	Troup	DOONE, John G.	3	Chatham
DODSON, Lott	1	Harris	DOPIN, John D.	3	Dooly
DODSON, M.	5	Henry	DOPSON, A. T.	5	Telfair
DODSON, Samuel	4	Muscogee	DORCANS?, Garland	1	Muscogee
DODSON, W.	30	Henry	DORCH, Mary	12	Franklin
DODSON, Saml.	21	Chattooga	DORCH, Walter	1	Washington
DOE, J. F.	1	Chatham	DORMAN, L. B.	6	Sumter
DOGGET, Thos. J.	2	Harris	DORMAN, Thomas	1	Sumter
DOGIT, Jesse	6	Jones	DORMAN?, Felix G.	23	Cass
DOILE?, F. M.	12	Pike	DORMINY, Mrs.	2	Irwin
DOLES, Benjamin	11	Muscogee	DOROUGH, Jas. P.	2	Wilkes

Name	Number	County	Name	Number	County
DOROUGH, Joshua	2	Wilkes	DOSTER, Jas.	1	Coweta
DOROUGH, N. L.	1	Oglethorpe	DOTSON, Mathew	5	Chatham
DOROUGH, Richmond	3	Oglethorpe	DOTSON, Charles	4	Butts
DOROUGH, J.	16	Crawford	DOTSON, Richard	2	Chatham
DOROUGH, Rebeca	1	Oglethorpe	DOTSON, Tilman	2	Butts
DORRIS, James	10	Cherokee	DOTSON, Zachariah	15	Chatham
DORRIS, Mc. M	1	Carroll	DOTTERY, James	1	Clarke
DORSAY, Edward	16	Columbia	DOTY, Mary	2	Chatham
DORSE, Wm. B.	1	Fayette	DOTY, Morris	3	Chatham
DORSETT, James	4	Jones	DOUGHERTY, Charles	37	Clarke
DORSETT, Jas.	1	Henry	DOUGHERTY, John	10	Columbia
DORSETT, Andrew	1	Campbell	DOUGHERTY, William	15	Muscogee
DORSETT, E.	8	Chattooga	DOUGHERTY, James	5	Columbia
DORSEY, (?)	3	Columbia	DOUGHERTY, Mike	22	Columbia
DORSEY, J. M.	23	Henry	DOUGHETY, Bryant	1	Houston
DORSEY, John	4	Hall	DOUGHTRY, Joshua	5	Early
DORSEY, Mathew	27	Houston	DOUGLAS, Alexander	11	Appling
DORSEY, Mathew	1	Houston	DOUGLAS, George W.	6	Muscogee
DORSEY, Sarah	1	Pike	DOUGLAS, John	7	Merriwether
DORSEY, Solomon D.	17	Fayette	DOUGLAS, John C.	23	Pike
DORSEY, Wm. H.	5	Clarke	DOUGLAS, Robert	42	Morgan
DORSEY, John	2	Bibb	DOUGLAS, Robert M.	10	Merriwether
DORSEY, John	28	Stewart	DOUGLAS, William A.	2	Muscogee
DORSEY, Madison	26	Columbia	DOUGLAS, A.	28	Decatur
DORTCH, D. J.	1	Washington	DOUGLAS, C. G.	2	Bibb
DORTCH, P. D.	1	Franklin	DOUGLAS, Dr. Tilman	1	Burke
DORTIE, Germain	10	Richmond	DOUGLAS, Elizabeth	4	Burke
DOSEY, Lenney	7	Taliaferro	DOUGLAS, James	3	Decatur
DOSIER, Abner C.	13	Jasper	DOUGLAS, John	3	Decatur
DOSIER, Albert	17	Columbia	DOUGLAS, John	3	Talbot
DOSIER, B.	5	Bibb	DOUGLAS, Sarah	6	Butts
DOSIER, Ignatius	6	Columbia	DOUGLAS, Thomas	36	Randolph
DOSIER, James F.	10	Columbia	DOUGLAS, Thomas L.	9	Randolph
DOSIER, Lemuel W.	11	Stewart	DOUGLASS, Elisha	3	Early
DOSIER, Lovett A.	2	Sumter	DOUGLASS, James	1	Bibb
DOSIER, Nathan B.	14	Troup	DOUGLASS, John	5	Troup
DOSIER, Richard	6	Columbia	DOUGLASS, John M.	1	Jefferson
DOSIER, Thomas	4	Sumter	DOUGLASS, Frederick	1	Tatnall
DOSIER, William	11	Columbia	DOUGLASS, George	6	Talbot
DOSIER, Wilson	10	Columbia	DOUGLASS, William	1	Talbot
DOSLEY?, Thomas	16	Habersham	DOUNAR, T. P.	15	Elbert
DOSS, Azariah	13	Fayette	DOUTHET, Davis	5	Gilmer
DOSS, Edward	1	Gwinnett	DOUTHET, Davis	1	Gilmer
DOSS, J.	2	Muscogee	DOUTHIL, Wm.	1	Cass
DOSS, James	2	Stewart	DOVE, Jacob A.	16	Richmond
DOSSET, Charles	8	Newton	DOW, John R.	4	Richmond
DOSSETT, William	1	Stewart	DOWD, Wm. C.	1	Marion
DOSSEY, J.	34	Henry	DOWD, Joseph	6	Stewart
DOSSEY, S. G.	23	Henry	DOWDELL, Crawford	46	Harris
DOSSIN, William R.	2	Dooly	DOWDELL, James	61	Harris
DOSTER, Isaac	1	Cherokee	DOWDELL, James	45	Harris
DOSTER, James W.	3	Jasper	DOWDING?, Wm. M.	2	Lowndes
DOSTER, Pheletus	4	Houston	DOWDY, F. U. M.	7	Oglethorpe
DOSTER, Stephen	3	Macon	DOWDY, J. M.	10	Oglethorpe

Name	Number	County	Name	Number	County
DOWDY, James	8	Lumpkin	DRAKE, James B.	9	Oglethorpe
DOWDY, Richard	19	Oglethorpe	DRAKE, James B.	2	Oglethorpe
DOWDY, Richard	7	Oglethorpe	DRAKE, John	14	Hancock
DOWDY, Jas. W.	14	Randolph	DRAKE, John C.	7	Upson
DOWELL, Thomas	3	Chatham	DRAKE, John C.	23	Upson
DOWLES?, Morris G.	33	Pike	DRAKE, Frances	3	Coweta
DOWLING, Michael	1	Dooly	DRAKE, William	4	Burke
DOWNER, Jno.	20	Wilkes	DRANDY, William	1	Wayne
DOWNER, Joseph	15	Muscogee	DRANE, Casey	41	Columbia
DOWNES, Jas.	21	Camden	DRANE, Hiram	22	Talbot
DOWNES, Robt.	9	Camden	DRANE, Stephen	19	Columbia
DOWNES, Winifred	3	Camden	DRANE, William	29	Talbot
DOWNING, L. T.	3	Muscogee	DRANE, William	16	Talbot
DOWNING?, George H.	2	Greene	DRAPER, W. G.	1	Oglethorpe
DOWNMAN, W. P.	3	Pulaski	DRAUGHON, T. T.	1	Crawford
DOWNS, Shelly	2	Newton	DREIGHER, A.	1	Crawford
DOWNS, Dennis	2	Talbot	DREW, Joseph	6	Thomas
DOWNS, Sarah	1	Bryan	DREW, N. B.	19	Floyd
DOWSE, Gideon	55	Burke	DREW, Nancy	8	Emanual
DOWSE, John	21	Burke	DREW, Thomas	4	Emanual
DOWSE, Samuel	89	Burke	DREW, William	1	Stewart
DOWSE, Samuel	42	Burke	DREWRY, Eliza	15	Pike
DOYAL, L. T.	2	Henry	DREWRY, John	43	Jones
DOYL, D. D.	1	Monroe	DREWRY, F. H.	3	Coweta
DOYLE, John	2	Chatham	DREWRY,		
DOYLE, Benjamin R.	17	Baldwin	Mrs, Catharene	10	Stewart
DOYLE, James	1	Chatham	DRICK, And.	1	Henry
DOYLE, William	14	Richmond	DRIGGERS, Daniel	2	Bibb
DOZIER, Augustus	14	Oglethorpe	DRINKARD, Jas. T.	1	Wikes
DOZIER, E. A.	7	Wilkes	DRISKALL, J.	12	Putnam
DOZIER, Edward	1	Muscogee	DRISKELL, J. W.	9	Henry
DOZIER, George A. B.	13	Harris	DRISKELL, James	4	Butts
DOZIER, H.	1	Oglethorpe	DRISKIL, George	1	Monroe
DOZIER, Isaac	1	Clarke	DRISKILL, James C.	3	Troup
DOZIER, James L.	2	Warren	DRIVER, Giles	23	Pike
DOZIER, John B.	38	Muscogee	DRIVER, Jordan	18	Pike
DOZIER, Nancy	3	Warren	DRIVER, M.	10	Carroll
DOZIER, Pryor	1	Muscogee	DRIVER, Daniel	3	Sumter
DOZIER, Richard	14	Harris	DROUGHON, Robert	2	Jones
DOZIER, Richard	18	Muscogee	DRUMMOND, William	8	Gwinnett
DOZIER, Seaborn	8	Warren	DRUMMOND,		
DOZIER, Thos. J.	39	Harris	William J.	7	Gwinnett
DOZIER, Tillman F.	12	Wilkes	DRUMMOND, George W.	6	Walton
DOZIER, Green	39	Columbia	DRUPREE, Lewis J.	16	Oglethorpe
DOZIER, John	11	Columbia	DRUPREE, W. H.	12	Oglethorpe
DOZIER, Thomas	6	Stewart	DRURY, E. H.	2	Coweta
DRAKE, A.	39	Oglethorpe	DuBERGIC, Joseph	1	Chatham
DRAKE, A.	1	Oglethorpe	DUBERY, W.	1	Morgan
DRAKE, Alford	5	Monroe	DUBIGNON, Felicite	10	Glynn
DRAKE, B. F.	3	Clarke	DUBIGNON, Henry	58	Glynn
DRAKE, Beverly	3	Hancock	DUBOSE, Asa	2	Early
DRAKE, Cargal	1	Cobb	DUBOSE, J. W.	16	Elbert
DRAKE, E.	4	Oglethorpe	DUBOSE, Jas. R.	99	Wilkes
DRAKE, Emilia	9	Emanual	DUBOSE, John E.	8	Cherokee

Name	Number	County	Name	Number	County
DUBOSE, Mary	7	Camden	DUKE, Green R.	41	Jackson
DUCK, David	3	Muscogee	DUKE, Henry	19	Butts
DUCK, John (hired)	1	Muscogee	DUKE, James	17	Marion
DUCK, Robert	1	Walton	DUKE, Jas. H.	5	Troup
DUCKS, Jonathan	16	Troup	DUKE, James J.	4	Heard
DUCKWORTH,			DUKE, John E.	2	Pike
William G.	10	Warren	DUKE, Joseph	7	Upson
DUDLEY, Enoch	3	Muscogee	DUKE, Meredith	3	Marion
DUDLEY, James S.	3	Madison	DUKE, Sarah	4	Marion
DUDLEY, Susan	32	Washington	DUKE, Tapley ?	1	Walton
DUDLEY, Thomas	20	Hancock	DUKE, Thomas	16	Newton
DUDLEY, E.	2	Gordon	DUKE, William	5	Jackson
DUDLEY, George A.	5	DeKalb	DUKE, William G.	4	Pike
DUDLEY, George M.	11	Sumter	DUKE, Chas.	2	Carroll
DUDLEY, James H.	3	Campbell	DUKE, Elisha	2	Burke
DUDLEY, R. S.	3	Chatham	DUKE, Isiah	2	Crawford
DUDLY, John D.	1	Baker	DUKE, J. S.	1	Bibb
DUDNEY, Abraham	11	Stewart	DUKE, R. G.	11	Butts
DUFELL, James	5	Oglethorpe	DUKE, Saml.	7	Crawford
DUFFEE, John	9	Henry	DUKE, Saraah	2	Butts
DUFFEE, Robert L.	3	Henry	DUKE, T. C.	1	Butts
DUFFEE, J. N.	5	Butts	DUKE, W.	2	Butts
DUFFEE, Samuel	15	Butts	DUKE, W.	13	Randolph
DUFFIE, Anna	3	Columbia	DUKES, Edward C.	17	Lowndes
DUFFY, Thomas	3	Richmond	DUKES, Joel B.	3	Thomas
DUFOUR, John	25	Camden	DUKES, Joseph W.	2	Burke
DUFOUR, Mary	10	Camden	DUKES, Mary	5	Burke
DUGAS, Leon C.	8	Richmond	DUKES, W.	1	Troup
DUGAS, Lewis A.	15	Richmond	DUKES, William	2	Jasper
DUGAS, Pauline	14	Richmond	DULIN, Adison	4	DeKalb
DUGDON, Elijah	2	Appling	DUMAS, Benjamin	11	Monroe
DUGER, John	7	Monroe	DUMAS, David	20	Franklin
DUGGAN, Archelus	14	Washington	DUMAS, Edmond	13	Jones
DUGGAN, John	12	Washington	DUMAS, Edmond	10	Monroe
DUGGAN, John H.	14	Washington	DUMAS, James	6	Monroe
DUGGAN, John M.	5	Washinngton	DUMAS, John C.	10	Jones
DUGGAN, Martha	3	Chatham	DUMAS, Matilda	10	Jones
DUGGAN, Michael	2	Chatham	DUMAS, Moses	7	Monroe
DUGGAR, Sampson	4	Troup	DUMAS, Moses	1	Monroe
DUGGEN, Asa	4	Washington	DUMAS, Nancy	18	Jones
DUGGER, Chesley	1	Chatham	DUMAS, Nehemiah	13	Pike
DUGGER, John	6	Thomas	DUMAS, Thomas	13	Monroe
DUGGER, John	1	Thomas	DUMAS, William H.	3	Pike
DUGGER, William	1	Gordon	DUN ?, Ellis	3	Upson
DUGGER, Chesly	1	Chatham	DUNAGAN, John	3	Walker
DUGLASS, G. L.	7	Sumter	DUNAHOO, James	17	Clarke
DUKE, Albert M.	6	Liberty	DUNAVENT, Mann	6	Warren
DUKE, Amos	2	Monroe	DUNAWAY, Isaac	1	Clarke
DUKE, David D.	3	Floyd	DUNAWAY, Saml.	1	Wilkes
DUKE, Edmond	5	Troup	DUNBAR, John W.	8	Pike
DUKE, Elizabeth	5	Muscogee	DUNBAR, B.	5	Richmond
DUKE, Ferdinand	4	Newton	DUNBAR, Thomas L.	7	Richmond
DUKE, Francis A.	1	Marion	DUNCAN, Davis	2	Jones
DUKE, Green	24	Monroe	DUNCAN, George	11	Jones

Name	Number	County	Name	Number	County
DUNCAN, Hugh	1	Gwinnett	DUNN, A. B.	3	Hancock
DUNCAN, J.	7	Pike	DUNN, Daniel	2	Gwinnett
DUNCAN, James	9	Upson	DUNN, Daniel	1	Walker
DUNCAN, James E.	37	Dooly	DUNN, David	3	Oglethorpe
DUNCAN, James E.	13	Houston	DUNN, Drury	2	Oglethorpe
DUNCAN, John	6	Jackson	DUNN, Gatewood	4	Harris
DUNCAN, John	5	Muscogee	DUNN, Harrison K.	9	Harris
DUNCAN, John P.	4	Monroe	DUNN, Hiram	18	Greene
DUNCAN, Lee	11	Jones	DUNN, Ismael	34	Fayette
DUNCAN, Martha	6	Jones	DUNN, J. A.	5	Henry
DUNCAN, Marvel	1	Walker	DUNN, James	21	Greene
DUNCAN, Mildred	1	Greene	DUNN, John	2	Troup
DUNCAN, Moses	1	Franklin	DUNN, John	4	Walker
DUNCAN, Nancy	1	Hancock	DUNN, Martin M.	3	Harris
DUNCAN, Robert	5	Gwinnett	DUNN, Moses	6	Walker
DUNCAN, Samuel	3	Newton	DUNN, Obedience	21	Monroe
DUNCAN, Simson	2	Newton	DUNN, William	1	Merriwether
DUNCAN, Thomas	32	Meriwether	DUNN, William C.	6	Meriwether
DUNCAN, Walker	11	Merriwether	DUNN, William G.	12	Jasper
DUNCAN, Elias	2	Coweta	DUNN, Willliam S.	20	Harris
DUNCAN, Frances	5	Talbot	DUNN, Wm.	4	Cobb
DUNCAN, G. S.	1	Coweta	DUNN, Wm.	4	Hancock
DUNCAN, George A.	48	Dooly	DUNN, Charles	2	Baldwin
DUNCAN, James	2	Baldwin	DUNN, Elizaeth	9	Randolph
DUNCAN, Robert	13	Talbot	DUNN, Ephraim	2	Baldwin
DUNCAN, Robert	3	Talbot	DUNN, Jacob	2	Randolph
DUNCAN, William	6	Chatham	DUNN, James	2	Baldwin
DUNCAN, William	16	Sumter	DUNN, Jos.	3	Crawford
DUNEGAN, A. F.	1	Hall	DUNN, Kate	26	Columbia
DUNEGAN, J. R.	1	Hall	DUNN, Lemmon	19	Randolph
DUNEGAN, Joseph	1	Hall	DUNN, Martin	9	Talbot
DUNHAM, Adam C.	1	Liberty	DUNN, Walter	28	Columbia
DUNHAM, Charles D.	1	Merriwether	DUNN, William	26	Columbia
DUNHAM, George	2	McIntosh	DUNN, Wm.	10	Crawford
DUNHAM, George W.	18	Liberty	DUNN, Wm.	20	Randolph
DUNHAM, Thos. J.	11	Liberty	DUNNAHOO, John B.	6	Madison
DUNHAM, William	38	Liberty	DUNNAHOO?, John W.	13	Floyd
DUNHAM, J. C.	44	Putnam	DUNNAWAY, Benj.	1	Wilkes
DUNHAM, James H.	3	Houston	DUNNING, Priscilla	5	Chatham
DUNHAM, Jno.	11	Putnam	DUNNING, Sheldon C.	10	Chatham
DUNHAM, Josiah	4	Putnam	DUNNY ? , Charles	4	Stewart
DUNHAM, Nathaniel	13	Putnam	DUNSON, John H.	12	Wilkes
DUNHAM, Wm. H.	3	Putnam	DUNSON, Permelia	3	Jackson
DUNING, Charles	4	Stewart	DUNSON, W.	19	Troup
DUNKIN, A. B.	35	Lee	DUNSON, Wm.	3	Troup
DUNKIN, J.	22	Elbert	DUNSON, Wm.	6	Troup
DUNLAP, Archibald	3	Gwinnett	DUNSON, Wm.	2	Troup
DUNLAP, Elizabeth K.	5	Gwinnett	DUNSTON, Joseph	13	Lowndes
DUNLAP, James	6	Campbell	DUNWIDDIE, D. M.	34	Bibb
DUNLAP, James C.	8	Gwinnett	DUNWODY, James	4	Houston
DUNLAP, Joseph	33	Merriwether	DUNWOODY, John	33	Cobb
DUNLAP, Robert L.	18	Merriwether	DUNWOODY, John Jr.	6	Cobb
DUNLEY, Thomas	1	Cass	DUNWOODY,		
DUNMAN, Joseph	4	Harris	William E.	6	Cobb

Name	Number	County	Name	Number	County
DUNWOODY,			DURR, Lewis M.	5	Muscogee
William J.	100	McIntosh	DURRANCE, Jesse	3	Tatnall
DUPON, J.P.A.	9	Chatham	DURRANCE, John	1	Tatnall
DUPON, Stephen F.	5	Chatham	DURRENT, R. J. D.	49	Elbert
DUPREE, Charles L.	23	Pike	DUSLER, Mary M.	5	Chatham
DUPREE, Drewry	3	Merriwether	DUTTON, Mrs. R.	6	Muscogee
DUPREE, Ira E.	5	Twiggs	DUTTON, Henry	6	Bullock
DUPREE, John	1	Wilkinson	DUTTON, Mann	19	Bullock
DUPREE, William B.	1	Houston	DUTTON, Sam	2	Bullock
DUPREE, Augustus N.	1	Cobb	DUVAL, Echols	15	Floyd
DUPREE, C. S.	13	Forsyth	DUVAL, James C.	2	Floyd
DUPREE, E.	7	Putnam	DUVAL, Nancy	3	Columbia
DUPRIEST, Green	7	Stewart	DUVANT, James	47	Greene
DURDAN, A.	2	Crawford	DWIGHT, Samuel J.	25	Murray
DURDEN, Dennis	2	Emanual	DYALL, David	2	Telfair
DURDEN, Eleazor	4	Emanual	DYAR?, F. L.	138	Early
DURDEN, Hannah	1	Houston	DYASS, Aquilla	3	Stewart
DURDEN, Lewis	7	Washington	DYASS, Elizabeth	5	Stewart
DURDEN, J. W.	8	Butts	DYE (?), Margaret	1	Columbia
DURDIN, John	37	Morgan	DYE ?, William	15	Wilkes
DURHAM, H.	36	Twiggs	DYE, G. J.	6	Elbert
DURHAM, Hardy	24	Twiggs	DYE, G. W.	23	Elbert
DURHAM, Lindsey	24	Clarke	DYE, J.	4	Elbert
DURHAM, Nancy	4	Twiggs	DYE, Mary A.	5	Jefferson
DURHAM, ? R.	21	Twiggs	DYE, Martin P.	14	Troup
DURHAM, Abner	8	Merriwether	DYE, T.	17	Elbert
DURHAM, Abram M.	1	Greene	DYE, T. B.	2	Elbert
DURHAM, George	8	Cobb	DYE, William	4	Burk
DURHAM, Hardy	42	Houston	DYER, Anthony	11	Jasper
DURHAM, Isbel Estate	5	Greene	DYER, Edwin	17	Walker
DURHAM, John	4	Cobb	DYER, Hezekiah	1	Habersham
DURHAM, Levi	5	Cherokee	DYER, Elizabeth	1	Columbia
DURHAM, Lyndsey	2	Clarke	DYER, Elizt.	13	Coweta
DURHAM, M.S.	15	Oglethorpe	DYER, John B.	6	Baldwin
DURHAM, Saml. D.	12	Greene	DYER, Thomas	15	Warren
DURHAM, Thomas	3	Gordon	DYER, Wm. A.	1	Taliaferro
DURHAM, Thomas S.	22	Jones	DYERS, Gresham	13	Richmond
DURHAM, William	1	Harris	DYESS, Christopher	11	Monroe
DURHAM, Hadin	2	Randolph	DYESS, Wm.	3	Macon
DURHAM, James	18	Columbia	DYESS, Mrs.	3	Tatnall
DURHAM, John L.	8	Taliaferro	DYKES, B. B.	27	Pulaski
DURHAM, John P.	2	Stewart	DYKES, Benj. B.	3	Floyd
DURHAM, Lucus	13	Stewart	DYKES, Faithy?	4	Pulaski
DURHAM, Michael	1	Stewart	DYKES, George J.	5	Floyd
DURHAM, Sanders W.	18	Talbot	DYKES, Jacob	3	Pulaski
DURHAM, Sanders W.	3	Talbot	DYKES, Allen	4	Cass
DURHAM, Sarah	7	Columbia	DYKES, George	8	Sumter
DURHAM, William	9	Columbia	DYKES, James	3	Sumter
DURHAM, Willis	1	Dooly	DYKES, Sarah	3	Sumter
DURIN?, W. W.	1	Elbert	DYKES, Wiloughby	3	Cass
DURKIN, John	1	Muscogee	DYNE, Elisha	3	Cherokee
DURMOND ?,			DYNE, Simpson C.	6	Cherokee
William P.	22	Richmond	DYRES, Martin M	7	Richmond
DURNAM, S.	28	Greene	DYSON, Thomas	56	Monroe

Name	Number	County	Name	Number	County
DYZART, Joseph	2	Cass	EBERHART, Abel	16	Madison
EADES, E.	12	Elbert	EBERHART, Abel	24	Oglethorpe
EADS, Elizabeth	2	Oglethorpe	EBERHART, Adam	3	Madison
EADS, John	1	Oglethorpe	EBERHART, Eli	6	Madison
EADS, Ranny	1	Oglethorpe	EBERHART, Francis P.	24	Madison
EADY, John	4	Wilkinson	EBERHART, George	15	Madison
EAKIN, Wm.	29	Putnam	EBERHART, J.	4	Elbert
EALEY, Osborn	24	Harris	EBERHART, Jacob	3	Hall
EALEY, A.	5	Randolph	EBERHART, Jacob	40	Madison
EALEY, H.S.	10	Randolph	EBERHART, Jacob	1	Madison
EALEY, Saml.	1	Randolph	EBERHART, Robert	27	Elbert
EALEY, Seaborn	2	Randolph	EBERHART, Robert	14	Oglethorpe
EANES, John	8	Bibb	EBERHART, Samuel	35	Madison
EARLE, Saml. M.	16	Cass	EBERHART, William	12	Madison
EARLY, Almyra	41	Troup	EBERHART, William	8	Madison
EARLY, Joel	60	Greene	EBESHAR, John	12	Oglethorpe
EARNEST, L. W.	6	Murray	ECHOLAS, Milner	1	Walton
EARNEST, Mary	1	Murray	ECHOLAS, Thomas J.	2	Walton
EARNEST, A. E.	19	Bibb	ECHOLDS, James C.	9	Taliaferro
EARP, Wm	6	Cass	ECHOLS, B.	16	Chattooga
EASLY, D. N.	11	Walton	ECHOLS, Capt. Samuel	2	Gwinnett
EASLEY, Priscilla	2	Newton	ECHOLS, Elijah	2	Wilkes
EASLEY, Benjamin	29	Dade	ECHOLS, Francis	4	Habersham
EASLEY, ISAAC	1	Randolph	ECHOLS, Peter	17	Hancock
EASOM, (?)	22	Crawford	ECHOLS, Robert	11	Gwinnett
EASOM, Andrew J.	2	Sumter	ECHOLS, Robert	6	Gwinnett
EASOM, Harrison	4	Coweta	ECHOLS, Robt. P.	5	Floyd
EASON, A. J.	2	Morgan	ECHOLS, Samuel D.	27	Heard
EASON, Felix R.	1	Appling	ECHOLS, T. M.	7	Oglethorpe
EASON, George	1	Appling	ECHOLS, Winston W.	8	Carroll
EASON, John	3	Fayette	ECHOLS, R.	4	Chattooga
EASON, Martha	6	Houston	ECKER, W. B.	19	McIntosh
EASON, Moses S.	11	Appling	ECKLES, Douglas	5	Walton
EASON, P. manager	26	Henry	ECKLES, Jas.	1	Meriwether
EASON, Parker	41	Henry	ECKLES, Sterling	5	Walton
EASON, Rice	4	Fayette	ECOLS, Phillip	7	Monroe
EASON, Abraham D.	9	Tatnall	ECOLAS, Mary	9	Walton
EASON, E. D.	1	Sumter	ECTSON ?, George	39	Talbot
EASON, Erily	1	Burke	EDDING, Daniel	1	Bibb
EASON, Michael M.	8	Tatnall	EDDINS, E. C.	4	Franklin
EASON, William	4	Tatnall	EDDLEMAN, William	1	Newton
EAST, William	3	Murray	EDDLEMAN, Francis	2	DeKalb
EASTERLIN, Benj. F.	2	Richmond	EDEN, Thomas	1	Chatham
EASTERLING, J. M.	6	Chattooga	EDGARS, Thomas A.	1	Muscogee
EASTERLING, J.C.	1	Chattooga	EDGE, Garland	31	Monroe
EASTERLING, Robt. C.	2	Richmond	EDGE, John M.	5	Cobb
EASTERLY, Henry W.	14	Walton	EDGE, Joseph	2	Merriwether
EASTERS, John	4	Stewart	EDGE, Marlin	12	Macon
EASTES, A.	7	Henry	EDGE, Simpson	6	Macon
EASTIN, S. G.	9	Fayette	EDGE, James	3	Taliaferro
EASTON, C. F. K.	2	Fayette	EDGE, Reason	14	Talbot
EASTON, Elisha H.	5	Franklin	EDGEWORTH, A. S.	43	Houston
EATON, T. H.	1	Bibb	EDINFIELD, Richard	2	Emanual
EAVES, James	5	Talbot	EDINGS, Wm.	7	Cass

Name	Number	County
EDMANSON, Wm.	1	Twiggs
EDMOND, Briant	1	Harris
EDMONDS, Jas.	2	Wilkes
EDMONDSON, William O.	10	Jasper
EDMONDSON, David	8	Lowndes
EDMONDSON, E. C.	11	Fayette
EDMONDSON, Henry	4	Oglethorpe
EDMONDSON, James	9	Lowndes
EDMONDSON, James	9	Murray
EDMONDSON, James	20	Muscogee
EDMONDSON, John	1	Fayette
EDMONDSON, John	4	Lowndes
EDMONDSON, John	1	Twiggs
EDMONDSON, John	13	Upson
EDMONDSON, Malinda	9	Oglethorpe
EDMONDSON, Griffin	1	Richmond
EDMONDSON, H. D. C.	3	Chattooga
EDMONDSON, Zachariah	71	Putnam
EDMONSON, Benjamin	1	Houston
EDMONSON, James	4	Muscogee
EDMONSON, Richard	1	Union
EDMONSON, A. V.	9	Cass
EDMONSON, John	50	Putnam
EDMONSON, Mary	1	DeKalb
EDMONSON, Susan	10	Cass
EDMONSON, W. S.	5	Troup
EDMUNDS, Jno.	8	Henry
EDMUNDS, Rosco	5	Henry
EDMUNDSON, Joseph	2	Walker
EDMUNDSON, Letta	5	Lumpkin
EDMUNDSON, Wm.	29	Greene
EDMUNDSON, Wm. L.	2	Wilkes
EDMUNDSON, Jos.	20	Coweta
EDSON, John	3	Wilkes
EDWARD, L. B.	2	Forsyth
EDWARD, Marshall	26	Oglethorpe
EDWARD, Joseph A.	10	Richmond
EDWARD, Nathan Bass	44	Putnam
EDWARDS (?), William	2	Columbia
EDWARDS, Gresham	6	Oglethorpe
EDWARDS, Alen	1	Effingham
EDWARDS, Asa	8	Harris
EDWARDS, B. S.	2	Cherokee
EDWARDS, Beal	7	Effingham
EDWARDS, C. M.	13	Monroe
EDWARDS, Charles	1	Effingham
EDWARDS, E.	4	Cherokee
EDWARDS, Edward K.	1	Murray
EDWARDS, Edwin	1	Effingham
EDWARDS, Elias	12	Lowndes
EDWARDS, Elizabeth	5	Murray
EDWARDS, Enoch	3	Habersham

Name	Number	County
EDWARDS, Faithfull	1	Chatham
EDWARDS, George C.	2	Lee
EDWARDS, George W.	3	Monroe
EDWARDS, Henry	1	Cherokee
EDWARDS, Henry	13	Effingham
EDWARDS, J. C.	14	Lee
EDWARDS, J. J.	2	Elbert
EDWARDS, J. W.	6	Henry
EDWARDS, James	1	Effingham
EDWARDS, James	5	Habersham
EDWARDS, James	1	Jasper
EDWARDS, James	15	Lincoln
EDWARDS, James	4	Walton
EDWARDS, James T.	1	Houston
EDWARDS, Jesse	1	Burke
EDWARDS, Jesse E.	4	Marion
EDWARDS, Johantla C.	8	Upson
EDWARDS, John	14	Harris
EDWARDS, John	3	Walker
EDWARDS, John W.	2	Jasper
EDWARDS, John W.	1	Muscogee
EDWARDS, Joseph	9	Effingham
EDWARDS, Joseph	1	Greene
EDWARDS, Joseph W. B.	15	Troup
EDWARDS, Jourden	6	Walton
EDWARDS, Lemuel	3	Oglethorpe
EDWARDS, Lewis	3	Meriwether
EDWARDS, Linsey	8	Walker
EDWARDS, Mahaly	14	Macon
EDWARDS, Mordica	35	Oglethorpe
EDWARDS, Mrs. S. A.	12	Meriwether
EDWARDS, Mrs. P.	4	Muscogee
EDWARDS, Nancy	13	Franklin
EDWARDS, Obadiah	6	Effingham
EDWARDS, Obadiah	3	Effingham
EDWARDS, Richard	2	Clarke
EDWARDS, Reuel	7	Walker
EDWARDS, Robt. M.	1	Forsyth
EDWARDS, S. A.E.	7	Elbert
EDWARDS, Sarah	6	Clarke
EDWARDS, Sarah	15	Muscogee
EDWARDS, Sophia A.	4	Chatham
EDWARDS, Sophiah	1	Franklin
EDWARDS, T. J.	7	Henry
EDWARDS, Thomas	3	Monroe
EDWARDS, Thomas A.	10	Troup
EDWARDS, W. H.	2	Elbert
EDWARDS, William	4	Effingham
EDWARDS, William H.	6	Warren
EDWARDS, Wm.	1	Heard
EDWARDS, Wm.	3	Henry
EDWARDS, Wm.	16	Oglethorpe
EDWARDS, Ambrose J.	2	Talbot

Name	Number	County	Name	Number	County
EDWARDS, D. G.	11	Baldwin	ELDER, Edmund G.	2	Clarke
EDWARDS, Daniel	2	Tatnall	ELDER, Edward A.	14	Jasper
EDWARDS, David M.	10	Baldwin	ELDER, Howell	3	Fayette
EDWARDS, Elison	10	Bibb	ELDER, John L.	32	Clarke
EDWARDS, Ethelred	39	Taliaferro	ELDER, Joshua	3	Fayette
EDWARDS, F. G.	31	Elbert	ELDER, Joshua	24	Henry
EDWARDS, H. M.	2	Sumter	ELDER, Joshua P.	2	Clarke
EDWARDS, Henry	4	Bryan	ELDER, Josiah H.	8	Fayette
EDWARDS, J.	1	Randolph	ELDER, Permelia	2	Clarke
EDWARDS, J. C.	5	Bibb	ELDER, Philip T.	7	Clarke
EDWARDS, Jas. J.	6	Putnam	ELDER, Saml. E.	3	Fayette
EDWARDS, Jesse H.	12	Putnam	ELDER, Sarah	2	Clarke
EDWARDS, Jno.	14	Putnam	ELDER, Thos. P.	12	Clarke
EDWARDS, Jno. C.	2	Talbot	ELDER, W.	15	Clarke
EDWARDS, John	4	Jones	ELDER, W. M.	2	Pike
EDWARDS, John	18	Talbot	ELDER, David	3	Butts
EDWARDS, John M.	8	Bryan	ELDER, Ed`	27	Clarke
EDWARDS, M.	1	Coweta	ELDER, George	5	Talbot
EDWARDS, Maria	36	Chatham	ELDER, John P.	20	Clarke
EDWARDS, Maria trust	9	Chatham	ELDER, Joseph	11	Clarke
EDWARDS, Martin E.	9	Baldwin	ELDER, N. T.	3	Clarke
EDWARDS, O.	5	Stewart	ELDER, Rebecca	18	Coweta
EDWARDS, Peter	3	Cherokee	ELDER, W. A.	3	Butts
EDWARDS, Posey	8	Talbot	ELDER, W. H.	21	Coweta
EDWARDS, R. H.	1	Butts	ELDERS, Charles	4	Monroe
EDWARDS, R. H.	4	Coweta	ELDRIDGE, Sarah	2	Bibb
EDWARDS, Ruben N.	2	Putnam	ELEBY, Isam	4	Camden
EDWARDS, Thomas	38	Taliaferro	ELEBY ?, Jane	4	Upson
EDWARDS, W. L.	1	Bibb	ELEERHGHST?, Jacob	2	Oglethorpe
EDWARDS, William H.	15	Tatnall	ELEY, B. H.	27	Lee
EDWARDS, Zechariah	3	Cass	ELEY, Samuel	5	Heard
EDWARDS. Henry	4	Tatnall	ELINGTON, David	9	DeKalb
EDWIN?, Thomas	1	Oglethorpe	ELIOTT, Richard L.	5	Talbot
EGARTON, William	2	Columbia	ELIOTT, Turner	2	Stewart
EGERTON, Mary	2	Burke	ELKINS, John	7	Effingham
EHRLICH, Geo.	2	Bibb	ELKINS, Saml.	6	Marion
EIDSON, James	1	Greene	ELKINS, Thomas	69	Effingham
EIDSON, John R.	3	Greene	ELKINS, Thos. P.	10	Effingham
EIDSON, Lewis	1	Clarke	ELKINS, Jas.	2	Coweta
EILAND, Absalom	5	Harris	ELLBECK, Henry J.	9	Muscogee
EILLOSS?, Henry	28	Harris	ELLEBY, James	4	Bullock
EINSTEIN, A.	1	Chatham	ELLEN, Mrs.	3	Muscogee
EINSTEIN, R.	2	Chatham	ELLERBEE, John	1	Baker
ELAM, W. F.	33	Lincoln	ELLERSON, James	55	Talbot
ELAM, A. G.	5	Stewart	ELLERSON, James	4	Talbot
ELAM, Hadikah	2	Stewart	ELLERSON, John	4	Talbot
ELAY, (?)	1	Dade	ELLERSON, Joohn	27	Talbot
ELBERT, Sarah	4	Richmond	ELLETT, Joseph	5	Warren
ELBURY, Benj.	5	Oglethorpe	ELLINGTON, Ann	9	Wilkinson
ELDER, Wm. T.	18	Clarke	ELLINGTON, Archibald	5	Walton
ELDER, D. Y.	1	Morgan	ELLINGTON, Archibald	22	Walton
ELDER, David	13	Clarke	ELLINGTON, Huldah	18	Wilkes
ELDER, David	4	Fayette	ELLINGTON, James	2	Newton
ELDER, David R.	9	Clarke	ELLINGTON, Jane C.	10	Greene

Name	Number	County
ELLINGTON, Joel	3	Newton
ELLINGTON, Josiah	43	Laurens
ELLINGTON, K. C.	1	Henry
ELLINGTON, Lewis D.	1	Gilmer
ELLINGTON, R. C.	20	Fayette
ELLINGTON, S. C.	11	Wilkes
ELLINGTON, W. B. Estate	36	Greene
ELLINGTON, W. H.	1	Henry
ELLINGTON, Amos	5	Taliaferro
ELLINGTON, E. C.	1	Randolph
ELLINGTON, Stephen	9	Taliaferro
ELLIOT, Andrew	18	Upson
ELLIOT, J. H.	11	Monroe
ELLIOT, Thomas	13	Newton
ELLIOT, Hetty	36	Bryan
ELLIOT, Ralph	40	Bryan
ELLIOTT, A. C.	2	Henry
ELLIOTT, Andrew	7	Lincoln
ELLIOTT, Bishop by agent	73	Monroe
ELLIOTT, Burrage	2	Marion
ELLIOTT, H. C.	2	Henry
ELLIOTT, J.	21	Henry
ELLIOTT, M. B.	4	Henry
ELLIOTT, R. H.	16	Henry
ELLIOTT, Ralph E.	182	Chatham
ELLIOTT, T. C.	1	Elbert
ELLIOTT, William	4	Pike
ELLIOTT, William M.	5	Cobb
ELLIOTT, Alexr.	14	Burke
ELLIOTT, Benjamin	19	Chatham
ELLIOTT, Jas. R.	34	Wilkes
ELLIOTT, James S.	12	DeKalb
ELLIOTT, Jesse M.	13	Warren
ELLIOTT, Jesse M.	13	Warren
ELLIOTT, Nancy	3	Burke
ELLIOTT, Nancy	14	Morgan
ELLIOTT, Thos.	6	Wilkes
ELLIOTT, Wm.	2	Taliaferro
ELLIS, A. E.	3	Cobb
ELLIS, Austin	8	Houston
ELLIS, Byrom	4	Upson
ELLIS, Calib	3	Forsyth
ELLIS, Daniel R.	1	Henry
ELLIS, Edward	3	Gordon
ELLIS, Henry	1	Jasper
ELLIS, J. T.	9	Pike
ELLIS, James	17	Floyd
ELLIS, James H.	2	Greene
ELLIS, John	53	Oglethorpe
ELLIS, John	1	Oglethorpe
ELLIS, John A.	23	Henry
ELLIS, Joseph	4	Houston

Name	Number	County
ELLIS, KINDRICK & REDD	1	Muscogee
ELLIS, L. H.	6	Hancock
ELLIS, Mathew V.	1	Floyd
ELLIS, Miram	4	Merriwether
ELLIS, Nathan	2	Pike
ELLIS, R.	1	Troup
ELLIS, Radford	5	Floyd
ELLIS, Richd.	12	Henry
ELLIS, Robt.	6	Forsyth
ELLIS, Thomas	11	Glynn
ELLIS, Thomas	10	Henry
ELLIS, Thos. W.	4	Lowndes
ELLIS, W. J.	3	Henry
ELLIS, William	18	Pike
ELLIS, William A.	4	Henry
ELLIS, William J.	1	Pike
ELLIS, Willis	2	Oglethorpe
ELLIS, Benjamin	23	Bullock
ELLIS, Ephraim	12	Randolph
ELLIS, J. W.	4	Crawford
ELLIS, James	2	Talbot
ELLIS, James P.	1	Stewart
ELLIS, John	12	Chattooga
ELLIS, Joseph B.	1	Randolph
ELLIS, Mary	1	Bibb
ELLIS, R. M.	3	Crawford
ELLIS, Thomas	67	Stewart
ELLIS, Thos. M.	3	Bibb
ELLIS, W.	2	Chattooga
ELLIS, William	15	Stewart
ELLIS, Wm.	6	Bibb
ELLISON, James	16	Franklin
ELLISON, Matthew	22	Jackson
ELLISON, Thomas T.	26	Houston
ELLISON, Benjamin	7	Stewart
ELLISON, Benjamin J.	14	Burke
ELLISON, J.B.M.	4	Bibb
ELLISON, John	3	Talbot
ELLISON, Robert J.	11	Burke
ELLISON, Samuel J.	11	Burke
ELLISON, Sarah	10	Burke
ELLISON, W. H.	25	Bibb
ELLLIS, Nathan	13	Merriwether
ELLS, Nathan	1	Chatham
ELMER, Jeremiah	2	Cobb
ELMORE, Elijah	3	Coweta
ELMORE, Thomas	3	Burke
ELROD, Abraham	5	Hall
ELROD, John	4	Hall
ELSBERRY, Lindley	5	Cobb
ELUM, George	5	DeKalb
ELVET?, Thomas M.	1	Cobb
ELY, J. H.	7	Hancock

Name	Number	County	Name	Number	County
ELY, James J.	8	Greene	ENGRAM, Robert B.	16	Houston
ELY, James J.	35	Hancock	ENGRAM, S. T.	10	Houston
EMANUAL, David	1	DeKalb	ENGRAM, William F.	7	Houston
EMANUEL, Benj. T.	76	Talbot	ENLOW, Barbary	1	Merriwether
EMBRE, (?)	24	Columbia	ENNIS, George	1	Marion
EMBRY, Johnnannah	11	Harris	ENNIS, James	2	Muscogee
EMBRY, Martha	2	Harris	ENNIS, Pleasant	2	Baldwin
EMBRY, T. J.	2	Henry	ENNIS, William	8	Wilkinson
EMERSON, Henry	5	Cherokee	EPPERSON, John	2	Franklin
EMFINGER, Amanda	2	Pike	EPPES, George W.	14	Harris
EMLIN, Chas.	1	Coweta	EPPING, H. H.	5	Muscogee
EMMERSON, James	3	Jones	EPPINGER, James	33	Pike
EMMERSON, Sarah	3	Jones	EPPS, D. T.	7	Twiggs
EMMERSON, James R.	1	DeKalb	EPPS, John C.	28	Twiggs
EMORY, Joseph	2	Troup	EPPS, James	7	Newton
EMORY, S.	8	Troup	EPPS, Thos. N.	1	Clarke
EMRY, Jasper	2	Harris	EPPS, William	20	Clarke
ENDLOW, Daniel	4	Pike	EPPS, Joshua	1	Columbia
ENDSBY, Joseph	3	Campbell	ERENTT, Jas.	1	Bibb
ENDSLEY, John	8	Coweta	ERSLY ?, Richar	2	Walton
ENFINGER, George	36	Dooly	ESTES, Jas.	2	Troup
ENGLAND, J. S.	3	Clarke	ESTES, M. H.	1	Troup
ENGLAND, Martom	4	Union	ESTES, Z.	9	Troup
ENGLAND, Mararett?	4	Habersham	ERVIN, Thos. M.	2	Gordon
ENGLAND, Martin	1	Campbell	ERWIN, Alexander	4	Habersham
ENGLAND, Thomas	5	Oglethorpe	ERWIN, Arthur	8	Forsyth
ENGLAND, Thos.	7	Oglethorpe	ERWIN, James M.	31	Gordon
ENGLAND, W. G.	9	Oglethorpe	ERWIN, Obediah	1	Gordon
ENGLAND, John E.	1	Rabun	ERWIN, C. A.	3	Bibb
ENGLISH, Aaron	16	Warren	ERWIN, Jared	3	Bibb
ENGLISH, Elijah	1	Lowndes	ERWIN, L. A. agt.	18	Bibb
ENGLISH, Elizabeth	34	Greene	ERWIN?, William R.	2	Clarke
ENGLISH, Georg	7	Monroe	ESKEN?, Isaac R.	3	Pike
ENGLISH, Green	16	Monroe	ESON, John	10	Floyd
ENGLISH, Joel	11	Warren	ESPEY, F. B.	20	Carroll
ENGLISH, John	1	Campbell	ESPY, Calvin J.	1	Jackson
ENGLISH, John	8	Monroe	ESPY, James W.	4	Pike
ENGLISH, John	2	Muscogee	ESPY, Robert	10	Jackson
ENGLISH, John	17	Warren	ESTERS, John A.	5	Jasper
ENGLISH, Robert H.	1	Macon	ESTERS, Philip	2	Jasper
ENGLISH, Sampson	11	Macon	ESTES, Henry	14	Marion
ENGLISH, Sarah T.	10	Campbell	ESTES, James B.	2	Meriwether
ENGLISH, Stephen	6	Greene	ESTES, John W.	4	Merriwether
ENGLISH, Thomas	7	Warren	ESTES, Joel	18	Marion
ENGLISH, W. N.			ESTES, Wm.	19	Decatur
(overseer?)	51	Lee	ESTES, Josephus	3	Putnam
ENGLISH, William	4	Greene	ESTIS, Micajah	3	Franklin
ENGLISH, William	18	Warren	ETCHASON, Benjamin	10	Troup
ENGLISH, Wm. W.	2	Macon	ETETUSON ?, William	1	Walton
ENGLISH, Barbary	11	Lowndes	ETHEREDGE, J. T.	3	Wilkinson
ENGLISH, Benson	8	Bibb	ETHEREDGE, Edmund	1	Wilkinson
ENGLISH, John D.	8	Greene	ETHERIDGE, James	2	Butts
ENGRAHM, William	5	Monroe	ETHERIDGE, J. K.	15	Wilkinson
ENGRAM, Elizabeth	18	Houston	ETHERIDGE, Shely P.	1	Wilkinson

Name	Number	County	Name	Number	County
ETHRIDGE, Elijah	19	Monroe	EVANS, Miram	1	Harris
ETHRIDGE, Frances	1	Upson	EVANS, Ozekiel	11	Houston
ETHRIDGE, Luis	11	Butts	EVANS, Philip	1	Jefferson
ETHRIDGE, Robert H.	5	Monroe	EVANS, Pleman	2	Merriwether
ETHRIDGE, William D.	44	Jones	EVANS, Rachel	1	Monroe
ETHRIDGE, Aaron	7	Randolph	EVANS, Rivel	15	Thomas
ETHRIDGE, Caswell	1	Butts	EVANS, Robert	1	Houston
EUBANKS, Alfred	6	Morgan	EVANS, Robert	4	Newton
EUBANKS, D. T.	5	Lincoln	EVANS, Robt.	2	Lumpkin
EUBANKS, C.	6	Bibb	EVANS, Sterling G.	26	Hancock
EUBANKS, E.	1	Crawford	EVANS, Thomas	51	Monroe
EUBANKS, W. J.	20	Columbia	EVANS, Thomas	5	Monroe
EULLS?, C. A.	6	Bibb	EVANS, Thomas J.	7	Lumpkin
EULLS?, M. W.	2	Bibb	EVANS, W. R.	1	Pike
EVANS, Phillip J.	3	Cherokee	EVANS, William	1	Jasper
EVANS, A. L.	32	Jefferson	EVANS, William	5	Meriwether
EVANS, A. M.	6	Hall	EVANS, William H.	1	Houston
EVANS, Aaron	2	Troup	EVANS, Wm. H.	1	Wilkes
EVANS, Arden B.	13	Marion	EVANS, William M.	1	Monroe
EVANS, Arden Sr.	25	Troup	EVANS, Z.	6	Early
EVANS, Augustus W.	7	Newton	EVANS, C.	21	Screven
EVANS, B. T.	10	Fayette	EVANS, C. W.	6	Chattooga
EVANS, Benj. J.	4	Clarke	EVANS, Chas. G.	2	Coweta
EVANS, Charles T. P.	18	Houston	EVANS, D. T.	5	Butts
EVANS, Cullin	3	Harris	EVANS, D. T.	2	Butts
EVANS, Daniel	7	Walker	EVANS, David	2	Madison
EVANS, Davenport	15	Upson	EVANS, Frances J.	24	Burke
EVANS, David	3	Muscogee	EVANS, George	7	Talbot
EVANS, Edward	28	Monroe	EVANS, George W.	78	Burke
EVANS, Elijah	16	Merriwether	EVANS, George W.	12	Richmond
EVANS, Elizabeth	11	Monroe	EVANS, H.	4	Columbia
EVANS, Fields	12	Newton	EVANS, Hezekiah	27	Screven
EVANS, George Ann	4	Twiggs	EVANS, Humphrey	24	Columbia
EVANS, H. E.	1	Walton	EVANS, James W.	1	Screven
EVANS, Henry	4	Pulaski	EVANS, Jesse	7	Columbia
EVANS, Isabella	6	Chatham	EVANS, John	11	Columbia
EVANS, Isom W.	1	Fayette	EVANS, John	2	Columbia
EVANS, J. E. B.	3	Franklin	EVANS, John	9	DeKalb
EVANS, J. P.	20	Morgan	EVANS, John	28	Taliaferro
EVANS, J. W.	4	Gordon	EVANS, John	21	Taliaferro
EVANS, James	16	Monroe	EVANS, John L.	12	DeKalb
EVANS, James E.	5	Chatham	EVANS, John P.	4	Bibb
EVANS, Jas. W.	10	Troup	EVANS, John R.	2	Screven
EVANS, John	29	Troup	EVANS, Joseph L.	16	Taliaferro
EVANS, John	1	Troup	EVANS, L. G.	7	Crawford
EVANS, John	17	Troup	EVANS, Lunedy ? Y.	7	Taliaferro
EVANS, John A.	76	Hancock	EVANS, N. P.	1	Decatur
EVANS, John B.	1	Fayette	EVANS, R. R.	24	Bibb
EVANS, John J.	3	Harris	EVANS, Rebecca	3	Taliaferro
EVANS, John Q.	9	Harris	EVANS, Robert agt for		
EVANS, John W.	2	Murray	MARTIN, Mrs.	79	Houston
EVANS, Llewellin	8	Lincoln	EVANS, Robert H.	7	Richmond
EVANS, Marcus A.	34	Jefferson	EVANS, Robert R.	6	Dooly
EVANS, Martha	7	Muscogee	EVANS, Starling	28	Stewart

Name	Number	County	Name	Number	County
EVANS, Thomas	3	Richmond	EVINGYSON, G.	4	Elbert
EVANS, Thomas	5	Screven	EVINS, Cain	3	Cherokee
EVANS, William	60	Burke	EVINS, Thos. D.	3	Cherokee
EVANS, William	21	Burke	EVINS, William H.	1	Cherokee
EVANS, William J.	20	Columbia	EVRETT, John C.	21	Dade
EVANS, William J.	2	Richmond	EWING, James	5	Dooly
EVANS, Wm.	26	Taliaferro	EXUM, Sterling W.	5	Houston
EVATT, James N.	1	Walker	EZELL, Brackston	22	Jasper
EVE, Edward A.	4	Richmond	EZELL, G. G.	5	Hancock
EVE, John C.	13	Floyd	EZELL, Henry	2	Hancock
EVE, John P.	55	Floyd	EZELL, William	1	Pike
EVE, Paul T.	15	Richmond	EZELL, H. W.	3	Carroll
EVE, William J.	77	Richmond	EZZEL, Levi	20	Houston
EVE, William J.	37	Richmond	FAGAN, Edward	9	Houston
EVERARD, John	1	Chatham	FAGAN, Thomas V.	2	Houston
EVERET, James M.	9	Dooly	FAGAN, H. G.	32	Stewart
EVERET, Sherod	4	Gwinnett	FAGAN, S.	1	Chatham
EVERETT, Alexander	36	Houston	FAGG, G. J.	6	Decatur
EVERETT, Antony	1	Effingham	FAGLE, Jacob agent	7	Muscogee
EVERETT, E.	1	Henry	FAHM, Mary A.	17	Chatham
EVERETT, J. A.	132	Houston	FAIGAN, T.	14	Crawford
EVERETT, M. B.	13	Pulaski	FAIGAN, Thos.	6	Crawford
EVERETT, Mrs. Mary E.	28	Houston	FAIL, Edna	3	Pulaski
EVERETT, Turner C.	14	Houston	FAIN, Abram	13	Cass
EVERETT, W. W.	4	Oglethorpe	FAIN, Greenberry	4	Paulding
EVERETT, Canay ?	1	Stewart	FAIN, Joel	8	Gordon
EVERETT, Charles C.	3	Dooly	FAIN, Robert C.	9	Paulding
EVERETT, David	4	Coweta	FAIN, William C.	1	Gilmer
EVERETT, Edwin	19	Screven	FAIN, William P.	2	Paulding
EVERETT, Hardy	39	Screven	FAIN?, J. W.	1	Habersham
EVERETT, Henry E.	3	Twiggs	FAINE, Wm.	17	Floyd
EVERETT, James	10	Thomas	FAIR, John	2	Decatur
EVERETT, Jasia	1	Thomas	FAIR, Peter	7	Baldwin
EVERETT, Jesse S.	17	Thomas	FAIRCHILD, F. A.	2	Muscogee
EVERETT, John W.	27	Thomas	FAIRCHILD, J. L.	1	Chatham
EVERETT, Joshua B.	9	Thomas	FAIRCHILD, Lewis J. B.	7	Chatham
EVERETT, Josiah	29	Thomas	FAIRCHILD, Samuel	6	Decatur
EVERETT, Mary	13	Twiggs	FAIRCLOTH, Etheldred	1	Dooly
EVERETT, Nancy	4	Thomas	FAIRCLOTH, Etheldsia	1	Thomas
EVERETT, Thomas	12	Stewart	FAIRCLOTH, Fred	1	Laurens
EVERETT, Thomas	11	Stewart	FAIRCLOTH, Green B.	1	Baker
EVERETT, W.	26	Decatur	FAIRCLOTH, Malinda	2	Randolph
EVERINGHAM, Mary	11	Marion	FAIRCLOTH, Reddin	15	Baker
EVERINGHAM, Phebe	4	Marion	FAIRCLOTH, Susan	1	Baker
EVERINGHAM, Thomas	10	Marion	FALKENBERRY, Mrs.	3	Muscogee
EVERITT, Elizabeth	6	Bullock	FALKNER, Peter	5	Jasper
EVERITT, Jehue	5	Bullock	FALKNER, Thomas	21	Jasper
EVERITT, Sarah	19	Bullock	FALL, C. J.	16	Henry
EVERS, William	25	Monroe	FALLAN, John	2	Chatham
EVERS, Frances	1	Screven	FALLEN, John	3	Talbot
EVERTT, Maston	9	Stewart	FALLIGANT, Louis N.	3	Chatham
EVES, Jane B.	22	Jackson	FALLIGANT, John G.	16	Chatham
EVINGSON, ?	5	Elbert	FALLIN, John H.	2	Taliaferro
EVINGSON, M.	5	Elbert	FALLIN, Salit?	8	Taliaferro

99

Name	Number	County	Name	Number	County
FALLIN, Sarah	11	Upson	FARMER, James M.	3	Washington
FAMBRO, W. M.	13	Walton	FARMER, Jared L.	2	Greene
FAMBROU, Anderson	10	Oglethorpe	FARMER, Joel	9	Floyd
FAMBROUGH, Alen G.	25	Monroe	FARMER, John G. O.	4	Wilkes
FAMBROUGH, Allen L.	3	Greene	FARMER, Lucy	2	Morgan
FAMBROUGH, Elizabeth	4	Greene	FARMER, R. F.	4	Jefferson
FAMBROUGH, Gac ?	4	Walton	FARMER, R. J.	15	Jefferson
FAMBROUGH, James B.	5	Greene	FARMER, Robert	1	Newton
FAMBROUGH, John	11	Clarke	FARMER, Robert H.	2	Oglethorpe
FAMBROUGH, John A.	5	Oglethorpe	FARMER, Thomas	6	Franklin
FAMBROUGH, John E.	3	Walton	FARMER, Thos.	1	Effingham
FAMBROUGH, John S.	4	Greene	FARMER, Thos.	11	Oglethorpe
FAMBROUGH, John W.	6	Monroe	FARMER, William	6	Harris
FAMBROUGH,			FARMER, Berien B.	10	Burke
Pendleton	2	Oglethorpe	FARMER, C. D.	17	Coweta
FAMBROUGH,			FARMER, Henry J.	10	Burke
Roberson	35	Monroe	FARMER, James	14	Taliaferro
FAMBROUGH, T. M.	16	Greene	FARMER, Jordan	7	Burke
FAMBROUGH, Wm. L.	25	Monroe	FARMER, Susan	4	Burke
FAMBROUGH, Wm.	7	Coweta	FARMER?, Henry	13	Oglethorpe
FANE, Amarantha	9	Early	FARMOR, C.	2	Elbert
FANE, Elizabeth	3	DeKalb	FARNALD, Wm.	2	Cobb
FANN, Thomas	3	Muscogee	FARNEL, William	11	Dooly
FANNIN, J. A.	28	Morgan	FARNOL, Thomas	2	Burke
FANNIN, Augustus B.	7	Troup	FARR, L.	1	Muscogee
FANNIN, Augustus B.	24	Troup	FARR, William	25	Columbia
FANNIN, James H.	24	Troup	FARR, Wm. W.	10	Screven
FANNIN, Joseph D.	16	Baldwin	FARRALL, James	3	DeKalb
FANNIN, Wm. F.	45	Troup	FARRAR, Abel	24	Putnam
FANNING, Jno. C.	7	Wilkes	FARRAR, Jesse C.	2	DeKalb
FANNING, Welcome	47	Wilkes	FARRAR, John	23	Putnam
FARBER, P.	1	Pike	FARRAR, William	39	Putnam
FARGEN ?, John	3	Taliaferro	FARREL, Mike	1	Chatham
FARGO, Herman W.	2	Richmond	FARRELL, John	1	Clarke
FARGO, Jordan	20	Richmond	FARRER, A.	1	Henry
FARGO, Jordon	2	Richmond	FARRER, John	18	Jones
FARGUSON, E. S.	2	Henry	FARRIER, J. H.	17	Floyd
FARGUSON, J.	34	Henry	FARROW, Thos.	1	Troup
FARGUSON, M. A.	2	Henry	FAUCETT, Anderson	6	Columbia
FARIES, George G.	1	Chatham	FAULK, Charles R.	30	Twiggs
FARLEY, John J.	4	Jasper	FAULK, Henry	16	Twigs
FARLEY, Mathew	33	Harris	FAULK, Henry	29	Twiggs
FARLEY, William	36	Harris	FAULK, Nancy	61	Twiggs
FARLEY, Mathew	54	Putnam	FAULK, William	5	Twiggs
FARLOW, Sarah	13	Greene	FAULK, Wm.	81	Twiggs
FARLY, Mathew	10	Monroe	FAULKNER, John	17	Jasper
FARMER, John J.	2	Jefferson	FAULKNER, John M.	2	Fayette
FARMER, Benjamin	1	Effingham	FAULKNER, Masten	1	Jasper
FARMER, Elam	11	Franklin	FAUST, John	25	Oglethorpe
FARMER, Enoch	11	Jefferson	FAUST, Peter	2	Sumter
FARMER, Frederick	3	Greene	FAUST, William	1	Sumter
FARMER, G. W.	1	Oglethorpe	FAVER, S. W.	25	Heard
FARMER, George W.	4	Jefferson	FAVER, S. W.	1	Heard
FARMER, J.E.	1	Henry	FAVISH, Samuel	17	Walkers

Name	Number	County	Name	Number	County
FAVOR, C. M.	17	Merriwether	FELTS, James W.	4	Houston
FAVOR, Nancy	20	Merriwether	FELTS, John B.	1	Houston
FAVOR, Thomas	78	Wilkes	FELTS, John H.	10	Warren
FAVOR, William R.	19	Merriwether	FELTS, Lewis F.	6	Warren
FAVORS, John	35	Coweta	FELTS, William H.	11	Gwinnett
FAY, Joseph S.	2	Chatham	FELTS, William T.	2	Cobb
FAY, Mary	2	Jefferson	FELTS, Martha	7	Putnam
FAY, Allen	17	Talbot	FELTS, William	3	Talbot
FAY, Sampson T.	11	Talbot	FEMBY, Obediah	2	Newton
FAY, William	18	Baker	FENCH, T. H.	17	Coweta
FAY, William	10	Talbot	FENDALL, Sarah	2	DeKalb
FAYETTE, Thomas	1	Habersham	FENN, Eli	7	Dooly
FEAGAN,			FENN, John H.	13	Dooly
Miss Missouri	34	Houston	FENNELL, George AW.	1	Chatham
FEAGIN, Michael J.	7	Macon	FENTRESS, J. C.	3	Randolph
FEAGIN, Wm. H.	17	Sumter	FERDON(?), John	4	Columbia
FEARS, A. B.	1	Henry	FERGASON, James	12	Muscogee
FEARS, Ezekiel	24	Jasper	FERGASON, Elizabeth	3	DeKalb
FEARS, James	30	Morgan	FERGERSON, Eliza	1	Chatham
FEARS, John P.	13	Jasper	FERGUSON, Augustus	8	Jefferson
FEARS, Oliver Z.	19	Troup	FERGUSON, D.	2	Henry
FEARS, Richd.	6	Hancock	FERGUSON, E. J.	1	Henry
FEARS, Riley	10	Jasper	FERGUSON, Jno.	17	Henry
FEARS, Thos.	3	Harris	FERGUSON, Wm. S.	1	Henry
FEARS, Thos.	10	Henry	FERGUSON, Anguish	3	Campbell
FEARS, W. L.	11	Henry	FERGUSON, Grief	29	Talbot
FEARS, Wiley M.	1	Henry	FERGUSON, J.	20	Decatur
FEARS, Zachariah	67	Morgan	FERGUSON, S. B.	1	Carroll
FEATHERSTONE, L. H.	18	Heard	FERGUSSON, John	19	Lincoln
FEAY, William T.	2	Chatham	FERINGSIDE, H.	2	Dooly
FELDER, Calvin	21	Houston	FERREL, Celia	6	Thomas
FELDER, Calvin W.	4	Houston	FERREL, Jabis	1	Thomas
FELDER, Henry B.	10	Houston	FERREL, Jas. A.	1	Coweta
FELDER, J. F.	35	Houston	FERRELL, F. M.	1	Pike
FELDER, Samuel	11	Houston	FERRELL, Blount C.	34	Thomas
FELDER, S.	48	Houston	FERRELL, James H.	1	Hancock
FELEK ?, Floyd M.	1	Richmond	FERRELL, John M.	14	Thomas
FELL, Mary	2	Chatham	FERRELL, Richard	5	Talbot
FELL, R. R.	3	Chatham	FESLER, Charles	1	Hall
FELLOWS, George P.	13	Clarke	FETCHCHAN, S.	6	Walton
FELKER, John	1	Walton	FETHN?, William	4	Houston
FELKER, Peter J.	3	Walton	FETZER, J. G.	13	Effingham
FELKER, Stephen	35	Walton	FETZER, Joshua	1	Effingham
FELT, Joseph	3	Chatham	FETZER, N. S.	9	Effingham
FELT, Allen	12	Crawford	FEW, James T.	2	Morgan
FELT, G. B.	6	Crawford	FEW, Mary	6	Morgan
FELT, Wm. H.	8	Richmond	FEW, Seaborn	2	Morgan
FELTON, John G.	10	Cobb	FEW, Wm.	2	Clarke
FELTON, John R.	23	Macon	FICKET, Robert	2	Newton
FELTON, Sam H.	5	Macon	FICKLAND?, Fielding	55	Taliaferro
FELTON, Shadrick	27	Macon	FICKLEN, F.	7	Wilkes
FELTON, William	54	Macon	FICKLING, Barnard	31	Warren
FELTON, John	38	Cass	FICKLING, James	8	Chatham
FELTS, David	2	Warren	FICKLING, Jeremiah	9	Muscogee

Name	Number	County	Name	Number	County
FICKLING, C. F.	30	Crawford	FINCHER, Elias	5	Forsyth
FICKLING, Samuel	1	Richmond	FINCHER, H. C.	1	Forsyth
FIELD, Elias E.	4	Cherokee	FINCHER, Isaac	5	Troup
FIELD, Elijah M.	14	Cherokee	FINCHER, John	5	Upson
FIELD, Jas. M.	28	Gordon	FINCHER, Joseph	2	Pike
FIELD, Jeremiah	39	Cherokee	FINCHER, Joseph T.	1	Pike
FIELD, John D.	16	Lumpkin	FINCHER, Wm.	1	Forsyth
FIELD, L.	1	Muscogee	FINCHER, Joseph	1	Stewart
FIELD, Lawson	9	Cherokee	FINDLEY, James	8	Henry
FIELD, Samuel	13	Clarke	FINDLEY, James T.	17	Greene
FIELD, William	2	Murray	FINDLEY, S. M.	8	Greene
FIELD, J. M.	8	Bibb	FINDLY, Mason	2	Randolph
FIELD, Peyton H.	2	Campbell	FINLEY, Amaniel	11	Merriwether
FIELDER, Elizabeth	7	Putnam	FINLEY, Anna	1	Houston
FIELDER, Marion	1	Merriwether	FINLEY, Charles H.	9	Morgan
FIELDER, Obediah	25	Jasper	FINLEY, John	12	Troup
FIELDER, S. L.	1	Cherokee	FINLEY, Jon	43	Wilkes
FIELDER, T.B.	10	Morgan	FINLEY, Joseph	3	Camden
FIELDER, Terrel	9	Merriwether	FINLEY, J. T.	7	Chattooga
FIELDER, Eliza	7	Butts	FINLEY, R.	2	Bibb
FIELDER, Mary Estate	35	Putnam	FINLEY, Saml.	40	Chattooga
FIELDING, Charles	6	Morgan	FINLY, Madison	16	Newton
FIELDING, Jonathan	15	Walker	FINLY, Riley	3	Merriwether
FIELDING, Saml.	1	Clarke	FINN, Francis	3	Campbell
FIELDS, Boling	1	Lumpkin	FINN, John	10	Richmond
FIELDS, Charles	1	Jefferson	FINNEY, Benjamin F.	21	Jones
FIELDS, Thompson	1	Houston	FINNEY, Benjamin T.	4	Jones
FIELDS, W. B.	5	Pike	FINNEY, Benjamin W.	12	Jones
FIELDS, William B.	4	Pike	FINNEY, Eupheny	18	Washington
FIELDS, Aquilla	1	Stewart	FINNEY, Ezekiel	17	Washington
FIELDS, Jackson	1	Talbot	FINNEY, Ferdinand P.	12	Jones
FIELDS, James	10	Stewart	FINNEY, James H.	19	Jones
FIETOR ?, William	2	Washington	FINNEY, Mrs. Harriett	3	Houston
FILESONE?, Elias	1	Muscogee	FINNEY, Nancy	15	Jones
FILLER, John P.	3	Oglethorpe	FINNEY, Sarah	15	Jones
FILLINGAM, A.	2	Randolph	FINNIE, James T.	82	Morgan
FILLINGHAM, B. M.	6	Paulding	FINNY, Margaret H.	4	Chatham
FILLINGHAM, J. W.	1	Greene	FINNY, Samuel B.	4	Jones
FILMAN ?, James	16	Walton	FISH, Vines	21	Jasper
FILORD, Everet	3	Radolph	FISH, G. W.	8	Bibb
FINAZY, F.	23	Oglethorpe	FISH, G. W.	39	Washington
FINCH, Burdit	2	Macon	FISH, Sarah	8	Baldwin
FINCH, Charles B.	9	Jackson	FISHBUM, B.	8	Muscogee
FINCH, Delia	8	Twiggs	FISHBURN,	60	Lee
FINCH, F.	1	Troup	FISHBURNE, Edward	10	Muscogee
FINCH, Gabriel	3	Franklin	FISHER, Charles	79	Muscogee
FINCH, Terre?	9	Oglethorpe	FISHER, J.R.	1	Chatham
FINCH, Thos. B.	1	Jackson	FISHER, John	4	Washington
FINCH, William	7	Monroe	FISHER, M. D.	12	Washington
FINCH, Wm. C.	17	Twiggs	FISHER, William	4	Wilkinson
FINCH, John	44	Screven	FITCH, Charles	9	Oglethorpe
FINCH, Susan	3	Bullock	FITCH, William	13	Stewart
FINCHEN, Jos.	4	Floyd	FITTEN(?), John	26	Columbia
FINCHER, Christopher	2	Jasper	FITTEN, John H.	14	Richmond

102

Name	Number	County	Name	Number	County
FITZ, James O.	2	Madison	FLEMING, William G.	3	Harris
FITZGAIRES, M.	1	Irwin	FLEMING, William W.	1	Harris
FITZGAIRES, P.	1	Irwin	FLEMING, Wily	8	Monroe
FITZGAIRES, Mrs.	8	Irwin	FLEMING, G. W.	1	Coweta
FITZGERALD, Ann	3	Fayette	FLEMING, Geo.	6	Camden
FITZGERALD,			FLEMING, J.	3	Coweta
Catherine	10	Baldwin	FLEMING, J. P.	4	Coweta
FITZGERALD, Mary	39	Morgan	FLEMING, James	20	Columbia
FITZGERALD, Phillip	27	Fayette	FLEMING, James P.	28	Columbia
FITZGERALD, Silas	4	Columbia	FLEMING, John	3	Jefferson
FITZGERALD, James	14	Houston	FLEMING, John P.	1	Richmond
FITZJARREL, David	5	Stewart	FLEMING, Pertn ? , F.	18	Richmond
FITZJARRELL, John	8	Stewart	FLEMING, Robt.	17	Coweta
FITZJARRELL, Matilda	1	Stewart	FLEMING, Thomas W.	2	Richmond
FITZPATRIC, Joseph	18	Harris	FLEMING, William B.	10	Chatham
FITZPATRICK, Zena	52	Morgan	FLEMING, Wm.	4	Coweta
FITZPATRICK, N.	5	Crawford	FLEMING, Wm.	5	Coweta
FITZSIMONS, D. P.	61	Jefferson	FLEMISTER, Aley	5	Jasper
FLANAGAN, John	10	Jackson	FLEMISTER, James	1	Merriwether
FLANDERS, F. E.	8	Laurens	FLEMISTER, John	18	Merriwether
FLANDERS, James M.	2	Chatham	FLEMISTER, Richard	8	Merriwether
FLANDERS, Susan	1	Bibb	FLEMISTER,		
FLANDERS, Wm.	5	Laurens	William L.	10	Jasper
FLANDERS, David	19	Bibb	FLEMMING, John	8	Pulaski
FLANDERS, Jas.	3	Bibb	FLEMMING, John S.		
FLANEGHAN, Nancy	2	Habersham	estate	40	Liberty
FLANIGAN, Gameell P.	14	Lincoln	FLEMMING, Peter W.	42	Liberty
FLANNIGAN, Joel L.	3	Paulding	FLEMMING, Thos. W.	28	Liberty
FLEEMAN, Henry G.	9	Oglethorpe	FLEMMING, W. G.	2	Pulaski
FLEEMAN, John S.	8	Oglethorpe	FLEMMING, Wm. B.	34	Liberty
FLEEMAN, Thos.	19	Oglethorpe	FLEMMING, C. P.	2	Dooly
FLEEMAN?, James P.	1	Oglethorpe	FLENNA, James	4	Harris
FLEEMING, Jesse	1	Harris	FLETCHER, B.	11	Meriwether
FLEETWOOD, Green	5	Chatham	FLETCHER, D.	7	Irwin
FLEETWOOD, William	22	Greene	FLETCHER, Effy	13	Monroe
FLEETWOOD, John	1	Chatham	FLETCHER, Henry B.	8	Monroe
FLEMESTING?, F.	3	Bibb	FLETCHER, James	9	Monroe
FLEMING ?, Anderson	1	Stewart	FLETCHER,		
FLEMING, A.	2	Pike	Mrs. Blaney	17	Meriwether
FLEMING, Benj. F.	2	Macon	FLETCHER,		
FLEMING, F. F.	27	Lincoln	no other name	3	Irwin
FLEMING, H.	10	Elbert	FLETCHER, R. M.	1	Henry
FLEMING, John A.	8	Harris	FLETCHER, Charles	4	Bullock
FLEMING, Lard	3	Jefferson	FLETCHER, Dix	6	Cobb
FLEMING, M. T.	6	Elbert	FLETCHER, John V.	20	Sumter
FLEMING, Martha	1	Franklin	FLETCHER, Mark H.	6	Sumter
FLEMING, R. M.	22	Oglethorpe	FLETCHER, R. M.	1	Carroll
FLEMING, Robert	13	Lincoln	FLETCHER, Wiley	7	Telfair
FLEMING, Robert A.	10	Harris	FLEUK?, Wm. M.	5	Habersham
FLEMING, S.	19	Elbert	FLEURY, Joseph	1	Hancock
FLEMING, Samuel	29	Jefferson	FLEWELEN, Wm. H.	3	Monroe
FLEMING, Sely	5	Monroe	FLEWELLEN, Abner		
FLEMING, Susan	3	Lincoln	estate	14	Muscogee
FLEMING, William	4	Jefferson	FLEWELLEN, James	64	Muscogee

Name	Number	County	Name	Number	County
FLEWELLEN, James T.	5	Muscogee	FLOYD, Mathus	4	Dooly
FLEWELLEN, Thomas	36	Upson	FLOYD, P.	3	Lee
FLEWELLEN, Wm. W.	1	Muscogee	FLOYD, Robert	1	Madison
FLICKLIN, William	6	Washington	FLOYD, Stewart	38	Morgan
FLING, Daniel	13	Merriwether	FLOYD, Thos. B.	7	Troup
FLINT, John	14	Monroe	FLOYD, Wilhelmina	1	Clarke
FLINT, John	1	Walton	FLOYD, Alexander	7	Campbell
FLINT, Joshua	1	Walton	FLOYD, Andrew	4	Burke
FLINT, Aquilla	15	Columbia	FLOYD, Goodwin	4	Talbot
FLINT, Thomas	3	Bibb	FLOYD, Jacin	9	Bullock
FLOERCH, J.	1	Murray	FLOYD, Jesse	1	Liberty
FLOID, Henry	1	Pike	FLOYD, John S.	3	Campbell
FLOOD, John P.	1	Franklin	FLOYD, Newport	5	Cass
FLOOD, Rebecca	2	Camden	FLOYD, R. T.	8	Butts
FLORANE, W. A.	3	Elbert	FLOYD, Sam	44	Camden
FLORENCE, G. W.	18	Wilkes	FLOYD, Shadrick agt		
FLORENCE, Gibson	4	Wilkes	for COOPER, Wm.	38	Houston
FLORENCE, John W.	6	Merriwether	FLOYD, Stephen	2	Cass
FLORENCE, Jno.	26	Wilkes	FLOYD, Thos.	3	Putnam
FLORENCE, John	2	Upson	FLUGER, Sarah	2	Chatham
FLORENCE, Thos.	6	Harris	FLUKER, W. N.	9	Greene
FLORENCE, W.	17	Meriwether	FLUKER, John	10	Taliaferro
FLORENCE, Elizabeth	3	Richmond	FLUKER, Robert	29	Washington
FLORENCE, Toliver			FLUKER, Sarah	12	Bibb
Agent	86	Randolph	FLUKER, Wm. T.	14	Taliaferro
FLORNEY, S. W.	5	Muscogee	FLYNN, Isabella	4	Harris
FLORNOY, Edward	6	Monroe	FLYNN, James	1	Upson
FLORNOY, Joseph	1	Monroe	FLYNN, John	22	Muscogee
FLOURENCE, J. A.	4	Lincoln	FLYNN, John	3	Columbia
FLOURENCE, Obediah	12	Lincoln	FLYNT, Augustus W.	24	Taliaferro
FLOURENCE, Thomas	24	Lincoln	FLYNT, George W.	17	Taliaferro
FLOURENCE, Wiliam	8	Lincoln	FLYNT, Jas. H.	38	Wilkes
FLOURNEY, William F.	18	Jasper	FLYNT, John B.	2	Taliaferro
FLOURNOY, J. J.	25	Jackson	FOGGERSON, Lorenzo	6	Oglethorpe
FLOURNOY, Howell C.	1	Clarke	FOLDS, Ann	1	Jasper
FLOURNOY, James	17	Talbot	FOLDS, Edward J.	8	Dooly
FLOURNOY, Robert W.	74	Washington	FOLDS, Jefferson	3	Putman
FLOURNOY, Thomas	16	Richmond	FOLDS, Thos.	7	Butts
FLOWERS, James	9	Gwinnett	FOLDS, Zackariah	5	Putnam
FLOWERS, James M.	41	Troup	FOLEY, Owen	2	Chatham
FLOWERS, William	1	Wayne	FOLKER, James	5	Chatham
FLOY, Thaddeus S.	1	Richmond	FOLKES, Celia	1	Jefferson
FLOYD, Allen O.	6	Liberty	FOLKNER?, Susan	2	Oglethorpe
FLOYD, Charles B.	1	Pike	FOLKS, Solomon	35	Dooly
FLOYD, David	21	Newton	FOLSOM, Elijah	3	Lowndes
FLOYD, Dolpin	5	Monroe	FOLSOM, G. A.	2	Wilkinson
FLOYD, Edwin	2	Newton	FOLSOM, James	24	Lowndes
FLOYD, J. N.	3	Wilkinson	FOLSOM, John	6	Lowndes
FLOYD, J. W.	27	Meriwether	FOLSOM, Maston	2	Lowndes
FLOYD, J.A.	40	Morgan	FOLSOM, Randal	17	Lowndes
FLOYD, James U.	18	Washington	FOLSOM, Thomas	20	Lowndes
FLOYD, John J.	9	Newton	FOLSOM, Wm.	15	Lowndes
FLOYD, Julia	8	Camden	FOLSOM, Israel	9	Lowndes
FLOYD, Larkin	9	Troup	FOLTSOM, James T.	9	Harris

Name	Number	County	Name	Number	County
FOMBEY, M. B.	21	Troup	FOREHAND, W. W.	8	Sumter
FOMBY, Aaron	5	Troup	FOREHAND, William A.	7	Dooly
FOMBY, Nathan	8	Heard	FOREHAND, William J.	5	Emanual
FOMBY, R.	20	Troup	FOREMAN, Frederick	13	Cherokee
FOMBY, Rowland	19	Heard	FOREMAN, Glover	10	Glynn
FOMBY, S. R.	2	Troup	FOREMAN, James	3	Stewart
FONDSUE ?, John G.	124	Thomas	FOREST, Sugar	13	Thomas
FONERDON, Wm. H.	1	Murray	FORISTER, Joel	14	Muscogee
FONTAINE, John	8	Muscogee	FORMAN, Thos. M.	36	Glynn
FOOT, E.	25	Bibb	FORMELL, Charlotte	2	Chatham
FOOTE, George W.	2	Cobb	FORMWALT, M. W.	8	DeKalb
FOOTE, George W.	1	Cobb	FORREST, Wm .	6	Laurens
FOOTE, James	8	Cobb	FORRESTER, Bailley	8	Glynn
FOOTE, Reubin	2	Cobb	FORRISTER, J. T.	2	Habersham
FORACRES, Nathan	1	Camden	FORRISTER, Jesse M.	14	Paulding
FORBES, Gilbert	2	Troup	FORSON, Wiley G.	8	Thomas
FORBES, John M.	19	Troup	FORSON, William J.	2	Thomas
FORBES, Margary	24	McIntosh	FORSYTH, J.	17	Twiggs
FORBS, James	12	Harris	FORSYTH, James	8	Murray
FORBS, George N.	12	Talbot	FORSYTH, James	1	Paulding
FORBS, Joseph	6	Washington	FORSYTH, John	11	Muscogee
FORCE, M. S.	6	Chattooga	FORSYTH, John	13	Twiggs
FORD, Elizabeth	8	Floyd	FORSYTH, Ambrose	2	DeKalb
FORD, Ann A.	13	Early	FORT, Benjamin F.	3	Dooly
FORD, Henry	3	Franklin	FORT, Elias	10	Wayne
FORD, James	7	Franklin	FORT, Henry R.	7	Camden
FORD, John I.	4	Cherokee	FORT, Dr. Tomlinson	21	Baldwin
FORD, Jos.	19	Floyd	FORT, John	53	Wayne
FORD, Meric H.	16	Cherokee	FORT, Jno.	27	Randolph
FORD, Richard	2	Upson	FORT, Maranda	3	Talbot
FORD, Richard F.	4	Marion	FORT, Mary E.	63	Stewart
FORD, Sarah	2	Gwinnett	FORT, Mrs. Laura estate	19	Houston
FORD, Zadoc	2	Heard	FORT, William A.	14	Stewart
FORD, Abraham	17	Baldwin	FORTH, Francis W.	13	Burke
FORD, Edward E.	3	Richmond	FORTH, Louis E.	6	Burke
FORD, Eudecia	12	Baldwin	FORTNER, Peter	15	Henry
FORD, G. G.	11	Dooly	FORTNER, Swain M.	1	Emanaul
FORD, James	4	Talbot	FORTSOM, Benj. R.	5	Harris
FORD, James N.	2	Dooly	FORTSON, B.W.	48	Wilkes
FORD, John	30	Talbot	FORTSON, Peter	6	Hall
FORD, John P.	4	Richmond	FORTSON, Thomas	15	Muscogee
FORD, Keziah	25	Talbot	FOSDICK, B. W.	3	Chatham
FORD, Lewis D.	7	Richmond	FOSET, Early	3	Pike
FORD, R. G.	18	Dooly	FOSSET, C. F.	1	Clarke
FORD, Thomas	2	Chatham	FOSTER, Ransum Jr.	2	Forsyth
FORD?, J.	2	Irwin	FOSTER, A. G.	29	Morgan
FORDHAM, Benj.	10	Wilkinson	FOSTER, Absalom	5	Murray
FORDHAM, T.	1	Wilkinson	FOSTER, Ann	12	Troup
FORDHAM, W.	9	Wilkinson	FOSTER, Arthur	44	Bibb
FORDHAM, Zenith	3	Wilkinson	FOSTER, Charles	5	Heard
FOREHAND, Berrien A.	5	Burke	FOSTER, Collier	8	Monroe
FOREHAND, John A.	4	Dooly	FOSTER, E.	1	Henry
FOREHAND, Solomon	16	Houston	FOSTER, E. G.	6	Harris
FOREHAND, William R.	1	Burke	FOSTER, E. G.	5	Pike

Name	Number	County	Name	Number	County
FOSTER, Elizabeth	4	Forsyth	FOUNTAIN, James	1	Chatham
FOSTER, Fletcher	24	Clarke	FOUNTAIN, J. H.	24	Wilkinson
FOSTER, Hannah	17	Greene	FOUNTAIN, Tabitha	5	Houston
FOSTER, Henry T.	2	Burke	FOUNTAIN, Wm.	19	Pulaski
FOSTER, Ira R.	9	Forsyth	FOUNTAIN, Wm. T.	1	Wilkinson
FOSTER, James	3	Walker	FOUNTAIN, Janet	5	Chatham
FOSTER, James F.	61	Greene	FOUNTAIN, John	65	Stewart
FOSTER, Jno. B.	4	Harris	FOUNTAIN, Mitchel	5	Wilkinson
FOSTER, Jno. B.	3	Harris	FOURSTON, J. M.	7	Elbert
FOSTER, John	6	Walker	FOURTSON, B.	6	Elbert
FOSTER, Joel	27	Cass	FOURTSON, B. G.	1	Elbert
FOSTER, John	3	Chatham	FOURTSON, E.	44	Elbert
FOSTER, John	16	Hancock	FOURTSON, E. K.	2	Elbert
FOSTER, Joseph A. J.	3	Troup	FOURTSON, H.	7	Elbert
FOSTER, Lewis	6	Heard	FOURTSON, R.	2	Elbert
FOSTER, Moses	11	Greene	FOURTSON, Richard	12	Elbert
FOSTER, Mrs. E. G.	36	Harris	FOUSE?, John	1	Heard
FOSTER, N.	1	Muscogee	FOUT?, Noah	5	Floyd
FOSTER, Newet	5	Lee	FOUTS, Solomon	7	Murray
FOSTER, Newton M.	4	Gilmer	FOWLER, James S.	10	Warren
FOSTER, Rachel	2	Forsyth	FOWLER, Jeremiah	1	Early
FOSTER, Ransum Sr.	5	Forsyth	FOWLER, Levi	14	Warren
FOSTER, Richard	2	Jasper	FOWLER, Mark	6	Cherokee
FOSTER, Robert K.	7	Pike	FOWLER, Robert T.	3	Jackson
FOSTER, Robt. S.	2	Floyd	FOWLER, S. W.	5	Forsyth
FOSTER, Stephen	5	Monroe	FOWLER, Sarah W.	11	Warren
FOSTER, Thomas	4	Gwinnett	FOWLER, Thomas	6	Cobb
FOSTER, W.	1	Muscogee	FOWLER, William	1	Cherokee
FOSTER, Wiley J.	8	Monroe	FOWLER, William	22	Warren
FOSTER, William	6	Thomas	FOWLER, A.	4	Crawford
FOSTER, Andrew	7	Campbell	FOWLER, Alford	8	DeKalb
FOSTER, F. W.	1	Screven	FOWLER, Cody	8	Clarke
FOSTER, Fleming	2	Talbot	FOWLER, H. J.	4	DeKalb
FOSTER, Harriet	34	Sumter	FOWLER, Harriette L.	12	Burke
FOSTER, J.	20	Crawford	FOWLER, Joel	11	DeKalb
FOSTER, J. G.	3	Randolph	FOWLER, John W.	9	DeKalb
FOSTER, James R.	4	Stewart	FOWLER, Mary V.	11	DeKalb
FOSTER, John	5	Columbia	FOWLER, N.	12	Crawford
FOSTER, John	23	Richmond	FOWLER, Thos.	3	DeKalb
FOSTER, Moses	1	Stewart	FOWLER, William W.	1	Dade
FOSTER, Ried	17	Randolph	FOWLER, Y.	2	Crawford
FOSTER, Robert	9	Talbot	FOX, Franklin estate	17	Chatham
FOSTER, Saml.	8	Randolph	FOX, Joseph	1	Hall
FOSTER, Sterling	25	Putnam	FOX, R. W.	5	Muscogee
FOSTER, Thomas	12	Butts	FOX, Daniel	33	Chatham
FOSTER, Thomas	1	Campbell	FOX, Martha H.	7	Richmond
FOSTER, William	17	Butts	FOX, R. D.	4	Camden
FOSU?, Sarah	1	Lee	FOXWORTH, John	23	Pike
FOTTSEM, James T.	4	Harris	FOY, George	8	Effingham
FOUCH, George W.	5	Monroe	FOY, James M.	11	Thomas
FOUCHE, Daniel	7	Wilkes	FOY, William	8	Talbot
FOUCHE, S.	26	Cass	FOY, Wilmouth	1	Talbot
FOUK, Jarret	6	Lincoln	FOZWILLE?, S. S.	2	Harris
FOUNTAIN, B.	1	Wilkinson	FRALEY, George	3	Hancock

Name	Number	County	Name	Number	County
FRALEY, William	10	Hancock	FRAZIER, Permelia	1	Lincoln
FRALIX, Martin	2	Murray	FRAZIER, J.	3	Randolph
FRAMBOUGH, J. H.	5	Oglethorpe	FRAZIER, Martha	15	Taliaferro
FRAMMEL, Dan	4	Pulaski	FRAZUR, India	3	DeKalb
FRAMMILL, John	4	Habersham	FREBON, James	1	Chatham
FRANCIS, Cordy	31	Washington	FREDERICK, Austin M.	13	Houston
FRANCIS, Mary A.	38	Jefferson	FREDERICK, C.	1	Muscogee
FRANCIS, Nancy	29	Washington	FREDERICK, Daniel	34	Macon
FRANCISCO, Peter	1	Cass	FREDERICK, Martin	5	Richmond
FRANFORT, S.	1	DeKalb	FREDRICK ?, Augustus	12	Richmond
FRANKLIN, Benj. C.	2	Glynn	FREE, Henry	21	Houston
FRANKLIN, Benjamin	1	Franklin	FREE, Isaac	1	Houston
FRANKLIN, David	1	Upson	FREEMAN, Bailey	22	Jasper
FRANKLIN, Elizabeth	20	Merriwether	FREEMAN, Beasley	1	Greene
FRANKLIN, Francis	6	Upson	FREEMAN, Benjamin	1	Walker
FRANKLIN, George T.	12	Washington	FREEMAN, Beverley A.	3	Gilmer
FRANKLIN, John	8	Newton	FREEMAN, Charles	15	Troup
FRANKLIN, John	13	Upson	FREEMAN, Drury	7	Henry
FRANKLIN, John	3	Walton	FREEMAN, Edith	2	Habersham
FRANKLIN, Joseph	1	Jones	FREEMAN, Elizabeth	10	Jasper
FRANKLIN, Mary G.	8	Cherokee	FREEMAN, Fleming	28	Merriwether
FRANKLIN, Rebecca	1	Gordon	FREEMAN, George	3	Jasper
FRANKLIN, Samuel O.	33	Washington	FREEMAN, H. D.	1	Cherokee
FRANKLIN, Semides?	7	Clarke	FREEMAN, Hawkins	6	Jasper
FRANKLIN, Singleton	17	Marion	FREEMAN, Henry	14	Franklin
FRANKLIN, W. L.	4	Henry	FREEMAN, Henry	26	Lincoln
FRANKLIN, William	3	Gordon	FREEMAN, Henry	7	Upson
FRANKLIN, William	2	Upson	FREEMAN, Hopson	28	Jasper
FRANKLIN, Wm.	5	Monroe	FREEMAN, Isaac	4	Jefferson
FRANKLIN, Wm. F.	7	Greene	FREEMAN, J.	12	Troup
FRANKLIN, Benjamin	3	Chatham	FREEMAN, J. S.	4	Meriwether
FRANKLIN, James	8	Cass	FREEMAN, J. T.	3	Henry
FRANKLIN, M. A.	20	Bibb	FREEMAN, Jacob	2	Greene
FRANKLIN, Mary G.	31	Cherokee	FREEMAN, Jacob	1	Wilkinson
FRANKLIN, Pernell	1	Bullock	FREEMAN, James	53	Gordon
FRANKS, Robert	8	Franklin	FREEMAN, James	80	Jones
FRANKS, Robert	2	Morgan	FREEMAN, James	15	Merriwether
FRANKS, Wiley	28	Jones	FREEMAN, James C.	10	Pike
FRASEL, Green B.	3	Jasper	FREEMAN, James G.	1	Wilkinson
FRASER, W. M.	11	Pulaski	FREEMAN, Jas.	2	Troup
FRASER, S. M.	1	Pulaski	FREEMAN, Jane	5	Greene
FRASER, Simon	17	Liberty	FREEMAN, John	7	Franklin
FRASER, Simon A.	27	Liberty	FREEMAN, John	5	Meriwether
FRASIER, J.	17	Meriwether	FREEMAN, John	29	Wilkinson
FRASIER, Emeline	27	Sumter	FREEMAN, John F.	5	Greene
FRASIER, Simon	1	Cobb	FREEMAN, John J.	2	Greene
FRASIER, Thos.	2	Wilkes	FREEMAN, John M.	12	Wilkinson
FRAYOR, David	6	Richmond	FREEMAN, John W.	1	Wilkinson
FRAZER, George R.	1	Richmond	FREEMAN, Johnson	9	Merriwether
FRAZER, James	1	Richmond	FREEMAN, Joseph W.	6	Jasper
FRAZIER, Alexander	32	Lincoln	FREEMAN, Josiah	13	Butts
FRAZIER, Edward	10	Lincoln	FREEMAN, Lavany	2	Franklin
FRAZIER, John B.	1	Greene	FREEMAN, Malinda	11	Meriwether
FRAZIER, Permelia	2	Lincoln	FREEMAN, Moses	1	Jefferson

Name	Number	County	Name	Number	County
FREEMAN, Nancy	4	Merriwether	FRYER, Joshua	13	Telfair
FREEMAN, Robt.	2	Henry	FRYER, Mary E.	6	Richmond
FREEMAN, Robt.			FRYER?, Z. L.	29	Pike
(overseer?)	80	Lee	FUDGE, Daniel C.	5	Houston
FREEMAN, Samuel	12	Franklin	FUDGE, Jacob	10	Houston
FREEMAN, Susan	3	Clarke	FUDGE, Mrs. Jane	18	Houston
FREEMAN, William	1	Muscogee	FUDGE, Solomon	29	Houston
FREEMAN, Wm.	13	Pike	FUDGE, Benjamin	1	Dooly
FREEMAN, Wm. H.	1	Cherokee	FUGERSON, Aaron	10	Muscogee
FREEMAN, A. R.	11	Bibb	FULCHER ?, Mary	15	Richmond
FREEMAN, Anderson	2	Talbot	FULCHER, James A.	3	Burke
FREEMAN, Centity?	8	Screven	FULCHER, James L.	9	Burke
FREEMAN, Fleming	3	Talbot	FULCHER, John C.	21	Burke
FREEMAN, H.	13	Coweta	FULCHER, Amistead	4	Richmond
FREEMAN, Hannah	2	Decatur	FULCHER, Vincent W.	13	Burke
FREEMAN, J. T.	2	Coweta	FULCHER. Ann C.	18	Richmond
FREEMAN, Jacob	5	Baker	FULFORD, Bryan B.	7	Washington
FREEMAN, Jesse	3	Screven	FULFORD, Jas.	4	Marion
FREEMAN, John	3	Putnam	FULFORD, Stephen	1	Talbot
FREEMAN, John A.	4	Dooly	FULGAM, E.	1	Decatur
FREEMAN, Mitchell T.	1	Talbot	FULGAM, Mathew	2	Washington
FREEMAN, Roberson	1	Talbot	FULGHUM, Wm.	4	Monroe
FREEMAN, Thomas W.	5	Richmond	FULLE, Saml.	33	Bibb
FREEMAN, William	1	Talbot	FULLER, Alfred	9	Merriwether
FREEMAN?, Robert	39	Early	FULLER, Alpheus	12	Warren
FREEMOND, Thomas	8	Monroe	FULLER, E. W.	2	Merriwether
FREEMONT, Thomas Jr.	1	Monroe	FULLER, Elbert A.	1	Morgan
FREMONT, John agent	14	Monroe	FULLER, Green	13	Merriwether
FRENCH, John	16	Marion	FULLER, Hyram	3	Muscogee
FRENCH, Tilman	6	Marion	FULLER, Israel	1	Merriwether
FREWIN, James	4	Glynn	FULLER, James	13	Harris
FRIAR, J.	1	Henry	FULLER, James A.	6	Merriwether
FRIAR, Benjamin	4	Stewart	FULLER, John	3	Habersham
FRICKS, John	6	Walker	FULLER, John B.	21	Merriwether
FRICKS, Michael	10	Gordon	FULLER, John	4	Warren
FRICKS, Pleasant	6	Cass	FULLER, Marion	3	Harris
FRIEND, Jacob	3	Chatham	FULLER, Martha	30	Morgan
FRIERSON, George S.	5	Chatham	FULLER, Mrs. M.	7	Liberty
FRITH Thos. J.	4	Randolph	FULLER, Nancy F.	2	Henry
FRITTS, Levi	1	Newton	FULLER, Peter	7	Meriwether
FRITZJARREL, James	15	Stewart	FULLER, Simeon	2	Heard
FRITZPATRICK,			FULLER, Simion	4	Walton
Elizabeth	5	Twiggs	FULLER, Spivey	19	Warren
FRITZPATRICK, John	75	Twiggs	FULLER, Tilman	1	Pike
FRITZPATRICK, p.	4	Wilkes	FULLER, W. A.	1	Henry
FROCKTOR, Wm.	24	Camden	FULLER, William	9	Monroe
FROST, Eli	2	Floyd	FULLER, William A.	1	Merriwether
FROST, F. A.	3	Muscogee	FULLER, William J.	2	Gordon
FROST, Jacob W.	2	Muscogee	FULLER, Alsey	4	Meriwether
FROST, Johnston	2	Troup	FULLER, Benjamin	4	Talbot
FRYER, James H.	2	Pike	FULLER, Francis M.	5	Columbia
FRYER, A. G. estate	5	Burke	FULLER, Henry	1	Talbot
FRYER, Aaron G.	6	Telfair	FULLER, Margaret	9	Columbia
FRYER, Henderson	1	Telfair	FULLER, Pendleton	1	Meriwether

Name	Number	County	Name	Number	County
FULLER, Samuel	20	Talbot	FUTCH, Jesse	3	Bryan
FULLER, Solomon	4	Cherokee	FUTREL, J.	9	Crawford
FULLER, Spivy	9	Putnam	FUTRELL, Micagy	23	Effingham
FULLER, Wade H.	4	Talbot	FUTREN		
FULLER, William	2	Talbot	(or FUTREL), W.	35	Crawford
FULLERLOVE, Francis	1	Walton	GA. R. R. Company	5	DeKalb
FULLERTON, W. R.	3	Butts	GAAREY, Hetly	10	Chatham
FULLIGANT, Sarah	3	Chatham	GABLE, David	4	Coweta
FULLILOVE, B. P.	1	Clarke	GADACE, Thos.	9	Troup
FULLILOVE, Henry	5	Clarke	GADBEE, Robert	1	Burke
FULLOS, Stephen	1	Effingham	GAFFIN, George	8	Newton
FULLYLOVE, L. N.	4	Coweta	GAFFIS, Joel	1	Ware
FULMER, Geo.	1	Coweta	GAFFIS, Samuel	2	Ware
FULMER, Jacob	8	Coweta	GAILY, Joseph	2	Hall
FULMORE, Joseph	12	Cass	GAIN, John D.	1	Newton
FULTON, John G.	1	Liberty	GAINER, Benjamin	1	Lowndes
FULTON, William J.	1	Liberty	GAINER, James	12	Washington
FULTON, Catharine E.	5	Chatham	GAINER, James	23	Wasshington
FULTON, James	4	Dade	GAINER, James J.	7	Washington
FULTON, James	8	Randolph	GAINER, Samuel	21	Early
FULTON, John	13	Sumter	GAINER, Samuel	4	Early
FULTON, Silas	4	Bryan	GAINER, William	21	Washington
FULTON, William P.	10	Chatham	GAINES, Aaron	1	Cass
FULWOOD,			GAINES, Aaron	1	Cass
Mrs. Elizabeth	3	Houston	GAINES, Duncan	2	Burke
FULWOOD, James	14	Ware	GAINES, James	8	Cass
FUNDERBURK, Bryant	1	Jones	GAINES, John	5	Richmond
FUNDERBURK, David	1	Talbot	GAINES, M.	1	Cass
FUNDERBURK, Jacob	1	Talbot	GAINES, Reuben	4	Cass
FUQUA, A. A.	6	Laurens	GAINES, Richard	9	Chattooga
FUQUA, H. C.	30	Laurens	GAINEY, C.	1	Decatur
FUQUA, Thos. B.	9	Laurens	GAINEY, Jacob	3	Telfair
FURESOM, Sarah	6	Oglethorpe	GAINEY, M.	1	Wilkinson
FURGERSON, Ed.	3	Forsyth	GAINEY, N.	11	Decatur
FURGERSON, Isaac	2	Monroe	GAINEY, W.	7	Decatur
FURGERSON, David	13	Randolph	GAINS, F.	7	Elbert
FURGERSON, Dougal	5	Chatham	GAINS, George	11	Elbert
FURGERSON, Patrick	3	Randolph	GAINS, J. B.	1	Elbert
FURLOW & BIVINS	17	Sumter	GAINS, James	5	Elbert
FURLOW, C. M.	21	Morgan	GAINS, R. T.	10	Elbert
FURLOW, James W.	18	Houston	GAINS, R.S.	14	Elbert
FURLOW, Timothy M.	58	Sumter	GAINS, Wm.	9	Elbert
FURMAN, Dr. Samuel	34	Camden	GAINS, R.	12	Elbert
FUSSELL, David	1	Marion	GAISSERT, John M.	7	Greene
FUSSELL, John	1	Muscogee	GAITHER, Margaret	22	Walton
FUSSELL, Morris	5	Marion	GAITHER, William E.	1	Walton
FUSSELL, Jacob	3	Telfair	GALAGER, Bridget H.	8	Richmond
FUTAIL, Benj.	2	Henry	GALDING, Charles S.	4	Stewart
FUTCH, Isaac	29	Thomas	GALE, Mary A.	1	Chatham
FUTCH, John	1	Lowndes	GALLAUDET, James	3	Chatham
FUTCH, Reuben	1	Lowndes	GALLIA, John B.	17	Chatham
FUTCH, Thomas	7	Lowndes	GALLMAN, H.	1	Henry
FUTCH, Zach	1	Bryan	GALLON, Alexander H.	1	Baker
FUTCH, Eli	2	Bryan	GALLOWAY, Alexander	2	Chatham

Name	Number	County	Name	Number	County
GALLOWAY, Thomas	1	Newton	GARALS?, D. F.	3	Irwin
GALLOWAY, Thomas	2	Walton	GARDELLE, Adolphus	4	Richmond
GALLOWAY, William	4	Newton	GARDEN, Alexander	1	Pike
GALLOWY, Mary	1	Walton	GARDENER, Arthur	5	Muscogee
GALOWAY, John J.	3	Pike	GARDINER,		
GALMORE ?, John	13	Twiggs	Leonidas B.	7	Jones
GALMORE, J.	39	Twiggs	GARDNER, B. R.	4	Hancock
GALPIN, Wm.	1	Chatham	GARDNER, Celia	1	Washington
GALT, Edward M.	3	Murray	GARDNER, Elijah	1	Pike
GALT, Jabez	5	Cherokee	GARDNER, Ezekiel	4	Monroe
GALT, John M.	3	Richmond	GARDNER, Fedrick	27	Monroe
GAMAGE, James	6	Jones	GARDNER, Hilley	5	Gordon
GAMAGE, George W.	1	Talbot	GARDNER, James	61	Jefferson
GAMAGE, Nancy	1	Taliaferro	GARDNER, James	4	Monroe
GAMBLE, J.	13	Chattooga	GARDNER, John	12	Monroe
GAMBLE, John	1	Murray	GARDNER, John	17	Pike
GAMBLE, R. L.	67	Jefferson	GARDNER, Lewis	2	Pike
GAMBLE, R. L.	42	Jefferson	GARDNER, Robert B.	7	Pike
GAMBLE, R. L.	17	Jefferson	GARDNER, Samuel B.	2	Pike
GAMBLE, Wm.	3	Bibb	GARDNER, Delia A.	2	Chatham
GAMBLE, Adam	13	Talbot	GARDNER, Elizabeth	27	Richmond
GAMBLE, James	5	Dooly	GARDNER, James Jr.	9	Richmond
GAMBLE, Jas.	2	Bibb	GARDNER, James T.	2	Richmond
GAMBLE, John	11	Talbot	GARDNER, John	1	Crawford
GAMBLE, Robert	16	Talbot	GARDNER, Mrs.Thomas	15	Richmond
GAMBRELL, L.	8	Muscogee	GARDNER, N. E.	8	DeKalb
GAME?, John	11	Clarke	GARDNER, Robt. H.	4	Richmond
GAME?, William	5	Clarke	GARDOW,		
GAMMAGE, Davis	18	Macon	Wm. W. estate	7	Chatham
GAMMAGE, Milton	2	Macon	GARFIELD ?, Jacob	14	Richmond
GAMMAY, William	3	Gwinnett	GARINE, Emanuel	2	Lowndes
GAMMELL, George	6	Talbot	GARLAND, Henry	19	Upson
GAMMIL, A.	5	Muscogee	GARLAND, John	8	Jasper
GAMMIL, Mrs.	3	Muscogee	GARLAND, Mary	8	Upson
GAMMILL, William	6	Muscogee	GARLAND, William	4	Upson
GAMMON, Benjamin	1	Chatham	GARLAND, William H.	2	Chatham
GAMMON, Joseph	10	Chatham	GARLECK, Edward	3	Burke
GAN(?), J.P.	36	Decatur	GARLINGTON, J. L.	2	Newton
GANDER, Joseph B.	36	Hancock	GARLLA ?, Zelpa Mrs.	6	Stewart
GANDEY, Gocen ? B.	3	Thomas	GARMAN, James	3	Cobb
GANDY, Andrew J.	1	Baldwin	GARMANY, Capt. H.	8	Gwinnett
GANDY, James B.	1	Baldwin	GARMANY, Geo. W.	3	Forsyth
GANES, Ann B.	11	Monroe	GARMANY, William	5	Gwinnett
GANETT, Riley	1	Randolph	GARNER, Elizabeth	4	Jackson
GANIS, Hiram	7	Monroe	GARNER, Gideon	41	Murray
GANN, John	4	Cobb	GARNER, J. P.	1	Murray
GANN, Nathan	17	Paulding	GARNER, Jas. T.	2	Forsyth
GANNAY?, Dr. James	8	Gwinnett	GARNER, John	2	Franklin
GANNEAN, William	10	Baldwin	GARNER, John	1	Harris
GANRY ?, John	11	Twiggs	GARNER, John F.	7	Pike
GANT, Elizabeth	7	Putnam	GARNER, Lewis J.	1	Forsyth
GANTT, Henry	3	Jones	GARNER, M. G.	3	Jackson
GANTT, John	5	Jasper	GARNER, William H.	7	Monroe
GANTT, Robt.	1	Putnam	GARNER, James	1	Stewart

Name	Number	County	Name	Number	County
GARNER, Lemuel	12	Murray	GARRISON, Jas.	19	Coweta
GARNER, Thomas J.	1	Coweta	GARRISON, Levi	3	Stewart
GARNER, Thos.	8	Randolph	GARRITT, Harritt	10	Walton
GARNER, Wm.	9	Randolph	GARRITT, Henry B.	9	Muscogee
GARNETT, Eli	21	Lincoln	GARROTT, John	1	Washington
GARNETT, Jabez	1	Lincoln	GARTRELL, Joseph	62	Wilkes
GARNETT, Maryetta	4	Lincoln	GARTRELL, L. J.	13	Wilkes
GARNETT, James	3	Chatham	GARUIN, John	2	Lee
GARNETT, Paul	4	Screven	GARVEN, Ignatious P.	25	Richmond
GARR, John A.	2	Pike	GARVIN, David	11	Lumpkin
GARR, L.	8	Henry	GARVIN, James	1	Bibb
GARR, Thomas W.	19	Houston	GARWOOD, Johnson	7	Morgan
GARR, M. D.	13	Butts	GARWOOD, C. B.	2	Putnam
GARR, M. D. Jun.	4	Butts	GARY, ?	6	Elbert
GARR, Michael A.	2	DeKalb	GARY, Abner M.	4	Hancock
GARR, R. W.	3	DeKalb	GARY, William	14	McIntosh
GARRARD, S.	1	Henry	GARY, Henry	21	Baldwin
GARRARD, Jno.	16	Putnam	GARY, J. L.	15	Randolph
GARRARD, Wm.	20	Putnam	GASKILL, Jos.	7	Henry
GARRET, Charles	1	Meriwether	GASKINS, David	9	Telfair
GARRET, Hiram	15	Newton	GASS, David	4	Chatham
GARRET, Isaac	7	Campbell	GASS, Jesse H.	19	Troup
GARRET, Thos.	1	Henry	GASTEN, Wm. T.	15	Greene
GARRETT, -----	55	Camden	GASTIN, James	1	Heard
GARRETT, Benj.	13	Floyd	GASTIN, Wm.	2	Heard
GARRETT, D. A.	4	Muscogee	GASTON, Henry W.	4	Jasper
GARRETT, Elizabeth	2	Chattooga	GASTON, John	9	Merriwether
GARRETT, Elizabeth	20	Heard	GASTON, John T.	4	Troup
GARRETT, G. W.	8	Heard	GASTON, Joseph H.	14	Merriwether
GARRETT, H.	2	Chattooga	GASTON, Mathew	28	Butts
GARRETT, Henry	5	Jefferson	GATCHEL, E. H.	1	Camden
GARRETT, James R.	4	Walton	GATES, B. H. H.	5	Troup
GARRETT, Jesse	11	Troup	GATES, B. K.	20	Merriwether
GARRETT, John	4	Heard	GATES, Benjamin	72	Meriwether
GARRETT, Thomas C.	7	Jasper	GATES, Benjamin M.	2	Meriwether
GARRETT, Thomas D.	32	Heard	GATES, Charles	11	Troup
GARRETT, Thos. J.	8	Forsyth	GATES, James	42	Meriwether
GARRETT. T. W.	8	Troup	GATES, James	1	Meriwether
GARRETT, William	2	Merriwether	GATES, P.	11	Walker
GARRETT, William	1	Muscogee	GATES, Samuel K.	25	Meriwether
GARRETT, William	29	Wilkinson	GATES, Thomas	1	Houston
GARRETT, W. M.	1	Walker	GATES, James	30	Bibb
GARRETT, E.	6	Chattooga	GATES, Mary	11	Bibb
GARRETT, Greenberry	1	Chattooga	GATES, Thomas R.		
GARRETT, James	18	Stewart	agt for GRESHAM	28	Houston
GARRETT, Wm. T.	1	Chattooga	GATEWOOD, John H.	28	Putnam
GARRISON, George M.	3	Paulding	GATEWOOD, Rebbeca	65	Putnam
GARRISON, James J.	10	McIntosh	GATHRIGHT, William	2	Newton
GARRISON, Jas. F.	3	Carroll	GATHWRIGHT,		
GARRISON, Lovick	4	Paulding	Wm. M. Jun.	4	Jackson
GARRISON, Melas	4	Carroll	GATLIN, L. M.	1	Upson
GARRISON, Thomas W.	1	Franklin	GATT, Joel L.	5	Cherokee
GARRISON, Wm.	4	Carroll	GATTEN, Edward	4	Talbot
GARRISON, Darius	2	Telfair	GATTEN, Thomas M.	66	Thomas

Name	Number	County	Name	Number	County
GAUDECHONGE,			GEESLING, Samuel	5	Warren
Felicity	13	Chatham	GEIGER, Harmon	1	Hancock
GAUDFOY, Gazelle	3	Chatham	GEIGER, Harmon	20	Jasper
GAUDRY, Ann C.	5	Chatham	GEIGER, Jacob S.	2	Jasper
GAULDEN, Jonathan	59	Lowndes	GEIGER, David	4	Bryan
GAULDING, James	1	Chatham	GEIGER, James M.	9	Jasper
GAULDING, John N.	4	Troup	GEIGHER ?, James F.	3	Taliaferro
GAULDING, Rech.	20	Oglethorpe	GELL, G. W.	1	Heard
GAULDING, C. S.	26	Stewart	GELLENEAU, John	1	Chatham
GAUSE, J. R.	12	Randolph	GELMAN, William M.	9	Washington
GAUTHEN ?, Wylie S.	3	Walton	GEMKINS, Horace	1	Stewart
GAVIN, William	1	Clarke	GENDELL, William B.	4	Richmond
GAY, Allen	7	Early	GENLY, James	3	Habersham
GAY, Ann	1	Merriwether	GENTRY, Burgess	?	Fayette
GAY, Berry D.	1	Emanual	GENTRY, James H.	3	Troup
GAY, Elbert H.	25	Houston	GENTRY, N.	2	Hancock
GAY, Elbert H.	25	Jasper	GENTRY, Samuel	16	Hancock
GAY, Francis	10	Newton	GENTRY, Isaac L.	5	Stewart
GAY, George	5	Cass	GENTRY, Wm.	1	Coweta
GAY, Gilbert	19	Fayette	GEO. RAILROAD		
GAY, Gilbert	4	Fayette	& CO.	7	Greene
GAY, Isack B.	32	Fayette	GEO. R. ROAD & CO.	4	Greene
GAY, Jacob	10	Laurens	GEOGH, George	8	Burke
GAY, James	1	Jefferson	GEONOPOLY, Benjamin	1	Chatham
GAY, Joel	11	Newton	GEORGE, Alfred M.	29	Jones
GAY, John	1	Laurens	GEORGE, D.	6	Henry
GAY, Joseph Jr.	4	Monroe	GEORGE, David	1	Appling
GAY, Joseph Sen.	16	Monroe	GEORGE, Franklin	4	Jasper
GAY, Josiah	2	Laurens	GEORGE, Jesse	20	Heard
GAY, L. H.	9	Fayette	GEORGE, Joseph	4	Chatham
GAY, Lewis	5	Early	GEORGE, Joseph Jr.	9	Chatham
GAY, Richard	2	Emanual	GEORGE, Mary H.	8	Jones
GAY, Sherod H.	48	Jasper	GEORGE, William B.	15	Jones
GAY, Thomas B.	2	Fayette	GEORGE, E.	3	Crawford
GAY, Wiley J.	7	Fayette	GEORGE, Febath	6	Baker
GAY, Winston	4	Fayette	GEORGE, James	3	Baker
GAY, Ball	1	Bullock	GEORGE, James R.	18	DeKalb
GAY, Erasmus	17	Randolph	GEORGE, Mark A.	26	Talbot
GAY, Gasaway	11	Randolph	GEORGE, T. B.	2	DeKalb
GAY, Jas.	1	Randolph	GEORGIA RAILR.		
GAY, Joshua	4	Randolph	& BANK Co.	91	Richmond
GAY, Lewis	3	Randolph	GERALD, Isak	5	Coweta
GAY, Louis	1	Bullock	GERARD, Antoinette	1	Chatham
GAY, Richard	3	Randolph	GERARD, Georgia	3	Chatham
Gay, Solomon	11	Putnam	GERARD, Georgia A.	3	Chatham
GAY, William	1	Richmond	GERDTS, John	1	Chatham
GAYLORD, John A.	7	McIntosh	GERMANY, Mary	12	Pike
GAYNOR, Mary	1	Richmond	GERMANY, William	2	Pike
GAZAWAY, John C.	7	Harris	GERRALD, Anderson	8	Columbia
GEER, David	16	Greene	GERRALD, Erby	20	Columbia
GEER, J. F.	8	Greene	GERTMAN, John D.	14	Dooly
GEER, Levi	36	Troup	GERTMAN, David	40	Dooly
GEESLING, Benjamin	3	Warren	GERTMAN, Robert D.	7	Dooly
GEESLING, Flemming	11	Warren	GETER, Buck	2	Lincoln

Name	Number	County	Name	Number	County
GETER, Wiley	6	Lincoln	GIBSON, Springer	53	Paulding
GETTENGER, Phillip	11	Muscogee	GIBSON, Taylor F.	46	Jones
GEUDRON, Ellen	1	Richmond	GIBSON, William	10	Newton
GEURARD, Robert G.	58	Chatham	GIBSON, William	12	Warren
GHENT, Martha	4	Heard	GIBSON, (?)	10	Columbia
GHOLSON, John	4	Putnam	GIBSON, Augustus	32	Sumter
GHOLSON, Wm.	8	Putnam	GIBSON, Blanche	12	Stewart
GHOLSTON,			GIBSON, Eliza	3	Columbia
Col. Benjamin	21	Gwinnett	GIBSON, J. D. & J.	84	Decatur
GHOLSTON, James S.	4	Madison	GIBSON, Jacobus	20	Coweta
GHOLSTON, Nathaniel	13	Madison	GIBSON, Joseph C.	3	Campbell
GHOLSTON, Richard B.	3	Madison	GIBSON, L. A.	24	Columbia
GIBBINS, Andrew	2	Campbell	GIBSON, Luke	4	Coweta
GIBBONS, William	195	Chatham	GIBSON, Mary	52	Columbia
GIBBONS, Ann	5	Chatham	GIBSON, Polly	1	Richmond
GIBBONS, John	6	Coweta	GIBSON, Sarah	31	Columbia
GIBBONS, Joseph W.	1	Chatham	GIBSON, Wm. M.	1	Bibb
GIBBONS, William	147	Chatham	GICE, Jonas	12	Marion
GIBBONS, William	2	Chatham	GICE, Wm. H.	7	Harris
GIBBONS, William	60	Screven	GIDDENS, Francis	5	Jackson
GIBBS, J.	2	Irwin	GIDDENS, Hosea C.	1	Jackson
GIBBS, J. A.	4	Habersham	GIDDENS, Thomas M.	17	Muscogee
GIBBS, T. F.	16	Elbert	GIDDENS, Edward	14	Talbot
GIBBS, Thomas	9	Morgan	GIDDENS, Elizabeth	6	Talbot
GIBBS, Thomas	35	Walton	GIDDENS, Elizabeth	4	Talbot
GIBBS, Thomas	12	Walton	GIDDINGS, G. W.	3	Irwin
GIBBS, Thompson	1	Montgomery	GIDDINGS, Isham	6	Lowndes
GIBBS, Wm.	2	Floyd	GIDDINGS, Thomas	1	DeKalb
GIBBS, Elihu	1	Richmond	GIDEON, Barry	2	Gordon
GIBBS, John	7	Richmond	GIDEON ?, Chas. B.	19	Wilkinson
GIBLERT, Jackson	1	Dooly	GIGGER, Jerimiah	2	Effingham
GIBS, Matthew	8	Monroe	GIGNILLIAT, Henry G.	59	Glynn
GIBSON, Henry	9	Harris	GIGNILLIAT, N. P.	92	McIntosh
GIBSON, Henry	2	Warren	GIGNILLIAT,		
GIBSON, (?)	11	Decatur	William M.	42	Glynn
GIBSON, Albert	2	Harris	GIGNILLIAT, Wm. R.	80	McIntosh
GIBSON, Frances	23	Jones	GILBART, Amanda	2	Chatham
GIBSON, J. G.	3	Houston	GILBERT, A. G.	13	Henry
GIBSON, James	36	Upson	GILBERT, Drura	43	Upson
GIBSON, James	17	Wilkinson	GILBERT, Drury	14	Washington
GIBSON, James D.	1	Floyd	GILBERT, Edward	2	Walker
GIBSON, James W.	2	Houston	GILBERT, Elbert J.	7	Wilkinson
GIBSON, Jane	29	Paulding	GILBERT, Eliza H.	3	Hancock
GIBSON, Jemmimy	1	Upson	GILBERT, George	2	Murray
GIBSON, Joel	7	Troup	GILBERT, H. J.	2	Chatham
GIBSON, John Sen.	5	Wayne	GILBERT, Instant H.	7	Greene
GIBSON, John	9	Jasper	GILBERT, Isaac	10	Gwinnett
GIBSON, John C.	1	Merriwether	GILBERT, Isaac	1	Murray
GIBSON, Leroy	1	Monroe	GILBERT, J. C.	2	Henry
GIBSON, Littleton	1	Lincoln	GILBERT, James	2	Murray
GIBSON, Nancy	6	Newton	GILBERT, John B.	7	Chatham
GIBSON, O. C.	18	Upson	GILBERT, John B.	26	Lee
GIBSON, Richard T.	17	Chatham	GILBERT, John H.	1	Greene
GIBSON, Robert C.	34	Paulding	GILBERT, M.	4	Henry

Name	Number	County	Name	Number	County
GILBERT, Matthew	1	Morgan	GILLESPIE, Cleb G.	1	Cherokee
GILBERT, Michael E.	2	Dooly	GILLESPIE, D. L.	5	Lincoln
GILBERT, Ricd.	3	Wilkes	GILLESPIE, Daniel C.	3	Troup
GILBERT, Sarah	2	Clarke	GILLESPIE, James L.	1	Franklin
GILBERT, Thomas	21	Houston	GILLESPIE, John C.	8	Pike
GILBERT, William	14	DeKalb	GILLESPIE, Patterson R.	3	Franklin
GILBERT, William P.	18	Houston	GILLESPIE, Sarah	5	Oglethorpe
GILBERT, J. H.	9	Randolph	GILLESPIE, Thos.	2	Henry
GILBERT, Jno.	9	Randolph	GILLESPIE, William B.	2	Franklin
GILBERT, Lucinda	2	Bibb	GILLESPIE, Caleb	2	Cherokee
GILBERT, Nathan	1	Taliaferro	GILLESPIE, P. H.	2	Carroll
GILBERT, R. M.	22	Bibb	GILLIARD, Miss	1	Clarke
GILBERT, Robert	1	Bibb	GILLILAND, Allen	1	Cherokee
GILBERT, Thomas B.	39	Stewart	GILLILAND, David	1	Jackson
GILBERT, Wm. B.	17	Randolph	GILLILAND, Henderson	1	Jackson
GILBERT?, Edmund	20	Bibb	GILLILAND, Washn.	1	Jackson
GILBRATH (?), Tom	4	Columbia	GILLIS, John	8	Emanual
GILBREATH, Mary	1	Union	GILLIS, John D.	4	Emanual
GILDER, J. P.	5	Fayette	GILLIS, Norman	6	Montgomery
GILDER, U. M.	9	Fayette	GILLIS, Rodrick	7	Montgomery
GILDER, Irby	2	Randolph	GILLUM, Wm. H.	3	Greene
GILES, Alexander	5	Washington	GILMAN, George R.	12	Oglethorpe
GILES, B. M.	4	Houston	GILMAN, John H.	23	Lee
GILES, David	11	Houston	GILMAN, W. W.	5	Lee
GILES, Enoch	2	Fayette	GILMER, Francis	13	Hall
GILES, John M.	7	Houston	GILMORE, Alexander	4	Washington
GILES, John W.	3	Marion	GILMORE, James H.	5	Washington
GILES, Moses	3	Houston	GILMORE, John	31	Washington
GILES, William B.	23	Chatham	GILMON, John	1	Cherokee
GILES, John	4	Columbia	GILMORE ? , James	1	Talbot
GILES, John	9	Sumter	GILMORE, H.J. W.	1	Butts
GILES, John F.	2	Butts	GILMORE, R. F.	1	Butts
GILES, T. J.	2	Butts	GILMORE, Robert	2	Richmond
GILES, Thomas	1	Walton	GILMORE, Willaim	11	Butts
GILES, W.H.	3	Butts	GILNER, George W.	8	Pike
GILEY, Jackson B.	1	Walton	GILPIN, Joseph	3	Sumter
GILGORE?, Robt.	1	Carroll	GILREATH, James	1	Chattooga
GILHAM, E. M.	20	Oglethorpe	GILREATH, Nelson	1	Cass
GILHAM, R. L.	7	Troup	GILREATH, George	5	Cass
GILHAM, Thos. A.	1	Oglethorpe	GILSTRAP, Jeremiah M.	8	Jasper
GILHAM, W. C.	14	Oglethorpe	GILSTRAP, Wm.	4	Meriwether
GILL, Ellender	1	Jones	GILSTRAP, Wyly	3	Habersham
GILL, H. G.	1	Lee	GILSTRAP, Benjamin E.	61	Burke
GILL, J. H.	9	Floyd	GILSTRAP, Rial W.	13	Burke
GILL, John	4	Wayne	GIPSON, Obedience	1	Henry
GILL, Richard	6	Effingham	GIPSON, S.	4	Henry
GILL, Thos. Y.	5	Wilkes	GIPSON, Benj.	3	Randolph
GILL, Hillard	3	Chatham	GIPSON, Sylvanus	6	Upson
GILL, William	4	Meriwether	GIPSON, Thos.	4	Bibb
GILLAM, Horace	2	Chatham	GIRADEAUX, Wm. P.	7	Liberty
GILLAN, Patrick	2	Wilkes	GIRARD, Martha	6	Muscogee
GILLEAN?, Thos. H.	2	Oglethorpe	GIRARD, William N.	19	Muscogee
GILLEN, Joab	7	Baker	GIRTMAN, Andrew	7	Jefferson
GILLESPIE, Allen M.	2	Pike	GIRTMAN, Benjamin F.	7	Telfair

Name	Number	County	Name	Number	County
GIST, E. P.	4	Camden	GLENN, Dr. Sam	12	Oglethorpe
GIVINS, Mrs.	1	Bibb	GLENN, Francis A.	10	Floyd
GLADDEN, Elias	1	Walker	GLENN, John	7	Early
GLADDEN, Solomon	3	Washington	GLENN, John	2	Oglethorpe
GLADDIN, Jonatha.	4	Hancock	GLENN, John A.	6	Early
GLADING, James	3	Monroe	GLENN, John A.	5	Troup
GLANTON, Abner	64	Troup	GLENN, John C,.	6	Chatham
GLANTON, Dempsey	9	Marion	GLENN, John w.	18	Jackson
GLANTON, Luke	4	Troup	GLENN, Joshua N.	15	Clarke
GLANTON, Samuel	2	Troup	GLENN, L. J.	9	Henry
GLASCOCK,			GLENN, M.	1	Oglethorpe
Edmund B.	6	Richmond	GLENN, Mary	14	Oglethorpe
GLASS, Elijah	11	Fayette	GLENN, Patience	9	Washington
GLASS, J. D.	5	Henry	GLENN, R. M.	3	Oglethorpe
GLASS, J. T.	10	Henry	GLENN, Sarah	15	Early
GLASS, James	25	Newton	GLENN, Thos. L.	7	Oglethorpe
GLASS, James B.	14	Merriwether	GLENN, W. H.	9	Oglethorpe
GLASS, Joseph N.	2	Walton	GLENN, William	1	Muscogee
GLASS, Manson	24	Fayette	GLENN, William	4	Oglethorpe
GLASS, Mary	6	Troup	GLENN, William	4	Oglethorpe
GLASS, Thomas	9	Walker	GLENN, William Jun.	25	Oglethorpe
GLASS, William	13	Harris	GLENN, William B.	17	Washington
GLASS, William	3	Merriwether	GLENN, Wm. H.	19	Heard
GLASS, William P.	2	Meriwether	GLENN, George W.	6	Cass
GLASS, Zachariah	5	Newton	GLENN, J. N. for		
GLASS, Frederick	3	Fayette	Mr. Darracott	23	Clarke
GLASS, James	17	Sumter	GLENN, John	17	Butts
GLASS, Love	30	Coweta	GLENN, John	3	DeKalb
GLASS, Samuel B.	1	Sumter	GLENN, John	22	Stewart
GLASTON, George T.	1	Coweta	GLENN, Joseph	8	Stewart
GLATIGNY, John A.	2	Chatham	GLENN, Wm. W.	5	Randolph
GLAWSON, Jesse	8	Jones	GLESON, Jacob G.	16	Burke
GLAZE, John	6	Troup	GLESSON, Jno.	4	Randolph
GLAZE, Joseph L.	1	Cherokee	GLINAN ? , Mike	4	Taliaferro
GLAZE, Mary Ann	22	Marion	GLISSON, Evan C.	31	Burke
GLAZE, Samuel	5	Lincoln	GLOOMER, Joshua	1	Effingham
GLAZE, Susan	7	Lincoln	GLOVER, Eli	17	Jasper
GLAZE, T. G.	21	Lincoln	GLOVER, Eli T.	16	Jasper
GLAZE, W. D.	13	Lincoln	GLOVER, Elizabeth	10	Franklin
GLAZE, William	24	Harris	GLOVER, Henry	39	Houston
GLAZE, William	5	Harris	GLOVER, Henry J.	9	Jasper
GLAZE, William H. Sen.	4	Harris	GLOVER, James M.	1	Franklin
GLAZE, Thos.	4	Putnam	GLOVER, James T.	12	Twiggs
GLEASON, Patrick	1	Richmond	GLOVER, Jesse	17	Jefferson
GLEATON, Mary	1	Dooly	GLOVER, John	9	Jasper
GLEATON, Wm.	2	Dooly	GLOVER, John	16	Twiggs
GLEN, George	49	Chatham	GLOVER, John G.	1	Twiggs
GLENAFORD(?), H.	26	Decatur	GLOVER, John H.	33	Cobb
GLENDINNING, John	9	Richmond	GLOVER, Nathaniel S.	20	Jones
GLENDINNING,			GLOVER, Thomas	39	Twiggs
William	11	Richmond	GLOVER, Thos.	2	Twiggs
GLENN, George M.	7	Walker	GLOVER, Wiley	16	Jones
GLENN, James R.	9	Jackson	GLOVER, Wyley	1	Heard
GLENN, Charlott	16	Oglethorpe	GLOVER, B. G.	4	Coweta

Name	Number	County	Name	Number	County
GLOVER, Isham	28	Sumter	GODFREY, Susan	7	Chatham
GLOVER, J. J.	6	Putnam	GODIN, John	2	Dooly
GLOVER, J. P.	4	Crawford	GODKINS, James W.	6	Greene
GLOVER, J. P.	1	Decatur	GODWIN, B.	5	Meriwether
GLOVER, Job	4	Sumter	GODWIN, Jesse A.	1	Harris
GLOVER, Larkin	3	Sumter	GODWIN, John S.	1	Dooly
GLOVER, Robert D.	8	Richmond	GODWIN, Thos. G.	13	Lee
GLOVER, Sterling	1	Sumter	GODWIN, Alexander	2	Baker
GLOVER, Will	1	Stewart	GODWIN, Arnold	1	Sumter
GNANN, Benjamin	33	Effingham	GODWIN, Rufus L.	1	Sumter
GNANN, Christian	2	Effingham	GODWIN, Silas	3	Dooly
GNANN, Christopher	1	Effingham	GODWIN, William J.	9	Troup
GNANN, Elbert	1	Effingham	GOETCHUS, R. R.	17	Muscogee
GNANN, Jacob	14	Effingham	GOETCHY (?), (?)	43	Columbia
GNANN, Jonathan	1	Effingham	GOFF, Jacob W.	6	Houston
GNANN, Joseph	1	Chatham	GOFF, William	11	Laurens
GNANN, Joshua	2	Effingham	GOFF, William F.	1	Washington
GNANN, Joshua	1	Effingham	GOFF, David	15	Randolph
GOBER, Craddock	2	Franklin	GOGANS, John T.	6	Monroe
GOBER, Fanny	1	Gwinnett	GOGGANS, Madison	10	Monroe
GOBER, Francis	2	Gwinnett	GOGGINS, A. J.	3	Carroll
GOBER, John	1	Cobb	GOGGINS, Josiah	5	Carroll
GOBER, John	9	Franklin	GOHRAM, Jackson	9	Greene
GOBER, John F.	4	Jackson	GOING, Nancy	5	Columbia
GOBER, John M.	6	Forsyth	GOLATT, Charles	16	Troup
GOBER, William H.	4	Franklin	GOLATT, George	4	Harris
GOBER, Wm.	12	Jackson	GOLDEN, Francis	2	Muscogee
GOBER, Wm. C.	8	Meriwether	GOLDIN?, A. A.	3	Pike
GOBER, Thos. C.	1	DeKalb	GOLDING, Mary	2	Chatham
GOBER?, Robert H.	1	Cherokee	GOLDING, Pleasant	3	DeKalb
GODARD, Daniel	12	Monroe	GOLDING, Thomas	1	Stewart
GODARD, James	23	Jones	GOLDNELL?, R. Mc.	6	Bibb
GODARD, Simon	8	Jones	GOLDSBERRY,		
GODARD, Wiley F.	10	Jones	Alfred P.	2	Marion
GODBEE, Freeman	4	Burke	GOLDSBERRY, Robt.	6	Marion
GODBEE, Elizabeth	5	Burke	GOLDSMITH, William	8	DeKalb
GODBEE, Elizabeth	3	Burke	GOLDSMITH, T.	10	Cass
GODBEE, James	10	Burke	GOLDWINE, Wm. H.	6	Lowndes
GODBEE, James F.	2	Burke	GOLDWIRE,		
GODBEE, Martha	4	Burke	Henrietta O.	14	Lowndes
GODBEE, Martin	3	Burke	GOLDWIRE, James O.	19	Lowndes
GODBEE, S. & H.	12	Burke	GONARD, Joseph	1	Henry
GODBEE, Saml. estate	10	Burke	GONDER, Martha	4	Hancock
GODBEE, Simeon	15	Burke	GONEKE, L. A.	6	Randolph
GODBEE, Simeon S.	3	Burke	GONEKEE, John D.		Randolph
GODDARD, Thomas H.	10	Chatham	GONGT, Elis H.	2	Richmond
GODDARD, L. P.	2	Butts	GOOCHER, Wm. H.	4	Early
GODDARD, Lucius	8	Butts	GOOD, Nicolas	5	Newton
GODDARD, S. F.	7	Bibb	GOOD, Robt.	3	Randolph
GODDEN, Mrs. S.	2	Decatur	GOOD, Saml.	2	Bibb
GODFREY, George	9	Meriwether	GOODALL, Seaborn	3	Chatham
GODFREY, Charlotte	3	Burke	GOODARD, Henry	1	Pike
GODFREY, Ellen G.	3	Chatham	GOODBREAD, Thos.	16	Glynn
GODFREY, James S.	5	Thomas	GOODE, Benj.	5	Upson

Name	Number	County	Name	Number	County
GOODE, Hamilton	7	Warren	GOODWYN, George W.	4	Monroe
GOODE, John M.	10	Troup	GOODYEAR, T.	5	Bibb
GOODE, Thomas W.	16	Upson	GOOGE, J. W.	2	Floyd
GOODMAN, Aaron	39	Harris	GOOLBY, A.	18	Oglethorpe
GOODMAN, Aaron	9	Merriwether	GOOLBY, Kirby	13	Jasper
GOODMAN, Isaac	14	Jasper	GOOLBY, Nancy	10	Oglethorpe
GOODMAN, Isaac	1	Lowndes	GOOLBY, Nancy	32	Oglethorpe
GOODMAN, John	10	Butts	GOOLSBE, E.	1	Early
GOODMAN, John L.	3	Harris	GOOLSBY, A.	6	Oglethorpe
GOODMAN, John	6	Bullock	GOOLSBY, A.	5	Oglethorpe
GOODMAN, L. agent	10	Crawford	GOOLSBY, Allen	8	Oglethorpe
GOODMAN, Samuel	1	Stewart	GOOLSBY, Allen	1	Oglethorpe
GOODMAN, Sarah	11	Bullock	GOOLSBY, Ansen	1	Marion
GOODMAN?,			GOOLSBY, Artimus	8	Jasper
William H.	3	Cobb	GOOLSBY, Burgess	2	Jones
GOODRICH, Henry C.	1	Richmond	GOOLSBY, C. L.	29	Jasper
GOODRICH, William H.	62	Richmond	GOOLSBY, Cardin	86	Jasper
GOODRIGE?, E. R.	1	Pike	GOOLSBY, Jacob	14	Jasper
GOODROU, Jacob	2	Walker	GOOLSBY, James	1	Jasper
GOODRUM, James A.	4	Monroe	GOOLSBY, Levi	1	Jones
GOODRUM, John	33	Monroe	GOOLSBY, William	13	Jasper
GOODRUM, Thos. G.	1	Habersham	GOOLSBY, William	20	Oglethorpe
GOODRUM, Wm. G.	5	Habersham	GOOLSBY, William J.	32	Jasper
GOODSEN, William H.	3	Walton	GOOLSBY, Micajah	2	Talbot
GOODSON, Alexander	5	Marion	GOOP(?), Ephraim	3	Dade
GOODSON, Cordy	4	Houston	GORAIN, Madam	2	Clarke
GOODSON, Furney	1	Fayette	GORAM, Milton	1	Talbot
GOODSON, Jordan	10	Fayette	GORDAN, Henry	42	Jones
GOODSON, Michl.	2	Carroll	GORDAN, James	21	Walker
GOODSON, Noel	3	Jasper	GORDAN, James	14	Harris
GOODSON, Noel	4	Marion	GORDAN, Joseph	1	Harris
GOODSON, Andrw.	1	Carroll	GORDAN, Willis	6	Harris
GOODSON, Gordon J.	7	Bryan	GORDEN, Eleanor	7	Cobb
GOODSON, John w.	8	Baker	GORDIN, John	4	Elbert
GOODSON, M Cordy	4	Jasper	GORDON, A. G.	1	Harris
GOODSON, Thomas B.	1	Walker	GORDON, A. W.	2	Franklin
GOODWIN, Elmina	4	Gwinnett	GORDON, Agnes	1	Jefferson
GOODWIN, John S.	4	Twiggs	GORDON, Andrew G.	27	Walker
GOODWIN, Robt. M.	3	Habersham	GORDON, Dr. James M.	7	Gwinnett
GOODWIN, Solomon	2	DeKalb	GORDON, Ellinor	3	Jefferson
GOODWIN, Stertery?	3	DeKalb	GORDON, Few	7	Gwinnett
GOODWIN, Theodore	21	Baldwin	GORDON, Geo. W.	25	Walker
GOODWIN, Thos. D.	10	Coweta	GORDON, James H.	25	Walker
GOODWIN, W.	2	Henry	GORDON, James W.	6	Pike
GOODWIN, B.	7	Coweta	GORDON, John	13	Clarke
GOODWIN, G.	15	Talbot	GORDON, John	11	Jasper
GOODWIN, Harris	5	DeKalb	GORDON, John D.	153	Early
GOODWIN, J. H.	1	Crawford	GORDON, John V.	1	Pike
GOODWIN, Jas.	7	Coweta	GORDON, L. H.	19	Walker
GOODWIN, Joseph	1	Talbot	GORDON, Lavinia	3	Walker
GOODWIN, Josiah	8	Crawford	GORDON, Louisa	8	Jasper
GOODWIN, Ruffin	11	Talbot	GORDON, Robert		Cass
GOODWIN, Ruffin	4	Talbot	GORDON, Susan L.	3	Gwinnett
GOODWYN, Coalman G.	27	Monroe	GORDON, Thomas	12	Jefferson

Name	Number	County	Name	Number	County
GORDON, Thomas	11	Jones	GOULD, James F.	18	Glynn
GORDON, Thomas	2	Monroe	GOULD, John D.	16	Chatham
GORDON, Wiley C.	2	Pike	GOULD, Marion	8	Liberty
GORDON, William	3	Jones	GOULD, Thos. K. estate	23	McIntosh
GORDON, William	1	Marion	GOULD, Caleb	2	Carroll
GORDON, William	8	Murray	GOULD, William T.	4	Richmond
GORDON, Winston	6	Murray	GOULDEN, William B.	17	Liberty
GORDON, Wm.	10	Cass	GOULDS, John P.	2	Richmond
GORDON, J. W.	1	Coweta	GOULION, B.M.	1	Stewart
GORDON, John	19	Dooly	GOULL, Washington	2	Walker
GORDON, John E. D.	3	Richmond	GOULSBY, Jesse	1	Walton
GORDON, Peter	9	Coweta	GOWDER, Oliver	18	Hall
GORDON, Robert W.	1	Burke	GOWDLOCK, James	11	Hall
GORDON, Samuel	2	Burke	GOWEN, James	14	Glynn
GORDON, W. G.	7	Crawford	GOWEN, Barney	16	Camden
GORDY, Willson	14	Muscogee	GOWER, Robert	4	Gwinnett
GORE, Clement	1	Marion	GOYE, Johnathan H.	1	Houston
GORE, F.	6	Stewart	GRABILL, Mrs.	11	Muscogee
GORE, Henry	8	Walker	GRACE, Benj.	1	Bibb
GORE, Pharis	2	Stewart	GRACE, Joshua	4	Pike
GORHAM, John	5	Troup	GRACE, Mathew	3	Houston
GORLEY, Wm. A	40	Putnam	GRACE, Mrs.	1	Tatnall
GORMAN, J. B.	9	Bibb	GRACE, Samuel	16	Houston
GORMAN, John B.	48	Talbot	GRACE, Thomas	1	Warren
GORMAN, Wiliam H.	4	Campbell	GRACE, Thomas T.	9	Houston
GORMLY, Michael	9	Talbot	GRACE, William	2	Houston
GORMON, Claiborn	19	Campbell	GRACE, William A.	1	Houston
GORSE?, Jas. A.	1	Putnam	GRACE, Wm. H.	5	Muscogee
GORTCHEUS, R. ? Jr.	7	Richmond	GRACE, George	4	Crawford
GORUM, Jas.	1	Troup	GRACE, Thos. A.	11	Coweta
GORUM , Th.	10	Troup	GRACE, William	1	Talbot
GOSA, Bird	1	DeKalb	GRADDY, Calvin	9	Randolph
GOSHA?, Davis E.	9	DeKalb	GRADDY, Hays	8	Randolph
GOSLIN?, Charles	1	Habersham	GRADDY, Wm.	10	Randolph
GOSS, B.	9	Elbert	GRADIE, Lewis	3	Harris
GOSS, Benjamin	8	Lumpkin	GRADY, John W.	3	Lumpkin
GOSS, H. J.	24	Elbert	GRADY, William S.	6	Clarke
GOSS, H. J.	2	Elbert	GRADY, C.	1	Decatur
GOSS, Isham	3	Walton	GRADY, Haywood	19	Randolph
GOSS, Isham J. M.	4	Jackson	GRADY, J.	6	Decatur
GOSS, J. G.	4	Troup	GRAFTON, Daniel	4	Henry
GOSS, J. H.	2	Elbert	GRAGG, Robert G.	11	Pike
GOSS, Lucy	23	Merriwether	GRAGG, S. P.	12	Twiggs
GOSS, Nathaniel	4	Gilmer	GRAGG, Israel	9	Twiggs
GOSS, William P.	3	Franklin	GRAHAM, Abner	17	Clarke
GOSS, E. G.	2	Stewart	GRAHAM, D.	6	Wilkinson
GOSS, Joseph	2	Stewart	GRAHAM, David	8	Walker
GOSS, Stephen	4	Stewart	GRAHAM, Harriet W.	7	Madison
GOSS, Wm. G.	4	Camden	GRAHAM, Isiah	4	Hancock
GOSS, Z.	2	Stewart	GRAHAM, Jesse	1	Effingham
GOSSETT, John	2	Jones	GRAHAM, John	4	Chatham
GOULD, Horace B.	13	Glynn	GRAHAM, John T.	1	Lumpkin
GOULD, Jacob F.	25	Chatham	GRAHAM, John W.	1	Newton
GOULD, James	36	Glynn	GRAHAM, Martin	11	Hall

Name	Number	County	Name	Number	County
GRAHAM, Mary	14	Lowndes	GRAVES, B.	1	Lincoln
GRAHAM, Mary A.	2	Appling	GRAVES, Charles	1	Fayette
GRAHAM, W. H.	12	Lumpkin	GRAVES, Charles M.	1	Harris
GRAHAM, Alex.	1	Telfair	GRAVES, Frederick	1	Murray
GRAHAM, Daniel	2	Telfair	GRAVES, George W.	6	Newton
GRAHAM, David	2	Hall	GRAVES, G. W. -		
GRAHAM, David	3	Stewart	MITCHELL, George	8	Walton
GRAHAM, Duncan B.	6	Telfair	GRAVES, J. L.	26	Newton
GRAHAM, Emaline	3	Dooly	GRAVES, James	2	Fayette
GRAHAM, Ezekiel	6	Cass	GRAVES, James	1	Harris
GRAHAM, James	7	Stewart	GRAVES, Joel S.	1	Thomas
GRAHAM, Jas.	10	Coweta	GRAVES, John	3	Wilkes
GRAHAM, John	1	Richmond	GRAVES, John H.	4	Walton
GRAHAM, Robert	15	Upson	GRAVES, John S.	34	Newton
GRAHAM, Thompson	9	Upson	GRAVES, Joseph	1	Monroe
GRAHAM, William	11	Dooly	GRAVES, Major L.	2	Newton
GRAHAM, William	8	Stewart	GRAVES, Minton	2	Fayette
GRAHAM, William H.	3	Richmond	GRAVES, R.	7	Wilkinson
GRAHAM, Wm. H.	1	Randolph	GRAVES, Robert	4	Lincoln
GRAHAM?, Frances	7	Newton	GRAVES, Barzille	23	Randolph
GRANADE, Anna	2	Warren	GRAVES, Joseph A.	5	Burke
GRANADE, Feliz	2	Warren	GRAVES, Martha H.	8	Richmond
GRANADE, Stephen	1	Warren	GRAVES, Mary	7	Randolph
GRANADE, Susan	7	Warren	GRAVES, Solomon	40	Randolph
GRANBERRY, George	35	Harris	GRAVES, Thomas Estate	22	Walton
GRANBERRY, Joseph J.	3	Sumter	GRAVES, Thomas A.	6	Walton
GRANBERRY, Langley	6	Stewart	GRAVES, Unity	6	Putnam
GRANDE, Benjamin	1	Warren	GRAVES, Wm. B.	5	Randolph
GRANT, Alfred	2	Clarke	GRAVES?, Samuel	9	Madison
GRANT, Augustus l.	2	Muscogee	GRAVES?, William L.	2	Madison
GRANT, Charles	56	Glynn	GRAY, (?)	6	Decatur
GRANT, Daniel	1	Hancock	GRAY, A.	3	Pike
GRANT, Daniel	27	Upson	GRAY, A. W.	13	Henry
GRANT, Hugh F.	125	Glynn	GRAY, B.	37	Houston
GRANT, J. L.	9	Merriwether	GRAY, Benjamin	23	Houston
GRANT, James	5	Merriwether	GRAY, Davis	16	Harris
GRANT, John	1	Habersham	GRAY, Elizabeth	2	Washington
GRANT, John F.	41	Walton	GRAY, Geroge W.	1	Jackson
GRANT, John H.	3	Early	GRAY, J. F.	27	Elbert
GRANT, Joseph	1	Greene	GRAY, J. G.	4	Clarke
GRANT, Kenneth	6	Newton	GRAY, J. M.	5	Muscogee
GRANT, Pois?	1	Harris	GRAY, James	2	Carroll
GRANT, Rolin	1	Meriwether	GRAY, James	22	Talbot
GRANT, Lemuel P.	3	DeKalb	GRAY, James	6	Walker
GRANT, Nathan F.	4	Talbot	GRAY, James M.	41	Jones
GRANT, Susan	1	Crawford	GRAY, Jas.	1	Henry
GRANT, William	1	DeKalb	GRAY, John	7	Elbert
GRANTHAM, M.M.	2	Union	GRAY, John	1	Jones
GRANTHAM, Samuel	34	Upson	GRAY, John	4	Thomas
GRANTHAM, Thomas	1	Lumpkin	GRAY, John D. & Co.	23	Murray
GRANTLAND, S.	20	Baker	GRAY, William	2	Washington
GRANTLAND, Seataon	89	Baldwin	GRAY, Johnson	3	Butts
GRAPON, Thomas	1	Dade	GRAY, Joseph	3	Elbert
GRAVE, E.	3	Bibb	GRAY, Joshua	2	Early

Name	Number	County	Name	Number	County
GRAY, Martha S.	32	Chatham	GREEN, Benjamin	17	Cobb
GRAY, Mary Jane	1	Muscogee	GREEN, Benjamin	61	Lee
GRAY, N.	1	Muscogee	GREEN, Burrell	3	Monroe
GRAY, Nancy	1	Lincoln	GREEN, Burrell	15	Pike
GRAY, Nancy	3	Paulding	GREEN, C. C.	3	Early
GRAY, Rachel	1	Clarke	GREEN, Daniel F.	1	Pike
GRAY, Richard	2	Muscogee	GREEN, Edward H.	3	Newton
GRAY, Richard M.	2	Muscogee	GREEN, Elias	8	Gwinnett
GRAY, Saml.	9	Henry	GREEN, Francis A.	36	Pike
GRAY, Samuel	8	Marion	GREEN, Frederick M.	2	Cobb
GRAY, W. C.	1	Elbert	GREEN, Green B.	1	Jones
GRAY, William C.	3	Muscogee	GREEN, Harriet H.	9	Chatham
GRAY, Abram	14	Coweta	GREEN, Heartford	1	Pike
GRAY, Frank	1	Chattooga	GREEN, Hugh W.	6	Macon
GRAY, George	7	Columbia	GREEN, James	27	Jones
GRAY, George S.	33	Chatham	GREEN, James	16	Lee
GRAY, Hosea	2	Coweta	GREEN, James	1	Marion
GRAY, J. D.	5	Burke	GREEN, James	1	Muscogee
GRAY, J. P.	1	Decatur	GREEN, James P.	11	Jones
GRAY, Michael	1	Richmond	GREEN, James L.	4	Macon
GRAY, Mincvhi	5	Burke	GREEN, James R.	24	Monroe
GRAY, Mrs.	6	Tatnall	GREEN, Jas.	6	Camden
GRAY, P. W.	10	Crawford	GREEN, Jas. A.	1	Forsyth
GRAY, Rebbecca	3	Tatnall	GREEN, Jesse	2	Cherokee
GRAY, Rebecca	2	Decatur	GREEN, Joel A.	1	Cobb
GRAY, Richard	2	Burke	GREEN, John	1	Chatham
GRAY, Robert	1	Taliaferro	GREEN, John	1	Dooly
GRAY, Thos.	3	Coweta	GREEN, John	27	Lee
GRAY, Wm.	16	Bibb	GREEN, John	42	Monroe
GRAY?, Thomas	15	Talbot	GREEN, John	2	Monroe
GRAY, Zechariah	1	Washington	GREEN, John	16	Pike
GRAYBILL, John	47	Hancock	GREEN, John F.	32	Murray
GRAYBILL, Jas. S.	8	Bibb	GREEN, John H.	8	Habersham
GRAYBILL, John W.	4	Washington	GREEN, John O.	6	Franklin
GRAYBILL, Judith	19	Baldwin	GREEN, John W.	18	Emanual
GRAYBILL, M. L.	6	Bibb	GREEN, Joseph	3	Putnam
GRAYBILL, Tully	10	Washington	GREEN, Joseph P.	2	Cobb
GRAYHAM, David	1	Oglethorpe	GREEN, Leonard	46	Monroe
GREAVES, Thos. S.	4	Randolph	GREEN, Levi	1	Jasper
GREATHOUSE, Early	4	Troup	GREEN, Levi	1	Murray
GREEN, A. B.	4	Upson	GREEN, Miles S.	5	Houston
GREEN, B. G.	7	Troup	GREEN, Moses P.	23	Burke
GREEN, E.	1	Wilkinson	GREEN, Mountain	7	Pike
GREEN, Easm	1	Wilkinson	GREEN, Napoleon B.	1	Cobb
GREEN, H.H.	11	Troup	GREEN, Raleigh	20	Upson
GREEN, James T.	32	Lee	GREEN, Rice B.	7	Walton
GREEN, John	3	Troup	GREEN, Robert	4	Early
GREEN, John B.	9	Wilkes	GREEN, Robert H.	3	Muscogee
GREEN, Amos	7	Cherokee	GREEN, Samual	21	Emanual
GREEN, Anderson	1	Carroll	GREEN, Samuel	2	Marion
GREEN, Arthur A.	2	Greene	GREEN, Thomas	11	Chatham
GREEN, Augustus	18	Greene	GREEN, Thomas	28	Lee
GREEN, Benedict H.	12	Jones	GREEN, Thomas	3	Murray
GREEN, Benjamin	8	Chatham	GREEN, Thomas B.	31	Upson

Name	Number	County
GREEN, Thornberry	1	Jones
GREEN, W.	13	Troup
GREEN, W. A.	7	Hancock
GREEN, W. H.	32	Lee
GREEN, William	9	Monroe
GREEN, William	1	Monroe
GREEN, William M.	8	Jasper
GREEN, Wm.	2	Troup
GREEN, Wm. G.	50	Hancock
GREEN, Wm. H.	1	Habersham
GREEN, Wm. H.	13	Jefferson
GREEN, Wml	9	Macon
GREEN, A. H.	4	Carroll
GREEN, Abram	6	Richmond
GREEN, Allen	3	Richmond
GREEN, Bartlett G.	5	Stewart
GREEN, C. K.	6	Bibb
GREEN, Catherin	4	Richmond
GREEN, Charles	4	Chatham
GREEN, Cintha	19	DeKalb
GREEN, David	10	Richmond
GREEN, Frederick	30	Sumter
GREEN, G. D.	61	Coweta
GREEN, G. J.	3	Crawford
GREEN, George W.	1	Cass
GREEN, J. A.	2	Randolph
GREEN, J. V.	10	Bibb
GREEN, J. W.	12	Bibb
GREEN, James D.	2	Columbia
GREEN, Jesse P. estate	106	Burke
GREEN, John	1	Dooly
GREEN, John G.	36	Burke
GREEN, John T.	3	Richmond
GREEN, Mary	4	Richmond
GREEN, Mary J.	3	Chatham
GREEN, Robert D.	5	DeKalb
GREEN, Thomas	12	Talbot
GREEN, Thomas	11	Talbot
GREEN, Thomas H.	15	Baldwin
GREEN, Thos.	13	Randolph
GREEN, William	3	Richmond
GREEN, William	31	Screven
GREEN, William B.	32	Burke
GREEN, William B.	8	Richmond
GREEN, William T.	6	Baldwin
GREEN, Wm. E.	1	Campbell
GREENAWAY, William	15	Burke
GREENE, B. F.	7	Greene
GREENE, Burwell	7	Macon
GREENE, David	1	Warren
GREENE, J. M.	11	Henry
GREENE, Lemuel H.	9	Greene
GREENE, Richard A.	4	Macon
GREENE, W. H.	15	Henry
GREENE, William C.	13	Cobb
GREENE, Miller	15	Baldwin
GREENE, Phillip H.	8	Troup
GREENE, Phillip H.	25	Troup
GREENERWAY, J. H.	2	Elbert
GREENFIELD, Allen	8	Chatham
GREENLIEF, Luther H.	1	Campbell
GREENVILLE, Charles E.	5	Richmond
GREENWAY, John W.	1	Jackson
GREENWAY, M.	1	Troup
GREENWOLD, W. H.	1	Muscogee
GREENWOOD, E. S.	11	Muscogee
GREENWOOD, T. C.	4	Muscogee
GREENWOOD, Thomas B.	13	Troup
GREENWOOD, Thomas B.	39	Troup
GREENWOOD, George A.	13	Rabun
GREENWOOD, H. & U.	48	Burke
GREENWOOD, Sarah	26	Richmond
GREENWOOD, Thomas E.	12	Richmond
GREER, Alfred	3	Merriwether
GREER, Allen H.	1	Macon
GREER, Aquila	1	Greene
GREER, Benjamin F.	2	Muscogee
GREER, Crawford	27	Jasper
GREER, Francis M.	25	Merriwether
GREER, Gilbert	23	Merriwether
GREER, James	7	Troup
GREER, John C.	43	Clarke
GREER, John R.	3	Jasper
GREER, Joseph	8	Monroe
GREER, Thomas	51	Jasper
GREER, A. S.	22	Butts
GREER, A. S.	13	Butts
GREER, Archibald P.	4	Baker
GREER, Rebecca	7	Washington
GREER, Samuel	1	Butts
GREER, Thomas H.	2	Baldwin
GREER, W.	19	Troup
GREER, William	9	Talbot
GREER, William C.	2	Dooly
GREGG, Ann	3	McIntosh
GREGORY, Benj.	7	Clarke
GREGORY, Benjamin	1	Newton
GREGORY, G.	1	Clarke
GREGORY, H. B.	3	Jefferson
GREGORY, Jackson	16	Cobb
GREGORY, Ellen	21	Sumter
GREGORY, Henry	1	Bibb
GREGORY, J. M.	3	Chatham

Name	Number	County
GREGORY, J. W.	11	Stewart
GREGORY, John	1	Thomas
GREGORY, William	4	Butts
GREGORY, Wm.	21	Putnam
GREGRY, Susanna	2	Monroe
GREINER, John	39	Washington
GREINER, John P.	25	Burke
GRENBYS WAREHOUSE	4	Muscogee
GRESHAM ?, Susan	7	Taliaferro
GRESHAM, Catherine	15	Greene
GRESHAM, Chas.	27	Wilkes
GRESHAM, E. L.	19	Henry
GRESHAM, George	3	Wilkes
GRESHAM, George M.	8	Cobb
GRESHAM, Harris	1	Jones
GRESHAM, Hezekial	2	Upson
GRESHAM, Jane	6	Wilkes
GRESHAM, J. J.	28	Houston
GRESHAM, Jas. D.	1	Wilkes
GRESHAM, Jeptha J.	3	Pike
GRESHAM, John	13	Pike
GRESHAM, Joseph M.	4	Henry
GRESHAM, Kauffman	25	Wilkes
GRESHAM, Marion G.	8	Pike
GRESHAM, Rebecca	5	Wilkes
GRESHAM, Sterling A.	38	Greene
GRESHAM, Thos. S.	11	Oglethorpe
GRESHAM, V. D.	21	Greene
GRESHAM, William	4	Cobb
GRESHAM, William	29	Oglethorpe
GRESHAM, Absalom	2	Taliaferro
GRESHAM, Edmund	33	Burke
GRESHAM, Edmund B.	21	Burke
GRESHAM, Edmund B.	19	Burke
GRESHAM, J. J.	9	Bibb
GRESHAM, Lemuel	11	Sumter
GRESHAM, Nancy	22	Stewart
GRESHAM, Pleasant	8	Talbot
GRESON ?, P. C.	6	Walton
GREST, Valentine	23	Liberty
GREY, Albert	5	Walton
GREY, J. D.	8	Bibb
GRICE, Mrs. Sarah	1	Houston
GRICE, S.	16	Henry
GRIER, Moses	25	Early
GRIER, Robert	4	Paulding
GRIER, Thomas	2	Warren
GRIER, Thomas	2	Warren
GRIER, W.	30	Henry
GRIER, Aaran W.	21	Taliaferro
GRIER, James	69	Stewart
GRIER, Parillo	9	Butts
GRIER, S.	9	Randolph
GRIER, Thos.	14	Randolph
GRIEVES, Susan J.	14	Chatham
GRIEVES, Julia	1	Chatham
GRIFF, Fereby	1	Richmond
GRIFFET, Archer	48	Oglethorpe
GRIFFIN, Asa	15	Hall
GRIFFIN, Asy	15	Hall
GRIFFIN, Asy L.	1	Hall
GRIFFIN, Charles H.	17	Troup
GRIFFIN, Dan.	1	Pulaski
GRIFFIN, Daniel	6	Muscogee
GRIFFIN, Daniel	4	Muscogee
GRIFFIN, David	4	Emanual
GRIFFIN, E.	1	Henry
GRIFFIN, E.	24	Twiggs
GRIFFIN, E. B.	15	Meriwether
GRIFFIN, Ezekiel	10	Paulding
GRIFFIN, Hansford w.	6	Macon
GRIFFIN, J. J.	21	Hall
GRIFFIN, J. L.	6	Floyd
GRIFFIN, J. R.	22	Chattooga
GRIFFIN, James	27	Burke
GRIFFIN, James	1	Jackson
GRIFFIN, James	5	Ware
GRIFFIN, Jas. S.	4	Harris
GRIFFIN, Jno. C.	3	Henry
GRIFFIN, John	2	Fayette
GRIFFIN, John	1	Walton
GRIFFIN, John A.	9	Fayette
GRIFFIN, John H.	6	Monroe
GRIFFIN, John W.	8	Pike
GRIFFIN, M. D.	9	Houston
GRIFFIN, Mary	1	Chatham
GRIFFIN, Mary P.	1	Pike
GRIFFIN, Noah H.	2	Lowndes
GRIFFIN, N. M.	2	Troup
GRIFFIN, Robt. F.	8	Greene
GRIFFIN, S. H.	4	Pike
GRIFFIN, Thomas	1	Emanual
GRIFFIN, Thomas	1	Walton
GRIFFIN, Thos.	1	Lee
GRIFFIN, Walter	4	Greene
GRIFFIN, William	5	Twiggs
GRIFFIN, William Sr.	1	Gwinnett
GRIFFIN, Wm.	25	Henry
GRIFFIN, Wm.	12	Lee
GRIFFIN, Aaron	1	Burke
GRIFFIN, Ann	12	Burke
GRIFFIN, B. F.	3	Bibb
GRIFFIN, Baldy	1	Stewart
GRIFFIN, Bush	1	Stewart
GRIFFIN, Charles	3	Cass
GRIFFIN, Francis	1	DeKalb
GRIFFIN, Hardy	24	Baker

Name	Number	County	Name	Number	County
GRIFFIN, James	13	Decatur	GRIGGS, John W.	14	Troup
GRIFFIN, Joel	2	Bibb	GRIGGS, Maria L.	31	Harris
GRIFFIN, John	43	Coweta	GRIGGS, Maria L.	23	Harris
GRIFFIN, John B.	2	Talbot	GRIGGS, Rhodom	1	Carroll
GRIFFIN, Jonas	12	Stewart	GRIGGS, Robt.	10	Hancock
GRIFFIN, Jonas	3	Stewart	GRIGGS, Robert	26	Troup
GRIFFIN, Joseph	2	Burke	GRIGGS, Asa W.	6	Carroll
GRIFFIN, Joshua	42	Columbia	GRIGGS, C. W.	11	Putnam
GRIFFIN, L.	13	Decatur	GRIGGS, Jas.	18	Putnam
GRIFFIN, Leroy	12	DeKalb	GRIGGS, Jas.	9	Putnam
GRIFFIN, Madison	3	Taliaferro	GRIGGS, Robert	52	Putnam
GRIFFIN, Madison	1	Taliaferro	GRIGGS, Wesley	70	Putnam
GRIFFIN, Martha	37	Taliaferro	GRIMBELL, Mary A.	12	Chatham
GRIFFIN, Mrs. L.	21	Decatur	GRIMES, Harriet	3	Greene
GRIFFIN, Mrs. Sarah	5	Stewart	GRIMES, David L.	12	Heard
GRIFFIN, R.	14	Decatur	GRIMES, G.W.	59	Oglethorpe
GRIFFIN, Richard	29	Columbia	GRIMES, Lewis	1	Early
GRIFFIN, Richard	1	Putnam	GRIMES, S. F.	9	Muscogee
GRIFFIN, Robert H.	4	Chatham	GRIMES, Thomas C.	92	Hancock
GRIFFIN, Thos. M.	25	Coweta	GRIMES, Thomas C.	15	Hancock
GRIFFIN, W.	8	Coweta	GRIMES, Thomas W.	6	Muscogee
GRIFFIN, Washington	3	Burke	GRIMES, G. W.	1	Bibb
GRIFFIN, William	13	Decatur	GRIMES, John	1	Baldwin
GRIFFIN,			GRIMES, John	25	Bullock
William J. & Co.	2	Cobb	GRIMES, John	22	Stewart
GRIFFIN, Wm.	7	Taliaferro	GRIMES, M. A.	3	Coweta
GRIFFIT, James	1	Monroe	GRIMES, R.	1	Decatur
GRIFFITH, Benjamin	10	Gilmer	GRIMES, William D.	12	Washington
GRIFFITH, C. T.	2	Clarke	GRIMES?, Washigton	1	Madison
GRIFFITH, Caleb	6	Cherokee	GRIMS, W.	15	Elbert
GRIFFITH, D. H.	28	Clarke	GRIMSBY, Thos.	2	Twiggs
GRIFFITH, E. L. W.	3	Jackson	GRIMSLEY, Richard	2	Stewart
GRIFFITH, Frederick	1	Early	GRIMSLEY, William	13	Columbia
GRIFFITH, James B.	10	Madison	GRIMSLY, Jeremiah W.	5	Early
GRIFFITH, James L.	18	Clarke	GRIMSLY, Joseph	10	Early
GRIFFITH, John	9	Clarke	GRINDER, S.	1	Decatur
GRIFFITH, John	35	Madison	GRINDLE, John	1	Lumpkin
GRIFFITH, Lucy H.	4	Cobb	GRINER ? , Joshua	1	Tatnall
GRIFFITH, M. R.	2	Clarke	GRINER, B. W.	11	Tatnall
GRIFFITH, Oliver P.	9	Madison	GRINER, Elizabeth	6	Screven
GRIFFITH, Robert P.	15	Madison	GRINER, Martin	1	Bullock
GRIFFITH, Sarah	9	Madison	GRINER, Sarah	1	Bullock
GRIFFITH, Stephen	4	Cherokee	GRINER, William	11	Bullock
GRIFFITH, William	4	Madison	GRINER, William	2	Screven
GRIFFITH, William R.	4	Gilmer	GRINGER, James	2	Screven
GRIFFITH, A.D.E.	9	Clarke	GRINGER, John	2	Screven
GRIFFITH, Jas.	1	Crawford	GRINNELL, H. P.	1	Forsyth
GRIFFITH, L L.	5	Cherokee	GRINNET, A. J.	8	Henry
GRIFFITH, R. N .	2	Baker	GRINNETT, J. T.	5	Chattooga
GRIGGS, B. T.	7	Muscogee	GRISE ?, William	1	Tatnall
GRIGGS, Benj. R.	8	Hancock	GRISHAM, D. C.	11	Merriwether
GRIGGS, Dealina	3	Merriwether	GRISHAM, E.	7	Pike
GRIGGS, James O.	16	Paulding	GRISHAM, J. J.	33	Houston
GRIGGS, John	20	Jasper	GRISHAM, Nancy	24	Walton

Name	Number	County	Name	Number	County
GRISHAM, William	5	Cherokee	GROVER, Daniel R.	8	Bullock
GRISHAM, William	8	Stewart	GROVES, John J.	9	Stewart
GRISHAM, Willliam	14	Walton	GROVES?, Stephen C.	1	Madison
GRIST, F.	61	Early	GRUBBS, Ashford	1	Heard
GRISWOLD, Giles H.	42	Jones	GRUBBS, H.	4	Lee
GRISWOLD, Samuel	91	Jones	GRUBBS, James	81	Burke
GRISWOLD, E.	3	Camden	GRUBBS, Silas	3	Jasper
GRIZZARD?, Wm.	23	DeKalb	GRUBBS, Silas M.	5	Harris
GROCE, Alison	6	Pike	GRUBBS, Clarissa	2	Richmond
GROCE, Charles	2	Chatham	GRUGER, David	1	Chatham
GROCE, L.	4	Bibb	GRUHUND?, Elisha	3	Muscogee
GROCE, L. J.	6	Bibb	GRUMBLIS, Robert V.	1	Chatham
GROGAN, Thomas	4	Walker	GRUNNISS?, E. C.	2	Bibb
GROGAN, Thomas W.	1	Cobb	GUDGER, William	4	Gilmer
GROGAN, Wm.	9	DeKalb	GUERRY, Daniel	5	Houston
GROGG, John	1	Cobb	GUERRY, James	15	Houston
GROGHAN, Peter	1	Monroe	GUERRY, John M.	1	Harris
GRONBECK, Thomas	1	Muscogee	GUERRY, Mrs. T.	1	Muscogee
GROOMS, Benjamin	3	Tatnall	GUERRY, Peter N.	8	Muscogee
GROOMS, Joshua	1	Tatnall	GUERRY, James P.	33	Sumter
GROOMS, Mrs.	2	Tatnall	GUERRY, James P.	4	Sumter
GROOMS, Wiley	31	Thomas	GUERRY, Manassa M.	3	Sumter
GROOVER, Abner	16	Thomas	GUERRY, William B.	5	Sumter
GROOVER, Aley	4	Effingham	GUESS, Henry	2	Cobb
GROOVER, Charles	13	Thomas	GUESS, Joseph	1	Cobb
GROOVER, David	1	Bullock	GUESS, William	1	Murray
GROOVER, John	2	Bullock	GUEST, A.	1	Henry
GROOVER, James	45	Thomas	GUEST, W.	4	Henry
GROOVER, John	1	Thomas	GUEST, David	2	Franklin
GROOVER, Joshua S.	2	Thomas	GUEST, Jas. B.	1	Wilkes
GROOVER, Josiah	14	Thomas	GUEST, Jesse	2	Taliaferro
GROOVER, Martha	3	Bullock	GUEST, Miles G.	2	Ware
GROOVER, Samuel	6	Bullock	GUEST, N. Est.	8	Wilkes
GROOVER, William	9	Bullock	GUEST, Sarah	18	Burke
GROOVER, William W.	10	Thomas	GUFFIN, Andrew	1	Newton
GROSMAYER, Henry	1	Bibb	GUFFORD, William	3	Sumter
GROSS, L. D.	11	Merriwether	GUICE ?, Mrs. Jane	7	Stewart
GROSS, Mrs. Jane	1	Meriwether	GUICE, W. S.	7	Lincoln
GROSS, David	3	Screven	GUICE, William	3	Newton
GROSS, E. B.	8	Screven	GUICE, John B.	2	Richmond
GROSS, Thomas	14	Screven	GUILFORD ?, Jas. W.	13	Randolph
GROUGHTY, Domonic	2	Chatham	GUILFORD, Colson	23	Randolph
GROVE, John	6	Stewart	GUILFORD, Wm. M.	2	Randolph
GROVENSTEIN, Benjamin	11	Effingham	GUILLANS, Travis	23	Burke
GROVENSTEIN, Geo. W.	4	Effingham	GUILMARTIN, John F.	3	Chatham
GROVENSTEIN, J.	1	Chatham	GUIMYS?, Eliza C.	8	Newton
GROVENSTEIN, Lewis	8	Effingham	GUIN, Sarah	5	Muscogee
GROVENSTEIN, Shadrach	13	Effingham	GUIN, Thomas	8	Muscogee
GROVENSTINE, Henry	1	Camden	GUISE, Nicholas	13	Muscogee
GROVER, Edward	2	Cobb	GUISE, Rachael	3	Merriwether
GROVER, James	4	Macon	GULLATT, Absalom	16	Troup
			GULLATT, Peter	28	Wilkes
			GULLATT, William	22	Lincoln
			GULLETT, John M. T.	5	Marion

Name	Number	County	Name	Number	County
GUNBEY, Wm.	5	Lincoln	HA(?), Alexander	4	Dade
GUNBY, George	12	Cherokee	HAAMBRICK, Jas.	2	Carroll
GUNBY, John H.	1	Chatham	HABERSHAM, B. C.	5	Habersham
GUNBY, Mary	9	Columbia	HABERSHAM,		
GUNN, ?	5	Muscogee	Joseph Clay	5	Chatham
GUNN, Daniel G.	31	Morgan	HABERSHAM,		
GUNN, Green G.	8	Jones	Wm. Wyle	9	Chatham
GUNN, Jas. R.	7	Hancock	HABERSHAM, Robert	53	Chatham
GUNN, Jesse	15	Harris	HABERSHAM, Robert		
GUNN, Jesse	6	Harris	plantation no. 1	128	Chatham
GUNN, John	8	Jefferson	HABERSHAM, Robert		
GUNN, Larkin R.	2	Muscogee	plantation no. 2	80	Chatham
GUNN, Lewis F.	4	Jefferson	HABERSHAM, Stephen	225	Chatham
GUNN, Matilda	50	Houston	HABERSHAM, Susan	16	Chatham
GUNN, F.	1	Butts	HABERSHAM,		
GUNN, Jesse T.	29	Butts	William W.	3	Chatham
GUNN, John R.	8	Taliaferro	HABERSHEM, R. W.	5	Habersham
GUNN, Jonathan	27	Taliaferro	HABORRAN?, Catherin	2	Bibb
GUNN, Raford	18	Warren	HACHER, Sarah	1	Baker
GUNN, Richard	11	Taliaferro	HACK & DURAL	1	Richmond
GUNN, Robert	38	Wayne	HACK, Daniel D. B.	4	Richmond
GUNN, Sarah	5	Bibb	HACKELL, Eliza	2	Richmond
GUNN, Thomas	1	Talbot	HACKET, Maurice	1	Chatham
GUNN, Wm.	16	Taliaferro	HACKET, William	5	Harris
GUNN, Wm. N.	9	Taliaferro	HACKET, William P.	33	Harris
GUNN?, J. W. agt.	13	Bibb	HACKET, William	10	DeKalb
GUNNELS, Ethan	8	Franklin	HACKET?, David J.	3	Morgan
GUNTER ? , Isham	1	Walton	HACKETT, Drucilla	24	Habersham
GUNTOR, J. N.	1	Elbert	HACKETT, John T.	4	Habersham
GUNTOR, J. W .	7	Elbert	HACKETT, Sarah E.	7	Habersham
GUNTOR, James	2	Elbert	HACKETT, Wm. T.	12	Habersham
GUNTOR, John	20	Elbert	HACKNEY, Jas. M.	7	Wilkes
GUTHERY, N.	16	Walton	HACKNEY, Jas. T.	31	Wilkes
GUTHRIE, Simeon	5	Muscogee	HACKNEY, John O.	2	Wilkes
GUTTENDERGER,			HACKNEY, R. M.	7	Coweta
T. G.	3	Bibb	HACKNY, John O.	2	Paulding
GUY, Hinton J.	1	Talbot	HADDEN, Benjamin	9	Jefferson
GUY, William	2	Ware	HADDEN, Thomas	1	Jefferson
GUYTON, Archibald	13	Effingham	HADDOCK, Caswell	9	Jones
GUYTON, C. B.	3	Laurens	HADDOCK,		
GUYTON, Elmira	49	Laurens	Solomon M.	2	Houston
GUYTON, Moses	35	Laurens	HADDOCK, Jas.	3	Randolph
GUYTON, T. N.	7	Laurens	HADDOX, John	1	Harris
GUYTON, John	11	Cass	HADDOX, M. W.	1	Harris
GUYTON, N. F.	1	Cass	HADEN, Gorden	9	Stewart
GUYTON, Robt.	1	Cass	HADEN, Saml.	2	Stewart
GUYTON, Wm.	1	Cass	HADEN, Samuel	9	Stewart
GWALTNEY, E.	9	Henry	HADLEY, Joseph J.	1	Harris
GWENNUDD, Jane	1	Fayette	HADLEY, Lewis L.	12	Thomas
GWINN, D. T.	2	Henry	HADLEY, Samuel H.	87	Thomas
GWINN, Covington G.	1	Dade	HADLEY, Simon D.	21	Thomas
GWINN, John	2	Dade	HADLEY, Thos.	4	Harris
GWYN, John	3	Floyd	HADLEY, Davis B.	19	Burke
GWYN, W. S.	7	Floyd	HADLY, Davis B.	4	Richmond

Name	Number	County	Name	Number	County
HAGAN, Allen	5	Thomas	HAIRISON, Wm. B .	3	Bibb
HAGAN, Ethrael	5	Bullock	HAISE, William B.	4	Troup
HAGAN, J. S.	4	Bullock	HALE, Daniel	1	Troup
HAGAN, Jas.	3	Bullock	HALE, Elipha C.	4	Warren
HAGAN, Jeptha	13	Bullock	HALE, Henry	3	Heard
HAGAN, John C.	1	Bullock	HALE, James	3	Monroe
HAGAN, Malakiah	3	Bullock	HALE, James Revd.	3	Gwinnett
HAGAN, Margaret	39	Bullock	HALE, James	5	Upson
HAGAN, Wm.	1	Bullock	HALE, James	3	Walton
HAGARMON, Harrison	12	Talbot	HALE, Joel	10	Clarke
HAGGIA, Newton	24	Cobb	HALE, John	5	Newton
HAGGINS, Asa	1	Coweta	HALE, Joseph	3	Clarke
HAGGOOD, G. B.	4	Clarke	HALE, Obid	3	Walton
HAGGOOD, H.	10	Walton	HALE, Reedy C.	4	Greene
HAGGOOD, John	3	Newton	HALE, S. G.	2	Walton
HAGGOOD, Middleton	1	Washington	HALE, Silas	6	Clarke
HAGGOOD, Polly	7	Clarke	HALE, Silus G.	3	Walker
HAGGOOD, Thomas	6	Upson	HALE, Susan	1	Troup
HAGGOOD, Wiley	1	Cherokee	HALE, Thompson	1	Gwinnett
HAGGOOD, Wm. B.	3	Clarke	HALE, William	3	Monroe
HAGGOOD, F. M.	3	Cherokee	HALE, William O.	1	Warren
HAGIN, James	7	Pike	HALE, Wm. B.	1	Clarke
HAGINS, Nancy	1	Harris	HALE, Cornelius	2	Chatham
HAGINS, Robt. D.	1	Harris	HALE, J. M. agent	38	Crawford
HAGMAN, Elisha	2	Burke	HALE, N. H.	5	Crawford
HAGON, W.	1	Bibb	HALE, Tharp	8	Randolph
HAGSON, William B.	69	Chatham	HALE, Thos.	16	Decatur
HAHN, John	5	Richmond	HALES, John	7	Paulding
HAIL, Jno.	3	Henry	HALES, Thomas	7	Murray
HAIL, Mary	4	Monroe	HALEY, Jas. R.	9	Franklin
HAIL, Moab	13	Clarke	HALEY, Joel	18	Madison
HAIL, Benj.	1	Butts	HALEY, John J.	55	Pike
HAILE, James	9	Fayette	HALEY, Lucy	5	Franklin
HAILE, Lindsey	4	Pike	HALEY, M. B.	49	Lee
HAILES, John	7	Clarke	HALEY, S. L.	12	Putnam
HAILY, John	12	Elbert	HALEY, Wm. H.	6	Putnam
HAILY, W. R.	3	Elbert	HALIBURTON, D.	52	Houston
HAINE ?, William	10	Richmond	HALL, John T.	2	Harris
HAINE, Susan S.	1	Richmond	HALL, A. J.	1	Muscogee
HAINES, Alvin O.	10	Washington	HALL, A. J.	1	Muscogee
HAINES, David	11	Fayette	HALL, Alexander	31	Merriwether
HAINES, Eligah	6	Fayette	HALL, Almann	3	Clarke
HAINES, James	3	Fayette	HALL, Asa	9	Elbert
HAINES, James Sr.	5	Fayette	HALL, Christiana	5	Pike
HAINES, John M.	1	Fayette	HALL, Daniel G.	2	Emanual
HAINES, N. W.	15	Washington	HALL, Elihu	16	Greene
HAINS, James	3	Fayette	HALL, Enoch	2	Lowndes
HAINS, A. J.	1	Elbert	HALL, Gehu	3	Appling
HAINS, Bryhar?	16	Lee	HALL, George	19	Greene
HAINS, L.	3	Elbert	HALL, H. T.	2	Muscogee
HAINS, Jane	7	Washington	HALL, Harvey	7	Muscogee
HAINS, John	1	Sumter	HALL, Henry	7	Monroe
HAIR, William	1	Clarke	HALL, Hugh	36	Greene
HAIR, Roger	1	Baker	HALL, Hugh A.	6	Greene

Name	Number	County	Name	Number	County
HALL, Instance	8	Appling	HALL, George	1	Walker
HALL, Isaac L.	3	Laurens	HALL, H.	1	Decatur
HALL, J. M.	1	Henry	HALL, H. T.	10	DeKalb
HALL, James	16	Montgomery	HALL, J. M. B.	7	Wilkinson
HALL, Jeremiah T.	1	Madison	HALL, James	2	Burke
HALL, John	8	Cobb	HALL, James	4	Warren
HALL, John	25	Greene	HALL, James	32	Wilkinson
HALL, John	1	Laurens	HALL, James H.	8	Washington
HALL, John	14	Merriwether	HALL, James M.	2	Baldwin
HALL, John A.	1	Appling	HALL, Jane	1	Bibb
HALL, John E.			HALL, Jas. G.	4	Bibb
agt for BEAL, N. H.	40	Houston	HALL, Joel	23	Warren
HALL, John F.	8	Appling	HALL, John	1	Baker
HALL, John G.	8	Pike	HALL, John	23	Butts
HALL, John H.	45	McIntosh	HALL, John	39	Wilkinson
HALL, Levi	7	Harris	HALL, John M.	13	Warren
HALL, Limon	1	Emanual	HALL, Jonathan	7	Thomas
HALL, M. D.	4	Oglethorpe	HALL, Juniper	1	Thomas
HALL, Mariah	17	Elbert	HALL, Louisa	5	Richmond
HALL, Nancy	5	Appling	HALL, Lyman A.	1	Wilkinson
HALL, Nancy	1	Madison	HALL, Morgan	24	Sumter
HALL, Pleasant B.	6	Harris	HALL, Peter	1	Chatham
HALL, R. D.	4	McIntosh	HALL, R. P.	9	Bibb
HALL, R. P.	2	Elbert	HALL, Rebecca	6	Baldwin
HALL, R. S.	9	Hancock	HALL, Richard	5	Talbot
HALL, R. T.	3	Newton	HALL, Robt.	5	Troup
HALL, Saml.	16	Hancock	HALL, Saml.	9	Bibb
HALL, Sarah	14	Hancock	HALL, Samuel	38	Warren
HALL, Sarah	24	Marion	HALL, Samuel	7	Warren
HALL, Sebron	17	Appling	HALL, T. O.	2	Wilkinson
HALL, Thomas	8	Harris	Hall, Thomas J.	3	Richmond
HALL, Thomas	2	Harris	HALL, Todd	14	Wilkinson
HALL, Thomas	2	Murray	HALL, Wesley	1	Baldwin
HALL, U. J.	8	Oglethorpe	HALL, William	5	Screven
HALL, William	5	Emanual	HALL, William	1	Baker
HALL, William	4	Madison	HALL, William	8	Washington
HALL, William	19	Talbot	HALL, William	12	Washington
HALL, William K.	1	Macon	HALL, William G.	4	Richmond
HALL, William M.	4	Harris	HALL, William H.	2	Washington
HALL, Willis	1	Emanual	HALL, William J.	4	Richmond
HALL, Wm. B.	24	Hancock	HALL, William T.	2	Talbot
HALL, Wm. H. F.	1	Meriwether	HALL, William W.	17	Baker
HALL, Zelpha	16	Thomas	HALL, Young	19	Troup
HALL, Armija	42	Baker	HALL, Zachariah	26	Tatnall
HALL, Benjamin	7	Thomas	HALLEM?, George	1	Heard
HALL, Charles	3	Richmond	HALLIBURTON, David	33	Houston
HALL, Charles H.	16	Baldwin	HALLMAN, Geo. W.	1	Forsyth
HALL, E.	12	Crawford	HALLOWS, Miller	30	Camden
HALL, E. M.	4	Rabun	HALLS estate	17	Bullock
HALL, Ezekiel	42	Twiggs	HALMILTON, Adin	19	Houston
HALL, Frances	1	Sumter	HALMPTON, Jno.	8	Crawford
HALL, Francis	2	Sumter	HALSELY, C. S.	3	Chatham
HALL, Francis M.	2	Telfair	HALSELY, D. F.		
HALL, George	6	Richmond	executor	9	Chatham

Name	Number	County	Name	Number	County
HALSEY, A. G.	9	Newton	HAMILTON, Arthur	1	Monroe
HALSEY, E. S.	9	Henry	HAMILTON,		
HALSTEAD, John L.	2	Houston	Col. Mathew	2	Gwinnett
HALSTEAD, Willis S.	4	Muscogee	HAMILTON, Cyrus	3	Harris
HALSTON, Thomas	7	Newton	HAMILTON, Eliza	3	Wilkes
HALSY, D. F. executor	7	Chatham	HAMILTON, George	1	Harris
HALTEWAGER, George	4	Effingham	HAMILTON, Henrietta	12	Liberty
HALVESTON, Randolf	4	Camden	HAMILTON, Irwin	5	Pulaski
HAM, B.	14	Elbert	HAMILTON, Jas.	11	Pulaski
HAM, John	9	Monroe	HAMILTON, Jno.	5	Pulaski
HAM, Mary H.	8	Monroe	HAMILTON, John	1	Harris
HAM, Milton	2	Marion	HAMILTON, John	21	Murray
HAM, R. C.	2	Monroe	HAMILTON, John	2	Thomas
HAM, S.	7	Elbert	HAMILTON, John	15	Thomas
HAM, Stephen R.	8	Houston	HAMILTON, John	43	Thomas
HAM, W. R.	12	Elbert	HAMILTON, John G.	3	Montgomery
HAM, David	1	Baker	HAMILTON, Josiah	10	Montgomery
HAM, Jesse E.	8	Bryan	HAMILTON, Lucy	1	Newton
HAM, John B.	1	Dooly	HAMILTON, Mrs. S.	5	Muscogee
HAMACK, Wiley	104	Macon	HAMILTON, Mary	2	Warren
HAMACK, John	6	Taliaferro	HAMILTON, Nancy	8	Cass
HAMACK, M. W.	3	Crawford	HAMILTON, R.	9	Clarke
HAMACK, T. D.	18	Crawford	HAMILTON, Thos. N.	14	Clarke
HAMAK, Henry	1	Columbia	HAMILTON, Wade	5	Thomas
HAMAN, James	1	Upson	HAMILTON, William	1	Gwinnett
HAMAN, Martha	2	Upson	HAMILTON, William	5	Meriwether
HAMBRICH, R. B. agt.	2	Carroll	HAMILTON, Wm. C.	1	Gordon
HAMBRICK, James P.	2	Houston	HAMILTON, A.	4	Chattooga
HAMBRICK, James P.			HAMILTON, A. M.	7	Cass
agt for NESBIT	26	Houston	HAMILTON, Benjamin	23	Dooly
HAMBRICK, Harrison	1	Troup	HAMILTON, C. A.	15	Cass
HAMBRICK, Jeremiah	1	Monroe	HAMILTON, Cogdell	29	Dooly
HAMBRICK, Joseph	27	DeKalb	HAMILTON, Crozier	2	Richmond
HAMBRIGHT, Lawson	6	Walker	HAMILTON, Edley L.	2	Cass
HAMBY, D. C.	14	Walton	HAMILTON, George K.	4	DeKalb
HAMBY, Isaac	4	Newton	HAMILTON, J. J.	1	Chattooga
HAMBY, Jonathan	5	Meriwether	HAMILTON, J. M.	8	Chattooga
HAMBY, Thos. J.	3	Harris	HAMILTON, James	206	Columbia
HAMEL?, William S.	41	Dooly	HAMILTON, James	89	Columbia
HAMELL, George	3	Talbot	HAMILTON, James T.	8	Cass
HAMER, John	5	Harris	HAMILTON, M. H.	15	Chatham
HAMES, Joshua	1	Sumter	HAMILTON, Mary	9	Cass
HAMES, Robert T.	1	Sumter	HAMILTON, Robert	10	Sumter
HAMES, William	4	Sumter	HAMILTON, Robt.	8	Decatur
HAMES, Wm.	11	Troup	HAMILTON, S. G.	9	Cass
HAMIL, E. R.	2	Pike	HAMILTON, Saml.	2	Chattooga
HAMIL, George	1	Pike	HAMILTON, T. Lynch	58	Chatham
HAMIL, Hugh	1	Pike	HAMILTON, Thomas	49	Cass
HAMIL, James W.	3	Pike	HAMILTON, Thomas N.	45	Columbia
HAMILL, John	31	Talbot	HAMILTON, Thomas N.	32	Taliaferro
HAMILLON?, Mrs. N.	2	Meriwether	HAMILTON, Thos.	51	Columbia
HAMILTON, Andrew M.	4	Cass	HAMILTON, William G.	8	Dooly
HAMILTON, Archibald	11	Gwinnett	HAMLET, Jeptha	2	Stewart
HAMILTON, Archibald	4	Gwinnett	HAMLETT, John	4	Chatham

Name	Number	County	Name	Number	County
HAMLIN, William E.	6	Monroe	HAMMONDS, Abram	113	Walton
HAMLIN, James	2	Monroe	HAMMONS, Wm. P.	1	Cherokee
HAMLIN, John	7	Monroe	HAMMONS, E. H.	2	Putnam
HAMLIN, John C.	1	Upson	HAMOCK, Asa	2	Walton
HAMLIN, John C.	37	Upson	HAMON?, Charles	2	Lee
HAMLIN, Leonard	2	Monroe	HAMOND, C. C.	2	Murray
HAMM, S.	33	Elbert	HAMONS, Jesse	2	Cobb
HAMMACK, Charalotty	10	Jones	HAMPTON, A. Z.	60	Laurens
HAMMACK, Lewis	2	Sumter	HAMPTON, Ann J.	58	Laurens
HAMMEL, Elisha	18	Merriwether	HAMPTON, George	3	Madison
HAMMELL, Jno.	4	Randolph	HAMPTON, Henry	16	Oglethorpe
HAMMET, William	15	Troup	HAMPTON, John J.	52	Houston
HAMMETT, Elizabeth	1	Warren	HAMPTON, William	2	Houston
HAMMETT, Major F.	1	Troup	HAMPTON, Eliz.	2	Clarke
HAMMETT, Thomas J.	1	Warren	HAMPTON, Henry	24	Columbia
HAMMICK, Thomas B.	1	Cobb	HAMPTON, J.	1	Screven
HAMMIL, Clark	14	Butts	HAMPTON, Jacob	1	Crawford
HAMMIL, W. J.	1	Butts	HAMPTON, James	3	Burke
HAMMILL, Mrs. Mariah	7	Muscogee	HAMPTON,		
HAMMILL, Sarah	2	Talbot	James D. trustee	12	Baker
HAMMIT, Wm.	2	Heard	HAMPTON, Jas.	7	Crawford
HAMMND, Leroy	31	Cherokee	HAMPTON,		
HAMMOCK, D. F.	4	Heard	Simeon estate	19	Burke
HAMMOCK, James	1	Twiggs	HAMPTON, Wiliam L.	39	Baker
HAMMOCK, Jeptha J.	1	Jasper	HAMPTON, Wm.	1	Wilkes
HAMMOCK, Joseph	5	Muscogee	HAMRICK, T.	15	Henry
HAMMOCK, Moses	5	Wilkes	HAMRICK, W. T.	26	Lee
HAMMOCK, Simion	5	Macon	HAMS, Y.S.G.	17	Clarke
HAMMOCK, Benj.	1	Randolph	HAMS, Benj.	26	Macon
HAMMOCK, John	1	Tatnall	HAMS, J. W.	21	Randolph
HAMMOCK, John P.	2	Talbot	HANCELY, Wesly	5	Monroe
HAMMOCK, V. .D.	5	Randolph	HANCOCK, Armsted	1	Harris
HAMMOCK, Wm.	1	Randolph	HANCOCK, Charlotte	2	Murray
HAMMOND, A.	63	Elbert	HANCOCK, Durham	1	Thomas
HAMMOND, A. P.	3	Troup	HANCOCK, Hardy	4	Thomas
HAMMOND, Abner	10	Houston	HANCOCK, James	1	Upson
HAMMOND, Chas.	8	Henry	HANCOCK, Joel	5	Upson
HAMMOND, F.	3	Elbert	HANCOCK, John	5	Thomas
HAMMOND, J. W.	9	Monroe	HANCOCK, Jno. R.	1	Jackson
HAMMOND, John	2	Monroe	HANCOCK, John M.	5	Jackson
HAMMONG, John J.	16	Walton	HANCOCK, John W.	8	Lowndes
HAMMOND, Thomas	26	Morgan	HANCOCK, Margaret	5	Thomas
HAMMOND, W.A.	11	Morgan	HANCOCK, Mary	6	Houston
HAMMOND, William	10	Murray	HANCOCK, Richardson	25	Madison
HAMMOND, Wm. P.	3	Cherokee	HANCOCK, Richardson	4	Madison
HAMMOND, Abner	6	Bibb	HANCOCK, Robert	1	Jackson
HAMMOND, Abner	5	Richmond	HANCOCK, Thomas	16	Clarke
HAMMOND, Emanuel	1	Tatnall	HANCOCK, William D.	2	Murray
HAMMOND, Hope H.	14	Talbot	HANCOCK, Wm.	8	Jackson
HAMMOND, John	5	Baldwin	HANCOCK, A.	1	Coweta
HAMMOND, Moses	2	Tatnall	HANCOCK, A.	19	Randolph
HAMMOND, Sarah A.	17	Baldwin	HANCOCK, Clement	22	Putnam
HAMMOND?, William	1	Harris	HANCOCK, James	1	Tatnall
HAMMONDS, A. T.	1	Troup	HANCOCK, Morgan	1	Crawford

129

Name	Number	County	Name	Number	County
HANCOCK, Thomas	1	Talbot	HANSON, Columbus	9	Newton
HANCOCK, Wm.	4	Crawford	HANSON, Enoch	24	Monroe
HANCOCK?, W. F.	41	Lee	HANSON, James B.	1	Pike
HAND, Columbus W.	4	Houston	HANSON, Margaret	14	Wilkes
HAND, J. H.	2	Houston	HANSON, Michael	3	Washington
HAND, Jesse	3	Henry	HANSON, P. H.	51	Oglethorpe
HAND, Joseph R.	7	Macon	HANSON, S.	16	Henry
HAND, L.	5	Henry	HANSON, Simmons	7	Houston
HAND?, James B.	13	Richmond	HANSON, Thos. K.	36	Heard
HANDE?, Wright	5	Pulaski	HANSON, O. H.	1	Carroll
HANDELL, M.	1	Chatham	HANSON, Walter & Jno	8	Wilkes
HANDLEY, Mrs. Harriet	35	Liberty	HANSON, William	1	Columbia
HANDY, James	4	Bibb	HANYSON ?, David	1	Union
HANE, H. S.	3	Randolph	HARALSON, J.	2	Troup
HANES, Bennet	4	Hall	HARALSON, J. B.	19	Troup
HANES, Eaton	4	Hall	HARALSON, Lucy	2	Walker
HANES, John	6	Muscogee	HARALSON, Lucy	5	Walker
HANES, Wm. T.	6	Fayette	HARBEN, Samuel	2	Lumpkin
HANEY, Edward A.	16	Houston	HARBEN, Sarah	6	Gordon
HANEY, Milton	5	Meriwether	HARBER & SIMS	6	Newton
HANEY, Wilkins	2	Jackson	HARBER, Eli J.	6	Franklin
HANEY, William E.	1	Merriwether	HARBER, J. H.	4	Murray
HANEY, Amerlius	17	Columbia	HARBER, Talonon	19	Franklin
HANK, Jacob	33	Randolpph	HARBIN, Jesse	2	Cherokee
HANKERSON, J. T.	20	Crawford	HARBIN, John	3	Gwinnett
HANKERSON, William	28	Burke	HARBIN, Allen C.	1	Richmond
HANKS, A. B.	3	Houston	HARBOAR, S. J.	6	Coweta
HANKS, Henry	14	Oglethorpe	HARBOUR, Thomas	2	Cass
HANKS, James A. R.	1	Murray	HARBUCK, Nicholas	3	Warren
HANKS, Stephen	10	Harris	HARBY, Levi	13	Chatham
HANKS, Stephen L.	5	Harris	HARCROW, Jesse B.	1	Heard
HANKS, S. B.	1	Stewart	HARD, William J.	10	Richmond
HANLEY, John	1	Houston	HARDAGE, Wm.	5	Marion
HANLY, John	2	Merriwether	HARDAMAN, Elbert	8	Oglethorpe
HANLY, Charles S.	19	Baldwin	HARDAMAN, F. J.	9	Oglethorpe
HANNAH, Samuel	1	Jefferson	HARDAWAY,		
HANNAH, Thomas	21	Jefferson	Edmund C.	20	Warren
HANNAH, William	6	Jefferson	HARDAWAY,		
HANNAH, William	6	Jefferson	George W.	45	Warren
HANNAN, R.	8	Washington	HARDAWAY, James L.	11	Warren
HANNAY, John	1	Camden	HARDAWAY,		
HANNES, Thomas	2	Campbell	Thomas J.	24	Warren
HANNON, James H.	8	Macon	HARDAWAY, William	15	Meriwether
HANS, C.	1	Bibb	HARDAWY, J. M.	1	Butts
HANS ?, John	8	Thomas	HARDCASTLE,		
HANSBURY, Charles	1	McIntosh	George W.	5	Chatham
HANSELL, Andrew J.	7	Cobb	HARDEE, Geo. W.	29	Camden
HANSFORD, Benjamin	5	Monroe	HARDEE, Joseph P.	4	Early
HANSFORD, Charles P.	9	Upson	HARDEE, Noble A.	11	Chatham
HANSFORD, Robert	6	Monroe	HARDEE, Geo. W.	15	Camden
HANSILL, H. T. M.	11	DeKalb	HARDEMAN, C. M.	15	Elbert
HANSLEY, Samuel	5	Floyd	HARDEMAN, Robert V.	29	Jones
HANSOM, Wm.	4	Monroe	HARDEMAN, J. Thos.	7	Bibb
HANSON, Ann	2	Monroe	HARDEMAN, Thos.	19	Bibb

130

Name	Number	County	Name	Number	County
HARDEN, A. T.	8	Floyd	HARDISON, Wm. B.	30	Marion
HARDEN, B. B.	37	Wilkes	HARDMAN, ?	14	Elbert
HARDEN, Benjamin J.	17	Walton	HARDMAN, Alphonza	5	Jasper
HARDEN, Elizabeth	4	Walker	HARDMAN, Bibger	20	Wilkes
HARDEN, H. W.	3	Monroe	HARDMAN, John	2	DeKalb
HARDEN, J. M. estate	59	Liberty	HARDNETT, H. H.	10	Harris
HARDEN, James	46	Monroe	HARDUCK ?,		
HARDEN, John	6	Newton	William M.	4	Stewart
HARDEN, Margaret	2	Chatham	HARDWICK, Amos	6	Muscogee
HARDEN, Moses J.	5	Harris	HARDWICK, Jas.	16	Hancock
HARDEN, R. J.	8	Lincoln	HARDWICK, John B.	20	Newton
HARDEN, Thomas	34	Columbia	HARDWICK, John W,.	12	Jasper
HARDEN, William	17	Monroe	HARDWICK, Mary C.	5	Jasper
HARDEN, Charles A.	49	Bryan	HARDWICK, R.S.	30	Hancock
HARDEN, Edward J.	6	Chatham	HARDWICK, Thos.	5	Effingham
HARDEN, John	7	Columbia	HARDWICK, Charles	33	Stewart
HARDEN, R. M.	10	Bibb	HARDWICK, Daniel	5	Stewart
HARDEN, Thomas W.	5	Richmond	HARDWICK, Francis	7	Columbia
HARDEN, William	12	Bryan	HARDWICK, Redding C.	1	Burke
HARDEN, Wm.	1	Bryan	HARDWICK, Robert	39	Stewart
HARDEWAY, R. S.	12	Muscogee	HARDWICK, Robert	4	Stewart
HARDIE, C.	3	Troup	HARDWICK,		
HARDIE, Jas.	9	Troup	Thomas W.	12	Washington
HARDIE, Jas. D.	8	Troup	HARDWICK,		
HARDIE, Joel	6	Wilkinson	William P.	45	Washington
HARDIE, John	3	Troup	HARDY, Armstead	1	Franklin
HARDIE, Josiah	2	Troup	HARDY, Aron	4	Lincoln
HARDIE, Thomas	40	Troup	HARDY, Charles F.	1	Jackson
HARDIE, Thomas E.	12	Lowndes	HARDY, Cornelius	17	Jasper
HARDIE, Wm. A.	10	Troup	HARDY, Irwin	9	Jackson
HARDIGREE, H. G.	2	Clarke	HARDY, J. W.	1	Jackson
HARDIN, C.	4	Floyd	HARDY, John E.	1	Wilkinson
HARDIN, Danl.	7	Lee	HARDY, William	14	Monroe
HARDIN, Dorcus	2	Forsyth	HARDY, William P.	1	Jasper
HARDIN, Hudson W.	9	Heard	HARDY, Wm. D.	2	Wilkes
HARDIN, James	36	Warren	HARDY, A.	2	Coweta
HARDIN, James T.	4	Warren	HARDY, Jesse	5	Sumter
HARDIN, John	31	Troup	HARDY, Jesse	1	Sumter
HARDIN, Lawrence L.	15	Jones	HARDY, Josiah	7	Butts
HARDIN, Mary	5	Murray	HARDY, Lucy	2	Stewart
HARDIN, Mary A.	10	Clarke	HARDY, Rufus	1	Coweta
HARDIN, Silas	48	Jasper	HARDY, Samuel	9	Columbia
HARDIN, Thomas H.	4	Chatham	HARDY, Thomas	4	Stewart
HARDIN, Thos.	8	Carroll	HARDY, Thos.	2	Crawford
HARDIN, Thos. J.	5	Oglethorpe	HARDY, W. C.	7	Bibb
HARDIN, Thos. H.	59	Lee	HARDY, Wistern	6	Cass
HARDIN, William	3	Jasper	HARDYMAN, Flex	27	Newton
HARDIN, William	2	Warren	HARE, J. N,.	1	Habersham
HARDIN, Wm.	18	Cass	HARE, Robert	4	Lincoln
HARDINETT, Lovick	22	Troup	HARE, Simon	1	Marion
HARDINETT, Wm.	7	Troup	HARE, Wm. W.	5	Early
HARDISON, Henry G.	2	Houston	HARGINS ?, John	2	Union
HARDISON, James W.	18	Houston	HARGRAVES, Abraham	4	Ware
HARDISON, Thomas	2	Houston	HARGRAVES, George	16	Muscogee

Name	Number	County	Name	Number	County
HARGRAVES, John	8	Ware	HARMAN, William B.	4	Washington
HARGRAVES, Thomas	2	Ware	HARMEN, Anna	12	Newton
HARGROVE, Charles G.	26	Oglethorpe	HARMON, Baswell	5	Morgan
HARGROVE, George	1	Muscogee	HARMON, C.	8	Meriwether
HARGROVE, James	19	Jackson	HARMON, James M.	2	Elbert
HARGROVE, John W.	2	Jackson	HARMON, John C.	6	Jefferson
HARGROVE, Wineford	8	Murray	HARMON, John T.	2	Hall
HARGROVE, Wm. F.	2	Jackson	HARMON, Lewis	7	Newton
HARGROVE, B. W.	11	Carroll	HARMON, Luther M.	4	Meriwether
HARGROVE, Benj.	27	Putnam	HARMON, M.	7	Meriwether
HARGROVE, H.	2	Randolph	HARMON, Richard	14	Monroe
HARGROVE, Henry	21	Burke	HARMON, William	4	Merriwether
HARGROVE, James	4	Talbot	HARMON, Abram	27	Chatham
HARGROVE, John W.	13	Sumter	HARNESBERGER,		
HARGROVES, Oliver	1	Richmond	Adam	26	Lincoln
HARGROVES, ? R.	6	Walton	HAROLD, James	2	Upson
HARIS, WILLIS b.	6	Baker	HAROLD, John	3	Upson
HARISON, Hansal H.	1	Baker	HARP, Alphard	8	Upson
HARISON, John	7	Taliaferro	HARP, Dixon	34	Upson
HARISON, John	2	Taliaferro	HARP, George	1	Newton
HARISON, Tyler	6	Talbot	HARP, Lafayett	1	Muscogee
HARISON, Wm. M.	4	Taliaferro	HARP, Mrs.	48	Muscogee
HARIST, Archibald M.	1	Troup	HARP, Sidney	9	Muscogee
HARKEY, Martha	2	Cobb	HARP, Simon	2	Twiggs
HARKEY, Milas	1	Cobb	HARP, Thomas	3	Monroe
HARKINS, Andrew	14	Jackson	HARP, M. L.	16	Crawford
HARKINS, James	1	Jones	HARP, Robinson ? H.	2	Richmond
HARKINS, William	1	Jones	HARP. G. P.	23	Crawford
HARKINS, William	1	Monroe	HARPEN ?,	36	Richmond
HARKNESS, J.	9	Henry	HARPEN ?, William	19	Richmond
HARKNESS, J. H.	3	Forsyth	HARPER, A. S.	4	Clarke
HARKNESS, R. W.	3	Forsyth	HARPER, A. W.	8	Morgan
HARKNESS, J. B.	11	Butts	HARPER, Alexander	5	Harris
HARKNESS, J. WA.	23	Butts	HARPER, Alvis	5	Morgan
HARKNESS, Jas.	12	Butts	HARPER, B.	5	Troup
HARKNESS, Jas.	6	Butts	HARPER, B. J.	67	Elbert
HARKNESS, Jas. P.	3	Forsyth	HARPER, B. L.	7	Henry
HARKNESS, T. M.	15	Butts	HARPER, Benjamin F.	1	Pike
HARKNESS, W. S. B.	15	Butts	HARPER, C. H.	6	Elbert
HARLAN, James A.	3	Jackson	HARPER, E.	2	Newton
HARLAND, Joshua	2	Walker	HARPER, Elijah	4	Chattooga
HARLAND, Valentine	9	Walker	HARPER, George	14	Lincoln
HARLEY, James B. B.	7	Chatham	HARPER, Henry	2	Chatman
HARLEY, Joseph	1	Harris	HARPER, James	7	Chattooga
HARLEY, William J.	2	Hancock	HARPER, James	2	Troup
HARLOW, J.	1	Chattooga	HARPER, James	6	Wayne
HARLOW, Samuel	12	Jackson	HARPER, Jno.	9	Randolph
HARLOW, John A.	1	Burke	HARPER, John	6	Hancock
HARLOW, Wm. D.	6	Camden	HARPER, John	15	Lincoln
HARLY, Wm. J.	44	Taliaferro	HARPER, John	14	Newton
HARMAN, Emanuel	3	Lincoln	HARPER, John	5	Newton
HARMAN, Harriet	7	Monroe	HARPER, John	15	Pike
HARMAN, Z. E.	19	Monroe	HARPER, John F.	2	Fayette
HARMAN, John K.	2	Bibb	HARPER, Joseph	21	Houston

Name	Number	County
HARPER, Lucy	6	Morgan
HARPER, Mary	1	Hancock
HARPER, Meriwether	11	Lincoln
HARPER, N. G.	14	Greene
HARPER, Presly	40	Hancock
HARPER, R.	24	Henry
HARPER, R. H.	2	Henry
HARPER, R. S.	2	Henry
HARPER, Roda	5	Newton
HARPER, Thomas H.	1	Houston
HARPER, Thos.	11	Henry
HARPER, W. A.	14	Elbert
HARPER, Wiatt A.	2	Pike
HARPER, William	16	Lincoln
HARPER, Wm.	15	Chattooga
HARPER, Wm. H.	1	Marion
HARPER, Wyatt	40	Hancock
HARPER, Catherine	4	Sumter
HARPER, Elias	2	Randolph
HARPER, George R.	8	Sumter
HARPER, Hiram	2	DeKalb
HARPER, John	2	Richmond
HARPER, M.	1	Crawford
HARPER, Robert H.	16	Baldwin
HARPER, Robt.	1	Butts
HARPER, Vel	13	Cass
HARPER?, Micajah	18	Monroe
HARRAH, George	1	Harris
HARRALD, Dempsey	28	Early
HARRALL, Jane	1	DeKalb
HARRALL, John B.	2	Warren
HARRALL, John W. B.	13	Warren
HARRALL, Joseph	9	Warren
HARRALL, Matthew	1	Warren
HARRALL, Sarah	14	Warren
HARRALL, Sarah (guad.)	1	Warren
HARRALL, Simon	8	Warren
HARRALL, William	21	Telfair
HARRALL, William	6	Warren
HARRALSON, B.	1	Morgan
HARRALSON, H.	10	Troup
HARRALSON, Jesse	10	Newton
HARRALSON, P. A.	15	DeKalb
HARRALSON, T. J.	5	Union
HARREL, Andw.	4	Camden
HARRELL, Edward	24	Forsyth
HARRELL, Henry	6	Pulaski
HARRELL, J. B.	6	Henry
HARRELL, Jackson	8	Newton
HARRELL, Jane	9	Macon
HARRELL, Jesse	1	Newton
HARRELL, Joel	4	Macon
HARRELL, L. T.	67	Morgan
HARRELL, Levi	43	Pulaski

Name	Number	County
HARRELL, Loverd?	6	Pulaski
HARRELL, Margaret	18	Pulaski
HARRELL, Mary	7	Houston
HARRELL, Reuben	5	Pulaski
HARRELL, Robert	3	Houston
HARRELL, Wm.	15	Pulaski
HARRELL, C.	1	Randolph
HARRELL, Daniel	1	Randolph
HARRELL, David	35	Stewart
HARRELL, Isaac	1	Stewart
HARRELL, Jesse P.	14	Stewart
HARRELL, Jesse P.	8	Stewart
HARRELL, Mrs.	1	Burke
HARRELL, Solomon	18	Stewart
HARRELL, Thomas J.	6	Sumter
HARRELL, Wm.	6	Decatur
HARRELSON, H. E.	1	Walton
HARRILL, William	1	Muscogee
HARRILL, Elijah	5	Burke
HARRILL, Joseph	2	Burke
HARRINGTON, Jackson	5	Houston
HARRINGTON, John	3	Houston
HARRINGTON, John W.	1	Houston
HARRINGTON, Simon	6	Liberty
HARRINGTON, William	11	Houston
HARRINGTON, Jas.	6	Coweta
HARRIS, (?)	93	Columbia
HARRIS, A. E.	11	Lee
HARRIS, Absalom S.	42	Troup
HARRIS, Albert E.	9	Troup
HARRIS, Alston	9	Merriwether
HARRIS, Ann?	1	Muscogee
HARRIS, Ann	41	Washington
HARRIS, Archibald	3	Forsyth
HARRIS, Arthur	1	Jones
HARRIS, B. L.	2	Glynn
HARRIS, B. L.	3	Heard
HARRIS, B. T.	43	Hancock
HARRIS, B. T.	35	Hancock
HARRIS, Benj.	44	Morgan
HARRIS, Buckner	7	Gwinnett
HARRIS, Charles	5	Forsyth
HARRIS, Charles	38	Merriwether
HARRIS, Cordelia	1	Early
HARRIS, Daniel	8	Oglethorpe
HARRIS, Daniel	66	Washington
HARRIS, E. G.	25	Wilkes
HARRIS, Ebenezer	1	Wayne
HARRIS, Ebenezer H.	1	Fayette
HARRIS, Edmund S.	14	Troup
HARRIS, Edmund S.	75	Troup
HARRIS, Elias	2	Monroe
HARRIS, Eliz.	8	Clarke
HARRIS, Elizabeth	28	Morgan

Name	Number	County	Name	Number	County
HARRIS, Ezekell	11	Cobb	HARRIS, Mermoth?	5	Macon
HARRIS, Ezekiel	6	Forsyth	HARRIS, Mingard	1	Murray
HARRIS, G. R.	4	Murray	HARRIS, Morgan	8	Merriwether
HARRIS, George A.	2	Muscogee	HARRIS, Moris D.	1	Cobb
HARRIS, George R.	1	Murray	HARRIS, Morris	14	Fayette
HARRIS, Green B.	1	Gwinnett	HARRIS, Moses D.	12	Wayne
HARRIS, Guilford	5	Fayette	HARRIS, Moses S.	2	Wayne
HARRIS, H.	3	Troup	HARRIS, Mrs. E.	11	Muscogee
HARRIS, H. H.	1	Newton	HARRIS, Mrs. Mary A.	1	Liberty
HARRIS, H. R.	41	Merriwether	HARRIS, Myles G.	80	Hancock
HARRIS, Hancy	3	Cobb	HARRIS, Myles G.	2	Hancock
HARRIS, Handly ?	2	Walton	HARRIS, Nathan Jr.	1	Oglethorpe
HARRIS, Hardy	13	Warren	HARRIS, Nathan Sr.	37	Oglethorpe
HARRIS, Henry P.	9	Warren	HARRIS, Obediah	3	Macon
HARRIS, Hiram	6	Morgan	HARRIS, R. H.	5	Muscogee
HARRIS, Horace B.	1	Glynn	HARRIS, R. J.	11	Greene
HARRIS, Isaac	1	Twiggs	HARRIS, Raymond	5	Liberty
HARRIS, Isaac C.	5	Houston	HARRIS, Rebecca	6	Pulaski
HARRIS, J. D.	7	Morgan	HARRIS, Robt.	26	Morgan
HARRIS, J. P.	9	Houston	HARRIS, Robt. S.	11	Clarke
HARRIS, James	3	Forsyth	HARRIS, Sarah H.	13	Clarke
HARRIS, James	5	Jones	HARRIS, Seaborn	1	Fayette
HARRIS, James	2	Monroe	HARRIS, Simion	1	Twiggs
HARRIS, James J.	4	Paulding	HARRIS, Simon	14	Houston
HARRIS, James M.	2	McIntosh	HARRIS, Susan	9	Murray
HARRIS, James W.	13	Clarke	HARRIS, Theopolis	2	Morgan
HARRIS, James W.	88	Walton	HARRIS, Thomas	3	Cobb
HARRIS, Jane	2	Pike	HARRIS, Thomas	2	Greene
HARRIS, Jane	2	Twiggs	HARRIS, Thomas	5	Houston
HARRIS, Jas.	49	Wilkes	HARRIS, Thomas	38	Morgan
HARRIS, Jane M.	28	McIntosh	HARRIS, Thomas W.	12	Houston
HARRIS, Jas. M.	34	Hancock	HARRIS, Thos. O.	2	Morgan
HARRIS, Jeptha V.	16	Clarke	HARRIS, Treasey	2	Washington
HARRIS, Jesse D.	6	Houston	HARRIS, Treasey	10	Washington
HARRIS, John	9	Greene	HARRIS, Walton	4	Jackson
HARRIS, John	5	Merriwether	HARRIS, Wesley	13	Talbot
HARRIS, John	1	Muscogee	HARRIS, West	2	Newton
HARRIS, John	34	Newton	HARRIS, William	12	Cobb
HARRIS, John	1	Newton	HARRIS, William	14	Early
HARRIS, John	9	Washington	HARRIS, William	10	Forsyth
HARRIS, John A.	45	Greene	HARRIS, William	6	Forsyth
HARRIS, John D.	7	Oglethorpe	HARRIS, William	43	Houston
HARRIS, John E.	1	Cass	HARRIS, William	1	Walker
HARRIS, John N.	6	Murray	HARRIS, William	18	Walton
HARRIS, John R.	2	Housotn	HARRIS, William C.	2	Gwinnett
HARRIS, John R.	25	Merriwether	HARRIS, William R.	2	Houston
HARRIS, John W.	?	Thomas	HARRIS, William Y.	1	Jasper
HARRIS, Joshua	47	Early	HARRIS, Benjamin F.	39	Richmond
HARRIS, Joshua	2	Jones	HARRIS, E. A.	17	Crawford
HARRIS, Joseph	4	Washington	HARRIS, E. L.	17	Crawford
HARRIS, L. D.	10	Forsyth	HARRIS, Edmund	28	Stewart
HARRIS, M. B.	4	Merriwether	HARRIS, Elizabeth	5	Crawford
HARRIS, Margret M.	59	McIntosh	HARRIS, Gray	11	Stewart
HARRIS, Mary J.	2	Glynn	HARRIS, Henry	131	Merriwether

Name	Number	County	Name	Number	County
HARRIS, Henry B.	4	Talbot	HARRISON, John	2	Habersham
HARRIS, Iverson L.	20	Baldwin	HARRISON, John C..	1	Franklin
HARRIS, J. J.	2	Bibb	HARRISON, John H.	6	Floyd
HARRIS, J. L.	2	Crawford	HARRISON, John J.	3	Walker
HARRIS, J. V.			HARRISON, Joseph	1	Washington
see KEMP, E. C.	?	Floyd	HARRISON, Joseph	9	Washington
HARRIS, J. W.	7	Bibb	HARRISON, Kollach	7	Chatham
HARRIS, James	29	Columbia	HARRISON, Larkin	9	Franklin
HARRIS, James A.	2	Stewart	HARRISON, Lewis J.	3	Washington
HARRIS, James W.	16	Taliaferro	HARRISON, Manson J.	3	Gwinnett
HARRIS, Jas.	16	Crawford	HARRISON, Margaret	10	Jackson
HARRIS, Jesse C.	6	Baker	HARRISON, Martha	11	Merriwether
HARRIS, John	12	Columbia	HARRISON, Nathaniel	16	Campbell
HARRIS, John	11	Columbia	HARRISON, Reubin	3	Muscogee
HARRIS, Juriah	79	Burke	HARRISON, Thomas	12	Franklin
HARRIS, Lewis	1	Camden	HARRISON, Thomas	4	Franklin
HARRIS, Martha	2	Stewart	HARRISON, Thomas	1	Merriwether
HARRIS, Mary	6	DeKalb	HARRISON, Thomas	11	Troup
HARRIS, Maryann	14	Baldwin	HARRISON, Tilmon	17	Jackson
HARRIS, Math	2	Coweta	HARRISON, William	3	Henry
HARRIS, Nancy	7	Crawford	HARRISON, William	20	Monroe
HARRIS, Penelope	8	Talbot	HARRISON, William D.	4	Washington
HARRIS, Raymond	27	Bryan	HARRISON, Wm.	1	Henry
HARRIS, Robert Y.	29	Richmond	HARRISON, Wm.	5	Liberty
HARRIS, S.	3	Crawford	HARRISON, A. B.	20	Putnam
HARRIS, Sarah	17	Richmond	HARRISON, B. R.	3	Stewart
HARRIS, Stephen F.	6	Chatham	HARRISON, C.	13	Randolph
HARRIS, T. A.	6	Bibb	HARRISON, Colmore	6	Jackson
HARRIS, Tabitha(?)	2	Coweta	HARRISON, Daniel F.	3	Dooly
HARRIS, Thomas	5	Baldwin	HARRISON, G.	9	Bibb
HARRIS, Thomas	9	Stewart	HARRISON, Gabriel	13	Putnam
HARRIS, Thomas	1	Taliaferro	HARRISON, George P.	46	Chatham
HARRIS, Tyre	30	Coweta	HARRISON, J. M.	41	Dade
HARRIS, W. G.	14	Bibb	HARRISON, James	30	Randolph
HARRIS, W. T.	15	Crawford	HARRISON, Jas.	64	Randolph
HARRIS, W. T.	1	Putnam	HARRISON, John	5	Bryan
HARRIS, Wiley G.	17	Richmond	HARRISON, John	1	Chatham
HARRIS, William	1	Talbot	HARRISON, John B.	19	Sumter
HARRIS, William B.	15	Talbot	HARRISON, John Q.	1	Talbot
HARRIS, Wm. D.	2	Clarke	HARRISON, L. L.	12	Randolph
HARRISON, Benjamin	5	Warren	HARRISON, M.	5	Decatur
HARRISON, Mariah S.	20	Cherokee	HARRISON, Mary	5	Butts
HARRISON, Ailey	5	Harris	HARRISON, Presley	11	Talbot
HARRISON, Dunwoodie	2	Columbia	HARRISON, R. H.	9	Columbia
HARRISON, Ferrel P.	2	Franklin	HARRISON, Saml. E.	28	Coweta
HARRISON, George	15	Monroe	HARRISON, Sarah	5	Chatham
HARRISON, Henry	3	Monroe	HARRISON, Sol	5	Columbia
HARRISON, Hezekiah	1	Cobb	HARRISON, Sullivan	32	Columbia
HARRISON, J. H.	3	Walton	HARRISON, Wm.	12	Randolph
HARRISON, James	4	Monroe	HARRISSON, Friley J.	13	Jasper
HARRISON, James A.	4	Franklin	HARRISSON, Lorenzo D.	9	Jasper
HARRISON, James B.	7	Washington	HARRIST, Charles F.	1	Troup
HARRISON, Jas. G.	6	Hancock	HARRITT, John	17	Habersham
HARRISON, Jason C.	2	Jackson	HARRODSON, A. H.	11	Carroll

Name	Number	County
HARROLD, Jacob	1	Talbot
HARROLL, Thomas	1	Muscogee
HARRY, Thomas	4	Meriwether
HARSHAW, Sidney	13	Union
HART, Barnabas	16	Marion
HART, David	13	Marion
HART, Elizabeth	12	Jones
HART, Isaac	2	Marion
HART, Jesse	1	Monroe
HART, Joel	5	Madison
HART, Joel	41	Oglethorpe
HART, John	1	Chatham
HART, John	3	Monroe
HART, John	1	Thomas
HART, M.	2	Twiggs
HART, Mary	7	Madison
HART, Nancy	6	Washington
HART, R. W.	2	Hancock
HART, Randolph H.	3	Marion
HART, Saml.	4	Marion
HART, SAMUEL	23	Warren
HART, Solomon	7	Harris
HART, Thomas	22	Greene
HART, Thomas	15	Laurens
HART, Vincent T.	9	Marion
HART, Wiley	1	Lee
HART, William	12	Warren
HART, William S.	1	Washington
HART, Isaac	30	Sumter
HART, Isaac	2	Taliaferro
HART, Levy	3	Chatham
HART, Marshall	2	Bryan
HART, O. W.	25	Bryan
HART, S. S.	11	Bryan
HARTESFIELD, Middleton	8	Jasper
HARTFIELD, Bery	10	Oglethorpe
HARTISON, Harvey	4	Talbot
HARTLEY, F.	2	Bibb
HARTLEY, M.	1	Crawford
HARTMAN, C.	1	Crawford
HARTON, Alfred P.	20	Hancock
HARTON, Tabitha Mrs.	37	Hancock
HARTON, Wilkins J.	23	Hancock
HARTON, C. A.	11	Putnam
HARTRIDGE, Charles	6	Chatham
HARTRIDGE, Sarah	9	Baldwin
HARTSFIELD, A. J.	21	Henry
HARTSFIELD, G. M.	1	Monroe
HARTSFIELD, Green	9	Harris
HARTSFIELD, Moses A.	2	Cherokee
HARTSFIELD, S.	7	Henry
HARTSFIELD, Thomas J.	7	Pike
HARTSFIELD, W.	6	Henry
HARTSFIELD, Washington	13	Upson
HARTSFIELD, William	27	Harris
HARTSFIELD, William A.	4	Monroe
HARTSFIELD, D.	6	Decatur
HARTSFIELD, Daniel R.	3	Campbell
HARTSFIELD, Henry	5	Randolph
HARTSFIELD, Moses	1	Campbell
HARTY, William	2	Harris
HARVARD, John J.	7	Thomas
HARVARD, W. W.	4	Thomas
HARVEY, Albert	21	Monroe
HARVEY, Benjamin	2	Muscogee
HARVEY, Charlotte	1	Walton
HARVEY, David	1	Muscogee
HARVEY, Elizabeth	3	Harris
HARVEY, Evan J.	17	Jasper
HARVEY, H. C.	1	Monroe
HARVEY, H. H.	2	Newton
HARVEY, Hamilton	4	Houston
HARVEY, John	1	Gordon
HARVEY, Orran	1	Monroe
HARVEY, Robert	1	Chatham
HARVEY, Sarah	3	Chatham
HARVEY, Thomas J.	11	Jefferson
HARVEY, Edward	2	Talbot
HARVEY, Isaac	4	Camden
HARVEY, J. C.	69	Crawford
HARVEY, James	12	Talbot
HARVEY, John	6	Bryan
HARVEY, Joshua	6	Talbot
HARVEY, M.	9	Talbot
HARVEY, Richard	1	Bryan
HARVEY, Spencer	1	Campbell
HARVEY, Stephen	19	Talbot
HARVEY, Wright	3	Carroll
HARVIN, Thomas E.	6	Thomas
HARVIN, William N.	44	Thomas
HARVY, John P.	1	Thomas
HARVY?, Tabitha	17	Jones
HARWEK ?, Richard	19	Walton
HARWELL, Mark	6	Troup
HARWELL, Ransom	32	Jasper
HARWELL, Lewis P.	36	Putnam
HARWELL, T. B.	11	Putnam
HARWELL, Wm. F.	4	Troup
HARWILE?, Letty	4	Jackson
HASCALL, Francis R.	21	Jones
HASKINS, Attaway	11	Pulaski
HASLIM, George S.	31	Houston
HASLIM, William	28	Houston
HASLIP, John G.	5	Burke

Name	Number	County	Name	Number	County
HASLIP, Jonas	16	Burke	HAWES, Mosely	24	Lincoln
HASLIP, R. G.	9	Randolph	HAWK, Edward	1	Madison
HASS, George	1	Chatham	HAWK, Seabron	28	Jasper
HASS, Jacob	1	Baldwin	HAWK, Thomas D.	1	Madison
HASSETT, Dennis B.	1	Chatham	HAWK, Tillman	7	Jasper
HASSLER, William	2	Murray	HAWKING, Ridley A.	1	Baldwin
HASTINGS, Isaac A.	2	Fayette	HAWKINS		
HASTINGS, James E.	3	Fayette	& DURHAM	5	Murray
HATAWAY, Baton	1	Macon	HAWKINS, Alex	15	Walton
HATCH, Milo	2	Richmond	HAWKINS, B. F.	6	Floyd
HATCHCOCK, Jas.	9	Randolph	HAWKINS, G. W.	3	Cobb
HATCHELL, Hamel	2	Merriwether	HAWKINS, J. B.	1	Morgan
HATCHER, Isaac	3	Camden	HAWKINS, J. M.	10	Franklin
HATCHER, James M.	5	Jefferson	HAWKINS, Jas. M.	6	Wilkes
HATCHER, Jesse	1	Pike	HAWKINS, John	14	Floyd
HATCHER, John	8	Floyd	HAWKINS, Jno. L.	5	Wilkes
HATCHER, John G.	10	Burke	HAWKINS, John	2	Wallker
HATCHER, Josiah	11	Burke	HAWKINS, L. B.	1	Forsyth
HATCHER, P.	7	Troup	HAWKINS, L. B.	6	Paulding
HATCHER, Sam. J.	10	Muscogee	HAWKINS, Robt.	5	Cherokee
HATCHER, Valentine	6	Jefferson	HAWKINS, Saml.	4	Chattooga
HATCHER, Elias W.	4	Burke	HAWKINS, Thomas	5	Newton
HATCHER, J. B.			HAWKINS, Thos. H.	16	Oglethorpe
agt for TOOMBS, H.	11	Houston	HAWKINS, Thos. T.	34	Camden
HATCHER, Robt.	2	Crawford	HAWKINS, W. A.	2	Lee
HATCHER, W. L.	4	Randolph	HAWKINS, William	2	Jones
HATCHER, Wm. G.	2	Wilkinson	HAWKINS, Willis A.	15	Walton
HATFIELD, R. L.	1	Wilkinson	HAWKINS, Edward	5	Putnam
HATFIELD, S.	2	Wilkinson	HAWKINS, Ezekiel	8	Sumter
HATHAWAY, Mrs.	2	DeKalb	HAWKINS, J. T.	9	Chattooga
HATHCOCK, ---	1	DeKalb	HAWKINS, Jas. W.	3	Coweta
HATHORN, Jackson	3	Monroe	HAWKINS, John	4	Putnam
HATSON, William J.	10	Harris	HAWKINS, John A.	10	Putnam
HATTAWAY, Isabella	4	Morgan	HAWKINS, John T.	4	Sumter
HATTAWAY, John B.	4	Walton	HAWKINS, Nathan	30	Baldwin
HATTAWAY, Lacey	1	Campbell	HAWKINS, Pinckney	1	Sumter
HATTAWAY, Sterling	2	Morgan	HAWKINS, William	7	Talbot
HATTAWAY,			HAWKINS, William M.	2	Baker
Thomas L.	2	Morgan	HAWKINS, William M.	1	Baker
HATTEN, Abb. L.	8	Telfair	HAWKINS?, Sarah	5	Pike
HATTEN, William	2	Telfair	HAWKS ?, H.	21	Walton
HATTON, Robert	20	Merriwether	HAWKS, Henry	6	Oglethorpe
HATTON?, John	5	Muscogee	HAWKS, W.	3	Oglethorpe
HAUGABOOK, Harrit	78	Macon	HAWKS, Eliza	4	Cass
HAUGABROOK, Daniel	22	Macon	HAWLY, H. L.	3	Effingham
HAUGHTON, Nathan T.	10	Jasper	HAWS, Rebecca	21	Lincoln
HAUGHTON, William	9	Harris	HAWS, W. L.	4	Lincoln
HAUGHTON, Nancy	5	Putnam	HAWS, Samuel	18	Columbia
HAUPT, Eliza	7	Chatham	HAWTHORN, John	46	Troup
HAUPT, Henry	7	Chatham	HAWTHORN, Nancy	4	Marion
HAUPT, James L.	1	Chatham	HAWTHORN, Louisea	12	Gwinnett
HAUPT, John	5	Chatham	HAWTHORN, William	1	Stewart
HAUPT, Lamuel B.	5	Chatham	HAWTHORNE,		
HAWES, Elizabeth	3	Lincoln	Nathaniel	1	Cobb

Name	Number	County	Name	Number	County
HAWTHORNE, Thomas	14	Monroe	HAYS, Martha	3	Newton
HAWTHORNE, William	2	Monroe	HAYS, Mary	50	Early
HAWTHORNE, J. T.	8	Dade	HAYS, Nancy D.	1	Wilkinson
HAWTHORNE, Mrs. N.	4	Decatur	HAYS, Peter W.	6	Clarke
HAWTHORNE, W. B.	16	Decatur	HAYS, Robert	10	Muscogee
HAY, David R.	7	Merriwether	HAYS, S. J.	18	Clarke
HAY, John W.	2	Clarke	HAYS, Sarah	8	Jackson
HAY, Payton	3	Merriwether	HAYS, Thomas S.	2	Muscogee
HAY, William	5	Stewart	HAYS, Thos. S.	2	Muscogee
HAY, Wm.	3	Butts	HAYS, A. S.	45	Stewart
HAYES, Duke	19	Thomas	HAYS, Charlotte	1	DeKalb
HAYES, Edward	16	Cobb	HAYS, George W.	4	Sumter
HAYES, George	43	Thomas	HAYS, H.	17	Decatur
HAYES, Hendrix	1	Franklin	HAYS, Hiram	23	Clarke
HAYES, Jas. C.	1	Carroll	HAYS, James	13	Randolph
HAYES, James T.	58	Thomas	HAYS, Martin	2	Sumter
HAYES, Parmnus?	14	Oglethorpe	HAYS, Robert	5	Talbot
HAYES?, J. D.	18	Early	HAYS, Wesley	1	Talbot
HAYES, William	19	Thomas	HAYS, Wm.	1	Coweta
HAYGOOD, Benjamin	17	Monroe	HAYS, Wm.	17	Randolph
HAYGOOD, Mary	11	Monroe	HAYSE, Caborn	2	Camden
HAYLEHERST, L. M.	78	Camden	HAYSLIIP, Zorah B.	6	Sumter
HAYLES, W. A.	3	Jefferson	HAYSTY, Truman	1	Twiggs
HAYLEY, James	3	Cherokee	HAYWOOD, Joseph M.	6	Chatham
HAYMANS, Stouton	20	Liberty	HAYWOOD, Alfred	4	Chatham
HAYMIE, Adalline	6	Richmond	HAZELETT, Wm. A.	4	Elbert
HAYMON, Henry	4	Monroe	HAZELHURST,		
HAYNES, B. F.	3	Heard	Leighton W.	49	Glynn
HAYNES, Eli P.	2	Gordon	HAZELHURST, Robt.	131	Glynn
HAYNES, G. B.	6	Walton	HAZER, Sarah A.	4	Clarke
HAYNES, George P.	1	Walton	HAZIER, Mrs. Ruth	1	Meriwether
HAYNES, Henry	2	Carroll	HAZLETERE, Pinkney	20	Muscogee
HAYNES, James	7	Marion	HAZLETON, Mrs. Jane	2	Muscogee
HAYNES, James H.	2	Pike	HAZZARD, Thos. F.	33	Glynn
HAYNES, Jasper	15	Greene	HAZZARD, William W.	78	Glynn
HAYNES, John	13	Walker	HEAD, Andrew A.	17	Fayette
HAYNES, Martha	8	Walker	HEAD, B. J.	5	Macon
HAYNES, Richard M.	6	Cobb	HEAD, James	35	Pike
HAYNES, W. B. P.	10	Oglethrope	HEAD, James B.	1	Gwinnett
HAYNES, W. P.	1	Washington	HEAD, James D.	38	Monroe
HAYNES, Wm. P.	3	Washingrton	HEAD, James M.	1	Fayette
HAYNES, Emily	3	Screven	HEAD, James Sr.	37	Morgan
HAYNES, Reuben	5	DeKalb	HEAD, James Z.	5	Morgan
HAYNIE, Milton H.	7	Floyd	HEAD, Marshal	17	Morgan
HAYS, Ambrose	1	Warren	HEAD, Robt. A.	3	Fayette
HAYS, Elizabeth	1	Fayette	HEAD, Thomas M.	1	Pike
HAYS, George	2	Marion	HEAD, Thomas W.	11	Morgan
HAYS, Henry	16	Early	HEAD, W. C.	4	Elbert
HAYS, Hiram	11	Merriwether	HEAD, William	1	Jasper
HAYS, John	8	Clarke	HEAD, Wm. R.	1	Fayette
HAYS, John	40	Early	HEAD, Benjamin	2	Campbell
HAYS, John	1	Troup	HEAD, David	3	Carroll
HAYS, Jonathan	9	Muscogee	HEAD, Henry	5	Campbell
HAYS, Leonard B.	15	Walton	HEAD, Sarah	37	Putnam

Name	Number	County	Name	Number	County
HEAD, Sarah	3	Richmond	HEARNDON, B.	5	Elbert
HEAD, W. J.	27	Butts	HEARNDON, Benjamin	1	Jones
HEAD, Wm.	3	DeKalb	HEARNDON, T. J.	4	Elbert
HEADD, William W.	1	Dooly	HEARNDON, Edward	28	Columbia
HEADEN, Samuel	21	Franklin	HEARTSFIELD, Charles	9	Muscogee
HEALD, M. C.	9	McIntosh	HEATH, Abram	6	Meriwether
HEALEY, Michael M.	45	Jones	HEATH, Henry	4	Washington
HEAON?, John	17	Bryan	HEATH, Jos.	5	Meriwether
HEAR ?, Shapden ?	1	Walton	HEATH, Davison	11	Butts
HEARD, Caroline	21	Wilkes	HEATH, Epenetus	14	Campbell
HEARD, George	63	Troup	HEATH, George	10	Talbot
HEARD, George	14	Troup	HEATH, H. T.	1	Campbell
HEARD, James L.	9	Wilkes	HEATH, Henry	1	Burke
HEARD, Jno. A.	16	Wilkes	HEATH, Isaac I.	7	Burke
HEARD, Jno. W.	43	Wilkes	HEATH, John	1	Bibb
HEARD, Mary A.	11	Morgan	HEATH, John	35	Talbot
HEARD, Mrs.	8	Muscogee	HEATH, Jordan	19	Burke
HEARD, Nancy	2	Wilkes	HEATH, Lunsford	4	Walton
HEARD, S. T.	25	Elbert	HEATH, Moses	15	Burke
HEARD, T.	16	Newton	HEATH, Peterson	2	Warren
HEARD, T. J.	88	Elbert	HEATH, R. W.	9	Thomas
HEARD, Thos. A.	13	Wilkes	HEATH, W. B.	11	Bibb
HEARD, William	19	Greene	HEBBARD, E.	8	Camden
HEARD, William	40	Harris	HEBBERD, W. C. H.	4	Newton
HEARD, William J.	9	Thomas	HECKERBY, William	20	Monroe
HEARD, Wm. S.	2	Heard	HECKLE, Henry	1	Richmond
HEARD, Wm. S.	61	Wilkes	HECKS, J. H.	6	Wilkinson
HEARD, Wm. S.	2	Wilkes	HEDDINGTON, A. G.	9	Campbell
HEARD, C.A.	3	Chattooga	HEDDLESON,		
HEARD, Edmund	3	Richmond	William S.	5	Chatham
HEARD, Emily B.	5	Richmond	HEDGEPETH, Wm.	7	Harris
HEARD, Isaac F.	11	Richmond	HEDNAL, Jared	29	Early
HEARD, John W.	3	Richmond	HEDRICK, G. W.	1	Chatham
HEARD, John W. Jailer	13	Richmond	HEERY, Thomas	4	Chatham
HEARD, Stephen D.	6	Richmond	HEETH, Benjamin A.	4	Warren
HEARDEN, Stephen	12	Columbia	HEETH, Henry	39	Warren
HEARINGTON, W. S.	6	Pike	HEETH, Henry		
HEARIS?, B. estate	37	Elbert	(guardian)	3	Warrren
HEARN ?, Jordan Agt.	15	Upson	HEETH, Joel F.	1	Warren
HEARN, O.	2	Henry	HEETH, John	5	Warren
HEARN, T.	37	Elbert	HEETH, Wyatt	8	Warren
HEARN, F. L.	1	Putnam	HEFLIN, W. H.	1	Henry
HEARN, F. T. Jun.	12	Putnam	HEFTON ?, Will	2	Stewart
HEARN, Francis	34	Putnam	HEGGIE (?), James	40	Columbia
HEARN, John	4	Bryan	HEIDT, Emanual	3	Chatham
HEARN, Kendrick	6	Coweta	HEIDT, Samuel	7	Effingham
HEARN, Leverett ?	3	Twiggs	HEIDT, William	8	Effingham
HEARN, Lewis	12	Troup	HEIDT, Daniel	3	Chatham
HEARN, M. H.	2	Campbell	HEIGHT, S. D.	5	Newton
HEARN, O. R.	1	Campbell	HEINLY, Frederick	6	Effingham
HEARN, S.	13	Coweta	HEINLY, Joshua	8	Effingham
HEARN, Thomas	5	Bryan	HEIRSTEN, Alexander	2	Wilkinson
HEARN, Thomas T.	1	Campbell	HEISLER, Mary	1	Lee
HEARN, Wm.	26	Putnam	HEISLER, Elbert	7	Lee

Name	Number	County	Name	Number	County
HEISMAN, James	1	Pike	HENDERSON, James D.	2	Jackson
HELDERBRAND, M.	4	Carroll	HENDERSON, Jno. M.	7	Forsyth
HELFON, Isham	6	Carroll	HENDERSON, John	2	Jackson
HELLAM, W.	1	Henry	HENDERSON, John	5	Newton
HELLARTEN, David	1	Troup	HENDERSON, John S.	2	Walker
HELLOMS, Bales	3	Pike	HENDERSON,		
HELLUM, William	1	Madison	Lawson S.	24	Macon
HELMS, Charles	3	Muscogee	HENDERSON, M.	2	Irwin
HELMS, Elizabeth	5	Muscogee	HENDERSON, Mary	5	Early
HELMS, George	4	Muscogee	HENDERSON, Michael	1	Early
HELMS, Nathan	1	Muscogee	HENDERSON, Milton	34	Walton
HELMS, Noah G.	1	Muscogee	HENDERSON, Richard	6	Floyd
HELMS, Allen	4	Talbot	HENDERSON, Richd.	11	Henry
HELTER?, Thomas G.	17	Clarke	HENDERSON, Robert	19	Lincoln
HELTON, George W.	3	Pike	HENDERSON, Robert	11	Newton
HELTON, James M.	1	Jones	HENDERSON, Robert H.	1	Jones
HELTON, Francis	1	Baker	HENDERSON, S. B.	4	Houston
HELTON, Washington	5	Washington	HENDERSON, Saml.	8	Harris
HELVERSTON, Jas.	1	Camden	HENDERSON,		
HELVESTON, McGillis	2	Camden	Samuel S.	6	Houston
HELVINGSTON, Joseph	6	Lowndes	HENDERSON,		
HELVINSTON, John C.	29	Macon	Samuel S.	6	Jasper
HEMBREE, A. C.	3	Carroll	HENDERSON, Thomas	6	Fayette
HEMBREW,?, Annariah	3	Cobb	HENDERSON, Thomas	6	Fayette
HEMLY, Lewis	1	Early	HENDERSON, William	16	Harris
HEMP?, Harrison	11	Floyd	HENDERSON, William	3	Jackson
HEMPHILL, Alphonzo	21	Troup	HENDERSON, William	5	Newton
HEMPHILL, Sabrey	41	Jackson	HENDERSON,		
HEMPHILL, Alexr. H.	1	Richmond	William C.	12	Jasper
HEMPHILL, Wm.	3	Chattooga	HENDERSON, William H.	2	Paulding
HEMPHILL, Wm. S.	2	Clarke	HENDERSON, Wm.	2	Fayette
HENAL?, W.	1	Elbert	HENDERSON, Wm.	2	Gordon
HENARY, Robert	2	Thomas	HENDERSON, Wm.	32	Lee
HENDERSON, Abigal	8	Cass	HENDERSON, Wm.	13	Lowndes
HENDERSON, Anderson	5	Butts	HENDERSON, E.		
HENDERSON, Arch.	1	Cass	(or Hankerson)	12	Coweta
HENDERSON, Berrien	2	Ware	HENDERSON, Elijah	2	Chatham
HENDERSON, Charles	1	Jasper	HENDERSON, Ezekiel	4	Cass
HENDERSON, D.	1	Irwin	HENDERSON, George	3	Cass
HENDERSON, David	11	Troup	HENDERSON, Green	11	DeKalb
HENDERSON, Elisha	29	Walton	HENDERSON, Israel	2	Coweta
HENDERSON, Elizabeth	1	Newton	HENDERSON, J.		
HENDERSON, ? F.	1	Walton	(or Hankerson)	3	Coweta
HENDERSON, Francis	1	Gordon	HENDERSON, J. M.	8	Chatham
HENDERSON, G. C.	2	Lincoln	HENDERSON, J. M.	3	Coweta
HENDERSON, Henry M.	3	Houston	HENDERSON, M.	2	Coweta
HENDERSON, Henry M.	3	Jasper	HENDERSON, O. E.	3	Cass
HENDERSON, Isaac P.	47	Newton	HENDERSON, P.	2	Coweta
HENDERSON, J.	25	Troup	HENDERSON, Wm.	21	Cass
HENDERSON, J. J.	1	Newton	HENDERSON, Wm.	8	Coweta
HENDERSON, J. T.	1	Lee	HENDERSON, Wm. J C.	2	Coweta
HENDERSON, James	44	Jasper	HENDERSON?, H.	22	Pulaski
HENDERSON, James	1	Newton	HENDIN, Wm.	2	Cass
HENDERSON, James B.	11	Harris	HENDLEY, ?	2	Muscogee

Name	Number	County	Name	Number	County
HENDLEY, Milly	1	Pulaski	HENRY, Benjamin	19	Hancock
HENDLEY, Mrs.	1	Muscogee	HENRY, J. P.	13	Chattooga
HENDLEY, Wm.	6	Pulaski	HENRY, James B.	1	Gwinnett
HENDLEY, Wooten?	1	Pulaski	HENRY, John	5	Newton
HENDLY, Wright	1	Emanual	HENRY, John W.	5	Gilmer
HENDLY, Freeman	5	Bullock	HENRY, Joseph	4	Chattooga
HENDLY, Lovering	8	Bullock	HENRY, Joseph	7	Muscogee
HENDON, Elizabeth	4	Troup	HENRY, Lacy	11	Elbert
HENDON, Jas. W.	1	Clarke	HENRY, Margaret	5	Chattooga
HENDON, Margaret	2	Troup	HENRY, Mary	1	Hancock
HENDRICK ?, Gideon	8	Walton	HENRY, Mathew	5	Gwinnett
HENDRICK, A. F.	4	Troup	HENRY, William J.	5	Houston
HENDRICK, John J.	15	Heard	HENRY, William K.	6	Newton
HENDRICK, Stephen D.	4	Upson	HENRY, Wm.	16	Chattooga
HENDRICK, Willson	8	Pulaski	HENRY, Barney	1	Richmond
HENDRICK, Franklin	2	Butts	HENRY, George	6	Stewart
HENDRICK, G.	34	Butts	HENRY, Henderson	1	Taliaferro
HENDRICK, H.	7	Butts	HENRY, Isaac	23	Richmond
HENDRICK, Jno.	37	Randolph	HENRY, Jackson	1	Taliaferro
HENDRICK, M. D.	20	Randolph	HENRY, Josiah	1	Taliaferro
HENDRICKS,			HENRY, Martha	1	Richmond
Richmond R.	7	Pike	HENRY, P.	18	Decatur
HENDRICKS, W.	1	Elbert	HENRY, Wallis	1	Richmond
HENDRICKS,			HENRY?, Dr. Thomas	11	Muscogee
William P.	1	Cobb	HENSLEY, William B.	8	Sumter
HENDRICKS, Jemima	12	Bullock	HENSON, Elam	11	Twiggs
HENDRICKS, Seaborn	1	Bullock	HENSON, George W.	1	Monroe
HENDRICKSON,			HENSON, Jesse	14	Morgan
George R.	3	Chatham	HENSON, John A.	5	Morgan
HENDRIX, Andrew	1	Jackson	HENSON, John M.	33	Morgan
HENDRIX, H. C.	1	Hall	HENSON, Margaret	1	Carroll
HENDRIX, Moses	5	Jackson	HENSON, Thompson	1	Cass
HENDRIX, Thomas	8	Hall	HENSON, Henry	1	Rabun
HENDRIX, S.	2	Clarke	HENTZ, N. M.	1	Muscogee
HENDRY, John A.	8	Liberty	HERB, Frederick estate	41	Chatham
HENDRY, John Sen.	5	Lowndes	HERB, John F.	1	Chatham
HENDRY, L. B.	1	Liberty	HERD, George	8	Merriwether
HENDRY, Robert A.	1	Liberty	HERD, George	5	Merriwether
HENDRY, Robt. L.	6	Harris	HERD, Joseph B.	7	Merriwether
HENDRY, William H.	1	Lowndes	HERD, Eleanor	5	Butts
HENDRY, Alexander	44	Randolph	HERD, Hugh	7	Butts
HENGES, John	4	Chatham	HERD?, Roland D.	5	Meriwether
HENLEY, Jas.	2	Wilkes	HERINDON, M.	13	Walton
HENLEY, John S.	1	Franklin	HERING, H. H.	5	Twiggs
HENLY, Jesse	7	Henry	HERINGTON, Alexander	18	Baker
HENLY, John W.	2	Cobb	HERINGTON, Robert M.	13	Baker
HENLY, Micajah	5	Lincoln	HERMENDY, Joseph	1	Bibb
HENLY, Thos. H.	5	Greene	HERN, Caswell	2	Houston
HENLY, Elihu	1	Floyd	HERN, H.	3	Irwin
HENRICKS, Hester	1	Richmond	HERNANDEZ, Francis	1	Chatham
HENRY, Dexter	2	Wilkes	HERNANDEZ, John E.	2	Chatham
HENRY ?, Wm.	18	Taliaferro	HERNANDEZ, F. S.	4	Bibb
HENRY, Waness	1	Chattooga	HERNANDEZ,		
HENRY, Benj.	31	Harris	Thomas L.	2	Chatham

141

Name	Number	County
HERNDON, B. H.	2	Troup
HERNDON, Edward	14	Merriwether
HERNDON, F. M.	1	Walton
HERNDON, M	21	Elbert
HERNDON, R.	2	Floyd
HERNDON, W. T.	1	Elbert
HERNDON, D.	23	Elbert
HERNDON, George	13	Wilkinson
HERNDON, John P.	8	Troup
HERNDON, Love	5	Wilkinson
HERON, Felin	1	Morgan
HERRAGE, Jas. M.	1	Coweta
HERREN, Gresham	6	Walton
HERRING, Benjamin	2	Lowndes
HERRING, David	7	Walton
HERRING, James	18	Troup
HERRING, James	19	Troup
HERRING, Mary	2	Fayette
HERRING, Nancy	1	Harris
HERRING, (?)	1	Decatur
HERRING, C. W.	16	Decatur
HERRING, E. J.	4	Decatur
HERRING, Louisa	2	Baker
HERRING, W.	15	DeKalb
HERRING, Wm. G.	3	Coweta
HERRING, William	22	Twiggs
HERRINGDINE, Silas	16	Hancock
HERRINGTON, H. H.	3	Lee
HERRINGTON, John	2	Troup
HERRINGTON, Martin	73	Burke
HERRINGTON, Archibald	16	Burke
HERRINGTON, Berry	7	Burke
HERRINGTON, M.	31	Screven
HERRINGTON, R. M.	18	Screven
HERRINGTON, Robert M.	2	Burke
HERRINGTON, Simeon	6	Screven
HERRO N, Jesse	1	Clarke
HERRON, David	1	Greene
HESTER, Albert J.	12	Walton
HESTER, John	3	Walton
HESTER, S.	9	Wilkes
HESTER, Sarah	28	Troup
HERTER, Stephen C.	13	Clarke
HERTY, James	8	Baldwin
HESLEP, David D.	9	Paulding
HESTER, Stephen	6	Effingham
HESTER, Francis	18	Greene
HESTER, Jack	2	Heard
HESTER, Jasper	5	Laurens
HESTER, John	1	Heard
HESTER, M.	15	Morgan
HESTER, Martha	5	Clarke
HESTER, R.	12	Elbert
HESTER, William	3	Laurens
HESTER?, Wm. agt.	25	Bibb
HETWELL?, Leonard	14	Newton
HEWATT?, Thomas	6	DeKalb
HEWATT?,Micajah by Thomas Owen	13	Muscogee
HEWEL, John W.	3	Merriwether
HEWELL, Joseph A.	5	Muscogee
HEWETT, Armsted	1	Baker
HEWIT, N.	3	Chattooga
HEWITT, Ezekiel	2	Jackson
HEWLETT, William L.	2	Chatham
HEY, John H.	2	Pike
HEYS, Samuel	2	Muscogee
HEYWARD, Arthur	263	Chatham
HEYWARD, Margaret	6	Chatham
HIATT, Mrs. Hannah	2	Muscogee
HIBBERD, J.	6	Decatur
HICKEY, Joshua	5	Muscogee
HICKEY, William H.	4	Floyd
HICKEY, Wm.	7	Greene
HICKEY, Wm.	5	Stewart
HICKLE, Nancy	3	Richmond
HICKMAN, Louis	1	Monroe
HICKMAN, M. W.	18	Elbert
HICKMAN, Hamilton H.	7	Richmond
HICKMAN, Joseph	2	Sumter
HICKS, Charles F.	1	Upson
HICKS, Isaac W.	5	Meriwether
HICKS, J.	3	Troup
HICKS, James	38	Emanual
HICKS, John	5	Thomas
HICKS, Jones	16	Macon
HICKS, Samuel	14	Upson
HICKS, Thos. E.	5	Pike
HICKS, Toliver	1	Cobb
HICKS, Amos	8	Chattooga
HICKS, Daniel	15	Stewart
HICKS, E. H.	6	Crawford
HICKS, Grace	60	Crawford
HICKS, J. W.	4	Chattooga
HICKS, Jno.	2	Randolph
HICKS, L. F.	23	Crawford
HICKS, L. N.	8	Crawford
HICKS, Lucy A.	3	Coweta
HICKS, Mary	4	Crawford
HICKS, N.	7	Crawford
HICKS, Nat.	8	Columbia
HICKS, Sarah	1	Richmond
HICKSON, Seaborn	2	Pike
HICKY, Dollison	20	Coweta
HIGDON, A. D.	5	Lee
HIGDON, R.	45	Laurens

Name	Number	County
HIGDON, Robert	3	Laurens
HIGDON, J.	4	Decatur
HIGGANS, Robt .	2	Decatur
HIGGENBOTHAM,		
Alxr. W.	2	Glynn
HIGGENBOTHAN, John	4	Gordon
HIGGINBOTHAM,		
Sarah	2	Madison
HIGGINS, James	1	Oglethorpe
HIGGINS, Joseph	1	Oglethorpe
HIGGINS, David	16	Butts
HIGGINS, Patillo	1	Butts
HIGGENBOTHAM, ?	1	Wilkes
HIGGENBOTHAM,		
William	6	Walton
HIGGINBOTHAM, ?	9	Walton
HIGGONBOTHAM,		
James	3	Richmond
HIGGS, Southern J.	2	Cass
HIGH, John	6	Jasper
HIGH, Benj.	10	Monroe
HIGH, J. R.	4	Morgan
HIGH, Perkins	13	Morgan
HIGH, Thos.	5	Lee
HIGH, William L.	5	Murray
HIGH, W. H.	18	Bibb
HIGHHAM,		
Thomas H. Jr.	6	Chatham
HIGHNOTE, Philip	1	Stewart
HIGHSAW, James	11	Gwinnett
HIGHSMITH, Daniel	1	Marion
HIGHSMITH, J.	8	Elbert
HIGHSMITH, Thomas H.	7	Cobb
HIGHT, Fielding	5	Floyd
HIGHT, Henry	36	Warren
HIGHTOWER ESTATE	1	Richmond
HIGHTOWER,		
Arnold G.	15	Troup
HIGHTOWER, Daniel	4	Greene
HIGHTOWER, Daniel	16	Harris
HIGHTOWER, Daniel	1	Harris
HIGHTOWER, Daniel	13	Pike
HIGHTOWER, David?	10	Marion
HIGHTOWER, Elias D.	6	Paulding
HIGHTOWER, F. E.	7	Laurens
HIGHTOWER, Henry H.	5	Lownder
HIGHTOWER, Hilliard J.	6	Troup
HIGHTOWER, J. E.	8	Laurens
HIGHTOWER, James	10	Dooly
HIGHTOWER, James	27	Upson
HIGHTOWER, James	79	Upson
HIGHTOWER, Jas. F.	4	Harris
HIGHTOWER, Joel	27	Dooly
HIGHTOWER, Josh	17	Laurens

Name	Number	County
HIGHTOWER, Leroy	1	Harris
HIGHTOWER, Mrs.	3	Laurens
HIGHTOWER, Melissa	1	Upson
HIGHTOWER, Nancy	18	Marion
HIGHTOWER, Presley	15	Troup
HIGHTOWER, R.	12	Henry
HIGHTOWER, R. J.	2	Laurens
HIGHTOWER, Sarah	1	Greene
HIGHTOWER, Seaborn J.	2	Harris
HIGHTOWER, Simeon	12	Fayette
HIGHTOWER, Thos.	6	Greene
HIGHTOWER, William	2	Newton
HIGHTOWER, Winfield	9	Laurens
HIGHTOWER, Wm.	28	Greene
HIGHTOWER, H.	4	Bibb
HIGHTOWER, John	5	Stewart
HIGHTOWER, R. H.	3	DeKalb
HIGHTOWER,		
William P.	5	Campbell
HIGINBOTHAM, J. G.	4	Elbert
HILBERTS, Cornelius	1	Murray
HILBURN, L. J.	7	Floyd
HILDON ?, William H.	1	Sumter
HILEY, Jacob	6	Macon
HILEY, John	37	Macon
HILL, A. J.	2	Greene
HILL, Abner R.	9	Pike
HILL, Adam	6	Cass
HILL, Archibald	1	Marion
HILL, Asap	1	Lumpkin
HILL, B. M.	10	Clarke
HILL, Benjamin H.	7	Troup
HILL, Birdwell	6	Cherokee
HILL, Budcade	4	Warren
HILL, Carter	3	Walton
HILL, Churchwell	2	Warren
HILL, Daniel P.	15	Harris
HILL, David	3	Lumpkin
HILL, Dorothy C.	9	Warren
HILL, Edward Y.	12	Troup
HILL, Edward Y.	26	Troup
HILL, Elizabeth	5	Meriwether
HILL, Ely G.	24	Lee
HILL, Enos N.	2	Warren
HILL, Fredonia E.	1	Liberty
HILL, George	18	Columbia
HILL, Gracy	19	Warren
HILL, Green	43	Houston
HILL, Green B.	1	Pike
HILL, Hampton W.	13	Troup
HILL, Hampton W.	10	Troup
HILL, Henry P.	5	Pike
HILL, Hugh F.	1	Gwinnett
HILL, Isaac	9	Monroe

143

Name	Number	County	Name	Number	County
HILL, Isaac L.	12	Monroe	HILL, Barnard	2	Talbot
HILL, J. S.	1	Troup	HILL, Benjamin	1	Taliaferro
HILL, James	1	Monroe	HILL, Benjamin D.	18	Burke
HILL, James agent	24	Houston	HILL, Benjamin Jr.	8	Richmond
HILL, James H.	14	Thomas	HILL, Chas. B.	4	Richmond
HILL, James M.	1	Warren	HILL, Daniel H.	30	Richmond
HILL, Jasper	6	Harris	HILL, David B.	55	Baldwin
HILL, John	5	Cobb	HILL, Elizabeth	2	Sumter
HILL, John	6	Merriwether	HILL, Frances	5	Coweta
HILL, John	13	Murray	HILL, Geo.	1	Stewart
HILL, John	1	Wayne	HILL, Green	13	Stewart
HILL, John B.	1	Lowndes	HILL, Green	24	Sumter
HILL, John D.	45	Fayette	HILL, Henry B.	2	DeKalb
HILL, John S.	6	Troup	HILL, J.	4	Randolph
HILL, John W.	2	Cobb	HILL, John	13	Richmond
HILL, Jonah	2	Macon	HILL, John	4	Richmond
HILL, Joseph B.	10	Muscogee	HILL, John	3	Telfair
HILL, Joshua	21	Jasper	HILL, John M.	3	Richmond
HILL, Joshua	11	Morgan	HILL, Lee W.	1	Stewart
HILL, L. M.	214	Wilkes	HILL, Nancy	20	Telfair
HILL, Margaret F.	13	Walton	HILL, P. D.	18	Stewart
HILL, Martha P.	36	Wilkes	HILL, Robert D.	25	Baldwin
HILL, Martha R.	4	Troup	HILL, Samuel	2	DeKalb
HILL, Mary	1	Jackson	HILL, T. H.	16	Crawford
HILL, Mrs. E.	5	Jackson	HILL, Thomas E.	3	Richmond
HILL, Nancy	9	Clarke	HILL, W. C.	9	Bibb
HILL, Nancy	1	Lowndes	HILL, William	2	Richmond
HILL, Nancy S.	5	Murray	HILL, Wm.	1	Heard
HILL, Nathaniel C.	24	Houston	HILL, Wm. C.	12	Randolph
HILL, R. S.	8	Elbert	HILL, Wm. G.	37	Coweta
HILL, Reuben	9	Lumpkin	HILL, Wm. M.	4	DeKalb
HILL, Robert A.	14	Warren	HILLIARD, Thomas	17	Laurens
HILL, Robert C.	7	Warren	HILLIARD, L.	1	Stewart
HILL, Robert J.	7	Houston	HILLIARD, Thomas	9	Ware
HILL, Sarah	9	Troup	HILLIARD, ? W.	2	Ware
HILL, Sarah A.	3	Bibb	HILLIARD, William	6	Stewart
HILL, Slaughter	20	Macon	HILLIS, William	1	Burke
HILL, Tabitha	20	Oglethorpe	HILLLBURN, Vann	3	Laurens
HILL, Theophulus J.	25	Walton	HILLMAN, John F.	8	Warren
HILL, Thos.	46	Lee	HILLMAN, Josephus	3	Warren
HILL, Vincent	17	Harris	HILLMAN, Louis E.	7	Warren
HILL, W.	39	Troup	HILLMAN, Martha	1	Marion
HILL, Warren J.	35	Walton	HILLMAN, Samuel T.	6	Warren
HILL, Wiley	28	Monroe	HILLS, Dennis	12	Floyd
HILL, William	14	Lumpkin	HILLS, L. T.	1	Jackson
HILL, William	20	Warren	HILLSMAN, Barnet	32	Hancock
HILL, Wiley P.	69	Wilkes	HILLSMAN, H. H.	8	Morgan
HILL, Wm.	11	Monroe	HILLSMAN, Joshua	14	Talbot
HILL, A. S.	11	Clarke	HILLSMAN, Josiah	8	Talbot
HILL, Allen	44	Stewart	HILLY, F.	8	Elbert
HILL, Aralzaman M.	4	Burke	HILLY, T. M.	13	Elbert
HILL, Augustus S.	6	Richmond	HILLY, Thomas	22	Heard
HILL, B.	4	Talbot	HILLYARD, B.	1	Wilkes
HILL, Barnard	30	Talbot	HILLYER, S. G.	12	Greene

Name	Number	County	Name	Number	County
HILSMAN, Jeffrey E.	16	Hancock	HINSON, Caleb	1	Twiggs
HILSMON, Jeremiah	9	Lee	HINSON, Jas.	1	Pulaski
HILSON, William	1	Warren	HINSON, Saml. T.	6	Marion
HILTON, Elijah	5	Jones	HINSON, J. T.	2	Crawford
HINDS, Leroy B.	4	Greene	HINSON, James	1	Telfair
HINDS, Nathaniel	5	Greene	HINSON, R. A.	2	Crawford
HINDS, Little B.	5	Stewart	HINSON, Wm.	2	Twiggs
HINDS, William M	1	Stewart	HINTON, H. C.	8	Cherokee
HINDS, William M.	15	Stewart	HINTON, J. L.	5	Elbert
HINDSMAN, Peter	21	Henry	HINTON, J. S.	4	Elbert
HINES, Benjamin	7	Bryan	HINTON, Henry	2	Warren
HINES, C. T.	17	Washington	HINTON, Henry	1	Warren
HINES, Charlton	120	Liberty	HINTON, James M.	1	Warren
HINES, Elias D.	14	Harris	HINTON, Jesse	29	Merriwether
HINES, Frank?	4	Bibb	HINTON, Joab	3	Newton
HINES, Henry C.	51	Burke	HINTON, John	2	Wilkes
HINES, James	4	Chatham	HINTON, John agent	5	Muscogee
HINES, James	4	Effingham	HINTON, John W.	20	Newton
HINES, James	47	Meriwether	HINTON, Jos. R.	3	Wilkes
HINES, John W.	1	Troup	HINTON, M. F.	2	Jackson
HINES, Jno. D.	34	Bryan	HINTON, Mary	2	Chattooga
HINES, John	9	Jasper	HINTON, Seaborn A.	7	Walker
HINES, Littleberry	29	Jasper	HINTON, W. G.	12	Henry
HINES, Louis	12	Troup	HINTON, Wood	15	Jackson
HINES, Presley	67	Harris	HINTON, Bradford	5	Campbell
HINES, Robert C.	26	Liberty	HINTON, Robert	11	Talbot
HINES, Samuel	13	Troup	HINTON?, Elijah	11	Newton
HINES, Thomas	3	Troup	HISTERS?, A.	4	Irwin
HINES, Thomas	10	Warren	HITCH, Sylvanus	6	Jones
HINES, Thos. K.	28	Effingham	HITCHCOCK, Jas. M.	18	Hancock
HINES, Welcom	5	Lee	HITCHCOCK, John W.	4	Madison
HINES, Wm.	10	Lowndes	HITCHCOCK, Joseph	1	Hancock
HINES, Ann M.	7	Bryan	HITCHCOCK, Julia	10	Madison
HINES, Geo W.	5	Bibb	HITCHCOCK, Lucy	4	Paulding
HINES, Georgia C.	4	Bryan	HITCHCOCK,		
HINES, J. H.	5	Burke	Randford E.	16	Madison
HINES, James	5	Bryan	HITCHCOCK, Sarah	3	Washington
HINES, James J.	23	Burke	HITCHCOCK, Shad. L.	5	Hancock
HINES, Joseph H.	13	Burke	HITCHCOCK, D. L.	3	Putnam
HINES, Lewis	2	Bryan	HITTLER?, Nathaniel	14	Effingham
HINES, Mary J.	4	Bryan	HITOWER, Ephraim	2	Washington
HINES, Miss J.	2	Bibb	HIX, Elizabeth	9	Franklin
HINES, R. H.	3	Bibb	HIX, Hester	8	Newton
HINES, T. J.	29	Randolph	HIX, Uriah	10	Wallker
HINES, Thomas A.	5	Bryan	HIX, W. R.	1	Newton
HINES, Thos.	15	Decatur	HIX, William	1	Franklin
HINES, Thos.	9	Decatur	HIX, Mrs.	1	Decatur
HINES, Urssa	16	Bryan	HIXON, Seaborn	3	Marion
HINLEY, John M. C.	3	Pike	HIXON, Thomas	3	Harris
HINNARD, William	31	Walker	HIXON, Thos.	46	Harris
HINSLER, Ready	5	Floyd	HIXON, Sarah G.	5	Taliaferro
HINSLEY, Robert	17	Jones	HNDERSON, Israel	12	Coweta
HINSLOW, Levi	2	Jones	HOADLY, Henry S.	1	Richmond
HINSON, Asa	1	Lowndes	HOAGKINS, D. C.	4	Bibb

Name	Number	County	Name	Number	County
HOARD, J. M.	1	Butts	HODGES, S. H.	4	Wilkinson
HOARD, William	14	Butts	HODGES, Saml. J.	22	Marion
HOBBS, Benj.	4	Pulaski	HODGES, Samuel M.	2	Jones
HOBBS, David	14	Warren	HODGES, Sarah W.	8	Twiggs
HOBBS, David	2	Warren	HODGES, Stephen	9	Early
HOBBS, James	7	Warren	HODGES, William	8	Washington
HOBBS, John	1	Laurens	HODGES, Abel H.	2	Baldwin
HOBBS, John	5	Warren	HODGES, Asbury	6	Bullock
HOBBS, Joseph	1	Paulding	HODGES, Benjamin	1	Bullock
HOBBS, Jotham	32	Warren	HODGES, E. J.	2	Bibb
HOBBS, Moses	3	Warren	HODGES, Elias	4	Sumter
HOBBS, Nathan	1	Greene	HODGES, Elten	17	Burke
HOBBS, Richard	1	Warren	HODGES, Hardy B.	33	Bullock
HOBBS, Robert	2	Greene	HODGES, Henry	4	Sumter
HOBBS, Thomas F.	17	Warren	HODGES, John S.	15	Stewart
HOBBS, William	3	Warren	HODGES, John T.	1	Sumter
HOBBS, David	14	Columbia	HODGES, Joshua	14	Baker
HOBBS, Jacob	6	Stewart	HODGES, Joshua	3	Bullock
HOBBS, Joab	1	Randolph	HODGES, Lemuel	2	Sumter
HOBBS, John	6	Bryan	HODGES, Moses	1	Bullock
HOBBS, Martha	2	Bibb	HODGES, Mrs. Nancy	3	Burke
HOBBS, Nancy	6	Talbot	HODGES, Nathaniel	1	Bullock
HOBBS, Nancy	4	Talbot	HODGES, Rebecca	1	Bullock
HOBBY, J.	6	Irwin	HODGES, Robert J.	17	Sumter
HOBGOOD, Lewis	13	Fayette	HODGES, Seaborn R.	1	Tatnall
HOBGOOD, Samuel R.	2	Fayette	HODGES, Wiley	3	Stewart
HOBKIRK, Charlotte	4	Chatham	HODGSON & TELFAIR	234	Jefferson
HOBS, R.	1	Pike	HODGSON, Ed. R.	8	Clarke
HOBS, Thomas	33	Houston	HODGSON, William B.	135	Burke
HODGE, Alston	2	Greene	HODNET, James	2	Merriwether
HODGE, Andrew	9	Newton	HODNET, John	13	Merriwether
HODGE, David	4	Newton	HODNET, B. F.	7	Coweta
HODGE, Duke H.	3	Gordon	HODNITT, B.	2	Henry
HODGE, James	16	Newton	HODO, Dyer C.	25	Talbot
HODGE, Rachael	16	Newton	HOES, Bersheba	9	Houston
HODGE, William	5	Muscogee	HOFF, Henry	27	Oglethorpe
HODGE, Ambrose	1	Screven	HOFF, Richard	94	Oglethorpe
HODGE, Jane	11	Screven	HOFFMAN, J.	1	Muscogee
HODGES, A. G. W.	5	Washington	HOGAN, Elizabeth	22	Monroe
HODGES, Archibald	5	Liberty	HOGAN, Hannah	2	Jefferson
HODGES, Benjamin	18	Early	HOGAN, J. D.	2	Wilkinson
HODGES, Charlotte	9	Washington	HOGAN, James E.	3	Harris
HODGES, Edmund K.	38	Houston	HOGAN, John	8	Twiggs
HODGES, Isaac	1	Effingham	HOGAN, John G. R.	3	Wilkinson
HODGES, James H.	2	Houston	HOGAN, Thomas	6	Jones
HODGES, James O.	3	Houston	HOGAN, Tom M.	3	Muscogee
HODGES, Jesse	1	Lowndes	HOGAN, U. B. G.	1	Laurens
HODGES, John	13	Meriwether	HOGAN, Jas.	1	Coweta
HODGES, John	33	Washington	HOGAN, M.	4	Wilkes
HODGES, John W.	1	McIntosh	HOGAN, P.	5	Crawford
HODGES, Josiah	32	Houston	HOGAN, William	19	Campbell
HODGES, Madison M.	3	Madison	HOGAN, William	15	Troup
HODGES, Mrs.	13	Muscogee	HOGANS, Jas.	1	Camden
HODGES, Redding	6	Washington	HOGE, Robert W.	1	Floyd

146

Name	Number	County	Name	Number	County
HOGE, D. B.	7	Randolph	HOLEMAN, James T.	1	Sumter
HOGE, J. S.	4	Bibb	HOLEMAN, Warren	5	Richmond
HOGG, Ellen	6	Greene	HOLEMON, Mrs. Mary	17	Stewart
HOGG, Isaac	4	Greene	HOLENBECK, G.	1	Muscogee
HOGG, James E.	6	Chatham	HOLIDAY, William	11	Dooly
HOGG, James M.	13	Oglethorpe	HOLINGSWORTH,		
HOGG, John	26	Troup	P. V.	13	Irwin
HOGG, William	12	Paulding	HOLISFIELD, Willis R.	4	Heard
HOGG, William B.	7	Troup	HOLIWAY, H.	1	Troup
HOGG, John B.	2	Chatham	HOLLAND, Alexander	12	Jasper
HOGG, Samuel	1	Talbot	HOLLAND, Daniel	17	Twiggs
HOGON, Elizabeth	12	Lincoln	HOLLAND, Daniel	9	Twiggs
HOGON, John	3	Lincoln	HOLLAND, Eli	2	Thomas
HOGON, William	3	Lincoln	HOLLAND, F. W.	1	Jefferson
HOGSET, William W.	4	Dooly	HOLLAND, Jefferson	3	Franklin
HOGUE, Robert J.	1	Sumter	HOLLAND, Jesse	1	Murray
HOINES, Thomas	4	Chatham	HOLLAND, John	4	Houston
HOLADA, Thos. W.	4	Randolph	HOLLAND, John	5	Laurens
HOLAWAY, G. R.	7	Randolph	HOLLAND, John	2	Pulaski
HOLBROOK,			HOLLAND, Jonas H.	87	Jasper
Christopher	1	Forsyth	HOLLAND, Joseph L.	36	Jones
HOLBROOK, E. L.	3	Forsyth	HOLLAND, Lawson S.	21	Jasper
HOLBROOK, Hannah	6	Forsyth	HOLLAND, Lewis R.	3	Jasper
HOLBROOK, Mahala	1	Forsyth	HOLLAND, Margart	3	Jasper
HOLBROOK, Nathan	14	Clarke	HOLLAND, Mary	2	Jefferson
HOLBROOK, Pleasant	6	Franklin	HOLLAND, Mary A.	1	Forsyth
HOLBROOK, Sarah	1	Forsyth	HOLLAND, O. S.	2	Monroe
HOLBROOK, Thomas P.	3	Franklin	HOLLAND, Olanda	12	Monroe
HOLCOM, A. W.	1	Pike	HOLLAND, Randolph	19	Pike
HOLCOM, Henry	10	Newton	HOLLAND, Robert	2	Franklin
HOLCOMB, Nancy	6	Lumpkin	HOLLAND, Thomas	4	Franklin
HOLCOMB, W. P.	5	Oglethorpe	HOLLAND, A.	5	Coweta
HOLCOMB, H. C.	3	DeKalb	HOLLAND, C. S.	16	Coweta
HOLCOMB, Henry L.	17	Dooly	HOLLAND, Elizabeth	7	Burke
HOLCOMBE, A. K.	4	Meriwether	HOLLAND, G. W.	17	Coweta
HOLCOMBE, Jesse	5	Habersham	HOLLAND, Henry	4	Sumter
HOLCOMBE, Russel	1	Habersham	HOLLAND, J. R.	1	Bibb
HOLCOMBE, Eliza	8	Chatham	HOLLAND, James	7	Dooly
HOLCOMBE, James	30	Talbot	HOLLAND, Jethro	3	Sumter
HOLCOMBE, Thomas	3	Chatham	HOLLAND, Moses	3	Chattooga
HOLCOMBE?, Nancy	4	Habersham	HOLLAND, Tobias	12	Taliaferro
HOLDEN, Jane	4	Taliaferro	HOLLAND, William	20	Tatnall
HOLDEN, Thomas	13	Taliaferro	HOLLAND, Wm.	17	Decatur
HOLDER, James	24	Washington	HOLLENSHEAD,		
HOLDER, John	1	Wilkinson	Thomas	4	Lincoln
HOLDER, T.	12	Wilkinson	HOLLENWORTH, Mrs.	4	Bibb
HOLDER, Tapley	1	Clarke	HOLLEY, Elizabeth J.	4	Pike
HOLDER, Jos.	5	Camden	HOLLEY, Frederick	10	Franklin
HOLDER, Uriah	17	Stewart	HOLLEY, Henry F.	12	Troup
HOLDERFIELD, Mary	3	Jasper	HOLLEY, John A.	9	Franklin
HOLDERFIELD, Willis	3	Butts	HOLLEY, Nathaniel	17	Franklin
HOLDING, Lucy	3	Heard	HOLLEY, Pleasant	31	Franklin
HOLEMAN, T. G.	13	Wilkinson	HOLLEY, William	10	Franklin
HOLEMAN, Nathan	3	Houston	HOLLEY, Allen	3	Sumter

Name	Number	County
HOLLIDAY, Allen T.	9	Wilkes
HOLLIDAY, Ashley	1	Burke
HOLLIDAY, H. B.	1	Pike
HOLLIDAY, John M.	6	Jackson
HOLLIDAY, John S.	6	Fayette
HOLLIDAY, N.	10	Wilkes
HOLLIDAY, R. K.	3	Fayette
HOLLIDAY, Robert	4	Fayette
HOLLIDAY, Nathaniel	19	Stewart
HOLLIDAY, Wm. D.	15	Wilkes
HOLLIMAN, (?)	36	Columbia
HOLLIMAN, (?)	14	Columbia
HOLLIMAN, Benson	3	Columbia
HOLLIMAN, D.	4	Putnam
HOLLIMAN, David	7	Columbia
HOLLIMAN, Freeman	1	Columbia
HOLLIMAN, Louisa	13	Columbia
HOLLIMAN, Sam	19	Columbia
HOLLIN, J.	3	Randolph
HOLLINGSHEAD, T.	1	Coweta
HOLLINGSWORTH, J.	18	Henry
HOLLINGSWORTH, J. H.	3	Morgan
HOLLINGSWORTH, Levi	2	Heard
HOLLINGSWORTH, M.	1	Newton
HOLLINGSWORTH, William	6	Newton
HOLLINGSWORTH, J.	3	Bibb
HOLLINGSWORTH, Mary	1	DeKalb
HOLLINGSWORTH, Robert	1	DeKalb
HOLLINGSWORTH, W. T.	15	Bibb
HOLLINSHEAD, Anderson	15	Macon
HOLLINSHEAD, Ann	14	Macon
HOLLINSHEAD, James S.	39	Macon
HOLLINSHED, William	7	Houston
HOLLINSWORTH, Isaac	1	Screven
HOLLIS, Ezekiel	6	Marion
HOLLIS, Henry	8	Marion
HOLLIS, James M.	22	Marion
HOLLIS, John	16	Marion
HOLLIS, John	3	Morgan
HOLLIS, Joseph	3	Harris
HOLLIS, Joseph P.	1	Morgan
HOLLIS, Moses J.	13	Monroe
HOLLIS, Thomas	78	Monroe
HOLLIS, Thomas	15	Morgan
HOLLIS, William	4	Harris
HOLLIS, Wm.	9	Marion
HOLLIS, Edwin L.	4	Chatham
HOLLIS, George	2	Talbot
HOLLIS, Joseph	3	Talbot
HOLLIS, Marlin T.	6	Talbot
HOLLIS, Richard	30	Talbot
HOLLIS?, M. E. L.	7	Harris
HOLLISTER, R. B.	3	Chatham
HOLLOCK, Phineus M.	7	Chatham
HOLLODAY, Andrew	51	Chatham
HOLLODAY, John T.	1	Warren
HOLLOMAN, E. W.	28	Carroll
HOLLOWAY, Anthony	3	Troup
HOLLOWAY, Dabney P.	6	Jones
HOLLOWAY, Catharine	2	Bullock
HOLLOWAY, Eliza	2	Bullock
HOLLOWAY, Griffin	5	Thomas
HOLLOWAY, James	2	Thomas
HOLLOWAY, Jane	11	Richmond
HOLLOWAY, Martha	13	Upson
HOLLOWAY, Nancy	37	Upson
HOLLOWAY, Robert S.	11	Upson
HOLLOWAY, Stephen	4	Bullock
HOLLOWAY, William	10	Thomas
HOLLOWAY, Wm.	6	Bullock
HOLLY, Benj. J.	4	Marion
HOLLY, Garett	80	Stewart
HOLLY, James R.	11	Stewart
HOLLY, Ozwell	29	Stewart
HOLMAN ?, Francis	1	Richmond
HOLMAN, Thornton	1	Meriwether
HOLMAN, Christian	2	Coweta
HOLMAN, D.	20	Randolph
HOLMANSWORK?, Joseph	1	Pike
HOLMES, Adam T.	9	Houston
HOLMES, Amelia	3	Meriwether
HOLMES, Arthur G.	7	Gwinnett
HOLMES, C. L.	1	Laurens
HOLMES, David	9	Clarke
HOLMES, David M.	20	Houston
HOLMES, Edwin	1	Laurens
HOLMES, Henry	10	Gwinnett
HOLMES, J. R.	6	Troup
HOLMES, Isaac	34	Houston
HOLMES, J. M.	1	Pike
HOLMES, J. W.	2	Hancock
HOLMES, James C.	7	Pike
HOLMES, James G.	2	Pike
HOLMES, James P.	58	Early
HOLMES, John D.	7	Pike
HOLMES, Jonathan T.	16	Jones
HOLMES, Joseph	6	Hancock
HOLMES, Josiah	26	Pike
HOLMES, Margeret M.	2	Richmond

Name	Number	County	Name	Number	County
HOLMES, Robert W.	2	Wilkes	HOLT, Wilton	4	Merriwether
HOLMES, Sarah	8	Oglethorpe	HOLT, J. G.	10	Bibb
HOLMES, Vivion	25	Gwinnett	HOLT, John	20	Columbia
HOLMES, Washington	1	Gwinnett	HOLT, John H.	12	Richmond
HOLMES, Wiley T.	4	Wilkes	HOLT, P. T.	9	Bibb
HOLMES, G. W.	6	Early	HOLT, Peyton	77	Putnam
HOLMES, J.	3	Crawford	HOLT, Raleigh	30	Talbot
HOLMES, James	32	Talbot	HOLT, Ralleigh	4	Talbot
HOLMES, James S.	1	Chatham	HOLT, Robert	4	Stewart
HOLMES, W.	1	Gwinnett	HOLT, William	30	Talbot
HOLMES, William	12	Richmond	HOLT, William W.	64	Richmond
HOLMES, William T.	57	Talbot	HOLT, Wm.	4	Bibb
HOLMES, Wm.	5	Bibb	HOLTEN, Abel	4	Dooly
HOLMS, George P.	4	Talbot	HOLTON, Mary	13	Houston
HOLMS, James	22	Talbot	HOLTON, Frances F.	3	Appling
HOLOMON, Mark	8	Stewart	HOLTON, Margaret	9	Houston
HOLOWAY, David	1	Early	HOLTON, Nathaniel M.	8	Marion
HOLSCLAW, H.	1	Talbot	HOLTON, Robert O.	3	Houston
HOLSENBACK, (?)	1	Columbia	HOLTON, Sarah	2	Chatham
HOLSENBAKE, Ben	9	Columbia	HOLTZCLAW, Henry	3	Meriwether
HOLSENBAKE, Tom	4	Columbia	HOLTZCLAW, J. G.	14	Greene
HOLSENBAKE, W. D.	3	Sumter	HOLYMAN, Mrs.	1	Early
HOLSENDOF, John	7	Bibb	HOLZENDORF, Lewis	16	Camden
HOLSEY, Gideon	5	Hancock	HOLZENDORF, Pas.	29	Camden
HOLSEY, Hopkins	10	Clarke	HOLZENDORF, Alexr.	55	Camden
HOLSEY, James K.	18	Pike	HOLZENDORF,		
HOLSEY, Thos.	5	Pike	Jno. L. K.	29	Camden
HOLSOBAKE, Marshal	11	Columbia	HOLZENDORF, Wm. B.	15	Camden
HOLSOMBECK, Alfred	39	Jasper	HOMES, John	8	Oglethorpe
HOLSTEAD, Wm. B.	5	Bibb	HOMES, Mary	5	Washington
HOLSTEN, Elbert	2	Macon	HOMES, William	12	Oglethorpe
HOLSTEN, Jackson	2	Macon	HONEYCUT, .L. M.	10	Coweta
HOLSTEN, Seaborn J.	1	Macon	HONEYCUT, J. E. P.	9	Coweta
HOLSTIN, Stephen	30	Macon	HONET, M. D.	3	Wilkes
HOLSTON, T. M.	5	Chattooga	HONIKER, Robert	1	Chatham
HOLT, A. T. Esq	44	Houston	HONSELL, Marshall	1	Dooly
HOLT, Ann	4	Houston	HOOD, Andrew	4	Marion
HOLT, Asa	47	Jefferson	HOOD, Burwell	3	Wilkes
HOLT, Asy	6	Chatham	HOOD, Bynum	7	Heard
HOLT, Fowler	3	Houston	HOOD, Daniel	6	Muscogee
HOLT, Hines	17	Muscogee	HOOD, David	1	Pike
HOLT, James	5	Floyd	HOOD, E. C.	21	Harris
HOLT, John P.	8	Cobb	HOOD, Eli	13	Pike
HOLT, Kintchin	2	Monroe	HOOD, Harriett C.	3	Jackson
HOLT, Mary	12	Monroe	HOOD, James	4	Gwinnett
HOLT, P. S.	2	Monroe	HOOD, Joel	33	Merriwether
HOLT, Paton	11	Monroe	HOOD, John B.	3	Cass
HOLT, R. D.	8	Monroe	HOOD, Robert T.	1	Pike
HOLT, Raleigh	6	Marion	HOOD, Robin G.	7	Harris
HOLT, Richard	15	Gwinnett	HOOD, Saml.	1	Cass
HOLT, S. S.	31	Houston	HOOD, Sherrod	7	Washington
HOLT, T. G.	45	Houston	HOOD, Stephen R.	1	Jackson
HOLT, Tarpley	8	Marion	HOOD, William	1	Washington
HOLT, T. T. P.	18	Upson	HOOD, Alfred J.	1	Richmond

Name	Number	County	Name	Number	County
HOOD, Chas.	2	Wilkinson	HOPKINS, John A.	4	Campbell
HOOD, H.	5	Wilkinson	HOPKINS, John D.	9	Troup
HOOD, Hillary	12	Washington	HOPKINS, Lemuel	11	Madison
HOOD, Wm. C.	5	Heard	HOPKINS, Moses	4	Harris
HOOD, Z. C.	1	Randolph	HOPKINS, Mrs.	20	Camden
HOOK, Daniel	6	Jefferson	HOPKINS, Nancy	3	Oglethorpe
HOOK, Lewis M.	1	Cherokee	HOPKINS, O. C.	52	McIntosh
HOOK, Jacob	4	Cherokee	HOPKINS, Oliver P.	2	Madison
HOOKER, Nathaniel W.	2	Richmond	HOPKINS, Thos. S.	22	Glynn
HOOKER, R.	2	Bibb	HOPKINS, William	2	Harris
HOOKER, Samuel A.	14	Chatham	HOPKINS, William		
HOOKES, Jamea	2	Baker	Agent	23	Upson
HOOKES, Robert S.	17	Baker	HOPKINS, Adam	2	Richmond
HOOKS, James R.	3	Dooly	HOPKINS, Estate Thrs.	6	Richmond
HOOKS, L.	14	Lee	HOPKINS, J. F.	2	Chattooga
HOOKS, Hardy	5	Sumter	HOPKINS, Lambeth	8	Richmond
HOOKS, Henderson	1	Sumter	HOPKINS, Solomon	5	DeKalb
HOOKS, Homer	7	Sumter	HOPKINS, Susan	43	Camden
HOOKS, Hopewell	7	Washington	HOPKINS, W. T. estate	131	Camden
HOOKS, Jesse	8	Sumter	HOPKINS, Wiley	2	Campbell
HOOKS, John	3	Stewart	HOPKINS, Willis	1	Campbell
HOOKS, Jonathan	4	Wilkinson	HOPKINS, Wm.	17	Randolph
HOOKS, Raiford	2	Sumter	HOPPER, Jonathan	6	Oglethorpe
HOOKS, Sarah	40	Dooly	HOPPER, William	12	Gordon
HOOKS, Sarah	5	Washington	HOPPER, Saml.	1	Rabun
HOOKS, T.	1	Wilkinson	HOPPIN, E.S. Jr.	42	Clarke
HOOKS, William	20	Dooly	HOPPING, Ephraim S.	10	Clarke
HOOPER, Francis M.	8	Troup	HOPPS, Daniel	6	Appling
HOOPER, Harrison M.	10	Cobb	HOPSON, Edward	4	Wilkinson
HOOPER, Jane	6	Cass	HOPSON, Sabry	9	Troup
HOOPER, Lauton	4	Morgan	HOPSON, Willliam	29	Troup
HOOPER, M. B.	2	Franklin	HORA, Henry	8	Baker
HOOPER, Oban? R.	2	Pike	HORD, Gallant	1	Hall
HOOPER, R.	4	Muscogee	HORDEN, E. J.	5	Muscogee
HOOPER, Thomas	6	Cobb	HORETHEN?, ?	1	Elbert
HOOPER, Wm. A.	7	Gordon	HORN, Alford	1	Monroe
HOOPER, Benjamin	10	Stewart	HORN, Arthur B.	2	Houston
HOOPER, Enoch	1	DeKalb	HORN, B. H.	12	Laurens
HOOPER, Henry H.	6	Richmond	HORN, C. W.	27	Laurens
HOOPER, James	6	DeKalb	HORN, Crosby	8	Laurens
HOORS?, James	2	Oglethorpe	HORN, Elisha	1	Macon
HOOVER, John	6	Wilkinson	HORN, George	2	Murray
HOPE, Enoch J.	1	Liberty	HORN, Hendley F.	8	Liberty
HOPE, Wm.	10	Liberty	HORN, James M.	4	Thomas
HOPKINS, Charles H.	104	McIntosh	HORN, Jesse R.	17	Houston
HOPKINS,			HORN, Joab W. C.	21	Houston
Col. George H.	1	Gwinnett	HORN, John A. M.	1	Lowndes
HOPKINS, G. B.	2	Lincoln	HORN, Josiah	8	Laurens
HOPKINS, Henry J.	1	Cobb	HORN, Josiah	9	Pulaski
HOPKINS, Isiah	3	Madison	HORN, Thomas	1	Monroe
HOPKINS, Jackson P.	1	Madison	HORN, Thomas H.	1	Upson
HOPKINS, James	9	Meriwether	HORN, Whittington	1	Muscogee
HOPKINS, John	11	Madison	HORN, C. N.	12	Putnam
HOPKINS, John A.	4	Cambpell	HORN, Elijah	11	Talbots

Name	Number	County
HORN, J.	2	Chattooga
HORN, J. E. J.	12	Sumter
HORN, Jas.	2	Randolph
HORN, Joel	7	Sumter
HORN, Mary E.	17	Sumter
HORN, Thomas	8	Sumter
HORN, Wm. D.	26	Twiggs
HORN?, John	3	Marion
HORNADY, N. A.	2	Monroe
HORNE, Onun	6	Macon
HORNE, Q. U.	4	Baldwin
HORNE, Thos. E.	2	Coweta
HORNIDAY, Henry C.	1	Dooly
HORNING, Phillip	5	Effingham
HORNSBAY, Noah	6	DeKalb
HORNSBY, Joseph	14	Campbell
HORRELL, Mary W.	19	Hancock
HORSELY, James	15	Upson
HORSELY, John	4	Meriwether
HORSELY, Joseph	6	Randolph
HORSHAM, Moses	20	Habersham
HORSHEW?, M. M.	2	Habersham
HORSLEY, David	5	Randolph
HORTEN, Thomas	1	Emanual
HORTMAN, Jacob C. Agent	31	Bibb
HORTON, Hosia	3	Jackson
HORTON, Jeremiah	19	Troup
HORTON, John	25	Jackson
HORTON, John	3	Jasper
HORTON, John M.	4	Lowndes
HORTON, John R.	5	Campbell
HORTON, Labad	3	Newton
HORTON, Mrs. Nancy	2	Muscogee
HORTON, Paton F.	7	Pike
HORTON, Seaborn	1	Jasper
HORTON, Thomas G.	4	Gwinnett
HORTON, Turner	2	Newton
HORTON, Wm.	1	Henry
HORTON, Daniel	3	Stewart
HORTON, H. H.	1	Crawford
HORTON, J. agt.	23	Bibb
HORTON, John G.	107	Stewart
HORTON, W. F.	1	Chattooga
HORTON, Wiley B.	5	Stewart
HORWELL, T. ?	24	Putnam
HOSEH, Henry	4	Jackson
HOSKIN, Harris D.	8	Houston
HOSKINS, James	9	Lincoln
HOSKINS, Tabitha	1	Jones
HOSKINS, D.	7	Crawford
HOSLEY, Jas	2	Crawford
HOSTEN, Wm. B.	1	Randolph
HOTCHKISS, N. P.	49	Glynn

Name	Number	County
HOUG, James	2	Walker
HOUGH, A. S.	4	Morgan
HOUGH, James	12	Talbot
HOUGHTON, Ann R.	15	Greene
HOUGHTON, Jas. M.	39	Greene
HOUGHTON, Mary K.	28	Greene
HOUGHTON, John W.	39	Richmond
HOULAND, J.	1	Elbert
HOURAN, Ellen	2	Chatham
HOUSE, ? (Worthan)	11	Muscogee
HOUSE, Dennis	2	Lincoln
HOUSE, Leiston	4	Lincoln
HOUSE, Lewis	12	Lincoln
HOUSE, Lott	11	Lincoln
HOUSE, M. G.	1	Lincoln
HOUSE, Nancy W.	8	Clarke
HOUSE, Philip	5	Morgan
HOUSE, R.	2	Henry
HOUSE, Samuel	6	Cobb
HOUSE, Thomas P.	4	Franklin
HOUSE, Jacob	1	DeKalb
HOUSE, Paschal	2	DeKalb
HOUSE, Philip	4	DeKalb
HOUSE, Saml.	18	DeKalb
HOUSE, T.	8	Crawford
HOUSE, Thomas	18	Stewart
HOUSE, William	5	Cobb
HOUSE, William	2	Stewart
HOUSEMAN, J. J.	2	Carroll
HOUSER, David H.	12	Houston
HOUSER, Lewis M.	14	Houston
HOUSLEY, William	1	Richmond
HOUSTON, B. C.	28	Elbert
HOUSTON, George W.	8	Harris
HOUSTON, George W.	4	Harris
HOUSTON, James C.	35	McIntosh
HOUSTON, Thomas A.	12	McIntosh
HOUSTON, John Sen.	17	Coweta
HOUSTON, Martha	8	Coweta
HOUSTON, Sam	1	Early
HOUSTON, Sarah	17	Coweta
HOUSTOUN, Eliza	2	Chatham
HOUSTOUN, Patrick	23	Chatham
HOUSWORTH, Abram	3	DeKalb
HOUSWORTH, Michael	1	DeKalb
HOUSWORTH, Philip	12	DeKalb
HOVER, John	49	Chatham
HOVER, Lemuel	25	Chatham
HOVER, Agnes	6	Chatham
HOW, Mary	3	Bibb
HOWARD, Asa J.	14	Oglethorpe
HOWARD, Benj.	3	Monroe
HOWARD, Caroline	1	Cobb
HOWARD, Corodan H.	9	Jasper

Name	Number	County	Name	Number	County
HOWARD, D.	13	Laurens	HOWARD, Sarah	3	Chatham
HOWARD, Daniel	5	Pike	HOWARD, Stephen	9	Dooly
HOWARD, David	9	Monroe	HOWARD, T. C.	10	Crawford
HOWARD, Edward	4	Walker	HOWARD, Wm. F.	23	Oglethorpe
HOWARD, Ellis	5	Monroe	HOWARD, Wm. H.	10	Richmond
HOWARD, George	26	Early	HOWARD?, John F.	17	Lee
HOWARD, George	1	Muscogee	HOWE, George W.	78	Liberty
HOWARD, Green Berry	41	Meriwether	HOWE, John T.	8	Marion
HOWARD, Hardy	7	Jackson	HOWE, Wm.	7	Marion
HOWARD, Henry	11	Appling	HOWE, Wm. S.	12	Monroe
HOWARD, India	1	Dooly	HOWE, R.	18	Crawford
HOWARD, Jacob	9	Liberty	HOWE, William	2	Chatham
HOWARD, James W.	1	Pike	HOWEL, Evan Esq.	45	Gwinnett
HOWARD, James W.	4	Wilkes	HOWEL, H. H. Agent	20	Upson
HOWARD, John Jr.	7	Monroe	HOWEL, Henry	1	Macon
HOWARD, John Sen.	33	Monroe	HOWEL, Lewis	1	Lincoln
HOWARD, John G.	22	Morgan	HOWEL, Isaac	29	Campbell
HOWARD, John H.	8	Muscogee	HOWEL, John H.	2	Coweta
HOWARD, Joseph	27	Monroe	HOWEL, S.M.	1	Screven
HOWARD, Joseph	12	Monroe	HOWEL, Wm. M.	5	Screven
HOWARD, Joseph G. W.	2	Monroe	HOWELL, ?	5	Lowndes
HOWARD, Mary	6	Oglethorpe	HOWELL, ?E.	15	Thomas
HOWARD, Mrs. E.	9	Oglethorpe	HOWELL, Alexr. J.	27	Hancock
HOWARD, Nathan	2	Cass	HOWELL, Archibald	23	Cobb
HOWARD, Peter	5	Early	HOWELL, Burwell	7	Upson
HOWARD, Robert	26	Newton	HOWELL, Clark	24	Forsyth
HOWARD, Robert	20	Newton	HOWELL, D. W.	17	Troup
HOWARD, Robert	37	Oglethorpe	HOWELL, Egleert?	1	Oglethorpe
HOWARD, S.	3	Washington	HOWELL, Elisha	2	Emanual
HOWARD, Samuel	1	Pike	HOWELL, Elizabeth	40	Lowndes
HOWARD, Sarah	18	Lee	HOWELL, Green	11	Pulaski
HOWARD, Stephen	27	Jasper	HOWELL, H.	2	Merriwether
HOWARD, Theobald	2	Muscogee	HOWELL, H. H.	3	Upson
HOWARD, Thos.	11	Oglethorpe	HOWELL, H. W.	14	Forsyth
HOWARD, William	7	Jefferson	HOWELL, J. C.	10	Hancock
HOWARD, William	12	Thomas	HOWELL, J. L.	3	Muscogee
HOWARD, William N.	30	Harris	HOWELL, Jackson	2	Newton
HOWARD, Willis	17	Jefferson	HOWELL, James C.	17	Gordon
HOWARD, A. D.	6	Randolph	HOWELL, John	4	Upson
HOWARD, A. S.	7	Putnam	HOWELL, Jno.	4	Pulaski
HOWARD, A. W.	1	DeKalb	HOWELL, John	1	Fayette
HOWARD, C.	11	Cass	HOWELL, John	5	Muscogee
HOWARD, H. H.	16	Bibb	HOWELL, John J.	20	Hancock
HOWARD, H.J.	9	Putnam	HOWELL, Joseph	1	Jackson
HOWARD, Harriett	14	Baldwin	HOWELL, Joseph M.	20	Lowndes
HOWARD, John	49	Putnam	HOWELL, Mark	5	Oglethorpe
HOWARD, John	13	Talbot	HOWELL, McKinney	27	Greene
HOWARD, John T.	3	Talbot	HOWELL, Phillip	5	Troup
HOWARD, Louisa	7	Richmond	HOWELL, Thos.	12	Pulaski
HOWARD, Martha	3	Columbia	HOWELL, Thos. B.	15	Pulaski
HOWARD, Mrs. E. J.	6	Muscogee	HOWELL, William	1	Monroe
HOWARD, Nancy	8	Randolph	HOWELL, William	5	Troup
HOWARD, Penelope	13	Baldwin	HOWELL, William B.	1	Cobb
HOWARD, Samuel	1	Richmond	HOWELL, William J.	27	Early

Name	Number	County	Name	Number	County
HOWELL, Wm.	1	Henry	HUCKABY, Green	1	Muscogee
HOWELL, Wm. D. M.	7	Lowndes	HUCKABY, Seaborn	1	Muscogee
HOWELL, Wright	1	Twiggs	HUCKABY, John	2	Stewart
HOWELL, Absan K.	8	Taliaferro	HUCKABY, Wm. B.	3	Coweta
HOWELL, E.	5	Crawford	HUCKEBY, Green	2	Stewart
HOWELL, Elizabeth	17	Talbot	HUCKENS, Hugh	7	Gwinnett
HOWELL, James	7	Sumter	HUCKERBY, Nancy	2	Bibb
HOWELL, James	3	Talbot	HUCKEY (Hickey?),		
HOWELL, Jno.	7	Randolph	James	17	Muscogee
HOWELL, John	42	Decatur	HUCKEY (HIckey?),		
HOWELL, Richard H.	2	Chatham	James	14	Muscogee
HOWELL, Sarah	1	Chatham	HUCKEY (Hickey?),		
HOWELL, Thomas	8	Talbot	James	1	Muscogee
HOWELL, Thomas	1	Talbot	HUCKEY (Hickey?),		
HOWES, William	7	Stewart	John J.	6	Muscogee
HOWIK?, John D.	1	Muscogee	HUCTINGSON,		
HOWSE, John S.	3	Jackson	Nicholas	12	Harris
HOWZEN, John	8	Newton	HUD(?), T. B.	5	Decatur
HOY, James	4	Dooly	HUDDLESTON, J. F. N.	7	Monroe
HOY, James A.	11	Dooly	HUDDLESTON, John	19	Monroe
HOYE, James C.	7	Monroe	HUDGENS, Hamlen	5	Cobb
HOYL, Peter F.	25	DeKalb	HUDGENS, May	5	Habersham
HOYLE, Adam	19	Gwinnett	HUDGINS, Beverly	1	Hall
HOYLE, George S.	3	Cherokee	HUDGINS, F. S.	4	Chattooga
HOYT, Nathan	5	Clarke	HUDGINS, John	1	DeKalb
HUBBARD, B. M.	40	Greene	HUDLOW, Michael	1	Lumpkin
HUBBARD, B. W.	84	Oglethorpe	HUDSON, Alfred S.	9	Jefferson
HUBBARD, B. W.	4	Oglethorpe	HUDSON, Benjamin A.	9	Macon
HUBBARD, Benj. F.	36	Marion	HUDSON, Charles	10	Newton
HUBBARD, J.R.	10	Wilkinson	HUDSON, D. N.	7	Elbert
HUBBARD, Jacob	5	Cobb	HUDSON, David	4	Muscogee
HUBBARD, John T.	4	Oglethorpe	HUDSON, David	1	Wilkes
HUBBARD, Richard B.	30	Jasper	HUDSON, David	6	Wilkinson
HUBBARD, William	2	Hall	HUDSON, E.	7	Jefferson
HUBBARD, Wm.	28	Wilkes	HUDSON, E. J.	1	Henry
HUBBARD, S. H.	7	Coweta	HUDSON, Eason D.	19	Warren
HUBBARD, Stephen	1	Telfair	HUDSON, Elijah	2	Newton
HUBERT, Benjamin F.	11	Warren	HUDSON, George B.	1	Gwinnett
HUBERT, Harmon	35	Warren	HUDSON, George F.	8	Warren
HUBERT, Hiram	6	Warren	HUDSON, George W.	7	Franklin
HUBERT, John T.	14	Sumter	HUDSON, Henry B.	19	Houston
HUBERT, Matthew H.	27	Warren	HUDSON, James agent	64	Laurens
HUBERT, Robert W.	6	Warren	HUDSON, John F.	11	Warren
HUBERT, William	56	Sumter	HUDSON, Jno. P.	10	Forsyth
HUCHINGS, William	3	Jefferson	HUDSON, Joshua	1	Franklin
HUCHINS, James A.	5	Gwinnett	HUDSON, M.	23	Elbert
HUCHINSON, F.	12	Henry	HUDSON, Mary	8	Murray
HUCHINSON, Nathaniel	28	Harris	HUDSON, Mathew	3	Houston
HUCKABA, James B.	2	Muscogee	HUDSON, N.	7	Henry
HUCKABAY, C. P.	4	Lee	HUDSON, N. G.	4	Henry
			HUDSON, Noah L.	23	Jefferson
HUCKABAY,			HUDSON, Perry	10	Jefferson
George W.	2	Sumter	HUDSON, R. W.	8	Troup
HUCKABEE, James	4	Hall	HUDSON, Richard	8	Houston

Name	Number	County	Name	Number	County
HUDSON, Thomas P.	7	Gwinnett	HUGHES, D. G.	18	Twiggs
HUDSON, William A.	2	Muscogee	HUGHES, Eliza B.	16	Floyd
HUDSON, Wm. N.	3	Wilkinson	HUGHES, Elizabeth	4	Franklin
HUDSON, Wylanty	7	Jefferson	HUGHES, Hadin	20	Twiggs
HUDSON, C. F.	4	Bibb	HUGHES, Hadin	20	Twiggs
HUDSON, Cyrus	13	Burke	HUGHES, Hadin	61	Twiggs
HUDSON, F. M.	7	Coweta	HUGHES, Haywood	107	Twiggs
HUDSON, Hampton	35	Richmond	HUGHES, James	1	Floyd
HUDSON, Irby	26	Hancock	HUGHES, John	1	Forsyth
HUDSON, J. R.	2	Crawford	HUGHES, John	1	Twiggs
HUDSON, James M.	2	DeKalb	HUGHES, Rufus J.	1	Walton
HUDSON, John	30	Putnam	HUGHES, Thomas M.	2	Twiggs
HUDSON, John J.	5	Sumter	HUGHES, William	11	Gordon
HUDSON, Martha	35	Putnam	HUGHES, Wm. Jr.	3	Liberty
HUDSON, Martha	5	Putnam	HUGHES, Wm. Sr.	11	Liberty
HUDSON, Mary	1	Richmond	HUGHES, Samuel	8	Baldwin
HUDSON, Mrs. Mary	2	Burke	HUGHES, William	2	Randolph
HUDSON, Rebecca	1	Baldwin	HUGHES, William W.	99	Burke
HUEGUININ, Eliza	4	Chatham	HUGHEY, E. G. C.	1	Henry
HUETT, Edmond	4	Stewart	HUGHEY, Joseph	16	Clarke
HUEY, A. B.	15	Harris	HUGHEY, T.	5	Henry
HUEY, John	1	DeKalb	HUGHS, A.	33	Elbert
HUFF, Daniel	15	Muscogee	HUGHS, G. B.	9	Wilkinson
HUFF, Franklin	10	Pike	HUGHS, J. C.	3	Wilkinson
HUFF, George M.	15	Warren	HUGHS, J. T.	11	Wilkinson
HUFF, James M.	4	Harris	HUGHS, N.	10	Wilkinson
HUFF, James R.	3	DeKalb	HUGHS, N. W.	6	Wilkinson
HUFF, John	4	Muscogee	HUGHS, Beady	1	Appling
HUFF, John A.	1	Gwinnett	HUGHS, William Jr.	9	Muscogee
HUFF, Jonathan	17	Warren	HUGHS, Edward	7	Screven
HUFF, Joseph	3	Warren	HUGHS, Mathew	6	Bibb
HUFF, Leonidas	4	Wilkes	HUGHS, Sim	4	Coweta
HUFF, Leroy	1	Clarke	HUGHS, W. H., jailor	7	Bibb
HUFF, Robt.	1	Wilkes	HUGLE, John	4	Meriwether
HUFF, Travis	7	Bibb	HUGLEY, A. F.	10	Chattooga
HUFF, Whitfield	2	Pike	HUGLY, Mason	12	Monroe
HUFF, William	3	Harris	HUGLY, Zachariah	57	Monroe
HUFF, William H.	13	Walker	HUGUENIN, E. D.	134	Sumter
HUFF, Winny	15	Oglethorpe	HUGUENIN, Eliza	49	Chatham
HUFF, Daniel	7	Talbot	HUGULEY, Amos	58	Wilkes
HUFF, David	6	Carroll	HUGULEY, Charles	15	Harris
HUFF, Donaldson	19	Talbot	HUGULEY, George	15	Harris
HUFF, Green	6	Clarke	HUGULEY, George	23	Troup
HUFF, Green	11	Talbot	HUGULEY, Jno. A.	3	Wilkes
HUFF, J. C.	1	Randolph	HUGULEY, John	31	Wilkes
HUFF, Joseph	5	Talbot	HUGULEY, John T.	3	Wilkes
HUFF, L.C.	56	Cass	HUGULEY, Wm.	5	Wilkes
HUFFMAN, Henry	2	Cass	HUGULY, Henry	9	Harris
HUGDEN, Frances	3	Oglethorpe	HUGUNS, J. B.	1	Bibb
HUGEONS, John G.	1	Monroe	HUIE, James	3	Cobb
HUGER, T. P.	97	Glynn	HUIE, Robt.	1	Fayette
HUGGINS, John J.	9	Clarke	HUKEY, ?	7	Muscogee
HUGGINS, Jas.	16	Coweta	HUKEY, James	1	Muscogee
HUGH, Lelmual guard	1	Muscogee	HULBUT ?, James	13	Richmond

Name	Number	County	Name	Number	County
HULETT?, Henry	4	Lowndes	HUNGERFORD, Anson	3	Jasper
HULIN, Andrew	12	Harris	HUNGERFORD, C. H.	6	Randolph
HULIN, Andrew	5	Harris	HUNLEY, Ambrose	33	Harris
HULIN, Marcus A.	5	Harris	HUNLEY, J. W.	4	Muscogee
HULIN, Samuel	2	Harris	HUNLY, Abrose	4	Harris
HULING, James	61	Wilkes	HUNNICUT, Wm.	3	Bibb
HULL, Henry	38	Clarke	HUNNICUTT, Wm. P.	2	Gwinnett
HULL, Henry	23	Oglethorpe	HUNT, ?	9	Elbert
HULL, Henry Jr.	8	Clarke	HUNT, Adaline	3	Harris
HULL, Jos.	61	Camden	HUNT, Alexander J.	29	Jones
HULL, Thomas	10	Cobb	HUNT, Ann T.	14	Floyd
HULL, Arbury	49	Clarke	HUNT, Appleton	7	Fayette
HULL, Wm. W.	17	Camden	HUNT, Benjamin F.	1	Walker
HULLM, G. W.	7	Elbert	HUNT, D. R.	1	Lee
HULLM, H. B.	4	Elbert	HUNT, Daniel E.	1	Warren
HULLM, J. T.	11	Elbert	HUNT, Elisha	2	Union
HULLM, John	13	Elbert	HUNT, H. H.	28	Upson
HULLM, M.	1	Elbert	HUNT, Hellun	9	Habersham
HULSEY, Charles	3	Hall	HUNT, Henry	2	Harris
HULSEY, Elijah M.	5	Houston	HUNT, Hezekiah	4	Warren
HULSEY, Dicy	13	DeKalb	HUNT, Howell H.	7	Warren
HULSEY, Wm. M.	7	DeKalb	HUNT, J. M.	2	Clarke
HUMAN, H.D.	1	Putnam	HUNT, J. P.	1	Elbert
HUMBER, Charles C.	8	Troup	HUNT, James	8	Walker
HUME, George	1	Chatham	HUNT, James	1	Walker
HUMPHREY, Alexander	5	Thomas	HUNT, James M.	39	Hancock
HUMPHREY, Daniel	2	Lowndes	HUNT, Joel	5	Henry
HUMPHREY, Hellry	5	Thomas	HUNT, John	2	Washington
HUMPHREY, Jesse	1	Cobb	HUNT, John N.	1	Pike
HUMPHREY, John	1	Thomas	HUNT, John S.	3	Cobb
HUMPHREY, Joshua	1	Henry	HUNT, John S.	1	Henry
HUMPHREY, Mathew	4	Harris	HUNT, Joshua T.	1	Walton
HUMPHREY, Robert	13	Warren	HUNT, Judkins	16	Hancock
HUMPHREY, Wm. R.	1	Hancock	HUNT, Judkins	2	Hancock
HUMPHREYS, David	3	Murray	HUNT, L. R.	1	Murray
HUMPHREYS, David W.	1	Murray	HUNT, Mary	8	Muscogee
HUMPHREYS, Enoch	5	Murray	HUNT, R. C.	1	Elbert
HUMPHREYS, Joab	1	Murray	HUNT, Richard G.	1	Cobb
HUMPHREYS,			HUNT, Samuel M.	1	Cherokee
William Sen.	5	Chatham	HUNT, Thomas	37	Jones
HUMPHREYS, Wm. C.	3	Cass	HUNT, Thomas G.	5	Pike
HUMPHREYS,			HUNT, Thomas M.	54	Hancock
William trustee	2	Chatham	HUNT, Thos. W.	1	Forsyth
HUMPHRIES,			HUNT, W.	4	Elbert
Thomas S.	14	Jones	HUNT, W.	2	Elbert
HUMPHRIES, Charner	22	DeKalb	HUNT, William	5	Floyd
HUMPHRIES, Curtis	6	Screven	HUNT, William	4	Walton
HUMPHRIES, Geo. W.	6	DeKalb	HUNT, William	18	Washington
HUMPHRIES, J. T.	5	DeKalb	HUNT, William B.	37	Hancock
HUMPHRIES, Jas. T.	9	DeKalb	HUNT, William C.	2	Troup
HUMPHRIES, L.	1	Bibb	HUNT, William H.	3	Cobb
HUMPHRIES, Thomas	66	Baldwin	HUNT, William L.	8	Houston
HUMPHRY, A. W.	1	Pike	HUNT, Anderson	9	Baker
HUMPHURS?, S.	2	Bibb	HUNT, Daniel	4	Randolph

155

Name	Number	County	Name	Number	County
HUNT, Henry	2	Randolph	HURD, J. F.	5	Bibb
HUNT, Jno.	9	Randolph	HURLBURT, Roswell	5	Greene
HUNT, John	5	Bibb	HURLEY, Henry	17	Wilkes
HUNT, Joseph	6	Bibb	HURLEY, Sarah	2	Wilkes
HUNT, S. S.	2	Bibb	HURLY, Green B.	9	Stewart
HUNT, W. B.	1	Butts	HURST, Ann	4	Effingham
HUNT, William	9	Stewart	HURST, Benjamin F.	1	Murray
HUNT?, Turner	1	Lee	HURST, Charles B.	2	Burke
HUNTAR, A. D.	32	Elbert	HURST, Elizabeth	11	Effingham
HUNTER, Abel	2	Thomas	HURST, Franklin	3	Marion
HUNTER, Abraham Sen.	49	Lowndes	HURST, George J.	8	Walton
HUNTER, Abram Jun.	30	Lowndes	HURST, Henry	4	Screven
HUNTER, Absalom	3	Troup	HURST, James	1	Newton
HUNTER, Andrew heirs	3	Habersham	HURST, John	19	Newton
HUNTER, Boyd	10	Troup	HURST, Mary	7	Effingham
HUNTER, Charles	45	Twiggs	HURST, Mary	3	Effingham
HUNTER, E. H. W.	5	Jefferson	HURST, Nancy A.	2	Clarke
HUNTER, E. S.	18	Greene	HURST, Newton	2	Newton
HUNTER, Hardy	23	Houston	HURST, Pheby	13	Effingham
HUNTER, Hardy	30	Lowndes	HURST, William	22	Marion
HUNTER, Harriett	10	Chatham	HURST, William	3	Newton
HUNTER, James	49	Chatham	HURST, William	19	Washington
HUNTER, James	36	Chatham	HURST, Elizabeth	3	Burke
HUNTER, James	23	Meriwether	HURST, George W.	22	Burke
HUNTER, Jas.	4	Troup	HURST, Stephen	5	Baker
HUNTER, Jempsey B.	20	Marion	HURST, William S.	11	Burke
HUNTER, Jesse W.	10	Thomas	HURSTON, Jas.	9	Troup
HUNTER, John	3	Chatham	HURSTON, Wm.	10	DeKalb
HUNTER, John	14	Habersham	HURSTON, Wm.	2	DeKalb
HUNTER, John A.	19	Macon	HURT, Joel E.	11	Muscogee
HUNTER, John S.	1	Jackson	HURT, Wm. K.	1	Cass
HUNTER, Johnson	1	Union	HURT, Saml.	16	Carroll
HUNTER, Martha	2	Union	HURT, Sarah	33	Putnam
HUNTER, N. B.	8	Habersham	HURT, Spencer	22	Baldwin
HUNTER, Nathan	25	Oglethorpe	HURT, Spencer	13	Putnam
HUNTER, Saml. S.	1	Jackson	HURT, Thos.	4	Carroll
HUNTER, Starkey	20	Jackson	HUSAN, F. A.	4	Pike
HUNTER, William	2	Gwinnett	HUSCH, J.	3	Chattooga
HUNTER, Wm. R.	11	Lee	HUSK, Henry J.	8	Cobb
HUNTER, Alex.	21	Butts	HUSKEY, William F.	4	Warren
HUNTER, E.	26	Screven	HUSON, T. R.	3	Cobb
HUNTER, G. R.	11	Crawford	HUSON, Frances	16	Baldwin
HUNTER, H.	23	Putnam	HUSON, Marcus D.	59	Baldwin
HUNTER, Hardy H.	3	Baldwin	HUSS, James	1	Jasper
HUNTER, James W.	1	Screven	HUSSEY, Barbary	8	Merriwether
HUNTER, John	4	Coweta	HUSSEY, Hiram	15	Merriwether
HUNTER, Miles	38	Screven	HUSSEY, John H.	5	Merriwether
HUNTER, S. B.	34	Bibb	HUSTON, Jesse	4	Talbot
HUNTER, Seth	2	Talbot	HUSTON, Oliver	3	Coweta
HUNTER, William P.	7	Chatham	HUSTON?, J. L. B.	3	Newton
HUNTER, Wm. T.	1	Coweta			
HUNTER?, William	2	Marion	HUTCHENS,		
HUNTON, James	3	Muscogee	Col. Nathan L.	61	Gwinnett
HURD, Thos.	1	Greene			

Name	Number	County	Name	Number	County
HUTCHENS,			HYMAN, Henry	5	Hancock
Col. Nathan L. guardian	7	Gwinnett	HYST?, Pleasant	2	Newton
HUTCHENS, John P.	19	Gwinnett	IHENEN, Henry	1	Chatham
HUTCHERSON, Jesse T.	1	Monroe	IHLEY, Mary A.	3	Chatham
HUTCHERSON, P. W.	23	Oglethorpe	IKNER ?, Samson	2	Washington
HUTCHERSON,			IKNER, Philip	4	Washington
Peter W.	9	Oglethorpe	ILER, A.W.	1	Morgan
HUTCHESON, Ambrose	55	Greene	ILLGES, J. P.	5	Muscogee
HUTCHINGS, Charles	5	Jones	INABINET, Mary	4	Baker
HUTCHINGS, Robert R.	11	Jones	INGLES, Daniel	10	Clarke
HUTCHINGSON, J. A.	5	Harris	INGRAHAM, (?)	3	Decatur
HUTCHINS, A. G.	5	Forsyth	INGRAHAM, Porter	18	Harris
HUTCHINS, Matthew	13	Burke	INGRAHM, Francis	6	Monroe
HUTCHINS, R. C.	7	Habersham	INGRAM Wm.	15	Putnam
HUTCHINS, Samuel	16	Paulding	INGRAM, A.	1	Troup
HUTCHINS, Sarah	33	Early	INGRAM, A.	38	Wilkinson
HUTCHINS, Wiley	11	Meriwether	INGRAM, Anderson	4	Merriwether
HUTCHINS, Wiley B.	3	Forsyth	INGRAM, Anderson	70	Wilkinson
HUTCHINS, A.	1	Decatur	INGRAM, Ann S.	12	Jasper
HUTCHINS, Martha	3	Richmond	INGRAM, Benjamin F.	1	Pike
HUTCHINS,			INGRAM, Benj. T.	2	Washington
William N.W.	3	Burke	INGRAM, D. B.	1	Laurens
HUTCHINSON, (?)	3	Decatur	INGRAM, H. J.	8	Early
HUTCHINSON, A.			INGRAM, Hue	35	Laurens
decd.	12	Hancock	INGRAM, J.	7	Pike
HUTCHINSON, Charles	17	Upson	INGRAM, Lafayette	141	Hancock
HUTCHINSON, James	6	Campbell	INGRAM, Margaret	1	Laurens
HUTCHINSON,			INGRAM, Margaret	10	Marion
Maxmillian	9	Jasper	INGRAM, Nancy	19	Butts
HUTCHINSON, P. W.	35	Clarke	INGRAM, Benj.	33	Putnam
HUTCHINSON,			INGRAM, Bryant	15	Crawford
Richard P.	11	Lowndes	INGRAM, David	8	Taliaferro
HUTCHINSON,			INGRAM, Eliza	10	Richmond
Thomas S.	6	Jasper	INGRAM, Geo.	1	Randolph
HUTCHINSON, Abel	14	Columbia	INGRAM, James	2	Sumter
HUTCHINSON, Robert	20	Chatham	INGRAM, John	3	Randolph
HUTCHINSON, Seab	3	Columbia	INGRAM, Joseph	1	Talbot
HUTCHISON, John	14	Pike	INGRAM, Mildred	6	Sumter
HUTCINGTON,			INGRAM, R.	1	Crawford
Narthaniel	5	Harris	INGRAM, R.	19	Randolph
HUTEN, W.	27	Henry	INGRAM, S. H.	28	Putnam
HUTSON, Archibald	8	Harris	INGRAM, Thomas	2	Washington
HUTSON, Charles	1	Jackson	INGRAM, Thomas J.	6	Richmond
HUTSON, James M.	2	Cherokee	INGRAM, W.	4	Troup
HUTTLESON, Elza	18	Monroe	INGRAM, W.	23	Wilkinson
HUTTO, Marlin	10	Baker	INGRAM, Washington	19	Wilkinson
HUTTO, Meadelon	4	Thomas	INGRAM, Wm.	38	Randolph
HUTTON, Stephen	5	Newton	INGRAM, Wm. R. A.	16	Crawford
HYDE, Robert	2	Floyd	INGRIM, John S.	6	Floyd
HYDRAULIC			INICHELUTT, Margaret	2	Chatham
COTTON PRESS	11	Chatham	INMAN, Alfred	44	Burke
HYDRICK, Tillman	1	Columbia	INMAN, Allen	68	Burke
HYER, Thomas	2	Newton	INMAN, Daniel	25	Washington
HYLLIR ?, Junius	20	Walton	INMAN, Darcus	1	Walker

Name	Number	County	Name	Number	County
INMAN, Jeremiah	54	Burke	IVEY, Byrant	7	Warren
INMAN, William H. D.	1	Walker	IVEY, Chs.	1	Wilkes
IRBY, Abraham	7	Greene	IVEY, George W.	3	Warren
IRBY, D. R.	1	Jefferson	IVEY, Jesse	3	Warren
IRBY, H. J.	4	Muscogee	IVEY, Josiah B.	2	Warren
IRBY, Harrison B.	20	Houston	IVEY, Mrs. M.	4	Muscogee
IRBY, Samuel	1	Greene	IVEY, Martha	7	Warren
IRBY, William	17	Jefferson	IVEY, Mary	2	Warren
IRON STEAMBOAT			IVEY, Robert	1	Newton
CO.	17	Chatham	IVEY, Robert	15	Thomas
IRVIN, Alexander	33	Pike	IVEY, Sarah	3	Warren
IRVIN, Isaiah S.	129	Wilkes	IVEY, Sterling	43	Warren
IRVIN, J. T.	56	Lincoln	IVEY, Thomas	27	Warren
IRVIN, Josiah T.	62	Wilkes	IVEY, William A.	2	Thomas
IRVIN, Monroe	2	Pike	IVEY, William H.	7	Houston
IRVIN, S.	10	Lincoln	IVEY, Zaccheus	5	Warren
IRVIN, Sarah	8	Pike	IVEY, Charles	8	Baldwin
IRVIN, Thomas J.	7	Pike	IVEY, James	6	Baldwin
IRVIN, William	2	Merriwether	IVEY, R. D.	31	Baldwin
IRVIN, William B.	10	Pike	IVEY, Thomas	10	Columbia
IRVIN, John	13	Stewart	IVEY, W.	3	Screven
IRVINE, John R.	27	Thomas	IVEY, William	4	DeKalb
IRVINE, Thomas C.	6	Thomas	IVILY?, George D.	9	Muscogee
IRVINSON, Starkey	1	Laurens	IVINS, Mary	10	Oglethorpe
IRWIN, C. M.	17	Morgan	IVY, Allen	2	Walton
IRWIN, David	20	Cobb	IVY, Ephraim	14	Upson
IRWIN, John	4	Lowndes	IVY, George	9	Walton
IRWIN, John L.	40	Washington	IVY, Permelia	3	Walton
IRWIN, Josiah	2	Harris	IVY, Thomas	1	Walton
IRWIN, Josiah	1	Jones	IVY, Wilkins S.	11	Walton
IRWIN, S. D.	8	Lee	IVY, William S.	2	Walton
IRWIN, Francis	25	Cass	IVY, Z.	6	Clarke
IRWIN, J. R.	1	Coweta	IVY, Seaborn	8	Columbia
IRWIN, William A.	5	Washington	JACK, William C.	10	Merriwether
IRWIN, William A.	4	Washington	JACK, Patrick	20	Stewart
ISBEAL, Allen	4	Franklin	JACKS, Isaac	17	Clarke
ISBEAL, James	2	Franklin	JACKS, Lindsey	2	Clarke
ISBEL, Pendleton	2	Cass	JACKS, Mrs. E. C.	12	Oglethorpe
ISBELL, Robert	1	Habersham	JACKSON, A. M.	19	Walton
ISOM, F. M.	1	Pike	JACKSON, Aaron	1	Warren
ISOM, Hanah	8	Pike	JACKSON, Absalom	9	Warren
ISOME, Charles	2	DeKalb	JACKSON, Archibald M.	29	Warren
ISON, John F.	1	Pike	JACKSON, B. W.	20	Upson
IVANS, James	3	Walker	JACKSON, Carey W.	1	Walker
IVERSON, Alfred	4	Muscogee	JACKSON, Colden	9	Thomas
IVERSON, Alfred agent	14	Muscogee	JACKSON, Emanuel	1	Warren
IVERSON, B. V.	5	Muscogee	JACKSON, Erwin	12	Washington
IVEY, Adam	40	Warren	JACKSON, H.	1	Wilkinson
IVEY, Adam	1	Warren	JACKSON, H. G.	3	Upson
IVEY, Alexander	2	Warren	JACKSON, J. A.	25	Wilkinson
IVEY, Anderson	6	Warren	JACKSON, James	4	Walker
IVEY, Benjamin	26	Warren	JACKSON, Jesse M.	17	Wilkes
IVEY, Benjamin	1	Warren	JACKSON, John	11	Clarke
IVEY, Bithan	4	Jones	JACKSON, John B.	2	Clarke

Name	Number	County	Name	Number	County
JACKSON, John	26	Upson	JACKSON, John Sr.	30	Clarke
JACKSON, John F.	3	Wilkes	JACKSON, John W.	1	Marion
JACKSON, John W.	1	Warren	JACKSON, John W.	1	Morgan
JACKSON, Joseph	8	Wilkes	JACKSON, Jordan J.	20	Pike
JACKSON, ?	2	Macon	JACKSON, Joseph	5	Franklin
JACKSON, A. H.	4	Greene	JACKSON, Joseph	8	Heard
JACKSON, Abner	1	Clarke	JACKSON, Joseph	1	Jasper
JACKSON, Andrew	1	Effingham	JACKSON, Joseph	2	Liberty
JACKSON, Andrew B.	13	Clarke	JACKSON, Joseph W.	19	Chatham
JACKSON, Andrew M.	25	Oglethorpe	JACKSON, L. B.	23	Greene
JACKSON, Asher	3	Marion	JACKSON, L. B.	2	Murray
JACKSON, C. C.	8	Forsyth	JACKSON, Letitia	15	Clarke
JACKSON, Cavil	3	Harris	JACKSON, Lewis	7	Muscogee
JACKSON, Celia	2	Jasper	JACKSON, M. F.	2	Oglethorpe
JACKSON, E.	3	Hall	JACKSON, Marshall	9	Oglethorpe
JACKSON, Edmond	44	Monroe	JACKSON, Mercer	2	Oglethorpe
JACKSON, Edmond	13	Monroe	JACKSON, Miles G.	4	Pike
JACKSON, Elizabeth	14	Greene	JACKSON, Moses	2	Walker
JACKSON, Elizabeth R.	5	Paulding	JACKSON, N.	8	Henry
JACKSON, Fielding	9	Marion	JACKSON, Obediah	3	Clarke
JACKSON, Gabriel	1	Jackson	JACKSON, Phitetus	17	Merriwether
JACKSON, Green W.	2	Pike	JACKSON, Pleasant	19	Jasper
JACKSON, Hartwell	15	Clarke	JACKSON, R. H. Jr.	9	Greene
JACKSON, Hartwell	11	Clarke	JACKSON, Rebecca	1	Appling
JACKSON, Henry	2	Chattooga	JACKSON, Reddick	11	Monroe
JACKSON, Henry D.	14	Greene	JACKSON, Reuben	3	Heard
JACKSON, Henry F.	8	Pike	JACKSON, Robert M.	6	Monroe
JACKSON, Hillman	5	Clarke	JACKSON, Robt. H.	16	Greene
JACKSON, Hinson	21	Merriwether	JACKSON, Rollin	7	Pike
JACKSON, Isaac C.	8	Greene	JACKSON, S. D.	6	Lee
JACKSON, Isham	20	Merriwether	JACKSON, Samuel F.	4	Warren
JACKSON, J.	6	Henry	JACKSON, Sarah	6	Wilkes
JACKSON, J.	2	Henry	JACKSON, Stephen	7	Clarke
JACKSON, J.	2	Henry	JACKSON, Stephen	35	Greene
JACKSON, J. M.	5	Hancock	JACKSON, Stephen E.	1	Upson
JACKSON, J. S. K.	16	Liberty	JACKSON, Susan	8	Chatham
JACKSON, James	27	Greene	JACKSON, Susan	1	Lee
JACKSON, James W.	43	Greene	JACKSON, T. M.	2	Hall
JACKSON, Jane	7	Chatham	JACKSON, Tho.	1	Wilkinson
JACKSON, Jane	8	Clarke	JACKSON, Thompson	2	Jones
JACKSON, Jefferson	8	Merriwether	JACKSON, W.	7	Pike
JACKSON, Jeremiah	10	Harris	JACKSON, W ?	16	Wilkes
JACKSON, Job	4	Hancock	JACKSON, W. W.	7	Henry
JACKSON, John	6	Clarke	JACKSON, Warren	1	Laurens
JACKSON, John	21	Henry	JACKSON, Wilkins	2	Jasper
JACKSON, John	40	Jasper	JACKSON, William	45	Greene
JACKSON, John	2	Liberty	JACKSON, William	3	Murray
JACKSON, John	8	Newton	JACKSON, William	1	Newton
JACKSON, John	5	Newton	JACKSON, William	15	Pike
JACKSON, John Jr.	7	Jones	JACKSON, William	6	Walker
JACKSON, John B.	34	Oglethorpe	JACKSON, William D.	7	Greene
JACKSON, John E.	35	Greene	JACKSON, William E.	20	Richmond
JACKSON, John S.	16	Greene	JACKSON, William P.	1	Jones
JACKSON, John Sen.	32	Jones	JACKSON, Wm.	2	Clarke

Name	Number	County	Name	Number	County
JACKSON, Wm.	7	Lincoln	JAMES, Benjamin	1	Jones
JACKSON, Wm.	30	Wilkes	JAMES, D.	11	Henry
JACKSON, Wyche	20	Wilkes	JAMES, Daniel	7	Marion
JACKSON, Zadock	4	Lee	JAMES, Easom	1	Marion
JACKSON, A. M.	16	Clarke	JAMES, Elias	6	Twiggs
JACKSON, Ann E.	2	Richmond	JAMES, George V.	29	Paulding
JACKSON, Drury M.	2	Clarke	JAMES, J.	15	Henry
JACKSON, Ephraim	1	Carroll	JAMES, J. B.	6	Meriwether
JACKSON, Frances	27	Putnam	JAMES, John P.	60	Houston
JACKSON, Green	10	Talbot	JAMES, John S.	1	Gilmer
JACKSON, Green S.	2	Baker	JAMES, Jones	1	Twiggs
JACKSON, H. F.	11	Monroe	JAMES, Joseph	1	Appling
JACKSON, H. W.	2	Campbell	JAMES, M. S.	2	Henry
JACKSON, Henry R.	7	Chatham	JAMES, Orman	2	Thomas
JACKSON, J. M.	1	Randolph	JAMES, Sera E.	10	Oglethorpe
JACKSON, James B.	13	Talbot	JAMES, Sherard Sr.	3	Gilmer
JACKSON, James W.	1	Baker	JAMES, Spencer T.	1	Heard
JACKSON, Jesse	18	Sumter	JAMES, T. E.	2	Elbert
JACKSON, John	12	Baker	JAMES, W. E.	1	Elbert
JACKSON, John	18	Screven	JAMES, William	4	Floyd
JACKSON, John	25	Sumter	JAMES, William F.	27	Paulding
JACKSON, John K.	1	Richmond	JAMES, Wm.	12	Monroe
JACKSON, John S.	6	Taliaferro	JAMES, A. J.	4	Crawford
JACKSON, Joseph	1	Talbot	JAMES, D.	3	Crawford
JACKSON, M. A.	1	Chatham	JAMES, E.		
JACKSON, Mark	1	Cass	by J. CLARK	57	Lee
JACKSON, Mary	13	Sumter	JAMES, John	2	Campbell
JACKSON, N.	11	Crawford	JAMES, John	16	Crawford
JACKSON, N. A.	2	Cass	JAMES, John	5	Richmond
JACKSON, Paul E.	4	DeKalb	JAMES, John	1	Tatnall
JACKSON, Rober W.	1	Campbell	JAMES, Mary	1	Campbell
JACKSON, Robert	12	Campbell	JAMES, S.	1	Decatur
JACKSON, Robert	1	Chatham	JAMES, Thomas	1	Dade
JACKSON, Sam	5	Columbia	JAMES?, George B.	3	Pike
JACKSON, Samuel H.	3	Campbell	JAMESON, James	1	Lowndes
JACKSON, Sarah	1	Sumter	JAMESON, James J.	21	Talbot
JACKSON, Shadrich	8	Campbell	JAMESON, Seaborn	3	Talbot
JACKSON, Thomas	2	Talbot	JAMESON, S. Y.	5	Union
JACKSON, Thomas G.	11	Sumter	JAMESON, Thomas	2	Talbot
JACKSON, Thos. J.	1	Coweta	JAMISON, David	115	Houston
JACKSON, W. B.	2	Campbell	JAMISON, N. J.	9	Cherokee
JACKSON, Wilie	1	Taliaferro	JAMISON, N. J.	1	Cherokee
JACKSON, William B.	3	Campbell	JAMISON, Nancy	26	Talbot
JACKSON, Wm. E.	1	Richmond	JANES, David H.	42	Lee
JACOB, Dammison	1	Cobb	JAQUES, R. W.	4	Muscogee
JACOB, Timon	1	Hall	JARATT, James A.	6	Baldwin
JACOBS, Joseph	13	Lincoln	JARE, Thomas	1	Gilmer
JACOBS, Josiah	1	Heard	JARNAGAN, Margaret	6	Carroll
JACOBS, Thomas	4	Gwinnett	JARRATT, Alexander	18	Baldwin
JACOBS, Peter	4	Chatham	JARRATT, Anne	51	Baldwin
JACOBS, Tech	1	Randolph	JARRATT, William A.	65	Baldwin
JAMES STEAM			JARREL, Blake F.	19	Jones
BOAT Co.	51	Richmond	JARREL, Joseph	3	Pike
JAMES, Archibald G.	6	Richmond	JARRELL, E. P.	32	Greene

Name	Number	County	Name	Number	County
JARRELL, Elisha P.	6	Hancock	JENKINS, Edmond	1	Harris
JARRELL, Martha	9	Clarke	JENKINS, Edmond	31	Muscogee
JARRELL, Redden	30	Greene	JENKINS, Edmond	13	Muscogee
JARRELL, Stinson	11	Clarke	JENKINS, Jas. J.	6	Laurens
JARRELL, George	12	Clarke	JENKINS, James L.	35	Washington
JARRELL, Mary	5	Butts	JENKINS, John	6	Houston
JARRELL, William B.	6	Tatnall	JENKINS, John	20	Pike
JARRELL, Willis	2	Butts	JENKINS, John H.	4	Muscogee
JARRELL, Willis	1	Randolph	JENKINS, John W.	1	Houston
JARRET, A. B.	2	Campbell	JENKINS, Julie?	1	Pike
JARRETT, Arthur	2	Jackson	JENKINS, Lewis	1	Harris
JARRETT, Deveraux	33	Habersham	JENKINS, Lucy E.	17	Gwinnett
JARRETT, Devereaux	35	Habersham	JENKINS, Martha	5	Early
JARRETT, Devereaux			JENKINS, Mary	20	Pike
guardian	17	Habersham	JENKINS, Mrs. Ann	27	Houston
JARRETT, Howell	5	Jackson	JENKINS, Mrs. Margaret	12	Houston
JARRETT,			JENKINS, Newton	7	Merriwether
Mrs. James H.	20	Harris	JENKINS, Sterlin	6	Harris
JARRETT, Johnson T.	13	Wilkes	JENKINS, Sterling S.	12	Muscogee
JARRETT, Robert	24	Habersham	JENKINS, Stirling	5	Harris
JARRETT, Charles C.	7	Rabun	JENKINS, Susan	6	Jefferson
JARRETT, George W.	16	Taliaferro	JENKINS, William	1	Harris
JARRETT, Saml.	3	Decatur	JENKINS, William	4	Jasper
JARRETT, Thos. P.	27	Habersham	JENKINS, William D.	99	Glynn
JARRETT,?, John	19	Jones	JENKINS, Williamson	8	Fayette
JARROT, Joshua	3	Monroe	JENKINS, Charles J.	9	Richmond
JARVIS, Jas.	7	Pulaski	JENKINS, Elias	2	Bibb
JEAN, Robert M.	2	Heard	JENKINS, Franklin	26	Sumter
JEFFERS, Burkett M.	1	Jasper	JENKINS, H. M.	16	Stewart
JEFFERS, James D.	1	Burke	JENKINS, Izatus	4	Burke
JEFFERS, Eliza W.	6	Bibb	JENKINS, John	5	Stewart
JEFFERSON, Benjamin	8	Muscogee	JENKINS, Lee	9	Randolph
JEFFERSON, Richard G.	8	Harris	JENKINS, Marion A.	4	Sumter
JEFFREYS, Wm. O.	26	Camden	JENKINS, Mordecai	4	Sumter
JEFFREYS, Wm. O.	3	Camden	JENKINS, Robert B.	10	Sumter
JEFFRIES, Boling	8	Jasper	JENKINS, Robert C.	36	Sumter
JEFFRIES, Colbert	1	Jasper	JENKINS, Sarah	4	Sumter
JEFFRIES, Thomas	26	Jasper	JENKINS, William	8	Burke
JEFFRIES, William J.	2	Paulding	JENKINS, William	5	Screven
JEFFRIES, Sarah	6	Randolph	JENNA, J.	5	Muscogee
JEGEAM?, John M.	4	Merriwether	JENNENERA?, David	4	Bibb
JELKS, J. O.	4	Pulaski	JENNINGS, Giles	7	Clarke
JELKS, Wm. C.	3	Pulaski	JENNINGS, Henry	18	Clarke
JEMMISON, Georgia A.	1	Chatham	JENNINGS, James	22	Lincoln
JENCER, Thomas T.	2	Cass	JENNINGS, James	8	Lincoln
JENELL, James	14	Oglethorpe	JENNINGS, James R.	10	Harris
JENKE ?, William	1	Talbot	JENNINGS, John	4	Lincoln
JENKENS, Charles	2	Paulding	JENNINGS, Lewis W.	16	Pulaski
JENKINS, Cyrus R.	26	Troup	JENNINGS, Nancy	8	Lincoln
JENKINS, William	16	Effingham	JENNINGS, Robert A.	7	Troup
JENKINS, Charles	2	Hancock	JENNINGS, Robert M.	5	Troup
JENKINS, Clark E.	5	Early	JENNINGS, Solomon	25	Oglethorpe
JENKINS, David	2	Harris	JENNINGS, Solomon Jr.	30	Oglethorpe
JENKINS, Dr. John	39	Burke	JENNINGS, Synthia	25	Fayette

Name	Number	County	Name	Number	County
JENNINGS, Thomas	64	Troup	JOHNS, Charles	4	Jackson
JENNINGS, Thos.	6	Harris	JOHNS, Enock	16	Lee
JENNINGS, William	1	Fayette	JOHNS, George R.	2	Merriwether
JENNINGS, Jno.	2	Bibb	JOHNS, Jeremiah	4	Camden
JENNINGS, Robt.	10	Clarke	JOHNS, John	9	Camden
JENNINGS, Thomas J.	7	Richmond	JOHNS, L. J.	2	Harris
JENNINGS, Traves M.	21	Richmond	JOHNS, Leah W.	9	Marion
JENNINS, John J.	3	Fayette	JOHNS, M.	8	Wilkinson
JENNINS, William	29	Fayette	JOHNS, William J.	1	McIntosh
JERKINS?, E. B.	3	Floyd	JOHNS, Alexander	1	Bibb
JERNAGAN, Ptolemy	7	Marion	JOHNS, Andw.	1	Camden
JERNIGAN, Albert	11	Greene	JOHNS, David	1	Burke
JERNIGAN, Francis	11	Monroe	JOHNS, Geo.	10	Camden
JERNIGAN, Lewis A.	15	Washington	JOHNS, John	8	DeKalb
JERNIGAN, Margaret	12	Greene	JOHNS, John B.	2	DeKalb
JERNIGAN, Wm. H.	3	Richmond	JOHNS, Rebecca	8	Wilkinson
JERNIGAN, Zeptha K.	13	Washington	JOHNS, William	19	Wilkinson
JESSE, John	1	Wilkes	JOHNS, William Jr.	16	Wilkinson
JESSEE, J. D.	1	Chatham	JOHNSON, James P.	13	Fayette
JESSUP, G. R.	65	Morgan	JOHNSON, Joseph A.	1	Early
JESSUP, G. L.	3	Wilkinson	JOHNSON, (?)	1	Decatur
JESSUP, Isaac	5	Macon	JOHNSON, A. G.	1	Murray
JESSUP, J. agent	69	Crawford	JOHNSON, A. N.	9	Harris
JESSUP, James	22	Twiggs	JOHNSON, A. P.	1	Henry
JESTER, Abner	21	Butts	JOHNSON, Absalom	4	Laurens
JESTER, Henry	28	Butts	JOHNSON, Alexander	5	DeKalb
JETER, Augustus	1	Houston	JOHNSON, Alexander	14	Newton
JETER, Augustus			JOHNSON, Allen	1	Bibb
agt for TOOK, Allen	36	Houston	JOHNSON, Allen A.	16	McIntosh
JETER, Francis	28	Meriwether	JOHNSON, Amos	1	Hancock
JETER, James A.	17	Meriwether	JOHNSON, Asberry	6	Harris
JETER, John R.	20	Greene	JOHNSON, Augustus	4	Cobb
JETER, Lovick H.	1	Merriwether	JOHNSON, B. A.	2	Cobb
JETER, Thomas	1	Meriwether	JOHNSON, B. B.	5	Forsyth
JETER, William L.	7	Muscogee	JOHNSON, B. C.	9	Harris
JETT, Rich	2	DeKalb	JOHNSON, Benj.	20	Harris
JETY?, Mose	5	Lumpkin	JOHNSON, Benjamin	2	Baker
JEWELL, James	2	Murray	JOHNSON, Benjamin	5	Gilmer
JEWELL, William	24	Oglethorpe	JOHNSON, Bennett W.	1	Marion
JEWELL, William	22	Oglethorpe	JOHNSON, Berry Ann	7	Emanual
JEWETT, Susan	10	Bibb	JOHNSON, Berry D.	19	Heard
JEWETT, Eliza	6	Chatham	JOHNSON, Burton	12	Oglethorpe
JEWITT, H. L.	3	Bibb	JOHNSON, C. H.	4	Pike
JIMISON, Robert T.	1	Muscogee	JOHNSON, Carroll	2	Lee
JIMMERSON, Robert	5	Upson	JOHNSON, Cary	30	Oglethorpe
JIMMERSON, Robert	19	Upson	JOHNSON, Chandler	1	Morgan
JINKS, Gales	12	Butts	JOHNSON, Charles	4	Gwinnett
JOBSON, Francis W.	2	Houston	JOHNSON, D. M.	1	Cherokee
JOBSON, John S.	2	Houston	JOHNSON, D. M.	3	Elbert
JODIN?, A. G.	27	Pike	JOHNSON, Danel D.	20	Oglethorpe
JOHN & JARBO	2	Newton	JOHNSON, Daniel	3	Lumpkin
JOHN B. MATHEWS			JOHNSON, Daniel A.	4	Pike
CO.	1	Richmond	JOHNSON, David	1	Henry
JOHN, John M.	8	Houston	JOHNSON, David	21	Oglethorpe

Name	Number	County	Name	Number	County
JOHNSON, Dennis	15	Gordon	JOHNSON, James T.	39	Oglethorpe
JOHNSON, Duncan	2	Appling	JOHNSON, Jas. D.	4	Jackson
JOHNSON, E.	8	Henry	JOHNSON, Jesse	15	Jefferson
JOHNSON, E. B.	1	Meriwether	JOHNSON, John	8	Emanual
JOHNSON, E. M.	2	Hall	JOHNSON, John	3	Floyd
JOHNSON, E. W.	35	Jefferson	JOHNSON, John	2	Harris
JOHNSON, E. W.	16	Oglethorpe	JOHNSON, John	27	Morgan
JOHNSON, Edward	1	Cobb	JOHNSON, John	1	Morgan
JOHNSON, Eli	5	Hancock	JOHNSON, John	7	Muscogee
JOHNSON, Elizabeth C.	5	Cobb	JOHNSON, John	4	Muscogee
JOHNSON, Ellender	1	Cobb	JOHNSON, John A.	23	Floyd
JOHNSON, Ezra	4	Pike	JOHNSON, John E.	2	Chatham
JOHNSON, Francis S.	13	Jones	JOHNSON, John F.	3	Jackson
JOHNSON, Furney	1	Emanual	JOHNSON, John F.	1	Morgan
JOHNSON, G. B.	3	Pike	JOHNSON, John J.	11	Clinch
JOHNSON, G.D.	3	Pike	JOHNSON, John s.	1	Clinch
JOHNSON, Gabriel	14	Houston	JOHNSON, John S.	5	Lee
JOHNSON, Geo.	10	Chattooga	JOHNSON, Joshua	5	Chattooga
JOHNSON, George	2	Marion	JOHNSON, Kindred B.	1	Emanual
JOHNSON, Gooley A.	8	Early	JOHNSON, L. M.	14	Oglethorpe
JOHNSON, H.	10	Chattooga	JOHNSON, Lancelott	103	Morgan
JOHNSON, H.	12	Lee	JOHNSON, Lewis	10	Warren
JOHNSON, H. C.	13	Henry	JOHNSON, Littleberry	33	Emanual
JOHNSON, H. V.	60	Jefferson	JOHNSON, Luke	2	Gwinnett
JOHNSON, Harrith R.	4	Pike	JOHNSON, Luke G.	6	Oglethorpe
JOHNSON, Isaac	13	Harris	JOHNSON, M.	2	Chattooga
JOHNSON, Isaac	11	Macon	JOHNSON, M.	1	Henry
JOHNSON, Isaac N.	43	Muscogee	JOHNSON, M.	1	Henry
JOHNSON, Isaac W.	76	Oglethorpe	JOHNSON, M.	1	Muscogee
JOHNSON, Isabell	1	Montgomery	JOHNSON, M. A.	4	Elbert
JOHNSON, J.	7	Henry	JOHNSON, M. R.	4	Henry
JOHNSON, J.	1	Henry	JOHNSON, Malcolm	50	Hancock
JOHNSON, J. A. W.	5	Murray	JOHNSON, Mary	9	Houston
JOHNSON, J. C.	20	Clarke	JOHNSON, Mary	13	Jasper
JOHNSON, J. E.	1	Pike	JOHNSON, Mary Ann	20	Emanual
JOHNSON, J. F.	21	Morgan	JOHNSON, Mary Ann	5	Emanual
JOHNSON, J. H.	9	Henry	JOHNSON, Mordaci	7	Meriwether
JOHNSON, J. J.	1	Harris	JOHNSON, N.	11	Elbert
JOHNSON, J. S. C.	1	Elbert	JOHNSON, Nancy	2	Murray
JOHNSON, J. T.	1	Pike	JOHNSON, Nathan	6	Emanual
JOHNSON, J. W.	1	Henry	JOHNSON, Nathan	29	Oglethorpe
JOHNSON, J. W.	1	Morgan	JOHNSON, Peter	2	Greene
JOHNSON, J. W.	35	Oglethorpe	JOHNSON, Posey	2	Heard
JOHNSON, J.W.	1	Henry	JOHNSON, R. W.	22	Jefferson
JOHNSON, James	20	Bryan	JOHNSON, Richard	18	Houston
JOHNSON, James	5	Madison	JOHNSON, Richard	7	Jasper
JOHNSON, James	18	Murray	JOHNSON, Riley J.	7	Floyd
JOHNSON, James	13	Muscogee	JOHNSON, Robert D.	3	Gwinnett
JOHNSON, James	34	Newton	JOHNSON, Robert G.	15	Muscogee
JOHNSON, James	7	Oglethorpe	JOHNSON, Robert G.	15	Oglethorpe
JOHNSON, James C.	8	Lowndes	JOHNSON, S.	1	Elbert
JOHNSON, James D.	2	Muscogee	JOHNSON, S. J.	14	Floyd
JOHNSON, James H.	10	Liberty	JOHNSON, Samuel	6	Muscogee
JOHNSON, James L.	3	Pike	JOHNSON, Samuel	3	Newton

Name	Number	County	Name	Number	County
JOHNSON, Sanford	9	Clarke	JOHNSON, C. G.	10	Twiggs
JOHNSON, Sarah	34	Emanual	JOHNSON, Cephas	5	Troup
JOHNSON, Sarah	13	Heard	JOHNSON, Charles C.	9	Warren
JOHNSON, Scott A.	3	Oglethorpe	JOHNSON, Charles H.	10	Thomas
JOHNSON, Silas	14	Newton	JOHNSON, Daniel	5	DeKalb
JOHNSON, Simeon	1	Emanual	JOHNSON, Daniel	2	DeKalb
JOHNSON, Stephen	1	Hancock	JOHNSON, David	9	Ware
JOHNSON, Stephen	5	Macon	JOHNSON, Dr.	27	Wilkinson
JOHNSON, T.	5	Henry	JOHNSON, E.	1	Bibb
JOHNSON, T. D.	10	Pike	JOHNSON, E.	6	Crawford
JOHNSON, Thomas	2	Gwinnett	JOHNSON, E. J.	8	Bibb
JOHNSON, Thomas	3	Jackson	JOHNSON, Frances	14	Warren
JOHNSON, Thomas	6	Pike	JOHNSON, Freeman	6	Warren
JOHNSON, Thomas T.	26	Houston	JOHNSON, Galer	14	DeKalb
JOHNSON, Thos.	9	Heard	JOHNSON, Green	26	Putnam
JOHNSON, Thos. B.	11	Henry	JOHNSON, H. B.	9	Walker
JOHNSON, Thos. R.	4	Oglethorpe	JOHNSON, Henry	11	Richmond
JOHNSON, Toby	1	Cobb	JOHNSON, Henry	3	Taliaferro
JOHNSON, W. T.	6	Morgan	JOHNSON, Herschel V.	7	Baldwin
JOHNSON, W. W.	1	Murray	JOHNSON, Hershall L.	2	Richmond
JOHNSON, Wiley G.	2	Greene	JOHNSON, Hyram	7	Cherokee
JOHNSON, William	2	Emanual	JOHNSON, Isaac	5	Tatnall
JOHNSON, William	5	Gwinnett	JOHNSON, Isham f.	4	Ware
JOHNSON, William	6	Harris	JOHNSON, Ivy	2	Crawford
JOHNSON, William	4	Harris	JOHNSON, J. C.	1	Bibb
JOHNSON, William	10	Jones	JOHNSON, Jacob	1	Randolph
JOHNSON, William	4	Morgan	JOHNSON, James	38	Warren
JOHNSON, William	3	Murray	JOHNSON, James E.	1	Taliaferro
JOHNSON, William	7	Newton	JOHNSON, James M.	1	Warren
JOHNSON, William A.	8	Houston	JOHNSON, James R.	5	Baker
JOHNSON, William C.	13	Pike	JOHNSON, Jas.	7	Randolph
JOHNSON, William G.	2	Muscogee	JOHNSON, Jas. W.	2	Randolph
JOHNSON, William L.	1	Merriwether	JOHNSON, Jeptha V.	2	Troup
JOHNSON, Wm.	6	Cass	JOHNSON, Jeremiah	14	Twiggs
JOHNSON, Wm. B.	9	Greene	JOHNSON, Jesse	2	Stewart
JOHNSON, Wm. J.	14	Early	JOHNSON, Jesse Jr.	6	Richmond
JOHNSON, Wyatt	1	Chattooga	JOHNSON, Jesse	8	Troup
JOHNSON, Aaron	9	Warren	JOHNSON, John	5	Baker
JOHNSON, Aaron	3	Warren	JOHNSON, John	2	Burke
JOHNSON, Abraham	12	Jones	JOHNSON, John F.	19	Warren
JOHNSON, Alexander	5	Stewart	JOHNSON, John H.	52	Coweta
JOHNSON, Alexander	7	Talbot	JOHNSON, John S.	3	Warren
JOHNSON, Allin	16	DeKalb	JOHNSON, John W.	2	Talbot
JOHNSON, ALLIS	19	Twiggs	JOHNSON, Jno. P.	24	Wilkes
JOHNSON, Amos	7	Warren	JOHNSON, Jos.	20	Putnam
JOHNSON, Andrew	8	Walker	JOHNSON, Laughlin	12	DeKalb
JOHNSON, Asa	1	Warren	JOHNSON, Lemuel	7	Cass
JOHNSON, B. W.	32	Putnam	JOHNSON, Levina	2	Crawford
JOHNOSN, Bailey	16	Troup	JOHNSON, Lindsay	49	Cass
JOHNSON, Benj.	14	Cass	JOHNSON, Luke	11	Troup
JOHNSON, Benj.			JOHNSON, M.	4	Bibb
agt for THOMPSON,C.	55	Houston	JOHNSON, M. B.	1	Carroll
JOHNSON, Benjamin F.	2	Troup	JOHNSON, M. S.	10	Bibb
JOHNSON, Bryant	3	Troup	JOHNSON, Margarett	2	Stewart

Name	Number	County	Name	Number	County
JOHNSON, Margaret	25	Troup	JOHNSON?, M.	16	Oglethorpe
JOHNSON, Mark M.	9	Cass	JOHNSTON, Ahab	1	Monroe
JOHNSON, Matchet	5	Sumter	JOHNSTON, Alexander	3	Lincoln
JOHNSON, Mercer	6	Walker	JOHNSTON, B. C.	4	Troup
JOHNSON, Morgan	13	Bibb	JOHNSTON, Bellerne	13	Chatham
JOHNSON, Moses	34	Burke	JOHNSTON, Bryant	9	Early
JOHNSON, Moses D.	5	Upson	JOHNSTON, Darling	1	Pulaski
JOHNSON, Nicholas	1	Thomas	JOHNSTON, Elizabeth	8	Monroe
JOHNSON, P. H.	21	Bibb	JOHNSTON, Fleming	2	Jasper
JOHNSON, Rev.William	6	Baldwin	JOHNSTON, Gidion	10	Monroe
JOHNSON, Randolph	38	Warren	JOHNSTON, Hiram G.	4	Randolph
JOHNSON, Richard	16	Talbot	JOHNSTON, Isaac	6	Pulaski
JOHNSON, Robert	1	Walker	JOHNSTON, Isaac	2	Pulaski
JOHNSON, Rufus	2	Troup	JOHNSTON, James H.	14	Jasper
JOHNSON, Rufus M.	6	Troup	JOHNSTON, James R.	10	Chatham
JOHNSON, S. C.	1	Crawford	JOHNSTON, Jane E.	9	Chatham
JOHNSON, S. R.	9	Bibb	JOHNSTON, Jasper	1	Gilmer
JOHNSON, Samuel	1	Bullock	JOHNSTON, John	11	Monroe
JOHNSON, Samuel	29	Taliaferro	JOHNSTON, John	3	Walton
JOHNSON, Sankey T.	16	Troup	JOHNSTON, Martha	39	Jasper
JOHNSON, Sarah	6	Twiggs	JOHNSTON, Mary	20	Hancock
JOHNSON, Seaborn	1	Talbot	JOHNSTON, Mary	16	Monroe
JOHNSON, Seaborn	10	Warren	JOHNSTON, Mary A.	2	Chatham
JOHNSON, Seborn A.	22	Troup	JOHNSTON, Micajah	44	Pulaski
JOHNSON, Silas M.	5	Taliaferro	JOHNSTON, P. P.	9	Troup
JOHNSON, Smith	1	Columbia	JOHNSTON, R. A.	3	Walton
JOHNSON, T.	1	Chattooga	JOHNSTON, Rachael	5	Chatham
JOHNSON, Thomas	1	Decatur	JOHNSTON, Richd. M.	20	Hancock
JOHNSON, Thomas J.	32	Baker	JOHNSTON, Ruben	23	Monroe
JOHNSON, Thos.	27	Putnam	JOHNSTON, Seaborn	7	Hancock
JOHNSON, Thos.	1	Wilkes	JOHNSTON, Theodre	1	Walker
JOHNSON, Tyre	1	Wilkes	JOHNSTON, Thomas	9	Elbert
JOHNSON, Vinson	71	Warren	JOHNSTON, William	17	Jasper
JOHNSON, Vinson A.	21	Warren	JOHNSTON, William	78	Morgan
JOHNSON, W.	1	Decatur	JOHNSTON, William M.	24	Pike
JOHNSON, W. L.	1	Bibb	JOHNSTON, Wm.	12	Muscogee
JOHNSON, William	3	Bullock	JOHNSTON, Wm. P.	1	Troup
JOHNSON, William	22	Burke	JOHNSTON, Wm. W.	15	Chatham
JOHNSON, William	1	Columbia	JOHNSTON, Andrew	10	DeKalb
JOHNSON, William	31	Richmond	JOHNSTON, George H.	3	Chatham
JOHNSON, William	3	Troup	JOHNSTON, Jackson	2	DeKalb
JOHNSON, William	2	Warren	JOHNSTON, James	20	Randolph
JOHNSON, William	8	Washington	JOHNSTON, James B.	1	Randolph
JOHNSON, William A.	6	Campbell	JOHNSTON, Littleton	12	Randolph
JOHNSON, William G.	5	Warren	JOHNSTON, Mary	3	Talbot
JOHNSON, William H.	15	Walker	JOHNSTON, Richard	18	Randolph
JOHNSON, William L.	9	Talbot	JOHNSTON, Robert	5	Dooly
JOHNSON, Willis M.	3	Campbell	JOHNSTON, Thos	4	DeKalb
JOHNSON, Wm.	1	Bibb	JOHNSTON,		
JOHNSON, Wm.	1	Bibb	Waller E. Jr.	21	Richmond
JOHNSON, Wm.	12	Cass	JOHNSTON, William	25	DeKalb
JOHNSON, Wm.	26	Taliaferro	JOHNSTON, William	8	DeKalb
JOHNSON, Woodson	12	Putnam	JOHNSTON, William	14	Richmond
JOHNSON?, John	1	Lumpkin	JOHNSTON, William	6	Sumter

Name	Number	County	Name	Number	County
JOHNSTON, Wm. B.	2	DeKalb	JONES, Anthony	17	Warren
JOHNSTON, Wm. B.	4	Dooly	JONES, Arabella	20	Oglethorpe
JOHNSTON?, George W.	1	Muscogee	JONES, Arabella	11	Oglethorpe
JOHNSTON?, N. P.	2	Monroe	JONES, Augustus S.	19	Murray
JOICE, Sarah	2	Ware	JONES, Augustus	9	Thomas
JOINER & BULSELY ?	1	Richmond	JONES, B. A.	1	Morgan
JOINER, A. J.	19	Jefferson	JONES, B. O.	38	Fayette
JOINER, Absalom	21	Monroe	JONES, Baryel	4	Early
JOINER, Bennet	3	Laurens	JONES, Basil	1	Emanual
JOINER, Charles	3	Wayne	JONES, Benjamin	1	Muscogee
JOINER, Davis	6	Laurens	JONES, Benjamin H.	12	Hancock
JOINER, Elizabeth	2	Pike	JONES, Bennett	2	Twiggs
JOINER, Hamell	3	Troup	JONES, Bennington	1	Wilkes
JOINER, Huel A.	2	Washinngton	JONES, Berry	51	Lowndes
JOINER, Isaac	1	Newton	JONES, Bethena	5	Troup
JOINER, J. M.	1	Laurens	JONES, Burwell	2	Wayne
JOINER, John overseer	14	Madison	JONES, C. H.	2	Upson
JOINER, M.	2	Washington	JONES, Charles B.	31	Liberty
JOINER, Mary	3	Monroe	JONES, Charles B.	15	McIntosh
JOINER, Meredith	11	Houston	JONES, Charles C.	107	Liberty
JOINER, Moses	4	Washington	JONES, Christopher	3	Wilkes
JOINER, Rebecca	4	Laurens	JONES, Clarrisa	13	Franklin
JOINER, Sarah	5	Marion	JONES, Clayton	4	Harris
JOINER, Uriah	3	Wayne	JONES, Col. Samuel L.	2	Gwinnett
JOINER, Wells	2	Campbell	JONES, Daniel	1	Lumpkin
JOINER, Asa	2	Stewart	JONES, Daniel L.	1	Jones
JOINER, Bennett	10	Sumter	JONES, Darling	1	Pulaski
JOINER, Burwell	2	Sumter	JONES, David	1	Early
JOINER, John	1	Sumter	JONES, David C.	1	Jasper
JOINER, Mose	4	Sumter	JONES, David E.	19	Monroe
JOINER, Wm.	3	Decatur	JONES, Dr. T.	4	Wilkinson
JOLLEY, John P.	2	Franklin	JONES, Dudley	21	Wilkes
JOLLEY, Joseph	1	Jones	JONES, Dudley M.	9	Madison
JOLLY, Anderson C.	1	Baker	JONES, Dudley M. exc.		
JOLLY, Asa	11	Macon	of JORDAN,T.	?	Madison
JOLLY, Hays	3	Talbot	JONES, E.	21	Twiggs
JOLLY, Jesse	7	Butts	JONES, E. A.	12	Elbert
JOLLY, Joseph	11	Randolph	JONES, E. E.	116	Morgan
JONES ?, Elom	2	Stewart	JONES, E. M.	12	Elbert
JONES, Jno. F.	1	Forsyth	JONES, Early T.	16	Troup
JONES, (none)	1	Muscogee	JONES, Edmond	5	Hancock
JONES, ?, S.	8	Muscogee	JONES, Elford	4	Morgan
JONES, A. Estate	57	Greene	JONES, Elijah	11	Elbert
JONES, A. S.	10	Franklin	JONES, Elizabeth	4	Effingham
JONES, Abner W.	2	Early	JONES, Elizabeth	1	Paulding
JONES, Adam	7	Bullock	JONES, Ezekiel	4	Macon
JONES, Adam	15	Warren	JONES, F. G.	17	Harris
JONES, Agnes	1	Merriwether	JONES, Francis	14	Muscogee
JONES, Alfred	1	Heard	JONES, Francis M.	2	Fayette
JONES, Alfred A.	7	Chatham	JONES, G. H.	1	Troup
JONES, Allen	6	Lowndes	JONES, G. W.	2	Forsyth
JONES, Allen	3	Walton	JONES, Ga.	6	Wilkinson
JONES, Allen J.	9	Merriwether	JONES, Gabrael	30	Floyd
JONES, Ann	2	Fayette	JONES, George	48	Chatham

Name	Number	County	Name	Number	County
JONES, George	117	Jefferson	JONES, John	8	Macon
JONES, H. B.	5	Pike	JONES, John	87	Meriwether
JONES, H. G.	4	Wilkinson	JONES, John	1	Union
JONES, H. P.	73	Laurens	JONES, John A.	20	Muscogee
JONES, H. T.	10	Twiggs	JONES, John A.	100	Paulding
JONES, Harriett	14	Chattooga	JONES, John B.	3	Pike
JONES, Hartwell	20	Cobb	JONES, John E.	3	Chatham
JONES, Henry	2	Clarke	JONES, John H.	4	Early
JONES, Henry	6	Heard	JONES, John J.	3	Marion
JONES, Henry	1	Monroe	JONES, John K.	2	Muscogee
JONES, Henry	22	Pike	JONES, John M.	21	Hancock
JONES, Henry	2	Warren	JONES, John R.	27	Lee
JONES, Henry A.	13	Warren	JONES, John R.	19	Merriwether
JONES, Henry H.	26	Liberty	JONES, John R.	13	Merriwether
JONES, Henry T.	2	Cobb	JONES, John W.	1	Houston
JONES, Howel	5	Washington	JONES, Jonathan	13	Heard
JONES, J.	2	Elbert	JONES, Jos. estate	130	Liberty
JONES, J. B.	7	Early	JONES, Joseph	3	Jasper
JONES, J. H.	33	Elbert	JONES, Joseph H.	16	Franklin
JONES, J. H.	5	Wilkinson	JONES, Josiah	1	Washington
JONES, J. W.	8	Greene	JONES, Josiah G.	2	Early
JONES, J.W.	11	Elbert	JONES, Leroy	11	Walton
JONES, James	28	Elbert	JONES, Lewis	2	Merriwether
JONES, James	15	Elbert	JONES, Lurana	14	Muscogee
JONES, James	2	Fayette	JONES, M. E.	3	Wilkes
JONES, James	8	Ware	JONES, Macon H.	9	Clarke
JONES, James	2	Warren	JONES, Malake	2	Thomas
JONES, James D.	2	Clarke	JONES, Mannam	10	Warren
JONES, James D.	9	Jackson	JONES, Margaret	1	Jones
JONES, James H.	7	Muscogee	JONES, Martha	1	Emanual
JONES, James H.	3	Muscogee	JONES, Mary	1	Fayette
JONES, James H.	6	Paulding	JONES, Mary	5	Houston
JONES, James H. Sen.	92	Muscogee	JONES, Mary	1	Monroe
JONES, James J.	1	Greene	JONES, Mary	5	Twiggs
JONES, James J.	2	Houston	JONES, Mary	23	Wilkes
JONES, James J.			JONES, Mary B.	9	Warren
agt for WIMBERLY	27	Houston	JONES, Mason	11	Heard
JONES, James M.	3	Jefferson	JONES, Mason	1	Heard
JONES, James M.	12	Merriwether	JONES, Micajah	3	Newton
JONES, James N.	20	Liberty	JONES, Mitchell	30	Thomas
JONES, James R.	34	Muscogee	JONES, Mitchell	1	Thomas
JONES, James S.	12	Elbert	JONES, Moses	30	Harris
JONES, James S.	1	Merriwether	JONES, Moses	26	Harris
JONES, James S.	6	Pike	JONES, Moses	1	Heard
JONES, James S.	11	Warren	JONES, Moses L.	103	Liberty
JONES, James T.	2	Franklin	JONES, Mrs.		
JONES, James V.	29	Burke	Elizabeth S. L.	19	Liberty
JONES, Jesse	3	Fayette	JONES, N.	6	Randolph
JONES, Jno.	21	Carroll	JONES, Nancy	16	Twiggs
JONES, John	1	Clarke	JONES, Nancy	3	Walker
JONES, John	8	Cobb	JONES, Nancy L.	6	DeKalb
JONES, John	6	Early	JONES, Nathan	90	Monroe
JONES, John	6	Houston	JONES, Nathan L.	18	Muscogee
JONES, John	1	Laurens	JONES, Osborn	6	Houston

Name	Number	County
JONES, Peter	19	Monroe
JONES, Phebe	4	Wilkes
JONES, Pleasant	2	Newton
JONES, Presley	1	Newton
JONES, R.	3	Muscogee
JONES, R. W.	4	Hancock
JONES, Rachel	66	Lowndes
JONES, Randal	6	Muscogee
JONES, Rev. J.	28	Liberty
JONES, Richard	10	Troup
JONES, Richard	2	Walton
JONES, Richard W.	7	Murray
JONES, Robert	2	Houston
JONES, Robt.	1	Wilkes
JONES, S. S.	10	Elbert
JONES, Saml.	6	Marion
JONES, Saml.	12	Randolph
JONES, Samuel	5	Gilmer
JONES, Samuel	36	Muscogee
JONES, Sarah D.	4	Jones
JONES, Seaborn	56	Muscogee
JONES, Seaborn	4	Pulaski
JONES, Seaborn	36	Washington
JONES, Serena	9	Early
JONES, Stephen	10	Morgan
JONES, Stephen	25	Pike
JONES, Stephen	26	Warren
JONES, Stephen B.	16	Morgan
JONES, Susannah	13	Lowndes
JONES, Tarplay	9	Murray
JONES, Tho.	1	Lee
JONES, Thomas	11	Burke
JONES, Thomas	6	Elbert
JONES, Thomas	1	Houston
JONES, Thomas	28	Newton
JONES, Thomas	73	Thomas
JONES, Thomas	24	Twiggs
JONES, Thomas D.	11	Monroe
JONES, Thomas F.	3	Lowndes
JONES, Thomas F.	18	Newton
JONES, Thomas H.	38	Gwinnett
JONES, Thomas H.	5	Twiggs
JONES, Thomas J.	23	Troup
JONES, Thomas P.	3	Warren
JONES, Thos.	10	Hancock
JONES, Thos.	6	Harris
JONES, Thos.	1	Harris
JONES, Thos.	11	Pike
JONES, Thos. H.	3	Randolph
JONES, Thos. P.	36	Greene
JONES, Thos. W.	9	Oglethorpe
JONES, Toliver	73	Harris
JONES, Toliver	29	Harris
JONES, Toliver	19	Harris
JONES, Toliver	6	Wilkes
JONES, Uriah	7	Houston
JONES, V. & H.	13	Washington
JONES, W. S.	2	Elbert
JONES, W.M.	28	Lincoln
JONES, Wade H.	21	Troup
JONES, Walton	42	Floyd
JONES, Wheaton Jr.	1	Houston
JONES, Wiley	7	Monroe
JONES, Wiley	15	Paulding
JONES, Wiley A.	1	Clarke
JONES, Wiley E. agent	19	Muscogee
JONES, William	1	Greene
JONES, William l	1	Jasper
JONES, William	1	Lincoln
JONES, William	3	Marion
JONES, William	3	Muscogee
JONES, William	2	Muscogee
JONES, William	1	Newton
JONES, William	3	Walker
JONES, William	1	Union
JONES, William L.	1	Jasper
JONES, William R.	1	Pike
JONES, Willis	7	Harris
JONES, Wm.	2	Elbert
JONES, Wm.	1	Henry
JONES, Wm.	45	Lee
JONES, Wm.	80	Liberty
JONES, Wm. B.	10	Floyd
JONES, Wm. H.	9	Clarke
JONES, Wright Sr.	5	Houston
JONES, A.	1	Dade
JONES, A. S.	115	Screven
JONES, A. S.	37	Burke
JONES, Alexander	1	Crawford
JONES, Augustus S.	60	Burke
JONES, Bagil	5	Bullock
JONES, Batt	16	Burke
JONES, Benjamin	27	Taliaferro
JONES, Benjamin C.	3	Taliaferro
JONES, Bridger	1	Bullock
JONES, Charles F.	6	Richmond
JONES, D. J.	10	Crawford
JONES, D. P.	15	Coweta
JONES, Daniel B.	28	Dooly
JONES, David	2	Randolph
JONES, David	1	Randolph
JONES, David	3	Richmond
JONES, E. F.	4	Carroll
JONES, E. M.	1	Bibb
JONES, Edward	20	Columbia
JONES, Edward	12	DeKalb
JONES, Edward	40	Screven
JONES, Elizabeth	1	Baker

Name	Number	County	Name	Number	County
JONES, Elizabeth A.	7	Burke	JONES, Polly	1	Chatham
JONES, Fendoc F.	6	Newton	JONES, R.	2	Dade
JONES, Francis A.	31	Burke	JONES, Robert	1	DeKalb
JONES, G. H.	7	DeKalb	JONES, Robert J.	11	Burke
JONES, George W.	5	Talbot	JONES, Robt.	9	Camden
JONES, Gus	30	Columbia	JONES, Robt.	3	Coweta
JONES, H. M.	11	Clarke	JONES, Robt. W.	3	Telfair
JONES, Harley	9	Camden	JONES, Ruben	19	Stewart
JONES, Henry	5	Stewart	JONES, S. Augustus	25	Burke
JONES, Henry	2	Stewart	JONES, Samuel P.	15	Dooly
JONES, Henry	7	Talbot	JONES, Sarah	2	Chatham
JONES, Henry	12	Taliaferro	JONES, Sarah	2	Taliaferro
JONES, Henry L. B.	6	Paulding	JONES, Sarah H.	8	Coweta
JONES, Henry P.	67	Burke	JONES, Seaborn	8	Randolph
JONES, Henry W.	19	Burke	JONES, Seaborn	4	Talbot
JONES, Hezekiah	5	Putnam	JONES, Seaborn H.	30	Burke
JONES, Ivan	8	Camden	JONES, Sophia	16	Sumter
JONES, J.	25	Chattooga	JONES, T. agt.	20	Bibb
JONES, J.	32	Crawford	JONES, Thos. M.	13	Cass
JONES, J. J.	3	Randolph	JONES, Thos. M.	5	DeKalb
JONES, J. L.	9	Bibb	JONES, Tom	23	Columbia
JONES, James	3	Cass	JONES, Vincent G.	11	Burke
JONES, James	3	Richmond	JONES, Welliby agt.	45	Bibb
JONES, James	4	Stewart	JONES, Wiley K.	4	Columbia
JONES, James	9	Stewart	JONES, William	17	Burke
JONES, James A.	17	Burke	JONES, William	73	Columbia
JONES, James V.	8	DeKalb	JONES, William	4	Dooly
JONES, James W.	1	Richmond	JONES, William	2	Rabun
JONES, Jas.	2	Randolph	JONES, William	5	Richmond
JONES, Jesse	2	Rabun	JONES, William A.	2	Talbot
JONES, John	42	Bibb	JONES, William B.	5	DeKalb
JONES, John	4	Bryan	JONES, William H.	8	Richmond
JONES, John	6	Chatham	JONES, William P.	5	Sumter
JONES, John	12	Columbia	JONES, William S.	14	Richmond
JONES, John	11	Crawford	JONES, Willie	3	Coweta
JONES, John	1	DeKalb	JONES, Wm.	1	DeKalb
JONES, John	5	Talbot	JONES, Wm. T.	6	Richmond
JONES, John	1	Taliaferro	JONSTON, Jonithan	8	Monroe
JONES, John H.	6	Randolph	JORDAN, A. W.	2	Wilkinson
JONES, John H.	1	DeKalb	JORDAN, Abagal	1	Twiggs
JONES, John H.	6	Richmond	JORDAN, Abraham	3	Marion
JONES, Jonas	1	Stewart	JORDAN, Alexander	4	Cobb
JONES, Joseph B.	61	Burke	JORDAN, B. G.	34	Lee
JONES, Kearbro	1	Decatur	JORDAN, Benjamin	54	Jasper
JONES, Lewis N.	1	Rabun	JORDAN, Burrell	57	Pulaski
JONES, M. L.	4	Taliaferro	JORDAN, Catherin	4	Washington
JONES, Martha	5	Bullock	JORDAN, Charles	6	Jefferson
JONES, Martha	2	Talbot	JORDAN, Charles S.	6	Jasper
JONES, Mary	5	Columbia	JORDAN, Cornelius	16	Washington
JONES, Melford	1	Talbot	JORDAN, Dempsey Agt.	32	Upson
JONES, Miles	25	Coweta	JORDAN, E. D.	10	Washington
JONES, Mitchel	18	Columbia	JORDAN, Elizabeth	2	Jefferson
JONES, Mrs. Francis	15	Stewart	JORDAN, Elisha W.	6	Washington
JONES, P. L.	6	Talbot	JORDAN, Elisha W.	9	Washington

169

Name	Number	County	Name	Number	County
JORDAN, Fleming	44	Jasper	JORDAN, W.	3	Randolph
JORDAN, Fleming	14	Jasper	JORDAN, William	1	DeKalb
JORDAN, G. H.	9	Twiggs	JORDAN, William B.	13	Stewart
JORDAN, G. H.	33	Twiggs	JORDAN, William P.	2	Dooly
JORDAN, Isaac G.	10	Thomas	JORDAN, Wm.	32	Crawford
JORDAN, James	2	Washington	JORDAN?, Benj. F.	94	Lee
JORDAN, Jno.	43	Wilkes	JORDEN, Eldred T.	9	Oglethorpe
JORDAN, John	3	Houston	JORDEN, Elilzabeth	14	Oglethorpe
JORDAN, John	15	Jefferson	JORDEN, John M.	51	Lee
JORDAN, John	5	Upson	JORDEN, Josiah G.	44	Monroe
JORDAN, John J.	33	Washington	JORDEN, Mary	8	Lee
JORDAN, John M.	1	Harris	JORDEN, Reuben Sen.	67	Jasper
JORDAN, Joshua	16	Jefferson	JORDEN, Hamlin	1	Talbot
JORDAN, Lorenzo H.	3	Fayette	JORDON, Benj. F.	31	Greene
JORDAN, Mathew	19	Monroe	JORDON, James	1	Monroe
JORDAN, Matthew	20	Jefferson	JORDON, Alfred	2	Richmond
JORDAN, Nick	1	Marion	JORDON, Solomon	2	DeKalb
JORDAN, Reuben	46	Jasper	JORNAGAN, A.	1	Irwin
JORDAN, Reubin	7	Habersham	JOSEPH, Dennis	1	Richmond
JORDAN, Robert	12	Jefferson	JOSEY, John W.	1	Washington
JORDAN, S. G.	9	Jefferson	JOSEY, Robert J.	2	Gwinnett
JORDAN, Sylvester F.	6	Hancock	JOSEY, Henry	2	Stewart
JORDAN, Thomas decd.	6	Madison	JOSEY, J. W.	10	Stewart
JORDAN, Thomas	15	Washington	JOSEY, James W.		
JORDAN, Thomas G.	8	Jefferson	agt for POWERS, A.	33	Houston
JORDAN, Thomas M.	25	Jasper	JOSEY, Malchi	7	Stewart
JORDAN, Wiley	1	Marion	JOSEY, Mary	1	Washington
JORDAN, William D.	8	Washington	JOSEY, R. J.	13	Washington
JORDAN, William T.	38	Jefferson	JOSEY, Samuel	12	Washington
JORDAN, Wm. M.	39	Wilkes	JOSEY?, Andrew	3	Habersham
JORDAN, Willis A.	18	Fayette	JOSSEY?, John H.	9	Pike
JORDAN, Wm.	1	Coweta	JOURDAIN, Henry T.	4	Macon
JORDAN, A.	3	Bibb	JOURDAN, Benj.	83	Morgan
JORDAN, B.S. by			JOURDAN, Robert	4	Gilmer
agt. ALFORD, K.	54	Morgan	JOURDAN, Thomas	2	Muscogee
JORDAN, Benjamin	85	Baker	JOURDEN, E. R.	3	Greene
JORDAN, Benjamin	77	Baldwin	JOURDEN, Elvis	15	Pike
JORDAN, Duncan	5	Randolph	JOURDEN, B. P.	7	Putnam
JORDAN, E.	1	Randolph	JOURDEN, W.	7	Putnam
JORDAN, E. T.	14	Crawford	JOURDIN, James	1	Cobb
JORDAN, Edman	8	Taliaferro	JOURDIN, John	7	Pike
JORDAN, George W.	23	Talbot	JOURDIN, Josiah	2	Stewart
JORDAN, Green H.	81	Baldwin	JOURDON, E. B.	3	Early
JORDAN, J. R.	14	Crawford	JOURNAGIN estate	1	Muscogee
JORDAN, J. W.	3	Crawford	JOURNEGAN, S. F.	12	Hancock
JORDAN, Jane	13	Chatham	JOYCE, James J.	14	Lowndes
JORDAN, Jesse	5	DeKalb	JOYCE, William	2	Montgomery
JORDAN, Joshua	19	Dooly	JOYCE, Washington	4	Randolph
JORDAN, M. J.	13	Crawford	JOYCE, William	18	Tatnall
JORDAN, Miles C.	1	Dooly	JOYNER, A. L.	8	Twiggs
JORDAN, Nathan	3	Baker	JOYNER, Margaret	9	Upson
JORDAN, Rebecca	4	Richmond	JOYNER, Richard W.	18	Cobb
JORDAN, Sarah	1	Coweta	JOYNER, William A.	12	Upson
JORDAN, Seaborn	6	Taliaferro	JUDSON, David N.	2	Greene

Name	Number	County	Name	Number	County
JUHAN, Stephan D.	1	Jones	KELEY, Wm. G.	4	Randolph
JULIAN, Baily F.	4	Forsyth	KELEY, Wm. H.	10	Coweta
JULIAN, Geo. H.	5	Forsyth	KELGON, John L.	10	Walton
JULIAN, Jno. S.	1	Forsyth	KELL, Mazey	76	McIntosh
JULIAN, Saml.	12	Forsyth	KELL, Phineas	6	Butts
JUSTICE, Allen	3	Jackson	KELLAM, Mrs. T.	42	Laurens
JUSTICE, Isaac	1	Pulaski	KELLEBREW, Lindsey	11	Marion
JUSTICE, James	10	Pike	KELLER, Charles A.	8	Chatham
JUSTICE, John	12	Hancock	KELLER, Paul	34	Chatham
JUSTICE, D.	3	Decatur	KELLER, Thos. M.	3	Effingham
JUSTICE, Wm.	5	Decatur	KELLER, Edward	2	Chatham
JUSTISS, William	18	Troup	KELLER, Henry	2	Coweta
KADER, Martha	1	Ware	KELLER, John P.	6	Chatham
KADLE, J. J.	2	Monroe	KELLER, Stephen F.	19	Chatham
KAIGLER, R.	3	Crawford	KELLETT, Martin	5	Chattooga
KAPPEL, Dianah	3	Wilkes	KELLEY, Allen	2	Warren
KARGLER, David	103	Randolph	KELLEY, Hugh P.	1	Oglethorpe
KAY, William D.	8	Baldwin	KELLEY, Isham	2	Newton
KEAN, Alexr.	2	Camden	KELLEY, James	7	Warren
KEAN, Philip	1	Chatham	KELLEY, James M.	3	Warren
KEATON, Benjamin O.	93	Baker	KELLEY, John W.	2	Muscogee
KEATON, James J.	20	Baker	KELLEY, M.	2	Muscogee
KEBLER, Thos.	2	Effingham	KELLEY, R.	8	Washington
KEE, Hezekiah	1	Marion	KELLEY, Thomas	1	Rabun
KEEBLER, Harriet	30	Chatham	KELLEY, William H.	7	Chatham
KEEBLER, Richard	1	Chatham	KELLIBREW, P. P.	4	Heard
KEEL, Arden	1	Bibb	KELLINGSWORTH, G.	3	Bibb
KEEL, Nathaniel C.	12	Baldwin	KELLOGG, Geo.	24	Forsyth
KEEL, William	5	Baker	KELLUM, Gabriel	5	Thomas
KEEN, Ann T.	38	Jasper	KELLUM, Mary	8	Greene
KEEN, Young	5	Laurens	KELLUM, A. R.	2	DeKalb
KEEN, A. V.	30	Dade	KELLUM, George	4	Talbot
KEENE, J.	1	Henry	KELLUM, Seth	11	Dooly
KEENN ?, William	7	Richmond	KELLY, B. A.	2	Walton
KEEVER, James	1	Cass	KELLY G. M.	6	Randolph
KEIFER, Ephrain	14	Effingham	KELLY, J. L.	2	Union
KEIFER, Mary	2	Chatham	KELLY, Abner	3	Hancock
KEILER, John J.	2	Effingham	KELLY, Allen	15	Jasper
KEITH, George	13	Hall	KELLY, Amos	6	Gwinnett
KEITH, Cornelius	10	Lumpkin	KELLY, B. M.	1	Henry
KEITH, Daniel	16	Merriwether	KELLY, Beverly A.	8	Jasper
KEITH, David M.	11	Meriwether	KELLY, Elbert G.	1	Hancock
KEITH, George W.	6	Meriwether	KELLY, Ezekiel B.	6	Jasper
KEITH, George W.	8	Murray	KELLY, Hiram	1	Forsyth
KEITH, George W.	4	Walker	KELLY, J.	1	Elbert
KEITH, J. L.	1	Cherokee	KELLY, Jackson Agent	13	Upson
KEITH, John	11	Lumpkin	KELLY, James	13	Muscogee
KEITH, Martin	6	Murray	KELLY, James	1	Walker
KEITH, Mathew	8	Walker	KELLY, James	1	Upson
KEITH, P. G.	34	Merriwether	KELLY, James B.	1	Washington
KEITH, Reubin W.	5	Meriwether	KELLY, John	1	Early
KEITH, W. J.	7	Pike	KELLY, John	8	Greene
KEITH, M. A.	12	Cherokee	KELLY, John J.	2	Chatham
KEITHISON?, Thos. D.	10	Oglethorpe	KELLY, John N.	5	Jefferson

Name	Number	County	Name	Number	County
KELLY, John R.	9	Jasper	KENAN, Owen H.	37	Murray
KELLY, John W.	10	Campbell	KENAN, Augustus H.	9	Baldwin
KELLY, Miles	6	Jones	KENAN, M. D.	18	Baldwin
KELLY, Mrs. Anna	9	Houston	KENDALL, Charles	4	Muscogee
KELLY, Phoebe	11	Walker	KENDALL, David	81	Upson
KELLY, R. B.	7	Henry	KENDALL, Elizabeth	1	Muscogee
KELLY, Washington	6	Jones	KENDALL, Elizabeth P.	10	Muscogee
KELLY, William O.	4	Jones	KENDALL, Jeremiah	13	Upson
KELLY, W. S.	9	Twiggs	KENDALL, Mrs. Mary	22	Merriwether
KELLY, C. R.	9	Randolph	KENDALL, Reubin	30	Wilkes
KELLY, John	3	Burke	KENDALL, William	2	Fayette
KELLY, John	1	Taliaferro	KENDALL, Isaac	14	Fayette
KELLY, John	25	Dade	KENDALL, James	5	Fayette
KELLY, M.	28	Decatur	KENDELL, Henry H.	7	Marion
KELLY, Wade	5	Decatur	KENDER, David	2	Lincoln
KELLY, William	5	Burke	KENDER, Johnston	2	Lincoln
KELLY, Wm.	3	Camden	KENDRIC, William	37	Columbia
KELSY, Clay	18	Monroe	KENDRICK, Aaron T.	28	Warren
KELSY, Lafayette	4	Monroe	KENDRICK, Burrel J.	2	Merriwether
KELVIN, James	7	Muscogee	KENDRICK, J. A.	45	Houston
KEMBALL, Christr.	14	Henry	KENDRICK, J. A.	6	Houston
KEMBALL, D. T.	3	Henry	KENDRICK, J. K.	2	Merriwether
KEMBALL, William	4	Henry	KENDRICK, Jonathan	12	Heard
KEMEY, Wm.	11	Bibb	KENDRICK, Jonathan	3	Heard
KEMP, A. J.	1	Forsyth	KENDRICK, Jones	51	Houston
KEMP, Aaron	1	Forsyth	KENDRICK, Martin	10	Houston
KEMP, Alsey	5	Cherokee	KENDRICK, Robert	1	Meriwether
KEMP, Benjamin	1	Wilkinson	KENDRICK, Susan	1	Heard
KEMP, Etheldred	1	Wilkinson	KENDRICK, William M.	1	Pike
KEMP, Henry	1	Cobb	KENDRICK, A.	19	Crawford
KEMP, John	1	Wilkinson	KENDRICK, Elenar	2	Taliaferro
KEMP, John	2	Marion	KENDRICK, James	6	Sumter
KEMP, John A.	2	Emanual	KENDRICK, Melton	3	Talbot
KEMP, Joseph	12	Houston	KENDRICK, Robert	2	Talbot
KEMP, Mark agt for			KENDRICK, Robert F.	2	Taliaferro
COMER, A.	81	Houston	KENDRICK, Thomas	4	Lincoln
KEMP, Morgan	1	Marion	KENDRICK, Wiley	7	Talbot
KEMP, Reuben	1	Marion	KENDRICK, William	3	Baker
KEMP, Soloman	9	Cobb	KENEBREW, C. D.	42	Oglethorpe
KEMP, Alexander	13	Screven	KENEDA?, Ambrose	4	Hall
KEMP, Benjamin	2	Sumter	KENEDAY, J. M.	1	Sumter
KEMP, E. C. agt for			KENEDY, A. B.	1	Crawford
J. V. HARRIS	25	Floyd	KENMORE?, Mary G.	9	Harris
KEMP, Jacob H.	2	Baker	KENNADA, Wm.	1	Coweta
KEMP, John	2	Sumter	KENNAN, John	9	Lumpkin
KEMP, Kendred agt for			KENNDY?, Xenophin	13	Newton
HOBS, Thomas	33	Houston	KENNEDAY, James	6	Jefferson
KEMP, Lewis	2	Taliaferro	KENNEDAY, Thomas	11	Jefferson
KEMP, Thomaas	2	Chatham	KENNEDY ?, LLuciusC.	1	Richmond
KEMPTON, Ann V.	26	Chatham	KENNEDY, James	2	Chatham
KENADAY, Jas. M.	3	Lee	KENNEDY, James	2	Gordon
KENADY, James	3	DeKalb	KENNEDY, James A. R.	12	Hancock
KENADY, Thomas	8	DeKalb	KENNEDY, James B.	1	Emanual
KENADY, Thomas A.	1	DeKalb	KENNEDY, John	4	Cass

Name	Number	County	Name	Number	County
KENNEDY, Samuel	2	Emanual	KERLIN, Peter	2	Talbot
KENNEDY, William L.	3	Houston	KERR, John	5	Richmond
KENNEDY, Arthur	8	Columbia	KERR, R. N.	2	Cass
KENNEDY, Edward	18	Tatnall	KERSE, George	8	Dooly
KENNEDY, Gideon H.	4	Emanual	KERSEY, ?	1	Lee
KENNEDY, Harrison	1	Cass	KERSEY, Calvin	1	Lee
KENNEDY, Henry	1	Tatnall	KERSEY, Wm.	3	Coweta
KENNEDY, Jesse J.	4	Sumter	KERST, Mary	1	Chatham
KENNEDY, Jimison	4	Tatnall	KERWICK, Ellen	1	Chatham
KENNEDY, Jno.	16	Columbia	KESLER, George	1	Franklin
KENNEDY, John	1	Chatham	KESLER, William	2	Franklin
KENNEDY, Nancy	5	Richmond	KESTERSON, Thomas	1	Stewart
KENNEDY, Robert J.	1	Walton	KETTAN?, Hiram	4	Hall
KENNEDY, Samuel	3	Burke	KETTERER?, P.	1	Laurens
KENNEDY, Solomon	2	Tatnall	KEY, Abraham	13	Meriwether
KENNEDY, Stephen	4	Tatnall	KEY, Burrel	2	Emanual
KENNER, Thomas J.			KEY, Burrel P.	9	Jasper
Agt.	1	Richmond	KEY, C. W.	5	Morgan
KENNEY, Isaac M.	1	Clarke	KEY, G.	11	Henry
KENNEY, James	16	Clarke	KEY, George W.	9	Merriwether
KENNEY, John F.	1	Clarke	KEY, Henry	8	Harris
KENNEY, Joseph	7	Clarke	KEY, John B.	1	Merriwether
KENNIBREW, Edwin	10	Oglethorpe	KEY, Mary	7	Jefferson
KENNON, Addison	13	Newton	KEY, N.	1	Henry
KENNON, Meriwether	3	Newton	KEY, P. C.	2	Franklin
KENNON, Richard	8	Newton	KEY, Pierce	7	Franklin
KENNON, Charles	12	Talbot	KEY, Pleasant A.	5	Dooly
KENNON, Henry	3	Richmond	KEY, Thomas D.	51	Jefferson
KENNON, Richard	14	Talbot	KEY, H. M.	7	Dooly
KENT, Andrew	5	Emanual	KEY, J. L.	11	Butts
KENT, Daniel	26	Emanual	KEY, J.P.	25	Putnam
KENT, Elias	6	Oglethorpe	KEY, Jesse B.	7	Randolph
KENT, John L.	1	Madison	KEY, Joel	3	Randolph
KENT, Larkin	2	Oglethorpe	KEY, Joseph	16	Butts
KENT, Lewis	1	Morgan	KEY, Joshua Junr.	50	Burke
KENT, Thomas	9	Warren	KEY, Joshua Senr.	101	Burke
KENT, Wiley	10	Houston	KEY, M.H.	1	Sumter
KENT, William	1	Walton	KEY, W. M.	13	Randolph
KENT, Wm.	2	Early	KEY, William S.	2	Burke
KENT, Ezra	3	Chatham	KEYTON, John	9	Talbot
KENT, Gilbert	23	Taliaferro	KEYTON, Rebecca	8	Putnam
KENT, Isaac C.	3	Taliaferro	KICKLIGHTER, Andrew	4	Bullock
KENT, Jesse	25	Richmond	KIDD, Carter	6	Jackson
KENT, Penelopy	27	Screven	KIDD, Daniel	2	Bibb
KER, James	13	Chatham	KIDD, G. W.	29	Monroe
KERBOW, Charles H.			KIDD, George	34	Troup
agt for DAVIS,W.	60	Houston	KIDD, James	1	Merriwether
KERBOW, Francis M.	2	Jackson	KIDD, James B.	18	Oglethorpe
KERBY, Arthur	10	Bullock	KIDD, Royton?	1	Oglethorpe
KERBY, John	1	Bullock	KIDD, Thos. J.	1	Jackson
KERBY, Robert	2	Bullock	KIDD, Webb	7	Oglethorpe
KERIAN, A. H.	199	McIntosh	KIDD, Webb	1	Oglethorpe
KERLEY, Nicholas	1	Chatham	KIDD, William	3	Lumpkin
KERLIN, D.	9	Elbert	KIDD, William	22	Oglethorpe

Name	Number	County
KIDD, William	2	Oglethorpe
KIDD, Zaacaiah	7	Oglethorpe
KIDD, Edward	15	Burke
KIDD, George	4	Stewart
KIDD, Richard	13	Stewart
KIDDOO, D.	10	Randolph
KIKER, Charles	1	Gordon
KIKER, Joshua L.	4	Cobb
KILCREASS, James	1	Marion
KILE?, John	2	DeKalb
KILGORE, James Sr.	1	Walton
KILGORE, John H.	4	Walton
KILGORE, John T.	1	Pike
KILGORE, S.	6	Crawford
KILGORE, William	23	Troup
KILGORE, Willis	10	Walton
KILLEBREW, Jeremiah	1	Warren
KILLEBREW, John	2	Columbia
KILLEBREW, John	30	Warren
KILLEBREW, M. N.	9	Sumter
KILLEN, No first name	66	Houston
KILLEN, Samuel D.	4	Houston
KILLEN, Theodore W.	4	Houston
KILLGORE, Chas. A.	17	Wilkes
KILLIAN, Daniel	6	Morgan
KILLIAN, L. A.	2	Lumpkin
KILLINGSWORTH, Jane	3	Washington
KILLINGSWORTH, S.	10	Forsyth
KILLINGSWORTH, Wesley T.	1	Warren
KILLPATRICK, Thomas S.	1	Muscogee
KILPATRIC, George	13	Harris
KILPATRICK, Elisha	3	Harris
KILPATRICK, Elizabeth	7	Merriwether
KILPATRICK, John D.	9	Burke
KILPATRICK, Martha	1	Newton
KILPATRICK, William G.	5	Jones
KILPATRICK, Wm.	20	Bibb
KILPATRICK, Elizabeth	3	Burke
KILPATRICK, James H.	15	Richmond
KILPATRICK, Madison	17	Putnam
KILPATRICK, Rev. J. H. T.	53	Burke
KILPATRICK, Thos. J.	15	Putnam
KIMBELL, Benj.	7	Henry
KIMBELL, W. L .	4	Henry
KIMBERLY, William C.	5	Talbot
KIMBERLY, J. W.	1	Richmond
KIMBERLY, Louis	25	Talbot
KIMBLE, Charles	14	Early
KIMBLE, F. M.	11	Butts
KIMBLE, J. T.	2	Butts
KIMBOROUGH, B. S.	6	Stewart
KIMBRAL, William	23	Burke
KIMBREL, John	2	Walton
KIMBROUGH, Alexander	7	Greene
KIMBROUGH, Archibald	36	Muscogee
KIMBROUGH, Bradly	17	Greene
KIMBROUGH, Edith	4	Murray
KIMBROUGH, Henry C.	37	Harris
KIMBROUGH, J. R.	20	Harris
KIMBROUGH, James W.	26	Muscogee
KIMBROUGH, Jesse	27	Harris
KIMBROUGH, Jesse L.	6	Greene
KIMBROUGH, John	23	Greene
KIMBROUGH, John W.	22	Greene
KIMBROUGH, S. P.	27	Greene
KIMBROUGH, Sarah	24	Muscogee
KIMBROUGH, Thomas	18	Harris
KIMBROUGH, Wm. G.	7	Greene
KIMBROUGH, Beloved	16	Stewart
KIMMELL, Sarah	2	Talbot
KIMPSON, B.	10	Merriwether
KIMSEY, Thomas R.	2	Walker
KINABREW, J.	10	Elbert
KINABREW, Jordan W.	2	Jefferson
KINARD, John H.	9	Jasper
KINBOUGH, Mary	15	Randolph
KINCHEN, William	3	Houston
KINCHEON, J. T.	1	Laurens
KINCHLEY, Ann	3	Richmond
KINDEY ?, Elijah	2	Union
KINDRED, Burk	2	Talbot
KINDRICK, L. L.	6	Pike
KINDRICK, Manuel T.	2	Clarke
KINDRICK, Mary	8	Pike
KINDRICK, N. M.	33	Wikes
KINDRICK, Paten	3	Upson
KINDRICK, R. B.	3	Monroe
KINDRICK, Sylvanus	8	Pike
KINDRICK, Thomas C.	2	Pike
KINDRICK, William O.	12	Pike
KINDRICK, Wm.	1	Chattooga
KINDRICK, Samuel	3	Butts
KINDRICK, Zinamon	1	Talbot
KINDRIDS, Alexander F.	6	Pike
KINE, William	21	Chatham
KINEBREW, Newton	6	Floyd
KING, ?	1	Newton
KING, Alex.	28	Greene
KING, Alfred	2	Monroe
KING, Alfred J.	7	Floyd

174

Name	Number	County	Name	Number	County
KING, Allen	3	Houston	KING, Joseph	6	Muscogee
KING, Angus	21	Monroe	KING, Joseph	16	Twiggs
KING, B. B.	28	Liberty	KING, Levi	7	Houston
KING, Barrington	70	Cobb	KING, Mary E.	33	Troup
KING, Benjamin	28	Monroe	KING, Michael	12	Jefferson
KING, Brady R.	3	Hancock	KING, Mitchell	201	Chatham
KING, Butler B.	21	Upson	KING, Mrs. Julia K.	33	Liberty
KING, Charles	20	Muscogee	KING, N.	21	Merriwether
KING, Charles	8	Muscogee	KING, Nancy	4	Habersham
KING, Charles	1	Muscogee	KING, Nathaniel	4	Fayette
KING, Charles	5	Washington	KING, Richard	3	Newton
KING, Charles P.	1	Muscogee	KING, Roswell	140	Liberty
KING, Comfort	2	Franklin	KING, Ruben	42	McIntosh
KING, D. K.	6	Hall	KING, Samuel	3	Murray
KING, E.	6	Floyd	KING, Samuel F.	10	Gordon
KING, Elizabeth	1	Newton	KING, Stephen C.	114	Glynn
KING, Frances	5	Greene	KING, Stephen c.	40	Wayne
KING, Frederick J.	2	Macon	KING, Stephen H.	6	Fayette
KING, Geo. W.	10	Houston	KING, T. D.	12	Fayette
KING, George W.	3	Jasper	KING, Thomas	22	Houston
KING, Geraldus	3	Monroe	KING, Thomas	5	Houston
KING, H.	2	Wilkinson	KING, Thomas	4	Houston
KING, H. James	2	Muscogee	KING, Thomas	2	Houston
KING, Hannah	28	Franklin	KING, Thomas	6	Muscogee
KING, Henry	21	Muscogee	KING, Thomas R.	10	Jasper
KING, Henry W.	6	Greene	KING, Thomas W.	5	Monroe
KING, Isaac	3	Muscogee	KING, Thos. Butler	112	Glynn
KING, Isabel	1	Early	KING, Westley (Wesley)	26	Wilkinson
KING, Isham	1	Murray	KING, William	9	Harris
KING, J.	4	Floyd	KING, William	1	Houston
KING, J. P.	4	Lincoln	KING, William	13	Lee
KING, Jacob	223	Upson	KING, William	1	Monroe
KING, James	9	Chatham	KING, William	3	Muscogee
KING, James	4	Houston	KING, William D.	6	Pike
KING, James	4	Jackson	KING, William J.	75	McIntosh
KING, James	5	Thomas	KING, William P.	3	Franklin
KING, James F.	15	Wayne	KING, Wm.	3	Troup
KING, James W.	2	Greene	KING, Wm. C.	17	Greene
KING, Jas.	3	Henry	KING, Wm. C.	8	Marion
KING, Jeremiah	7	Monroe	KING, W. K.	1	Union
KING, Jesse	3	Muscogee	KING, Yelverson P.	10	Greene
KING, Joel	10	Marion	KING, A. E.	7	Camden
KING, John	1	Gordon	KING, A. H.	11	Butts
KING, John	1	Gordon	KING, Albert	8	Taliaferro
KING, John	11	Gwinnett	KING, Benjamin	1	Houston
KING, John	6	Houston	KING, C. C.	28	Decatur
KING, John	9	Jasper	KING, Elijah	1	Baldwin
KING, John	2	Murray	KING, Elisha	1	Cass
KING, John	1	Newton	KING, Elizabeth	13	Talbot
KING, John	4	Washington	KING, Elizabeth	5	Talbot
KING, John ?	4	Wilkinson	KING, Frances	1	Bibb
KING, John AW.	1	Chatham	KING, Francis	4	Butts
KING, John B.	3	Madison	KING, G. W.	4	Randolph
KING, John M.	14	Jasper	KING, Geo. D.	1	Camden

Name	Number	County	Name	Number	County
KING, H.	1	Decatur	KINSEY, Roland	2	Walker
KING, Henry	11	Muscogee	KINSEY, Syrenew	1	Wilkinson
KING, Hiram	4	Stewart	KINSMAN, Joseph	3	Talbot
KING, Hugh M. D.	5	Sumter	KINSY, James M.	1	Upson
KING, J. L.	5	Butts	KINZEY, Wm.	3	Chattooga
KING, J. P.	4	Richmond	KIRBY, E.	2	Chattooga
KING, James	12	Talbot	KIRBY, F.	22	Chattooga
KING, Jas.	24	Camden	KIRBY, F. A.	3	Chattooga
KING, John J.	6	Stewart	KIRK, Daniel	1	Walker
KING, John M.	6	Camden	KIRK, Elijah H.	14	Heard
KING, John P.	54	Richmond	KIRK, George	3	Gwinnett
KING, Joseph	35	Stewart	KIRK, Hudson	26	Pike
KING, Laura	1	Chatham	KIRK, John	1	Cobb
KING, M. C.	76	Chatham	KIRK, John	1	Pike
KING, Margaret	17	Baldwin	KIRK, Lawrence T.	1	Pike
KING, Martin	10	Talbot	KIRK, Martha	3	Henry
KING, Mary	11	Camden	KIRK, Thomas	1	Pike
KING, N. G.	5	Crawford	KIRK, William	1	Murray
KING, Newton	4	Muscogee	KIRK, Wm.	1	Heard
KING, Richard	10	Taliaferro	KIRKHAM, Michael	1	Gordon
KING, Rufus	1	Camden	KIRKLAND, A. J.	80	Early
KING, Rufus	3	Stewart	KIRKLAND, Abraham L.	10	Emanual
KING, Stephen	116	Camden	KIRKLAND, Ann M.	9	Jefferson
KING, Tamplin	3	Talbot	KIRKLAND, Caylor	5	Emanual
KING, Thos.	20	Bibb	KIRKLAND, Irvin	2	Emanual
KING, W.	2	Cass	KIRKLAND, D. B.	21	Randolph
KING, William	2	Bibb	KIRKLAND, Richard	8	Bullock
KING, William	11	Chatham	KIRKLAND, Saml.	3	Fayette
KING, William	3	Jasper	KIRKPATRICK, John	2	Clarke
KING, William	1	Stewart	KIRKPATRICK, H. P.	8	Pike
KING, William A.	4	Richmond	KIRKPATRICK,		
KING, Willlis	46	Lowndes	Thos. M.	16	Cobb
KING, Wm. H.	4	Cass	KIRKPATRICK, Danl.	33	Richmond
KINGMAN, Asbury	4	Jones	KIRKPATRICK, J. W.	6	DeKalb
KINGSBURY, Henry	1	Paulding	KIRKPATRICK, James	2	Cass
KINION, Solomon	4	Talbot	KIRKPATRICK, James	56	Columbia
KINKEAD, Margaret	3	Murray	KIRKPATRICK, James	3	Columbia
KINMAN, Samuel	4	Talbot	KIRKPATRICK, James	7	Stewart
KINMAN, William	2	Talbot	KIRKPATRICK, M. A.	1	Bibb
KINMON, Robert	1	Talbot	KIRKSEY, E. F.	3	Stewart
KINNAN, M.	9	Chattooga	KIRKSEY, Isiah	16	DeKalb
KINNE, Jesse	1	Greene	KIRKSEY, West H.	3	Randolph
KINNEBREW, Jordan	4	Warren	KIRTLAnd, Timothy	2	Ware
KINNEY, Charles	9	Jackson	KIRTLAND, Timothy	17	Ware
KINNEY, David	28	Jackson	KIRVEN, James H.	1	Floyd
KINNEY, George	3	Jackson	KISER, M. P.	2	Cobb
KINNEY, Margaret	4	Cherokee	KISER, Wiley J.	8	Cobb
KINNEY, Mary	2	Jackson	KITCHEN, Wm. K.	6	Richmond
KINNEY, Robert	1	Jackson	KITCHENS, Augustus	1	Warren
KINNY, Chesley	2	Newton	KITCHENS, Bose	13	Hancock
KINNY, James	1	Wilkinson	KITCHENS, Boze	8	Jones
KINSEY, John F.	38	Warren	KITCHENS, Charles	1	Jasper
KINSEY, Martin	3	Marion	KITCHENS, Charles H.	1	Jones
KINSEY, L.	8	Talbot	KITCHENS, Elizabeth	1	Warren

Name	Number	County	Name	Number	County
KITCHENS, G.	14	Lee	KNIGHT, Lavina	3	Burke
KITCHENS, John	10	Warren	KNIGHT, Robt. W.	5	Burke
KITCHENS, John U.	2	Lee	KNIGHT, Thomas	4	Bibb
KITCHENS, Matthew	12	Warren	KNIGHT, Thomas	2	Talbot
KITCHENS, Stephen	1	Lumpkin	KNIGHT, William W.	1	Richmond
KITCHENS, Urias	1	Jones	KNIGHT?, Alexander	14	Bullock
KITCHENS, William	2	Jones	KNIGHTON, A. M.	2	Randolph
KITCHENS, William	3	Warren	KNIGHTON, Moses	13	Randolph
KITCHENS, Wm. F.	12	Baker	KNIGHTON, R.L.	7	Randolph
KITCHINGS, William	1	Pike	KNIGHTON, Thos. C.	5	Randolph
KITE, John	1	Heard	KNOTT, James	3	Henry
KITE, Wm. J.	3	Heard	KNOTT, Malinda	2	Campbell
KITERELL, Noah	1	Washington	KNOTT, David	4	Stewart
KITRIDGE, Watson	24	DeKalb	KNOTTS, J. W.	6	Bibb
KITTLES, John R.	36	Screven	KNOWELS, Charles	4	Floyd
KITTLER, Martha	1	Wilkinson	KNOWLAND, Elizabeth	4	Richmond
KITTRELL, John	10	Washington	KNOWLES, B. B.	1	Hancock
KLECKLEY, Daniel	4	Macon	KNOWLES, C. R.	10	Hancock
KLECKLEY, Jacob	29	Macon	KNOWLES, James M.	7	Hancock
KLIFER, Samuel	42	Effingham	KNOWLES, Jas. P.	10	Hancock
KLIN?, Robert T.	1	Floyd	KNOWLES, Joshua	4	Floyd
KLOTZ, John P.	2	Greene	KNOWLES, R. P.	4	Hancock
KLUTZ, Jacob	8	Clarke	KNOWLES, George	13	Baker
KNAPP, Hanford	2	Chatham	KNOWLES, Joseph E.	8	Baker
KNAPP, N. B.	20	Chatham	KNOWLS, J. B.	2	Chattooga
KNIGHT, Allen H.	6	Washington	KNOWLS, S. R.	1	Meriwether
KNIGHT, Cofield	4	Houston	KNOWLS, A.	7	Talbot
KNIGHT, James	11	Randolph	KNOWLTON, Hiram	16	Talbot
KNIGHT, James	7	Wilkinson	KNOX, Eleanor	10	Gwinnett
KNIGHT, Jane M.	2	Wilkes	KNOX, H. M.	8	Chattooga
KNIGHT, Jno.	3	Henry	KNOX, J. G.	5	Lincoln
KNIGHT, John	7	Lincoln	KNOX, John	5	Wayne
KNIGHT, John	1	Lowndes	KNOX, Oscar F.	12	Upson
KNIGHT, Jonathan	5	Ware	KNOX, Samuel	45	Franklin
KNIGHT, Levi J.	6	Lowndes	KNOX, Samuel	11	Franklin
KNIGHT, Lewis	2	Washington	KNOX, Samuel	4	Gwinnett
KNIGHT, Peter	7	Henry	KNOX, W. M.	2	Lincoln
KNIGHT, Rufus	13	Emanual	KNOX, C. C.	3	Chattooga
KNIGHT, Thomas H.	7	Meriwether	KNOX, George	4	Columbia
KNIGHT, Thos. S. F.	4	Lowndes	KNOX, Hugh	1	Baldwin
KNIGHT, William	4	Pike	KNOX, J. B.	5	Chattooga
KNIGHT, Wm. A.	3	Lowndes	KNOX, James	4	Columbia
KNIGHT, Wm. C.	1	Lowndes	KNOX, Peter	30	Columbia
KNIGHT, Wm. F.	4	Heard	KNOX, Samuel	45	Chattooga
KNIGHT, A. C.	1	Campbell	KOKER, P. T.	1	Henry
KNIGHT, E.	3	Crawford	KOLB, David	4	Jasper
KNIGHT, E. agent	14	Crawford	KOLB, Martin	60	Campbell
KNIGHT, Elizabeth	4	Richmond	KOLB, Wilds	65	Morgan
KNIGHT, Elizabeth	2	Richmond	KOLB, Philip	2	Chatham
KNIGHT, Jas.	7	Bibb	KOLLACK, George J.	43	Chatham
KNIGHT, Jno.	1	Bibb	KOLLOCK, George J.	16	Habersham
KNIGHT, John	6	Burke	KOLLOCK?, P. M.	78	Liberty
KNIGHT, John	5	Crawford	KOLLY, David	6	Forsyth
KNIGHT, Joseph	1	Bullock	KORNEGAY, Basil	6	Lowndes

Name	Number	County	Name	Number	County
KORNEGAY, Daniel	14	Thomas	LAMAR, H.	29	Houston
KOUTZ, E.	1	Bibb	LAMAR, H. G.	11	Clarke
KRAPPIER, Calab	6	Muscogee	LAMAR, Henry G.	40	Monroe
KRAUS, Peter	1	Chatham	LAMAR, James	66	Monroe
KREIT, Frederick	5	Chatham	LAMAR, James J.	12	Burke
KRENSON, F.	5	Chatham	LAMAR, John	9	Macon
KROG, F.	1	DeKalb	LAMAR, Mary L.	47	Jones
KRUGER, Thomas H.	3	Chatham	LAMAR, Sarah	12	Newton
KYLE, David	2	Muscogee	LAMAR, William H.	1	Muscogee
KYLE, John	6	Muscogee	LAMAR, Basil	16	Sumter
KYLE, Joseph	9	Muscogee	LAMAR, Charles A. L.	23	Chatham
KYLE, Robt. B.	1	Muscogee	LAMAR0, E. B.	9	Bibb
KYLE, Thomas	4	Gwinnett	LAMAR, Gazaway	4	Richmond
KYZER, Geo.	1	Carroll	LAMAR, George W.	39	Burke
LAAWHORN, Daniel	14	Lee	LAMAR, Gus	49	Columbia
LAAWSON, Robert R.R.	25	Burke	LAMAR, J. B.	117	Bibb
LABOON ?, Mason C.	2	Walton	LAMAR, John B.	57	Sumter
LACHLISON, James	2	Chatham	LAMAR, John B.	41	Sumter
LACKEY, Chas.	9	Walton	LAMAR, M. L.	12	Bibb
LACKEY, Samuel	10	Walton	LAMAR, Thomas	7	Sumter
LACKWELL, Thomas	3	Paulding	LAMAR, Thomas B.	60	Baldwin
LACKWELL,			LAMAR, Thos.	2	Bibb
William W.	1	Paulding	LAMAR, Uriah	2	Bibb
LACKY, Noah	4	Walton	LAMAR. George M.	22	Richmond
LACOSTE, Charles A.	2	Chatham	LAMAS, William	2	Newton
LACOUNT, Joseph	10	Bibb	LAMB, A. H.	2	Floyd
LACOURT, William	2	Gwinnett	LAMB, Celia	15	Glynn
LACY, Elizabeth	10	Butts	LAMB, Green	14	Muscogee
LACY, Freeman W.	9	Burke	LAMB, H. U.	5	Marion
LADD, Robt. A.	17	Putnam	LAMB, Henry	8	Twiggs
LADSON, Joseph	12	Chatham	LAMB, Isham	1	Early
LAEN, William	5	Camden	LAMB, Jacob	14	Muscogee
LAFBURROW, H. M.	16	Screven	LAMB, Jas. M.	12	Laurens
LAFEVER, Mrs.	3	Laurens	LAMB, Jno.	2	Henry
LAFILLE, Augustus	3	Richmond	LAMB, John P.	5	Glynn
LAFILLE, Genevive	3	Richmond	LAMB, Lawrence	1	Dooly
LAIDLER, Hamilton A.	16	Houston	LAMB, Luke	18	Dooly
LAIDLER, John Jr.	12	Houston	LAMB, Mathew	3	Emanual
LAIDLER, John Sr.	25	Houston	LAMB, Meady.	15	Twiggs
LAIDLER, John Sr.			LAMB, R.	6	Henry
agt for JAMISON, D.	115	Houston	LAMB, Reubin	34	Twiggs
LAIDLER, Watkins	13	Houston	LAMB, William	12	Lowndes
LAMAR, Mary A.	31	Walton	LAMB, William	1	Walker
LAIN, Daniel N.	3	Chatham	LAMB, Burwell	1	Camden
LAIRAMORE, S.	7	Elbert	LAMB, Elijah	5	Burke
LAKE, Abraham	16	Monroe	LAMBACK, Frederick	21	Richmond
LAKE, James	10	Floyd	LAMBERT, (?)	1	Decatur
LAKE, William	6	Chatham	LAMBERT, S. R.	1	Habersham
LALTHAM, Thomas A.	22	Campbell	LAMBERT, Wm. M. D.	3	Habersham
LALTIMER, H.W.	10	Hancock	LAMBERT, Anderson	3	Burke
LAMA, John	4	Chatham	LAMBERT, B.	6	Coweta
LAMAAR, Zach.	16	Houston	LAMBERT, Green	1	Burke
LAMAR & HARPER			LAMBERT, John	5	Columbia
Agt.	4	Richmond	LAMBERT, Thos.	6	Burke

Name	Number	County	Name	Number	County
LAMBERT, William	10	Screven	LANDRUM, Jane	3	Warren
LAMBERTH, J. L.	1	Morgan	LANDRUM, James	3	Fayette
LAMBERTH, William	3	Morgan	LANDRUM, Jas. B.	1	Greene
LAMBETH, J.			LANDRUM, Joel	1	Warren
adm of John RUSSELL	7	Floyd	LANDRUM, John W.	9	Floyd
LAMDRUM, Whitfield	6	Oglethorpe	LANDRUM, Joseph	4	Oglethorpe
LAMKIN, Benj. H.	2	Floyd	LANDRUM, Sarah	1	Jackson
LAMKIN, Magella	2	Hall	LANDRUM, Silas	3	Warren
LAMKIN, Augustus	67	Columbia	LANDRUM, William	4	Oglethorpe
LAMKIN, Betsy	116	Columbia	LANDRUM, Wm. J.	2	Greene
LAMKIN, James & sister	137	Columbia	LANE, A. J.	33	Hancock
LAMKIN, Robert	28	Columbia	LANE, Albert M.	5	Troup
LAMKINS, Jas.	23	Pulaski	LANE, Augustus W.	23	Jasper
LAMKINS, Jno. L.	20	Pulaski	LANE, Benjamin	4	Houston
LAMKINS, Levi	47	Floyd	LANE, Benjamin	12	Liberty
LAMKINS, George	17	Floyd	LANE, Benjamin	31	Lowndes
LAMPEE, Christian	14	Chatham	LANE, Benjamin L.	13	Emanual
LAMPKIN, Edward	64	Clarke	LANE, Bryant	22	Houston
LAMPKIN, Joseph	1	Jackson	LANE, Bryant	1	Muscogee
LAMPKIN, Wm. H.	2	Jackson	LANE, Darrone B.	18	Morgan
LAMPKIN, Philip	7	Stewart	LANE, Edward	23	Emanual
LANAHAN, C.	2	Decatur	LANE, Elizabeth	6	Monroe
LANAHAN, S.	2	Decatur	LANE, Elizabeth	2	Troup
LANCAR, David	9	Harris	LANE, Elizabeth	6	Troup
LANCASTER, Wm. H.	11	Heard	LANE, Harriet	7	Newton
LANCASTER, James	1	Talbot	LANE, Henry	9	Newton
LANCASTER, John	3	Talbot	LANE, Isaac H.	6	Troup
LANCASTER, Lemuel	7	Putnam	LANE, J. W.	2	Early
LANCEFORD, Henry	4	Newton	LANE, Jacob	1	Lumpkin
LANCY, P. K.	34	Effingham	LANE, James H.	6	Wilkes
LAND, G. A.	1	Habersham	LANE, John	2	Houston
LAND, Henry	19	Twiggs	LANE, John A.	36	Thomas
LAND, J. Estate	15	Twiggs	LANE, Jonathan	1	Heard
LAND, John	4	Warren	LANE, Joseph F.	2	Heard
LAND, Thomas	6	Warren	LANE, Joseph M.	6	Heard
LAND, Thos. B.	4	Harris	LANE, Lewis L.	12	Jasper
LAND, William	2	Monroe	LANE, Mark A.	12	Cobb
LAND, Benj. F.	1	Randolph	LANE, M. A.	7	Wilkes
LAND, Jas.	3	Coweta	LANE, Mary M.	5	Fayette
LAND, L. E.	2	Randolph	LANE, Mrs. Worthy?	7	Houston
LAND, Mrs. L.	10	Decatur	LANE, Richard	1	Houston
LAND, N.	10	Cass	LANE, Richard A.	35	Walker
LANDALL, Luke	5	Oglethorpe	LANE, Richd.	6	Hancock
LANDERS, James B. M.	4	Paulding	LANE, S. G.	13	Troup
LANDERS, Jas. B.	1	Wilkes	LANE, Sanders	27	Houston
LANDERS, John	8	Lincoln	LANE, Thomas M.	2	Emanual
LANDERS, John	8	Madison	LANE, Turner	4	Habersham
LANDING, John	4	Burke	LANE, W.	15	Oglethorpe
LANDINGHAM, John V.	1	Wilkinson	LANE, W. H. C.	6	Morgan
LANDINGHAM, Wm. V.	7	Wilkinson	LANE, Wiley	5	Houston
LANDROM, Jeptha	10	Fayette	LANE, William	4	Jasper
LANDRUM, C. J.	2	Oglethorpe	LANE, William S.	2	Jones
LANDRUM, H. T.	3	Oglethorpe	LANE, Wm.	2	Heard
LANDRUM, Hay F.	25	Oglethorpe	LANE, Wm. G.	42	Lowndes

Name	Number	County	Name	Number	County
LANE, Emma A.	3	DeKalb	LANGSTON, Alexander	1	Franklin
LANE, John H.	2	Bibb	LANGSTON, James	4	Jackson
LANE, M. J.	4	Putnam	LANGSTON, Jesse	3	Madison
LANE, Richard	24	Bullock	LANGSTON, John	1	Campbell
LANE, Sarah	2	Baldwin	LANGSTON, John	5	Gilmer
LANE, Thos. estate	6	Burke	LANGSTON, Betty	7	Columbia
LANE, William	9	Dooly	LANGSTON, Celia	2	Columbia
LANER, Benj. A.	2	Walton	LANGSTON, J. Agt.	21	Bibb
LANER, Jefferson	4	Walton	LANGSTON, James	7	Columbia
LANEY, John	8	Henry	LANGSTON, Martha	1	Columbia
LANEY, Thomas	1	Henry	LANGSTON, W.	3	Chattooga
LANFORD, Curles C.	3	Gwinnett	LANGSTON, William	3	Columbia
LANFORD, Hazam?	5	Gwinnett	LANIER, Allen Jr.	1	Emanual
LANG, David	4	Randolph	LANIER, Burrel	1	Emanual
LANG, Eller	2	Twiggs	LANIER, Elizabeth	1	Greene
LANG, Elvira	1	Early	LANIER, George M.	5	Clarke
LANG, Henry C.	2	Washington	LANIER, James M.	1	Clarke
LANG, Henry J.	2	Lincoln	LANIER, Margaret	6	Gwinnett
LANG, James	20	Liberty	LANIER, Murphey	1	Thomas
LANG, Jno. A.	26	Camden	LANIER, Nicholas	18	Hancock
LANG, Mrs. Lyia	15	Liberty	LANIER, Philip	2	Marion
LANG, Nancy	40	Camden	LANIER, William	14	Clarke
LANG, David	8	Camden	LANIER, Aaron	8	Randolph
LANG, Elizabeth	10	Camden	LANIER, Augustus	4	Bullock
LANG, Geo.	14	Camden	LANIER, Augustus	1	Bullock
LANG, Isaac	19	Camden	LANIER, Benj.	2	Bullock
LANG, James	1	Randolph	LANIER, Isaac	1	Screven
LANG, Nancy	53	Camden	LANIER, James	3	Bullock
LANG, Nathaniel	9	Tatnall	LANIER, Louis	4	Bullock
LANG, Robt.	15	Camden	LANIER, Mitchell	3	Bullock
LANG, Thos. agent	22	Crawford	LANIER, Nowel	12	Screven
LANGDEN, John B.	3	Taliaferro	LANIER, Patrick	1	Bullock
LANGFORD, Bedford	4	Clarke	LANIER, Providence	1	Bryan
LANGFORD, Benjamin	3	Marion	LANIER, S.	15	Bibb
LANGFORD, J. M.	28	Henry	LANIER, Samuel	2	Bullock
LANGFORD, James	9	Marion	LANIER, Thomas C.	1	Bullock
LANGFORD, James W.	1	Marion	LANIER, Walter	19	Cass
LANGFORD, Uriah	1	Warren	LANKFORD, Edmund	3	Upson
LANGFORD, William	1	Harris	LANKFORD, Hampton	2	Cass
LANGFORD, Wm. H.	4	Marion	LANKFORD, J.	1	Stewart
LANGFORD, Albert	1	Talbot	LANLEY(?), Frances	1	Coweta
LANGFORD, Chatham	4	Monroe	LANNEAR, John	4	Cobb
LANGFORD, Edmond	1	Talbot	LANOIR, Francis	10	Gwinnett
LANGFORD, J. W.	8	DeKalb	LANOIR, John W.	3	Gwinnett
LANGFORD, John	4	Bibb	LANON ?, B. A.	20	Twiggs
LANGLEY, Benjamin	10	Chatham	LANSDALE, Alfred M.	4	Greene
LANGLEY, Isiah	7	Houston	LANSFORD, John B.	2	Walker
LANGLEY, Oswell B.	1	Cobb	LANSFORD, Vincent	6	Greene
LANGLEY, William	6	Gwinnett	LANSON, Hugh	119	Houston
LANGLEY, L.	4	Crawford	LANSON, Peter	21	Chatham
LANGLY, Jackson	1	Monroe	LANTERN, Theopalus	2	Stewart
LANGLY, William	4	Monroe	LANY?, Jackson	6	Merriwether
LANGMAID, E. S.	33	Washington	LANZLOTTE, Frances	1	Stewart
LANGMAID, John T.	20	Washington	LAPHAM, L.	4	Muscogee

Name	Number	County	Name	Number	County
LARAMAR, James	1	Lee	LASSSITER, J.	5	Bibb
LARAMAR?, James	31	Lee	LASTER, Thomas	1	Dooly
LARAMORE, John L.	8	Lee	LASTINGER, Wm.	3	Lowndes
LARANCE, Oliver	1	Monroe	LATHAM, George	3	Hall
LARANCE, Z.	11	Monroe	LATHAM, Mary	2	Cherokee
LARASY, Wm. B.	4	Screven	LATHAM, Richard	1	Cherokee
LARK, Mary	7	Richmond	LATHROP ?, Joseph T.	2	Richmond
LARK, Matilda A.	5	Richmond	LATHROP, J. W.	7	Pulaski
LARKEY, John	5	Telfair	LATHROP, James K.	1	Chatham
LARKIN, Eli	1	Marion	LATIMER, A. J.	12	Hancock
LARKIN, Hugh	1	Chatham	LATIMER, B. F.	22	Hancock
LARKIN, John	41	Columbia	LATIMER, George	12	Oglethorpe
LARKIN, Julia	1	Richmond	LATIMER, H.	4	Cobb
LARKIN, Leazer	12	Stewart	LATIMER, J. S.	16	Hancock
LARKIN, Patsy	7	Columbia	LATIMER, J. W.	1	Oglethorpe
LARKINS, John L.	6	Floyd	LATIMER, James L.	27	Warren
LARKINS, T. J.	8	Morgan	LATIMER, John B.	19	Hancock
LARLIE, John	1	Harris	LATIMER, John P.	19	Oglethorpe
LARNAR, Henry J.	66	Bibb	LATIMER, M. E.	8	Hancock
LaROCHE, Oliver A.	21	Chatham	LATIMER, Perkin	1	Franklin
LaROUCHE, Isaac D.	12	Chatham	LATIMER, T. W.	7	Hancock
LaROUCHE, Mary	3	Chatham	LATIMER, Thomas H.	17	Hancock
LARRENCE, Leroy	14	Jasper	LATIMER, Thomas L.	56	Warren
LARRIMORE, W. P.	4	Lee	LATIMER, Thomas L.		
LARY, Archibald	26	Monroe	(guardian)	18	Warren
LARY, James	10	Monroe	LATIMER, Thos. J.	5	Oglethorpe
LASELTER, James	5	Campbell	LATIMER, Wiley B.	8	Cobb
LASETER, James	9	Pike	LATIMER, William M.	1	Troup
LASETER, Jas. H.	1	Carroll	LATIMER, Wm.	4	Cass
LASETER, Joel	1	Walton	LATIMER, Wm.	17	Hancock
LASETER, W.	1	Pike	LATIMER, H. B.	10	DeKalb
LASETER, William	33	Burke	LATIMORE, Saml.	15	Stewart
LASETTER, Mary	2	Monroe	LATIMORE, Charles	13	DeKalb
LASH, Alex.	5	Lee	LATIMORE, J.	6	Chattooga
LASHLEY, Hugh	1	Harris	LATIMUR, Reubin	9	Cobb
LASIETER, Elisha M.	3	Pike	LATROP, B.	4	Chatham
LASITER, J. S.	2	Morgan	LAUDEASTON?, Wash.	13	Pulaski
LASITER, William	29	Pike	LAUGHTER, Jane	6	Wilkes
LASITER, Orin	1	Burke	LAUGHTER, John	2	Wilkes
LASITER?, Amos	7	Pulaski	LAUGIND, James F.	6	Troup
LASSER, Thomas	9	Thomas	LAUNIUS, Jacob	1	Morgan
LASSETER, William	4	Sumter	LAUNIUS, John	8	Morgan
LASSETER, John A.	3	Upson	LAURENCE, James W.	7	Hall
LASSIER, Mary	1	McIntosh	LAURENCE, Seaborn	90	Hancock
LASSITER, Amos	8	Houston	LAURENER, Z.	3	Upson
LASSITER, James	1	Clarke	LAUSING, Francis	3	Henry
LASSITER, Terrel	20	Merriwether	LAVENDER, Charles	1	Jackson
LASSITER, Vincent	17	Monroe	LAVENDER, Jas.	25	Henry
LASSITER, C.	2	Decatur	LAVENDER, John	4	Wilkinson
LASSITER, Elizabeth	6	Sumter	LAVENDER, John A.	16	Houston
LASSITER, Henry	8	Sumter	LAVENDER, Mary A.	5	Chatham
LASSITER, J.	15	Decatur	LAVENDER, W. R.	2	Henry
LASSITTER, Mrs. E.	10	Stewart	LAVENDER, George W.	2	Chatham
LASSSETER, Elizabeth	8	Merriwether	LAVENDER, J. agent	26	Crawford

Name	Number	County
LAVENTINE, John P.	5	Richmond
LAVIN, George W.	1	Baker
LAW, Charles R.	4	Houston
LAW, Daniel S.	9	Gordon
LAW, George	17	Macon
LAW, Hugh D.	2	Walton
LAW, John C.	3	Cobb
LAW, Jos.	13	Liberty
LAW, Josiah S.	25	Liberty
LAW, Mary	16	Hall
LAW, Mary	9	Macon
LAW, Mrs. Sarah	39	Liberty
LAW, Richard	1	Macon
LAW, William	46	Chatham
LAW, William	5	Macon
LAW, William A.	4	Walton
LAW, Wiley	5	Sumter
LAW, William	24	Bryan
LAW, William F.	3	Chatham
LAWANCE, Thos. J.	12	Oglethorpe
LAWERY, F. G.	13	Twiggs
LAWFORD, Robert	5	Greene
LAWHORN, A.	1	Troup
LAWHORN, Allen	5	Cherokee
LAWHORN, Henry	3	Muscogee
LAWHORN, Sarah	2	Lee
LAWHORN, Adam	5	Richmond
LAWLESS, Sara	4	Hall
LAWNIUS, Thos. G.	5	Morgan
LAWRENCE, A. G.	2	Muscogee
LAWRENCE, Allen	1	Emanual
LAWRENCE, Cynthia	7	Greene
LAWRENCE, Frank	9	Muscogee
LAWRENCE, H. A.	8	Morgan
LAWRENCE, Heartwell	6	Merriwether
LAWRENCE, Homer	3	Washington
LAWRENCE, Homey	3	Washington
LAWRENCE, James	15	Jasper
LAWRENCE, John	1	Gordon
LAWRENCE, Peyton	14	Pike
LAWRENCE, Richard	4	Pike
LAWRENCE, Samuel	8	Cobb
LAWRENCE, W. G.	3	Lumpkin
LAWRENCE, Allen Jr.	16	Putnam
LAWRENCE, Allen Sen.	58	Putnam
LAWRENCE, David	25	Putnam
LAWRENCE, E.	5	Talbot
LAWRENCE, Eliza	8	Richmond
LAWRENCE, J.	1	Chattooga
LAWRENCE, James M	47	Baldwin
LAWRENCE, John	19	Baldwin
LAWRENCE, Joseph	14	Putnam
LAWRENCE, M.	11	Chattooga
LAWRENCE, M. J.	5	Putnam

Name	Number	County
LAWRENCE, Newton D.	3	Baldwin
LAWRENCE, S. A. T.	3	Chatham
LAWRENCE, Seaborn see HUTCHINSON		Hancock
LAWRY, Allis	19	Twiggs
LAWRY, B. F.	7	Twiggs
LAWRY, John H.	11	Twiggs
LAWSHE, Lewis	2	DeKalb
LAWSHE, Wm. C.	6	Bibb
LAWSON, Alexander E.	38	Washington
LAWSON, Arthur	14	Butts
LAWSON, Ashley	4	Lowndes
LAWSON, John	2	Lowndes
LAWSON, John R.	8	Harris
LAWSON, Lrien?	3	Lowndes
LAWSON, Nancy	26	Hancock
LAWSON, Sion	3	Forsyth
LAWSON, Thos.	6	Floyd
LAWSON, W.	10	Gordon
LAWSON, William	3	Merriwether
LAWSON, William B.	2	Walton
LAWSON, Alex. J.	15	Burke
LAWSON, Alexander J.	107	Burke
LAWSON, James	10	Stewart
LAWSON, Robt.	10	Butts
LAWSON, Thos.	13	Stewart
LAWTON, Alexander R.	5	Chatham
LAWTON, Alexander B.	60	Baker
LAWTON, W. J.	37	Screven
LAWTON, W. S.	2	Bibb
LAWTON, William S.	54	Baker
LAWTON, Winborn	7	Chatham
LAY, Charles	3	Gordon
LAY, Charles F.	9	Cherokee
LAY, Elijah	7	Jackson
LAY, Elisha	2	Jackson
LAY, John	14	Gordon
LAY, Littleton	1	Troup
LAY, Richd.	2	Jackson
LAY, S.	11	Troup
LAYFIELD, Lowdy	2	Harris
LAYTON, James M.	1	Early
LAZENBWRY, John	12	Jasper
LAZENBY, A.	5	Coweta
LAZENBY, Elias	7	Columbia
LAZENBY, Elias	7	Warren
LAZENBY, Elizabeth	9	Warren
LAZENBY, John M.	24	Warren
LAZENBY, Maria	5	Warren
LAZENBY, Richard S.	20	Warren
LAZENBY, Robert H.	5	Warren
LAZENBY, Robert S.	1	Warren
LAZENBY, Robt.	1	Putnam
LAZENBY, Samuel J.	22	Warren

Name	Number	County	Name	Number	County
LAZENBY, Thomas G.	2	Warren	LEE, Green	1	Pulaski
LAZENBY, William	1	Columbia	LEE, J. H.	3	Henry
LEACH, A. B.	14	Floyd	LEE, James	10	Appling
LEACH, Edward	1	Fayette	LEE, James	2	Early
LEACH, Langford	1	Pike	LEE, James	9	Effingham
LEACH, Martha	2	Chatham	LEE, James	1	Heard
LEACH, Wm.	2	DeKalb	LEE, James M.	3	Walker
LEAK, Armsted C.	6	Cass	LEE, Jas.	12	Pulaski
LEAK, B. T.	17	Cass	LEE, John	12	Newton
LEAK, Garlington	11	Pike	LEE, John	10	Pulaski
LEAK, John	1	Pike	LEE, John	9	Thomas
LEAK, Robert	14	Pike	LEE, Joseph	6	Early
LEAK, W. M.	3	Pike	LEE, Joseph A. L.	23	Muscogee
LEAK, Wesley	2	Pike	LEE, Joshua	7	Ware
LEAK, Armsted	13	Cass	LEE, Moses	14	Troup
LEAK, R. T.	7	Cass	LEE, Moses C.	2	Lowndes
LEAK, Sally	28	Cass	LEE, Mrs. Sarah	2	Muscogee
LEAPTROT, Bolin P.	7	Washington	LEE, Nancy	25	Walton
LEAPTROT, Hilbrod	2	Washington	LEE, Nathan P.	43	Newton
LEAPTROT, Southern	1	Murray	LEE, Noah	28	Troup
LEAPTROT, Jesse A.	21	Burke	LEE, O. P.	6	Henry
LEARRY, Pearcey	21	Dooly	LEE, Peter	11	Early
LEARY, Curtis	13	Houston	LEE, Robert	18	Gwinnett
LEARY, Cornelius	21	Baker	LEE, W. C.	2	Henry
LEASH?, Edmond B.	2	Pike	LEE, W. C.	2	Meriwether
LEATH, William C.	11	Early	LEE, W. W.	7	Wilkinson
LEATHERS, Elizabeth	3	Cass	LEE, William	5	Early
LEBEVENELL, Harman	1	Clarke	LEE, William	13	Newton
LeCONTE, John	35	Liberty	LEE, William F.	4	Harris
LeCONTE, Joseph	48	Liberty	LEE, William H.	1	Houston
LeCONTE, Lewis	34	Liberty	LEE, William M.	6	Muscogee
LeCONTE, Wm. L.			LEE, Wm.	3	Pulaski
estate	66	Liberty	LEE, Wm. C. H.	6	Laurens
LEDBETTER, Jane	9	Upson	LEE, Abigail	15	Putnam
LEDBETTER, John	1	Paulding	LEE, Benjamin	3	Bullock
LEDBETTER, Jonathan	5	Lumpkin	LEE, C.	1	Dade
LEDBETTER, L. J.	1	Forsyth	LEE, David M.	14	Screven
LEDBETTER, L. L.	3	Henry	LEE, H. J.	1	Screven
LEDBETTER, John	12	Putnam	LEE, Henry	50	Stewart
LEDDIK?, Susan G.	1	Gwinnett	LEE, Henry	15	Stewart
LEE Jr., General	3	Bullock	LEE, J. H.	1	Putnam
LEE, A. L.	18	Muscogee	LEE, J. S.	22	Crawford
LEE, Alexander	3	Houston	LEE, James	7	Bullock
LEE, Allen	4	Monroe	LEE, James	1	Bullock
LEE, Augustus	7	Newton	LEE, James M.	2	Screven
LEE, B. F.	13	Murray	LEE, Jesse	11	Screven
LEE, Benj. T.	4	Floyd	LEE, John	5	Bullock
LEE, Benjamin	1	Early	LEE, Lewis	8	Stewart
LEE, Bryant	5	Pike	LEE, Mary	1	Bibb
LEE, David	5	Early	LEE, Oliver H.	9	Richmond
LEE, Elam	10	Early	LEE, R.W.	4	Butts
LEE, Elias	5	Early	LEE, Reuben	2	Screven
LEE, Elizabeth	18	Clarke	LEE, S.	8	Henry
LEE, G. B.	11	Pulaski	LEE, Sanders W.	31	Coweta

Name	Number	County	Name	Number	County
LEE, Sarah	1	Screven	LEON, Lewis	1	Richmond
LEE, Sen., General	14	Bullock	LEONARD, James	5	Cherokee
LEE, Stephen	10	Randolph	LEONARD, Joseph	2	Warrren
LEE, Thomas	1	Baldwin	LEONARD, Van	11	Muscogee
LEE, Will	3	Stewart	LEONARD, W. A.	5	Morgan
LEE, William	14	Bullock	LEONARD, W. P. W.	26	Lee
LEE, William	3	Screven	LEONARD, Alexander	62	Talbot
LEE, William	11	Stewart	LEONARD, Henry	12	Talbot
LEE, William Jun.	7	Bullock	LEONARD, Jno. H.	5	Randolph
LEE, Z. J.	1	DeKalb	LEONARD, L.	24	Talbot
LEEK, Elizabeth	5	Newton	LEONARD, Patrick	4	Talbot
LEEK, Mitson	2	Newton	LEONARD, S. D.	1	Cherokee
LEEK, Newton	2	Newton	LEPHANE?, Daniel	7	Heard
LEEK, Washington	2	Newton	LEPHAW, Frances A.	19	Wilkes
LEET, A. R.	24	Walker	LEPURE?, S. J.	8	Elbert
LEEVES, George	19	Baldwin	LEREY, C. P.	4	Bibb
LEEVY, James	5	Newton	LEROY, Henry M.	23	Fayette
LEFFILS, Armend	6	McIntosh	LEROY, James M.	4	Fayette
LEFTRIDGE, Wm.	2	Troup	LEROY, Jas. M.	2	Fayette
LEGAN, Thomas	10	Merriwether	LESETER, Benjamin	5	Campbell
LEGETT, Wiley G.	1	Early	LESEUER, Harison	7	Monroe
LEGGET, Mathew H.	24	Macon	LESEUER, Mead	47	Monroe
LEGGETT, Mahala	2	Muscogee	LESIEL, M.	4	Crawford
LEGGETT, Gil. D.			LESLIE, Daniel	4	Jones
agt for WOOLFOLK	32	Houston	LESLIE, David	27	Greene
LEGGETT, Lewis	1	Putnam	LESLIE, Felix	15	Troup
LEGGITT, Martha	4	Muscogee	LESLIE, George G.	1	Wilkinson
LEGRIEL, Leocade	6	Chatham	LESLIE, Jonathan B.	5	Troup
LEGUIRE, Lott M.	11	Clarke	LESLIE, Jos.	5	Coweta
LEIGH, Richard	8	Floyd	LESLIE, Peter W.	17	Troup
LEIGH, Absalum	6	Coweta	LESLIE, Robt. A.	1	Coweta
LEIGH, Ansalem B.	19	Coweta	LESLIE, Thos.	2	Coweta
LEIGH, Benjamin	12	Coweta	LESLIE, Thos.	4	Troup
LEIGH, J.T.	1	Putnam	LESLLIE, Silas	2	Wilkinson
LEIGH, William M.	33	Chatham	LESLY?, James M.	4	Pike
LEIGH, Wm. D.	12	Coweta	LESSEURE, Susan	14	Bibb
LEITNER, John	3	Muscogee	LESTER, David	48	Jones
LEMAN, Abraham	10	Butts	LESTER, Dennis	55	Jones
LEMMON, Mary	8	Cobb	LESTER, Eliza W.	5	Newton
LEMON, A. A.	25	Henry	LESTER, James D.	14	Monroe
LEMON, Robert	4	Cobb	LESTER, Jas. T.	13	Clarke
LEMON, Smith	3	Cobb	LESTER, John	2	Campbell
LEMONS, William	1	Butts	LESTER, John	7	Monroe
LENCLUS ?, Jesse	13	Twiggs	LESTER, John E.	30	Jones
LENDLY, Mary	1	Cobb	LESTER, Josiah	5	Clarke
LENDSEY, J. D.	1	Butts	LESTER, Lewis	51	Clarke
LENICK, R. B.	6	Morgan	LESTER, Mrs.	1	Muscogee
LENIER, L.	5	Pike	LESTER, Nancy	5	Madison
LENNARD, Francis	31	Talbot	LESTER, Patman	6	Clarke
LENNARD, James C.	39	Talbot	LESTER, Robert	18	Walton
LENNARD, William	6	Talbot	LESTER, Sarah	26	Oglethorpe
LENNICK, Benj. C.	2	Richmond	LESTER, Sarah	13	Pulaski
LENSON?, James	10	Muscogee	LESTER, Servis	5	Clarke
LEON, Henry L.	2	Richmond	LESTER, Thomas J.	9	Walton

Name	Number	County	Name	Number	County
LESTER, Winnifred	8	Warren	LEWIS, David	4	Early
LESTER, Wm. M.	11	Clarke	LEWIS, David H.	1	Heard
LESTER, A. J.	3	Sumter	LEWIS, Davis W.	9	Hancock
LESTER, Geo.	1	Stewart	LEWIS, Edward G.	2	Washington
LESTER, George	2	Newton	LEWIS, Elam B.	9	Burke
LESTER, German	2	DeKalb	LEWIS, Elizabeth	3	Wilkinson
LESTER, H. P.	18	Baldwin	LEWIS, Elph	3	Wilkinson
LESTER, J. J.	24	Decatur	LEWIS, Freeman	19	Greene
LESTER, James	1	Bullock	LEWIS, George M.	5	Heard
LESTER, James D.	11	Dooly	LEWIS, H. C.	1	Henry
LESTER, Lewis	3	Coweta	LEWIS, Harret	46	Troup
LESTER, Pleasant	17	Coweta	LEWIS, Harriet	16	Troup
LESTER, William	1	Bullock	LEWIS, Henry	54	Burke
LESTERJETT?, Mrs. C.	1	Muscogee	LEWIS, Howell	19	Harris
LESUER, Stephen S.	11	Pike	LEWIS, J. R.	6	Wilkinson
LESUER, Mhalah	6	Stewart	LEWIS, J. P.	4	Wilkinson
LESUEUR, Cary S.	8	Monroe	LEWIS, James agt.	19	Bibb
LESURE, Andrew J.	6	Pike	LEWIS, James A.	1	Marion
LESURE, Lucinda	1	Madison	LEWIS, James F.	9	Upson
LESUREUR, Drue	3	Randolph	LEWIS, James W.	4	Cass
LETHRIDGE, Jas. H.	9	Troup	LEWIS, Jas.	2	Troup
LEVEL, Chas.	19	Coweta	LEWIS, John	1	Chatham
LEVER, John	1	Screven	LEWIS, John	9	Cobb
LEVERETT, Francis	1	Greene	LEWIS, John L.	1	Cass
LEVERETT, Handy	35	Lincoln	LEWIS, John W.	64	Cherokee
LEVERETT, Joel P.	8	Washington	LEWIS, John W.	2	Hancock
LEVERETT, John	4	Lincoln	LEWIS, Joseph	2	Warren
LEVERETT, William C.	17	Jasper	LEWIS, Josiah	3	Hancock
LEVERETT, Elizabeth	11	Stewart	LEWIS, M. J.	2	Early
LEVERETT, Feriba	1	Burke	LEWIS, Major J.	1	Forsyth
LEVERETT, John E.	1	DeKalb	LEWIS, Mrs. Ellen	3	Meriwether
LEVERETT, Wiley	1	Putnam	LEWIS, Nancy	1	Greene
LEVERETTE, Billington	7	Meriwether	LEWIS, Nathan G.	10	Houston
LEVERIT, H. J.	8	Harris	LEWIS, Noah	5	Newton
LEVERMAN, Elizabeth	2	Richmond	LEWIS, Philip	5	Jasper
LEVINGSTON,			LEWIS, Prior	10	Thomas
William M.	4	Dooly	LEWIS, R. G.	12	Troup
LEVINS, Robert	1	Heard	LEWIS, Rebecca	19	Warren
LEVINT, Jesse	3	Heard	LEWIS, Richard	3	Greene
LEVRETT, Gideon	22	Troup	LEWIS, Slates	4	Muscogee
LEVY, Isaac	3	Richmond	LEWIS, T. L.	20	Newton
LEVY, James	7	Gordon	LEWIS, Thomas	1	Greene
LEVY, Lewis	3	Richmond	LEWIS, Thomas	15	Houston
LEVY, Samuel	3	Richmond	LEWIS, W.	1	Morgan
LEWALLING, Jonathan	6	Walton	LEWIS, Walker	26	Greene
LEWIS ?, Joseph E.	1	Stewart	LEWIS, William B.	2	Washington
LEWIS, B.	5	Wilkinson	LEWIS, Adkin	3	Burke
LEWIS, E.	3	Wilkinson	LEWIS, Alexander	35	Burke
LEWIS, Aaron	1	Morgan	LEWIS, Barnett	2	Burke
LEWIS, Augustus A.	38	Burke	LEWIS, Baylis W.	10	Cass
LEWIS, Barthend	4	Morgan	LEWIS, Benjamin	38	Burke
LEWIS, Benjamin	1	Houston	LEWIS, David F.	7	Cass
LEWIS, Cephus	1	Greene	LEWIS, Ebert	6	Stewart
LEWIS, Curtis	11	Pike	LEWIS, Elbert	11	Stewart

Name	Number	County	Name	Number	County
LEWIS, Eliza	3	Burke	LIGHTFOOT, T.J.	2	Bibb
LEWIS, Elizabeth	2	Dooly	LIGHTFOOT, W. S.	6	Bibb
LEWIS, F. A.	4	Randolph	LIGHTFOOT, W. T.	8	Bibb
LEWIS, F. B.	1	Randolph	LIGNER, William L.	13	Meriwether
LEWIS, Fielding	37	Baldwin	LIGNOR, Young F.	3	Marion
LEWIS, G. B.	1	Randolph	LIGON ?, Sarah	2	Talbot
LEWIS, Green	4	Stewart	LIGON, Branch	13	Harris
LEWIS, Hanson	1	Tatnall	LIGON, Frances M.	11	Harris
LEWIS, James	23	Dooly	LIGON, J. M.	4	Heard
LEWIS, James	5	Dooly	LIGON, James	1	Muscogee
LEWIS, John	2	Burke	LIGON, James L.	1	Harris
LEWIS, John	6	Columbia	LIGON, John	3	Muscogee
LEWIS, John A.	2	Burke	LIGON, William	3	Muscogee
LEWIS, John N.	17	Chatham	LIGON, T. H.	8	Cass
LEWIS, John W.	2	Baldwin	LIGURUN?, Franklin	1	Newton
LEWIS, Josiah	10	Burke	LIKINS, Samuel	1	Troup
LEWIS, Lillie	7	Columbia	LILES ?, R. B. Agent	37	Upson
LEWIS, Lydia	3	Burke	LILES, Benjamin	9	Wayne
LEWIS, Mary	1	Stewart	LILES, Charles	6	Marion
LEWIS, Milton	1	Burke	LILES, D.	2	Henry
LEWIS, Mrs. Rebecca	2	Burke	LILES, Thomas	1	Twiggs
LEWIS, N.	2	Crawford	LILES, Thomas T.	1	Wayne
LEWIS, Nelson	4	Sumter	LILLEY, William F.		
LEWIS, Rachel	9	Burke	agt THREAT, Jas.	26	Houston
LEWIS, Ransome	20	Burke	LILLIBRIDGE, Oliver	16	Chatham
LEWIS, Robert A.	14	Chatham	LILLY, John C.	3	Houston
LEWIS, Robert A.	8	Chatham	LILLY, John E.		
LEWIS, Robert A.	7	Chatham	agt for TOOMER, Henry	3	Houston
LEWIS, Samuel	7	Campbell	LILLY, John F.	3	Lumpkin
LEWIS, T. R.	2	Dooly	LILLY, Thomas	8	Lumpkin
LEWIS, Tarlton	21	Cass	LIMONTON, Theophalus	1	Gwinnett
LEWIS, Thomas	9	Sumter	LINCH, George	4	Harris
LEWIS, W. J.	1	Butts	LIND?, George Phason	2	Muscogee
LEWIS, W. S.	21	Dooly	LINDAY, William	31	Richmond
LEWIS, Warren	1	Randolph	LINDEN, Jacob T.	14	Laurens
LEWIS, William	4	Baldwin	LINDER, Lewis	21	Laurens
LEWIS, William	9	Stewart	LINDER, Lewis	8	Laurens
LEWIS, William H.			LINDER?, George F.	28	Morgan
agt for TOOMBS, J.	28	Houston	LINDLEY, Elisha	14	Cobb
LIDDELL, Moses	15	Gwinnett	LINDLEY, Elisha	12	Cobb
LIDDELL, Moses W.	4	Gwinnett	LINDLEY, James	1	Cobb
LIDDELL, Wm. C. P.	3	Gwinnett	LINDSALY, Parham	10	Butts
LIGHT, Jno. R.	3	Forsyth	LINDSAY, J. C. W.	37	Upson
LIGHT, Y. K.	1	Forsyth	LINDSAY, John	1	Jasper
LIGHT, Chas. E.	8	Coweta	LINDSAY, John	9	Newton
LIGHTFOOT, E. B.	8	Early	LINDSAY, C.W.		
LIGHTFOOT, John W.	8	Jones	agt for HOLT, A. T.	44	Houston
LIGHTFOOT, Archa	3	Burke	LINDSAY, H. C .	6	Bibb
LIGHTFOOT, B.	9	Crawford	LINDSAY, Samuel	1	Richmond
LIGHTFOOT, Carolus	1	Burke	LINDSEY, Benjamin F.	43	Troup
LIGHTFOOT, H.	5	Bibb	LINDSEY, Benjamin T.	5	Troup
LIGHTFOOT, Jas.	1	Crawford	LINDSEY, Caleb	6	Macon
LIGHTFOOT, John A.	18	Taliaferro	LINDSEY, Claiborn	1	Greene
LIGHTFOOT, Richard	8	Washington	LINDSEY, D.	1	Troup

Name	Number	County	Name	Number	County
LINDSEY, David	9	Pulaski	LISLE, Ephraim	2	Walker
LINDSEY, J. M.	6	Henry	LISTER, Henry	7	Cobb
LINDSEY, Jacob	9	Jones	LITTERALL?, Richard	2	Cherokee
LINDSEY, James	4	Jackson	LITTLE, (?)	7	Dade
LINDSEY, Letitia	30	Wilkes	LITTLE, A.	1	Wilkes
LINDSEY, Lucy	1	Greene	LITTLE, Anderson	1	Greene
LINDSEY, S.	5	Henry	LITTLE, Francis	6	Paulding
LINDSEY, Sherod	1	Jasper	LITTLE, Henry H.	8	Harris
LINDSEY, Sherwood	1	Muscogee	LITTLE, K. J. T.	1	Troup
LINDSEY, Sherwood C.	27	Muscogee	LITTLE, James	19	Washington
LINDSEY, T.	1	Lee	LITTLE, James H.	17	Franklin
LINDSEY, Thomas	4	Cobb	LITTLE, James M.	1	Franklin
LINDSEY, Thomas	9	Jones	LITTLE, John	13	Oglethorpe
LINDSEY, B. F. agent	32	Crawford	LITTLE, John H.	13	Franklin
LINDSEY, Dolphin	11	Butts	LITTLE, John H.	10	Hancock
LINDSEY, Wm.	1	Wilkes	LITTLE, John J.	17	Harris
LINER, Mrs. Mary	2	Meriwehter	LITTLE, John M.	18	Monroe
LINES?, R. B.	5	Lumpkin	LITTLE, Kinchen	28	Hancock
LINGO, Elijah H.	3	Twiggs	LITTLE, L. L.	13	Hancock
LINGO, John R. T.	6	Marion	LITTLE, Lewis	1	Union
LINGO, R. T.	13	Twiggs	LITTLE, R. T.	23	Jefferson
LINGO, Talafaro	11	Stewart	LITTLE, Thomas	6	Forsyth
LINGO, W. S.	8	Twiggs	LITTLE, William	2	Franklin
LINN, John	14	Warren	LITTLE, William	10	Jefferson
LINN, Reese	7	DeKalb	LITTLE, William	17	Jones
LINNEBARGER, John	1	Floyd	LITTLE, William	10	Walker
LINNY, Isaac	6	Meriwether	LITTLE, Willis	1	Cass
LINNY, J. C.	1	Merriwether	LITTLE, Z.	13	Henry
LINNY, Joseph	1	Meriwether	LITTLE, Alexander	7	Sumter
LINSAY, Dennis	1	Talbot	LITTLE, Allen	42	Baldwin
LINSEY, Cullen	2	DeKalb	LITTLE, Benjamin	1	DeKalb
LINSEY, Jacob	2	Troup	LITTLE, Cecelia	4	Chatham
LINSLEY, William	68	Merriwether	LITTLE, D. S.	6	Bibb
LINTON ?, Samuel D.	7	Richmond	LITTLE, Drury	7	DeKalb
LINTON, Benjamin	18	Thomas	LITTLE, F. L.	1	Carroll
LINTON, John S.	39	Oglethorpe	LITTLE, F. M.	2	Carroll
LINTON, Moses W.	75	Thomas	LITTLE, George	1	Dade
LINTON, Sarah	20	Greene	LITTLE, J. C.	4	Butts
LINVILLE, John	8	Heard	LITTLE, J. H.	15	Lincoln
LINZEY, C.	2	Floyd	LITTLE, James	3	Randolph
LIONS, Edmon I.			LITTLE, John	1	Dade
(overseer)	6	Lincoln	LITTLE, Joseph	18	Carroll
LIONS, James	65	Monroe	LITTLE, Kinchem	65	Putnam
LIONS, John G.	13	Monroe	LITTLE, L. F.	14	Putnam
LIPPITT, Samuel C.	23	Dooly	LITTLE, Lewis	18	Putnam
LIPPMAN, Joseph	4	Chatham	LITTLE, Nath.	1	Putnam
LIPSCOMB, Hariet	24	Heard	LITTLE, Robert	26	Putnam
LIPSCOMB, Minor	3	Jackson	LITTLE, Robert	1	Stewart
LIPSCOMB, Nathan S.	1	Jackson	LITTLE, Ruben	2	Campbell
LIPSCOMB, Smith	2	Hall	LITTLE, Saml. B.	1	Carroll
LIPSEY, Barbary	3	Burke	LITTLE, Thomas	9	Talbot
LIPSEY, Rasco	3	Macon	LITTLE, Thos.	3	Bibb
LIPTROT, John	14	Houston	LITTLE, Tolbert	1	Bullock
LISH (Tish?), Jesse	4	Muscogee	LITTLE, W. G.	5	Bibb

Name	Number	County
LITTLE, William	7	Bullock
LITTLE, William	2	Dade
LITTLE, Wm.	9	Putnam
LITTLE, Wm.	8	Taliaferro
LITTLEFIELD, Samuel	20	Screven
LITTLETON, E.	3	Wilkes
LITTLETON, Edward	11	Talbot
LIVELY, Geo. W.	4	Muscogee
LIVELY, Mark	15	Burke
LIVELY, Elizabeth	3	Burke
LIVELY, Mary	5	DeKalb
LIVELY, Milton	4	DeKalb
LIVINGSTON ?, Samuel	29	Morgan
LIVINGSTON, Alferd	7	Newton
LIVINGSTON, Frances A.	17	Heard
LIVINGSTON, Henry	2	Harris
LIVINGSTON, James	6	Harris
LIVINGSTON, James	5	Harris
LIVINGSTON, James	6	Walton
LIVINGSTON, John	8	Harris
LIVINGSTON, John Jr.	1	Harris
LIVINGSTON, Joseph	1	Newton
LIVINGSTON, Joseph	2	Walton
LIVINGSTON, Lewis	4	Muscogee
LIVINGSTON, Robert	8	Newton
LIVINGSTON, Thomas	18	Muscogee
LIVINGSTON, Wm. T.	2	Laurens
LIVINGSTON, John	2	Richmond
LIVINGSTON, John	4	Sumter
LIVINGSTON, John	9	Sumter
LLOYD, James M.	7	Muscogee
LLOYD, John	2	Muscogee
LLOYD, Thomas E. Estate	72	Chatham
LLOYD, William H.	19	Chatham
LLOYD, Betsy	1	Chatham
LLOYD, Eliza	7	Chatham
LLOYD, Hannah	4	Chatham
LLOYD, James	24	DeKalb
LMURDEN, Wm. H.	32	Greene
LOAGG, Brinson	2	Jefferson
LOCHLIN, Sarah G.	6	Clarke
LOCK, James	7	Dooly
LOCK, Sarah	6	Morgan
LOCK, William	11	Merriwether
LOCK, William R.	1	Washington
LOCK, E. W.	5	Putnam
LOCK, Joseph L.	3	Chatham
LOCK, Lenard	1	Dooly
LOCK, Thomas	12	Laurens
LOCKET, Hetty	12	Jones
LOCKETT, Jas. R.	1	Wilkes

Name	Number	County
LOCKETT, Reuben	14	Marion
LOCKETT, Solomon	9	Marion
LOCKETT, Rebecca	11	Crawford
LOCKETT, Royal	48	Crawford
LOCKETT, Thomas	5	Warren
LOCKETT, Wm.	27	Crawford
LOCKEY, Dingley	18	Warren
LOCKEY, James	1	Lee
LOCKHART, E.	5	Richmond
LOCKHART, Franklin	2	Marion
LOCKHART, Jesse	43	Hancock
LOCKHART, Jno.	8	Henry
LOCKHART, John	7	Lincoln
LOCKHART, LayFayette	20	Marion
LOCKHART, M. M.	3	Henry
LOCKHART, B. J.	1	Carroll
LOCKHART, David	18	Talbot
LOCKHART, Eliel	90	Lincoln
LOCKHART, Julius	3	Talbot
LOCKHART, Lemuel	3	Talbot
LOCKHART, Lemuel D.	2	Talbot
LOCKHART, M.	9	Talbot
LOCKHART, Rhoda	8	Burke
LOCKHEART, L. T.	12	Sumter
LOCKLIER, Hamilton	6	Burke
LOCKRIDGE, A. Y.	9	Chattooga
LOCKRIDGE, Jas.	3	Cass
LOCKWOOD, D. B.	3	Bibb
LOCKLEAR, Obadiah	1	Thomas
LOCKLIN ?, James A.	6	Walton
LOCKLIN ?, Samuel	13	Walton
LODGE, John	1	Chatham
LODGE, S.	1	Decatur
LOFLEY, William	6	Macon
LOFLIN, James	12	Lincoln
LOFTEN, James	17	Meriwether
LOFTEN, James H.	18	Wilkinson
LOFTEN, William L.	17	Meriwether
LOFTICE, W.	1	Elbert
LOFTIN, Isaac	12	Houston
LOFTIN, Joel	15	Houston
LOFTIN, W. J.	6	Henry
LOFTON, James	45	Elbert
LOFTON, R. Y.	29	Meriwether
LOFTON, James B.	9	DeKalb
LOFTON, John	15	Butts
LOGAN, A. J.	5	Lumpkin
LOGAN, J. H.	2	Pike
LOGAN, John	1	Houston
LOGAN, John agt for HOLT, T. G.	45	Houston
LOGAN, Thomas	3	Merriwether
LOGAN, G. M.	7	Bibb

Name	Number	County	Name	Number	County
LOGAN, L. B.	5	Union	LONGFORD, Joseph	1	Marion
LOGUE, Calvin	1	Warren	LONGINO, Absolem	5	Campbell
LOGUE, Charles	16	Warren	LONGINO, James W.	5	Campbell
LOITER, R. C.	12	Union	LONGINO, John T.	9	Campbell
LOKEY, John E.	8	Muscogee	LONGSHORE, David	1	DeKalb
LOMERS ?, George W.	10	Richmond	LONGSTOCK, Herman	6	Chatham
LOMINAC, M.	1	Elbert	LONGSTREET &		
LOMINS, Richard	1	Richmond	CARMICHAEL	30	Burke
LONDEN, John H.	5	Morgan	LONLIP, Jas.	3	Cherokee
LONG, Battle A.	22	Muscogee	LOONEY, Noah	2	Franklin
LONG, Crawford	2	Hancock	LOOPER, J. W.	4	Lumpkin
LONG, David	2	Jasper	LORAN, John	2	Chatham
LONG, Davis	4	Hancock	LORD, George W.	1	Wilkinson
LONG, G. T.	8	Henry	LORD, John	1	Wilkinson
LONG, George	1	Jasper	LORD, Stephen	7	Wilkinson
LONG, Henry	51	Talbot	LORD, Stephen	47	Wilkinson
LONG, Henry	51	Troup	LORD, William	3	Merriwether
LONG, Henry	1	Troup	LORD, William	18	Wilkinson
LONG, Henry R. J.	19	Madison	LORD, Windsor	1	Baldwin
LONG, James	39	Madison	LOTT, Alpea	3	Lumpkin
LONG, James L.	4	Pike	LOTT, Daniel	3	Ware
LONG, James S.	4	Madison	LOTT, Elisha	2	Ware
LONG, John A.	1	Jackson	LOTT, Enoch	4	Forsyth
LONG, John B.	13	Troup	LOTT, Ensley	2	Muscogee
LONG, John J.	71	Washington	LOTT, H. J.	1	Hall
LONG, John P.	4	Jackson	LOTT, J.	4	Irwin
LONG, John S.	2	Liberty	LOTT, Jane	9	Jackson
LONG, Jonathan	2	Paulding	LOTT, Jas. M.	1	Gordon
LONG, Joseph B.	3	Madison	LOTT, Jesse	9	Hall
LONG, Margaret	1	Paulding	LOTT, Jno. G.	10	Forsyth
LONG, Mathew	3	Hall	LOTT, Joel	2	Ware
LONG, Rufus	4	Floyd	LOTT, Moses	1	Hall
LONG, Samuel	40	Madison	LOTT, Daniel	12	Telfair
LONG, Solomon	9	Heard	LOTT, John	1	Telfair
LONG, Thomas	6	Madison	LOTT, Mark	4	Telfair
LONG, William T.	4	Warren	LOTT, Mark	2	Ware
LONG, Willis	1	Jackson	LOTT, Michael	9	Baker
LONG, Wm.	30	Monroe	LOTT, Robert	1	Richmond
LONG, Wm. E.	15	Chatham	LOUD, ?	6	Morgan
LONG, A.	1	Crawford	LOUDEN, Henry	1	Muscogee
LONG, Alexander	13	Chattooga	LOUDERMILK, J. J.	8	Morgan
LONG, Ann	2	Screven	LOUGHRIDGE,		
LONG, G.	13	Decatur	Benjamin	13	Murray
LONG, George	3	Camden	LOUIS, George G.	5	Upson
LONG, James	1	Talbot	LOVE, Albert G.	1	Paulding
LONG, Jas.	10	Crawford	LOVE, Charles	7	Pulaski
LONG, Jas.	3	Crawford	LOVE, Elizabeth	58	Laurens
LONG, Jesse	2	Crawford	LOVE, Henry	3	Effingham
LONG, Lott	6	Decatur	LOVE, Hugh R.	9	Walker
LONG, R. S. Y.	16	Coweta	LOVE, James	13	Bryan
LONG, Thos. L.	2	Carroll	LOVE, John	1	Gordon
LONG, Wm. W.	2	Cass	LOVE, Mrs.	4	Muscogee
LONG, Young T.	14	Coweta	LOVE, N. B.	3	Muscogee
LONG?, Benjamin	10	Early	LOVE, Peter E.	19	Thomas

Name	Number	County
LOVE, S. B.	3	Henry
LOVE, W. A.	4	Floyd
LOVE, John H.	6	Talbot
LOVE, Louisa	7	Chatham
LOVEJOY, Amerson R.	6	Meriwether
LOVEJOY, D. M.	11	Henry
LOVEJOY, J. L.	5	Henry
LOVEJOY, Pleasant P.	16	Jasper
LOVEJOY, W. C.	5	Meriwether
LOVEJOY, Welcome	2	Jasper
LOVEL, Jesse	1	Rabun
LOVELACE, Jas.	13	Troup
LOVELACE, L. B.	27	Troup
LOVELACE, Wm. R.	2	Troup
LOVELESS, John M.	2	Troup
LOVELESS, Levi	2	Gwinnett
LOVELESS, Hazall	1	Cass
LOVELL, Payne	4	Chatham
LOVELL, Delilah	2	Richmond
LOVELL, Edward	2	Chatham
LOVELL, James	7	Richmond
LOVERETT, Burrel	3	Jasper
LOVETT, Hinton	1	Campbell
LOVETT, Nancy	5	Monroe
LOVETT, Aaron B.	2	Thomas
LOVETT, Anthony B.	11	Burke
LOVETT, Augustus L. L.	3	Burke
LOVETT, Catherine	4	Thomas
LOVETT, James C.	17	Burke
LOVETT, John F.	25	Screven
LOVETT, Nomand	2	Thomas
LOVETT, R. W.	39	Screven
LOVETT, Robert W.	8	Screven
LOVETT, T.	8	Screven
LOVETT, Thomas	25	Screven
LOVETT, W. H.	19	Screven
LOVETTE, N. B.	41	Merriwether
LOVIN, Gabriel	1	Newton
LOVIN, Jonathan	1	Newton
LOVINGOOD, A. H.	2	Elbert
LOVINGOOD, H.	16	Elbert
LOVINGOOD, Samuel	4	Union
LOVLESS, Senna	2	Gordon
LOW, Hixon C.	1	Houston
LOW, J. H.	25	Henry
LOW, Jesse	6	Gwinnett
LOW, John	4	Forsyth
LOW, John R.	6	Jefferson
LOW, Levenia	6	Chatham
LOW, Lunsford	15	Laurens
LOW, Samuel	2	Houston
LOW, Andrew	11	Chatham
LOW, Caroline	4	Bibb
LOW, Charles	7	Columbia
LOW, Christopher	3	Richmond
LOW, James M. N.	6	Baker
LOW, John	43	Bibb
LOW, Mary G.	9	Columbia
LOWDEN, William	6	Macon
LOWDER, Samuel S.	4	Sumter
LOWE, Benj.	1	Harris
LOWE, Benj. T.	103	Harris
LOWE, Cader W.	19	Jones
LOWE, Curtis	27	Warren
LOWE, Curtis G.	31	Warren
LOWE, David	8	Morgan
LOWE, David W.	15	Warren
LOWE, Elizabeth	9	Morgan
LOWE, Henry H.	65	Harris
LOWE, Henry H.	35	Harris
LOWE, James	19	Harris
LOWE, James H.	7	Morgan
LOWE, Jeremiah	4	Jones
LOWE, John	33	Jones
LOWE, John	20	Jones
LOWE, John H. Jr.	34	Clarke
LOWE, John M.	13	Clarke
LOWE, John W. Sr.	23	Clarke
LOWE, L.	9	Henry
LOWE, Patrick	6	Burke
LOWE, William	22	Jones
LOWE, William	24	Upson
LOWE, William R.	14	Warren
LOWE, Wm. H.	18	Marion
LOWE, Isiah	1	Dade
LOWE, J.	19	Crawford
LOWE, James P.	14	Stewart
LOWE, John	5	Crawford
LOWERY, William C.	1	Jefferson
LOWERY, Andrew	1	Laurens
LOWERY, E. & M.	18	Jefferson
LOWERY, Eliza	43	Jefferson
LOWERY, Isaac H.	4	Jefferson
LOWERY, William C.	1	Jefferson
LOWERY, A. P.	2	Stewart
LOWERY, John	15	Stewart
LOWLES, James	1	Cherokee
LOWMAN, William	6	Houston
LOWMAN, G.	10	Crawford
LOWREY, David	1	Walker
LOWREY, David P.	11	Jefferson
LOWREY, Mark	1	Walker
LOWREY, W. S.	25	Jefferson
LOWREY, William	2	Walker
LOWRIE, David C.	1	Glynn
LOWRIE, William	4	Glynn
LOWRY, Martha	14	Jackson
LOWRY, Osborn M.	9	Jackson

Name	Number	County	Name	Number	County
LOWRY, David	7	Cass	LUFBURROW, Mathew	14	Chatham
LOWRY, S. R.	5	Cass	LUKE, James	37	Columbia
LOWRY, Willis B.	28	Burke	LUKER, Benj.	3	Wilkes
LOWTHER, A. A.	5	Muscogee	LUMAN?, Robt.	7	Bibb
LOWTHER, Eliza	18	Camden	LUMBERLAKE, J. L.	4	Wilkinson
LOWTHER, Elizabeth	91	Jones	LUMDEN, J. G.		
LOWTHER, Hampton	15	Camden	see CARTER, Wm.		Floyd
LOYAL, Tinsey	32	Newton	LUMIS?, Bayulis M.	10	Cass
LOYALL, Jesse	5	Jasper	LUMMERB?, Lazarus	17	Heard
LOYD, James	10	Troup	LUMPIN, John B.	8	Richmond
LOYD, Milton	1	Fayette	LUMPKIN, A. D.	3	Walker
LOYD, Charles	11	Harris	LUMPKIN, Ann R.	30	Oglethorpe
LOYD, Green B.	1	Newton	LUMPKIN, B. H.	8	Oglethorpe
LOYD, Jeremiah	2	Jones	LUMPKIN, Edward	20	Greene
LOYD, Sarah	8	Fayette	LUMPKIN, George	41	Oglethorpe
LOYD, J. C.	1	Crawford	LUMPKIN, H. J.	3	Oglethorpe
LOYD, John	3	Talbot	LUMPKIN, Henry H.	31	Marion
LOYD, Susannah	1	Richmond	LUMPKIN, John B.	11	Burke
LOYD, W.	1	Richmond	LUMPKIN, John H.	18	Floyd
LOYLESS, Chesterfield	3	Houston	LUMPKIN, Joseph	3	Oglethorpe
LOYLESS, Elliot	3	Stewart	LUMPKIN, Joseph H.	18	Clarke
LUCAS, Charles	19	Newton	LUMPKIN, Joseph H.	17	Oglethorpe
LUCAS, F. W.	6	Clarke	LUMPKIN, P.	1	Floyd
LUCAS, Mary M.	1	Fayette	LUMPKIN, Samuel	38	Oglethorpe
LUCAS, William	2	Newton	LUMPKIN, Susan	37	Oglethorpe
LUCAS, C. M.	23	Crawford	LUMPKIN, Wilson	20	Clarke
LUCAS, Isaac	8	Talbot	LUMPKIN, Dickerson	3	Talbot
LUCAS, John M.	8	Screven	LUMPKIN, Edmund W.	1	Burke
LUCAS, L. B.	52	Crawford	LUMPKIN, Henry H.	9	Sumter
LUCAS, Martha	10	Crawford	LUMPKIN, Jack C.	8	Coweta
LUCAS, Richard	2	Screven	LUMPKIN, John	7	Talbot
LUCE, A. B.	7	Chatham	LUMPKIN, Leroy C.	3	Taliaferro
LUCE, A. B., Atty.	2	Chatham	LUMPKIN, Washington	2	Chattooga
LUCEFORD, Sarah	14	Monroe	LUMPKIN, William H.	15	Richmond
LUCIUS, James	1	Dooly	LUNCEFORD, Peter	5	Wilkes
LUCK, Archibald	3	Gwinnett	LUNCEFORD,		
LUCK, John	2	Gwinnett	William L.	2	Newton
LUCKER, Crawford	1	Cobb	LUNCEFORD, Wm.	9	Wilkes
LUCKEY, R. H.	6	Thomas	LUNDAY, Mc.	20	Lee
LUCKEY, Abram	3	Jefferson	LUNDAY, Robert	34	Baker
LUCKEY, John	1	Jefferson	LUNDY, James	1	Harris
LUCKEY, John	14	Monroe	LUNDY, Lewis W.	1	Greene
LUCKEY, Samuel	3	Jefferson	LUNDY, Robert	32	Jones
LUCKIE, Nancy	5	Greene	LUNDY, John	8	Coweta
LUCKIE, W. D.	3	Newton	LUNDY, Robert	1	Taliaferro
LUCKIE, William F.	16	Greene	LUNDY, Wm.	36	Bibb
LUCKY, Alexr.	5	DeKalb	LUNLEY, Jesse	3	Stewart
LUCKY, Nancy	1	Columbia	LUNSFORD, Henry	1	Houston
LUCKY, J. B.	9	DeKalb	LUNSFORD, Isaac	7	Walton
LUCY, Wm. E.	4	Coweta	LUNSFORD, Geo.	2	Bibb
LUDDELL, Isabella	12	Gwinnett	LUNSFORD, George W.	2	Baker
LUDDELL, Thomas H.	2	Gwinnett	LUNSFORD, John	3	Stewart
LUDICUS, Edwin	1	Chatham	LUNSFORD, John	8	Taliaferro
LUDOWICK	1	Gwinnett	LUNSFORD, Mrs. P.	3	Bibb

Name	Number	County	Name	Number	County
LUNSFORD, Peter H.	1	Taliaferro	LYON, Jonathan	9	Washington
LUNSFORD, Rubin	12	Taliaferro	LYON, Richard F.	4	Baker
LUNSFORD, Wm.	5	Taliaferro	LYON, Thomas	1	DeKalb
LUNSFORD, Wm. M.	1	Taliaferro	LYONS, F. R.	1	Liberty
LUPO, Giles	1	Houston	LYONS, James	12	Upson
LURQUEST?, John M.	1	Pike	LYONS, Jane	34	Harris
LUSK, John	1	Cass	LYONS, John P.	25	Thomas
LUSTER?, Jas. M.	1	Floyd	LYONS, John W.	9	Jefferson
LUTES, David	1	Murray	LYONS, Jordan	3	Jefferson
LYIESSEGGAR?,			LYONS, Jordan	17	Upson
Samuel	6	Chatham	LYONS, Thos.	2	Pike
LYKES, John P.	47	Hancock	LYONS, Wm. G.	3	Jefferson
LYKES, William B.	2	Hancock	LYONS, Frederick	1	Liberty
LYLE, James	1	Gilmer	LYONS, J. E.B.	16	Butts
LYLE, Dilmus R.	26	Jackson	LYONS, Thomas L.	1	Bryan
LYLE, J.	5	Henry	LYONS?, James R.	3	Pike
LYLE, James	10	Newton	LYTLE?, Robert Y.	9	Jones
LYLE, James B.	1	Jackson	M. & R. RAILROAD	4	DeKalb
LYLE, Katherine	6	Jackson	MAAXEY, Lewis M.	6	Greene
LYLE, Pleasant	4	Floyd	MABIN, Henry	7	Randolph
LYLE, Wm.	13	Jackson	MABLER, Robert	12	Cobb
LYLE, Chas.	7	Coweta	MABRY, C. W.	7	Heard
LYLE, Hugh	17	Stewart	MABRY, Daniel S.	2	Monroe
LYLE, M.	1	Coweta	MABRY, Daniel W.	30	Monroe
LYLE, Robt.	1	Coweta	MABRY, H. B.	13	Upson
LYLE, Wm. M.	1	Coweta	MABRY, James	2	Newton
LYLS, Jas.	10	Wilkes	MABRY, Jemerson	29	Lincoln
LYMAN, A.	1	Muscogee	MABRY, Joel B.	2	Newton
LYME, Thomas A.	31	Taliaferro	MABRY, Nancy	6	Paulding
LYN, Charles	2	Newton	MABRY, Woodford	19	Glynn
LYNAH, Edward T.	31	Warren	MABRY, A.	2	Randolph
LYNCH, Asa	27	Muscogee	MABRY, B. M.	8	Carroll
LYNCH, Benjamin	1	Lumpkin	MABRY, Seth W.	11	Carroll
LYNCH, G. G.	6	Putnam	MACHAL, George	30	Stewart
LYNCH, James	2	Fayette	MACK, Charles	4	Columbia
LYNCH, Jarrot	10	Jasper	MACK, John	6	Walton
LYNCH, Cornelius	1	Stewart	MACK, Samuel	2	Thomas
LYNCH, David	15	Coweta	MacKAY, Eliza	17	Chatham
LYNCH, Jas. N.	12	Putnam	MacKAY, William estate	86	Chatham
LYNCH, John	11	Putnam	MacKELSEY, Wm.	1	Bibb
LYNCH, Lewis	38	Putnam	MacMATH, J. H.	9	Merriwether
LYNCH, Lewis	8	Putnam	MacNEELEY, Mary A.	1	Bibb
LYNCH, Osbern	5	Coweta	MACKEY, J.	10	Wilkinson
LYNCH, Seaborn	1	Putnam	MACOMSON, Andrew	3	DeKalb
LYNCH, Wilkins	6	Putnam	MACON, L. A.	12	Greene
LYNN, J.	1	Muscogee	MACON, Thos. G.	10	Clarke
LYNN, William	14	Jasper	MACON, C. D.	3	Baker
LYNN, R.	1	Bibb	MADARD, Eliza	12	Monroe
LYNN, Sarah E.	7	Wilkes	MADDAX, Mark W.	1	Monroe
LYNN, William	2	Tatnall	MADDEN, James M.	5	Pike
LYON, Emmanual	3	Paulding	MADDEN, John H.	4	Muscogee
LYON, J. T.	4	Heard	MADDEN, Saml.	6	Fayette
LYON, J. T.	1	Heard	MADDOX, David	1	Butts
LYON, George	13	DeKalb	MADDOX, E.	21	Troup

Name	Number	County	Name	Number	County
MADDOX, H. J.	4	Newton	MAGBEE, Hiram	5	Heard
MADDOX, Jane	4	Clarke	MAGEE, Eli K.	2	Monroe
MADDOX, Jas. A.	4	Cherokee	MAGEE, William	10	Stewart
MADDOX, Jesse J.	12	Jones	MAGINES, Pamelia	2	Cobb
MADDOX, John	7	Butts	MAGRUDER, C. B.	12	Monroe
MADDOX, Joseph	21	Newton	MAGRUDER, Joseph	7	Monroe
MADDOX, Joseph A.	1	Newton	MAGRUDER, L. S.	15	Merriwether
MADDOX, Joseph D.	1	Jackson	MAGRUDER, Geo.	48	Columbia
MADDOX, Mary	3	Jackson	MAGUIRE, Thomas	22	Gwinnett
MADDOX, N. W.	2	Newton	MAGUIRE, Thomas	1	McIntosh
MADDOX, Nottey	21	Harris	MAHAFFEE, James	5	Cobb
MADDOX, W.	10	Henry	MAHAFFEE, John	1	Cobb
MADDOX, William G.	15	Jones	MAHAFFEY, William	3	Muscogee
MADDOX, William L.	2	Newton	MAHARRY, Charity	4	Richmond
MADDOX, Wm. D.	9	Greene	MAHARRY, Wm. H.	9	Richmond
MADDOX, Alexander	22	Putnam	MAHON, Mary A. B.	6	Macon
MADDOX, G.B.T.	5	Chattooga	MAHONE, Dickson	2	Baldwin
MADDOX, J. P.	1	Butts	MAHONE, Peeter F.	46	Talbot
MADDOX, Jackson	1	Columbia	MAHONE, Peter F.	11	Talbot
MADDOX, John C.	27	Putnam	MAHONE, Rowland	53	Talbot
MADDOX, Wm.	1	Butts	MAHONE, Tilman	15	Talbot
MADDOX, Wm. Sen.	32	Putnam	MAHONEY, C. O.	7	Wilkes
MADDOX?, Lott	1	Irwin	MAHONY, James	1	Lincoln
MADDUX, Abram B.	8	Jasper	MAHONY, Daniel	4	Columbia
MADDUX, BenjaminW.	2	Walker	MAILEY, J.	8	Elbert
MADDUX, Chapman F.	20	Marion	MAIN, Mathew	4	Hall
MADDUX, D. R.	11	Laurens	MAINE, Robert W.	3	Lowndes
MADDUX, David N.	10	Marion	MAINES, Elbert	2	Talbot
MADDUX, Emory M.	3	Jasper	MAJOR, Daniel	10	Walker
MADDUX, James L.	26	Jasper	MAJORS, Daniel	13	Marion
MADDUX, Jas. R.	1	Laurens	MAJORS, John	2	Marion
MADDUX, John	23	Jasper	MAJORS, Nancy	1	Cass
MADDUX, John C.	2	Jasper	MAKIN, E.	7	Camden
MADDUX, Lucius Q.	4	Marion	MALCOM, John G.	9	Morgan
MADDUX, Mary	3	Warren	MALCOM, G.	9	Walton
MADDUX, Meshack	2	Jasper	MALCOM, George Sr.	9	Walton
MADDUX, Patrick N.	16	Warren	MALCOM, George A.	3	Walton
MADDUX, Posey	1	Cobb	MALCOM, John	38	Walton
MADOCKS, William B.	7	Dooly	MALCOM, Margaret	16	Morgan
MADOWS, Joseph	5	Harris	MALCOM, Thos. J.	5	Walton
MADOWS, William	2	Harris	MALCOM, William	3	Walton
MADOX, James G.	1	Jackson	MALCOM, Wilson	1	Morgan
MADOX, J. R.	5	Randolph	MALCOMB, Alexander	35	Merriwether
MADRY, George	17	Burke	MALDEN, Alexander	8	Habersham
MAFFET, Samuel	9	Troup	MALDIN, A.	2	Irwin
MAFFETT, E. C.	9	Meriwether	MALLARD, Cyrus	31	Liberty
MAG, J. T.	2	Crawford	MALLARD, John B.	11	Liberty
MAGAHEE, Andrew J.	1	Columbia	MALLARD, Lazarous J.	17	Liberty
MAGAHEE, Betsey	7	Columbia	MALLARD, T. S.	45	Liberty
MAGAHEE, David	2	Columbia	MALLARD, Thos.	84	Liberty
MAGAHEE, John	9	Columbia	MALLETT, Jeremiah	29	Effingham
MAGAHEE, William	18	Columbia	MALLETT, Lewis	1	Effingham
MAGAHEE, William	3	Columbia	MALLETT, Geo. A.	1	Camden
MAGARITY, M.	1	Carroll	MALLETTE, Abraham	3	Bullock

Name	Number	County	Name	Number	County
MALLORY, E.	3	Troup	MALTBIE, John W.	3	Gwinnett
MALLORY, John	5	Chatham	MALTBIE, William	10	Gwinnett
MALLORY, John	3	Troup	MALTON, John	1	Walton
MALLORY, Mary	2	Chatham	MAN, Leroy C.	2	Merriwether
MALLORY, W. B.	1	Morgan	MAN, Lucy	7	Newton
MALLORY, William	3	Troup	MAN, Moses	6	Newton
MALLORY, Charles E.	50	Baker	MAN, Robert	4	Newton
MALLORY, Zachariah	7	Troup	MAN, William	2	Newton
MALONE, Agnes	8	Franklin	MANARD, William	7	Monroe
MALONE, Amanda M.	3	Meriwether	MANCE, John O.	1	Richmond
MALONE, Ann	1	Jones	MANDERVILLE, C. G.	21	Randolph
MALONE, Cader	14	Jasper	MANEGAULT, J.	84	Chatham
MALONE, Cherry	7	Washington	MANER, ?	1	Screven
MALONE, D. R.	11	Murray	MANER, Geo. H.	104	Screven
MALONE, Floyd	7	Jasper	MANER, John. S.	18	Screven
MALONE, Frank	2	Muscogee	MANERY, John	1	Madison
MALONE, Franklin	13	Jasper	MANES, Benj.	17	Talbot
MALONE, George	1	Cobb	MANES, E.	1	Bullock
MALONE, Jarret	2	Jasper.	MANEY, Caleb G.	1	Lowndes
MALONE, Jeptha	10	Jasper	MANEY, Richard	1	Pike
MALONE, John	6	Jones	MANGHAM, James P.	6	Pike
MALONE, John	3	Merriwether	MANGHAM, Jas. C.	14	Glynn
MALONE, John	4	Murray	MANGHAM, John C.	16	Muscogee
MALONE, John W.	5	Paulding	MANGHAM, John C.	22	Pike
MALONE, Ludford B.	1	Pike	MANGHAM, John N.	22	Pike
MALONE, Maranday	13	Gwinnett	MANGHAM, Wiley	14	Pike
MALONE, Martha	4	Jasper	MANGHAM, Henry	39	Talbot
MALONE, Mary	3	Paulding	MANGRAM, Jas.	5	Butts
MALONE, Spencer	5	Meriwether	MANGUM, Arthur	4	Jackson
MALONE, Thompson	31	Greene	MANGUM, G. M.	1	Franklin
MALONE, William	7	Jasper	MANGUM, Howell	10	Franklin
MALONE, Wm.	11	Henry	MANGUM, James	1	DeKalb
MALONE, Wm.	6	Muscogee	MANGUM, Nathaniel	2	DeKalb
MALONE, Ann H.	25	Richmond	MANGUM, R. C.	2	DeKalb
MALONE, C. B.	4	Butts	MANING, Martin	4	Wayne
MALONE, Chas. J.	21	Sumter	MANING, Moses	3	Wayne
MALONE, Martha	2	Butts	MANIS, Edmond	4	Talbot
MALONE, Rachel	4	Stewart	MANLEY, J. P.	28	Henry
MALONE, Y.S.	12	Randolph	MANLEY, R. J.	10	Henry
MALONEY, S. V.	10	Cobb	MANLEY, K. A.	1	Dooly
MALONEY, William	1	Cobb	MANLY, G. W.	5	Henry
MALONEY, William P.	9	Cobb	MANN, Asa	7	Harris
MALONS, Stith B.	7	Pike	MANN, B. J.	1	Elbert
MALORY, Allen b.	2	Upson	MANN, Baker	15	Merriwether
MALORY, Allen B.			MANN, Ephrain	3	Houston
Agent	24	Upson	MANN, Henry	3	Appling
MALORY, Elizabeth	1	Burke	MANN, J.B.	1	Meriwether
MALORY, John	8	Upson	MANN, J. H.	7	Troup
MALOY, Hugh	5	Telfair	MANN, Jesse	6	Campbell
MALAPAS, K. F.	18	Washington	MANN, Joel	9	Floyd
MALPAS, John	2	Talbo	MANN, Joel W.	5	Houston
MALRY, W. J.	1	Heard	MANN, John E.	23	Liberty
MALSLEY, Lott	5	Bibb	MANN, John. T.	27	Morgan
MALSLEY, Maria	2	Bibb	MANN, M.	1	Henry

Name	Number	County	Name	Number	County
MANN, Mary	5	Monroe	MAPP, Wm. F.	8	Monroe
MANN, R. F. M.	1	Pike	MAPP, Wm. T.	21	Hancock
MANN, Reuben	69	Morgan	MAPP, Wm. L.	14	Taliaferro
MANN, Robert B.	8	Upson	MAPPIN, Willis	7	Putnam
MANN, Thomas	17	Monroe	MARABLE, Robt.	13	Clarke
MANN, William L.	1	Jackson	MARABLE, Wm.	18	Clarke
MANN, Z.	5	Henry	MARAH, Thos.	4	Harris
MANN, E. L.	17	Butts	MARAN, Washington	1	Monroe
MANN, Elizabeth	16	Sumter	MARAN, A.	8	Crawford
MANN, John H.	12	Richmond	MARANT, S.	3	Bibb
MANN, Joseph	4	Sumter	MARBLE, William	15	Oglethorpe
MANN, Luke for			MARBLE, Wm.	1	Oglethorpe
S. E. MANN	12	Bryan	MARBUT, Eucledus	2	DeKalb
MANN, Sarah	7	Sumter	MARCHAND, Mrs.	2	Decatur
MANN, William	18	Tatnall	MARCHANT estate	35	Chatham
MANN, Wm. J.	7	DeKalb	MARCHERSON, John	9	Chatham
MANNING, Alexander	12	Houston	MARCHMAN,		
MANNING, Ambrose	11	Cherokee	Alphred G.	4	Paulding
MANNING, Benjamin	1	Lumpkin	MARCHMAN, Boswell	7	Paulding
MANNING, Benjamin	6	Thomas	MARCHMAN,		
MANNING, Eppy	4	Pulaski	Cornelius P.	9	Troup
MANNING, J. W.	2	Newton	MARCHMAN, Elizabeth	3	McIntosh
MANNING, Joseph	3	Wayne	MARCHMAN, Franklin		
MANNING, Leary C.	14	Houston	agt HALIBURTON	52	Houston
MANNING, LIttleton	1	Newton	MARCHMAN, G.	1	Hancock
MANNING, Mary	3	Cherokee	MARCHMAN, James	2	Houston
MANNING, Penelope	2	Houston	MARCHMAN, Thomas	4	Greene
MANNING, Riley	7	Houston	MARCHMAN, William	2	Harris
MANNING, Seabron	3	Pulaski	MARCHMAN,		
MANNING, Shadrac	2	Wayne	William R.	15	Troup
MANNING, Thomas	3	Walker	MARCUS, Morris	2	Wilkes
MANNING, Solomon	6	Cherokee	MARCUS, S.	26	Troup
MANNING, Col. Wm. R.	64	Telfair	MAREBLE, Joel	6	Floyd
MANNING?, John J.	1	Houston	MARGARUM?, Jarrett	4	Cobb
MANNORS, William R.	1	Dooly	MARKEE, Lawrence	1	Richmond
MANRAN?, P. P.	3	Lee	MARKET, John	9	Sumter
MANSELL, Samuel	5	Cherokee	MARKET, Joseph	2	Sumter
MANSFIELD, James	2	Baker	MARKHAM, Timothy	1	Muscogee
MANSFIELD, John	2	Baker	MARKHAM, W.	14	Henry
MANSFIELD, L.	4	Stewart	MARKS, Isaac	1	Upson
MANSFIELD, W. S.	2	Stewart	MARKS, J. C.	1	Newton
MANSOME?, E.	4	Bibb	MARKS, Robt.	8	Newton
MANSON, F. E.	26	Henry	MARKS, Samuel	4	Newton
MANSON, Margaret	12	Wilkinson	MARKS, R. T.	12	Harris
MANSON, Richard	2	Jefferson	MARLER, Peterson T.	2	Jackson
MANSON, William	13	Wilkinson	MARLIN, John S.	1	Gilmer
MANVILLE, Harriet	2	Thomas	MARLOW, Joseph	6	Cobb
MAP, James	2	Muscogee	MARLOW, Mary	1	Wilkes
MAPLES, Israel	7	Baker	MARLOW, Tabitha	13	Effingham
MAPLES, Temperance	2	Baker	MARLOW, Rebecca	13	Burke
MAPP, Lucretia	5	Greene	MARNDERILLE?, A.	4	Carroll
MAPP, Mary	51	Greene	MARONEY, Wm.	1	Chattooga
MAPP, Mary	23	Hancock	MARPUT, Joshua	4	Newton
MAPP, R. H.	7	Hancock	MARPUT, Robert	1	Newton

Name	Number	County
MARR, Jos.	1	Camden
MARR, John	1	Camden
MARRELE ?, G. W. H.	19	Walton
MARRINER, A. S.	1	Muscogee
MARSH, J.	2	Troup
MARSH, John	10	Jones
MARSH, John	2	Warren
MARSH, Mrs.	3	Irwin
MARSH, Mulford	13	Chatham
MARSH, Martin	15	Screven
MARSH, Mulford	19	Burke
MARSH, Spencer	12	Walker
MARSH, T.	18	Troup
MARSHAL, Mrs. Margaret	1	Houston
MARSHAL, Danl.	18	Columbia
MARSHAL, Danl. P.	15	Columbia
MARSHAL, John A.	20	Columbia
MARSHAL, Joseph	13	Columbia
MARSHALL, James	12	Macon
MARSHALL, Abr.	9	Houston
MARSHALL, Alex.	3	Early
MARSHALL, Alexander	1	Early
MARSHALL, Benjamin T.	18	Houston
MARSHALL, Edward B.	3	Houston
MARSHALL, Elizabeth	3	Jefferson
MARSHALL, Elizabeth	13	Pike
MARSHALL, Francis A.	8	Clarke
MARSHALL, Jackson	3	Newton
MARSHALL, James	1	Pike
MARSHALL, James M.	22	Harris
MARSHALL, Joseph	1	Chatham
MARSHALL, Joseph	8	Jefferson
MARSHALL, Madison	23	Houston
MARSHALL, Martha	16	Jones
MARSHALL, Mary	56	Chatham
MARSHALL, Mary	1	Jefferson
MARSHALL, Mary M.	13	Chatham
MARSHALL, P. R.	1	Gordon
MARSHALL, Polly	1	Chatham
MARSHALL, Andrew	8	Chatham
MARSHALL, Asa	13	Crawford
MARSHALL, Bursheba	13	Talbot
MARSHALL, Daniel L.	21	Columbia
MARSHALL, David	9	Talbot
MARSHALL, J.	8	Decatur
MARSHALL, Joseph E.	4	Richmond
MARSHALL, M.	4	Crawford
MARSHALL, Margaret W.	12	Chatham
MARSHALL, Peter	4	Sumter
MARSHALL, Solomon	1	Talbot
MARSHALL, Solomon	1	Talbot
MARSHALL, Stephen	94	Putnam
MARSHALL, Thos. C.	8	Wilkes
MARSHALL, W. H.	2	Columbia
MARSHALL, W. W.	1	Bibb
MARSHALL, William	3	Troup
MARSHALL, William B.	94	Talbot
MARSTON, John B.	11	Murray
MARTEN, John	16	Oglethorpe
MARTIAL, A. E.	20	Hall
MARTIN ?, Samuel C.	1	Richmond
MARTIN, A.	8	Twiggs
MARTIN, Abraham	8	Walker
MARTIN, Absalom	20	Hall
MARTIN, Alex.	10	Pulaski
MARTIN, Angus	34	Liberty
MARTIN, Ann A.	2	Troup
MARTIN, Archibald	7	Macon
MARTIN, C. W.	3	Oglethorpe
MARTIN, Conard	11	Morgan
MARTIN, Crawford	7	Upson
MARTIN, Daniel	6	Liberty
MARTIN, David	1	Hall
MARTIN, E. F.	6	Pike
MARTIN, E. H.	13	Lee
MARTIN, Elisha	2	Jackson
MARTIN, Elizabeth	5	Chattooga
MARTIN, G. S.	7	Franklin
MARTIN, George	21	Greene
MARTIN, George	5	Morgan
MARTIN, George T.	1	Jackson
MARTIN, George W.	1	Pike
MARTIN, Green	11	Washington
MARTIN, Hopson	2	Oglethorpe
MARTIN, J. R.	1	Pike
MARTIN, Jacob	8	Forsyth
MARTIN, James	9	Meriwether
MARTIN, James	9	Randolph
MARTIN, John	4	Monroe
MARTIN, John	15	Oglethorpe
MARTIN, John	4	Pike
MARTIN, John	6	Washington
MARTIN, John	1	Washington
MARTIN, John A.	3	Clarke
MARTIN, John F.	59	Gwinnett
MARTIN, John L.	11	Chatham
MARTIN, John L.	5	Monroe
MARTIN, John T.	5	Hancock
MARTIN, John W.	2	Habersham
MARTIN, Jonathan	2	Hall
MARTIN, Josiah	1	Walker
MARTIN, Lewis	4	Twiggs
MARTIN, L. O. H.	50	Elbert
MARTIN, Levi	2	Pike
MARTIN, Linson A.	1	Warren
MARTIN, Lovin	5	Cass

Name	Number	County	Name	Number	County
MARTIN, M. C.	3	Floyd	MARTIN, J. H.	6	Randolph
MARTIN, Marshal C.	53	Merriwether	MARTIN, James	3	Sumter
MARTIN, Martha C.	39	Pike	MARTIN, John	5	Baldwin
MARTIN, Mary	1	Gordon	MARTIN, John	27	Decatur
MARTIN, Mary	4	Jackson	MARTIN, John	1	Randolph
MARTIN, Mathew A.	13	Oglethorpe	MARTIN, John C.	1	Coweta
MARTIN, Micajah	4	Franklin	MARTIN, John c.	13	Talbot
MARTIN, Mrs.	79	Houston	MARTIN, Joshua	2	Randolph
MARTIN, Nathaniel	14	Liberty	MARTIN, Joshua F.	6	Putnam
MARTIN, Oden	1	Macon	MARTIN, Kinchen	7	Crawford
MARTIN, Phillip	3	Habersham	MARTIN, M. H.	24	Decatur
MARTIN, Phillip			MARTIN, Martin	8	Richmond
guardian for free person	16	Habersham	MARTIN, Mary	12	Richmond
MARTIN, Priscilla	8	Washington	MARTIN, Maurice	10	Baldwin
MARTIN, Robert D.	10	Macon	MARTIN, Patrick	2	Chatham
MARTIN, Robt. E.	8	Greene	MARTIN, Pleasant	2	Coweta
MARTIN, Samuel	3	Gwinnett	MARTIN, Robert	24	Cobb
MARTIN, Seaborn J.	9	Marion	MARTIN, Robert	51	Columbia
MARTIN, Simeon	8	Jackson	MARTIN, Robt.	1	Randolph
MARTIN, Stephen H.	19	Lowndes	MARTIN, W. B.	1	Campbell
MARTIN, T. H.	16	Monroe	MARTIN, William	24	Columbia
MARTIN, T. O.	1	Henry	MARTIN, William	22	Fayette
MARTIN, William	6	Upson	MARTIN, William	1	Talbot
MARTIN, William	3	Upson	MARTIN, Wm G.	56	Liberty
MARTIN, William	2	Warren	MARTLEAR?, George	9	Marion
MARTIN, William D.	49	Meriwether	MARTN, Samuel	2	Gwinnett
MARTIN, William T.	1	Franklin	MARTN, William	4	Lumpkin
MARTIN, William W.	4	Muscogee	MARTON, John	6	Cobb
MARTIN, Willis	3	Lee	MASABLE, Benj.	1	Randolph
MARTIN, Wm. D.	9	Jackson	MASATH ?, George	41	Walton
MARTIN, Wm. H.	10	Liberty	MASENGALE, (?)	4	Columbia
MARTIN, Z.	11	Henry	MASEY, James	6	Muscogee
MARTIN, A. estate	62	Burke	MASEY, John R.	1	Muscogee
MARTIN, A. C.	3	Coweta	MASH, J. J.	8	Thomas
MARTIN, A. P.	5	Rabun	MASH, Nathan	2	Fayette
MARTIN, Angus	22	Columbia	MASK, B.	1	Henry
MARTIN, Angus	3	Richmond	MASK, John B.	1	Sumter
MARTIN, Ann	13	Richmond	MASOBLE, B.	5	Randolph
MARTIN, Bird	2	Randolph	MASON, Benjamin	13	Jones
MARTIN, C. C.	1	Randolph	MASON, Charles	2	Gwinnett
MARTIN, Charles B.	3	Richmond	MASON, Charles	1	Jackson
MARTIN, Charles E.	3	Richmond	MASON, Churchill	5	Paulding
MARTIN, E. B.	5	Carroll	MASON, Henry	4	Washington
MARTIN, E. J.	14	Bibb	MASON, J. F. heirs of	8	Washington
MARTIN, Elias	2	Bullock	MASON, J. M.	21	Hancock
MARTIN, Elijah	26	Coweta	MASON, J. W.	1	Henry
MARTIN, G. W.	3	Randolph	MASON, James	26	Laurens
MARTIN, Gabr(?)	2	Columbia	MASON, James	7	Laurens
MARTIN, George W.	6	Cobb	MASON, L.B.	1	Henry
MARTIN, Henry	5	Stewart	MASON, M.	3	Henry
MARTIN, Irwin	7	Cass	MASON, M. H.	3	Washington
MARTIN, Isaac	2	Randolph	MASON, Michael agt		
MARTIN, J. E.	18	Decatur	for FORT, Laura	19	Houston
MARTIN, J. G.	3	Bibb	MASON, Morris	2	Laurens

Name	Number	County
MASON, R.S.	1	Henry
MASON, William	1	Clarke
MASON, William	20	Laurens
MASON, Alfred	5	Putnam
MASON, Chas. N.	9	Cass
MASON, James	22	Talbot
MASON, James L.	6	DeKalb
MASON, Silas	2	Cass
MASON, Thos.	2	Bibb
MASON, William	7	DeKalb
MASON, Wm. C.	3	DeKalb
MASON, Y. M.	16	Bibb
MASSEE, Nedham W.	16	Baker
MASSEY, Cordey	6	Muscogee
MASSEY, Drewry W.	5	Houston
MASSEY, Elizabeth	1	Washington
MASSEY, George	31	Macon
MASSEY, George W.	5	Washington
MASSEY, Henry	2	Cobb
MASSEY, Jeremiah	2	Muscogee
MASSEY, John B.	1	Washington
MASSEY, Kinchen W.	6	Washington
MASSEY, Nancy	3	Twiggs
MASSEY, Nathan	20	Morgan
MASSEY, Needham	39	Macon
MASSEY, Ruth	9	Jones
MASSEY, Sophia	11	Morgan
MASSEY, William	7	Morgan
MASSEY, Gideon	2	Stewart
MASSEY, Nathan M.	10	Dooly
MASSEY, W. T.	9	Bibb
MASSINGALE, Thos.	2	Columbia
MASSINGEL, Wright	2	Merriwether
MASSISNGALE, W. H.	16	Columbia
MASSSINGALE, Alfred	2	Columbia
MASSY, E. J.	10	Wilkinson
MASSY, Pleasant	1	Harris
MASSY, Robt.	1	Harris
MASSY, O. W.	17	Bibb
MASTERS, S. C.	1	Henry
MATEY, C. J.	1	Houston
MATHER, Samuel	2	Chatham
MATHERSON, Wm.	4	Muscogee
MATHES, Thomas	21	Fayette
MATHEW, Andrew	1	Marion
MATHEW, John C.	4	Pike
MATHEW, John W.	1	Oglethorpe
MATHEWS, Caroline	5	Cobb
MATHEWS, Charity	2	Gwinnett
MATHEWS, Charles	2	Muscogee
MATHEWS, D. R.	1	Pulaski
MATHEWS, Dan	10	Pulaski
MATHEWS, Elijah	5	Walker
MATHEWS, Frances A.	7	Muscogee
MATHEWS, Friar	14	Upson
MATHEWS, Griffin	5	Wilkes
MATHEWS, Henry	4	Harris
MATHEWS, Jas.	2	Pulaski
MATHEWS, Joel	3	Upson
MATHEWS, John	1	Macon
MATHEWS, John	5	Upson
MATHEWS, John A.	1	Clarke
MATHEWS, John R.	4	Clarke
MATHEWS, L. B.	2	Muscogee
MATHEWS, Lanford	2	Oglethorpe
MATHEWS, Mary	11	Morgan
MATHEWS, Mary	4	Walton
MATHEWS, Mrs. Ann	3	Muscogee
MATHEWS, Nancy	6	Marion
MATHEWS, Numan S.	6	Lincoln
MATHEWS, Robert C.	7	Madison
MATHEWS, Rolley	3	Oglethorpe
MATHEWS, S. C.	9	Jefferson
MATHEWS, Sarah	7	Pike
MATHEWS, W. D.	6	Meriwether
MATHEWS, William	2	Oglethorpe
MATHEWS, William	2	Walker
MATHEWS, Alfred L.	1	Columbia
MATHEWS, C.	10	Crawford
MATHEWS, C.	15	Randolph
MATHEWS, E.	2	Crawford
MATHEWS, J. B. see WHITE, Wm.		Habersham
MATHEWS, J. D.	21	Clarke
MATHEWS, J. M.	3	Crawford
MATHEWS, Jacob	14	Stewart
MATHEWS, Jas.	23	Crawford
MATHEWS, Josiah N.	3	Stewart
MATHEWS, M.	1	Crawford
MATHEWS, Martha	28	Bibb
MATHEWS, Mrs. B.	30	Stewart
MATHEWS, Mrs. Priscilla	9	Stewart
MATHEWS, Nicholas	1	Muscogee
MATHEWS, P.	4	Crawford
MATHEWS, R. N.	9	Crawford
MATHEWS, W. W.	8	Crawford
MATHEWS, William	49	Clarke
MATHEWS, Wm. L.	4	Screven
MATHIAS, Richard	10	Stewart
MATHINSON, Daniel	8	Stewart
MATHIS, D.	8	Randolph
MATHIS, Dr. A.	1	Oglethorpe
MATHIS, E. Y.	5	Elbert
MATHIS, Lewis	9	Marion
MATHIS, Littleton	16	Washington
MATHIS, P.	19	Elbert
MATHIS, Sherwood	4	Floyd

Name	Number	County	Name	Number	County
MATHIS, Thomas	6	Gwinnett	MATTHIS, Andrew J.	1	Burke
MATHIS, William	12	Cobb	MATTHIS, Charles	2	Burke
MATHIS, Wm. W.	15	Fayette	MATTHIS, Elisha	4	Cass
MATHIS, Charles B.	6	Baldwin	MATTHIS, Elizabeth	4	Burke
MATHIS, Jacob	2	Randolph	MATTHIS, James R.	1	Burke
MATHIS, S. (Matthews)	10	Putnam	MATTOX, Benjamin	4	Pike
MATHIS, T. D.	10	Baker	MATTOX, Daniel	2	Gwinnett
MATHIS, Thos.	1	DeKalb	MATTOX, David	41	Oglethorpe
MATHISON, Eliz.	2	Richmond	MATTOX, Davis W.	7	Pike
MATLOCK, Stephen	11	Montgomery	MATTOX, Elijah	17	Ware
MATLOCK, Stephen	44	Tatnall	MATTOX, John	13	Murray
MATLOCK, Wm.	9	Randolph	MATTOX, John W.	28	Oglethorpe
MATOX, H. P.	36	Elbert	MATTOX, John W.	5	Oglethorpe
MATTHEW, Elijah	1	Morgan	MATTOX, Nathan	52	Oglethorpe
MATTHEW, Allen	16	Talbot	MATTOX, Samuel	11	Pike
MATTHEW, Sarah	6	Warren	MATTOX, Thos.	2	Oglethorpe
MATTHEWS, Abram M.	27	Merriwether	MATTOX, W.	3	Oglethorpe
MATTHEWS, Aquilla	4	Merriwether	MATTOX, Candee	2	Bryan
MATTHEWS, Benj.	6	Marion	MATTOX, Hiram	4	Bryan
MATTHEWS, Catherine S.	8	Jefferson	MATTOX, Jno.	12	Randolph
MATTHEWS, Elizabeth	7	Warren	MATTOX, John A.	9	Tatnall
MATTHEWS, Emaline L.	13	Greene	MATTOX, Joseph a.	4	Tatnall
MATTHEWS, Ezekiel	2	Warren	MATTOX, Michael	7	Tatnall
MATTHEWS, Isaac	11	Marion	MATTOX, P. W. W.	4	Tatnall
MATTHEWS, J. H.	26	Habersham	MAUGHAM, Thos. H.	70	Lee
MATTHEWS, J. H.	25	Lincoln	MAUK?, John	8	Marion
MATTHEWS, James	31	Jefferson	MAUK, Mathias	8	Upson
MATTHEWS, James	8	Jefferson	MAULDEN, Caleb	1	Bibb
MATTHEWS, James	1	Macon	MAULSBY, M.	5	Putnam
MATTHEWS, James	1	Merriwether	MAULDIN, Frances	19	Upson
MATTHEWS, James A.	1	Paulding	MAULDIN, Martha	8	Upson
MATTHEWS, Jeremiah	6	Upson	MAUND, John C.	9	Talbot
MATTHEWS, John	4	Warren	MAXEY, Barnebas	14	Oglethorpe
MATTHEWS, John T.	12	Marion	MAXEY, Boaz	1	Clarke
MATTHEWS, Milo B.	17	Merriwether	MAXEY, G. W.	3	Oglethorpe
MATTHEWS, Milton	11	Jackson	MAXEY, Garland	42	Jasper
MATTHEWS, Thomas	3	Jefferson	MAXEY, James	6	Oglethorpe
MATTHEWS, William	7	Jackson	MAXEY, Jeremiah	5	Oglethorpe
MATTHEWS, Wm.	1	Cass	MAXEY, Jesse	3	Oglethorpe
MATTHEWS, Wm.	48	Marion	MAXEY, John H.	3	Oglethorpe
MATTHEWS, Wm. R.	2	Heard	MAXEY, Josiah	2	Clarke
MATTHEWS, Wm. T.	3	Meriwether	MAXEY, Pouny	12	Monroe
MATTHEWS, Green	12	Talbot	MAXEY, Samuel	9	Monroe
MATTHEWS, Green	5	Talbot	MAXFIELD, R.	3	Washington
MATTHEWS, John D.	13	Talbot	MAXLEY, Lewis	1	Burke
MATTHEWS, Josiah	96	Talbot	MAXWELL, ?	8	Elbert
MATTHEWS, Josiah	4	Talbot	MAXWELL, ?	3	Elbert
MATTHEWS, Marion	5	Talbot	MAXWELL, Alexander	20	Chatham
MATTHEWS, William	19	Talbot	MAXWELL, Benjamin	4	Franklin
MATTHEWS, William	11	Talbot			
MATTHIS, C. B.	3	Greene	MAXWELL, Dr. George T.	18	Liberty
MATTHIS, John	1	Lowndes	MAXWELL, George	1	Meriwether
			MAXWELL, J.	2	Elbert

Name	Number	County	Name	Number	County
MAXWELL, J. B.	8	Elbert	MAYES, Allen N.	9	Franklin
MAXWELL, J. E.	16	Clarke	MAYES, Thomas	26	Monroe
MAXWELL, James	24	Pike	MAYES, William	29	Warren
MAXWELL, Joel	9	Elbert	MAYES, Wm.	10	Cobb
MAXWELL, Joseph G.	10	Liberty	MAYFIELD, E. W.	51	Franklin
MAXWELL, L. E.			MAYFIELD, Battle	3	Cobb
& C. E.	39	Liberty	MAYFIELD, Stephen	1	Newton
MAXWELL, S. R.	13	Oglethorpe	MAYFIELD, T. W.	12	Forsyth
MAXWELL, William	7	Franklin	MAYFIELD, William	6	Gordon
MAXWELL, William	29	Liberty	MAYFIELD, Robt.	21	Butts
MAXWELL, William P.	3	Cobb	MAYISE?, Mars F.	7	Cobb
MAXWELL, Wm.	4	Wilkes	MAYNARD, James M.	3	Jones
MAXWELL, Wm. A.	89	Lee	MAYNARD, Jonathan D.	5	Jones
MAXWELL, B.	6	Decatur	MAYNARD, Robt. J.	1	Clarke
MAXWELL, Benson	28	Talbot	MAYNE, John W.	36	Clarke
MAXWELL, Benson	3	Talbot	MAYO, D.	1	Wilkes
MAXWELL, D. P.	2	Decatur	MAYO, Elisha	13	Walton
MAXWELL, J.	9	Decatur	MAYO, G. B.	2	Lee
MAXWELL, James H.	13	Richmond	MAYO, Hillman	1	Marion
MAXWELL, John F.			MAYO, Jesse	18	Marion
children	4	Bryan	MAYO, John	8	Dooly
MAXWELL, Martin	4	Cass	MAYO, John	1	Marion
MAXWELL, Mary	3	Chatham	MAYO, Lewis A.	2	Walton
MAXWELL, T.	5	Decatur	MAYO, M.	13	Floyd
MAXWELL, T.	3	Decatur	MAYO, William	93	Early
MAXWELL, T. J.	2	Decatur	MAYO, Wm.	21	Pulaski
MAXWELL, Thomas B.	1	Chatham	MAYO, Burrel	3	Stewart
MAY ?, Robert H.	20	Richmond	MAYO, Crawford M.	13	Baker
MAY, Daniel	1	Murray	MAYO, J. M.	2	Butts
MAY, Drewry B.	18	Fayette	MAYO, James M.	37	Baker
MAY, Edmund	2	Forsyth	MAYO, Wilie	2	Taliaferro
MAY, Edmund	10	Washington	MAYO, Wm. S.	6	Coweta
MAY, Hardy	1	Harris	MAYS, A. G.	7	Harris
MAY, Horatio	2	Jones	MAYS, Blair R.	5	Murray
MAY, James C.	1	Warren	MAYS, James	9	Monroe
MAY, James E.	15	Fayette	MAYS, James H.	28	Monroe
MAY, Jeptha V.	3	Fayette	MAYS, John	1	Lumpkin
MAY, John	10	Camden	MAYS, Morris	27	Muscogee
MAY, L.	1	Harris	MAYS, Mrs. Sarah	5	Harris
MAY, Nancy	4	Jones	MAYS, Robert	20	Monroe
MAY, P. L. J.	5	Macon	MAYS, Stephen T.	3	Gordon
MAY, Reuben	48	Warren	MAYS, H. S.	12	Butts
MAY, Stephen	1	Macon	MAYS, Robert	1	Lumpkin
MAY, William	24	Fayette	MAYS, Ruben	1	Stewart
MAY, William	28	Washington	MAZO, Daniel	2	Tatnall
MAY, Wm.	7	Fayette	Mc(?), S. G.	5	Decatur
MAY, Zero B.	3	Troup	McADAM, Thomas	13	Cass
MAY, Benj.	23	Bibb	McAFEE, Jesse	4	Washington
MAY, James	13	Crawford	McAFEE, John M.	43	Cherokee
MAY, K.	11	Bibb	McAFEE, Joseph	4	Harris
MAY, Warren	24	Stewart	McAFEE, Robert B.	16	Cobb
MAYBERRY, Ephrim	9	Walker	McAFEE, Tillman G.	8	Cobb
MAYBERRY, Joel	3	Walker	McAFEE, W. M.	9	DeKalb
MAYBERRY, Alfred	13	Warren	McAFIE, Mary M.	12	Gwinnett

Name	Number	County	Name	Number	County
McALFINE?, Henry	1	Effingham	McCALL, Francis	4	Franklin
McALISTER, Jas.	10	Greene	McCALL, Francis H.	5	Clinch
McALISTER, Samuel	6	Montgomery	McCALL, Francis S.	16	Lowndes
McALISTER, W. J.	14	Muscogee	McCALL, Geo. R.	9	Lowndes
McALISTER, Geo. W.			McCALL, Jacob	2	Hancock
estate	194	Bryan	McCALL, Marhamed?	2	Muscogee
McALISTER, Jas. D.	1	Carroll	McCALL, McKeen G.	1	Lowndes
McALISTER, Wesley G.	2	Baker	McCALL, Moses N.	3	Lowndes
McALLESTER, J. G.	1	Cass	McCALL, Nancy	3	Appling
McALLIAN, Arch	40	Twiggs	McCALL, Thomas F.	6	Lowndes
McALLISTER, James	1	DeKalb	McCALL, William	7	Lowndes
McALPIN, Alexander	9	Morgan	McCALL, Charles	1	Tatnall
McALPIN, Henry	28	Effingham	McCALL, E.	7	Bibb
McALPIN, Floyd	1	DeKalb	McCALL, Francis	2	Tatnall
McALPIN, Henry	199	Chatham	McCALL, Moses	17	Screven
McALPIN, Joseph	11	Upson	McCALL, Stephen	12	Camden
McARTHA, P.P.	2	Randolph	McCALLA, James	1	Walker
McARTHER, Peter	7	Randolph	McCALLA, James R.	30	Newton
McARTHUR, John	22	Montgomery	McCALLAR, Joseph	2	Bryan
McARTHUR, L. A.	9	Hall	McCALLEY, James	7	Troup
McARTY, William B.	9	Macon	McCALLEY, Susan	11	Troup
McAULAY, Angus	3	Lowndes	McCALPIN, J. W.	1	Henry
McAULEY, Donald N.	8	Thomas	McCALLS, Mathew	2	Walker
McAULEY, John	3	Thomas	McCAMEY, Robert	6	Murray
McAULEY, Tonquil	13	Thomas	McCAMY, Samuel R.	3	Murray
McBAIN, Norman	15	Sumter	McCAN, Joshua	23	Thomas
McBAIN, T. J.	6	Thomas	McCANN, Nancy	1	Burke
McBEAN, Daniel	2	Newton	McCANTS, Eli	18	Henry
McBRAYER, Nancy	1	Murray	McCANTS, Robt. A.	1	Harris
McBRIDE, ?	33	Muscogee	McCANTS, Samuel	2	Harris
McBRIDE, Andrew	4	Fayette	McCANTS, Andrew	3	Talbot
McBRIDE, Benjamin	1	Fayette	McCANTS, Jeremiah	12	Talbot
McBRIDE, George	1	Montgomery	McCANTS, Margaret	4	Talbot
McBRIDE, James	6	Muscogee	McCARDELL, A. V.	1	Wilkinson
McBRIDE, Jane	3	Jefferson	McCARDLE, Chas.	8	Bibb
McBRIDE, Robert B.	2	Jefferson	McCARN, PHILIP	1	Richmond
McBRIDE, Thomas	5	Jefferson	McCARN, William	3	Upson
McBRIDE, William G.	18	Washington	McCARTER, J. D.	3	Harris
McBRIDE, Wm.	1	Fayette	McCARTER, John E.	2	Franklin
McBRIDE, James H.			McCARTER, William	2	Harris
agt for GRISHAM	33	Houston	McCARTER, James R.	2	Sumter
McBRIDE, Thomas	6	Sumter	McCARTIN, C.	15	Troup
McBRYDE, Mancel	2	Talbot	McCARTHA, H.	13	Bibb
McBRYDE, Robert	7	Talbot	McCARTHA, Saml.	4	Bibb
McBURNETT, Nancy	5	Carroll	McCARTHY, John	3	Muscogee
McBURTONE, Thos.	10	Carroll	McCARTHY, A.	10	Bibb
McCABE, D. M.	1	Pulaski	McCARTY, B. F.	1	Pike
McCAFFRITY, James N.	4	Richmond	McCARTY, E. F.	3	Pike
McCAHEY, W.	1	Muscogee	McCARTY, Allen	2	Walton
McCAHY, Patrick N.	1	Richmond	McCARTY, Jesse	7	Walton
McCAIN, J. H.	2	Chattooga	McCARTY, Sherrod	5	Clarke
McCAIN, J. N.	18	Chattooga	McCARTY, Thomas	2	Muscogee
McCAIN, W. B.	8	Troup	McCARTY, Alexander	2	McIntosh
McCALL, Charles H.	24	Marion	McCARTY, George	5	Richmond

Name	Number	County
McCARTY, Madison	7	Burke
McCARVER, John	24	Floyd
McCASKIN, Murdock	43	Houston
McCASON, Jas.	8	Hancock
McCAUL, William P.	2	Franklin
McCAULA, Hugh	5	Harris
McCAULA, John	2	Harris
McCAULA, Robt.	2	Harris
McCAULEY, Lanna	3	Greene
McCAULEY, M.	24	Troup
McCAULEY, Mary A.	4	Warren
McCAULLEY, Mrs. E.	1	Houston
McCAULLEY, Mrs. Elizabeth	19	Houston
McCAW, David	2	Jefferson
McCAW, James	4	Newton
McCAY, Charles F.	3	Clarke
McCAY, John A.	21	Houston
McCAY, John B.	5	Houston
McCHUGH, James	7	Morgan
McCLANAHAN, M.	4	Elbert
McCLASKY, G. L.	2	Walton
McCLELAND, Rufus	1	Murray
McCLELAND, Wm.	1	Butts
McCLELLAN, James	7	Greene
McCLELLAND, J.	1	Henry
McCLELLAND, Mary M.	3	Lowndes
McCLENAN, Francis	3	Newton
McCLENDON, Benniah	18	Heard
McCLENDON, C.	7	Henry
McCLENDON, Dennis	1	Houston
McCLENDON, Freeman	53	Merriwether
McCLENDON, H. W.	2	Henry
McCLENDON, J.	4	Henry
McCLENDON, Jesse	9	Troup
McCLENDON, Jas.	1	Butts
McCLENDON, Joseph t.	18	Monroe
McCLENDON, Mack W.	22	Marion
McCLENDON, Nancy	1	Burke
McCLENDON, Needham	8	Early
McCLENDON, Stephen W.	10	Jasper
McCLENDON, William	13	Merriwether
McCLENDON, Willis	11	Merriwether
McCLENDON, O. H. P.	4	Butts
McCLENDON, Willis	26	Talbot
McCLESKEY, B. G.	5	Hall
McCLESKEY, D. H.	2	Hall
McCLESKEY, David G.	1	Cherokee
McCLESKEY, James R.	22	Jackson
McCLESKEY, Thomas J.	12	Chatham
McCLINDON, J.	1	Henry
McCLISTER, James	24	Muscogee
McCLOUD ?, Jacob	22	Richmond
McCLOUD, Daniel A.	8	Houston
McCLOUD, Daniel	2	Stewart
McCLUNG, David	4	Newton
McCLUNG, Jonas	1	Chattooga
McCLUNG, Mary	1	Newton
McCLUNG, Reuben	1	Cobb
McCLURE, John	6	Murray
McCLURE, Robert	16	Lumpkin
McCLURE, Chas.	9	Forsyth
McCLUSKY, Thadious H.	6	Cobb
McCOBITT, Henry	5	Putnam
McCOLER, Mrs. P.	1	Stewart
McCOLERISS, Jas. D.	1	Pulaski
McCOLLUM, Catherine	9	Monroe
McCOLLUM, George B.	5	Houston
McCOLLUM, George W.	1	Cherokee
McCOLLUM, James	10	Newton
McCOLLUM, John	1	Monroe
McCOLLUM, John B.	1	Cherokee
McCOLLUM, Joseph	2	Newton
McCOLLUM, John	6	Coweta
McCOLLUM, Nathan	14	Burke
McCOLOUGH, James S.	14	Liberty
McCOLOUGH, Mathew C.	15	Emanual
McCOMAC, H.	1	Meriwether
McCOMASK?, Mathias	34	Pulaski
McCOMB, M. B.	10	Merriwether
McCOMBS, Robert	47	Baldwin
McCOMBS, Wm.	9	Coweta
McCOMMON, James	4	Monroe
McCOMMON, R. C.	17	Oglethorpe
McCOMMONS, Thomas	6	Monroe
McCONN, P. H.	2	Dooly
McCONNEL, Mary	7	Walker
McCONNEL, Joshua	6	Walker
McCONNEL, W.	2	Henry
McCONNELL, Clark O.	2	Washington
McCONNELL, Edgar M.	7	Chatham
McCONNELL, Eli	4	Cherokee
McCONNELL, H.	1	Gordon
McCONNELL, J.	29	Henry
McCONNELL, James	8	Floyd
McCONNELL, John	20	Cherokee
McCONNELL, John C.	13	Franklin
McCONNELL, Joshua	5	Cherokee
McCONNELL, Thomas	25	Franklin
McCONNELL, Wm. P.	14	Liberty
McCONNELL, Isaac	3	Cobb
McCONNELL, Joseph	4	Cherokee
McCONNELL, Samuel M.	3	Cherokee

Name	Number	County	Name	Number	County
McCONNELL,			McCRARRY,		
Samuel M.	3	Cherokee	Timothy G.	1	Muscogee
McCONNELL, Wm.	20	Chattooga	McCRARRY, John T.	6	Sumter
McCONNELL, Wm.	1	DeKalb	McCRARY, J. W.	1	Hall
McCOOK, D.	5	Wilkinson	McCRARY, Ezra	12	Warren
McCOOK, Joshua R.	34	Muscogee	McCRARY, Isaac	3	Wilkes
McCORD, Bassel	8	Lincoln	McCRARY, James	13	Monroe
McCORD, Elisha	11	Monroe	McCRARY, James M.	7	Wilkes
McCORD, J. M.	12	Lincoln	McCRARY, John B.	11	Talbot
McCORD, James	7	Lincoln	McCRARY, Mathew	4	Muscogee
McCORD, James E.	3	Monroe	McCRARY, R. H.	1	Hall
McCORD, John	8	Butts	McCRARY, Sara	9	Hall
McCORD, John	17	Lincoln	McCRARY, Gilliah	1	Talbot
McCORD, John	1	Monroe	McCRARY, H.	5	Crawford
McCORD, John Agent	45	Warren	McCRARY, James	30	Baldwin
McCORD, John N.	1	Lincoln	McCRARY, John	33	Talbot
McCORD, Robert	3	Monroe	McCRARY, John	9	Talbot
McCORD, Robert B.	4	Walton	McCRARY, Johnathan	9	Talbot
McCORD, William S.	11	Newton	McCRARY, Malissa	2	Sumter
McCORD, George	2	Richmond	McCRARY, Matthew	24	Talbot
McCORD, J. AW.	12	Butts	McCRARY, Sterling T.	3	Sumter
McCORD, J. R.	13	Butts	McCRARY, W. C.	27	Crawford
McCORD, William	10	Talbot	McCRARY, William	16	Talbot
McCORKLE, Archibald	1	Lincoln	McCRAY, C.	2	Chattooga
McCORKLE, J. M.	22	Lincoln	McCRAY, Eppa	1	Hancock
McCORKLE, Robt.	2	Marion	McCRAY, Colon	2	Talbot
McCORKLE, John	1	Columbia	McCRAYER, Andrew E.	2	Paulding
McCORKLE, Quincy	4	Carroll	McCREARY, Asa M.	8	Warren
McCORMACK, Jas.	12	Pulaski	McCREARY, Jasper	4	Warren
McCORMICK, David	2	Columbia	McCREARY, Nancy	2	Warren
McCORQUODALE, R.	4	Early	McCRIMMON, Charles	2	Montgomery
McCOUGHINS,			McCRIMMON, Duncan	1	Montgomery
Margaret	4	Newton	McCRIMMON,		
McCOWEN, Duncan	36	Monroe	George W.	8	Montgomery
McCOY, A. H.	2	Troup	McCRIMON, Archy	6	Telfair
McCOY, Abner	10	Upson	McCROAN, Eli	22	Jefferson
McCOY, Benj.	14	Morgan	McCROAN, Rhesa	5	Bullock
McCOY, Charles M.	6	Houston	McCRORY, James	21	Talbot
McCOY, Henry	3	Muscogee	McCRORY, William	4	Talbot
McCOY, J. H.	3	Muscogee	McCROY?, Matthew	1	Lee
McCOY, James	18	Upson	McCUE, Patrick	3	Richmond
McCOY, Jeremiah	16	Muscogee	McCULLEN, J. C.	3	Laurens
McCOY, O. G.	6	Twiggs	McCULLER, Uriah	1	Warren
McCOY, Robert A.	15	Newton	McCULLERS, Calvin	15	Burke
McCOY, Sarah	20	Morgan	McCULLEY, J.	2	Henry
McCOY, Charles	22	Richmond	McCULLOCK, J. J.	8	Jackson
McCOY, Jane	1	Dooly	McCULLOCK, John S.	2	Newton
McCOY, John T.	6	Coweta	McCULLOH, Dempsey	4	Talbot
McCOY, Mrs. Charlotte	8	Burke	McCULLOH, Joseph P.	38	Walker
McCOY, Thomas	14	Campbell	McCULLOUGH, Hiram	1	Harris
McCRACKEN, James	4	Habersham	McCUNE, J. A.	45	Butts
McCRACKIN, James	5	Campbell	McCUNE, W. A.	15	Butts
McCRANE, John D.	1	Lowndes	McCURDEY, James	4	Cobb
McCRANIE, Daniel M.	1	Lowndes	McCURDY, Francis W.	9	Murray

Name	Number	County	Name	Number	County
McCURDY, Clarrissa	1	DeKalb	McDONALD, Alxr.	53	Glynn
McCURLEY, M.	14	Elbert	McDONALD, Barbara	3	Fayette
McCURRY, J.	3	Elbert	McDONALD, Charles J.	14	Cobb
McCURRY, J. G.	3	Elbert	McDONALD, Collins	1	Murray
McCURRY, James	5	Pike	McDONALD, Daniel	523	Glynn
McCURRY, John	10	Elbert	McDONALD, Daniel	12	Monroe
McCURY, Reuben	1	Talbot	McDONALD, Donald J.	3	Ware
McCUTCHEM, Robt.	6	Henry	McDONALD, G. B.	3	Heard
McCUTCHEON,			McDONALD, George A.	23	McIntosh
Benjamin R.	6	Walker	McDONALD, J. C.	2	Henry
McCUTCHINS, W. W.	2	Troup	McDONALD, J. H.	2	Muscogee
McCUTCHINS, Wm.	5	Troup	McDONALD, James	1	Thomas
McDADE, ?	9	Richmond	McDONALD, James M.	2	Franklin
McDADE, David	14	Monroe	McDONALD, Joshua	43	Early
McDADE, William	6	Monroe	McDONALD, Mary J.	4	Cobb
McDADE, John	33	Richmond	McDONALD, Mc.G.	13	Camden
McDANIEL, ?	1	Upson	McDONALD, Mrs.	4	Muscogee
McDANIEL, Andrew	3	Merriwether	McDONALD, Richard	2	Baker
McDANIEL, Arch	1	Cass	McDONALD, Randal	4	Ware
McDANIEL, B. M.	1	Merriwether	McDONALD, William	24	McIntosh
McDANIEL, Benj. F.	1	Harris	McDONALD, William	4	Murray
McDANIEL, Carson	14	Butts	McDONALD,		
McDANIEL, Comfor A.	1	Wilkinson	William A.	13	McIntosh
McDANIEL, Darling	5	Gwinnett	McDONALD,		
McDANIEL, E.	4	Elbert	William A.	2	Ware
McDANIEL, Eli J.	6	Gwinnett	McDONALD, Alexander	33	Chatham
McDANIEL, Elizabeth	3	Washington	McDONALD, C.	8	Henry
McDANIEL, Geo. W.	6	Forsyth	McDONALD, E..	3	Randolph
McDANIEL, James	4	Gwinnett	McDONALD, G.	2	Bibb
McDANIEL, John	1	Jones	McDONALD, Jackson M.	7	Tatnall
McDANIEL, Mary	5	Pulaski	McDONALD, James	1	Richmond
McDANIEL, Matthew	4	Pike	McDONALD, M. G.	80	Camden
McDANIEL, Neill	1	Merriwether	McDONALD, Mary	10	Baldwin
McDANIEL, Noah	2	Jefferson	McDONALD, Middleton	4	Bibb
McDANIEL, Redick	14	Upson	McDONALD, Philip C.	4	DeKalb
McDANIEL, Sarah	4	Gwinnett	McDONALD, T. O.	7	DeKalb
McDANIEL, Samuel	9	Upson	McDONALD, Wm. A.	1	Putnam
McDANIEL, William	1	Newton	McDONNELL,		
McDANIEL, George	23	Talbot	George W.	11	McIntosh
McDANIEL, James	5	Bullock	McDONNELL, Jane	21	McIntosh
McDANIEL, James	2	Sumter	McDONNELL, Edgar	5	Chatham
McDANIEL, James M.	16	Talbot	McDONOUGH, J.	4	Pike
McDANIEL, John	27	Talbot	McDOUGALD,		
McDANIEL, Lovick	25	Talbot	Alexander	13	Muscogee
McDANIEL, M. R.	10	Butts	McDOUGALD,		
McDANIEL, Margaret	5	Butts	Mrs. E. A.	18	Muscogee
McDANIEL, Margaret	2	Butts	McDOUGLAS, Duncan	68	Muscogee
McDANIEL, R.	1	Decatur	McDOW, Jonathan	10	Cass
McDANIEL, William	1	Columbia	McDOW, Saml.	11	Cass
McDERMENT, Owen	1	Jefferson	McDOWAL, George	1	Macon
McDERMONT, John	3	Wilkes	McDOWAL, William	1	Macon
McDILL, Newton	3	Forsyth	McDOWAL, John	107	Stewart
McDILLDA, Elias	1	Tatnall	McDOWEL, Charles	7	Pike
McDONALD, Alexander	19	Early	McDOWEL, Patrick H.	8	Pike

Name	Number	County	Name	Number	County
McDOWELL, Daniel	40	Jasper	McEVER, Andrew	3	Madison
McDOWELL, James	2	Marion	McEVER, Synthia	4	Madison
McDOWELL, Joel C.	10	Jasper	McEWEN, W. P.	6	Washington
McDOWELL, John M.	8	Jasper	McFAIL, D. C.	2	Pulaski
McDOWELL, Joseph	3	Murray	McFAIL, Eli	28	Liberty
McDOWELL, William T.	7	Jasper	McFARLAND, C. D.	11	Walker
McDOWELL, James	13	Talbot	McFARLAND, J. B.	15	Harris
McDUFFEE, Mrs.	14	Irwin	McFARLAND, James M.	20	Troup
McDUFFIE, Daniel	5	Thomas	McFARLAND, John R.	3	Harris
McDUFFIE, George	3	Marion	McFARLAND, Nancy M.	36	Troup
McDUFFIE, N.	21	Pulaski	McFARLAND, Saunders G.	5	Walker
McDUFFIE, Archy	1	Telfair	McFARLAND, Thomas G.	12	Walker
McDUFFIE, Samuel	1	Telfair	McFARLAND, Washington	23	Lowndes
McDURMON?, L. D.	2	Muscogee	McFARLAND, Mack	1	Talbot
McEACHERN, B.	1	Troup	McfARLAND, Mary	1	Richmond
McEACHOM, David N.	3	Cobb	McFARLANE, John	19	Chatham
McELHANEY, Mrs. A.	11	Harris	McFARLANE, William	1	Chatham
McELHANNON, Fr.	4	Jackson	McFARLIN, Charles	19	Muscogee
McELHANNON, Hez.	2	Jackson	McFARLIN, John	10	Franklin
McELHANNON, Hugh	13	Jackson	McFARLIN, Thomas J.	3	Upson
McELHANNON, Steward	2	Jackson	McFARLIN, William M.	20	Muscogee
McELHANY, John	11	Jasper	McGANGHEY, ?	3	Walton
McELHANY, Mary	4	Wilkes	McGANGHEY, James	8	Walton
McELMORE, (?)	11	Decatur	McGANGHEY, James H.	3	Walton
McELMURRAY, John G.	11	Burke	McGANGHEY, Mary	4	Walton
McELMURRAY, Minus H.	11	Burke	McGANGHEY, Robert	4	Walton
McELMURRAY, Richard H.	6	Burke	McGANGHEY, Thomas	4	Walton
McELMURRY, J. R.	9	Bibb	McGAHEE, Isaac M.	4	Meriwether
McELRAY, R. B.	1	Harris	McGAHEE, Willis	1	Meriwether
McELROY, Need.	4	Clarke	McGAHEE, Willis	1	Meriwether
McELROY, Peter E.	1	Fayette	McGAR, Edward	7	Emanual
McELROY, Thos.	1	Harris	McGAR, Owen	1	Emanual
McELROY, A. M.	4	Decatur	McGARATY, Solomon	8	DeKalb
McELROY, Dawson	2	Butts	McGARER, James	10	Sumter
McELROY, H.	11	Decatur	McGARER, Thomas	7	Sumter
McELROY, James	10	Decatur	McGARITY, J.	3	Elbert
McELROY, Wm.	15	Wilkes	McGARRAH, Mary	2	Marion
McELVAIN, Daniel	1	Dooly	McGAUGH, Thos.	4	Butts
McELVAN, James	9	Bryan	McGAULEY, William	7	Appling
McELVEEN, John	1	Bullock	McGEE, G. W.	18	Troup
McELVY, Robert	13	Early	McGEE, James	3	Pike
McELVY, Wm.	4	Cass	McGEE, John F.	1	Pike
McELVY, Wm.	15	Early	McGEE, John W.	18	Troup
McELWIN, W. M.	13	Decatur	McGEE, William L.	8	Warren
McENTEE, James	23	Floyd	McGEE, D.	2	Crawford
McENTIRE, James L.	11	Murray	McGEHEE, Jacob	8	Upson
McENTIRE, Joseph A.	4	Murray	McGEHEE, (none)	1	Muscogee
McENTIRE, Nancy B.	11	Franklin	McGEHEE, C. T.	28	Houston
McENTIRE, William M.	11	Murray	McGEHEE, E. J.	29	Houston
McENTIRE, Wm.	1	Gordon			

Name	Number	County	Name	Number	County
McGEHEE, G. L.	12	Muscogee	McGOVERN, Fariel	3	Cass
McGEHEE, J. C.	13	Harris	McGOWEN, ?	1	Wilkinson
McGEHEE, J. C.	4	Harris	McGOWEN, Gideon	7	Liberty
McGEHEE, Dorcas	16	Troup	McGOWEN, Jenssey	4	Wilkinson
McGEHEE, James	25	Harris	McGOWEN, Jos. F.	14	Liberty
McGEHEE, James M.	8	Muscogee	McGOWEN, Joseph	10	Muscogee
McGEHEE, John	20	Morgan	McGOWEN, William	9	Wilkinson
McGEHEE, John	1	Muscogee	McGRADY, Silas	3	Muscogee
McGEHEE, Mark	1	Harris	McGRADY, Isaac N.	6	Stewart
McGEHEE, Robert M.	1	Jones	McGRADY, Robt.	8	Butts
McGEHEE, Sarah	9	Harris	McGRADY, William B.	1	Stewart
McGEHEE, T. F.	29	Merriwether	McGRAN, Philip Estate	7	Richmond
McGEHEE, William	54	Harris	McGRAW, H.	4	Bibb
McGEHEE, James Jun.	3	Harris	McGREGGOR, Daniel	2	Montgomery
McGENEY, Nathan C.	39	Baldwin	McGREGOR, John	3	Lee
McGENEY, James J.	1	DeKalb	McGREGOR, Rhuse	10	Paulding
McGHEE, Bartley	1	Lumpkin	McGREGOR, Samuel D.	6	Paulding
McGHEE, E.	1	Elbert	McGREGOR, A.	13	Bibb
McGHEE, Hugh M.	3	Floyd	McGRIFF, William	11	Early
McGHEE, James M.	2	Murray	McGRIFF, Edw.	1	DeKalb
McGHEE, Nathaniel	1	Murray	McGRIFF, Mrs.	13	Decatur
McGHEE, Doras	8	Screven	McGRIFF, Mrs. S.	30	Decatur
McGHEE, H. H.	22	Screven	McGRIPP, Jas.	20	Pulaski
McGHEE, Theopulus	1	Talbot	McGRIPP, Thos.	23	Pulaski
McGILL, A.	3	Muscogee	McGRUDER, Archibald	39	Muscogee
McGILLIS, Ellen	1	Bryan	McGRUDER, H.	16	Merriwether
McGILLIS, Henry	1	Liberty	McGRUDER, James A.	93	Burke
McGILLIS, Faith Ann	1	Bryan	McGRUDER, J. T.	6	Randoph
McGILVARY, John	13	Hancock	McGRUGAN, John	1	Early
McGINNES, Osbon	5	Forsyth	McGUIN, James	2	Muscogee
McGINNES, Sarah	4	Forsyth	McGUIRE, Abner	2	Upson
McGINNES, Jas. M.	1	Cass	McGUIRE, Absalom B.	1	Thomas
McGINNIS, Patrick	2	Lincoln	McGUIRE, Diannah H.	2	Cobb
McGINNIS, Stephen	8	Gwinnett	McGUIRE, Green	4	Lumpkin
McGINNIS, William B.	1	Paulding	McGUIRE, Nancy	24	Oglethorpe
McGINNIS, James	11	Cass	McGUIRE, Susan	25	Floyd
McGINTY, Enoch	1	Monroe	McGUIRE, Thomas	6	Cobb
McGINTY, Joet T.	3	DeKalb	McGUIRE, Thompson	1	Greene
McGINTY, John	4	Hancock	McGUIRE, A.	6	Butts
McGINTY, John A.	7	Warren	McGUIRE, Ann	1	Taliaferro
McGINTY, Rabun E.	18	Warren	McGUIRE?, Lewis	5	Baker
McGINTY, Richard	1	Warren	McGYLL, Sarah	6	Richmond
McGINTY, Robert	4	Monroe	McGYRE, Larkin	2	Warren
McGINTY, Thomas	20	Muscogee	McHANN, A.	4	Cherokee
McGINTY, William	13	Monroe	McHANN, Allison	1	Murray
McGINTY, George W.	2	Sumter	McHARGUE, Martha	6	Greene
McGIVINCHY?, H. J.	4	Habersham	McHARGUE, Wm. T.	16	Greene
McGLAMERY, Nancy	4	Warren	McHENRY, Sarah A.	14	Greene
McGLAWN, David	20	Marion	McHENRY, Peter	5	Putnam
McGLAWN, John	13	Muscogee	McINFEE, A. J.	12	Upson
McGOINES, William	10	Pike	McINNY, Travis	6	Monroe
McGOMERY?, Elizabeth	3	DeKalb	McINTERE, Daniel	1	Montgomery
McGOUGH, Robert	23	Monroe	McINTIRE, Thomas C.	5	Harris
McGOUGH, Wm. T.	2	Marion	McINTIRE, Emma	5	Chatham

Name	Number	County	Name	Number	County
McINTIRE, James	3	Chatham	McKEE, William	8	Richmond
McINTIRE ?, Mary	4	Wilkinson	McKENNE, John	37	Burke
McINTIRE, Robert	5	Chatham	McKENNE, John	13	Richmond
McINTOSH, J. J.	3	Morgan	McKENNEY, Patience	6	Monroe
McINTOSH, James M.	46	McIntosh	McKENZIE, Danl. J.	3	Chatham
McINTOSH, John A.	7	Thomas	McKENZIE, Hardy	4	Macon
McINTOSH, Lacklin	12	McIntosh	McKENZIE, Henry	7	Lee
McINTOSH, Mary	2	Montgomery	McKENZIE, James W.	6	Houston
McINTOSH, M. E.	2	Fayette	McKENZIE, Kenith	2	Muscogee
McINTOSH, Murdoch	14	Thomas	McKENZIE, Alexander	15	Burke
McINTOSH, Roderick	1	Thomas	McKENZIE, George M.	1	Stewart
McINTOSH, W. M.	18	Elbert	McKENZIE, Jas.	1	Coweta
McINTOSH, Alxr. D.	1	Glynn	McKEVANS?, Jesse	5	Houston
McINTOSH, Eliza	1	Chatham	McKEY, John	6	Merriwether
McINTOSH, William J.	34	Chatham	McKEY, Jonathan	56	Henry
McINTYRE, Archy	1	Telfair	McKEY, Lewis	16	Putnam
McINTYRE, Hugh	8	Telfair	McKEY, William G.	4	Talbot
McINTYRE, John	1	Telfair	McKIBIN, Thomas	27	Butts
McINTYRE, ?T.	33	Thomas	McKIE, Andrew W.	5	Franklin
McINVAIL, Robert	6	Houston	McKIE, John	2	Franklin
McINVAIL, Robt			McKIE, Mary	9	Franklin
agt for SHANNON, C.J	37	Houston	McKIE, Thomas	5	Franklin
McIVER, Monroe	23	Liberty	McKIGNEY, B.	1	Troup
McIVER, Wm.	2	DeKalb	McKIGNEY, James	12	Jefferson
McIVEY, A.	6	Coweta	McKINDREE, J. J.	5	Muscogee
McJENKINS, D. W.	25	Wilkes	McKINLEY, A. C.	13	Oglethorpe
McJUNKIN, John S.	5	Stewart	McKINLEY, F. C.	11	Greene
McKAMIE, Sarah	23	Troup	McKINLEY, John	1	Troup
McKAMIE, John	5	Troup	McKINLEY, William	55	Baldwin
McKAMIE, Robert P.	3	Troup	McKINLEY, Wm	7	Putnam
McKAMIE, William M.	10	Troup	McKINLY, ?	12	Upson
McKAY, Benjamin	2	Newton	McKINLY, E. D.	10	Coweta
McKAY, George W. F.	28	Jones	McKINLY, George	3	Upson
McKAY, Hugh D.	14	Jones	McKINLY, Robert	4	Upson
McKAY, John	45	Harris	McKINNE, Ann	17	Richmond
McKAY, John F.	7	Cobb	McKINNE, John	59	Burke
McKAY, Archy	13	Telfair	McKINNE, John Agent	2	Richmond
McKAY, Daniel	3	Tatnall	McKINNEL?, James	3	Muscogee
McKAY, Duglass	1	Sumter	McKINNEY, Benjamin	1	Houston
McKAY, George	2	Columbia	McKINNEY, Charles	2	Gwinnett
McKAY, H.K.	8	Sumter	McKINNEY, George	5	Pike
McKAY, J. R.	3	Sumter	McKINNEY, Geo.	25	Wilkes
McKAY, John	5	Dade	McKINNEY, Henry	25	Warren
McKEE, A. D.	1	Chattooga	McKINNEY, James	4	Cherokee
McKEE, Archil.	1	Harris	McKINNEY, John	3	Gwinnett
McKEE, Arthur A.	4	Troup	McKINNEY, John	1	Houston
McKEE, Benj.	21	Clarke	McKINNEY, John	8	Monroe
McKEE, David A.	1	Harris	McKINNEY, Kinchen	20	Marion
McKEE, H. C.	8	Muscogee	McKINNEY, Mary	5	Macon
McKEE, John	13	Clarke	McKINNEY, Mary A.	1	Wilkes
McKEE, Rebecca	5	Clarke	McKINNEY, Preston	8	Gilmer
McKEE, Rowan	6	Clarke	McKINNEY, Samuel	10	Gwinnett
McKEE, T. M.	4	Harris	McKINNEY, David	10	Rabun
McKEE, Thos.	5	Harris	McKINNEY, H.	3	Bibb

207

Name	Number	County	Name	Number	County
McKINNEY, Henry	11	Talbot	McLARRIN, Peter	6	Muscogee
McKINNEY, Valentine	1	Sumter	McLARTY, Alexander	2	Campbell
McKINNEY, William	1	Rabun	McLARTY, George W.	3	Campbell
McKINNON ?, John	1	Richmond	McLARTY, John	2	Campbell
McKINNON, A.	2	Irwin	McLARTY, S. H.	9	Campbell
McKINNON, Alexander	6	Telfair	McLARTY, Samuel W.	11	Campbell
McKINNON, Ann	6	Thomas	McLAUCHLIN,		
McKINNON, Cornelius	1	Telfair	Daniel M.	5	Telfair
McKINNON, Daniel	7	Thomas	McLAUGHLIN, ? M.	4	Richmond
McKINNON, Duncan	10	Thomas	McLAUGHLIN, George	6	Oglethorpe
McKINNON, John	5	Thomas	McLAUGHLIN, J. T.	10	Meriwether
McKINNON, John C.	4	Stewart	McLAUGHLIN, A. R.	8	Bibb
McKINNON, Kenneth	3	Thomas	McLAUGHTON, James	2	Jasper
McKINNON, Malcom	8	Thomas	McLAUGHTON, C.	4	Decatur
McKINNON, Margaret	4	Telfair	McLAWS, Abram H.	8	Richmond
McKINNON, Margaret	1	Telfair	McLAWS, James	10	Richmond
McKINNON, Margaret	13	Thomas	McLAWS, James	1	Richmond
McKINNON, Mary	7	Thomas	McLAWS, Louisa A.	2	Richmond
McKINNON, Murdock	4	Thomas	McLAWS, William R.	3	Richmond
McKINNON, Neel	22	Thomas	McLEAN, Archy	4	Telfair
McKINNON, William	1	Telfair	McLEAN, Ewin	17	Thomas
McKINNY, John	41	Jefferson	McLEAN, John	10	Telfair
McKINNY, Joshua	8	Upson	McLEAN, W. B.	7	Cass
McKINNY, William	12	Upson	McLEAN, W. B.	1	Cass
McKINSEY, Jas.	3	Putnam	McLEAN?, Hugh	2	Cass
McKINSEY, Joseph H.	7	Dooly	McLEARY, Robert	24	Baker
McKINVY, Chas. G.	6	Coweta	McLEARY, Robert	22	Baker
McKINZEE, Milton S.	3	Macon	McLEARY, Samuel	21	Baker
McKINZEY, John	12	Macon	McLELAN, Clarissa	13	Hancock
McKINZEY, Andrew C.	3	Sumter	McLEMORE, Chesley B.	7	Emanual
McKINZIE, Duncan	18	Columbia	McLEMORE, Ira T.	2	Emanual
McKINZIE, Mary	2	Richmond	McLEMORE, Sarah	1	Emanual
McKIPACKE?, Arch.	4	Carroll	McLENDEN, Francis	36	Wilkes
McKISACK, John W.	3	Coweta	McLENDON, Burrell	1	Lee
McKISSACK, John	9	Jasper	McLENDON, Elizabeth	8	Thomas
McKISSACK, Duncan	2	Jasper	McLENDON, Freeman	1	Pike
McKISSACK, John			McLENDON, Henry	6	Laurens
agt for McKISSICK	2	Jasper	McLENDON, Henry	4	Thomas
McKISSACK, Rebecca L.	7	Troup	McLENDON, Isaac A.	5	Wilkes
McKISSICK, Thomas	15	Jones	McLENDON, Jacob	12	Pike
McKLEROY, Wm.	4	Randolph	McLENDON, Jesse	4	Troup
McKNIGHT, J. L.	12	Chattooga	McLENDON, John	7	Laurens
McKNIGHT, James F.	10	Talbot	McLENDON, John	14	Lee
McKOWN, James M.	2	Fayette	McLENDON, John	2	Lee
McKOWN, Hugh	3	Fayette	McLENDON, Josiah	1	Lee
McKUTCHEON,			McLENDON, L.	1	Early
Saml. K.	1	Cherokee	McLENDON, M.	4	Lee
McLANE, Elizabeth C.	19	Jones	McLENDON, Need?	15	Laurens
McLANE, John	5	Fayette	McLENDON, Rebecca	4	Monroe
McLANE, Mary	8	Murray	McLENDON, Robert P.	3	Pike
McLANE, Wm.	5	Lincoln	McLENDON, William	5	Lee
McLANE, John	7	Burke	McLENDON,		
McLARIN, Harrison	22	Campbell	William M.	3	Houston
McLARIN, William	5	Campbell	McLENDON, Wm.	27	Laurens

Name	Number	County	Name	Number	County
McLENDON, Wm.	11	Lee	McMAKER, Peter	2	Richmond
McLENDON, Wylly	16	Laurens	McMALSON, Mrs. M.	2	Bibb
McLENDON, Amos	5	Randolph	McMAN, Turquil	14	Pulaski
McLENDON, Edmund L.	1	Dooly	McMANUS, Jackson	1	Talbot
McLENDON, J.	7	Crawford	McMANUS, Leroy	7	Bibb
McLENDON, J. J.	6	Coweta	McMANUS, Thos.	6	Putnam
MCLENDON, Lucinda	9	Stewart	McMATH, Lena	1	Warren
McLENDON, Mary	8	Talbot	McMATH, Philip	6	Thomas
McLENDON, O. H. P.	17	Butts	McMATH, William	3	Sumter
McLENDON, Olive	4	Coweta	McMATH?, John	1	Cobb
McLENDON, S.D.	3	Randolph	McMEKIN, A. C.	18	Wilkes
McLENDON, Simpson	4	Randolph	McMEKIN, N. L.	20	Wilkes
McLENDON, W.	2	Talbot	McMEKIN, Thomas	8	Paulding
McLENNAN, Alex.	1	Telfair	McMICCLE, Peter	8	Monroe
McLEOD, Alexander	1	Pike	McMICEL, William	16	Monroe
McLEOD, Alexr. T.	5	Montgomery	McMICHAEL, Burton J.	10	Jasper
McLEOD, Archd.	1	Lowndes	McMICHAEL, Green L.	3	Jasper
McLEOD, Daniel	4	Muscogee	McMICHAEL, Griffin C.	6	Murray
McLEOD, Duncan	8	Emanual	McMICHAEL, J. G.	7	Butts
McLEOD, George T.	4	Montgomery	McMICHAEL, John	19	Fayette
McLEOD, J. F.	10	Pulaski	McMICHAEL, John	11	Marion
McLEOD, J.W.	6	Lee	McMICHAEL, John L.	20	Jasper
McLEOD, John	2	Montgomery	McMICHAEL, Levi	17	Butts
McLEOD, Lodowick J.	2	Walker	McMICHAEL, Pollard B.	15	Jasper
McLEOD, Murdoch M.	2	Lowndes	McMICHAEL, Seaborn	33	Marion
McLEOD, Nancy	3	Montgomery	McMICHAEL, Shadrick	35	Jasper
McLEOD, Nancy C.	3	Montgomery	McMICHAEL, Silas	1	Muscogee
McLEOD, Niell	1	Emanual	McMICHAEL, J. B.	11	Butts
McLEOD, Norman	20	Thomas	McMICHAEL, J. G.	2	Butts
McLEOD, William L.	1	Montgomery	McMICHAEL, John	15	Butts
McLEOD, F. H.	211	Chatham	McMICHAEL, Joseph	7	Randolph
McLEROY, Andrew	1	Monroe	McMICHAEL, Leroy	7	Butts
McLEROY, Edward J.	9	Pike	McMICHAEL, Ruben	8	Stewart
McLEROY, Edward M.	30	Pike	McMICHAEL, T. J.	3	Butts
McLEROY, Isaac	14	Pike	McMICHAEL, W. G.	7	Butts
McLEROY, Tabitha	4	Madison	McMICKLE, John M.	3	Cass
McLEROY, W. J.	1	Walton	McMIKIN, John	4	Cherokee
McLESKEY, James W.	3	Jackson	McMILLAN, Angus	1	Montgomery
McLESTER, Jas. G	3	Jackson	McMILLAN, Archibald	4	Montgomery
McLESTER, Joseph	24	Jackson	McMILLAN, Archibald	55	Thomas
McLIN, George A.	4	Walker	McMILLAN, Daniel	4	Montgomery
McLISTER, N.	13	Muscogee	McMILLAN, Daniel	2	Troup
McLOUD, Daniel	6	Jones	McMILLAN, J.	1	Irwin
McLOUD, Norman	11	Jones	McMILLAN, M.	1	Irwin
McLOUD, Norman E.	23	Lee	McMILLAN, Mary	3	Montgomery
McLOUD, D.	3	Randolph	McMILLAN, R.	8	Elbert
McLOWER, John	3	Campbell	McMILLAN, I.	1	Early
McLURE, James	5	Lumpkin	McMILLEN, A.	1	Twiggs
McLURE, John	4	Lumpkin	McMILLEN, Adolphus	1	Laurens
McLURE, Elizabeth	4	Campbell	McMILLEN, Lavina	8	Thomas
McLURE, J. B.	1	Coweta	McMILLEN, William	3	Thomas
McLURE, James	14	Coweta	McMILLON, A.	1	Irwin
McLURE, William L.	4	Campbell	McMINN, Richard	1	Bibb
McMAHAN, Woodred	3	Walton	McMULLAN, J.	6	Elbert

Name	Number	County
McMULLAN, John	27	Lowndes
McMULLAN, Lorenzo D.	6	Macon
McMULLAN, Mark J.	5	Macon
McMULLAN, P.	7	Elbert
McMULLEN, ?	5	Macon
McMULLEN, James Jun.	24	Lowndes
McMULLEN, Nail	16	Monroe
McMULLEN, Randolph	1	Macon
McMULLEN, Sinclair	18	Cass
McMULLEN, William F.	5	Thomas
McMULLIN, G. W.	8	Henry
McMULLIN, John	1	Murray
McMULLIN, Anor	2	Carroll
McMULLON, J. F.	3	Elbert
McMULLON, S.	12	Elbert
McMULLON, W.	8	Elbert
McMURRAIN, John	14	Muscogee
McMURRAIN, John W.	3	Muscogee
McMURRAY, James	9	Muscogee
McMURRAY, James B.	4	Houston
McMURRAY, Frances	4	Talbot
McMURRIN, Thomas	1	Sumter
McMURRY, John	9	Morgan
McNAIR, Daniel	1	Marion
McNAIR, John	2	Newton
McNAIR, John A.	5	Lowndes
McNAIR, L. L.	12	Jefferson
McNAIR, Saml.	1	Marion
McNAIR, Wm. G.	6	Lowndes
McNAIR, Daniel	3	Richmond
McNAIR, G.	6	Decatur
McNAIR, James	4	Richmond
McNAIR, R. M.	2	Decatur
McNAIR, Robert	7	Warren
McNAIR, William	29	Wilkinson
McNATT, Adam	62	Burke
McNAUGHTON, Wm.	1	Clarke
McNEAL, John	7	Hall
McNEAL, Michael	1	Hall
McNEAL, Willliam	1	Hall
McNEAL, Elizabeth	5	Talbot
McNEAL, James	4	DeKalb
McNEAL, Mary	1	Talbot
McNEAL, William W.	2	Talbot
McNEALY, J. E.A.	2	Henry
McNEALY, James	4	Pike
McNEASE, Vincin	3	Dooly
McNEASE, William T.	4	Dooly
McNEEL, A. J.	3	Henry
McNEER, James	10	Floyd
McNEIL, John T.	37	Morgan
McNEIL, R.	9	Muscogee
McNEIL, Francis	2	Chatham
McNEIL, William	5	Talbot
McNELTY, P.	3	Chatham
McNEVER, Martin	7	Richmond
McNICE, Emanual	5	Houston
McNIEL, J. B.	4	Randolph
McNIGHT, B. N.	15	Henry
McNIGHT, M.	5	Henry
McNISH, John	2	Chatham
McNORRELL, James	12	Burke
McNORRELL, Lafayette	5	Burke
McNORRILL, Mackey	25	Burke
McNORTON, J. G.	5	Butts
McNUTT, Robt.	13	Putnam
McOWEN, P. C.	7	Murray
McPHERSON, George	1	Walker
McPHERSON, Jno. M.	1	Talbot
McPHERSON, Mahala	3	Sumter
McPHERSON, Riley	2	Talbot
McPOLLACK, Jonah	24	Screven
McQUEEN, Rachel	2	Screven
McRAE, Christopher	11	Montgomery
McRAE, Cornelius W.	4	Lowndes
McRAE, Daniel F.	1	Appling
McRAE, Danl. W.	7	Lowndes
McRAE, Farquhard	8	Montgomery
McRAE, Isabel	7	Montgomery
McRAE, John	12	Montgomery
McRAE, John.	4	Montgomery
McRAE, Phillip	4	Lowndes
McRAE, William	3	Montgomery
McRAE, Duncan M.	15	Telfair
McRAE, Duncan M. Jr.	15	Telfair
McRAE, Effy	7	Telfair
McRAE, John F.	2	Telfair
McRAE, Malcom N.	7	Telfair
McREA, E. L.	23	Sumter
McREA, Gus	22	Twiggs
McREA, William L.	22	Sumter
McREYNOLDS, Martha A.	5	Cass
McSWAIN, Peter	1	Merriwether
McSWAN ?, David	3	Rabun
McTIER, John	7	Columbia
McTYRE, Kendall	10	Warren
McTYRE, Reddick	2	Warren
McVAIR, E.	2	Henry
McWADE, Stewart	3	Burke
McWATTY, Thomas	11	Jefferson
McWHISTER?, D. W.	1	Hall
McWHORTER, Eli	2	Hancock
McWHORTER, Frederick	5	Greene
McWHORTER, James H.	26	Oglethorpe
McWHORTER, John	4	Hancock

Name	Number	County	Name	Number	County
McWHORTER, John	4	Walker	MEADOWS, Harison	13	Taliaferro
McWHORTER, M. E.	10	Clarke	MEADOWS, J. C.	1	Coweta
McWHORTER, Saml.	3	Chattooga	MEADOWS, J. M.	3	Coweta
McWHORTER, William M.	61	Oglethorpe	MEADOWS, Pearson S.	1	Dade
			MEADOWS, Wm.	11	Taliaferro
McWHORTER, William P.	3	Greene	MEALER, James	2	Muscogee
McWHORTER, M. A.	4	Carroll	MEAN ?, Lucius S.	3	Richmond
McWHORTER, Robert	18	Taliaferro	MEANS, Alexander	20	Newton
McWILLIAMS, A. J.	5	Meriwether	MEANS, Jacob	3	Franklin
McWILLIAMS, Andrew	5	Merriwether	MEANS, James	6	Upson
McWILLIAMS, Eliza	3	Chatham	MEANS, James	2	Upson
McWILLIAMS, George W.	6	Walker	MEANS, John	4	Pike
			MEANS, John S.	30	Walton
McWILLIAMS, John	3	DeKalb	MEANS, Mathew H.	7	Houston
McWILLIAMS, John	1	Walker	MEARCER, Griffin	2	Emanual
McWILLIAMS, John G.	1	DeKalb	MEARRETT, N.	7	Elbert
McWILLIAMS, Margarett	6	Randolph	MEARS, H. D.	8	Screven
			MEARS, J. W.	7	Screven
McWILLIAMS, Mitilda	2	Walker	MEBLEY, C. W.	8	Screven
			MECHAM, Elijah	18	Merriwether
McWILLIAMS, Thomas N.	25	Randolph	MECHAM, James M.	1	Heard
McWILLIAMS, William	2	Walker	MECHAM, Thomas	6	Merriwether
McWRIGHT, J. B.	3	Henry	MECHAM, Willis	1	Merriwether
MdDANIEL, Wm.	6	Dooly	MECKELBERRY, W. H. C.	4	Butts
MEACHAM, R. B.	5	Heard	MEDDLETON, James	7	Appling
MEACHUM, James	54	Muscogee	MEDDLETON, Stephen	1	Appling
MEAD, J. H.	5	DeKalb	MEDDOWS, John J.	6	Walker
MEADERS, Benj. J.	9	Madison	MEDISON, Francis S.	3	Richmond
MEADERS, David	2	Madison	MEDLING, Green	1	Baldwin
MEADOR, Simeon	5	Heard	MEDLOCK, B. F.	18	Hancock
MEADOR, J. T.	2	Carroll	MEDLOCK, James J.	1	Gwinnett
MEADOR, Vashti	9	DeKalb	MEDLOCK, John W.	5	Gwinnett
MEADORS, Noah W.	5	Oglethorpe	MEDLOCK, M. S.	20	Hancock
MEADOUS, Morris?	1	Macon	MEDLOCK, John W.	6	DeKalb
MEADOUS, Richard	8	Houston	MEDLOCK, Thos. L.	3	DeKalb
MEADOUS, William A. agt KENDRICK	45	Houston	MEDWAY, Joseph	2	Muscogee
			MEEK, Charles	4	Appling
MEADOW, Margaret	4	Walker	MEEK, Homery	1	Appling
MEADOWS, Barney	8	Franklin	MEEKER, Wm. T.	2	Habersham
MEADOWS, Bartholemew	2	Harris	MEEKS, (?)	8	Decatur
			MEEKS, E.	2	Floyd
MEADOWS, Daniel	2	Hall	MEEKS, B.	6	Decatur
MEADOWS, G.	5	Wilkinson	MEEKS, H.	2	Cass
MEADOWS, Green w.	7	Wilkinson	MEEKS, Allen	2	Wilkinson
MEADOWS, James W.	3	Oglethorpe	MEER, A. D.	1	Coweta
MEADOWS, Jeremiah	1	Franklin	MEERER, H. W.	9	Chatham
MEADOWS, Milus R.	7	Upson	MEGAHEE, Michael	4	Jefferson
MEADOWS, Vincent	1	Troup	MEGEN ?, John A.	2	Richmond
MEADOWS, William	1	Franklin	MEGGS, Henry V.	11	Muscogee
MEADOWS, D.	9	Coweta	MEIGGS, Daniel Estate	14	Richmond
MEADOWS, Edward	14	Taliaferro	MEIGGS, Eliza L.	9	Richmond
MEADOWS, Elijah	1	Taliaferro	MEIGGS, Jonathan	9	Richmond
			MELDRIM, James	1	Chatham

Name	Number	County	Name	Number	County
MELDRIUM, Ralph	1	Chatham	MERCER, George F.	2	Taliaferro
MELFORD, James	5	Forsyth	MERCER, L.	25	Randolph
MELING, John H.	8	Muscogee	MERCER, M.	1	Randolph
MELING, William E.	14	Muscogee	MERCER, Malakiah	14	Bullock
MELL, James B.	16	Liberty	MERCER, R.	1	Randolph
MELL, Miss Mary	4	Liberty	MERCER, Riley	5	Bullock
MELL, P. H.	4	Greene	MERCER, S.	7	Troup
MELL, William	20	Newton	MERCER, William A.	4	Walton
MELL, Allethea J.	7	Chatham	MERCHISON, K.	2	Carroll
MELL, Charles C.	2	Chatham	MERCIER, Thomas D.	16	Troup
MELL, William	4	Chatham	MERCUR, George W.	28	Early
MELLER, Obadiah	1	Cass	MERCY, Jas.	7	Coweta
MELLON, William E.	5	Troup	MERDOC, B.	7	Chattooga
MELLOWIN, Martin R.	2	Jones	MERELL?, Allen	32	Bullock
MELSON, William A.	3	Monroe	MEREDITH, Cyrus B.	5	Walker
MELTON, Benjamin	5	Thomas	MEREDITH, Noah	1	Walker
MELTON, David T.	2	Troup	MEREDITH, S.	4	Wilkinson
MELTON, Elbert	13	Marion	MEREDITH, Wiott	32	Wilkinson
MELTON, F.	16	Newton	MERIDITH, Joseph	7	Murray
MELTON, Hardy	19	Morgan	MERIDITH, James W.	1	Richmond
MELTON, Josiah T.	2	Troup	MERIMON, Haley	11	Laurens
MELTON, Matthew	13	Marion	MERIMON, Wm. B.	9	Laurens
MELTON, Nathaniel	14	Thomas	MERIT, Elizabeth	2	Pike
MELTON, Thomas	2	Newton	METIT, John Agent	9	Upson
MELTON, W. S.	2	Meriwether	MERIT, Miccleberry	46	Monroe
MELTON, David R.	6	Burke	MERIWEATHER,		
MELTON, E. A.	3	Carroll	Alexnder	1	Dooly
MELTON, Hez.	1	Randolph	MERIWEATHER, Jas.	23	Coweta
MELTON, James M.	1	Burke	MERIWEATHER, P. L.	5	Coweta
MELTON, Jno.	1	Randolph	MERIWETHER, Charles	70	Oglethorpe
MELTON, Moses	2	Newton	MERIWETHER, Thomas	29	Newton
MELTON, William	6	Stewart	MERIWETHER, V. H.	70	Oglethorpe
MELVIN, John	11	Wilkinson	MERIWETHER, C. S.	10	Clarke
MEMAHAM ?, John	12	Taliaferro	MERIWETHER, Jas. A.	12	Putnam
MENDELL, E.	1	Chatham	MERIWITHERS, Frances	72	Oglethorpe
MENDHAM, Benj.	3	Muscogee	MERK, George	1	Jackson
MENEFEW, Richard	9	Talbot	MERKE, John	2	Hall
MENIFEE, W. P.	39	Campbell	MERKE, John	1	Hall
MENTER, John	1	Jasper	MERNSON?, Daniel	17	Madison
MEPPIN, J. A. P.	19	Randolph	MERONEY, Rufus M.	2	Madison
MERATE, F.	8	Irwin	MERRELL, Henry	10	Greene
MERAWETHER, David	6	Jasper	MERRETT, Isham	6	Franklin
MERAWETHER,			MERRETT, Joseph	6	Franklin
George F.	75	Jasper	MERRETT, Wiley	3	Franklin
MERCEIR, H. H.	25	Lincoln	MERRIL, Benjm.	1	Carroll
MERCER, Ann	1	Lee	MERRILL, Joseph	2	Carroll
MERCER, Garner	3	Twiggs	MERRILL, Patrick	1	Carroll
MERCER, J.	1	Lee	MERRILL, J. S.	12	Chattooga
MERCER, Jno. W.	5	Henry	MERRILL, Robt.	1	Carroll
MERCER, John	14	Lee	MERRIT, Hiram	5	Merriwether
MERCER, Leonedus B.	38	Lee	MERRIT, S.	7	Meriwether
MERCER, Levi	8	Newton	MERRIT, George	13	Burke
MERCER, Addison	1	Sumter	MERRITT, Benjamin	7	Greene
MERCER, Elizabeth	8	Sumter	MERRITT, E. W.	14	Hall

Name	Number	County	Name	Number	County
MERRITT, H. C.	26	Henry	MICHELL, Thomas	13	Taliaferro
MERRITT, J. A.	1	Forsyth	MICHOLSON, Nathaniel	30	Stewart
MERRITT, James	5	Greene	MICKEJOHN, George	1	Bibb
MERRITT, John C.	7	Greene	MICKLEJOHN, Robert	1	Baldwin
MERRITT, John T.	1	Jones	MIDDLEBANKS, E. C.	1	Harris
MERRITT, Lovett	22	Greene	MIDDLEBROOK,		
MERRITT, Thomas	32	Greene	Alford	15	Monroe
MERRITT, William B.	8	Monroe	MIDDLEBROOK,		
MERRITT, Frederick	5	Burke	James	23	Upson
MERRITT, John W.	5	Chatham	MIDDLEBROOKS,		
MERRITT, Wm .	4	Bibb	A. B.	7	Henry
MERRITTE, Sarah	1	Baker	MIDDLEBROOKS,		
MERRIWEATHER,			Anderson J.	9	Jones
William	43	Columbia	MIDDLEBROOKS,		
MERRON, Thos.	1	Camden	Andr.	33	Clarke
MERRY, Mrs. C.	1	Wilkes	MIDDLEBROOKS,		
MERSHON, John B.	1	Talbot	David	7	Henry
MESSER, John R.	32	Jones	MIDDLEBROOKS, E.	1	Newton
MESSER, Joseph	30	Jones	MIDDLEBROOKS,		
MESSER, J. C.	1	Butts	Edward	2	Harris
MESSER, John	10	Columbia	MIDDLEBROOKS,		
MESSEX, Elly	1	Burke	Elisha	2	Jones
MERTZ, Charles	2	Thomas	MIDDLEBROOKS, Isaac	18	Harris
METCALF, Thomas S.	13	Richmond	MIDDLEBROOKS, Isaac	17	Newton
METCALF, Thomas S.	3	Richmond	MIDDLEBROOKS,		
METHVIN, Sam	16	Twiggs	Isaac R.	16	Jones
METHVIN, William	20	Twiggs	MIDDLEBROOKS, J. H.	29	Hancock
METTROZIER, Jno.	10	Wilkes	MIDDLEBROOKS, J. H.	4	Hancock
METS, Joseph	12	Henry	MIDDLEBROOKS,		
METSGER, ?	2	Effingham	Jas. W.	3	Henry
METTS, Nathan	9	Laurens	MIDDLEBROOKS, John	5	Newton
METZGER, Mary	9	Effingham	MIDDLEBROOKS,		
METZGER, John	14	Effingham	John A.	3	Harris
METZGER, John	6	Effingham	MIDDLEBROOKS,		
METZGER, Moses	26	Effingham	John S.	8	Jones
MEUBORN, T. M.	1 ·	Elbert	MIDDLEBROOKS, M.	9	Troup
MEWBOURN, A.	1	Elbert	MIDDLEBROOKS,		
MEYER ? , Henry	5	Richmond	Marundae	2	Newton
MEYER, M. W.	1	Chatham	MIDDLEBROOKS,		
MICHAEL, Amy	4	Walton	Mary	2	Monroe
MICHAEL, Breton	4	Walton	MIDDLEBROOKS,		
MICHAL, John	8	Oglethorpe	Nancy	11	Jones
MICHAL, William	4	Oglethorpe	MIDDLEBROOKS,		
MICHEL, David	2	Walton	Rachael	8	Troup
MICHEL, William ?	5	Walton	MIDDLEBROOKS,		
MICHELL, Elizabeth	24	Harris	T. A.	15	Harris
MICHELL, L. S.	3	Harris	MIDDLEBROOKS,		
MICHELL, Robert	3	Jasper	Thomas J.	9	Jones
MICHELL, William	2	Franklin	MIDDLEBROOKS,		
MICHELL, George	2	Taliaferro	Williamson P.	12	Jones
MICHELL, Jacob W. H.	5	Taliaferro	MIDDLEBROOKS, Zary	29	Newton
MICHELL, John G.	1	Taliaferro	MIDDLEBROOKS, Jas.	4	Putnam
MICHELL, John G.	1	Taliaferro	MIDDLETON, Augustus	1	Chatham
MICHELL, Joseph	3	Taliaferro	MIDDLETON, David	8	Monroe

Name	Number	County
MIDDLETON, John M.	7	Bryan
MIDDLETON, Robert	1	McIntosh
MIDDLETON, William	9	McIntosh
MIDDLETON, Geo. M.	3	Bryan
MIDDLETON, J. M.	93	Chatham
MIDDLETON, J. P.	47	Bryan
MIDDLETON, Nancy	5	Putnam
MIDDLETON, P. T.	7	Bryan
MIDDLETON, S.	6	Stewart
MIDDLETON, William	2	Dade
MIDDLETON, William	2	Dade
MIDLEMS, Frances	4	Richmond
MIERE, M. L. M.D.	3	Oglethorpe
MIFFLIN, L. F.	1	DeKalb
MIFFLIN, Mary	3	Richmond
MILAN, William	1	Fayette
MILER, S. A.	13	Jefferson
MILES, Asa	4	Henry
MILES, George	7	Henry
MILES, James M. overseer	3	Habersham
MILES, Jesse	1	Dooly
MILES, Milton	1	Campbell
MILES, William	5	Harris
MILES, Wm.	1	Carroll
MILES, Wm.	15	Fayette
MILES, M.	1	Bibb
MILES, Mary	3	Columbia
MILET?, Dudley	3	Harris
MILEY, Daniel R.	5	Lowndes
MILLEN, Archy M.	1	Telfair
MILLEN, Cornelia M.	20	Chatham
MILLEN, Martin L.	1	Ware
MILLEN, Mcpherson B.	1	Burke
MILLENER, Johnathan G.	16	Oglethorpe
MILLENOR, A.	2	Randolph
MILLER, A. G.	1	Henry
MILLER, A. L.	18	Wilkinson
MILLER, Alvin N.	16	Chatham
MILLER, Andrew J.	22	Jones
MILLER, Ann	1	Newton
MILLER, Archibald	7	Harris
MILLER, Asa R.	3	Franklin
MILLER, Ashburn	1	Jones
MILLER, Benjamin	11	Harris
MILLER, Brazil	3	Pulaski
MILLER, Burel	1	Hall
MILLER, Burwell S.	3	Jones
MILLER, Charles	3	Emanual
MILLER, Charles	5	Jefferson
MILLER, Charles	3	Muscogee
MILLER, Charles F.	6	Glynn
MILLER, D.	2	Gordon

Name	Number	County
MILLER, Daniel W.	3	Macon
MILLER, David	6	Gordon
MILLER, David A.	26	Liberty
MILLER, Dennis	10	Harris
MILLER, Dr. B. B.	118	Burke
MILLER, E.	2	Wilkinson
MILLER, Edward	1	Gordon
MILLER, Eliz.	12	Henry
MILLER, Emson	13	Marion
MILLER, Fanny	9	Jefferson
MILLER, Frederick	3	Muscogee
MILLER, Gadi S.	1	Chatham
MILLER, George	3	Oglethorpe
MILLER, George	2	Stewart
MILLER, Goodwin	3	Walton
MILLER, H. V.	8	Henry
MILLER, H. V. M.	3	Floyd
MILLER, Henry	1	Thomas
MILLER, Hugh H.	1	Cobb
MILLER, Inda	10	Jackson
MILLER, Ira M.	1	Warren
MILLER, J.	4	Henry
MILLER, J. Q.	4	Thomas
MILLER, Jacob	2	Chatham
MILLER, Jacob	7	Meriwether
MILLER, James	3	Laurens
MILLER, James	3	Thomas
MILLER, James R.	12	Emanual
MILLER, Jane	2	Jefferson
MILLER, Jeremiah H.	43	Jones
MILLER, Jerome	1	Jackson
MILLER, Jesse	4	Murray
MILLER, Jesse N.	6	Murray
MILLER, John	9	Harris
MILLER, John	1	Heard
MILLER, John	1	Lumpkin
MILLER, John	30	Montgomery
MILLER, John	1	Murray
MILLER, John A.	6	Greene
MILLER, John B.	1	Muscogee
MILLER, John M.	1	Henry
MILLER, Jona.	7	Hancock
MILLER, Jonathan	1	Hancock
MILLER, Jonathn. D.	2	Hancock
MILLER, Joseph	13	Harris
MILLER, Joseph	39	Heard
MILLER, Joseph	1	Montgomery
MILLER, Joseph	8	Thomas
MILLER, Joshua C.	1	Pike
MILLER, Margt.	7	Camden
MILLER, Mark	5	Gwinnett
MILLER, Morris	2	Chatham
MILLER, N.	9	Henry
MILLER, Nathan	4	Randolph

Name	Number	County	Name	Number	County
MILLER, P. A.	22	Cobb	MILLER, Thomas	13	Stewart
MILLER, P. S.	1	Effingham	MILLER, Thomas G.	6	Chatham
MILLER, Rachel	3	Early	MILLER, Thomas W.	5	Richmond
MILLER, Rebecca	1	Effingham	MILLER, Thos.	85	Camden
MILLER, Richard	1	Hall	MILLER, Thos.	10	Crawford
MILLER, Sarah	15	Wilkinson	MILLER, Tom	36	Columbia
MILLER, Solomon	10	Warren	MILLER, Wiley	28	Randolph
MILLER, T. C.	13	Troup	MILLER, William	14	Decatur
MILLER, T. M.	2	Walker	MILLER, William	2	Sumter
MILLER, T. W.	2	Floyd	MILLER, William	3	Tatnall
MILLER, Thom. V.	15	Muscogee	MILLER, William H.	60	Chatham
MILLER, Thomas H.	25	Cobb	MILLER, Wm. R.	22	Crawford
MILLER, Uriah	2	Madison	MILLICAN, A.	2	Chattooga
MILLER, W. G.	3	Henry	MILLICAN, James	6	Jackson
MILLER, William P.	2	Jackson	MILLICAN, John	7	Jackson
MILLER, Willis	12	Troup	MILLICAN, R. J.	1	Jackson
MILLER, Wm.	3	Henry	MILLICAN, Thomas	1	Madison
MILLER, Andrew J.	20	Richmond	MILLICAN, James	3	DeKalb
MILLER, Bright	6	Stewart	MILLIGAN, Joseph	3	Richmond
MILLER, C.	2	Decatur	MILLIN, James	3	Thomas
MILLER, Elijah	2	Stewart	MILLINER, James	10	Cass
MILLER, Elisabeth	1	Dooly	MILLION, George M.	4	Cobb
MILLER, Francis	27	Henry	MILLIRONS, Jesse	1	Murray
MILLER, G. G.	1	Bibb	MILLS, D.	1	Randolph
MILLER, Irna	32	Richmond	MILLNER, L. B.	5	Harris
MILLER, Isham	2	Crawford	MILLS, ?	6	Muscogee
MILLER, Israel	2	DeKalb	MILLS, ?	1	Pike
MILLER, J.	1	Camden	MILLS, A. S.	2	Elbert
MILLER, J. A.	84	Crawford	MILLS, Isham R.	1	Early
MILLER, J. L.	3	Stewart	MILLS, James	1	Chatham
MILLER, J. M.	27	Screven	MILLS, James	8	Washington
MILLER, James	3	Bullock	MILLS, James H.	2	Early
MILLER, James	9	Burke	MILLS, Jas. S.	20	Twiggs
MILLER, James	7	Richmond	MILLS, Jesse	2	Washington
MILLER, James M.	1	Burke	MILLS, John	34	Washington
MILLER, Joel	1	Stewart	MILLS, M. E.	6	Elbert
MILLER, John	6	Talbot	MILLS, Margaret	2	Camden
MILLER, John A.	3	Richmond	MILLS, Morgan M.	1	Jones
MILLER, John H.	7	Burke	MILLS, Seth M.	2	Jones
MILLER, John J.	43	Baldwin	MILLS, Stephen	16	Washington
MILLER, John R.	1	Bullock	MILLS, Thomas	4	Washington
MILLER, Jonathan W.	8	Richmond	MILLS, William	7	Thomas
MILLER, Joseph	1	Baldwin	MILLS, William	4	Washington
MILLER, Joseph	23	Bibb	MILLS, Wm.	4	Cass
MILLER, Lemuel	10	Talbot	MILLS, Wm.	25	Elbert
MILLER, Levi	2	Stewart	MILLS, A. T.	6	Decatur
MILLER, Lucy	12	Screven	MILLS, Abraham	1	Campbell
MILLER, Mary	4	Stewart	MILLS, Anthony	13	Burke
MILLER, Mason	4	Crawford	MILLS, Archebald	8	Burke
MILLER, Mathias	3	Merriwether	MILLS, Charles F.	9	Chatham
MILLER, Matthew F.	6	Talbot	MILLS, Frederick	5	Baker
MILLER, N. S.	11	Camden	MILLS, Green	7	Crawford
MILLER, Pamelia	2	Baldwin	MILLS, H. M.	5	Chattooga
MILLER, Robert	1	Campbell	MILLS, Henry F.	17	Screven

Name	Number	County	Name	Number	County
MILLS, Isaac	5	Crawford	MIMS, John F.	10	DeKalb
MILLS, J.	1	Chattooga	MIMS, Martin G.	3	Sumter
MILLS, James	1	Talbot	MIMS, Mary A. Estate	2	Richmond
MILLS, John	1	Bibb	MIMS, Thos. S.	33	Screven
MILLS, Nancy	11	Decatur	MIMS, William	6	Sumter
MILLS, S.	4	Crawford	MIMS, William J.	33	Richmond
MILLS, Sarah S.	2	Chatham	MIMS, Wright	4	Sumter
MILLS, Stephen	9	Burke	MINCEY, Abraham	4	Burke
MILLS, Thomas	18	Bulock	MINCHEW, M.	7	Bibb
MILLS, Thomas R.	4	Chatham	MINCHEW, Nathan	7	Baker
MILLS, W.H.C.	2	Chatham	MINCHEW, R. R.	6	Bibb
MILLS, William H.	4	Burke	MINCY, Absalom	15	Bullock
MILLS, Wm.	1	Burke	MINCY, James	15	Bullock
MILLS, Wm.	2	Decatur	MINCY, John	4	Screven
MILLSAPP, Larkin	5	Fayette	MINGLEDORF, N.	1	Bullock
MILLSAPS, Marvel	21	Jackson	MINGLEDORFF,		
MILLSAPS, F.	5	Chattooga	Edmond	3	Effingham
MILNER, Arnold	23	Cass	MINGLEDORFF, James	2	Effingham
MILNER, Arnold	15	Cass	MINGLEDORFF,		
MILNER, B. F.	30	Pike	John G.	25	Effingham
MILNER, Elizabeth	1	Pike	MINGLEDORFF,		
MILNER, Hopson	1	Harris	Robt. P.	1	Effingham
MILNER, J. A.	6	Henry	MINGLEDORFF,		
MILNER, John D.	27	Oglethorpe	William	3	Effingham
MILNER, John H.	38	Pike	MINIFER, Richard	8	Talbot
MILNER, Jonathan G.	7	Pike	MINIS, Hetty	4	Chatham
MILNER, Jonathan P.	3	Pike	MINIS, S. A.	6	Murray
MILNER, O. E.	1	Wilkes	MINIS, Abaraham	1	Chatham
MILNER, Pitt	18	Pike	MINIS, Dinah	18	Chatham
MILNER, Pitt	7	Pike	MINOR, Daniel	1	Gwinnett
MILNER, R. A.	15	Cass	MINOR, Daniel	1	Gwinnett
MILNER, Thomas J.	4	Fayette	MINOR, Frances	2	Hancock
MILNER, Willis I.	45	Pike	MINOR, Henry	23	Gwinnett
MILNER, Wm.	17	Cass	MINOR, Nancy	1	Hancock
MILNER, George W.	5	Cass	MINOR, Rachel	6	Gwinnett
MILSAP, Precilia	1	Fayette	MINOR, William W.	1	Gwinnett
MILSAP, Rubin	1	Fayette	MINOR, Wm. W.	2	Gwinnett
MILTON, Lewis	6	Muscogee	MINOR, Sarah	6	Bibb
MILTON, Allen	2	Stewart	MINOR, Zazarous	9	DeKalb
MILURN?, Wiley	6	Campbell	MINSCHEW, George A.	9	Baker
MIMMS, David D.	3	Fayette	MINSON, John D.	23	Walton
MIMMS, Elias	5	Houston	MINTER, Elizabeth	5	Early
MIMMS, J. A.	6	Gordon	MINTER, Jeremiah	2	Jasper
MIMMS, James E. T.	7	Houston	MINTER, John M.	19	Marion
MIMMS, R. S.	8	Houston	MINTER, Joseph J.	3	Marion
MIMMS, Williamson	84	Houston	MINTER, L. D.	2	Merriwether
MIMMS, Needham	89	Bibb	MINTER, Oliver H.	4	Marion
MIMMS, Wm. D.	22	Bibb	MINTER, Robert	1	Jasper
MIMS, Abner	12	Washington	MINTER, Robt.	6	Marion
MIMS, C. E.	3	Muscogee	MINTER, G. G.	2	Henry
MIMS, Elizabeth	2	Pike	MINTON, Jacksn	1	Jefferson
MIMS, B. R.	21	Screven	MINTON, Mills	2	Upson
MIMS, Calvin	1	Stewart	MINTON, Nancy	3	Hancock
MIMS, James L.	3	Richmond	MINTON, Wm.	1	Randolph

216

Name	Number	County	Name	Number	County
MINTZ, Michael M.	6	Jackson	MITCHELL, Stephen	21	Pulaski
MINTZ, William	14	Jackson	MITCHELL, Stephen	3	Pulaski
MINYARD, Sandford	1	Jones	MITCHELL, Thomas	23	Clarke
MIRA, Anthony F.	1	Chatham	MITCHELL, Thomas G.	49	Thomas
MIRACK, Nathaniel	24	Monroe	MITCHELL, Thos.	1	Pulaski
MIRAULT, Asphasia	6	Chatham	MITCHELL, Uriah	2	Jones
MIRAULT, Simon	5	Chatham	MITCHELL, W.	7	Henry
MITCHAM, James	7	Troup	MITCHELL, W. S.	23	Clarke
MITCHAM, Mrs. Mary	7	Meriwether	MITCHELL, Walter	3	Jackson
MITCHAM, N. J.	1	Cobb	MITCHELL, Walter H.	16	Baldwin
MITCHEL, George	3	Greene	MITCHELL, Wiley	6	Franklin
MITCHEL, Hugh C.	21	Greene	MITCHELL, Wiley M.	15	Franklin
MITCHEL, John G.	10	Greene	MITCHELL, William	14	Franklin
MITCHEL, Johnathan	5	Hall	MITCHELL, William	4	Newton
MITCHEL, Madison R.	19	Gwinnett	MITCHELL, William	1	Walton
MITCHEL, Margaret	10	Greene	MITCHELL, William W.	8	Franklin
MITCHEL, William	4	Gilmer	MITCHELL, Wm.	4	Macon
MITCHEL, William	34	Meriwether	MITCHELL, Wm. S.	10	Clarke
MITCHEL, William J.	10	Merriwether	MITCHELL, Wilson L.	1	Walton
MITCHEL, A. P.	2	Randolph	MITCHELL, A. W.	12	DeKalb
MITCHELL, Alexander	17	McIntosh	MITCHELL, B. H.	1	Coweta
MITCHELL, B.	2	Pulaski	MITCHELL, B. H. H.	1	Coweta
MITCHELL, Daniel R.	45	Floyd	MITCHELL, Barney	1	Cass
MITCHELL, Drewry	10	Marion	MITCHELL, Calvin	5	Talbot
MITCHELL, George -			MITCHELL, Frances	6	Putnam
GRAVES, G. W.	8	Walton	MITCHELL, G. B.	1	Chatham
MITCHELL, Geo. M.	3	Lowndes	MITCHELL, Isaac	3	DeKalb
MITCHELL, Giles	19	Jackson	MITCHELL, James W.	1	DeKalb
MITCHELL, Hartwell R.	9	Thomas	MITCHELL, John M.	3	Campbell
MITCHELL, Irwin A.	1	Franklin	MITCHELL, John Q.	11	Baldwin
MITCHELL, Isaac	6	Muscogee	MITCHELL, L.	3	Bibb
MITCHELL, Isaac	2	Muscogee	MITCHELL, Rebecca	5	DeKalb
MITCHELL, Isaac	1	Muscogee	MITCHELL, Robert	21	Talbot
MITCHELL, Isaac	30	Wilkinson	MITCHELL, Robert	10	Talbot
MITCHELL, Isaac W.	80	Thomas	MITCHELL, U.	1	Bryan
MITCHELL, J. V.	10	Pulaski	MITCHELL, William	34	Talbot
MITCHELL, J. W. H.	29	Hancock	MITCHELL, William	2	Talbot
MITCHELL, James C.	1	Franklin	MITCHELL, Wm.	29	Decatur
MITCHELL, James H.	1	Walton	MITCHENER, W. B.	20	Randolph
MITCHELL, Jane	1	Muscogee	MITCHER, James	9	Merriwether
MITCHELL, Jane L.	37	Pike	MITCHUM, Hendrick	4	Newton
MITCHELL, Jesse	6	Walton	MITCHUM, Merrell	4	Morgan
MITCHELL, John	2	Meriwether	MIXEN, Asbury	1	Jasper
MITCHELL, John W.	14	Macon	MIXON, Elijah	2	Newton
MITCHELL, John W. H.	37	Thomas	MIXON, William W.	1	Emanual
MITCHELL, Mathew A.	17	Jasper	MIXON, Wm.	1	Marion
MITCHELL, Mrs. Nancy	3	Muscogee	MIXON, George	2	Burke
MITCHELL, Nathaniel	52	Thomas	MIXON, George Sen.	3	Burke
MITCHELL, Richard	6	Jasper	MIXON, James	2	Burke
MITCHELL, Richard	82	Thomas	MIXON, Michael	33	Burke
MITCHELL, Richard D.	1	Pulaski	MIZE, Clackston	9	Franklin
MITCHELL, Robert	23	Hancock	MIZE, John J.	2	Franklin
MITCHELL, Robt. G.	1	Muscogee	MIZE, Thomas	4	Franklin
MITCHELL, S. C.	41	Henry	MIZE, Warren	4	Franklin

Name	Number	County	Name	Number	County
MIZE, William	2	Harris	MOMON, John	23	Merriwether
MIZELL, Jackson	3	Camden	MONAGHAN, Peter	13	Warren
MIZELL, William	3	Telfair	MONCRIEF, Caleb J.	3	Meriwether
MIZZELL, John	16	Camden	MONCRIEF, David U.	4	Walton
MIZZELL, Joshua	6	Camden	MONCRIEF, Marshall	1	Greene
MIZZELL, Mary	1	Camden	MONCRIEF, William	13	Greene
MIZZELL, Owen K.	5	Camden	MONCRIEF, William M.	6	Troup
MIZZELL, Perry	5	Camden	MONCRIEF, Eli J.	7	Coweta
MIZZELL, William	15	Talbot	MONCRIF, Thos. J.	3	Greene
MOAD, James	2	Walker	MONDAY, Reuben	1	Fayette
MOBLEY, J.	8	Henry	MONGEN, Eliza C.	5	Chatham
MOBLEY,			MONGER, Edwin	12	Randolph
Alexander J. L.	1	Burke	MONGERS, John A.	3	Oglethorpe
MOBLEY, B.	5	Irwin	MONGIN, Ann	16	Chatham
MOBLEY, Benjamin	11	Burke	MONGIN, William H.	164	Chatham
MOBLEY, Biggers	5	Appling	MONGIN, John D.	19	Richmond
MOBLEY, Bird P.	8	Appling	MONGIN, William H.	10	Chatham
MOBLEY, Elizabeth	4	Appling	MONGIN?, W. H.	123	McIntosh
MOBLEY, Fleming	12	Jasper	MONK, Pearson B.	5	Taliaferro
MOBLEY, G. C.	9	Harris	MONOHAN, James	3	Chatham
MOBLEY, G. C.	8	Harris	MONROE ?, A. B.	9	Richmond
MOBLEY, J. B.	3	Irwin	MONROE, Daniel	11	Thomas
MOBLEY, James	8	Harris	MONROE, James	2	Murray
MOBLEY, Jesse	9	Appling	MONROE, Joseph	13	Murray
MOBLEY, Mrs.	11	Irwin	MONROE, Lorenzo D.	13	Muscogee
MOBLEY, Richard H.	1	Murray	MONROE, Malcom	14	Thomas
MOBLEY, Solomon	5	Appling	MONROE,		
MOBLEY, William	4	Jasper	Richard W. Z.	2	Muscogee
MOBLEY, Hester	20	Coweta	MONROE, William A.	2	Murray
MOBLEY, James H.	7	Burke	MONROE, William H.	1	Muscogee
MOBLEY, Jas. R.	12	Burke	MONROE, James	10	Stewart
MOBLEY, N. H.	20	Crawford	MONROE, N. C.	7	Bibb
MOBLEY, Peyton	10	Murray	MONROE, Robert	4	Bibb
MOBLEY, Thomas	5	Dooly	MONROW, M. E.	5	Pike
MOBLEY, W. P.	4	Troup	MONT, Christopher L.	2	Gwinnett
MOBLEY, Warren R.	8	Coweta	MONTEEK, Robert	5	Oglethorpe
MOBLEY, William L.	6	Burke	MONTFORD, Loyd	7	Laurens
MOBLY, D. A.	7	Walton	MONTFORT, E.	30	Crawford
MOBLY, Iverson D.	1	Walton	MONTFORT, J. E.	5	Crawford
MOBLY, James	1	Walton	MONTFORT, John		
MOBLY, John	23	Tatnall	see MORRISON	38	Greene
MOCK, D.	5	Decatur	MONTFORT, T. W.	6	Crawford
MOCK, Joel	1	Randolph	MONTGOMERY,		
MOCK, John J.	1	Decatur	William	30	Floyd
MODE, Adolph	2	Chatham	MONTGOMERY,		
MODISETT, Samuel J.	1	Heard	Abner P.	1	Pike
MODISIT, Samual	2	Heard	MONTGOMERY, Anna	2	Warren
MOEL, William, trustee	1	Chatham	MONTGOMERY, Bartly	6	Floyd
MOFFAT, Thomas	3	Richmond	MONTGOMERY, D.	24	Newton
MOFFET, John	1	Gwinnett	MONTGOMERY, David	3	Jasper
MOFFITT, Henry	8	Muscogee	MONTGOMERY, David	1	Pike
MOLDER, Saml. W.	11	Stewart	MONTGOMERY,		
MOLINA, Emanuel	1	Chatham	David P.	5	Warren
MOMAN, Thos.	6	Harris	MONTGOMERY, Hugh	9	Chattooga

218

Name	Number	County	Name	Number	County
MONTGOMERY, Hugh	4	Floyd	MOODY, P. L.	31	Morgan
MONTGOMERY, James F.	10	Warren	MOODY, Robert	5	Glynn
MONTGOMERY, James H.	9	Jasper	MOODY, Selah	16	Oglethorpe
MONTGOMERY, Jno.	5	Forsyth	MOODY, Simeon S.	12	Liberty
MONTGOMERY, John	10	Chattooga	MOODY, Thomas J.	2	Macon
MONTGOMERY, John L.	5	Thomas	MOODY, Thomas J.	2	Monroe
MONTGOMERY, John N.	14	Madison	MOODY, William	4	Pike
MONTGOMERY, Joseph T.	9	Troup	MOODY, William L.	3	Houston
MONTGOMERY, M.	9	Chattooga	MOODY, William L.	4	Jasper
MONTGOMERY, M. C. B.	7	Gwinnett	MOODY, J.	10	Crawford
MONTGOMERY, Martha	3	Madison	MOODY, Manging ?, J.	13	Tatnall
MONTGOMERY, N. W.	8	Clarke	MOODY, Thomas	5	Stewart
MONTGOMERY, Robert	6	Warren	MOON, Alfred B.	14	Baldwin
MONTGOMERY, Rufus	2	Newton	MOON, Archibald	25	Jackson
MONTGOMERY, S. A.	10	Meriwether	MOON, Charles	9	Merriwether
MONTGOMERY, Seaborn	9	Sumter	MOON, Cash C.	1	Walton
MONTGOMERY, William S.	8	Newton	MOON, Elijah	10	Walton
MONTGOMERY, F. M.	1	Floyd	MOON, George R.	3	Thomas
MONTGOMERY, Hugh	3	Stewart	MOON, J.	1	Troup
MONTGOMERY, James	8	Crawford	MOON, J. B.	5	Elbert
MONTGOMERY, Jennette	7	Richmond	MOON, J. D.	4	Elbert
MONTGOMERY, John	10	Baker	MOON, Jacob	16	Meriwether
MONTGOMERY, Mrs. S.	6	Decatur	MOON, James	5	Chattooga
MONTGOMERY, P. F.	8	Talbot	MOON, James	1	Greene
MONTGOMERY, Robt.	13	Forsyth	MOON, James	2	Warren
MONTGOMERY, Samuel	10	Talbot	MOON, Jeremiah	8	Cobb
MONTMOLLEN, John S.	20	Chatham	MOON, Jesse	2	Pike
MOODY, Charles B.	5	Wayne	MOON, John	2	Chattooga
MOODY, Dr. Thos.	1	Oglethorpe	MOON, John	3	Meriwether
MOODY, Elias B.	1	Greene	MOON, John W.	4	Cobb
MOODY, Isaac	12	Appling	MOON, John W.	10	Heard
MOODY, Isham J.	1	Pike	MOON, Nancy	1	Heard
MOODY, J. M.	9	Oglethorpe	MOON, Rauleigh	5	Heard
MOODY, Jacob	3	Appling	MOON, Robert	26	Jackson
MOODY, James	1	Liberty	MOON, Thomas	6	Meriwether
MOODY, James A.	5	Greene	MOON, Thomas P.	9	Jackson
MOODY, Joel	8	Upson	MOON, W. B.	5	Meriwether
MOODY, John	3	Washington	MOON, Wood A.	1	Muscogee
MOODY, John W.	23	Oglethorpe	MOON, Amelia	3	Richmond
MOODY, Mrs. Rachael	3	Liberty	MOON, Jas. H.	1	Coweta
			MOON, John M.	10	Walton
			MOON, John R.	3	Walton
			MOON, Joseph	3	Walton
			MOON, Lewis S. Jr.	1	Walton
			MOON, Lewis S. Sr.	2	Walton
			MOON, Mary	30	Bibb
			MOON, M. E.	1	Walton
			MOON, Madison	3	Walton
			MOON, Matthew	7	Washington
			MOON, Thomas	2	Walton
			MOON, Zach	1	Walton
			MOONEY, Alford	2	DeKalb
			MOONEY, J. G.	4	Cass
			MOONOUGH, E. H.	4	Randolph

Name	Number	County	Name	Number	County
MOONY, Martin D.	2	Liberty	MOORE, James T.	1	Monroe
MOOR, James B.	2	Harris	MOORE, Jesse J.	1	Greene
MOOR, John	16	Oglethorpe	MOORE, Jno.	8	Henry
MOOR, Joseph	7	Merriwether	MOORE, John	24	Cobb
MOOR, Precilla	17	Oglethorpe	MOORE, John B.	7	Madison
MOOR, William	2	Merriwether	MOORE, John C.	4	Glynn
MOORE, Alsa	9	Clarke	MOORE, John S.	2	Murray
MOORE, Thomas	21	Clarke	MOORE, Kilby	1	Upson
MOORE, ?	1	Elbert	MOORE, Leah	1	Forsyth
MOORE, A. R.	3	Pike	MOORE, Luis	4	Butts
MOORE, Abram	2	Gwinnett	MOORE, Martha	1	Warre
MOORE, Ann G.	13	Chatham	MOORE, Mary	7	Jones
MOORE, Anna	10	Clarke	MOORE, McLany	2	Jefferson
MOORE, Archilus D.	5	Madison	MOORE, O. F.	1	Upson
MOORE, Barnet	12	Oglethorpe	MOORE, Owen W.	1	Jones
MOORE, Benjamin F.	3	Jones	MOORE, Phily	11	Walton
MOORE, Benning	15	Macon	MOORE, Rebecca	37	Greene
MOORE, Bernard D.	9	Greene	MOORE, Resdon	30	Upson
MOORE, C. J.	5	Elbert	MOORE, Richard	16	Fayette
MOORE, C. J.	5	Elbert	MOORE, Richard D.	11	Clarke
MOORE, Cassander	3	Wilkes	MOORE, Robert	7	Cherokee
MOORE, Charles w.	7	Upson	MOORE, Robert H.	21	Lumpkin
MOORE, D. W.	12	Morgan	MOORE, S.	1	Henry
MOORE, David	17	Monroe	MOORE, Saml.	1	Harris
MOORE, David B.	12	Troup	MOORE, Samuel L.	1	Thomas
MOORE, Drusilla	7	Warren	MOORE, Sarah	5	Hancock
MOORE, Edward	2	Fayette	MOORE, Sarah	12	Jones
MOORE, Edward	1	Walker	MOORE, Sarah	2	Washington
MOORE, Elias	2	Ware	MOORE, Shelton W.	2	Troup
MOORE, Elijah Revd.	1	Gwinnett	MOORE, Simpson	3	Jones
MOORE, Elliotte	1	Cass	MOORE, T.	2	Henry
MOORE, Frances T.	14	Clarke	MOORE, Thomas	9	Harris
MOORE, Francis b.	3	Houston	MOORE, Thomas	9	Twiggs
MOORE, G.	2	Oglethorpe	MOORE, Thomas J.	3	Houston
MOORE, George	4	Chatham	MOORE, Thomas W.	2	Jones
MOORE, George	1	Troup	MOORE, Thompson	11	Gwinnett
MOORE, George W.	18	Wilkes	MOORE, W. A.	3	Oglethorpe
MOORE, Gilly	11	Troup	MOORE, W. J.	6	Elbert
MOORE, Greene	79	Greene	MOORE, W. T.	2	Hancock
MOORE, H. J.	2	Henry	MOORE, William	13	Greene
MOORE, Henry	5	Pike	MOORE, William A.	4	Troup
MOORE, Hiram	2	Henry	MOORE, William S.	9	Houston
MOORE, Isabella	5	Wilkes	MOORE, William S.	4	Madison
MOORE, J. C.	13	Morgan	MOORE, Wm. A.	3	Floyd
MOORE, J. N.	1	Elbert	MOORE, Wm. B.	9	Taliaferro
MOORE, J. J.	2	Upson	MOORE, Wm. H.	16	Troup
MOORE, Jackson	4	Greene	MOORE, Wm. W.	10	Greene
MOORE, Jacob W.	9	Glynn	MOORE, Zachariah	22	Effingham
MOORE, James	3	Emanual	MOORE, A. J.	2	Chattooga
MOORE, James	1	Floyd	MOORE, Augustus	5	Carroll
MOORE, James	43	Greene	MOORE, B. B.	30	Lincoln
MOORE, James	2	Meriwether	MOORE, Blitch	3	Bullock
MOORE, James M.	2	Greene	MOORE, Edward	1	Tatnall
MOORE, James M.	2	Gwinnett	MOORE, Edwin M.	37	Chatham

Name	Number	County	Name	Number	County
MOORE, Elija	12	DeKalb	MOOTY, Alexander	4	Troup
MOORE, Elijah	4	Coweta	MOOTY, James	6	Troup
MOORE, Elisha	4	Taliaferro	MOOTY, James	19	Troup
MOORE, Eliz.	9	Richmond	MOOTY, John	11	Troup
MOORE, Elizabeth	11	Taliaferro	MOOTY, William	6	Troup
MOORE, G.	1	Randolph	MORAGNE, I. M.	5	Lincoln
MOORE, George	4	Coweta	MORAN, James	3	Baldwin
MOORE, George	51	Crawford	MORAN, William	?	Baldwin
MOORE, Henry	4	Taliaferro	MORAN, William A.	3	Baldwin
MOORE, Isaac	20	Taliaferro	MORE, Israel	6	Troup
MOORE, J. & Lester R.	13	Burke	MORE, Jesse	1	Lee
MOORE, J. K.	9	Chattooga	MORE, Jesse J.	4	Lee
MOORE, J. L.	8	Butts	MORE, Robert	10	Paulding
MOORE, J. R.	3	Carroll	MORE, Sarah	1	Paulding
MOORE, James	6	DeKalb	MORE, Wm. M.		
MOORE, James	7	Taliaferro	(overseer?)	156	Lee
MOORE, James R.	4	Burke	MORE, D.	4	Putnam
MOORE, Jas. D.	15	Carroll	MORE, West E.	2	Dooly
MOORE, Jef &			MORE, William	2	Columbia
GONES, Wm.	8	Richmond	MORE, William J.	2	Sumter
MOORE, Jesse	19	Bullock	MOREFIELD, Willis W.	1	Troup
MOORE, Jesse	2	Taliaferro	MOREHEAD, M. L.	1	Forsyth
MOORE, Jno. S.	1	Randolph	MOREL, Andrew	3	Chatham
MOORE, John	4	Taliaferro	MOREL, Ann	4	Chatham
MOORE, John	3	Richmond	MOREL, Bryan M.	67	Chatham
MOORE, John Estate	1	Richmond	MOREL, Sarah M.	6	Chatham
MOORE, John G.	22	Taliaferro	MOREL, William	12	Chatham
MOORE, John L.	3	Baldwin	MORELAN, Tucker	11	Merriwether
MOORE, John R.	8	Baldwin	MORELAND, Asberry F.	1	Muscogee
MOORE, John T.	10	Sumter	MORELAND, B. S.	1	Lee
MOORE, Jonathan F.	14	Baldwin	MORELAND, Halson	25	Upson
MOORE, Lewico	15	Baldwin	MORELAND, Hosea	11	Jasper
MOORE, Lovel	6	Randolph	MORELAND, Isaac H.	23	Houston
MOORE, Lucretia	7	Screven	MORELAND, J. A.	3	Meriwether
MOORE, Mary	1	Baldwin	MORELAND, J. C.	5	Heard
MOORE, Mrs. Mary	18	Burke	MORELAND, J. F.	16	Heard
MOORE, Owen	6	Carroll	MORELAND, John	13	Lee
MOORE, Penina	4	Butts	MORELAND, John F.	14	Troup
MOORE, R. L.	2	Randolph	MORELAND, N. A.	19	Heard
MOORE, Thomas	1	DeKalb	MORELAND, Robt. C.	34	Meriwether
MOORE, Whittington S.	6	Telfair	MORELAND, Robert K.	21	Warren
MOORE, William	11	Burke	MORELAND, Sintha	19	Merriwether
MOORE, William	39	Stewart	MORELAND, Susan	21	Jasper
MOORE, William	7	Tatnall	MORELAND, William	6	Jones
MOORE, William	13	Screven	MORELAND, William	2	Lee
MOORE, Wm.	1	Carroll	MORELAND, William	5	Merriwether
MOORE, Wm.	1	Putnam	MORELAND, J. F.	3	Putnam
MOORE, Wm. M.	4	Taliaferro	MORELAND, John	14	Putnam
MOORE, Wm. M.	2	Taliaferro	MORELAND, P.	13	Coweta
MOORE, Wm. R.	4	Randolph	MORELL, William T.	4	Harris
MOORE, Wyatt	1	Carroll	MORELY, Samuel	4	Cobb
MOORE?, Pleasant	9	Madison	MORENGER, John C.	8	Dooly
MOOREHOUSE, A. C.	14	Bibb	MOREMAN, Chas. M.	13	Wilkes
MOORELAND, Alfred	3	Merriwether	MORGAN, Ann	7	Effingham

Name	Number	County	Name	Number	County
MORGAN, B. F.	13	Paulding	MORGAN, Betsy W.	19	Columbia
MORGAN, C. L.	8	Effingham	MORGAN, Chas. W.		Sumter
MORGAN, Christian	14	Effingham	MORGAN, Daniel	4	Coweta
MORGAN, David	4	Hall	MORGAN, George W.	7	Richmond
MORGAN, David W.	26	Troup	MORGAN, H. M.	2	Cass
MORGAN, Davis	3	Effingham	MORGAN, Hardy	11	Sumter
MORGAN, E.	1	Morgan	MORGAN, Henry	6	Bibb
MORGAN, Eli	5	Oglethorpe	MORGAN, J. S.	2	DeKalb
MORGAN, Elihue	18	Clinch	MORGAN, John	6	Newton
MORGAN, Frances	14	Jones	MORGAN, John	10	Screven
MORGAN, George W.	4	Paulding	MORGAN, Joseph	1	Sumter
MORGAN, H.	1	Henry	MORGAN, Joshay	35	Taliaferro
MORGAN, H. C.	8	Merriwether	MORGAN, L.	11	Crawford
MORGAN, H. F.	1	Troup	MORGAN, M. A.	6	Coweta
MORGAN, Harper	4	Cobb	MORGAN, M.J.	11	Sumter
MORGAN, Hiram	5	Meriwether	MORGAN, P. N.	2	Chattooga
MORGAN, Isaac N.	3	Lowndes	MORGAN, Pleasant	6	Dooly
MORGAN, James B.	4	Meriwether	MORGAN, Seth	1	DeKalb
MORGAN, Jesse	2	Jefferson	MORGAN, Thomas	17	Chattooga
MORGAN, John	6	Madison	MORGAN, Thos. G.	1	Chattooga
MORGAN, John estate	12	Jefferson	MORGAN, W.	1	Decatur
MORGAN, John E.	50	Troup	MORGAN, William	4	Stewart
MORGAN, John H.	1	Jefferson	MORGAN, Wm.	3	Coweta
MORGAN, John L.	11	Clinch	MORGAN, Wm. G.	6	Clarke
MORGAN, John R.	2	Chattooga	MORGAN, Wm. L.	3	Coweta
MORGAN, Johnathan	2	Franklin	MORIN, Margaret A.	5	Chatham
MORGAN, Joseph	5	Paulding	MORIS, Wm.	1	Troup
MORGAN, Joseph D.	4	Paulding	MORK, Julia	10	Camden
MORGAN, Joseph L.	2	Clinch	MORN, Mrs. Eliza	5	Muscogee
MORGAN, Lewis	12	Effingham	MORNING, John H.	2	Sumter
MORGAN, Luke J.	4	Floyd	MORNINGSTAR, Susan	10	Chatham
MORGAN, Mark	5	Meriwether	MORR, James	3	Gordon
MORGAN, Mark	5	Meriwether	MORREL, William	9	Stewart
MORGAN, Mary	13	Monroe	MORRELL, Isaac W.	9	Chatham
MORGAN, N. M.	1	Harris	MORRELL, Jesse	3	Marion
MORGAN, Nicholas	8	Harris	MORRELL, John	11	Effingham
MORGAN, Randle	6	Harris	MORRELL, Joseph	3	Effingham
MORGAN, Randle	3	Harris	MORRELL, Samuel	4	Chatham
MORGAN, Sampson	1	Floyd	MORRIS, (?)	10	Columbia
MORGAN, Samuel	1	Jones	MORRIS, A. J.	1	Henry
MORGAN, Solomon	6	Clinch	MORRIS, A. J.	1	Henry
MORGAN, Thomas	25	Appling	MORRIS, A. P.	2	Henry
MORGAN, Thomas R.	13	Troup	MORRIS, Ann	32	Jones
MORGAN, Wilis	9	Campbell	MORRIS, Benj.	1	Henry
MORGAN, William	8	Effingham	MORRIS, Boling G.	8	Jones
MORGAN, William	1	Greene	MORRIS, C.	4	Floyd
MORGAN, William	1	Merriwether	MORRIS, D.	11	Randolph
MORGAN, William	6	Newton	MORRIS, Dury	3	Cobb
MORGAN, William B.	4	Appling	MORRIS, E.	2	Henry
MORGAN, William G.	2	Jones	MORRIS, E. W.	12	Franklin
MORGAN, William M.	3	Paulding	MORRIS, Franklin B.	2	Murray
MORGAN, Wm.	7	Jackson	MORRIS, J. H.	17	Union
MORGAN, Wm. N.	1	Greene	MORRIS, H. T.	10	Hall
MORGAN, A. A.	10	Dooly	MORRIS, Isam	4	Pike

Name	Number	County	Name	Number	County
MORRIS, J. B.	4	Henry	MORRIS, Mrs. Delah	4	Stewart
MORRIS, J. H.	17	Union	MORRIS, Nancy	12	DeKalb
MORRIS, James	4	Jackson	MORRIS, Rebecca	13	Columbia
MORRIS, James	1	Marion	MORRIS, Renly N.	6	DeKalb
MORRIS, James	22	Murray	MORRIS, Richard	16	Talbot
MORRIS, James S.	19	Cobb	MORRIS, Robert	1	Richmond
MORRIS, Jas. M.	2	Henry	MORRIS, William S.	41	Burke
MORRIS, Jas. M.			MORRIS, Wm.	1	Carroll
manager	3	Henry	MORRISON, Azra	27	Monroe
MORRIS, Jesse	8	Morgan	MORRISON, Blansel	2	Lowndes
MORRIS, Joel E.	4	Cobb	MORRISON, Daniel	3	Appling
MORRIS, John	16	Franklin	MORRISON, Hugh	4	Marion
MORRIS, John	23	Monroe	MORRISON, Isaac	5	Greene
MORRIS, John J.	12	Jasper	MORRISON, Isaac agt.	2	Greene
MORRIS, Joseph	3	Cobb	MORRISON, J. J.	23	Elbert
MORRIS, N. J.	10	Hall	MORRISON, James	2	Gilmer
MORRIS, Nancy	5	Henry	MORRISON, Lauchline	6	Thomas
MORRIS, R.	17	Henry	MORRISON, Nancy	25	Jones
MORRIS, R. J.	1	Early	MORRISON, Thos. J.	1	Jackson
MORRIS, R. L.	96	McIntosh	MORRISON, Eliza	9	Chatham
MORRIS, S. D.	8	Henry	MORRISON, Geo.	27	Camden
MORRIS, Sarah	9	Franklin	MORRISON, Henry	3	Camden
MORRIS, Sarah	30	Hancock	MORRISON, Isaac		
MORRIS, Sherod	4	Gwinnett	adm MONFORT	38	Greene
MORRIS, Taylor	49	Jones	MORRISON, Robert J.	34	Burke
MORRIS, Thomas	6	Franklin	MORRISON, Robert J.	7	Burke
MORRIS, Thomas	7	Muscogee	MORRISON, William J.	1	Upson
MORRIS, Thomas	8	Warren	MORROW, David	4	Gordon
MORRIS, Thomas M.	3	Cobb	MORROW, Elizabeth	3	Gwinnett
MORRIS, Thompson	1	Cobb	MORROW, H.	5	Henry
MORRIS, William	8	Cobb	MORROW, James	6	Hall
MORRIS, William	6	Jones	MORROW, James H.	15	Jones
MORRIS, William	4	Merriwether	MORROW, John	3	Franklin
MORRIS, William H.	1	Walton	MORROW, Peter J.	25	Walton
MORRIS, Wm.	6	Forsyth	MORROW, R. E.	3	Henry
MORRIS, Alexander	18	Taliaferro	MORROW, R. W.	1	Henry
MORRIS, Bartholomeu	1	Richmond	MORROW, Thomas	10	Oglethorpe
MORRIS, C. P.	2	Columbia	MORROW, V. P.	1	Henry
MORRIS, Delila	1	Stewart	MORROW, Joseph E.	17	Heard
MORRIS, Garnett S.	1	DeKalb	MORROW, William	9	Stewart
MORRIS, H.	1	Bibb	MORRY, William N.	9	Stewart
MORRIS, J.	2	Crawford	MORSE, B. C.	2	Murray
MORRIS, James B.	12	Chatham	MORSE, Oliver	5	Monroe
MORRIS, Jas.	6	Bibb	MORSE, J. K.	1	Dooly
MORRIS, Jas.	27	Randolph	MORSE, William H.	1	Tatnall
MORRIS, Jas.	1	Randolph	MORSE?, Elick	26	Muscogee
MORRIS, Jeremiah ?	3	Richmond	MORTEN, Achsah	24	Troup
MORRIS, Jesse	7	Bibb	MORTIN, William M.	22	Clarke
MORRIS, Jesse	16	Columbia	MORTON, David	8	Effingham
MORRIS, John	5	Columbia	MORTON, Harrel	8	Washington
MORRIS, John A.	3	Stewart	MORTON, J. L.	7	Muscogee
MORRIS, John H.	3	DeKalb	MORTON, James O.	7	Lowndes
MORRIS, Joseph	22	Columbia	MORTON, Joel J.	11	Clarke
MORRIS, Lucy A.	2	Bibb	MORTON, John	20	Clarke

Name	Number	County	Name	Number	County
MORTON, John	10	Muscogee	MOSS, Barrell	17	Newton
MORTON, Joseph	46	Clarke	MOSS, Elizabeth	54	Lincoln
MORTON, Matilda	6	Jones	MOSS, Francis	25	Troup
MORTON, William	27	Oglethorpe	MOSS, Henry	3	Greene
MORTON, William M.	20	Clarke	MOSS, I. D.	20	Lincoln
MORTON, E. L.	1	Coweta	MOSS, J. D.	1	Oglethorpe
MORTON, Henry	32	Putnam	MOSS, John D.	68	Oglethorpe
MORTON, Henry	27	Screven	MOSS, John E.	6	Merriwether
MORTON, L. B.	13	Stewart	MOSS, John H.	4	Newton
MORTON, M.	5	Coweta	MOSS, John S.	12	Wilkes
MORTON, Silas	36	Screven	MOSS, M.	2	Elbert
MORTON, Simson	3	Screven	MOSS, T. G.	4	Habersham
MORTON, T. R.	3	Chattooga	MOSS, W.	8	Elbert
MOSEHOM?, William	62	Baker	MOSS, Wm. R.	52	Hancock
MOSELEY, Jos. L.	2	Floyd	MOSS, A.	1	Chattooga
MOSELEY, B.	38	Henry	MOSS, Albert	2	Campbell
MOSELEY, Benj.	13	Putnam	MOSS, Felix	3	Cherokee
MOSELEY, Cuyler	7	Montgomery	MOSS, Hudson	2	Campbell
MOSELEY, John H.	1	Montgomery	MOSS, Hutson	19	Habersham
MOSELEY, John P.	9	Lincoln	MOSS, James	1	Dooly
MOSELEY, Joseph	5	Newton	MOSS?, R. H.	11	Hancock
MOSELEY, M. F.	4	Harris	MOSTILLA, A.	3	Chattooga
MOSELEY, Priscilla	10	Newton	MOTE, John	7	Newton
MOSELEY, R.	5	Henry	MOTE, Lucy	7	Habersham
MOSELEY, S.	33	Henry	MOTE, Silas	1	Murray
MOSELEY, Seborn	35	Lincoln	MOTE, William A.	3	Murray
MOSELEY,			MOTE, Asbury	3	Newton
Benjamin Sen.	72	Putnam	MOTHERSHED,		
MOSELEY, E.	4	Crawford	William	13	Jasper
MOSELEY, Henry F.	1	Rabun	MOTLEY, Benjamin	8	Muscogee
MOSELEY, J. A.	4	Putnam	MOTLEY, Thomas	48	Muscogee
MOSELEY, J. A.			MOTT, Hiram	3	Washington
by Hawk, John	15	Putnam	MOTT, Joseph	18	Macon
MOSELEY, Jas.	15	Bibb	MOTT, Nat.	1	Clarke
MOSELEY, T. M.	2	Bibb	MOTT, Nathan	1	Macon
MOSELEY, Wm. R.	2	Bibb	MOTT, R.	5	Muscogee
MOSELY, Benjamin T.	16	Paulding	MOTT, Randolph	20	Muscogee
MOSELY, Jesse B.	1	Early	MOTT, John	2	Chatham
MOSELY, R. P.	8	Morgan	MOTT, William A.	22	Baker
MOSELY, Rebecca	3	Greene	MOTT, William A.	16	Baldwin
MOSELY, Thos. J.	2	Clarke	MOUGHON, Thomas	84	Jones
MOSELY, William A.	16	Lincoln	MOULDER, H.W.	1	Forsyth
MOSES, A. J.	4	Clarke	MOULDER, Irvin	1	Cherokee
MOSES, Isaac	1	Muscogee	MOULDER, Jacob	8	Gwinnett
MOSES, R. J.	16	Muscogee	MOULTON, James G.	3	Macon
MOSES, Nancy	3	Coweta	MOULTON, John	1	Macon
MOSLEY, Clemond	3	Emanual	MOULTRIE, B. H.	6	Bibb
MOSLEY, Daniel	1	Franklin	MOULTRIE, John B.	16	Screven
MOSLEY, Edmond w.	1	Emanual	MOULTRIE, T. J.	2	Bibb
MOSLEY, William	1	Henry	MOUNCH, L.	1	Bibb
MOSLEY, William S.	3	Emanual	MOUNT, Jesse	53	Chatham
MOSLEY, C.	19	Chattooga	MOUNT, Mathias	4	Houston
MOSLY, Thomas	3	Montgomery	MOUNT, T. H.	3	Lee
MOSLY, Benj.	1	Putnam	MOUNT, William	35	Early

Name	Number	County
MOUNT, Wm. P.		
agent for FELDER, J.	35	Houston
MOUNTAIN, Francis B.	10	Jefferson
MOUNTJOY, John W.	1	Meriwether
MOWER, B. F.	2	Habersham
MOY, Durin G.	15	Washington
MOY, John E.	4	Washington
MOYE, B. A.	35	Jefferson
MOYE, Issac	13	Washington
MOYE, John E.	22	Washington
MOYE, Obediah	20	Lowndes
MOYE, S. J.	28	Randolph
MOYE, Thomas E.	9	Washington
MOYERS, Samuel W.	2	Merriwether
MOYERS, Wm.	13	Chattooga
MOYNE, Jas. P.	31	Clarke
MOZE, Thomas W.	7	Pike
MRHAM Estate	2	Muscogee
MUCLEHANNON,		
Josiah	3	Walker
MUDD(?), Herman	2	Bibb
MUDGE, Wm.	8	Coweta
MUKEN, H. N.	10	Stewart
MULBUAL?, Isaac	4	Gilmer
MULFORD, Thomas	1	Screven
MULHOLLAND, C.	2	Bibb
MULIER, Wm. P.	2	Fayette
MULIKIN, Josiah	4	Taliaferro
MULIN, Elbert	1	Emanual
MULKEY, Felix G.	1	Jones
MULKEY, Isaac	5	Marion
MULKEY, Enoch	7	Burke
MULKY, Freeman	4	Burke
MULKY, Littlebury	9	Macon
MULLIN, Lloyd	4	Heard
MULLING, James A.	1	Jefferson
MULLING, Jesse	4	Jefferson
MULLINS, Autain	1	Monroe
MULLINS, Budd	2	Cobb
MULLINS, Elijah	3	Harris
MULLINS, Elizabeth	2	Hancock
MULLINS, Green	1	Harris
MULLINS, James	4	Harris
MULLINS, John	4	Greene
MULLINS, John	10	Muscogee
MULLINS, William	2	Hall
MULLINS, William	5	Muscogee
MULLINS, Harvey	11	Hancock
MULLINS, Jesse	19	Talbot
MULLINS, P. J.	33	Putnam
MULLINS, Philip	2	Richmond
MULLINS, William	7	Talbot
MULLINS?, Elisha	4	Harris
MULLIS, Chas.	5	Pulaski

Name	Number	County
MULLIS, Solomon	3	Pulaski
MUMFORD, Robert	12	Lincoln
MUMFORD, Sylvester	5	Wayne
MUMFORD, Wm. E.	16	Early
MUN, Thomas	13	Randolph
MUND, John	3	Macon
MUND, Angus	3	Macon
MUNDAY, Andrew J.	4	Fayette
MUNDY, John B.	3	Hall
MUNFORD, Lewis	8	Cass
MUNGIN?, John D.	20	Jefferson
MUNN, John	2	Muscogee
MUNNENLYNN, (?) C.	71	Dade
MUNNENLYNN, C.	77	Decatur
MUNNERLYN, C.	8	Decatur
MUNRO?, G. W. C.	6	Lee
MUNROE, ?	2	Muscogee
MUNSON, Owen	2	Richmond
MURCHISON, C.	15	Crawford
MURCHISON, J.	1	Crawford
MURDEN ?, Henry	7	Taliaferro
MURDEN ?, Redman	8	Taliaferro
MURDOC, J.	1	Chattooga
MURDOC, James M.	1	Stewart
MURDOCK, Robt. Z.	3	Muscogee
MURDOCK, D.	1	Chattooga
MURDOCK, F. H.	6	Crawford
MURDOCK, Thomas J.	9	Burke
MURKEE, Edw.	3	Camden
MURNAN, Wm.	4	Bibb
MURPEY, John	14	Harris
MURPH, Conrad	25	Houston
MURPH, Jacob	27	Lincoln
MURPH, John	5	Lincoln
MURPH, George	26	Baldwin
MURPHEY, Ambrose	24	Monroe
MURPHEY, J. H.	3	Fayette
MURPHEY, John	8	Wilkes
MURPHEY, John S.	1	Wilkes
MURPHEY, Josiah	11	Twiggs
MURPHEY, Rebeccah	4	Fayette
MURPHREE, James A.	16	Burke
MURPHREE, Wright	65	Burke
MURPHREE, James A.	7	Burke
MURPHREE, Josiah	15	Burke
MURPHREE, William	28	Burke
MURPHREE, William J.	2	Burke
MURPHREY,		
Milledgeville	6	Jefferson
MURPHY, Alexander	45	Burke
MURPHY, Cullen	15	Washington
MURPHY, Dr. I. B.	3	Baldwin
MURPHY, G. D.	10	Habersham
MURPHY, J. B.	1	Meriwether

225

Name	Number	County	Name	Number	County
MURPHY, Jeptha M.	1	Fayette	MUSGROVE,		
MURPHY, John	7	Cass	Millington	4	Lincoln
MURPHY, John M.	13	Fayette	MUSGROVE, Harison	56	Columbia
MURPHY, Lemuel M.	7	Fayette	MUSHIAN?, John L.	37	Merriwether
MURPHY, Mary	14	Washington	MUSTER ?, Eli	2	Richmond
MURPHY, Robert	3	Fayette	MYER?, Lewis	5	Effingham
MURPHY, S. B.	8	Wilkinson	MYERS, James	19	Glynn
MURPHY, S. H.	11	Merriwether	MYERS, Margaret	32	Chatham
MURPHY, Batts W.	1	Sumter	MYERS, Michael	8	Lowndes
MURPHY, Charles	15	DeKalb	MYERS, George W.	1	Cass
MURPHY, Edmund	1	Richmond	MYERS, M. V.	1	Chatham
MURPHY, H.	1	Decatur	MYGATT, George	2	Jasper
MURPHY, L. H.	4	Richmond	MYHAND, Alvin	5	Harris
MURPHY, Malcomb	5	Sumter	MYHAND, James	4	Harris
MURPHY, Nicholas	9	Richmond	MYHAND, John B.	2	Harris
MURPHY, Nicholas	5	Richmond	MYIRES, Mordaci	27	Cobb
MURPHY, William R.	48	Monroe	MYRECK, S. P.	36	Twiggs
MURRAY, Arza	5	Marion	MYRES, Francis M.	1	Muscogee
MURRAY, Daniel	9	Houston	MYRES, James	6	Monroe
MURRAY, Edward	5	Muscogee	MYRES, E. H.	4	Bibb
MURRAY, Elias B.	2	Franklin	MYRES, Stephen	1	Wayne
MURRAY, Ezekiel	4	Houston	MYRES, William	3	Walker
MURRAY, James	12	Houston	MYRICK, Josiah	18	Warren
MURRAY, James	30	Marion	MYRICK, Josiah H.	6	Pike
MURRAY, James J.	4	Houston	MYRICK, Richard	8	Pike
MURRAY, John	10	Houston	MYRICK, Septimus	10	Marion
MURRAY, John	4	Marion	MYRICK, William R.	7	Pike
MURRAY, John H.	6	Houston	MYRICK, B. H.	32	Baldwin
MURRAY, John N.	1	Walker	MYRICK, David	13	Putnam
MURRAY, John P.	10	Upson	MYRICK, G. T. W.	28	Baldwin
MURRAY, John T.	2	Harris	MYRICK, Jas.	31	Bibb
MURRAY, Nancy	1	Madison	MYRICK, John W.	42	Baldwin
MURRAY, William	24	Clarke	MYRICK, M. H.	42	Crawford
MURRAY, William	5	Murray	MYRICK, S.	46	Crawford
MURRAY, Drewry	12	Sumter	MYRICK, S. P.	90	Baldwin
MURRAY, James	1	Cass	MYRICK, William J.	30	Baldwin
MURRAY, Moses M.	6	Baker	NABERS, James B.	7	Jackson
MURRELL, Joseph M.	7	Newton	NABERS, William	2	Clarke
MURROW, John	1	Effingham	NAIL, Elizabeth	2	Appling
MURRY, A. G.	6	Pike	NAIL, Morris	7	Tatnall
MURRY, J. W.	16	Lincoln	NALER, Dixon	4	Murray
MURRY, Jane	16	Lincoln	NALER, Joseph	1	Murray
MURRY, John B.	3	Oglethorpe	NALL, A.	3	Pike
MURRY, Lucy	1	Oglethorpe	NALL, Nathan	5	Meriwether
MURRY, Ex.	52	Columbia	NALOR, Robt.	1	Forsyth
MURRY, Mary A.	32	Screven	NANCE, Fleming B.	8	Harris
MURRY, William	12	Columbia	NANCE, H. W.	3	Muscogee
MURY, Nancy	11	Lincoln	NANCE, Harvey	10	Muscogee
MURY, Thomas J.	104	Lincoln	NANCE, M. M.	1	Muscogee
MUSE, D.	3	Hancock	NANCE, Wesley	11	Jackson
MUSE, T. E.	8	Chatham	NANCE, William J.	3	Troup
MUSE, Wm. P.	6	Wilkes	NANCE, William N.	7	Murray
MUSGROVE,			NANN, A.	48	Thomas
Edward W.	1	Gwinnett	NANSANT?, S.	2	Merriwether

Name	Number	County	Name	Number	County
NAPIER, J. T.	3	Bibb	NEAL, Thales M.	15	Franklin
NAPIER, Leroy	39	Bibb	NEAL, Thomas	43	Warren
NAPIER, Shelton	81	Putnam	NEAL, Thomas M.	3	Warren
NAPIER, Skelton	59	Putnam	NEAL, W. W.	1	Fayette
NAPIER, Skitten?	10	Bibb	NEAL, B. F.	3	DeKalb
NAPIER, Thomas	26	Walker	NEAL, Charity	8	Bibb
NAPIER, William J.	27	Baldwin	NEAL, J. C.	6	Chattooga
NAPPIER, J.	26	Houston	NEAL, Jno.	15	Talbot
NAPPIER, S.	44	Houston	NEAL, John	45	Talbot
NARUM, Silvester	2	Harris	NEAL, Jourdan	2	DeKalb
NASH, A.	1	Elbert	NEAL, Mrs. S.	18	Decatur
NASH, Ariel	1	Madison	NEAL, Perry	4	Crawford
NASH, E. C.	2	Henry	NEAL, Richard	11	Columbia
NASH, F.	4	Elbert	NEAL, S. H.	8	Campbell
NASH, Francis H.	1	Madison	NEAL, Sarah	25	Columbia
NASH, J.	3	Henry	NEAL, William	5	Talbot
NASH, Jacob B.	8	Wilkes	NEAL, William M.	14	Warren
NASH, James	1	Elbert	NEALEY, Nancy	21	Oglethorpe
NASH, James	2	Jackson	NEALY, Francis	3	Newton
NASH, Jeremiah	43	Twiggs	NEALY, George W.	2	Fayette
NASH, John W.	1	Gwinnett	NEALY, Thomas	7	Newton
NASH, Lewis	1	Gwinnett	NEASE, Frederick	8	Effingham
NASH, Margaret	12	Jackson	NEASE, George	1	Effingham
NASH, R.A.	20	Twiggs	NEASE, Robert	2	Effingham
NASH, T.	7	Henry	NEASE, J. N.	4	Crawford
NASH, Thos.	10	Oglethorpe	NEAVES, John	3	Early
NASH, Thomas	6	Walker	NEEL, Elijah	17	Thomas
NASH, Wm.	1	Jackson	NEEL, Thomas	46	Hancock
NASH, Hillary H.	1	Talbot	NEELAND, Elizabeth	5	Washington
NASH, Leroy	7	Columbia	NEELY, Hugh J.	4	Pike
NASH, Reuben	18	Habersham	NEELY, J. T.	17	Washington
NASWORTHY, George	8	Burke	NEELY, Jackson	15	Coweta
NASWORTHY, Urias	3	Burke	NEELY, Jane	6	Jefferson
NASWORTHY, William	27	Burke	NEELY, Sarah	4	Newton
NAUGHTON, James	6	Oglethorpe	NEELY, Jas. J.	10	Coweta
NAUGHTON, Mary	7	Oglethorpe	NEELY, Julia	2	Washington
NAVVEE, Thomas	2	Chatham	NEFFER, Jno.	9	Henry
NAVY ?, John E.	2	Richmond	NEILL, Joseph	5	Monroe
NEAK?, Michael	2	Burke	NEILL, Adam	4	Chattooga
NEAL, B.	8	Elbert	NELMS, ?	1	Elbert
NEAL, B. A. R.	14	Franklin	NELMS, J. C.	12	Elbert
NEAL, C.	5	Elbert	NELMS, N.	2	Elbert
NEAL, David J.	2	Franklin	NELMS, Presly	7	Monroe
NEAL, Dickey	4	Franklin	NELMS, Thomas	6	Newton
NEAL, George V.	20	Warren	NELMS, W. B.	14	Elbert
NEAL, Harral	7	Warren	NELMS, W..	4	Elbert
NEAL, J. B.	18	Lincoln	NELSON, Abel	10	Harris
NEAL, James	123	Pike	NELSON, Abel F.	5	Harris
NEAL, Jno.	16	Carroll	NELSON, Alfred	11	Houston
NEAL, John	23	Pike	NELSON, Allison	16	Cobb
NEAL, John M.	51	Franklin	NELSON, Appling	1	Newton
NEAL, Lindsay	7	Gordon	NELSON, Drury A.	4	Warren
NEAL, Luvenia	10	Franklin	NELSON, James F.	9	Campbell
NEAL, Older	51	Greene	NELSON, John	18	Harris

Name	Number	County	Name	Number	County
NELSON, John	2	Heard	NEVEL, William	1	Chatham
NELSON, John	1	Troup	NEVILLE, Jacob Sen.	1	Bullock
NELSON, John	60	Twiggs	NEVILLE, Jas.	2	Cass
NELSON, John H.	3	Burke	NEVILLE, Jacob	1	Bullock
NELSON, John Jun.	2	Harris	NEVILLE, Thomas	4	Bullock
NELSON, N. H.	14	Morgan	NEVILLS, John	4	Bullock
NELSON, Noble	1	Harris	NEVIN, Mary	3	Richmond
NELSON, Perry	1	Greene	NEVITT, Louisa	13	Chatham
NELSON, Thomas M.	12	Muscogee	NEW, A.B.S.	1	Chattooga
NELSON, Wade	1	Wilkinson	NEW, Elijah	3	Newton
NELSON, Washington	2	Twiggs	NEW, Jarrell	1	Carroll
NELSON, William	7	Harris	NEW, William	4	DeKalb
NELSON, William D.	1	Pike	NEWBERRY, C. L.	5	Muscogee
NELSON, William N.	3	Muscogee	NEWBERRY, James Jr.	8	Marion
NELSON, William P.	10	Monroe	NEWBERRY, James P.	9	Marion
NELSON, A. P.	4	Coweta	NEWBERRY, Isaac J.	3	Dooly
NELSON, A. W.	11	Coweta	NEWBERRY, James Sr.	17	Marion
NELSON, Andrew	3	Chatham	NEWBERRY, Zelpha	1	Stewart
NELSON, Gideon	9	Talbot	NEWBORNE, Wm. C.	4	Lowndes
NELSON, Gideon	1	Talbot	NEWBURY, J.	1	Early
NELSON, Horace	13	Columbia	NEWBY, Daniel J.	8	Jones
NELSON, James	2	Bibb	NEWBY, Esom	1	Twiggs
NELSON, James	35	Putnam	NEWBY, Jesse	9	Talbot
NELSON, Jesse	2	Talbot	NEWEL, E. A.	9	Coweta
NELSON, John H.	1	Richmond	NEWELL, C.	6	Henry
NELSON, John P.	47	Baker	NEWELL, Isaac	29	Baldwin
NELSON, John W.	8	Screven	NEWELL, P. J.	2	Bibb
NELSON, Joshua	8	Stewart	NEWELL, Thomas M.	12	Chatham
NELSON, R.	6	Bibb	NEWELL, Warren S.	13	Talbot
NELSON, Thos.	4	Talbot	NEWHART, Henry D.	1	Richmond
NELSON, Wall	39	Stewart	NEWLANDS,		
NELSON, William	4	Talbot	Adam L. Jr.	3	Richmond
NELSON, William H.	1	Richmond	NEWMAN, (?).	6	Coweta
NELUMS, Curtis	3	Baker	NEWMAN, Arthur	11	Pulaski
NELUY, James A.	1	Lee	NEWMAN, John	4	Pulaski
NESBET, Alex	5	Wilkinson	NEWMAN, N.	6	Monroe
NESBIT, Agnes A.	4	Clarke	NEWMAN, N.	5	Wilkes
NESBIT, E. A.	26	Houston	NEWMAN, Richard	5	Heard
NESBIT, Joseph H.	2	Gwinnett	NEWMAN, H. J.	2	Coweta
NESBIT, Thomas	67	Jefferson	NEWMAN, James	3	Columbia
NESBIT, J. A.	3	Bibb	NEWMAN, O. T. M.	8	Coweta
NESBIT, John A.W.	6	Cobb	NEWMAN, Randal	2	Columbia
NESBITT, William	26	Gwinnett	NEWMAN, Thomas J.	1	Columbia
NESBITT, H.O.P.	105	Early	NEWMAN, Thomas J.	8	Coweta
NESMITH, Charles	9	Burke	NEWMAN, Thomas W.	2	Columbia
NESMITH, Charles	6	Thomas	NEWMAN, Thos. E.	9	Columbia
NESMITH, Elijah	1	Thomas	NEWMAN, William	3	Columbia
NESMITH, John	24	Burke	NEWNAN, Daniel	5	Walker
NESSMITH, Elizabeth	1	Bullock	NEWSHART?, Daniel	28	Effingham
NETHERLAND, Jempsey	5	Burke	NEWSOM, A.	9	Washington
NETTLES, L. A. E. P.	6	Paulding	NEWSOM, Benjamin F.	2	Macon
NETTLES, Williamg.	2	Appling	NEWSOM, Daniel	1	Marion
NETTLY, James agent	1	Muscogee	NEWSOM, David	5	Lowndes
NEUFVILLE, Edward	12	Chatham	NEWSOM, David	2	Morgan

Name	Number	County
NEWSOM, Gideon	23	Crawford
NEWSOM, H. K.	8	Washington
NEWSOM, Joel D.	14	Troup
NEWSOM, Joseph W. A.	1	Jones
NEWSOM, R.	1	Washington
NEWSOM, Richard A.	3	Greene
NEWSOM, Robert	22	Greene
NEWSOM, Ruben D.	1	Lincoln
NEWSOM, Seaborn	4	Washington
NEWSOM, Solomon	62	Washington
NEWSOM, Thomas H.	1	Marion
NEWSOM, William	7	Harris
NEWSOM, Wm.	9	Lee
NEWSOM, D. A.	3	Coweta
NEWSOM, Jas.	2	Crawford
NEWSOM, Jno.	3	Crawford
NEWSOM, L. L.	2	Randolph
NEWSOM, Martha	21	Crawford
NEWSOME, Carter	5	Warren
NEWSOME, David	12	Warren
NEWSOME, Green	1	Warren
NEWSOME, Jesse	1	Bullock
NEWSOME, Solomon	13	Warren
NEWSOME, Solomon	17	Warren
NEWSOME, William	4	Warren
NEWSON, Joel	5	Morgan
NEWSON, A. T.	23	Stewart
NEWSON, J. F.	4	Randolph
NEWSON, Jno.	6	Randolph
NEWSON, John	35	Putnam
NEWSON, L.	32	Randolph
NEWTON ?, David K.	1	Richmond
NEWTON, A. D.	2	Greene
NEWTON, Aris	23	Jasper
NEWTON, Barnette	17	Effingham
NEWTON, Benjamin L.	5	Emanual
NEWTON, Chancery	1	Floyd
NEWTON, Chancery	1	Floyd
NEWTON, Crawford	1	Jones
NEWTON, Daniel	1	Macon
NEWTON, Ebenezar	22	Troup
NEWTON, Elizur L.	9	Clarke
NEWTON, Giles	2	Fayette
NEWTON, Henry	2	Franklin
NEWTON, Isaac	1	Jones
NEWTON, James M.	7	Jasper
NEWTON, John H.	24	Clarke
NEWTON, John L.	3	Emanual
NEWTON, Josiah	1	Clarke
NEWTON, Marcus L.	3	Jasper
NEWTON, Nathan J.	2	Cherokee
NEWTON, Phillip	11	Emanual
NEWTON, W. H.	11	Morgan
NEWTON, William	3	Lowndes
NEWTON, Ben. Lee	1	Bullock
NEWTON, C. F.	12	Butts
NEWTON, George M.	13	Richmond
NEWTON, James	2	Screven
NEWTON, T. F.	4	Bibb
NEWTON, William	5	Screven
NEX, Edward	17	Newton
NEYLAND, John P.	11	Chatham
NEYLAND, Elizabeth	2	Richmond
NEYLAND, Mary	4	Richmond
NIBLACK, Margaret	7	Jackson
NIBLACK, Samuel J.	3	Jackson
NICELER, Hugh	15	Clarke
NICHOLDS, John	2	Cherokee
NICHOLLS, Wright	8	Richmond
NICHOLS, Adam	1	Union
NICHOLS, Andrew J.	1	Habersham
NICHOLS, Charles C.	2	Richmond
NICHOLS, George	5	Harris
NICHOLS, Henry J.	96	Glynn
NICHOLS, J. C.	14	Merriwether
NICHOLS, J. R.	1	Clarke
NICHOLS, James	1	Habersham
NICHOLS, James C.	5	Clarke
NICHOLS, John	1	Hall
NICHOLS, Jonathan	3	Merriwether
NICHOLS, Martha	7	Pike
NICHOLS, Ransom	5	Clarke
NICHOLS, Simon W.	1	Ware
NICHOLS, Travis	2	Fayette
NICHOLS, Wm. P.	1	Habersham
NICHOLS, Abba	17	Baldwin
NICHOLS, Wm.	1	DeKalb
NICHOLSON, James	5	Newton
NICHOLSON, N.	8	Cass
NICHOLSON, Nathaniel	13	Marion
NICHOLSON, S. C.	3	Wilkinson
NICHOLSON, Thomas	5	Dooly
NICHOLSON, Archbale	4	Stewart
NICHOLSON, Duncan	2	Stewart
NICHOLSON, Duncan S.	8	Stewart
NICHOLSON, G.	3	Decatur
NICHOLSON, Jas.	13	Putnam
NICHOLSON, William	1	Rabun
NICKLESOM, Jas. B.	42	Greene
NICKOLSEN, J.	17	Decatur
NICKS, Anderson	2	Talbot
NICOLAN, Elizabeth	27	Glynn
NICOLL, John C.	14	Chatham
NICOLL, John C.	5	Chatham
NIGHT, George	10	Harris
NIGHT, James M.	1	Newton
NIGHT, Nathaniel	1	DeKalb
NIGHTENGALE, P. N.	8	Camden

Name	Number	County	Name	Number	County
NIGHTENGALE, P. M.	12	Sumter	NORMAN, G. G.	8	Wilkes
NIGHTINGALE, P. M.	129	Baker	NORMAN, Geo. Agent	11	Wilkes
NISBET, Robert	1	Newton	NORMAN, George	31	Wilkes
NISBET, A. M.	6	Baldwin	NORMAN, H. W.	4	Wilkes
NISBET, E. A.	13	Bibb	NORMAN, J. W.	5	Elbert
NIVEN, Daniel	15	Jones	NORMAN, James	3	Muscogee
NIVINS, William H. C.	2	Jones	NORMAN, James	1	Muscogee
NIX, B. J.	1	Newton	NORMAN, John	3	Wilkes
NIX, David	1	Newton	NORMAN, John H.	15	Wilkes
NIX, David E.	1	Cobb	NORMAN, John L.	3	Wilkes
NIX, Herain?	3	Walton	NORMAN, Johnson	14	Wilkes
NIX, J.	9	Henry	NORMAN,		
NIX, J. T.	2	Newton	Mrs. Mary W.	3	Liberty
NIX, John	3	Habersham	NORMAN, P. W.	32	Lincoln
NIX, Thos. T.	1	Jackson	NORMAN, P. W.	13	Lincoln
NIX, Uriah	1	Cherokee	NORMAN, W. H.	17	Lincoln
NIX, William H.	1	Muscogee	NORMAN, William	1	Wilkinson
NIX, Edward	2	Campbell	NORMAN, Wm.	5	Wilkes
NIX, Larkin	1	Stewart	NORMAN, Wm. B.	2	Wilkes
NIXON, Frances S.	11	Houston	NORMAN, Wm. B.	1	Wilkes
NIXON, George H.	3	Clarke	NORMAN, Wm. S.	34	Liberty
NIXON, Mary S.	2	Fayette	NORMAN, Wm. S.	20	Monroe
NIXON, Mrs. P.	30	Houston	NORMAN, Alexander	1	Stewart
NIXON, Mrs. Priscilla	8	Houston	NORRELL, J. B.	2	Bibb
NIXON, William	9	Talbot	NORRELL, Richd.	19	Richmond
NIXON, Martha	10	Coweta	NORRELL, William	1	Stewart
NIXON, S.	1	Coweta	NORRIS, (?)	2	Decatur
NIXON, Wm.	1	Cass	NORRIS, Abner	2	Warren
NO NAME	72	Early	NORRIS, Elihu T.	13	Jasper
NO NAME	5	Fayette	NORRIS, George A.	2	Muscogee
NOBLE, H.	2	Muscogee	NORRIS, Isaac	1	Emanual
NOBLE, Mary H.	12	Floyd	NORRIS, Isaac	10	Twiggs
NOBLES, Amos	1	Monroe	NORRIS, James	5	Monroe
NOBLET, Jehu	6	Murray	NORRIS, James	17	Warren
NOCK, Mary	1	Chatham	NORRIS, Jeptha M.	1	Warren
NOEL, James F.	10	Oglethorpe	NORRIS, Joel	5	Harris
NOELL, Azarial	1	Gwinnett	NORRIS, John Q. A.	2	Clarke
NOELL, Hoe	5	Oglethorpe	NORRIS, Jos.	7	Floyd
NOELL, Huldah	15	Oglethorpe	NORRIS, Mary E.	9	Chatham
NOELL, Sopha	10	Oglethorpe	NORRIS, Simion	1	Monroe
NOLAN, James	70	Wilkes	NORRIS, William P.	7	Meriwether
NOLAN, Q. R.	19	Henry	NORRIS, Christopher	1	Campbell
NOLAN, Rich.	20	Butts	NORRIS, James A.	8	Chatham
NOLAND, Thomas	36	Morgan	NORRIS, L. H.	1	Randolph
NOLAND, William	28	Newton	NORRIS, Martha	2	Butts
NOLAS, Jas.	5	Butts	NORRIS, Rebecca	29	Taliaferro
NOLES, W.	1	Wilkinson	NORRIS, Robert	1	Washington
NOLLEY, D.	18	Henry	NORRIS, Ruth	4	Sumter
NOMILL ?, William W.	7	Walton	NORRIS, Thos.	28	Bibb
NORCROSS, J.	2	DeKalb	NORRIS, William T.	1	Walton
NORCROSS, J. N.	3	DeKalb	NORTH, E.	1	Coweta
NORLAND, Joseph	6	Morgan	NORTH, John J.	5	Ware
NORMAN, John S.	14	Liberty	NORTH, Leah	8	Coweta
NORMAN, B.	35	Elbert	NORTH, Wm.	5	Coweta

Name	Number	County	Name	Number	County
NORTH, A.	10	Coweta	NUNELLY, John G.	10	Pike
NORTH, Allen	4	Coweta	NUNGAZER, Ann	6	Chatham
NORTH, Anthony	24	Coweta	NUNGAZER, Nathaniel	17	Chatham
NORTH, Besy	1	Coweta	NUNN, Hawkins H.	3	Sumter
NORTH, M. D.	14	Coweta	NUNN, James	1	Madison
NORTH, R. W.	6	Coweta	NUNN, James	9	Warren
NORTH, W. W.	1	DeKalb	NUNN, John	2	Warren
NORTHCUT, Wm.	1	Cass	NUNN, Rachel	14	Warren
NORTHCUTT, J. J.	3	Cobb	NUNN, Samuel	1	Warren
NORTHCUTT, John R.	1	Cobb	NUNNALLY, Jacob G.	3	Oglethorpe
NORTHEN, B. A.	12	Houston	NUNNALLY, John A.	3	Oglethorpe
NORTHEN, Peter	24	Greene	NUNNALLY, A. F.	25	Clarke
NORTHERN, B.	1	Coweta	NUNNELLY, Wm. H.	8	Screven
NORTHERN, W. T.	13	Crawford	NUNNEZ, Charles	2	Burke
NORTHINGTON,			NUSOM, Wm. D.	1	Bibb
James R.	1	Washington	NUSOM, Henry	43	Bibb
NORTHON, Robert S.	1	Merriwether	NUTT, Andrew	11	Marion
NORTON, C. R.	3	Morgan	NUTT, J. B.	7	Henry
NORTON, Elizabeth	4	Gwinnett	NUTT, James	12	Marion
NORTON, Hiram	1	Pike	NUTT, John T.	7	Heard
NORTON, James H.	2	Pike	NUTT, Saml. M.	6	Marion
NORTON, John	47	Chatham	NUTT, Samuel R.	7	Marion
NORTON, John	3	Fayette	NUTT, W. B.	10	Henry
NORTON, Melidda	1	Fayette	NUTT, Wm. C.	7	Marion
NORTON, R. S.	3	Floyd	NUTT, Samuel	4	Butts
NORTON, R. S.	1	Newton	NUTTING, C. A.	6	Butts
NORTON, Thomas	6	Murray	NYE, Bainhard	2	Hancock
NORTON, Wm.	12	Heard	O"CONNER, Dennis	1	Chatham
NORTON, Jesse	7	Stewart	OAKLEY, J. E.	2	Pulaski
NORTON, R. S.	6	Chatham	OAKMAN, W. H.	22	Columbia
NORTON, William T.	3	Baker	OAKMAN, Wm. H. Jr.	4	Richmond
NORWOOD, Andrew P.	10	Troup	OATES, William W.	7	Chatham
NORWOOD, Amasa	5	Jackson	OATS, Jethro	6	Harris
NORWOOD, Calab	16	Monroe	OATS, Wyatt	11	Sumter
NORWOOD, Croxton	1	Franklin	OATTIS, Zah	5	Randolph
NORWOOD, Daniel	18	Troup	OBANNON, Brian A.	6	Wilkinson
NORWOOD, James	3	Franklin	OBAR, William	1	Franklin
NORWOOD, Lorenzo D.	11	Houston	OBRIANT, T.	5	Elbert
NORWOOD, William C	16	Troup	OBRIEN, Andrew W.	2	Houston
NOSTRANCE, George	5	Chatham	OBRIEN, Jeremiah	1	Richmond
NOTTINGHAM, A. B.	7	Bibb	O'BRIEN, Michael	10	Baldwin
NOUIS?, Willes	1	Newton	O'BRIEN, Phoebe	2	Baldwin
NOWEL, Isham	1	Macon	O'BRIEN, William	15	Baldwin
NOWEL, James	5	Upson	OBRYAN, M.	3	Coweta
NOWELL, James A.	6	Walton	O'BRYNE, Domonic	17	Chatham
NOWELL, L. J.	10	Bibb	O'BRYNE, Edward	2	Chatham
NOWLAND, Wm. M.	7	Richmond	OCONNER, John	1	Murray
NUCKELS, N.	9	Muscogee	O'CONNER, Patrick	1	Chatham
NUCKLES, Alexander	6	Hall	OCONNER, David	2	Chatham
NUCKOLLS, Alex	24	Forsyth	OCONNER, Dolin ?	1	Richmond
NUCKOLLS, J. T.	4	Forsyth	ODELL, John	1	Murray
NUNALLY, John	6	Walton	ODELL, Solomon	1	Henry
NUNALLY, Josiah E.	9	Pike	ODEM, Arch	3	Pulaski
NUNALLY, William B.	22	Walton	ODEM, D. W.	1	Pulaski

Name	Number	County
ODEN, Hezekiah	2	Richmond
ODEN, William	2	Richmond
ODEN, Wilson	7	Chatham
ODEN, Wilson	2	Chatham
ODENGSELL, Mary A.	1	Chatham
ODINGSELL, W.	2	Chatham
ODINGSELL, Anthony	10	Chatham
ODOM, Aaron	9	Muscogee
ODOM, Deldatha	23	Early
ODOM, J. M.	1	Pulaski
ODOM, Jackson	22	Muscogee
ODOM, John Sen.	37	Muscogee
ODOM, John Junion	18	Muscogee
ODOM, W. L.	1	Pulaski
ODOM, Zadock	7	Early
ODOM, B.B.	37	Putnam
ODOM, Beverly R.	9	Burke
ODOM, James P.	2	Burke
ODOM, Labon	2	Burke
O'DRISCOLL, W. C.	5	Chatham
ODUM, Aron	7	Laurens
ODUM, James S.	6	Dooly
ODUM, Mrs.	3	Bibb
ODWINE, A. C.	5	Bibb
OFFILL, John H.	6	Bibb
OGBURN, E.	7	Wilkinson
OGBURN, Littlebury	10	Macon
OGDEN, Elisha	1	Merriwether
OGDEN, Jonathan	1	Cherokee
OGDEN, J. H.	2	Sumter
OGILBY, G. S.	4	Morgan
OGILBY, H. J.	34	Morgan
OGILVIE, Eliza	4	Oglethorpe
OGILVIE, William H.	8	Jones
OGILVIE, William J.	13	Oglethorpe
OGILVIE, Artemus W.	18	Coweta
OGILVIER, William J.	10	Oglethorpe
OGLEBAY, Clara A.	1	Chatham
OGLESBEY, G.	3	Henry
OGLESBY, G. T.	13	Hancock
OGLESBY, G. T.	13	Hancock
OGLESBY, James	5	Emanual
OGLESBY, John	3	Emanual
OGLESBY, M. W.	6	Troup
OGLESBY, Martha	15	Pike
OGLESBY, Elijah	4	Screven
OGLESBY, G. S.	36	Lee
OGLESBY, Rachael	2	Emanual
OGLESVIE, Thomas	2	Newton
OGLETREE, B.	1	Henry
OGLETREE, C.	1	Muscogee
OGLETREE, David	19	Monroe
OGLETREE, Hope	1	Fayette
OGLETREE, John R.	35	Monroe
OGLETREE, Mars	6	Monroe
OGLETREE, Nancy	7	Twiggs
OGLETREE, Philimon	34	Merriwether
OGLETREE, Pierce	3	Fayette
OGLETREE, Absalem	6	Monroe
OGLETREE, Asberry	1	Taliaferro
OGLETREE, John	7	Stewart
OGLEVIE, James	1	Newton
OGLISBY, Shalun H.	2	Wilkes
OGLY, William	1	Newton
OHARA, Charles	7	Talbot
OHATLY, John W.	2	Chatham
OKEEFE, Pi	5	Troup
OKELLEY, Thomas	8	Walton
OKELLY, Benjamin	2	Gwinnett
OKELLY, Benjamin F.	3	Madison
OKELLY, Charles	2	Madison
OKELLY, Delila	9	Gwinnett
OKELLY, Frances	1	Walton
OKELLY, Frances D.	8	Walton
OKELLY, James	6	Walton
OKELLY, Linsay	1	Walton
OKELLY, Sarah	2	Madison
OKELLY, Welborn J.	2	Oglethorpe
OKELLY, James	11	Oglethorpe
OLAP?, Manson	27	Newton
OLCOTT, William B.	3	Chatham
OLEM?, Henry	12	Muscogee
OLIFF, Benjamin	2	Dooly
OLIN, W. Milo	2	Richmond
OLIPHANT, Jospeh	19	Jefferson
OLIVAR, Alfred	25	Elbert
OLIVAR, Lucy	40	Elbert
OLIVE, A.	6	Oglethorpe
OLIVE, James	1	Meriwether
OLIVE, John	1	Oglethorpe
OLIVE, Littleton	1	Marion
OLIVE, Richard	3	Greene
OLIVE, Wendon	21	Oglethorpe
OLIVER, Andrew	13	Jackson
OLIVER, Charles S.	2	Clarke
OLIVER, E. G.	10	Monroe
OLIVER, Elijah	6	Jackson
OLIVER, Geo.	1	Lee
OLIVER, Jackson	15	Franklin
OLIVER, Jacob	1	Harris
OLIVER, James	2	Lee
OLIVER, James	4	Muscogee
OLIVER, James G. Sen.	18	Dooly
OLIVER, James L.	2	Chatham
OLIVER, Jas.	1	Troup
OLIVER, Jas. B.	1	Troup
OLIVER, John G.	8	Greene
OLIVER, Peter	1	Cobb

Name	Number	County	Name	Number	County
OLIVER, Robert E.	3	Jackson	ONEAL, John	2	Murray
OLIVER, Sarah	1	Laurens	ONEAL, Marshall	9	Harris
OLIVER, Shelton	42	Oglethorpe	ONEAL, Mary	15	Troup
OLIVER, Shelton	39	Oglethorpe	ONEAL, Seaborn	9	Harris
OLIVER, W. H.	3	Heard	ONEAL, T. C.	5	Walker
OLIVER, William	6	Chatham	ONEAL, Theopolis	1	Monroe
OLIVER, William	1	Greene	ONEAL, W. W.	20	Laurens
OLIVER, William	5	Lumpkin	ONEAL, Wooten Sen.	1	Greene
OLIVER, Willis J.	1	Greene	ONEAL, Edwin	17	Talbot
OLIVER, George	1	Chatham	ONEAL, Elizabeth	9	Putnam
OLIVER, George	99	Screven	ONEAL, G.	38	Crawford
OLIVER, Hampton	2	Burke	ONEAL, John	2	Talbot
OLIVER, James	5	Chatham	ONEAL, Zachariah	1	Dade
OLIVER, James	12	randolph	ONEEL, Daniel	6	Decatur
OLIVER, James G.	9	Dooly	ONEIL, Hough	9	Richmond
OLIVER, Jas. M.	5	Randolph	ONEIL, John C.	1	Richmond
OLIVER, John A.	6	DeKalb	ONEILL, J. H.	7	Murray
OLIVER, Joseph	6	Randolph	OPRY, Amos	17	Houston
OLIVER, Joseph	6	Screven	OQUIN, John	9	Washington
OLIVER, Joshua B.	18	Dooly	ORD?, James J.	2	Habersham
OLIVER, Martha	8	Screven	ORIC, M.	21	Putnam
OLIVER, Mathew	1	Stewart	ORIN, William	3	Muscogee
OLIVER, McDavid	1	Screven	ORINBURG, M. J.	3	Floyd
OLIVER, Nancy	2	Bibb	ORME, Richard M.	48	Baldwin
OLIVER, Robt. J.	7	Screven	ORME, Wm. P.	3	DeKalb
OLIVER, Stephen H.	3	Richmond	O'ROURKE, Owen	19	Chatham
OLIVER, Thomas	8	Burke	ORR, Andrew	1	Gordon
OLIVER, Thos. W.	17	Screven	ORR, Burwell	4	Pike
OLIVER, Virgil	5	Screven	ORR, Freeman	1	Washington
OLIVER, W. W.	6	Screven	ORR, Gustavous	4	Newton
OLIVER, Zilpha	13	Burke	ORR, J. B.	4	Henry
OLIVERAS, Bartolo	2	Chatham	ORR, James	16	Jackson
OLLIFF, Joseph	1	Bullock	ORR, James M.	8	Gwinnett
OLLIVE, (?)	11	Columbia	ORR, John	2	Cobb
OLMSTEAD, Johanna	3	Chatham	ORR, Robert	1	Gilmer
OLMSTEAD, Jonathan	7	Chatham	ORR, Timothy	1	Heard
OLMSTEAD, E. H.	2	Chatham	ORR, Watkins	10	Heard
OLMSTEAD, Francis	1	Screven	ORR, A. J.	17	Bibb
OLMSTEAD, William	6	Chatham	ORR, Ann	3	Randolph
OLNER, William M.	4	Houston	ORR, John	2	Stewart
OLOVER, Henry	2	Campbell	ORR, Matthew T.	2	Carroll
OLSIN, S. S.	3	Crawford	ORR, N. W.	50	Coweta
ONAIL, E. M.	2	Butts	ORR, Robt.	9	Coweta
ONEAL, Alfred	1	Monroe	ORR, Robt.	6	DeKalb
ONEAL, Atlas	4	Merriwether	ORR, William F.	5	Columbia
ONEAL, B. P.	33	Lincoln	ORSBAN?, Lazarus	2	Newton
ONEAL, Charles	20	McIntosh	ORSBEUN? C. H.	4	Pike
ONEAL, Cullen	34	Laurens	ORSBORN, A.	4	Henry
ONEAL, Elizabeth	3	Morgan	ORSBORN, J. H .	10	Bibb
ONEAL, H.	3	Troup	ORSBURN, Elias	4	Newton
ONEAL, James	2	DeKalb	OSBERN, Martha	7	Jasper
ONEAL, Jesse H.	43	Greene	OSBERN, Nelson	1	Franklin
ONEAL, Joel	1	Greene	OSBERN, Reuben	3	Washington
ONEAL, John	2	Cobb	OSBERN, George	2	Stewart

Name	Number	County	Name	Number	County
OSBORN, Francis	3	Clarke	OVERSTREET, John D.	3	Jackson
OSBORN, George	11	Harris	OVERSTREET, C. C.	1	Chatham
OSBORN, George	1	Harris	OVERTON, Eliza	11	Greene
OSBORN, Jesse	13	Gwinnett	OVERTON, Gilerest	44	Taliaferro
OSBORN, John	2	Clarke	OVERTON, Wm. J.	18	Taliaferro
OSBORN, Priscilla	4	Jackson	OWEN, D. G.	1	Walton
OSBORN, William	2	Hancock	OWEN, George W.	3	Upson
OSBORN, William	33	Harris	OWEN, Glen	6	Monroe
OSBORN, William A.	7	Harris	OWEN, J.	13	Henry
OSBORNE, Green B.	2	Pike	OWEN, Mary	9	Monroe
OSBORNE, H. J.	4	Hancock	OWEN, Mary	23	Upson
OSBORNE, Isaac	1	Cobb	OWEN, Newton	4	Monroe
OSBORNE, Newman	3	Gilmer	OWEN, R. B. S.	10	Chattooga
OSBORNE, Nicholas R.	1	Gilmer	OWEN, S. C.	1	Henry
OSBURN, Mathew	8	Jasper	OWEN, V.	1	Henry
OSBURN, Sarah	2	Washington	OWEN, W. B.	1	Heard
OSGOOD, Albert G.	2	Baker	OWEN, Wm. D.	5	Wilkes
OSHAY, P. M.	1	Sumter	OWEN, Alexander	6	Talbot
OSLIN, Crosby W.	3	Henry	OWEN, Allen F.	5	Talbot
OSLIN, John	8	Troup	OWEN, Daniel	18	Talbot
OSMOND, Jesse	1	Richmond	OWEN, Davis	29	Coweta
OSMOND, John W.	1	Richmond	OWEN, James	19	Talbot
OSMORE, Thos.	4	Randolph	OWEN, John	3	Burke
O'SULLIVAN, Florence	3	Glynn	OWEN, John D.	17	Talbot
OSWALD, ---	1	DeKalb	OWEN, John D.	7	Talbot
OSWALT, John	1	Franklin	OWEN, John H.	7	Coweta
OTT, George	3	Chatham	OWEN, Laben	6	Stewart
OUGALSBAY, D.	4	Elbert	OWEN, Stephen D.	1	Talbot
OUGLESBAY, A.	9	Elbert	OWEN, William	6	Burke
OUGLESBAY, D.	2	Elbert	OWEN, William W.	14	Talbot
OUGLESBAY, J.	2	Elbert	OWENBY, W. B.	7	Union
OUGLESBAY, James	2	Elbert	OWENBY, Porter	1	Union
OUGLESBAY, R.	5	Elbert	OWENBY, Powell	16	Lumpkin
OUGLESBAY, R.	1	Elbert	OWENS, Malachi	1	Heard
OUGLESBAY, W.	37	Elbert	OWENS, Coleman	1	Meriwether
OULAS, Daniel	2	Elbert	OWENS, Coleman	1	Meriwether
OUSLEY, N.	3	Bibb	OWENS, Daniel	1	Marion
OUSLEY, P.	5	Bibb	OWENS, Daniel	8	Troup
OUSLEY, Robt.	3	Bibb	OWENS, Francis F.	1	Pike
OUTLAW, Allen	1	Laurens	OWENS, Geo. W. agent	4	Habersham
OUTLAW, M. N. B.	9	Lee	OWENS, George	4	Merriwether
OUTLAW, Morgan	15	Emanual	OWENS, J. T.	6	Meriwether
OUTLAW, Morgan A.	3	Emanual	OWENS, Jesse	6	Marion
OUTLAW, Mrs. Jane	2	Houston	OWENS, John	11	Burke
OUTLAW, Jordan	5	Washington	OWENS, John	6	Walker
OUTLAW, William L.	11	Dooly	OWENS, Joshua	1	Franklin
OUTMAN, David	2	Cherokee	OWENS, Martha	6	Franklin
OVERBY, B. H.	6	Newton	OWENS, R.	3	Muscogee
OVERBY, H.	23	Jackson	OWENS, Susan	1	Marion
OVERBY, B. M.	6	Stewart	OWENS, William	2	Gordon
OVERBY, E. H.	11	Clarke	OWENS, Wm.	3	Newton
OVERBY, L. B. & T. J.	6	Coweta	OWENS, Edmond	5	Putnam
OVERBY, Thos.	17	Coweta	OWENS, Geo. W.	183	Camden
OVERBY, Wm.	12	Coweta	OWENS, George W.	107	Chatham

Name	Number	County	Name	Number	County
OWENS, J. W.	2	Decatur	PACE, Davis	40	Baker
OWENS, John	1	Putnam	PACE, Drury	3	DeKalb
OWENS, R.	14	Crawford	PACE, John	7	Baker
OWENS, William J.	2	Baldwin	PACE, Martha	2	Coweta
OWENS, William J.	12	Richmond	PACE, Solomon	7	DeKalb
OWENS?	none	Lee	PACE, Susan	34	Columbia
OWENSBY, Edwin	6	Heard	PACE, Thos.	1	Carroll
OWENSBY, Matthew	1	Heard	PACE?, Mathew	18	Oglethorpe
OWENSBY, Thomas	2	Heard	PACETTY, John	3	Camden
OWIN, Miner	7	Newton	PACETTY, Dennis	2	Camden
OWIN, T.	1	Elbert	PACKARD, C.	7	Murray
OWINGBY, T.	5	Henry	PACKARD, Erathus	21	Merriwether
OWINS, James	9	Meriwether	PADEN, M. W.	1	Cherokee
OWINS, Mary	1	Twiggs	PADEN, Samuel	1	Gwinnett
OWINS, Sarah	1	Jefferson	PADEN, James	8	DeKalb
OXFORD, E. B.	5	Henry	PADEN, Thomas	1	DeKalb
OXFORD, Edward	3	Marion	PADGETTE, Susan	2	Tatnall
OXFORD, John	7	Walker	PADJET, Elijah	1	Muscogee
OXFORD, Tilman	4	Monroe	PAGE, James J.	4	Washington
OXFORD, William	16	Monroe	PAGE, John	3	Washington
OXLEY, Hardy	1	Randolph	PAGE, Joseph H.	5	Washington
OZBURN, J. M.	1	Fayette	PAGE, Joseph H.	4	Washington
OZELY, J.	13	Elbert	PAGE, McKenneth	3	Macon
OZENCRAFT, W. T.	4	Morgan	PAGE, Mrs. N.	3	Meriwether
OZIER, Jacob	8	Randolph	PAGE, Solomon	5	Emanual
PACE, Alfred G.	1	Pike	PAGE, Ebenezar	21	Richmond
PACE, Alexander	7	Upson	PAGE, G. H.	41	Coweta
PACE, C. D.	23	Newton	PAGE, John W. R.	7	Richmond
PACE, C. D.	1	Newton	PAGE, Leonard	3	Sumter
PACE, Clement	21	Muscogee	PAGE, William T.	7	Richmond
PACE, Elcuna	16	Harris	PAGE, Wm. H.	6	Upson
PACE, Elizabeth	1	Houston	PAIN, Flan	3	Monroe
PACE, F.	5	Twiggs	PAIN, Mary	6	Elbert
PACE, Hardy	24	Cobb	PAINE, George M.	25	Clarke
PACE, John	1	Heard	PAINE, Milton	26	Clarke
PACE, John	21	Muscogee	PAINE, Samuel T.	13	Floyd
PACE, John C.	2	Washington	PAINE, Dr. Charles R.	33	Baldwin
PACE, Noel	13	Troup	PAINE, Eli	21	Clarke
PACE, Noel A.	5	Heard	PAINE, Martha	8	Talbot
PACE, Solomon	4	Upson	PAINE, O. E.	2	Floyd
PACE, Stephen	53	Harris	PAIR, W. M.	5	Henry
PACE, Stephen	7	Heard	PALIN, John M.	4	Chatham
PACE, Thomas B.	3	Twiggs	PALMER, Aaron	10	Lumpkin
PACE, Thomas T.	7	Harris	PALMER, D. B.	9	Glynn
PACE, Tyron	5	Effingham	PALMER, E. T.	1	Forsyth
PACE, Usel?	17	Oglethorpe	PALMER, Edmund	10	Clarke
PACE, W. H. C.	6	Newton	PALMER, George A.	8	Jefferson
PACE, William	2	Wilkinson	PALMER, Israel	26	Hancock
PACE, William H.	5	Upson	PALMER, James M.	4	Hancock
PACE, William Sen.	28	Muscogee	PALMER, Jesse	6	Lumpkin
PACE, William T.	7	Jasper	PALMER, John	3	Fayette
PACE, Bazel	8	Randolph	PALMER, Josiah	2	Heard
PACE, Bryant	1	Stewart	PALMER, Mary	10	Fayette
PACE, Charles	1	DeKalb	PALMER, Mary A.	10	Hancock

Name	Number	County	Name	Number	County
PALMER, Samuel	27	McIntosh	PARHAM, Robert N.	31	Merriwether
PALMER, Silas	3	Lumpkin	PARHAM, S. A.	19	Merriwether
PALMER, Benjamin	47	Burke	PARHAM, Seth	1	Pike
PALMER, Daniel	1	Stewart	PARHAM, Thomas S.	26	Merriwether
PALMER, David	13	Burke	PARHAM, J. S.	2	Crawford
PALMER, Edmund	48	Burke	PARHAM, John	3	Putnam
PALMER, Geo. W.	10	Wilkes	PARHAM, R. C.	17	Crawford
PALMER, George R.	14	Burke	PARHAM, Robt.	26	Putnam
PALMER, Isaac O.	4	Troup	PARHAM, W. T.	2	Crawford
PALMER, J. A.	12	Troup	PARHAM, William H.	1	Warren
PALMER, James	10	Richmond	PARIS, H. C.	2	Greene
PALMER, John B.	1	Richmond	PARIS, Isaac	5	Burke
PALMER, Jonathan	37	Richmond	PARIS, Parphenia	3	Sumter
PALMER, Richard	1	Dooly	PARISH, Jonathan	3	Camden
PALMER, Samuel B.	1	Washington	PARISH, Absalom	4	Bullock
PALMER, Wm. estate	25	Burke	PARISH, Ansel	14	Bullock
PALMER,			PARISH, Ansel	4	Bullock
(Wright Agent)	16	Warren	PARISH, C. A.	2	Richmond
PALMORE, Elijah	1	Walton	PARISH, G. F. Agt.	4	Richmond
PALMORE, Geo. H.	3	Carroll	PARISH, Hardy O.	4	Warren
PALMORE, F. D.	4	Carroll	PARISH, John S.	3	Taliaferro
PALMORE, George	4	Talbot	PARISH, Mary V.	5	Richmond
PALMORE, J. F.	3	Stewart	PARISH, Wm	18	Camden
PALMORE, Solomon	8	Carroll	PARK, A.	39	Meriwether
PALNUS, Caroline L.	2	Chaham	PARK, B. H.	2	Jackson
PALOMON ?, John	10	Wilkinson	PARK, C. M.	13	Greene
PANE, L. G.	2	Harris	PARK, Joseph	6	Meriwether
PANE, Rowana	30	Columbia	PARK, Josiah	1	Marion
PANNEL, E. J.	1	Columbia	PARK, Julia N.	9	Merriwether
PANUM?, John	1	Paulding	PARK, Mrs. Sarah	9	Merriwether
PAPAT, Samuel M.	3	Chatham	PARK, R. C.	4	Jackson
PAPE ?, Mary	2	Stewart	PARK, Richard S.	101	Morgan
PAPOT, R. D.	3	Chatham	PARK, Robert W.	5	Floyd
PARADICE, Margarett	6	Lincoln	PARK, Russel J.	11	Jackson
PARADICE, William	7	Lincoln	PARK, Samuel	12	Pike
PARADISE, Elizabeth	8	Jefferson	PARK, Sidenham R.	7	Newton
PARADISE, John D.	4	Washington	PARK, Thomas Y.	3	Walker
PARAMORE, Jas	13	Randolph	PARK, William	2	Meriwether
PARAMORE, Rolling	13	Stewart	PARK, Wm. L.	7	Marion
PARAMORE, S.	51	Decatur	PARK, J. G.	5	Butts
PARAMORE, William	1	Stewart	PARK, Lenard	2	Coweta
PARDUE, Reubin	1	Hancock	PARK, Lewis C.	9	Columbia
PARDUE, Samuel A.	10	Hancock	PARK, Susan	12	Baldwin
PARHAM, Augustus W.	2	Warren	PARK, Wm.	21	Jackson
PARHAM, Benjamin	28	Merriwether	PARKER, West	3	Clarke
PARHAM, Darling	8	Oglethorpe	PARKER, A.	15	Henry
PARHAM, Elijah	20	Warren	PARKER, Benj. B.	1	Franklin
PARHAM, Frances E.	3	Warren	PARKER, B. D.	21	Twiggs
PARHAM, Frances H.	4	Warren	PARKER, Chas.	1	Henry
PARHAM, J. J.	2	Elbert	PARKER, Christopher	14	Monroe
PARHAM, John A.	14	Monroe	PARKER, D. M .	2	Newton
PARHAM, Jonas	7	Harris	PARKER, Dudley H.	5	Floyd
PARHAM, Mary	1	Elbert	PARKER, Elizabeth	1	Walton
PARHAM, Nathaniel	11	Warren	PARKER, Emanual	1	Greene

Name	Number	County	Name	Number	County
PARKER, G. W .	3	Franklin	PARKER, James	2	Sumter
PARKER, George D.	5	Upson	PARKER, James	10	Talbot
PARKER, George W.	1	Monroe	PARKER, Jas.	12	Coweta
PARKER, Henry W.	3	Henry	PARKER, Jell	2	Bibb
PARKER, Hilliard J.	2	Newton	PARKER, Jeptha	2	Stewart
PARKER, Isaac	5	Newton	PARKER, John	4	Bibb
PARKER, Isaac L.	2	Jasper	PARKER, John	11	Campbell
PARKER, Isiah	7	Harris	PARKER, John	1	DeKalb
PARKER, J.	1	Henry	PARKER, John W.	9	Talbot
PARKER, J. M.	3	Lee	PARKER, Joseph R.	5	Taliaferro
PARKER, J. T.	13	Jefferson	PARKER, Mathew	7	Screven
PARKER, James	1	Harris	PARKER, O. C.	5	Chatham
PARKER, James	1	Houston	PARKER, R.	75	Decatur
PARKER, James	5	Marion	PARKER, Richard	21	Taliaferro
PARKER, James A.	21	Jefferson	PARKER, Robert	4	Stewart
PARKER, John	4	Monroe	PARKER, Samuel	3	Screven
PARKER, John	42	Twiggs	PARKER, Simeon	38	Talbot
PARKER, John P.	2	Franklin	PARKER, Thomas	6	Screven
PARKER, Jonathan	6	Laurens	PARKER, William	14	Jefferson
PARKER, Joseph C.	1	Monroe	PARKER, William	15	Talbot
PARKER, Lewis	1	Washington	PARKER, William	25	Telfair
PARKER, Lucy	7	Upson	PARKER, William J.	6	Lee
PARKER, M. E.	14	Hancock	PARKER, Wm. B.	11	Bibb
PARKER, Mary W.	5	Clarke	PARKER?, Benjamin	1	Lumpkin
PARKER, Mrs. Anna S.	1	Liberty	PARKES, J.	29	Wilkinson
PARKER, Mrs. Sarah	1	Houston	PARKINS, Walker	7	Morgan
PARKER, Peyton	5	Marion	PARKINSON, John W.	1	Cass
PARKER, Rachal	5	Monroe	PARKMAN, Daniel	5	Muscogee
PARKER, Robert	1	Walker	PARKMAN, Henry	5	Merriwether
PARKER, Robt. F.	1	Greene	PARKMAN, John	8	Muscogee
PARKER, Sheba	4	Twiggs	PARKMAN, Richard G.	1	Muscogee
PARKER, Stephen	1	Muscogee	PARKMAN, William	3	Muscogee
PARKER, Susannah	1	Warren	PARKMAN, Wand	4	Talbot
PARKER, Theophilus	4	Thomas	PARKS & DAY	5	Murray
PARKER, Thomas D.	3	Jefferson	PARKS, A.	4	Elbert
PARKER, Thos.	15	Wilkinson	PARKS, C. D.	13	Merriwether
PARKER, W. H.	2	Forsyth	PARKS, Dr. Richard	1	Gwinnett
PARKER, West	18	Marion	PARKS, Elizabeth	30	Coweta
PARKER, West S.	1	Marion	PARKS, John	1	Union
PARKER, William	2	Monroe	PARKS, H. H.	1	Franklin
PARKER, William	17	Troup	PARKS, J. W.	18	Lincoln
PARKER, William H.	5	McIntosh	PARKS, J. W.	3	Lincoln
PARKER, William R.	4	Fayette	PARKS, John	8	Gilmer
PARKER, Wm. C.	23	Wilkinson	PARKS, Lewis	33	Lincoln
PARKER, Zephaniah	4	Muscogee	PARKS, Lewis G.	9	Lincoln
PARKER, A. M.	2	DeKalb	PARKS, Ned	3	Greene
PARKER, Austin	4	Putnam	PARKS, Samuel C.	26	Muscogee
PARKER, Barney	1	Sumter	PARKS, Thos. H.	30	Coweta
PARKER, Elizabeth	4	Sumter	PARKS, William	9	Lincoln
PARKER, G.	2	Bibb	PARKS, William J.	9	Franklin
PARKER, Hardy	3	Screven	PARKS, William W.	1	Jasper
PARKER, Isiah	3	DeKalb	PARKS, Byrd	17	Coweta
PARKER, Jacob	2	Stewart	PARKS, Franklin	5	Coweta
PARKER, James	14	Screven	PARKS, Gabril	16	Monroe

Name	Number	County	Name	Number	County
PARMELER, A. C.	3	Upson	PASCHAL, William	60	Lincoln
PARMENTER, Henry	2	Camden	PASCHAL, William	1	Lincoln
PARMENTER, Sarah	4	Chatham	PASCHAL, Asa	40	Columbia
PARMER, Isabella	6	Washington	PASCHAL, Jerry	14	Columbia
PARMER, Rebecca	2	Monroe	PASCHALL, Benj.	1	Wilkes
PARR, Acy V.	12	Monroe	PASCHALL, Dennis	1	Wilkes
PARR, Daniel W.	16	Houston	PASCHALL, Dennis	28	Wilkes
PARR, Leonard	2	Monroe	PASCHALL, Saml.	10	Wilkes
PARR, Charles D.	1	DeKalb	PASCO, John	8	Cherokee
PARRAMORE, Adam	12	Thomas	PASEUR?, John U.	2	Clarke
PARRAMORE, Everett	20	Thomas	PASS ?, Henry	4	Taliaferro
PARRAMORE, John C.	7	Thomas	PASS, John	1	Gordon
PARRAMORE, Noash	14	Thomas	PASS, Edmund	12	Coweta
PARRETT, Frances	7	Jackson	PASSMORE, Abraham	2	Macon
PARRIS, N. H.	3	Oglethorpe	PASSMORE, Alex	2	Wilkinson
PARRIS, Robert M.	14	Dade	PASSMORE, James	4	Harris
PARRISH, Absalom	3	Lowndes	PASSMORE, John	45	Harris
PARRISH, Ansil	1	Lowndes	PASSMORE, John	5	Muscogee
PARRISH, Ezekiel M.	3	Lowndes	PASSMORE, Josephus	6	Marion
PARRISH, H.	2	Troup	PASSMORE, Miley	6	Macon
PARRISH, J. H.	1	Pulaski	PASSMORE, Nathan	17	Harris
PARRISH, James	1	Lowndes	PASSMORE, Rebecca	4	Pike
PARRISH, Jonathan	102	Jones	PASSMORE, Seabon	5	Stewart
PARRISH, Josiah	5	Lowndes	PASSMORE, Thomas J.	1	DeKalb
PARRISH, Matthew A.	2	Lowndes	PATE, Freeman	1	Warren
PARRISH, Wm.	1	Lowndes	PATE, J. W.	1	Washington
PARRISH, Hezekiah	13	Emanual	PATE, Jesse	7	Jackson
PARROT, George	6	Richmond	PATE, Jesse	5	Warren
PARROT, James	18	Stewart	PATE, Jesse A.	1	Jackson
PARROTT, Curtis	4	Greene	PATE, John F.	5	Walton
PARROTT, Mrs. L. B.	23	Hancock	PATE, John R. Agent	29	Warren
PARSONS, James M.	26	Monroe	PATE, Nathan	7	Warren
PARSONS, Matthew J.	5	Burke	PATE, Thomas	1	Fayette
PARSONS, Elisha	4	Chatham	PATE, Wm.,		
PARSONS, Mrs. Sarah	10	Burke	Louisa & M.	1	Fayette
PARSONS, Thos. A.	20	Burke	PATHILLO, James	2	Cobb
PARTAIN, Enoch	16	Thomas	PATILLO, Charles F.	7	Houston
PARTEE, Abner	10	Morgan	PATILLO, James	9	Muscogee
PARTEE, W. A.	6	Greene	PATILLO, John	15	Harris
PARTIN, Kindred	9	Laurens	PATILLO, Mrs.	2	Muscogee
PARTRIDGE, Isaac	8	Harris	PATILLO, Wesley H.	1	Cobb
PARTRIDGE, Jesse	11	Meriwether	PATMAN, David W.	11	Oglethorpe
PARTRIDGE, N.	16	Meriwether	PATMAN, Elias B.	5	Oglethorpe
PARTRIDGE, William	4	Meriwether	PATMAN, J. W.	3	Greene
PASCAL, Wm.	43	Putnam	PATMAN, Wm.	30	Clarke
PASCALL, W. W.	2	Putnam	PATMAN, James P.	2	Floyd
PASCALL, W.W.	1	Putnam	PATMON ?, Edmund	1	Richmond
PASCHAL, Dennis	8	Lincoln	PATNER, J. V.	5	Franklin
PASCHAL, Eliza	3	Upson	PATNER, James S.	2	Franklin
PASCHAL, Jeremiah	13	Lincoln	PATON, David	18	Pike
PASCHAL, John	31	Morgan	PATRIC, James	6	Newton
PASCHAL, John L.	29	Lincoln	PATRICK, James	19	Morgan
PASCHAL, Milton	28	Lincoln	PATRICK, John H.	25	Franklin
PASCHAL, Samuel	6	Heard	PATRICK, Josiah	7	Oglethorpe

Name	Number	County	Name	Number	County
PATRICK, Matthew	1	Murray	PATTERSON,		
PATRICK, Nedleston	6	Dooly	William J.	3	Sumter
PATRICK, R. N.	3	Walton	PATTESON, David	2	Oglethorpe
PATRICK, Reuben	5	Dooly	PATTILLO, J.	11	Henry
PATRICK, Wiley	3	Henry	PATTILLO, B. F.	2	Henry
PATRICK, Wm. S.	19	Marion	PATTILLO, Harrison	9	Columbia
PATRICK, Catherine	2	Talbot	PATTILLO, Leroy	1	Walton
PATRICK, Churchwell	8	Dooly	PATTMAN, A. C.	3	Jackson
PATRICK, Pernal	9	Dooly	PATTMAN, M. A.	4	Jackson
PATRIDGE, Jesse	7	Upson	PATTMON, Henry	5	Madison
PATRIDGE, M.	1	Troup	PATTON, ?	4	Lumpkin
PATRIE, Elizabeth	17	Newton	PATTON, A. K.	20	Floyd
PATTEN, Samuel	3	Madison	PATTON, A. L.	1	Floyd
PATTEN, Samuel	2	Monroe	PATTON, Elizabeth	28	Fayette
PATTEN, Thomas E.	5	Walker	PATTON, Elizabeth	3	Fayette
PATTEN, Nash	4	Richmond	PATTON, Emily J.	3	Chatham
PATTENT, George	4	Bibb	PATTON, J. N,.	6	Harris
PATTERSON, Amos	1	Gilmer	PATTON, Mathew P.	2	Madison
PATTERSON,			PATTON, Julius M.	7	Baldwin
Augustus L.	1	Burke	PATTON, Robert C.	7	Cass
PATTERSON, David	5	Monroe	PATTYSHAIl, N.	1	Wilkinson
PATTERSON, George	6	Franklin	PAUL, A. Y.	9	Henry
PATTERSON, Jesse	9	Troup	PAUL, Catherine	2	Marion
PATTERSON, Hearndon	15	Jones	PAUL, Charles	3	Jones
PATTERSON, James	25	Elbert	PAUL, Elizabeth	15	Lee
PATTERSON, James C.	11	Gwinnett	PAUL, James	2	Twiggs
PATTERSON, James P.	10	Merriwether	PAUL, John T.	4	Twiggs
PATTERSON, John	5	Cass	PAUL, Marshall	10	Marion
PATTERSON, John	1	Union	PAUL, Moses	15	Marion
PATTERSON, John T.	8	Monroe	PAUL, Moses	2	Marion
PATTERSON, John W.	10	Muscogee	PAUL, Robt.	4	Marion
PATTERSON, Joseph B.	8	Jones	PAUL, Robert	18	Twiggs
PATTERSON, Josiah	2	Gwinnett	PAUL, William	20	Jones
PATTERSON, Mary	7	Cass	PAULETT, Jesse	9	Morgan
PATTERSON,			PAULETT, Henry	11	Campbell
Nathaniel Jr.	12	Camden	PAULK, G.	7	Irwin
PATTERSON, Pleasant	1	Franklin	PAULK, H.	4	Irwin
PATTERSON, Robert	24	Jefferson	PAULK, J.	11	Irwin
PATTERSON, Robert C.	8	Muscogee	PAULK, J.	9	Irwin
PATTERSON, Robt.	1	Muscogee	PAULK, J.	6	Irwin
PATTERSON, W.	7	Elbert	PAULK, M.	4	Irwin
PATTERSON, Wiley	20	Jones	PAULK, M.	1	Wilkinson
PATTERSON, William	4	Monroe	PAUL, Micajah	1	Wilkinson
PATTERSON, D. S.	1	Butts	PAULK, Mrs.	5	Irwin
PATTERSON, Job	16	Stewart	PAULLIN, Ann	4	Chatham
PATTERSON, John	3	Decatur	PAULSON, Jonathan	9	Carroll
PATTERSON, Jas. W.	12	Decatur	PAXATON, Jas. M.	2	Camden
PATTERSON, M.	61	Crawford	PAXON, Benj. F.	4	Walton
PATTERSON, Miss Mary	1	Burke	PAYNE, Benjamin	2	Lumpkin
PATTERSON, N. J. Sen.	30	Camden	PAYNE, David H.	4	Cherokee
PATTERSON, Robert J.	11	Burke	PAYNE, Henry	1	Marion
PATTERSON, William	53	Bryan	PAYNE, James	3	Newton
PATTERSON, William	4	Burke	PAYNE, James B.	5	Newton
			PAYNE, James W.	5	Franklin

Name	Number	County	Name	Number	County
PAYNE, Jerry	1	Lumpkin	PEAK, William	2	Paulding
PAYNE, John H.	5	Troup	PEAKE, William	38	Baker
PAYNE, Mary	8	Franklin	PEAL, James	2	Stewart
PAYNE, Mary	4	Franklin	PEAMENS?, Mrs.	1	Clarke
PAYNE, Pollard	15	Marion	PEANCE, Newton	1	Richmond
PAYNE, Pollard	5	Marion	PEARCE, Alexander	1	Twiggs
PAYNE, R. L.	44	Lee	PEARCE, C.	10	Screven
PAYNE, Sarah	6	Franklin	PEARCE, Elias	19	Twiggs
PAYNE, Thomas	2	Chatham	PEARCE, Jacob	10	Houston
PAYNE, Thomas S.	9	Walker	PEARCE, Jacob	5	Twiggs
PAYNE, Uriah W.	1	Cherokee	PEARCE, Jesse F.	15	Greene
PAYNE, Wm.	1	Marion	PEARCE, John S.	8	Twiggs
PAYNE, Charles T.	1	Richmond	PEARCE, Levi	2	Cass
PAYNE, Edwin	12	DeKalb	PEARCE, Mary M.	17	Thomas
PAYNE, George	7	Bibb	PEARCE, Nancy	1	Greene
PAYNE, H. A.	2	Butts	PEARCE, Theophilus	1	Greene
PAYNE, Mary	1	Richmond	PEARCE, Theopalus	16	Twiggs
PAYNE, Thomas	2	Butts	PEARCE, Thomas	12	Harris
PAYNE, W. L.	6	Crawford	PEARCE, Wiley	1	Gwinnett
PAYSON, James	4	Newton	PEARCE, William	34	Upson
PEABODY, Mrs.	1	Muscogee	PEARCE, Nat.	10	Columbia
PEABODY, N. J.	8	Muscogee	PEARCE, Robert M.	1	Richmond
PEABODY, Wm.	1	Decatur	PEARCE, S. B.	2	Cass
PEACE, John R.	1	Houston	PEARCE, Sarah	2	Talbot
PEACE, Major	5	Hancock	PEARCE, Wiley	14	Decatur
PEACE, Humphrey	1	Columbia	PEARIMAN ?, Jas.	2	Putnam
PEACHECK, M. J.	2	DeKalb	PEARRIN, M.	6	Elbert
PEACOCK, Asa P.	19	Washington	PEARSE ?, G. T.	2	Richmond
PEACOCK, B.	59	Macon	PEARSEY, B. T.	17	Bibb
PEACOCK, Barnes	6	Macon	PEARSON, Christopher	2	Marion
PEACOCK, Benajah	7	Marion	PEARSON, Donald D.	7	Houston
PEACOCK, Dellemar C.	3	Thomas	PEARSON, Evan	4	Gordon
PEACOCK, Exum	3	Macon	PEARSON, James	6	Twiggs
PEACOCK, Howell	3	Thomas	PEARSON, H. A.	4	Henry
PEACOCK, Jesse	2	Wilkinson	PEARSON, James	12	Monroe
PEACOCK, John	14	Houston	PEARSON, Jeremiah	10	Harris
PEACOCK, L.	14	Wilkinson	PEARSON, Jeremiah	77	Jasper
PEACOCK, Moulton	5	Washington	PEARSON, Samuel	2	Wayne
PEACOCK, Raiford	4	Macon	PEARSON, Stephen	82	Hancock
PEACOCK, Richmond H.	1	Liberty	PEARSON, Stephen	1	Harris
PEACOCK, Robert	30	Lowndes	PEARSON, B. O.	10	Dooly
PEACOCK, Robert M. D.	6	Lowndes	PEARSON, Bennajah	8	Telfair
PEACOCK, Thomas P.	13	Morgan	PEARSON, Chesley	1	Talbot
PEACOCK, J. T.	7	DeKalb	PEARSON, Daniel B.	17	Putnam
PEACOCK, Raiford	3	Sumter	PEARSON, James N.	37	Baker
PEACOCK, S. E.	1	Randolph	PEARSON, John	7	Talbot
PEACOCK, W.	7	Washington	PEARSON, John	12	Tatnall
PEACOCK, Washington	70	Upson	PEARSON, John	6	Talbot
PEACOCK, William H.	3	Forsyth	PEARSON, L.	2	Talbot
PEAD, Henry	2	Talbot	PEARSON, Randolph	2	Stewart
PEAK, Henry	1	Paulding	PEARSONS, John	13	Monroe
PEAK, John C.	10	Macon	PEARSONS, Thomas G.	13	Heard
			PEASE, John W.	3	Muscogee
			PEASE, P. P.	8	McIntosh

Name	Number	County	Name	Number	County
PEAVY, David	3	Meriwether	PEGG, Samuel J.	7	DeKalb
PEAVY, Eli	1	Meriwether	PEIFFER, Joanna	4	Richmond
PEAVY, Eli	6	Dooly	PEIRCE, Obadiah	15	Jefferson
PEAVY, Thomas	1	Merriwether	PELLEN, Alexander	6	Cobb
PEAY, Henry T.	1	Richmond	PELOT, Mrs. H. L.	7	Wilkes
PECK, Sidney	5	Glynn	PEMBERTON, J. C.	11	Floyd
PECK, Fenn	2	Chatham	PEMBLE, Charles	1	Richmond
PECK, Ira	30	Twiggs	PEMO, Wm.	16	Chattooga
PECKIM, William	1	Dooly	PENDARUIS, Caleb	9	Wayne
PEDDY, Bradford	9	Muscogee	PENDARVIS, Rachel	9	Wayne
PEDDY, Bradford	3	Muscogee	PENDAVIS, Richard L.	9	Glynn
PEDDY, James H.	4	Washington	PENDERGAST,		
PEDDY, Nancy	11	Heard	Margaret A.	34	Chatham
PEDDY, Wiley	11	Jasper	PENDERGAST, Michail	9	Chatham
PEEBLES, Abram	5	Henry	PENDERGAST, Thos.	1	Chatham
PEEBLES, Delilah	2	Marion	PENDERGRASS, Edwin	2	Jackson
PEEBLES, Dudly	18	Merriwether	PENDERGRASS,		
PEEBLES, Ephraim	2	Jefferson	George H.	1	Newton
PEEBLES, Henry	8	Jefferson	PENDERGRASS, John	18	Jackson
PEEBLES, Henry	1	Marion	PENDERGRASS, Levi	11	Heard
PEEBLES, Howell	1	Jefferson	PENDERGRASS, N. H.	2	Jackson
PEEBLES, J. L.	12	Merriwether	PENDLETON, E. M.	4	Hancock
PEEBLES, Phebe	5	Marion	PENDLY, Wm. R.	1	DeKalb
PEEBLES, Thomas	4	Marion	PENFONTON?, Joseph	1	Oglethorpe
PEED, John	6	Lincoln	PENICK, Joseph	45	Morgan
PEEK, H.	9	Newton	PENICK, S. R.	13	Crawford
PEEK, Hart C.	9	Greene	PENINGTON, Thadius	13	Jasper
PEEK, Henry	1	Newton	PENINGTON, William	1	Pike
PEEK, James	1	Hancock	PENINGTON,		
PEEK, John F.	1	Newton	William R. R.	6	Jasper
PEEK, John M.	15	Hancock	PENLAND, John	1	Union
PEEK, L. C.	16	Hancock	PENN, A.J.	3	Troup
PEEK, Mary	7	Greene	PENN, Benj.	4	Cass
PEEK, Simpson T.	19	Greene	PENN, E.	6	Oglethorpe
PEEKE, Doctor	10	Taliaferro	PENN, James	9	Elbert
PEEKE, James	108	Taliaferro	PENN, James	9	Elbert
PEEKE, James H.	18	Taliaferro	PENN, James	7	Newton
PEEKE, Lockett	15	Taliaferro	PENN, Martha A.	7	Jasper
PEEKE, Thomas	1	Stewart	PENN, W. M.	1	Newton
PEEKE, Thomas J.	4	Taliaferro	PENN, William	5	Monroe
PEEKE, Wm.	109	Taliaferro	PENN, William C.	20	Jasper
PEEKE, Wm. T.	9	Taliaferro	PENN, Benj.	4	Cass
PEEL, Robert	3	Stewart	PENN, Francis	12	Coweta
PEEL, Thomas F.	2	Stewart	PENN, Richard T.	13	Coweta
PEEL, William	9	Talbot	PENNINGTON, C. M.	3	Floyd
PEELE, Robert A.	4	Troup	PENNINGTON, E.	9	Meriwether
PEELER, Berry	8	Hancock	PENNINGTON, H. M.	9	Morgan
PEEPLES, B. M.	81	Morgan	PENNINGTON, Ephraim	2	Campbell
PEEPLES, Drury	3	Gordon	PENNINGTON, F.	3	Randolph
PEEPLES, James D.	16	Jasper	PENNINGTON, Willliam	7	Sumter
PEEPLES, W. T.	3	Hall	PENROE, Martha	2	Burke
PEEPLES, Henry	3	Lowndes	PENROE, Sarah	2	Burke
PEGG, S. G.	1	Fayette	PENTICOST, R. W.	3	Jackson
PEGG, William H.	3	Jasper	PEOPLES, B. W.	2	Morgan

Name	Number	County
PEOPLES, H. B.	4	DeKalb
PEOPLES, Isam	2	Camden
PEOR, R. estate	21	Burke
PEOR?, Allen S. B.	28	Burke
PEPKIN, H. B.	5	Jefferson
PEPPER, F. L.	17	Lee
PEPPEER, John	1	Walton
PEPPER, Sarah P.	15	Lee
PEPPION, Bridges	2	Upson
PERDEN, Elizabeth	14	Upson
PERDEW, Green	6	Upson
PERDEW, Isaac	2	Monroe
PERDEW, J. P.	1	Pike
PERDEW, James	17	Monroe
PERDEW, John	7	Houston
PERDEW, John	8	Monroe
PERDEW, Thomas	2	Wayne
PERDUE, Alfred	3	Monroe
PERDUE, Beacham	7	Meriwether
PERDUE, Benjamin R.	6	Jefferson
PERDUE, Daniel	36	Greene
PERDUE, George L.	6	Jones
PERDUE, James M.	3	Jefferson
PERDUE, John	6	Jefferson
PERDUE, John G.	9	Jefferson
PERDUE, John T.	8	Greene
PERDUE, Linsey	13	Merriwether
PERDUE, Mary	9	Jefferson
PERDUE, Newton	2	Jefferson
PERDUE, Stephen J.	31	Morgan
PERDUE, Wm.	1	Cass
PEREZ, Littleton D.	4	Houston
PERKERSON, J. W.	4	Meriwether
PERKINS, A. L.	7	Monroe
PERKINS, Abraham	35	Greene
PERKINS, Alexander	35	Monroe
PERKINS, Ann	2	Lowndes
PERKINS, Franklin	4	Warren
PERKINS, James	28	Greene
PERKINS, James P.	2	Floyd
PERKINS, Mrs. Elizabeth	10	Houston
PERKINS, Newton	1	Burke
PERKINS, Nicholas	19	Hancock
PERKINS, S. T.	5	Jefferson
PERKINS, Susan	7	Greene
PERKINS, W.	26	Morgan
PERKINS, William	4	Pike
PERKINS, William H.	1	Troup
PERKINS, Zeno	6	Jackson
PERKINS, Absalom	5	Taliaferro
PERKINS, B. H.	3	Randolph
PERKINS, Brinson L.	20	Burke
PERKINS, David	3	Burke

Name	Number	County
PERKINS, Dempsey	8	DeKalb
PERKINS, J. F.	8	Randolph
PERKINS, James	3	Stewart
PERKINS, John B.	12	Dade
PERKINS, John B.	5	Dade
PERKINS, John T.	22	Coweta
PERKINS, Mary A.	2	Taliaferro
PERKINS, Newton	20	Burke
PERKINS, Sydney	15	Bibb
PERKINS, William	2	Talbot
PERKINS, Wm.	8	Stewart
PERKINS, Wm. C.	2	Randolph
PERKINS, Wm. R.	10	Coweta
PERKINS, Wright	2	Talbot
PERKINSON, William	10	Cherokee
PERMILIA?, Mrs.	1	Burke
PERMINTER, John	2	Houston
PERMINTON, Bennet	6	Dooly
PERON, Lewis	31	Merriwether
PERRIN, Susan	54	Columbia
PERRY, ----	5	Early
PERRY, Alen	5	Macon
PERRY, Alexander J.	2	Burke
PERRY, Barden J.	1	Bibb
PERRY, Clarise	39	Newton
PERRY, Edward	3	Laurens
PERRY, Jesse	5	Lincoln
PERRY, Jesse	1	Lincoln
PERRY, Jesse M.	21	Morgan
PERRY, Joel	5	Marion
PERRY, Joel W.	28	Early
PERRY, John	20	Laurens
PERRY, John	24	Liberty
PERRY, John	1	Pulaski
PERRY, John B.	1	Early
PERRY, John O.	6	Liberty
PERRY, John W.	1	Muscogee
PERRY, Joseph	3	Laurens
PERRY, Joseph	2	Marion
PERRY, Joshua	5	Early
PERRY, M. W.	67	Lee
PERRY, Mark A.	2	Marion
PERRY, Miles M.	2	Jasper
PERRY, N.	13	Merriwether
PERRY, Obed	3	Troup
PERRY, O. F.	12	Chattooga
PERRY, P. N.	5	Jefferson
PERRY, Paschal	1	Muscogee
PERRY, Reddock	2	Marion
PERRY, Terrel	23	Houston
PERRY, Washington	2	Monroe
PERRY, William	14	Muscogee
PERRY, William	10	Muscogee
PERRY, William A.	12	Jasper

Name	Number	County	Name	Number	County
PERRY, William M.	10	Harris	PESTLE, Jacob	8	Hall
PERRY, Bird	6	Columbia	PESTLE, John	4	Hall
PERRY, Brigs	37	Newton	PETERMAN, B.	9	Oglethorpe
PERRY, Calvin	3	Dooly	PETERMAN, Francis	2	Oglethorpe
PERRY, Charlton	16	Talbot	PETERMAN, Henry G.	11	Oglethorpe
PERRY, Elias	30	Bryan	PETERS, Balaam	6	Jones
PERRY, George S.	2	Burke	PETERS, James C.	1	Walton
PERRY, George W.	9	Newton	PETERS, Joseph C.	3	Macon
PERRY, Isaac	3	Bryan	PETERS, Lewis	30	Harris
PERRY, J. D.	4	Burke	PETERS, Lewis M.	1	Macon
PERRY, J. G.	27	Stewart	PETERS, Middleton	19	Harris
PERRY, James	2	Dooly	PETERS, Richard	9	DeKalb
PERRY, James C.	5	Columbia	PETERS, William	7	Lowndes
PERRY, James L.	4	Coweta	PETERS, William B.	3	Houston
PERRY, Jetson	4	Baldwin	PETERS, Jno.	2	Randolph
PERRY, Joel	4	Columbia	PETERSON, Alexander	1	Montgomery
PERRY, Joseph M.	1	Burke	PETERSON, Daniel	3	Randolph
PERRY, King W.	3	Coweta	PETERSON, Eliza	2	Burke
PERRY, Mary	14	Stewart	PETERSON, James	2	Clinch
PERRY, Mrs. Mary	1	Liberty	PETERSON, John	4	Montgomery
PERRY, Mrs. Sarah A.	6	Burke	PETERSON, Josiah S.	3	Clarke
PERRY, Oliver H.	10	Burke	PETERSON, Angelina	11	Randolph
PERRY, Sarah	9	Bibb	PETERSON, Charles	3	Randolph
PERRY, W. H. C.	15	Burke	PETERSON, Robt. B.	23	Randolph
PERRY, William B.	3	Stewart	PETOL, Stephen A.	2	Chatham
PERRY, Wm. R. agent	21	Crawford	PETTARD, Davis	1	Coweta
PERRYMAN, A. G.	4	Talbot	PETTEY, Littleton	22	Newton
PERRYMAN, Elisha	11	Richmond	PETTEY, Wiley	7	Cherokee
PERRYMAN, Elisha	72	Putnam	PETTIE, Mary Ann	5	Dooly
PERRYMAN, Elisha P.	3	Warren	PETTIE, A. R.	8	Dooly
PERRYMAN, Freeman	9	Putnam	PETTIE, B. G.	9	Dooly
PERRYMAN, Jeremiah	2	Warren	PETTIGREW, Wm	3	Putnam
PERRYMAN, J.S.	6	Putnam	PETTIS, Davis A.	1	Lee
PERRYMAN, James	15	Talbot	PETTIT, B.	4	Henry
PERSOLL, John	10	Newton	PETTIT, Nancy	5	Columbia
PERSON, Shadrick	7	Stewart	PETTUS, Ann	2	Wilkes
PERSONS, Benjamin	21	Jasper	PETTUS, Isabella	7	Chatham
PERSONS, Deanna	22	Upson	PETTUS, S. G.	84	Wilkes
PERSONS, Jeremiah	4	Monroe	PETTUS, S. G. Jun.	28	Wilkes
PERSONS, Lovett	11	Monroe	PETTY, Allen	3	Floyd
PERSONS, Pinkny	23	Monroe	PETTY, James T.	11	Oglethorpe
PERSONS, Sarah	14	Warren	PETTY, P. T.	1	Oglethorpe
PERSONS, Thomas	14	Heard	PETTY, Thomas	1	Cobb
PERSONS, Thomas F.	123	Warren	PETTY, Luke	1	Bibb
PERSONS, Amos J.	6	Coweta	PETTYJOHN, Jas.	3	Jackson
PERSONS, G. W.	77	Crawford	PETUL?, Simson	61	Meriwether
PERSONS, Nancy	9	Coweta	PEUREFOY, M. C.	10	Monroe
PERSONS, Thos. H.	16	Talbot	PEURIFOY,		
PERTEET, Elizabeth	12	Wilkes	Benjamin W.	30	Jasper
PERTEET, Martha	8	Wilkes	PEURIFOY, John	4	Jasper
PERTUS, Wm. K.	18	Wilkes	PEVERSON, Jas. N.	3	Gordon
PERULENTOR ?,			PEVY, Shadrick	1	Cobb
Wm. F.	5	Richmond	PEW, Elizabeth	6	Hall
PERVIS, William	2	Dooly	PEW, Martin	2	Hall

Name	Number	County	Name	Number	County
PEW, William	1	Upson	PHILIPS, S.	3	Crawford
PEY, Curtis	3	Troup	PHILIPS, S. J.	2	Campbell
PHARR, Alexandeer	50	Newton	PHILIPS, Stephen	1	Talbot
PHELPS, Aquilla	36	Jasper	PHELIPS, William	1	Sumter
PHELPS, Augustus	39	Warren	PHILLIPS, B.	6	Screven
PHELPS, D. S.	7	Hancock	PHILLIPS, Abner	2	Cherokee
PHELPS, Elizabeth	2	Jasper	PHILLIPS, Ann	9	Screven
PHELPS, Henry	37	Pulaski	PHILLIPS, Anthony	9	Emanual
PHELPS, O. C.	4	Monroe	PHILLIPS, Ashley	14	Lee
PHELPS, Sarah P.	1	Pulaski	PHILLIPS, Daniel	8	Harris
PHENEZY & CLAYTON	2	Richmond	PHILLIPS, David M.	12	Monroe
PHIFER, S.	2	Henry	PHILLIPS, David R.	2	Gwinnett
PHILBRICK, Samuel	5	Chatham	PHILLIPS, Dennis	3	Franklin
PHILIP, Alex.	1	Richmond	PHILLIPS, Drury	2	Emanual
PHILIP, Robert	3	Richmond	PHILLIPS, Edmund	10	Newton
PHILIPS, ?	2	Muscogee	PHILLIPS, Elijah	28	Meriwether
PHILIPS, Ambros	18	Harris	PHILLIPS, Ephraim	1	Emanual
PHILIPS, Exam. estate	32	Pulaski	PHILLIPS, George D.	38	Habersham
PHILIPS, Exaws?	33	Pulaski	PHILLIPS, Green	6	Monroe
PHILIPS, Frances	8	Jones	PHILLIPS, H.	10	Troup
PHILIPS, Gathara	1	Burke	PHILLIPS, Haden	17	Meriwether
PHILIPS, Henry	1	Chatham	PHILLIPS, H. D.	9	Troup
PHILIPS, J.	17	Troup	PHILLIPS, Hamit	6	Troup
PHILIPS, J. A. P.	11	Pulaski	PHILLIPS, Henry	3	Walton
PHILIPS, Jas.	7	Pulaski	PHILLIPS, J.	17	Troup
PHILIPS, John	11	Montgomery	PHILLIPS, J. C.	16	Meriwether
PHILIPS, Joseph	3	Montgomery	PHILLIPS, J. H.	19	Meriwether
PHILIPS, Leonard	13	Campbell	PHILLIPS, J. W.	18	Meriwether
PHILIPS, Levi	17	Campbell	PHILLIPS, James S.	20	Troup
PHILIPS, Mark	3	Montgomery	PHILLIPS, John	1	Early
PHILIPS, Micajah	1	Jefferson	PHILLIPS, John B. M.	6	Jasper
PHILIPS, Micajah	4	Montgomery	PHILLIPS, John B.	9	Troup
PHILIPS, Patrick	6	Montgomery	PHILLIPS, John H.	7	Meriwether
PHILIPS, Pleasant J.	18	Harris	PHILLIPS, Joseph	8	Laurens
PHILIPS, Polly	5	Cass	PHILLIPS, Joseph L.	9	Troup
PHILIPS, W. R.	11	Pike	PHILLIPS, Lancelot	15	Greene
PHILIPS, Wilder	7	Harris	PHILLIPS, Mark	8	Meriwether
PHILIPS, William	15	Jasper	PHILLIPS, Mark	2	Walton
PHILIPS, William L.	10	Jones	PHILLIPS, Nathan	25	Monroe
PHILIPS, Yarby	7	Harris	PHILLIPS, Noah	9	Newton
PHILIPS, Zacheus	1	Marion	PHILLIPS, Sherrod	9	Emanual
PHILIPS, Arington H.	11	Sumter	PHILLIPS, Thomas	9	Walton
PHILIPS, G.W.	7	Stewart	PHILLIPS, Uriah	1	Gordon
PHILIPS, J. D.	1	Cass	PHILLIPS, W. R.	21	Pike
PHILIPS, J. W.	1	Campbell	PHILLIPS, Wiley	27	Jasper
PHILIPS, James	16	DeKalb	PHILLIPS, William	10	Walton
PHILIPS, James R.	2	Campbell	PHILLIPS, William D.	11	Troup
PHILIPS, Jas			PHILLIPS, William S.	7	Chatham
for estate of PHILIPS, E.	32	Pulaski	PHILLIPS, Wm. A.	13	Meriwether
PHILIPS, John	8	Taliaferro	PHILLIPS, Wm. D.	14	Marion
PHILIPS, John M.	4	DeKalb	PHILLIPS, Ab	1	Columbia
PHILIPS, Lewellen	5	Sumter	PHILLIPS, Abraham	22	Stewart
PHILIPS, Rachal C.	9	DeKalb	PHILLIPS, Ashley	4	Sumter
PHILIPS, Robert	2	Cass	PHILLIPS, David T.	24	Screven

244

Name	Number	County	Name	Number	County
PHILLIPS, Ellis	7	Columbia	PICQUET, Antoine	20	Richmond
PHILLIPS, J.	2	Decatur	PICQUET, Autorn ?	5	Richmond
PHILLIPS, J. W.	8	Butts	PIERCE, Axom	1	Meriwether
PHILLIPS, John	1	Baker	PIERCE, E.	8	Walker
PHILLIPS, John	1	Campbell	PIERCE, Emilia	2	Wilkinson
PHILLIPS, Joseph	3	Columbia	PIERCE, George	10	Newton
PHILLIPS, Joseph B.	1	Baker	PIERCE, Lovick	31	Muscogee
PHILLIPS, Kizeah	10	Emanual	PIERCE, Lovick	8	Muscogee
PHILLIPS, Mathew	4	Columbia	PIERCE, Micajah	3	Meriwether
PHILLIPS, Stephen	5	Talbot	PIERCE, Milly	3	Jefferson
PHILLIPS, William	10	Columbia	PIERCE, Peter	4	Macon
PHILLIPS, William	2	Richmond	PIERCE, Thos.	52	Burke
PHILPOT, David A.	8	Richmond	PIERCE, Elijah	3	Stewart
PHILPOT, Enos M.	1	Troup	PIERCE, Haywood	2	Randolph
PHILPOT, Henry R.	2	Richmond	PIERCE, J.	1	Randolph
PHILPOT, James C.	1	Richmond	PIERCE, Neel	7	Baker
PHILPOT, Mary	6	Richmond	PIERCE, S. W.	3	Stewart
PHILPOTT, David	33	Heard	PIERCE, William G.	4	Baker
PHILPOTT, David A.	4	Heard	PIERCE, William H.	5	Baker
PHILPOTT, Reuben B.	11	Heard	PIERSON, James	3	Madison
PHILPS, John	1	Elbert	PIERSON, Nancy	1	Early
PHILPS, G. W.	4	Randolph	PIERSON, Wm.	1	Henry
PHINAZEE, Hiram	22	Monroe	PIERSON, Samuel	71	Putnam
PHINAZEE, John H.	16	Monroe	PIKE, John	8	Lowndes
PHINAZY, Jacob	21	Oglethorpe	PIKE, Henry	1	Bibb
PHINEZEE, James S.	3	Monroe	PIKE, Rebecca	9	Putnam
PHINEZY, R. M.	43	Jefferson	PIKE, William	10	Walton
PHINEZY, John Agt.	3	Richmond	PILCHER, James	16	Warren
PHINEZY, John Sr.	76	Richmond	PILCHER, Lewis	2	Washington
PHINIZEE, William	2	Jasper	PILCHER, Thomas P.	6	Warren
PHINIZY, Jacob	39	Clarke	PILES ?, Anderson	12	Thomas
PHINIZY, John F.	18	Clarke	PILES, James D.	10	Glynn
PHINIZY, Marco	27	Clarke	PILES, John	16	Glynn
PHINIZY, John	2	Richmond	PILES, John Jr.	19	Glynn
PHINIZY, Thomas B.	1	Richmond	PILES, Robt. S.	62	Glynn
PICKARD, Barkitall	2	Upson	PILES, S. M.	6	Chattooga
PICKARD, Sylus	17	Muscogee	PILGRIM, William B.	1	Cobb
PICKARD, William	1	Marion	PILKINGTON, Isaac	2	Upson
PICKENS, Alexr.	5	Richmond	PILKINTON, Laban	1	Carroll
PICKERING, Elizah	2	Baker	PILKINTON, Robert	15	Pike
PICKET, John	9	Pulaski	PINKSTON, James M.	2	Washington
PICKET, D. J.	3	Coweta	PINKSTON, Mary S.	1	Wilkes
PICKET, Wm. A.	1	Coweta	PINKSTON, Thos. M.	1	Wilkes
PICKETT, Jane	22	Pulaski	PILTCHER, John	1	Sumter
PICKETT, Charles	2	Sumter	PILTCHER, William	3	Sumter
PICKETT, Charles H.	1	Chatham	PILTCHER, Wilson	1	Sumter
PICKETT, Jeptha	16	Stewart	PINCHARD, John	17	Monroe
PICKETT, Jeptha B.	11	Stewart	PINCKARD, Daniel E.	25	Jasper
PICKETT, Micajah B.	15	Sumter	PINCKNEY, R. S.	3	Clarke
PICKETT, Musco	5	Stewart	PINDER, J. W.	28	Chatham
PICKETT, Musco P.	12	Stewart	PINDER, J. W.	4	Chatham
PICKINS ?, Wm. M.	2	Richmond	PINKERTON, David	1	Putnam
PICKLE, Richard	6	Early	PINKERTON, Jas.	12	Putnam
PICKREN, Elijah	3	Telfair	PINKSTON, J. M.	14	Hancock

Name	Number	County	Name	Number	County
PINKSTON, John	23	Hancock	PITTMAN, A. B.	1	Jackson
PINKSTON, Sousan	13	Stewart	PITTMAN, Alden	3	Lincoln
PINSON, Edward T.	2	Warren	PITTMAN, Daniel N.	4	Gwinnett
PINSON, James C.	1	Jackson	PITTMAN, Geo. T.	1	Jackson
PINSON, Joseph E.	8	Floyd	PITTMAN, James	5	Madison
PINSON, Mary	12	Oglethorpe	PITTMAN, Jas. F.	6	Jackson
PINSON, Matilda	1	Jackson	PITTMAN, Joseph	4	Cobb
PINSON, Shadrach	1	Jackson	PITTMAN, Joseph	12	Monroe
PINSON, Sturling	2	Franklin	PITTMAN, M. H.	10	Murray
PINSON, Thomas B.	21	Floyd	PITTMAN, Nancy	14	Wilkinson
PINSON, Jas. P.	2	Coweta	PITTMAN, Noah W.	11	Madison
PINSON, Jos. J.	6	Coweta	PITTMAN, Susannah	12	Jackson
PINSON, R.	8	Cass	PITTMAN, Ann	4	Lincoln
PINSON, Wm. B.	31	Coweta	PITTMAN, John	1	Tatnall
PINTUP?, Joseph J.	26	Gordon	PITTMAN, Samuel L.	5	Chatham
PINXTON, Green	3	Stewart	PITTS, Burton B.	4	Houston
PIOR, A. S. B.	14	Jefferson	PITTS, Columbus A.	4	Jones
PIOR, Mary	16	Jefferson	PITTS, D. L.	5	Pulaski
PIPKIN, Asa	2	Pulaski	PITTS, Geo. J.	14	Muscogee
PIPKIN, Edward	1	Pulaski	PITTS, Hardy A.	10	Warren
PIPPES, Littleton	7	Baker	PITTS, Isaac	14	Monroe
PIPPIN, Martha	3	Jones	PITTS, James W.	14	Harris
PIRKINS, James T.	1	Cobb	PITTS, Jesse	12	Jasper
PITCHFORD, H. P.	1	Oglethorpe	PITTS, Jesse	3	Macon
PITILLO, James	2	Marion	PITTS, Jno.	1	Carroll
PITMAN, Ann	3	Lincoln	PITTS, John	61	Jones
PITMAN, Elisha D.	6	Troup	PITTS, John W.	25	Newton
PITMAN, Joel	5	Floyd	PITTS, Lansford	16	Houston
PITMAN, John	1	Cherokee	PITTS, Lewis I.	20	Harris
PITMAN, Kimrod	16	Washington	PITTS, Nester	27	Jasper
PITMAN, McG. P.	3	Oglethorpe	PITTS, Nester	8	Newton
PITMAN, P. O.	2	Murray	PITTS, Peyton T.	51	Jones
PITMAN, R. M.	1	Cobb	PITTS, Priscilla	39	Warren
PITMAN, Sarah	2	Washington	PITTS, S.	2	Troup
PITMAN, William	1	Washington	PITTS, Samuel	53	Harris
PITMAN, Ana	9	Randolph	PITTS, Wm. H.	16	Marion
PITMAN, B. D.	1	Randolph	PITTS, Augustus S.	3	DeKalb
PITMAN, Delila	18	Randolph	PITTS, Coleman	26	Cass
PITMAN, Elizabeth	6	Richmond	PITTS, Frances M.	1	Campbell
PITMAN, Emaly C.	1	DeKalb	PITTS, Giles	4	Coweta
PITMAN, Jas. B.	10	Randplph	PITTS, Rebecca	3	Coweta
PITMAN, Jesse	3	Sumter	PITTS, S.	2	Decatur
PITMAN, Jno. R.	22	Randolph	PLASMAN, Mrs. N.	8	Muscogee
PITMAN, Joel S.	1	Sumter	PLASTER, Benjamin	12	DeKalb
PITMAN, Joseph	3	DeKalb	PLASTER, Edwin	12	DeKalb
PITMAN, Tim	10	Randolph	PLASTER, Sarah	6	DeKalb
PITNER, A. G.	5	Habersham	PLATT, George F.	12	Oglethorpe
PITNER, John	15	Murray	PLATT, Jonathan	10	Dooly
PITTARD, W. ?	3	Oglethorpe	PLATT, Charles A.	11	Richmond
PITTARD, William	14	Oglethorpe	PLATT, Ephraim H.	4	Baker
PITTARD, Wm.	15	Oglethorpe	PLATT, Susan	12	Chatham
PITTARD, Wm. S.	11	Oglethorpe	PLATT, William	7	Thomas
PITTARD, Sarah	28	Clarke	PLAYER, T.	2	Wilkinson
PITTARD, Wm.	2	Clarke	PLAYER, William	3	Houston

Name	Number	County	Name	Number	County
PLEDGER, James	5	Gordon	POLLHILL, Harriet	2	Baldwin
PLEDGER, K.	6	Elbert	POLLOCK, Lewis	15	Houston
PLEDGER, Thos.	8	Chattooga	POLLOCK, Morris	7	Houston
PLEDGER, Wm.	5	Monroe	POLLOCK, Thomas	8	Houston
PLESANT, Daniel B.	14	Richmond	POLLOCK, J. B.	4	Stewart
PLESS, George E.	13	Macon	POLLOCK, John	4	Baker
PLESS, Andrew	19	Merriwether	POLSOM, Mark	1	Newton
PLOTT, Hyram P.	3	Muscogee	POMEROY, John W.	2	Richmond
PLUMB, David	1	Wilkes	PONCE, Dimas	23	Hancock
PLUMER, Samuel	5	Jasper	PONCE, Antonio	4	Chatham
PLUNK, T. H.	4	Bibb	POND, A.	7	Muscogee
PLUNKETT, Elijah	1	Newton	POND, Priscilla	7	Richmond
PLUNKETT, John	1	Gwinnett	PONDER, Amos	33	Monroe
PLUNKETT, John	7	Newton	PONDER, D. H.	2	Henry
PLUNKETT, James J.	1	Sumter	PONDER, Daniel	64	Monroe
PLUNTS, J. C.	5	Bibb	PONDER, Dulane	15	Monroe
PLYTHRESS, John C.	84	Burke	PONDER, Ellen	9	Jefferson
POAGUE, John	1	Troup	PONDER, J. M.	3	Henry
POE, Alfred W.	3	Walker	PONDER, Jefferson	4	Walker
POE, B. W.	1	Pike	PONDER, James W. H.	3	Monroe
POE, David	3	Lumpkin	PONDER, John H.	6	Morgan
POE, John	14	Monroe	PONDER, Lucippi	1	Monroe
POE, Stephen	2	Lumpkin	PONDER, Mary A.	15	Monroe
POE, Sylvest	2	Chatham	PONDER, Oliver H.	9	Monroe
POE, Washington	17	Monroe	PONDER, S. M.	9	Randolph
POE, Robert F.	16	Richmond	PONDER, W. J.	2	Jefferson
POE, W.	8	Bibb	PONDER, Hezekiah	5	Burke
POESY, Henry	1	Baldwin	POOL, ?	3	Troup
POINDEXTER, William	8	Jones	POOL, Adam	5	Gwinnett
POINER, Laby	2	Wilkes	POOL, Henry	2	Warren
POLHIL, Thomas	14	Jefferson	POOL, James	8	Jefferson
POLHILL, Nathaniel	19	Jefferson	POOL, Jane	2	Newton
POLHILL, Frederick A.	5	Burke	POOL, John	16	Houston
POLHILL, Joseph	10	Burke	POOL, John agt for		
POLK, Archibald	3	Jasper	TOOK, J.	34	Houston
POLK, C. C.	3	Henry	POOL, John P.		
POLK, Charles S.	7	Campbell	agt for NAPPIER, S.	44	Houston
POLK, Daniel	1	Lowndes	POOL, John S.	24	Wilkes
POLK, Ezekiel	22	Madison	POOL, Michael	1	Jefferson
POLK, Ezekiel	8	Campbell	POOL, Middleton	22	Washington
POLK, M.	2	Decatur	POOL, Tilman	2	Warren
POLLAND, Martha	20	Columbia	POOL, Wiley	2	Newton
POLLAND, Zach	2	Columbia	POOL, Y. P.	1	Forsyth
POLLARD, Elizabeth	6	Paulding	POOL, Adam	16	DeKalb
POLLARD, J. J.	1	Meriwether	POOL, Allin J.	9	DeKalb
POLLARD, James	33	Harris	POOL, Eliza	3	Putnam
POLLARD, James L.	23	Harris	POOL, Hennitt	1	Richmond
POLLARD, Josiah	2	Paulding	POOL, Thomas	9	DeKalb
POLLARD, Mary	5	Heard	POOL, Wm.	11	Wilkes
POLLARD, Thomas	3	Paulding	POOLE, E. M.	8	Fayette
POLLARD, William P.	5	Harris	POOLE, John	4	Chatham
POLLARD, Wm. A.	7	Heard	POOLE, William	9	Franklin
POLLARD, Samuel	4	Columbia	POOLE, William B.	18	Franklin
POLLARD, Sarah	20	Taliaferro	POOLEN, Thomas	9	Emanual

Name	Number	County	Name	Number	County
POOLER, R. W. Sen.	20	Chatham	PORTER, Benj. F.	7	Floyd
POOLER, Robert W. Jun.	9	Chatham	PORTER, Benjamin	19	Effingham
POOR, D. M.	6	Harris	PORTER, E. S.	1	Walton
POOR, William T.	4	Harris	PORTER, H.	1	Hall
POORE, James M.	2	Gilmer	PORTER, J.	1	Troup
POPE, Alex Sr.	27	Wilkes	PORTER, J. M.	2	Henry
POPE, Alex Senr.	137	Wilkes	PORTER, J. N.	4	Wilkinson
POPE, Cadesmam	30	Pike	PORTER, James T.	2	Greene
POPE, Caroline T.	4	Pike	PORTER, Joel W.	19	Early
POPE, Elijah	4	Twiggs	PORTER, John W.	53	Morgan
POPE, Eliza S.	13	Clarke	PORTER, Josiah	1	Merriwether
POPE, Fredrick	1	Laurens	PORTER, L. B.	1	Pulaski
POPE, James	48	Houston	PORTER, R. T.	1	Wilkinson
POPE, Jesse	1	Pulaski	PORTER, Robt.	6	Henry
POPE, John	84	Oglethorpe	PORTER, T.	1	Muscogee
POPE, John	2	Oglethorpe	PORTER, W. A.	4	Morgan
POPE, John C.	6	Jasper	PORTER, William R.	1	Muscogee
POPE, John N.	36	Lee	PORTER, Anthony	5	Chatham
POPE, Josiah P.	4	Jasper	PORTER, Drewry	3	Sumter
POPE, M.	79	Oglethorpe	PORTER, John S.	6	Stewart
POPE, M. H.	47	Wilkes	PORTER, Vincent R.	1	Taliaferro
POPE, Micajah	4	Walker	PORTER, William	33	Stewart
POPE, Middleto n	43	Greene	PORTERFIELD, James	1	Madison
POPE, O. C.	26	Washington	PORTERFIELD,		
POPE, Sarah K.	12	Clarke	William	2	Madison
POPE, Urania	5	Clarke	PORTHRO, C.	5	Merriwether
POPE, W. R.	11	Merriwether	POSEY, John F.	4	Chatham
POPE, Wiley B.	3	Jones	POSEY, Thomas	1	Newton
POPE, Wiley M.	3	Washington	POSEY, Wm. R.	5	Floyd
POPE, William	4	Muscogee	POSEY, H.	1	Chattooga
POPE, William H.	8	Jasper	POSEY, Jane	5	Coweta
POPE, Wm. H.	46	Wilkes	POSEY, P. C.	1	Carroll
POPE, Wylie M.	27	Wilkes	POSS, Elijah	1	Wilkes
POPE, Britton	3	Talbot	POSS, Elijah S.	1	Wilkes
POPE, C.	7	Bibb	POSS, Elijah overseer	9	Madison
POPE, H. J.	72	Stewart	POSS, Henry	1	Wilkes
POPE, John H.	1	DeKalb	POSS, J. D.	13	Elbert
POPE, Mary	5	Burke	POSS, John M.	1	Wilkes
POPE, S. L.	4	Bibb	POSS, Uriah overseer	4	Madison
POPE, Wiley	31	Talbot	POST, Elizabeth	8	Troup
POPE?, Zedekiah	1	Pulaski	POST, James	2	Houston
POPWELL, Jordan	1	McIntosh	POST, Samuel C.	2	Jasper
PORCH, A.	3	Meriwether	POST, William M.	4	Jasper
PORCH, Davis J.	13	Monroe	POST, Allen	8	Coweta
PORCH, James	13	Meriwether	POSTELL, James C.	39	Houston
PORCH, Thomas	27	Meriwether	POSTELL, John	9	Chatham
PORCH, William M.	3	Gordon	POSTELL, William B.	2	Chatham
PORCHER, Mary J.	12	Chatham	POSTELL, William F.	13	Houston
PORE, David R.	2	Cobb	POSTELL, C. P.	14	Chatham
PORTER, Jeddithan	1	Franklin	POSTELL, Sarah C. P.	14	Chatham
PORTER, A. J.	8	Greene	POTHROU, Nathaniel	8	Stewart
PORTER, Alber t G.	33	Effingham	POTTER, George G.	1	Upson
PORTER, Anthony	51	Liberty	POTTER, Iva L.	5	Thomas
PORTER, B. F.	3	Hall	POTTER, Margaret	1	Harris

248

Name	Number	County
POTTER, Stephen	4	Newton
POTTER, Clinton	1	Sumter
POTTER, James	220	Chatham
POTTER, Riley	1	Sumter
POTTER, Thomas F.	210	Chatham
POTTER, Washington	5	Sumter
POTTLE, Edward H.	3	Warren
POTTLE, John	6	Camden
POTTS, John M.	1	Jackson
POTTS, Chris C.	4	Jackson
POTTS, J. M.	14	Troup
POTTS, James E.	7	Pike
POTTS, Labon	7	Carroll
POTTS, Moses H.	11	Jackson
POTTS, N.	3	Oglethorpe
POTTS, William E.	15	Monroe
POTTS, Wm. L.	10	Troup
POTTS, Saml.	2	DeKalb
POTTS, Thos.	3	Coweta
POU, Lewis H.	39	Jasper
POU, Joseph	28	Talbot
POU, Saml.	7	Chattooga
POUDER, James	24	Thomas
POUDER, William G.	18	Thomas
POUDRY, R. J.	2	Jefferson
POULAN, William B.	1	Lowndes
POULLAIN, Felix	17	Greene
POULLAIN, Thomas N. Sen.	178	Greene
POULLAIN, Antoin	13	Richmond
POULNOTT, John	2	Oglethorpe
POUND, Alva	6	Hancock
POUND, James	2	Talbot
POUND?, James	1	Houston
POUNDS, Daniel	1	Pike
POUNDS, Madison	23	Warren
POUNDS, Nancy	14	Merriwether
POUNDS, William D.	1	Pike
POUNDS, H. C.	59	Putnam
POUNDS, Robert	3	Columbia
POUNDS, Merimon	8	Putnam
POURNELL, John	11	Washington
POURNELL, William F.	2	Washington
POUNDS?, Isham J.	2	Merriwether
POWARS, C. M.	3	Irwin
POWEL, Evan	27	Jasper
POWEL, John Jr.	2	Jones
POWEL, John Sen.	16	Jones
POWEL, Lafayette	13	Murray
POWEL, Pleasant	2	Jones
POWEL, Seana	13	Randolph
POWEL, Wm.	5	Lincoln
POWEL, Gillis	3	Stewart
POWEL, John	28	Coweta

Name	Number	County
POWEL, John W.	3	Coweta
POWEL, L. P. G .	3	Coweta
POWEL, W. F. S.	6	Coweta
POWELL, ?	8	Elbert
POWELL, Asa	9	Newton
POWELL, Benjamin	12	Merriwether
POWELL, Benjamin M.	4	Walker
POWELL, Calvin G.	6	Emanual
POWELL, Caas N.	4	Thomas
POWELL, D. B.	1	Lee
POWELL, Flora	5	Lowndes
POWELL, Frank	13	Habersham
POWELL, Green B.	23	Burke
POWELL, Hardy R.	2	Houston
POWELL, Henry	2	Laurens
POWELL, Isaac	20	Walton
POWELL, J. S. P.	32	Murray
POWELL, James	11	Marion
POWELL, James L.	4	Marion
POWELL, Jas. D.	1	Carroll
POWELL, Jesse	8	Monroe
POWELL, Joseph	2	Marion
POWELL, Larkin	3	Cobb
POWELL, Louis R.	3	Walker
POWELL, Marquis	13	Hancock
POWELL, Mary	8	McIntosh
POWELL, N.	4	Pulaski
POWELL, Nancy	3	Upson
POWELL, Nathan	1	Warren
POWELL, Nathan D.	14	Lee
POWELL, Richard	1	Warren
POWELL, Richmond	3	Muscogee
POWELL, Richmond	1	Muscogee
POWELL, Roswell	20	Upson
POWELL, S. C.	7	Merriwether
POWELL, S. W.	4	Wilkinson
POWELL, Samuel J.	6	Marion
POWELL, Sarah	10	Houston
POWELL, Silas	5	Emanual
POWELL, Thos.	1	Chattooga
POWELL, Wain?	8	Muscogee
POWELL, William N.	1	Cobb
POWELL, Wm.	34	Marion
POWELL, A. J.	1	Dooly
POWELL, Abraham	2	Telfair
POWELL, C.	3	Bibb
POWELL, C.	2	Decatur
POWELL, C. R.	1	Burke
POWELL, Chapman	16	DeKalb
POWELL, Charles	4	Dooly
POWELL, Edley	3	Rabun
POWELL, H.	7	Crawford
POWELL, H. J.	6	Dooly
POWELL, H. T.	4	Bibb

Name	Number	County	Name	Number	County
POWELL, John	17	Monroe	PRATHER, James	1	Macon
POWELL, K.	20	Decatur	PRATHER, King	1	Troup
POWELL, Lewis	2	Screven	PRATHER, Thos.	12	Harris
POWELL, Mrs. P.	23	Decatur	PRATHER, Mrs. Emily	6	Stewart
POWELL, Robert	4	Cass	PRATHER, Pritchard	19	Stewart
POWELL, S.	6	Stewart	PRATHER, Wm. W.	9	Wilkes
POWELL, Thomas	16	Talbot	PRATHOR, W. C.	3	Elbert
POWELL, W. A.	1	DeKalb	PRATHOR, Wm.	4	Elbert
POWELL, Wm. G.	13	Putnam	PRATOR, John D.	11	Dooly
POWER, Elizabeth	2	Madison	PRATT, Allen	1	Troup
POWER, F. M.	2	Meriwether	PRATT, Henry	2	Monroe
POWER, Francis	2	Madison	PRATT, Jane	1	Troup
POWER, Francis E.	2	Madison	PRATT, James	2	Houston
POWER, Jesse	12	Madison	PRATT, Leonard	16	Harris
POWER, Kitty	1	Oglethorpe	PRATT, Nathaniel	9	Cobb
POWER, Margartt	2	Madison	PRATT, Selina	4	Monroe
POWER, Martha	8	Madison	PRATT, T. F.	5	Harris
POWER, Milton H.	17	Effingham	PRATT, A.	1	Camden
POWERS ? , Patrick M.	1	Stewart	PRATT, Abram	1	Camden
POWERS, Alex	7	Cass	PRATT, Absalem		
POWERS, Charles	1	Troup	agt for SMITH, James		Houston
POWERS, G. W.	3	Heard	PRATT, Sofy	2	Camden
POWERS, George	18	Fayette	PRAY, Ephram	2	Campbell
POWERS, Jno.	22	Pulaski	PRENDERGAST,		
POWERS, John	34	Monroe	Margaret	19	Chatham
POWERS, John H.	6	Houston	PRENTISS, Peter W.	1	Greene
POWERS, S. J.	1	Oglethorpe	PRENTISS, S. B .	3	Butts
POWERS, Sarah	1	Early	PRESCOTT, Eli W.	1	Clinch
POWERS, Virgil	6	Houston	PRESCOTT, Lemuel	5	Newton
POWERS, Wiley G.	67	Early	PRESCOTT, Anderson	1	Burke
POWERS, Zara	27	Effingham	PRESCOTT, Benj.	30	Screven
POWERS, A. P.	14	Bibb	PRESCOTT, J. R.	6	Washington
POWERS, A. P.	33	Houston	PRESCOTT, Nathan H.	3	Burke
POWERS, Godfrey	4	Chatham	PRESCOTT, Sarah	3	Richmond
POWERS, J.	1	Chattooga	PRESCOTT, Seaborn A.	2	Richmond
POWERS, John	17	Chattooga	PRESCOTT,Eliza	6	Richmond
POWERS, Wm. J.	1	Chattooga	PRESLEY, Elijah	2	Carroll
POWL, William	8	Baker	PRESLY, ?	1	Upson
POWLES ?, James A.	11	Upson	PRESLY, F. M.	8	Stewart
POWLRIGS?, John M.	4	Meriwether	PRESLY, Jas. M.	12	Putnam
POYTHRESS, George			PRESLY, Moses	10	Putnam
estate	36	Burke	PRESTON, Arch	6	Walton
POYTHRESS, Joseph	18	Troup	PRESTON, Arthur W.	3	Thomas
POYTHRESS, Joseph	77	Troup	PRESTON, D. B.	1	Muscogee
PRATER estate	1	Muscogee	PRESTON, William H.	19	Jasper
PRATER, Bolton ? O.	6	Upson	PRESTON, D.	20	Crawford
PRATER, J.	2	Henry	PRESTON, Elisha	1	Butts
PRATER, Andrew J.	4	Stewart	PRESTON, Jas.	1	Crawford
PRATER, Mrs. Ednay	1	Stewart	PRESTON, William S.	1	Sumter
PRATER, John A.	16	Upson	PREWETT, Alvin	5	Muscogee
PRATER, William	4	Upson	PREWETT, Jeremiah	2	Jackson
PRATHER, A. T.	18	Harris	PRICE, A.	25	Henry
PRATHER, Benajah	22	Wilkes	PRICE, Benjamin	5	Pike
PRATHER, Jackson	6	Troup	PRICE, Elizabeth	10	Fayette

Name	Number	County	Name	Number	County
PRICE, Garry H.	4	Floyd	PRIER, John	1	Walker
PRICE, Harriet H.	18	Washington	PRIER, Wm. M.	4	Walker
PRICE, J. L.	8	Walker	PRIMROSE, L.	11	Henry
PRICE, J. R.	8	Lee	PRIN, Abraham	5	Stewart
PRICE, James	48	Chattooga	PRINCE, Daniel	2	Morgan
PRICE, James A.	29	Clarke	PRINCE, G. W.	10	Henry
PRICE, James E.	10	Houston	PRINCE, Hiram	4	Walker
PRICE, John	7	Jasper	PRINCE, S.	6	Washington
PRICE, John	1	Walker	PRINCE, S.	8	Washington
PRICE, John H.	6	Jasper	PRINCE, Sylvanus	14	Muscogee
PRICE, John W.	2	Walker	PRINCE, John M.	1	Stewart
PRICE, Joseph	9	Jefferson	PRINCE, Noah F.	2	Stewart
PRICE, Joseph Jr.	13	Jefferson	PRINCE, Robert M.	1	DeKalb
PRICE, Leroy M.	1	Jasper	PRINCE, Saml.	4	Crawford
PRICE, P. W.	4	Oglethorpe	PRINE, Robert	7	Lowndes
PRICE, Robert B.	7	Jasper	PRINE, Daniel	4	Lowndes
PRICE, Thomas	1	Gilmer	PRINGLE, Barton F.	12	Pike
PRICE, Thomas R.	2	Jasper	PRINGLE, James A.	6	Houston
PRICE, Zacheus	27	Newton	PRINGLE, Josiah	5	Muscogee
PRICE, Charles	30	Chattooga	PRINTUP, Jacob	22	Warren
PRICE, E.	2	Bibb	PRIOR, A. W.	34	Pike
PRICE, G. W.	8	Bibb	PRIOR, Andrew J.	11	Paulding
PRICE, George S. J.	16	Burke	PRIOR, Asa	76	Paulding
PRICE, H. T.	14	Cass	PRIOR, Asa agent	2	Paulding
PRICE, J. V.	24	Stewart	PRIOR, Garland	17	Morgan
PRICE, John V.	3	Stewart	PRIOR, Haden M.	19	Paulding
PRICE, John W.	5	Coweta	PRIOR, Robert	21	Morgan
PRICE, L. D.	26	Randolph	PRIOR, Wade	21	Harris
PRICE, Patrick	1	Chatham	PRIOR, William H. C.	2	Paulding
PRICE, S. W.	28	Butts	PRIOR, Felix	49	Columbia
PRICE, William	4	Baker	PRIOR, Martha	13	Richmond
PRICE, Wm. T.	27	Floyd	PRITCHARD, Edward	2	Clarke
PRICHAN, Charles H.	3	Harris	PRITCHARD, Joshua	2	Cobb
PRICHARD, A. R.	1	Pike	PRITCHARD, Robt. S.	3	Glynn
PRICHARD, J. M.	1	Harris	PRITCHARD,		
PRICHARD, Roland	2	Monroe	Thomas T.	11	Murray
PRICHARD, W. H.	19	Pike	PRITCHARD, Ann	1	Richmond
PRICHARD, Wiley	2	Monroe	PRITCHARD, Presley E.	5	Putnam
PRICHARD, William	2	Monroe	PRITCHARD, William R.	50	Chatham
PRICHARD, Dr. Sen.	21	Decatur	PRITCHARD, Wm. H.	1	Richmond
PRICHARD, Frank	1	Crawford	PRITCHET, Benjamin	2	Hancock
PRICHARD, S. H.	20	Decatur	PRITCHIT, Cain M.	1	Emanual
PRICHET, James	5	Heard	PRITTLE?, Moses	9	Merriwether
PRICHETT, M.	3	Elbert	PRIZVANT, Margret	9	McIntosh
PRICHETT, Philip B.	12	Jasper	PROCTOR, Beder	32	Warren
PRICHETT, William	23	Jasper	PROCTOR, D. G.	2	Monroe
PRICHETT, William	1	Sumter	PROCTOR, David	8	Monroe
PRICKET, John N.	2	Franklin	PROCTOR, John	1	Heard
PRICKET, Nancy	1	Morgan	PROCTOR, Zachariah	14	Talbot
PRICKET, T.	3	Coweta	PRONDON, Joseph	1	Chatham
PRIDDY, R. T.	6	Troup	PROPER, James A.	4	Dooly
PRIDE, William	2	Muscogee	PROPER, Mary	1	Baldwin
PRIDGEON, Edward	3	Washington	PROPER, Samuel C.	3	Baldwin
PRIDGON, M.L.D.	1	Chatham	PROPER, Thomas	8	Baldwin

Name	Number	County	Name	Number	County
PROSPER, Eliza	18	Baldwin	PULLEN, George	16	Wilkes
PROUDFOOT, Hugh W.	1	Cobb	PULLEN, Guilford	3	Lincoln
PROUTY, Amelia M.	1	Richmond	PULLEN, J.	2	Meriwether
PRUDDEN, J. H.	3	Harris	PULLEN, Jas.	26	Wilkes
PRUDEN, Jos.	4	Muscogee	PULLEN, Mary	2	Wilkes
PRUDEN, William H.	2	Muscogee	PULLEN, Peter M.	4	Merriwether
PRUDEN, Sidney	7	Putnam	PULLEN, Robert C.	1	Meriwether
PRUDIN?, Mrs.	1	Muscogee	PULLEN, S. M.	1	Wilkes
PRUETT, Robert M.	22	Franklin	PULLEN, Tillman	6	Merriwether
PRUIT, Escay L.	1	Pike	PULLEN, (?)	43	Columbia
PRUIT, Newton	1	Harris	PULLEN, Elizabeth	3	Decatur
PRUITT, Bird	8	Harris	PULLEN, M.	11	Dade
PRUITT, John	8	Harris	PULLEN, Moses	10	Sumter
PRUITT, John W.	39	Franklin	PULLIAM, John	1	Franklin
PRUITT, Robert	8	Franklin	PULLIAM, Thomas	1	Franklin
PRUITT, Saml. W.	3	Franklin	PULLIAM, Thomas G.	4	Gwinnett
PRUNADE?, Timothy	1	Newton	PULLIN, J. G.	7	Henry
PRYON?, C. A.	1	Merriwether	PULLIN, William A.	11	Troup
PRYOR, Andrew J.	2	Pike	PULMAN, Willis	2	Hall
PRYOR, C. S.	1	Muscogee	PULSNER, J. E.	1	Newton
PRYOR, Delise W.	16	Morgan	PUMPHREY, R.	10	Decatur
PRYOR, James	2	Murray	PUNCH, John	1	Clarke
PRYOR, Josiah	9	Pike	PUNCH, Philip J.	3	Chatham
PRYOR, Mrs. A. C.	5	Muscogee	PURCELL, J.	2	Chattooga
PRYOR, Mrs. J.	3	Muscogee	PURCELL, James	2	Franklin
PRYOR, William	25	Pike	PURDY, John	3	Marion
PRYOR, William B.	3	Troup	PURIFOY, Carol	11	Monroe
PRYOR, Spencer	32	Sumter	PURIFOY, John	2	Upson
PRYOR, William	4	Screven	PURIFOY, Santly	23	Upson
PRYOR, E.	1	Wilkes	PURKINS, John E.	18	Union
PSALMOND, L. H.	8	Lincoln	PURNALL, Solomon	4	Sumter
PSALMOND, Sarah	4	Wilkes	PURSE, Thomas	13	Chatham
PUCKET, Edward	7	Cass	PURTLE, R. L.	2	Richmond
PUCKET, John	5	Gwinnett	PURVIS, Emanual	4	Emanual
PUCKET, E.	3	Bibb	PURVIS, Nancy	1	Jefferson
PUCKET, R.M.	2	Sumter	PURYEAR, Lucy	7	Clarke
PUCKETT, B. A.	1	Pike	PURYEAR, Seymour	5	Clarke
PUCKETT, Elijah B.	1	Gwinnett	PURYEAR, Wm. H.	37	Clarke
PUCKETT, John B.	1	Cherokee	PURYER, Wm. H. Jr.	4	Clarke
PUCKETT, Wm.	2	Cass	PUSSELY, J. W.	9	Chattooga
PUGH, J. E. H.	7	Thomas	PUTMAN, G. R.	5	Lincoln
PUGH, Jas.	1	Pulaski	PUTMAN, J. M.	3	Merriwether
PUGH, Thomas	10	Thomas	PUTNAM, Daniel	2	Cherokee
PUGSLEY, Robt. J.	6	Jefferson	PUTNAM, C. S.	3	Bibb
PUGSLEY, Sidney A.	15	Jefferson	PYAL, William W.	5	Appling
PULIN, Greenville	14	Cass	PYE, Benia	31	Monroe
PULLAM, George	12	Elbert	PYE, James	24	Jasper
PULLAM, J.	4	Elbert	PYE, John	8	Monroe
PULLAM, John	15	Habersham	PYE, Jordan	25	Jasper
PULLAM, Joseph	10	Habersham	PYE, Sarah F.	1	Jasper
PULLAM, M.	21	Elbert	PYE, Theophilus	19	Jasper
PULLEN, Attwall	17	Newton	PYLE, Samuel	1	Fayette
PULLEN, Dicy	32	Wilkes	PYLE, Abraham	12	Stewart
PULLEN, Elijah	6	Wilkes	PYNCHEON?, E. E.	1	Bryan

Name	Number	County
PYNCHON, Edward E.	90	Chatham
PYNE ?, Benjamin	13	Richmond
PYRON, Triry?	2	Greene
PYRON, William	14	Greene
QUANTOCK, James Sen.	5	Chatham
QUANTOCK, James Sen.	2	Chatham
QUANTOCK, James Jr.	13	Chatham
QUANTOCK, William	7	Chatham
QUANTOCK, Sarah	1	Chatham
QUARLES, David	5	Cass
QUARTERMAN, Edward W.	16	Liberty
QUARTERMAN, Hetty A.	8	Liberty
QUARTERMAN, John W.	6	Liberty
QUARTERMAN, Jos. M.	8	Liberty
QUARTERMAN, Joseph	59	Liberty
QUARTERMAN, Lafayette S.	9	Liberty
QUARTERMAN, Mrs. Sarah M.	17	Liberty
QUARTERMAN, R. minors of	24	Liberty
QUARTERMAN, Robert	5	Liberty
QUARTERMAN, Robert Y.	6	Liberty
QUARTERMAN, Thos.	77	Liberty
QUARTERMAN, Thos. W.	16	Liberty
QUARTERMAN, W. E. W.	9	Liberty
QUARTERMAN, W. G. M.	1	Glynn
QUEEN, Hugh	1	Rabun
QUILLAIN, C.	1	Murray
QUILLAN, Lewis	2	Lumpkin
QUILLAN, Milligan	4	Lumpkin
QUILLIAN, Bethel B.	2	Gilmer
QUILLIAN, George	2	Lumpkin
QUILLIN, Elizer ?	1	Walker
QUIN, Bryant	3	Burke
QUIN, Gara	5	Appling
QUIN, Hugh	1	Walker
QUIN, John	6	Lincoln
QUIN, Terry	4	Macon
QUINKEN?, Joseph	4	Bibb
QUINN, A. G.	4	Chattooga
QUINN, B.J.	1	Wilkes
QUINN, Frances	7	Floyd

Name	Number	County
QUINN, Wm.	4	Floyd
QUINN, Wm. D.	10	Wilkes
QUINN, Wm. S.	16	Floyd
QUINN, Calvin	16	Telfair
QUINN, P. W.	2	Camden
QUINNEY, Sarah	1	Jefferson
QUISENBERRY, James	1	Taliaferro
QUISENBERRY, James L.	1	Taliaferro
QUITMAN?, Henry	54	Newton
RABOURNE, R.	1	Bibb
RABUN, John W.	37	Chatham
RABURN, Willerford	1	Macon
RABURN, Zechariah	2	Warren
RACHEL, John	3	Hancock
RACHEL, Wm.	14	Hancock
RACHELS, Jacob	16	Coweta
RACHELS, Nathaniel	1	Richmond
RACHFORD, Ezekiel	11	Talbot
RACKLEY, A.	25	Dade
RACKLEY, A.	2	Decatur
RACKLEY, L.	5	Decatur
RACKLEY, N.	5	Dade
RACKLEY, Nathan	7	Baker
RACKLY, Jones	18	Dooly
RADCLIFF, Jackeline	11	Talbot
RADE, Lemual W.	1	Stewart
RADE, Samuel W.	34	Stewart
RADEN, Wm.	9	Oglethorpe
RADFORD, Eliza	14	Morgan
RADFORD, Henry	11	Lowndes
RADFORD, James	18	Houston
RADFORD, John P.	6	Walton
RADFORD, Kinchen	15	Lowndes
RADFORD, Damon	1	Bibb
RADFORD, R. W.	13	Twiggs
RADFORD, Robert	34	Twiggs
RADIN, George	1	Greene
RADNEY, John B.	3	Stewart
RADNEY, M. H.	3	Talbot
RADNEY, Wm. A.	4	Troup
RADSFORD, Joseph	7	Talbot
RAEFORD, Capel	7	Butts
RAFORD, Hamilton	3	Jefferson
RAGAN, A. B.	6	Muscogee
RAGAN, A. B.	6	Muscogee
RAGAN, Charles	7	Troup
RAGAN, David	31	Oglethorpe
RAGAN, Giken?	1	Newton
RAGAN, Jasa	4	Walton
RAGAN, Ibson H.	12	Oglethorpe
RAGAN, J.	5	Henry
RAGAN, J. H.	25	Lee
RAGAN, James	22	Pike

Name	Number	County
RAGAN, James J.	10	Pike
RAGAN, John	6	Newton
RAGAN, John J.	2	Lee
RAGAN, Joseph	4	Newton
RAGAN, Milton	9	Pike
RAGAN, Moses E.	15	Lee
RAGAN, Robert L.	3	Cobb
RAGAN, William	2	Newton
RAGAN, William A.	19	Pike
RAGAN, Jones	1	DeKalb
RAGEN, Thos.	3	Randolph.
RAGG, Richard	15	Floyd
RAGIN, William	3	Sumter
RAGINS, James W.	2	Sumter
RAGLAN, Edward	3	Merriwether
RAGLAN, Elizabeth	12	Merriwether
RAGLAN, John	22	Merriwether
RAGLAN, Richard	1	Merriwether
RAGLAND, ?	1	Muscogee
RAGLAND, A.	23	Merriwether
RAGLAND, A. M.	32	Troup
RAGLAND, B.	8	Henry
RAGLAND, L.	14	Henry
RAGLAND, Eve	14	Upson
RAGLAND, Thomas	6	Macon
RAGLAND, Thomas	20	Muscogee
RAGLAND, Thomas	7	Muscogee
RAGLAND, E.	1	Coweta
RAGLAND, William	7	Talbot
RAGN (?), William	7	Columbia
RAGSDALE, John	5	Jackson
RAGSDALE, Joseph	1	Cobb
RAGSDALE, Joseph S.	3	Cherokee
RAGSDALE, L. A.	2	Cherokee
RAGSDALE, Benj.	6	DeKalb
RAGSDALE, Elijah	1	DeKalb
RAGSDALE, John C.	1	DeKalb
RAHN, Amos	1	Effingham
RAHN, Christopher	1	Effingham
RAHN, Cletus	4	Effingham
RAHN, Clitus	4	Effingham
RAHN, Irwin	4	Liberty
RAHN, James	5	Effingham
RAHN, John	3	Effingham
RAHN, Naomi	1	Effingham
RAHN, William	14	Effingham
RAHN, Alexander	10	Chatham
RAIFORD, B.C.M.	2	Dooly
RAIL, W. T.	1	Elbert
RAILROAD COMPANY	3	Warren
RAILEY, John	4	Talbot
RAIN, Wm. K.	4	Camden
RAINES, Edmond	17	Upson
RAINES, Edmond Agent	23	Upson
RAINES(?), F.	2	Decatur
RAINES, Lucun	69	Thomas
RAINES, Mary S.	26	Upson
RAINES, Sarah T.	17	Thomas
RAINES, Nathaniel	71	Talbot
RAINES, Nathaniel	18	Talbot
RAINES, Thos.	18	Crawford
RAINEY, Benj.	1	Telfair
RAINEY, Bennet	4	DeKalb
RAINEY, Charles	7	DeKalb
RAINEY, John	6	Wilkinson
RAINEY, Woodson	20	Coweta
RAINS, James	1	Dooly
RAINS, Richard	6	Washington
RAINS, Susan.	13	Oglethorpe
RAINS, C. W.	15	Bibb
RAINS, Cadwallader	11	Baldwin
RAINS, Griffin	1	Dooly
RAINWATER, Abner	7	Hancock
RAINWATER, James	8	Campbell
RAINWATER, Sol.	15	Hancock
RAINWATER, Joseph	1	Campbell
RAKESTRAW, Robert	16	Newton
RAKESTRAW, Robert M.	2	Newton
RALEIGH, Richmond agent	14	Houston
RALEY, Abner	1	Bibb
RALEY, Jas. agent	39	Crawford
RALEY, Randal	5	Wilkinson
RALEY, S. B.	1	Bibb
RALL, Charles	1	Cobb
RALLS, Mrs.	2	Decatur
RALSTON, Alexander R.	12	Chatham
RALSTON, D. A.	2	Bibb
RALSTON, J. A.	18	Bibb
RAMBO, Cryrenins	10	Floyd
RAMBO, James M.	2	Harris
RAMBO, Jesse	18	Gwinnett
RAMBO, John	1	Montgomery
RAMBO, Kinchen	12	Floyd
RAMBO, D.	13	Decatur
RAMBO, Daniel	123	Decatur
RAMBO, Drury(?)	12	Decatur
RAMBO, Marcellos	11	Dooly
RAMBOUT, Thomas	2	Chatham
RAMBURT, Wm. P.	76	Elbert
RAMER, Martha	2	Bibb
RAMEY, Daniel	62	Walton
RAMEY, William	2	Jasper
RAMEY, William P.	3	Jasper
RAMEY?, Wm.	7	Floyd
RAMNEY, John J.	11	Cherokee

Name	Number	County	Name	Number	County
RAMSAY, George	11	Henry	RANDLE, Seaborn	5	Burke
RAMSAY, James N.	10	Harris	RANDLEMAN, John P.	2	Walker
RAMSAY, David B.	12	Richmond	RANDOLPH, Dorathy	11	Wilkes
RAMSEY(?), Thomas F.	7	Coweta	RANDOLPH, Hi. J.	5	Jackson
RAMSEY, Alferd	4	Newton	RANDOLPH, John	25	Jackson
RAMSEY, Allen C.	7	Troup	RANDOLPH, Joshua H.	4	Jackson
RAMSEY, Caswell	3	Murray	RANDOLPH, R H. estate	67	Morgan
RAMSEY, Elbert	6	Harris	RANDOLPH, R. R.	37	Wilkes
RAMSEY, Eliza	1	Clarke	RANDOLPH, Augustus	3	Baldwin
RAMSEY, H. A.	8	Lincoln	RANDOLPH, Dorothy	74	Taliaferro
RAMSEY, James	1	Cherokee	RANES, Fredick	9	Walton
RAMSEY, James	7	Murray	RANEY, Mathew	1	Jasper
RAMSEY, James W. H.	6	Muscogee	RANEY, Richard B.	9	Morgan
RAMSEY, John	3	Hall	RANEY, Thomas	6	Marion
RAMSEY, John	2	Walker	RANEY, William P.	1	Cobb
RAMSEY, Mary	3	Jones	RANEY, Frederick	28	Putnam
RAMSEY, Owen	6	Thomas	RANEY, John	1	Richmond
RAMSEY, Newton	11	Lincoln	RANEY, S.	7	Twiggs
RAMSEY, Priscilla	6	Muscogee	RANEY, Silas	18	Stewart
RAMSEY, R. A.	7	Walker	RANEY, Wm.	2	Bibb
RAMSEY, R. H.	13	Baldwin	RANEY, Wm. D.	8	Bibb
RAMSEY, R. R.	6	Chattooga	RANKIN, William	14	Muscogee
RAMSEY, Randle	9	Cass	RANKIN, William estate	4	Chatham
RAMSEY, Randolph	27	Lincoln	RANLERSON ?, Russel	1	Wayne
RAMSEY, Richard	16	Thomas	RANLERSON, David	1	Ware
RAMSEY, Saml.	2	Chattooga	RANSOM, B.B.	17	Walton
RAMSEY, Seaborn J.	1	Clarke	RANSOM, Evelina	4	Hancock
RAMSEY, Seth J.	3	Franklin	RANSOM, James	8	Walker
RAMSEY, Caleb	9	Columbia	RANSOM, Jas.	2	Pike
RAMSEY, Isaac	95	Columbia	RANSOM, John T.	2	Pike
RAMSEY, Isaac	22	Sumter	RANSOM, Milton B.	3	Pike
RAMSEY, Jacob	4	Stewart	RANSOM, Reubin	3	Paulding
RAMSEY, John D.	7	Richmond	RANSOM, Thos.	10	Harris
RAMSEY, Joseph B.	2	Richmond	RANSOME, J. B.	9	Hancock
RAMSEY, Phocian	18	Columbia	RANSOME, Lucinda	1	Heard
RAMSEY, Sarah	2	Richmond	RANSOME, Samuel	13	Heard
RAMSEY, William	8	Sumter	RANSOME, Uriah	2	Sumter
RAMSEY, William	11	Washington	RAPE, Israel	4	Henry
RAMSEY, William	1	Thomas	RASBERRY, John C.	1	Paulding
RAMSEY, William H.	2	Richmond	RASSON, W. A.	3	Stewart
RAMSEY, William H.	27	Thomas	RATCLIFF, James M.	7	Glynn
RAMSOUR, J. R.	2	Gordon	RATCLIFF, Richard R.	8	Glynn
RAMSOUR, Mary	3	Gordon	RATCLIFF, Geo. W.	1	Camden
RANDAL, C.	14	Lee	RATLIFF, Thomas	1	Sumter
RANDAL, Peter	24	Monroe	RAULERSON, Jacob	16	Wayne
RANDALL, Littlebury	2	Muscogee	RAULERSON, James	1	Wayne
RANDALL, J. R .		Coweta	RAUR, Frances	1	Bibb
RANDALL, James R.	1	Cobb	RAVENS, David E.	12	Monroe
RANDALL, L. R.	15	Coweta	RAVENS, James B.	4	Monroe
RANDALL, P. H.	12	DeKalb	RAVENS, David S.	5	Sumter
RANDALL, Thos. G.	20	Coweta	RAVES, Tyre	28	Meriwether
RANDLE, A. H.	16	Greene	RAVINS, William J.	4	Macon
RANDLE, Beverly	34	Burke	RAWLES, T. J.	2	Randolph
RANDLE, Amelia	47	Stewart	RAWLINS, Issac	5	Telfair

Name	Number	County	Name	Number	County
RAWLINS, James W.	6	Telfair	RAY, S. J.	4	Bibb
RAWLINS, Mathias	1	Telfair	RAY, Wm. A.	1	Taliaferro
RAWLINS, R.	1	Telfair	RAY, Y. M.	1	Coweta
RAWLS, Caroline	110	Pulaski	RAYLEY, James	3	Warren
RAWLS, D.	6	Pulaski	RAYNES, William	5	Columbia
RAWLS, Elisha	7	Laurens	REA, D.	6	Baker
RAWLS, H. M.	2	Lee	REA, William T.	7	Walker
RAWLS, Isaac	12	Jackson	READ, David	16	Harris
RAWLS, Milley	4	Laurens	READ, G. R.	10	Irwin
RAWLS, Sarah	10	Emanual	READ, James	20	Newton
RAWLS, Shadrach	5	Clarke	READ, Cullin	42	Putnam
RAWLS, Silas	11	Houston	READ, D. H.	33	Putnam
RAWLS, Allen	44	Bullock	READ, James B.	6	Chatham
RAWLS, C. M.	9	Bibb	READ, Jas.	36	Putnam
RAWLS, Jos.	2	Coweta	READ, Joseph L.	1	Richmond
RAWLS, Joseph	4	Sumter	READ, Lucy P.	6	Richmond
RAWLS, Thos.	11	Columbia	READ, Silas	72	Dooly
RAWSON, Charles W.	3	Baker	READ, Wm.	51	Troup
RAWSON, E.	4	Stewart	READE, Ed.	21	Putnam
RAY, A. J.	13	Hancock	READICK, William	2	Chatham
RAY, B. H.	9	Henry	READY, ?	1	DeKalb
RAY, Ben	3	Twiggs	REAGAN, John	6	Floyd
RAY, Ben	16	Twiggs	REALL, John	1	Upson
RAY, Duncan	26	Thomas	REARES?, D.	5	Irwin
RAY, Geo. W.	12	Houston	REATHAFORD, Jas.	15	Randolph
RAY, George A.	6	Meriwether	REAVES, Josiah F.	2	Fayette
RAY, George W.	11	Warren	REAVES, Jane	26	Screven
RAY, Henry S.	5	Houston	RED, Green B.	61	Richmond
RAY, Jackson	3	Troup	REDD, A. G.	16	Greene
RAY, James	22	Washington	REDD, A. G.	5	Muscogee
RAY, James C.	1	Laurens	REDD, James K.	11	Muscogee
RAY, John	1	Cobb	REDD, Jennett	3	Burke
RAY, John H.	6	Greene	REDD, Mrs. Elizabeth	11	Muscogee
RAY, Montreville	2	Thomas	REDD, William A.	6	Muscogee
RAY, N.	3	Henry	REDDEN, John W.	13	Merriweth
RAY, Nancy T.	13	Forsyth	REDDICK, Jacob	3	Burke
RAY, Peter	7	Habersham	REDDICK, Mrs. Sarah	8	Burke
RAY, Pharis?	5	Muscogee	REDDICK, Jacob	1	Screven
RAY, Pleasant	18	Dooly	REDDICK, Peter	3	Burke
RAY, Robert	8	Gilmer	REDDICK, Peter	24	Camden
RAY, Silas	1	Walton	REDDICK, Peter	21	Screven
RAY, W.	2	Elbert	REDDICK, Thos.	14	Screven
RAY, William	5	Jackson	REDDING, A. W.	19	Harris
RAY, William	2	Newton	REDDING, A. W.	7	Lumpkin
RAY, William J.	1	Murray	REDDING, Alexander H.	2	Emanual
RAY, Wm.	6	Henry	REDDING, Arthur	3	Harris
RAY, Betsy	12	Columbia	REDDING, Augustus	10	Muscogee
RAY, D.	5	Randolph	REDDING, Haney M.	26	Monroe
RAY, D. J.	3	Randolph	REDDING, James A.	6	Muscogee
RAY, J.	9	Crawford	REDDING, James P.	38	Monroe
RAY, James	5	Stewart	REDDING, Parum	15	Muscogee
RAY, John	59	Coweta	REDDING, Robert E.	56	Houston
RAY, Nancy	4	Taliaferro	REDDING, Thos.	10	Bibb
RAY, Neal	21	Talbot	REDDING, Thos. P.	6	Harris

256

Name	Number	County	Name	Number	County
REDDING, William D.	6	Monroe	REES, James M.	4	Columbia
REDDING, Wm.	34	Monroe	REES, Lycingus	21	Columbia
REDDING, Wm. C.	28	Monroe	REES, Vincent	10	Columbia
REDDINGER?, Samuel	6	Effingham	REESE, ?	7	Clarke
REDDISH, David	3	Appling	REESE, Alfred W.	3	Floyd
REDDISH, George	2	Appling	REESE, Charles A.	2	Warren
REDDISH, Isham	4	Appling	REESE, Charles M.	17	Clarke
REDDOCK, David	21	Marion	REESE, Cuthbert	30	Jasper
REDDY, Richard	2	Houston	REESE, David A.	9	Jasper
REDDY, Thomas J.	7	Baldwin	REESE, Elizabeth	6	Cobb
REDICH, Alexander	2	Upson	REESE, Harrison	9	Warren
REDICK, Nicholas	20	Dooly	REESE, Jeremiah	4	Harris
REDICK, John	5	Stewart	REESE, Joel	4	Warren
REDING, James T.	18	Monroe	REESE, John	1	Warren
REDISH, Sarah P.	14	Chatham	REESE, John C .	3	Muscogee
REDLEY, Jonathan	2	Wilkinson	REESE, Jordan	23	Merriwether
REDMAN, Mary	10	Butts	REESE, Milns	1	Floyd
REDWINE, John	1	Campbell	REESE, Prudence D.	6	Warren
REDWINE, Wm. C.	5	Heard	REESE, Rivers	21	Muscogee
REDWINE, Jacob	4	DeKalb	REESE, A. C.	4	Coweta
REDWINE, Lewis	26	Coweta	REESE, Ben	10	Columbia
REDWINE, Wm. P.	2	DeKalb	REESE, C.	18	Coweta
REECE, A. H.	4	Troup	REESE, Catherine	4	Stewart
REECE, Henry	2	Monroe	REESE, David	9	Putnam
REED, Edward	25	Putnam	REESE, J. J.	1	Putnam
REED, H.	1	Lee	REESE, Joel	23	Talbot
REED, James	1	Meriwether	REESE, Wm. M.	13	Wilkes
REED, John S.	2	Hancock	REESE?, Charles	1	Lumpkin
REED, Robert V.	5	Pike	REEVES, A. E.	16	Floyd
REED, Seaborn	3	Murray	REEVES, Archibald T.	6	Newton
REED, Thomas	1	Muscogee	REEVES, Benjamin F.	5	Monroe
REED, ? S.	48	Putnam	REEVES, Elizabeth	9	Hancock
REED, A.S.	57	Putnam	REEVES, Federick	18	Monroe
REED, Andrew	36	Putnam	REEVES, J. E.	1	Hall
REED, E.	24	Columbia	REEVES, James T.	10	Muscogee
REED, Edmund	12	Putnam	REEVES, Jas.	8	Carroll
REED, Edwd.	28	Putnam	REEVES, John	5	Pike
REED, Mike	27	Columbia	REEVES, John T.	1	Hall
REED, Robert A.	11	Richmond	REEVES, John W. L.	2	Jasper
REED, William N.	2	Stewart	REEVES, Joseph	11	Jasper
REEDE, J. B.	88	Pike	REEVES, Lee	63	Hancock
REEDE, James	21	Taliaferro	REEVES, Nancy	12	Jasper
REEDE, Wm.	40	Taliaferro	REEVES, Osborn	1	Gordon
REEDER?, N. P.	2	Forsyth	REEVES, R.	14	Lee
REEDY, William	2	Talbot	REEVES, Sabinah	14	Pike
REES, Augustus	25	Morgan	REEVES, Sarah	51	Merriwether
REES, H. K.	2	McIntosh	REEVES, Thos.	9	Harris
REES, Henry K.	12	Glynn	REEVES, William	8	Fayette
REES, J. C.	7	Morgan	REEVES, William	4	Monroe
REES, Jeremiah	6	Harris	REEVES, Willis B.	37	Pulaski
REES, Jeremiah	3	Lincoln	REEVES, Edison	1	Carroll
REES, T. B.	32	Morgan	REEVES, J. N.	1	Butts
REES, William J.	8	Harris	REEVES, James W.	23	DeKalb
REES, Albert	52	Sumter	REEVES, Joseph A.	2	DeKalb

Name	Number	County
REEVES, Philip	2	Telfair
REEVES, Riley	11	Burke
REEVES, Simeon	6	Burke
REEVES, Stephen G.	2	Columbia
REEVS, James F.	1	Campbell
REEVS, A. A.	1	Campbell
REEVS, Eli	3	Campbell
REGGAL, Mark	2	Lee
REGISTER, Samuel	5	Clinch
REGISTER, Samuel	3	Clinch
REGISTER, Wiley	1	Putnam
REGISTER, William	1	Ware
REICH, Augustus	1	Chatham
REID, (none)	3	Muscogee
REID, A.	1	Union
REID, Alfred B.	24	Walker
REID, Allen	10	Lincoln
REID, Augustus	13	Troup
REID, David N.	2	Troup
REID, Elias, trustee	4	Chatham
REID, Eliza	4	Franklin
REID, Elizabeth W.	47	Jasper
REID, Isaac A.	11	Troup
REID, J. C.	6	Walton
REID, J. T.	2	Lincoln
REID, Joffin	3	Hall
REID, John	3	Union
REID, John H.	12	Oglethorpe
REID, John L.	4	Gwinnett
REID, Joseph	5	Hall
REID, Robert A.	1	Gwinnett
REID, Samuel	25	Troup
REID, Samuel S.	13	Troup
REID, W. H.	22	Twiggs
REID, W. P.	3	Lumpkin
REID, W. S.	10	Lincoln
REID, Alexander	36	Putnam
REID, Alfred	12	Sumter
REID, Ann	5	Randolph
REID, Elias	10	Chatham
REID, Elizabeth	9	Richmond
REID, J. B. estate	9	Chatham
REID, Mary	18	DeKalb
REID, Wm. J.	2	DeKalb
REILLEY, John	4	Richmond
REILLEY, Richard	1	Richmond
REILLEY, Sarah	1	Richmond
REILLY, James	1	Chatham
REILLY, Margaret	2	Chatham
REILLY, Owen	2	Chatham
REILLY, Philip	4	Chatham
REILLY, James	1	Chatham
REINS, William	6	Jefferson
REMAGE, P.C.	4	Randolph
REMSHURT, William	9	Chatham
RENALDS (David)	5	Early
RENALS, Balos	1	Hall
REND, ?	9	Muscogee
REND, Jesse B.	6	Muscogee
RENDER, James	83	Merriwether
RENDER, Robert L.	37	Merriwether
RENEAU, J.	1	Floyd
RENEAU, R. R.	3	Newton
RENELS, Bartems?	7	Hall
RENFORD?, James M.	15	Muscogee
RENFRO, James B.	1	Baldwin
RENFROE, Briant	1	Houston
RENFROE, James	2	Washington
RENFROE, James F.	2	Hancock
RENFROE, James T.	1	Jones
RENFROE, Joel G.	1	Jones
RENFROE, Stephen	14	Jones
RENFROE, Morgan	1	Talbot
RENFROE, Nathaniel	4	Washington
RENNALS, Fielding	1	Dooly
RENNARD (RENNEAU?), Jesse	1	DeKalb
RENTFROW, Burket	1	Fayette
RENTFROW, Henry	2	Fayette
RENTZ, George	18	Houston
RENTZ, John A.	7	Houston
RENTZ, Samuel	2	Lowndes
RENWICK ?, Nathan	12	Troup
RENWICK, Nathan	4	Troup
RESLEY, William W.	3	Richmond
RESPASS, Richard R.	2	Marion
RESPESS, Thomas	34	Putnam
RESPIP ?, Nathan	40	Upson
RESPISS, John R.	8	Baldwin
RETHERFORD, William	39	Monroe
REVEL, Harrison	9	Merriwether
REVEL, M.	11	Talbot
REVELS, Jesse L.	2	Harris
REVIER, H. B.	2	Wilkes
REVIERE, Milton	5	Pike
REVUERE, T. W.	30	Upson
REVIERE, Vincent E.	19	Marion
REVIL, Mathew	3	Muscogee
REWAK, Lemual	13	Morgan
REWARK, Elias	2	Morgan
REYNOLD, Archibald	13	Muscogee
REYNOLDS, Charles	4	Twiggs
REYNOLDS, Coleman	6	Walton
REYNOLDS, Davis	29	Floyd
REYNOLDS, Abner M.	1	Jackson
REYNOLDS, Anstaties	3	Cobb
REYNOLDS, Benjamin	29	Floyd
REYNOLDS, George	1	Newton

Name	Number	County	Name	Number	County
REYNOLDS, Green B.	35	Walton	RHODES, Mrs.	1	DeKalb
REYNOLDS, H.	1	Twiggs	RHODES, Madison E.	2	Walker
REYNOLDS, Herbert	2	Upson	RHODES, Alex	5	Taliaferro
REYNOLDS, Hubbard	8	Jefferson	RHODES, Asa	19	Taliaferro
REYNOLDS, James	8	Greene	RHODES, Asa G.	1	Warren
REYNOLDS, James	6	Greene	RHODES, B. S.	2	Randolph
REYNOLDS, James	3	Hancock	RHODES, C.	1	Screven
REYNOLDS, James H.	1	Elbert	RHODES, Eleakin	3	Talbot
REYNOLDS, James M.	13	Jones	RHODES, Elizabeth	3	Warren
REYNOLDS, John	1	Clarke	RHODES, Jemima	11	Taliaferro
REYNOLDS, John	10	Hancock	RHODES, John	43	Taliaferro
REYNOLDS, John S.	4	Muscogee	RHODES, John A.	7	Richmond
REYNOLDS, Joseph D.	3	Marion	RHODES, John Jr.	5	Taliaferro
REYNOLDS, Levi	1	Marion	RHODES, Jno.	4	Wilkes
REYNOLDS, Martha	1	Warren	RHODES, Patsey	2	Screven
REYNOLDS, Martin	1	Clarke	RHODES, Robert	1	Chatham
REYNOLDS, Mrs.	2	Muscogee	RHODES, Robert H.	15	Chatham
REYNOLDS, Pennetus	64	Newton	RHODES, Sarah	18	Taliaferro
REYNOLDS, Peyton	12	Twiggs	RHODES, Saml.	8	Wilkes
REYNOLDS, Reuben	1	Marion	RHODES, Thomas R.	7	Richmond
REYNOLDS, Thomas	10	Monroe	RHODES, Thos. N.	2	Wilkes
REYNOLDS, Thomas	4	Paulding	RHODES, Wilie	9	Taliaferro
REYNOLDS, William	1	Jefferson	RHODES, William J.	68	Richmond
REYNOLDS, William	28	Jones	RHODES, Wm.	9	Taliaferro
REYNOLDS, William	1	Lumpkin	RHODES, Wm. W.	51	Wilkinson
REYNOLDS, William A.	18	Greene	RHONE, S.	9	Campbell
REYNOLDS, William H.	42	Thomas	RIALS, J. C.	1	Decatur
REYNOLDS, Wm.	2	Hancock	RICE, Atlas	1	Newton
REYNOLDS, Wm. B.	3	Lee	RICE, Benjamin	2	Newton
REYNOLDS, Benj.	34	Cass	RICE, George D.	3	Cobb
REYNOLDS, C. J.	18	Crawford	RICE, George L.	26	Houston
REYNOLDS, Dick	2	Columbia	RICE, George L.	1	Madison
REYNOLDS, Edmond	6	Talbot	RICE, James	1	Newton
REYNOLDS, Elza	5	DeKalb	RICE, John H.	1	Cass
REYNOLDS, James M.	71	Burke	RICE, Marth	11	McIntosh
REYNOLDS, James M.	50	Burke	RICE, Mrs. Jane E.	2	Houston
REYNOLDS, Jesse F.	9	Baker	RICE, Parker M.	7	Carroll
REYNOLDS, John	3	Greene	RICE, Saml. S.	2	Wilkes
REYNOLDS, John W.	17	Taliaferro	RICE, Van A.	7	Madison
REYNOLDS, Joseph	4	Columbia	RICE, William	30	Effingham
REYNOLDS, Martin	19	Columbia	RICE, Wilson P.	1	Clarke
REYNOLDS,			RICE, Wm. H.	5	Randolph
Mrs. Mary Jane	9	Burke	RICE, Aaron	2	Randolph
REYNONS, Wm.	1	Troup	RICE, B. H.	32	Randolph
RHAMES, Peter G.	17	Taliaferro	RICE, D. L.	11	Randolph
RHENEY, Elisha A.	7	Jefferson	RICE, Jas.	3	Randolph
RHENEY, Nancy	1	Jefferson	RICE, John	12	Stewart
RHENEY, Charles	6	Burke	RICE, Mary	2	DeKalb
RHENEY, John W.	12	Burke	RICE, William	10	Baldwin
RHIND, James	9	Richmond	RICH, Emanual	13	Muscogee
RHOBA ?, B.	2	Stewart	RICH, Green B.	2	Appling
RHODES, James	9	Clarke	RICH, John	1	Appling
RHODES, James	1	Madison	RICH, Samuel	11	Gwinnett
RHODES, M.	5	Newton	RICH, Daniel B.	3	Baker

Name	Number	County	Name	Number	County
RICH, G. W.	2	Decatur	RICHARDSON, Wm. B.	6	Lee
RICHARD, A.	17	Floyd	RICHARDSON, C. P.	19	Chatham
RICHARDS, ?. A.	3	Muscogee	RICHARDSON, Daniel	15	Stewart
RICHARDS, H. P.	2	Newton	RICHARDSON, Edw.	2	Camden
RICHARDS, R.	3	Elbert	RICHARDSON,		
RICHARDS, Willis	10	Greene	Elizabeth	9	Campbell
RICHARDS, A.	8	Bibb	RICHARDSON, J.	3	Bibb
RICHARDS, A. R.	7	Cherokee	RICHARDSON, J.	1	Crawford
RICHARDS, Anthony G.	6	Chatham	RICHARDSON, J. S.	7	Bibb
RICHARDS, Augustus	4	Talbot	RICHARDSON, Martha	4	Chatham
RICHARDS, Edward	2	Baker	RICHARDSON, W.	2	Crawford
RICHARDS, F. M.	1	Carroll	RICHARDSON, William	1	Bullock
RICHARDS, John J.	5	Camden	RICHES, S. K,	6	Pike
RICHARDS, T. J.	2	Bibb	RICHESON, Asa	1	Stewart
RICHARDS, Thomas	4	Richmond	RICHEY, William R.	3	Jones
RICHARDS, Thos.	3	Bibb	RICHISON, John	1	Washington
RICHARDSON, Allen	10	Merriwether	RICHISON, Nancy	17	Stewart
RICHARDSON, Allen	31	Upson	RICHMOND, Henry A.	2	Chatham
RICHARDSON, Benj.	2	Harris	RICHMOND, Wm. R.	5	Richmond
RICHARDSON, D. C.	5	Merriwether	RICHTER, Charles	4	Morgan
RICHARDSON, Daniel	1	Monroe	RICHTER, Edward F.	1	Upson
RICHARDSON,			RICKE (RIKE?),		
Everard H.	23	Paulding	Henry W.	4	Bryan
RICHARDSON,			RICKERSON, Gordin	9	Columbia
Henry H.	10	Walton	RICKETSON, Jane	7	Warren
RICHARDSON, J. V.	2	Elbert	RICKETSON, Jesse	14	Warren
RICHARDSON, Jane G.	6	Clarke	RICKETSON, William	6	Warren
RICHARDSON, Jas.	21	Walton	RICKINS, Martin	1	Harris
RICHARDSON, John	2	Houston	RICKOTS, John	6	Oglethorpe
RICHARDSON, John L.	19	Habersham	RICKS, Daniel H.	3	Emanual
RICHARDSON, John M.	2	Habersham	RICKS, R. G.	57	Randolph
RICHARDSON, John W.	5	Clarke	RIDDING, H. P.	8	Bibb
RICHARDSON,			RIDDLE, Anderson	23	Washington
Jonathan	11	Upson	RIDDLE, William C.	31	Washington
RICHARDSON, Joseph	2	Habersham	RIDDLESPURGER,		
RICHARDSON,			Elizabeth	1	Paulding
Joseph L.	1	Pike	RIDENHORN?, Daniel	13	Muscogee
RICHARDSON, M.	1	Chattooga	RIDER, John S.	2	Clarke
RICHARDSON, Mathis	2	Gwinnett	RIDGELY, Catharine	52	Burke
RICHARDSON, N.	10	Troup	RIDGEWAY, J. J.	13	Muscogee
RICHARDSON, Phillip	8	Harris	RIDGEWAY, L. T.	4	Elbert
RICHARDSON, Richd.	7	Clarke	RIDGEWAY, Nelson	7	Clarke
RICHARDSON,			RIDGEWAY, R.	3	Elbert
Robt. W.	1	Clarke	RIDGILL, William	6	Muscogee
RICHARDSON,			RIDGWAY, James E.	10	Troup
Robt. M.	5	Floyd	RIDGWAY, Samuel	10	Butts
RICHARDSON, William	6	Murray	RIDLEY, Charles L.	84	Jones
RICHARDSON,			RIDLEY, James B.	13	Jones
William H.	6	Upson	RIDLEY, Robert A. T.	60	Troup
			RIDLING, John M.	3	DeKalb
RICHARDSON,			RIED, Jacob	3	Wilkes
William N.	19	Walton	RIED, John W.	13	Pike
RICHARDSON, Wm.	2	Gwinnett	RIED, William H. C.	6	Pike
RICHARDSON, Wm.	22	Habersham	RIED, David	1	Bibb

Name	Number	County	Name	Number	County
RIEVES, Thos.	1	Putnam	RISH, Adam	4	Coweta
RIGBY, Lanson, agent	2	Houston	RITCHERSON, ?	1	Troup
RIGDEN, Mary	1	Bullock	RITTER, Henry	3	Chatham
RIGDON, Berry	2	Appling	RIVER ?, James	6	Wilkinson
RIGGIN, Wm. P.	2	Floyd	RIVERERE ?, Frances	16	Upson
RIGGINS, Stephen G.	11	Sumter	RIVERS, Jas.	2	Pike
RIGGS, Abraham	5	Bullock	RIVERS, Joel	3	Fayette
RIGHT, Samuel W.	3	Floyd	RIVERS, Joel	35	Wilkinson
RIGHT, Willime	3	Fayette	RIVERS, Joseph	15	Hall
RIGHT, William	5	Chatham	RIVERS, Mary Ann	3	Warren
RIGLEY, Caroline	2	Bibb	RIVERS, Robert	1	Fayette
RIGSBY, J.J.	1	Wilkinson	RIVERS, Thomas	1	Thomas
RILANDER, W. J.	4	Muscogee	RIVERS, Thomas J.	3	Warren
RILE, Wm. J. C.	1	DeKalb	RIVERS, W. M.	2	Henry
RILEY, Abraham	8	Newton	RIVERS, William	11	Harris
RILEY, Addison	3	Newton	RIVERS, William	7	Oglethorpe
RILEY, Bennet	5	Hall	RIVERS, William B.	6	Clarke
RILEY, Bennet	5	Hall	RIVERS, James C.	10	Randolph
RILEY, David H.	24	Houston	RIVERS, Lewis	12	Randolph
RILEY, Edward	76	Glynn	RIVERS, M.S.	1	Putnam
RILEY, Edward	5	Wayne	RIVES, George	44	Hancock
RILEY, Geo. F.	20	Houston	RIVES, George S.	41	Hancock
RILEY, Harrison	43	Lumpkin	RIVES, J. G.	7	Wilkes
RILEY, Jacob	21	Houston	RIVES, Jno. G.	27	Wilkes
RILEY, James	28	Hall	RIVES, Jno. G.	4	Wilkes
RILEY, James	18	Hall	RIVIERE, Jacob A. H.	1	Warren
RILEY, James G.	7	Greene	RIVIERE, John K.	1	Warren
RILEY, John	6	Floyd	RIVIERE, Sarah	1	Warren
RILEY, Miles	8	Early	RIVUS, John	5	Jefferson
RILEY, Nancy	3	Greene	RIZER, Jacob	16	Lowndes
RILEY, William J.	1	Cobb	ROACH, D. K.	7	Butts
RILEY, William M.	106	Glynn	ROACH, George W.	1	Campbell
RILEY, William M.	6	Pike	ROACH, Nicholas	3	Warren
RILEY, A. H.	20	Talbot	ROAN, B. S.	1	Henry
RILEY, David	5	Bibb	ROAN, Eliz.	6	Henry
RILEY, Edward	16	Franklin	ROBARDS, ?	5	Elbert
RILEY, James	2	Newton	ROBARDS, F.	5	Elbert
RILEY, James B.	1	Talbot	ROBARDS, Thos. H.	1	Carroll
RILEY, John P.	19	Talbot	ROBARTS, Eliza	10	Cobb
RILEY, John P.	4	Talbot	ROBB, Alexander	1	Stewart
RILEY, Joseph	29	Talbot	ROBB, Sarah	6	Stewart
RILEY, Peter E.	10	Talbot	ROBBS, Green J.	2	Walker
RILEY, Spencer	5	Bibb	ROBBINS, Jeremiah	6	Gordon
RILEY, T. J.	13	Talbot	ROBBINS, John	37	Greene
RILEY, Wm.	3	Bibb	ROBBINS, Susan A.	45	Jefferson
RILLY, William S.	2	Talbot	ROBBINS, Arthur	12	Screven
RIMES, W. J.	33	Morgan	ROBBINS, Elijah	1	Screven
RIMES, James	1	Bullock	ROBBINS, James	4	Screven
RINE, John L.	1	Chatham	ROBBINS, Sarah	9	Screven
RINGER, Jacob E.	1	Troup	ROBBINSON, Elizabeth	6	Jefferson
RINGER, William I.	5	Troup	ROBER, Fredrick	1	Chatham
RINGGOLD, C.	1	Bibb	ROBERD, James H.	27	Jasper
RINGLAND, George M.	2	Baldwin	ROBERDS, Jesse	17	Harris
RIPLEY, Elizabeth	8	Pulaski	ROBERDS, Millen	3	Harris

Name	Number	County	Name	Number	County
ROBERDS, William H.	1	Harris	ROBERTS, Jackson	8	Jones
ROBERDS, Grant	7	Campbell	ROBERTS, James	1	Paulding
ROBERSON, John	1	Newton	ROBERTS, James S.	7	Jones
ROBERSON, John L.	10	Jasper	ROBERTS, James T.	11	Walton
ROBERSON, Joseph	19	Harris	ROBERTS, Jas.	1	Carroll
ROBERSON, Joseph	3	Newton	ROBERTS, Jas. B.	2	Hancock
ROBERSON, Joseph L.	4	Appling	ROBERTS, Jefferson	5	Burke
ROBERSON, Margaret	1	Franklin	ROBERTS, Jesse M.	95	Warren
ROBERSON, Milos	3	Harris	ROBERTS, John	20	Cobb
ROBERSON, Richard	1	Muscogee	ROBERTS, John	3	Jones
ROBERSON, Wiley	13	Morgan	ROBERTS, John H.	7	Warren
ROBERSON, William	4	Appling	ROBERTS, John H.	9	Warren
ROBERSON, Wm.	4	Forsyth	ROBERTS, John R.	1	Clarke
ROBERSON, B. B.	11	Crawford	ROBERTS, John R.	2	Upson
ROBERSON, Bedford	4	Walton	ROBERTS, John T.	6	Ware
ROBERSON, Icnatius	7	Stewart	ROBERTS, John W.	18	Washington
ROBERSON, James	1	Talbot	ROBERTS, Joshua	4	Cherokee
ROBERSON, Silas	18	Walton	ROBERTS, Josiah	1	Dooly
ROBERSON, William	3	Stewart	ROBERTS, Martha	5	Washington
ROBERSON, William A.	5	Baldwin	ROBERTS, L. M.	7	Morgan
ROBERSON, William G.	2	Baldwin	ROBERTS, Luke Sen.	31	Jones
ROBERSON, Wm.	5	Crawford	ROBERTS, Luke Jr.	2	Jones
ROBERT, Henry	1	Muscogee	ROBERTS, M. estate of	14	Burke
ROBERT, James	1	Screven	ROBERTS, M. A.	13	Pike
ROBERT, Melton G.	17	Wilkes	ROBERTS, Marriam	6	Jones
ROBERT, U. M.	69	Baker	ROBERTS, Martin	4	Forsyth
ROBERT, William T.	2	Richmond	ROBERTS, Mary	5	Gwinnett
ROBERTS, A. C.	13	Walton	ROBERTS, Mary	4	Gwinnett
ROERTS, Alexander A.	15	Troup	ROBERTS, Nancy	4	Jones
ROBERTS, Benjamin F.	24	Warren	ROBERTS, Nathan P.	9	Jasper
ROBERTS, Elias	13	Thomas	ROBERTS, Noah	3	Murray
ROBERTS, Green	23	Washington	ROBERTS, R. F. G.	7	Greene
ROBERTS, Hany	1	Fayette	ROBERTS, Reuben	22	Jones
ROBERTS, Archd.	2	Henry	ROBERTS, Reuben	6	Lowndes
ROBERTS, Armsted	5	Heard	ROBERTS, Sherwood H.	3	Warren
ROBERTS, Benjamin	1	Hancock	ROBERTS, Tharpe	7	Clinch
ROBERTS, Benson	12	Pike	ROBERTS, Thomas G.	6	Upson
ROBERTS, Bridget	1	Glynn	ROBERTS, Thos.	2	Cherokee
ROBERTS, Bryan J.	8	Lowndes	ROBERTS, Wiley	18	Cobb
ROBERTS, Burrell	1	Early	ROBERTS, Wiley Sen.	7	Cobb
ROBERTS, Chas.	2	Early	ROBERTS, Wilis	21	Cobb
ROBERTS, Daniel	28	Laurens	ROBERTS, William	6	Jones
ROBERTS, Daniel C.	3	Paulding	ROBERTS, William J.	2	Troup
ROBERTS, Drewy	18	Early	ROBERTS, Wylie	5	Troup
ROBERTS, Edward	5	Marion	ROBERTS, Wm. B.	7	Greene
ROBERTS, Eli	4	Emanual	ROBERTS, Wm. P.	2	Chatham
ROBERTS, G. W.	9	Lincoln	ROBERTS, Wm. P.	4	Lowndes
ROBERTS, George	8	Columbia	ROBERTS, Wm. S.	10	Clinch
ROBERTS, Green	8	Jones	ROBERTS, A. G.	8	Dooly
ROBERTS, Hardin	4	Hall	ROBERTS, Abner P.	20	Richmond
ROBERTS, Henry	1	Early	ROBERTS, Aramint ? L.	2	Richmond
ROBERTS, Hiram	64	Chatham	ROBERTS, Augustus	4	Richmond
ROBERTS, Isaac	1	Merriwether	ROBERTS, Augustus R.	4	Burke
ROBERTS, Isaac	6	Murray	ROBERTS, Cullen	16	Stewart

Name	Number	County	Name	Number	County
ROBERTS, Daniel E.	4	Screven	ROBEY, M.	40	Lee
ROBERTS, Elijah	28	Screven	ROBEY, Mariah	16	Jasper
ROBERTS, Elijah D.	10	Richmond	ROBEY, Elizabeth	4	Putnam
ROBERTS, Elijah			ROBEY, Wm. M.	1	Putnam
for Bryan Est.	11	Screven	ROBEY, Wm. P.	16	Putnam
ROBERTS, G. B .	5	Bibb	ROBIDIER, Louis	1	Chatham
ROBERTS, G.T.	12	Butts	ROBINETT, G.	1	Muscogee
ROBERTS, George	4	Richmond	ROBINOR?, Alexander	1	Hall
ROBERTS, George	4	Richmond	ROBINS, Daniel	1	Effingham
ROBERTS, H.	25	Chatham	ROBINS, Samuel W.	1	Floyd
ROBERTS, H. R.	7	Screven	ROBINS, Sarah	9	Talbot
ROBERTS, J.	3	Crawford	ROBINSON, Alexander	1	Hall
ROBERTS, James	48	Screven	ROBINSON, Arthur	1	Fayette
ROBERTS, Jefferson	63	Screven	ROBINSON, B. H.	5	Early
ROBERTS, Jesse	12	Carroll	ROBINSON, Benj. H.	1	Marion
ROBERTS, John	9	Screven	ROBINSON, Blake	2	Muscogee
ROBERTS, John I.	4	Burke	ROBINSON, C. B.	1	Gordon
ROBERTS, Joseph	4	Talbot	ROBINSON, Catherine	1	Macon
ROBERTS, Luke	1	Bibb	ROBINSON, Dennis	2	Morgan
ROBERTS, Mary	7	Chatham	ROBINSON, Edmund M.	6	Houston
ROBERTS, Mary	2	Sumter	ROBINSON, Edward A.	5	Macon
ROBERTS, Nathan	1	Bullock	ROBINSON, Elsberry	2	Upson
ROBERTS, Richard	5	Sumter	ROBINSON, estate	8	Bullock
ROBERTS, Rutledge agt.	7	Bibb	ROBINSON, George	4	Troup
ROBERTS, Samuel estate	43	Chatham	ROBINSON, Gideon	10	Floyd
ROBERTS, Sherwood	25	Columbia	ROBINSON, Isaac J.	1	Jasper
ROBERTS, Susan	2	Chatham	ROBINSON, J. M. C.	22	Merriwether
ROBERTS, Thomas	1	Fayette	ROBINSON, James	3	Burke
ROBERTS, Thomas J.	10	Cobb	ROBINSON, James B.	16	DeKalb
ROBERTS, William	1	Baker	ROBINSON, James C.	3	Heard
ROBERTS, William	1	Dooly	ROBINSON, James C.	11	Jasper
ROBERTS, William S.	2	Screven	ROBINSON, James H.	19	Jasper
ROBERTS, Willis	31	Columbia	ROBINSON, Jeremiah	9	Walton
ROBERTS, Willis	1	DeKalb	ROBINSON, Jno.	18	Carroll
ROBERTS, Wm. M.	3	Bibb	ROBINSON, John	10	Floyd
ROBERTSN, Alvin	17	Oglethorpe	ROBINSON, John	1	Hall
ROBERTSN, Thomas	20	Clarke	ROBINSON, John	32	Jasper
ROBERTSON, Abner P.	113	Columbia	ROBINSON, John	3	Merriwether
ROBERTSON, Amy	22	Troup	ROBINSON, John B.	3	Clarke
ROBERTSON, C. B.	6	Oglethorpe	ROBINSON, John F.	3	Macon
ROBERTSON, James	3	Newton	ROBINSON, John S.	5	Clarke
ROBERTSON, John J.	25	Clarke	ROBINSON, John T.	15	Marion
ROBERTSON, John W.	10	Upson	ROBINSON, John W.	224	Troup
ROBERTSON, J. J.	4	Wilkes	ROBINSON, Jos. W.	4	Troup
ROBERTSON, Lake	8	Newton	ROBINSON,		
ROBERTSON, Mathew	7	Gordon	Jos. W. Agent	3	Wilkes
ROBERTSON, Pleasant	19	Oglethorpe	ROBINSON, L. P.	3	Early
ROBERTSON, R.	3	Troup	ROBINSON, Leroy	2	Gwinnett
ROBERTSON, Robt.	28	Hancock	ROBINSON, Littleberry	1	Greene
ROBERTSON, Wm.	2	Lowndes	ROBINSON, Matthew	19	Harris
ROBERTSON, Daniel	10	Chatham	ROBINSON,		
ROBERTSON, David	3	Coweta	Mrs. Martha	6	Meriwether
ROBERTSON, Turner	2	Burke	ROBINSON, N. M.	28	Muscogee
ROBESON, James F.	10	Lowndes	ROBINSON, P. J.	3	Meriwether

Name	Number	County	Name	Number	County
ROBINSON, Reuben	2	Harris	ROBSON, John	9	McIntosh
ROBINSON, Richard	1	Hall	ROBSON, John	6	Morgan
ROBINSON, Robert	6	Laurens	ROBSON, Stephen	1	Wayne
ROBINSON, Saml.	28	Fayette	ROBSON, William	8	Morgan
ROBINSON, Samuel	2	Cobb	ROBSONE, John	26	Morgan
ROBINSON, Thomas W.	2	Walton	ROBUCK, Wm.	1	Pulaski
ROBINSON, William	9	Chatham	ROBUCK, Julius	3	Stewart
ROBINSON, William	4	Merriwether	ROBY, Richard	34	Lee
ROBINSON, William	2	Walton	ROBY, Elizabeth	25	Putnam
ROBINSON, William B.	14	Muscogee	ROCKINBOUGH, Jacob	27	McIntosh
ROBINSON, William C.	15	Jasper	ROCKMORE, Elijah	1	Newton
ROBINSON, Wm.	1	Muscogee	ROCKMORE, John	13	Newton
ROBINSON, Wm. H.	17	Macon	ROCKMORE, Peter	1	Newton
ROBINSON, Wm. T.	2	Early	ROCKWALL, Stoddard	5	Stewart
ROBINSON, A.	3	Bibb	ROCKWELL, Wm. S.	10	Baldwin
ROBINSON, A. A.	19	Sumter	RODDEN, David	19	Jasper
ROBINSON, A. N.	11	Talbot	RODDENBERRY, Herny	1	Camden
ROBINSON, A.W.M.	1	Carroll	RODDENBERRY,		
ROBINSON, Alexandria	2	Talbot	Richard	1	Thomas
ROBINSON, Cyrus	47	Talbot	RODDENBERRY,		
ROBINSON, Frances	4	Stewart	Robert	14	Thomas
ROBINSON, J.	1	Decatur	RODDIN, Margarette	2	Pike
ROBINSON, J. E.	48	Coweta	RODDY, R. L.	10	Monroe
ROBINSON, James	10	Stewart	RODES, Joseph	1	Washington
ROBINSON, Jas.	4	Camden	RODGERS, Charles	3	Muscogee
ROBINSON, Jesse	11	Randolph	RODGERS, Jas. H.	10	Carroll
ROBINSON, John	4	Burke	RODGERS, John	1	Cass
ROBINSON, John	2	DeKalb	RODGERS, Martha E.	13	Chatham
ROBINSON, John	6	Richmond	RODGERS, Osburn	11	Newton
ROBINSON, Noah	5	Randolph	RODGERS, Wiley	3	Pike
ROBINSON, Philip	25	Burke	RODGERS, William	3	Newton
ROBINSON, R. L.	2	Sumter	RODGERS, Atha	1	Bullock
ROBINSON, Sarah	1	Taliaferro	RODGERS, B.		4 Decatur
ROBINSON, Syd?	1	DeKalb	RODGERS, B. F.	6	Decatur
ROBINSON, Thomas	4	DeKalb	RODGERS, David G.	4	Stewart
ROBINSON, Thomas	5	Talbot	RODGERS, Elijah	1	Stewart
ROBINSON, William	13	Richmond	RODGERS, Elizabeth	7	Randolph
ROBINSON, William	2	Talbot	RODGERS, Irvin G.	1	Bullock
ROBINSON, William A.	21	Burke	RODGERS, John C.	31	Macon
ROBINSON, Wm.	1	Bibb	RODGERS, L.	4	Decatur
ROBINSON, Zachariah	3	Sumter	RODGERS, S. G.	10	Randolph
ROBISON, A. J.	9	Muscogee	RODGERS, Uriah	1	Bullock
ROBISON, H.	1	Chattooga	RODNEY, Perry D.	2	Muscogee
ROBISON, W. W.	13	Muscogee	ROE & RELLAN	2	Oglethorpe
ROBISON, James	16	Washington	ROE, Nepha	1	Franklin
ROBISON, Moses	20	Washington	ROE, Augustus H.	7	Burke
ROBISON, Samuel	54	Washington	ROE, John	7	Randolph
ROBISON, William	2	Washington	ROEBUCK, E. W.	11	Elbert
ROBORDS, Kellis	12	Harris	ROEBUCK, W. J.	15	Elbert
ROBRDS, Jesse	3	Monroe	ROFF, Aaron	7	Gordon
ROBSON, Allen	9	Morgan	ROGDEN(?), S.	3	Crawford
ROBSON, Charles	16	Morgan	ROGER, Lucinda	1	Walton
ROBSON, J. R.	13	Morgan	ROGER, R.	30	Wilkinson
ROBSON, James	5	Morgan	ROGERS, Allelujah	14	Troup

Name	Number	County	Name	Number	County
ROGERS, Robt.	8	Forsyth	ROGERS, W. A .	2	Henry
ROGERS, ?	8	Muscogee	ROGERS, William	1	Meriwether
ROGERS, A. C.	6	Forsyth	ROGERS, William	3	Muscogee
ROGERS, A. C.	28	Monroe	ROGERS, William A.	2	Monroe
ROGERS, Abner	4	Fayette	ROGERS, Willis	1	Morgan
ROGERS, Augustus	10	Marion	ROGERS, Wm.	19	Forsyth
ROGERS, Augustus D.	2	Jefferson	ROGERS, Wm. H.	6	Lowndes
ROGERS, Benjamin	1	Hancock	ROGERS, Wm. S.	6	Jackson
ROGERS, Benjamin	9	Monroe	ROGERS, Abel	2	Sumter
ROGERS, C.	15	Upson	ROGERS, Ann W.	18	Bryan
ROGERS, David	3	Morgan	ROGERS, B. P.	1	DeKalb
ROGERS, Drury W.	13	Warren	ROGERS, Berry	25	Bibb
ROGERS, Edmond	1	Liberty	ROGERS, C. W. est.	277	Bryan
ROGERS, Elcanah	13	Jefferson	ROGERS, Carolen A.	8	Richmond
ROGERS, Eli	1	Monroe	ROGERS, Charles W.	125	Bryan
ROGERS, Elizabeth	8	Monroe	ROGERS, E. S.	27	Bibb
ROGERS, Ephraim	10	Walton	ROGERS, Ebenezer P.	3	Richmond
ROGERS, Geo. W.	2	Forsyth	ROGERS, Edward	3	Tatnall
ROGERS, Green	5	Monroe	ROGERS, Elisha	2	Richmond
ROGERS, Harrison	17	Murray	ROGERS, Geo. T.	8	Bibb
ROGERS, Henry	11	Hancock	ROGERS, Henry	1	Putnam
ROGERS, Henry	2	Jefferson	ROGERS, J. A.	2	Bibb
ROGERS, Jackson	4	Forsyth	ROGERS, J. A.	4	Putnam
ROGERS, Jacob	3	Hall	ROGERS, James	1	Campbell
ROGERS, James	1	Jackson	ROGERS, James A.	13	Telfair
ROGERS, James	1	Jackson	ROGERS, Jeremiah	6	Burke
ROGERS, James G.	43	Jasper	ROGERS, Jno.	3	Putnam
ROGERS, John	1	Warren	ROGERS, John	20	Burke
ROGERS, John	1	Walton	ROGERS, M.	2	Bibb
ROGERS, Jno.	6	Henry	ROGERS, Ozekiah	10	Baldwin
ROGERS, Jno.	2	Henry	ROGERS, R. D.	4	Crawford
ROGERS, Job	15	Floyd	ROGERS, Ransom	14	Screven
ROGERS, John	6	Forsyth	ROGERS, Richard W.	8	Burke
ROGERS, John	1	Jackson	ROGERS, Robert	7	Cass
ROGERS, Lutby?	3	Merriwether	ROGERS, Samual		
ROGERS, Joseph	1	Walker	agt for BARNES, B.	4	Houston
ROGERS, Lorenzo D.	6	Warren	ROGERS, Samuel	7	Cass
ROGERS, Martha A.	6	Warren	ROGERS, W. L.	1	Telfair
ROGERS, Mary	8	Burke	ROGERS, William	20	Chatham
ROGERS, Nancy	2	Muscogee	ROGERS, William S.	8	Baldwin
ROGERS, Noah	1	Marion	ROGERS, William W.	1	Tatnall
ROGERS, R.	3	Fayette	ROGERS, Wm. M.	126	Bryan
ROGERS, Richmond	4	Morgan	ROGGERS, Jas.	2	Putnam
ROGERS, Robert Y.	7	Washington	ROLAND, Wiley	4	Monroe
ROGERS, Samuel	5	Monroe	ROLF, A.	1	Screven
ROGERS, Sarah L.	9	Troup	ROLF, Grace J.	2	Chatham
ROGERS, Seth	1	Lee	ROLL, Jacob	3	Stewart
ROGERS, Sheppard	4	Houston	ROLL, Luther	27	Richmond
ROGERS, Simon	43	Upson	ROLLAND, Charles?	3	Muscogee
ROGERS, Sophia	1	Warren	ROLLANS, A. J.	1	Murray
ROGERS, Stephen	1	Upson	ROLLENS, Robert	2	Burke
ROGERS, Thomas	12	Burke	ROLLIN, Samuel	1	Burke
ROGERS, Thomas	4	Forsyth	ROLLINS, Green B.	5	Merriwether
ROGERS, Uriah	3	Lowndes	ROLLINS, James D.	2	Heard

Name	Number	County	Name	Number	County
ROLLINS, Jno. C.	1	Pulaski	ROSENBANE, J.	1	Chatham
ROLLINS, John	16	Burke	ROSENBAUM, M.	4	Elbert
ROLLINS, John	10	Merriwether	ROSES, T. M.	1	Chatham
ROLLINS, N. P.	8	Pulaski	ROSIER, (?)	3	Decatur
ROLLINS, Rachael	4	Merriwether	ROSIER, Freeman	4	Harris
ROLLINS, Wiliam	10	Burke	ROSIER, John	9	Pulaski
ROLLINS, B.	1	Screven	ROSIER, John A.	16	Burke
ROLLS, Jesse	1	Pike	ROSS, A. B.	1	Floyd
ROLLS, Pherby	4	Monroe	ROSS, B.	96	Houston
RONALDSON, A. G.	2	Sumter	ROSS, Charles E.	5	Floyd
RONALDSON, William	8	Sumter	ROSS, Daniel W.	1	Paulding
RONALDSON,			ROSS, Etheldred	19	Lincoln
William Sr.	14	Sumter	ROSS, James	6	Wilkinson
RONE, Thomas S.	10	Troup	ROSS, John	3	Jackson
RONEY, Thomas	5	Warren	ROSS, John	1	Wilkinson
ROOCKOOGY, Sam	17	Muscogee	ROSS, Joseph	1	Chatham
ROOFE, Richard W.	10	Talbot	ROSS, Larkin Agent	25	Upson
ROOKS, Defama	2	Wayne	ROSS, Mary	5	Harris
ROOKS, N.	1	Jackson	ROSS, Roland	9	Jones
ROOKS, Hiram	1	Wayne	ROSS, Syrus	7	Monroe
ROOKS, Isaac	1	Screven	ROSS, William	20	Jasper
ROOKS, Rufus N.	1	Sumter	ROSS, William	11	Monroe
ROOKS, Timothy	2	Sumter	ROSS, ?	55	Putnam
ROONEY, L.	2	Muscogee	ROSS, Andrew	1	Chatham
ROOSEVELT, C. J.	1	Muscogee	ROSS, B. F.	6	Bibb
ROOT, Evelina	1	Baldwin	ROSS, Benjamin	6	Talbot
ROOT, Sidney	3	Stewart	ROSS, Eliza	6	Chatham
ROP (Ross?), B. W.	4	Newton	ROSS, Eliza	1	Richmond
ROPER, Aaron	5	Lumpkin	ROSS, F. G.	1	Cass
ROPER, Joel C.	3	Cass	ROSS, Francis	3	Putnam
ROPER, John	3	Merriwether	ROSS, George	22	Bullock
ROPER, W. C.	5	Merriwether	ROSS, Henry H.	9	Dooly
ROPER, W. H.	1	Forsyth	ROSS, J. B.	14	Bibb
ROPER, Willey G.	3	Muscogee	ROSS, James L.	18	Randolph
ROPER, Emily	3	Randolph	ROSS, Jno.	26	Crawford
ROPER, James E.	1	Talbot	ROSS, John	1	Bibb
ROPER, James N.	1	DeKalb	ROSS, John C.	2	Dooly
ROQUEMORE,			ROSS, Martha	35	Putnam
estate of J.	13	Muscogee	ROSS, Sarah	15	Columbia
ROQUEMORE, James	1	Jones	ROSS, T. L.	5	Bibb
ROQUEMORE, Wm. B.	13	Muscogee	ROSS, Wm.	11	Crawford
ROQUEMORE?,			ROSS, Wm. A.	13	Bibb
James A.	11	Houston	ROSSEAU, William	3	DeKalb
ROSE, David	2	Chatham	ROSSER, Asa	9	Merriwether
ROSE, Elizabeth	22	Putnam	ROSSER, Benjamin	14	Meriwether
ROSE, Grantham	5	Upson	ROSSER, J. W.	4	Newton
ROSE, Jas. P. Admr.	11	Randolph	ROSSER, John	5	Meriwether
ROSE, Thomas E.	10	Upson	ROSSER, John O.	18	Hancock
ROSE, Thomas G.	20	Upson	ROSSER, S. D. S.	2	Meriwether
ROSE, William	4	Upson	ROSSER, Thos.	24	Meriwether
ROSEBERRY, William	2	Newton	ROSSER, William	11	Merriwether
ROSEBERRY, Richard	1	Newton	ROSSER, ?	13	Putnam
ROSEBURY, James D.	3	Stewart	ROSSER, Abner	8	Meriwether
ROSEN, Henry	6	Chatham	ROSSER, David	64	Putnam

Name	Number	County	Name	Number	County
ROSSER, E. L.	1	Chattooga	ROWE, James	9	Merriwether
ROSSER, Hix	12	Stewart	ROWE, James C.	10	McIntosh
ROSSER, Lewis	2	Stewart	ROWE, James S.	1	Merriwether
ROSSIGNAL, Paul	12	Richmond	ROWE, Sheldrake	13	Harris
ROSSIGNOT, James L.	4	Chatham	ROWE, Sheldrake Sen.	12	Harris
ROSSOU, Jule	2	Chatham	ROWE, T. H.	10	Laurens
ROSWELL MANU-			ROWE, E. A.	2	Richmond
FACTERORY & CO.	14	Cobb	ROWEL, Martha W.	1	Dooly
ROSY, Matilda	1	Chatham	ROWEL, Mary	1	Dooly
ROTHAMEN?, George	5	Muscogee	ROWEL, John R .	4	Dooly
ROUGHTON, Enoch	13	Washington	ROWEL, Margaret	1	Dooly
ROUGHTON, Z.	1	Putnam	ROWELL, Britian D.	1	Emanual
ROUND, Mrs. Susan	9	Muscogee	ROWELL, R.	6	Muscogee
ROUNDTREE,			ROWELL, George W.	110	Baldwin
Mrs. Elizabeth	23	Houston	ROWELL, Lawrence	24	Baldwin
ROUNDTREE, William	32	Telfair	ROWEN, ?, C.	6	Muscogee
ROUNSAVILLE, Gracy	6	Chattooga	ROWLAND, J. W.	8	Twiggs
ROUNTREE, Allen	1	Emanual	ROWLAND, James	27	Greene
ROUNTREE, George	12	Emanual	ROWLAND, Jas. J.	17	Greene
ROUNTREE, John	5	Emanual	ROWLAND, Joel T.	1	Cass
ROUNTREE, Joshua	7	Emanual	ROWLAND, John	4	Greene
ROUNTREE, William	2	Emanual	ROWLAND, John J.	5	Greene
ROUNTREE, James	6	Lowndes	ROWLAND, John S.	103	Cass
ROUNTREE, Weston	3	Lowndes	ROWLAND, Nathan	7	Macon
ROUNTREE, William	1	Chatham	ROWLAND, William	45	Greene
ROUSAU, George	21	Talbot	ROWLAND, William P.	4	Chatman
ROUSE, Benj. P.	2	Marion	ROWLAND, Joel	14	Cass
ROUSE, Benjamin	14	Lee	ROWLAND, John	8	Coweta
ROUSE, James	1	Hall	ROWLAND, John T.	8	Chatham
ROUSE, James	5	Houston	ROWLAND, Martha	2	Richmond
ROUSE, Joseph	9	Macon	ROWLAND, Rebecca	2	Richmond
ROUSE, Mrs. Mary	1	Houston	ROWLINGS, Daniel K.	1	Walker
ROUSE, B. P.	1	Sumter	ROWLY, Edward	14	Washington
ROUSE, James	19	Lee	ROWTAN, Shane	1	Coweta
ROUSE, Thomos	9	Burke	ROWZEE, Hiram	1	Greene
ROUSE, W. A.	3	Twiggs	ROYAL, Asa	6	Marion
ROUSEAU, George	7	Talbot	ROYAL, Ezekiel	1	Marion
ROUSSAU, John Sr.	11	Putnam	ROYAL, Isaac H.	9	Houston
ROUSSAW, John	1	Putnam	ROYAL, John	2	Clarke
ROUSSAW, Thos.	2	Putnam	ROYAL, John R.	1	Paulding
ROUSSEU, James P.	2	Talbot	ROYAL, John	4	Columbia
ROUZEE, T. M.	5	Elbert	ROYAL, William T.	4	Richmond
ROUZEE, W.	18	Elbert	ROYALE, Louis M.	1	Burke
ROW, Bernard	1	Richmond	ROYALE, William T.	2	Burke
ROW, J.	1	Decatur	ROYALL, H. J.	10	Chatham
ROW, J. J.	12	Troup	ROYALL, William	5	Wayne
ROWAN, G. W.	2	Henry	ROYALL, James H.	29	Burke
ROWAN, J.	3	Henry	ROYALS, John J.	1	Dooly
ROWAN, S.	12	Henry	ROYALS, John C.	10	Dooly
ROWDEN, Mathew	2	Merriwether	ROYALS, Raiford	5	Dooly
ROWE, Allen	7	Merriwether	ROYALS, Sarah	5	Dooly
ROWE, D.	3	Muscogee	ROYSTON, G. D.	36	Baker
ROWE, Elizabeth	15	Hancock	ROZAR, Wm.	8	Laurens
ROWE, Jacob	5	Hancock	ROZIER, M. M.	3	Pike

Name	Number	County
ROZIER, James	1	Talbot
ROZIER, R.F.	27	Wilkinson
ROZIER, Robert	14	Twiggs
RUCKER, A.	2	Elbert
RUCKER, Azmon	1	Franklin
RUCKER, George	12	Franklin
RUCKER, George	7	Franklin
RUCKER, John B.	1	Murray
RUCKER, John T.	5	Pike
RUCKER, Joseph	208	Elbert
RUCKER, Mastin H.	1	Pike
RUCKER, R.	11	Elbert
RUCKER, Simon B.	2	Cherokee
RUCKER, T. W.	53	Elbert
RUCKER, Wiley	3	Franklin
RUCKER, H. F.	5	Randolph
RUCKER, James R.	2	Randolph
RUCKER, Richard	30	Talbot
RUDELL?, M.	1	Irwin
RUDER, Elizabeth	3	Walton
RUDISEL, Levi	4	Cherokee
RUDISEL, John	31	Taliaferro
RUDISELL, John	22	Hancock
RUDISIL, Edward	10	Taliaferro
RUDISILL, John W.	4	Washington
RUDLIN, Rodrick	23	Monroe
RUDOLPH, Emily	2	Camden
RUDOLPH, Francis	19	Camden
RUFF, D.	1	Henry
RUFF, D.	1	Henry
RUFF, Lemon	25	Burke
RUFFIN, Albert	3	Columbia
RUGASON, John	1	Heard
RUMPH, John C.	11	Macon
RUMPH, John H.	17	Macon
RUMPH, John R.	2	Glynn
RUMPH, Lewis	64	Houston
RUMPH, D.	12	Randolph
RUMSEY, N.	2	Elbert
RUNNELS, James	3	Meriwether
RUNNELS, John	5	Macon
RUNNELS, Wesley	1	Meriwether
RUNNELS, Wiley	6	Merriwether
RUNNELS, Robert	5	Dooly
RUSAW, William R.	2	Stewart
RUSE, John C.	5	Muscogee
RUSE, Joseph L.	6	Merriwether
RUSH, Jackson	3	Harris
RUSH, W. W.	1	Elbert
RUSH, Jane	2	Talbot
RUSH, John	3	Talbot
RUSH, Leonard	17	Talbot
RUSHIN, James	10	Hancock
RUSHIN, James	7	Hancock
RUSHIN, Joel F.	17	Marion
RUSHIN, William	7	Macon
RUSHIN, Wm.	11	Hancock
RUSHING, Calvin	1	Bullock
RUSHING, James	3	Bullock
RUSHING, John B.	8	Bullock
RUSHING, William	1	Bullock
RUSHING, William	22	Stewart
RUSHING, William T.	4	Stewart
RUSHSAN ?, T.	14	Stewart
RUSHTON, Robert S.	1	Murray
RUSK, S. W.	2	Pike
RUSK, Thomas	3	DeKalb
RUSO, S.	6	Bibb
RUSSEL, Booker L.	9	Jones
RUSSEL, George	7	Jones
RUSSEL, J.	13	Irwin
RUSSEL, J.	13	Troup
RUSSEL, J. A.	5	Merriwether
RUSSEL, John	6	Meriwether
RUSSEL, Wm.	12	Irwin
RUSSEL, A.	2	Coweta
RUSSEL, Drayton	3	Coweta
RUSSEL, E.	5	Bibb
RUSSEL, Harris	8	Coweta
RUSSEL, J.	1	Bibb
RUSSEL, J. B.	5	Coweta
RUSSEL, J. L.	2	Coweta
RUSSEL, John	11	Cass
RUSSEL, Robert	1	Cass
RUSSEL, Robert	17	Coweta
RUSSEL, Wm.	10	Coweta
RUSSELL, J.	17	Henry
RUSSELL, Abel	9	Jefferson
RUSSELL, F.	4	Henry
RUSSELL, Jane	6	Cass
RUSSELL, James	4	Union
RUSSELL, Jas. L.	7	Gwinnett
RUSSELL, John H.	6	Forsyth
RUSSELL, John see LAMBETH, J.		Floyd
RUSSELL, Levi S.	5	Chatham
RUSSELL, P. G.	3	Henry
RUSSELL, R. B.	3	Henry
RUSSELL, Robert	3	Gordon
RUSSELL, Thos.	4	Henry
RUSSELL, W.	6	Henry
RUSSELL, William J.	17	Gwinnett
RUSSELL, William R.	15	Muscogee
RUSSELL, Benj. B.	2	Richmond
RUSSELL, Caroline	17	Camden
RUSSELL, David	4	Talbot
RUSSELL, H. T .by Agt. Hancock	7	Richmond

Name	Number	County	Name	Number	County
RUSSELL, Henry F.	4	Richmond	RYCKLEY, John E.	1	Muscogee
RUSSELL, Jane	10	DeKalb	RYDER, William	5	Houston
RUSSELL, Jas.	3	DeKalb	RYE, Luander	5	Bibb
RUSSELL, John	1	Cass	RYENE, Thomas	7	Fayette
RUSSELL, John R.	13	Talbot	RYERSON, Thomas	5	Chatham
RUSSELL, M. R.	13	Talbot	RYLANDER, M. E.	18	Bibb
RUSSELL, Philip M.	3	Chatham	RYLE, Robert	7	Muscogee
RUSSELL, Winright	7	Talbot	RYNEHART, William	1	Muscogee
RUSSIL, Jas.	19	Coweta	RYON, Birden	2	Muscogee
RUST, Joseph B.	7	Franklin	SABAL, Adolph	3	Richmond
RUST, Margaret	1	Clarke	SABBATTE, Clement	4	Chatham
RUSTAN, Nathan	1	DeKalb	SADAWHITE, E.	11	Troup
RUSTE, Yewel G.	5	Baker	SADDLER, T.	15	Henry
RUSTIN, Benj. W.	1	Liberty	SADDLER, C.W.	41	Putnam
RUSTIN, Wm.	1	Liberty	SADDLER, Jas.	1	Decatur
RUTHERFORD,			SADDLER, Nathaniel	18	Putnam
Benjamin H.	46	Houston	SADLOR, James R.	16	Elbert
RUTHERFORD, H. L.	6	Muscogee	SADLOR, John	11	Elbert
RUTHERFORD, John H.	36	Houston	SADLOR, W. B.	22	Elbert
RUTHERFORD, Saml.	1	Wilkinson	SAFFOLD, A. G.	71	Morgan
RUTHERFORD,			SAFFOLD, Daniel O.	2	Lowndes
Thomas B.	12	Houston	SAFFOLD, Isham H.	49	Washington
RUTHERFORD, William	18	Clarke	SAFFOLD, James	3	Pike
RUTHERFORD, Catha	1	Richmond	SAFFOLD, S. J.	14	Morgan
RUTHERFORD, Saml.	85	Crawford	SAFFOLD, Thomas P.	35	Morgan
RUTHERFORD, Wm.	16	Crawford	SAFFOLD, W. O.	13	Morgan
RUTHERFORD,			SAFFORD, Henry	1	Greene
Wm. Sen.	31	Crawford	SAGGUS, John	1	Wilkes
RUTLAND, John H.	1	Dooly	SAILERS, William	4	Madison
RUTLAND, B. B.	6	Dooly	SAILORS, Alex.	1	Jackson
RUTLEDGE, James	33	Troup	SAILORS, J.	2	Henry
RUTLEDGE, James Jr.	3	Troup	SALE, A.J.	4	Troup
RUTLEDGE, John	6	Troup	SALE, J. T.	2	Troup
RUTLEDGE, Joseph	13	Troup	SALE, L. C.	6	Randolph
RUTLIFF, W.	2	Chattooga	SALE, Leonard	11	Talbot
RUTRIDGE, William O.	26	Harris	SALES, Guiford	23	Wilkes
RYAL, Wm.	2	Wilkinson	SALISBURY, David G.	6	Richmond
RYALL, Isaiah B.	9	Lowndes	SALLENS, William A.	1	Glynn
RYALLS, David	1	Telfair	SALLERSTEAD,		
RYALLS, John	1	Telfair	Lawrence D.	3	Richmond
RYALLS, William	1	Telfair	SALLIS, George H.	4	Warren
RYALS, Elizabeth	7	Laurens	SALMON?, L. S.	6	Pike
RYALS, John B.	15	Montgomery	SALSBURY, J. S.	4	Bibb
RYALS, Jordan	9	McIntosh	SALTER, Charles	13	Washington
RYALS, Joseph	10	Montgomery	SALTER, Wm. G.	51	Jefferson
RYALS, Lewis E.	4	McIntosh	SALTER, James	19	Dooly
RYALS, William R.	1	Montgomery	SALTER, James	6	Stewart
RYAN, Abram	5	Clarke	SALTER, Richard	89	Stewart
RYAN, Ann	3	Jasper	SALTER, Thomas	17	Stewart
RYAN, John	1	Chatham	SALTER, Thomas	1	Washington
RYAN, Martha B.	5	Hancock	SAMMERLAND, A.	1	Bibb
RYAN, Patrick	17	Chatham	SAMMIS, R.	3	Muscogee
RYAN, Margarett	1	Taliaferro	SAMMONDS, Martha	1	Warren
RYAN, T. D. L.	10	Pulaski	SAMMONS, C. R.	7	Hall

Name	Number	County	Name	Number	County
SAMMONS, Edwin E.	2	Burke	SANDERS, James	3	Forsyth
SAMMONS, John C.	5	Newton	SANDERS, James N.	1	Upson
SAMMONS, Joshua	19	Hall	SANDERS, James R.	8	Greene
SAMMONS, Mary B.	10	Gwinnett	SANDERS, Jno.	5	Henry
SAMMONS, William	2	Gwinnett	SANDERS, John	3	Laurens
SAMMONS, E. W. Sen.	9	Putnam	SANDERS, Lovitt	7	Hancock
SAMMONS, Wm. T.	5	Putnam	SANDERS, Lucy	7	Wilkes
SAMONS, Benjamin	1	Jefferson	SANDERS, Mary	2	Upson
SAMPKIN, Lewis J.	16	Clarke	SANDERS, Micajah	2	Carroll
SAMPLES, John	8	Jefferson	SANDERS, Miles	16	Houston
SAMPLES, William	3	Jefferson	SANDERS, Minyard	14	Franklin
SAMPLES, John	12	Putnam	SANDERS, Samuel	8	Wilkinson
SAMPLES, Newton	15	Putnam	SANDERS, Stephen	3	Franklin
SAMPLES, U. C.	20	Troup	SANDERS, Thomas	14	Thomas
SAMPLES, W. M.	11	Troup	SANDERS, Thomas F.	1	Jones
SAMPSON?, Benjamin	13	Lumpkin	SANDERS, Thomas F.	10	Monroe
SAMS, Elvira	16	Newton	SANDERS, W. J.	28	Thomas
SAMS, James B.	1	Walton	SANDERS, Warren E.	29	Houston
SAMS, N.	2	Walton	SANDERS, William	52	Greene
SAMSON, James	1	Muscogee	SANDERS, William	2	Madison
SAMUEL, P. T.	1	DeKalb	SANDERS, Willis P.	5	Marion
SAMUELS, Antony	20	Lincoln	SANDERS, Wright	9	Thomas
SAMUELS, Benjamin	8	Lincoln	SANDERS, Carroll	10	Talbot
SAMUELS, Elizabeth	6	Lincoln	SANDERS, Emanuel	2	Sumter
SAMUELS, Josiah	3	Lincoln	SANDERS, H.	2	Coweta
SAMUELS, Mary	11	Lumpkin	SANDERS, J. M .	8	Crawford
SANBORN, J.	27	Decatur	SANDERS, J. M .	2	Crawford
SANCHES, Dorcas	7	Camden	SANDERS, James	3	Talbot
SANCHIE, Ann	1	Chatham	SANDERS, James	2	Talbot
SANDEFER, Jas.	1	Henry	SANDERS, Jas. B.	7	Putnam
SANDEFER, Robert	3	Henry	SANDERS, John	6	Bibb
SANDEFER, A.	1	Crawford	SANDERS, John H.	4	Stewart
SANDEFER, J.	1	Crawford	SANDERS, Peter	10	Talbot
SANDEFER, J. S.	9	Crawford	SANDERS, Richard	1	Putnam
SANDEFER, L. B.	2	Crawford	SANDERS, Robbin ?	12	Taliaferro
SANDEFER, L. J.	1	Floyd	SANDERS, S. J .	9	Crawford
SANDEFER, Thos.	3	Crawford	SANDERS, Thomas	9	Talbot
SANDEFER, Wm.	4	Crawford	SANDERS, Thos.	5	Columbia
SANDEFORD, Hill	3	Burke	SANDERS, Tilmon agt.	43	Bibb
SANDERFORD, E.	4	Crawford	SANDERS, W.	4	Bibb
SANDERLIN, Henry	1	Randolph	SANDERS, W.	1	Screven
SANDERLIN, James T.	2	Randolph	SANDERS, Wm.	26	Bibb
SANDERLIN, Wm.	1	Randolph	SANDERS, Wm. L.	12	Crawford
SANDERS, Aaron	11	Franklin	SANDERSON, A.	2	Talbot
SANDERS, B. M.	42	Greene	SANDFORD, Daniel	6	Monroe
SANDERS, C. H.	43	Newton	SANDFORD, Joseph	10	Putnam
SANDERS, Candy	5	Jones	SANDIFORD, James H.	6	Chatham
SANDERS, Edward L.	4	Madison	SANDRAGE, J. M.	12	Elbert
SANDERS, Gillen	2	Jones	SANDS, James	1	Tatnall
SANDERS, Hardy T.	9	Madison	SANDWICH, M. H.	11	Upson
SANDERS, Harris	17	Jackson	SANDWICH, Wm. S.	3	Upson
SANDERS, Henry	3	Chatham	SANE, H. G.	1	Clarke
SANDERS, Isaac	8	Upson	SANFORD, Adah	17	Hancock
SANDERS, James	8	Floyd	SANFORD, Daniel	8	Greene

Name	Number	County	Name	Number	County
SANFORD, Elam	16	Hancock	SARGEN ?, Wm.	12	Taliaferro
SANFORD, Elizabeth	4	Harris	SARLING, Isaac	3	Richmond
SANFORD, L. P.	5	Greene	SARRENCY, Allen P.	1	Tatnall
SANFORD, Lucinda	3	Hancock	SARTIN?, John	3	Madison
SANFORD, Obed P.	2	Troup	SARTZEN?, Edwin	1	Newton
SANFORD, B.W. Agt.	70	Putnam	SASNETT, Rhoda H.	4	Hancock
SANFORD, Benjamin F.	1	Baldwin	SASNETT, Richd. P.	35	Hancock
SANFORD, Sterling	23	Talbot	SASNETT, Richd. P.	18	Hancock
SANFORD, William	100	Baldwin	SASNETT, Wm. J.	38	Hancock
SANFORD, W. F.	19	Wilkinson	SASSER, E. R.	4	Walker
SANGER, Frederick H.	2	Richmond	SASSER, William	3	Early
SANKEY, Mrs. F.	7	Muscogee	SASSER, William	1	Merriwether
SANNORS?, G. T.	1	Elbert	SASSER, Howel	12	Screven
SANSOM, Glen H.	1	Morgan	SASSER, J. H.	1	Stewart
SANSOM, Micajah	5	Murray	SASSER, James	2	Stewart
SANSOM, Thomas	15	Clarke	SASSER, Jane	4	Stewart
SANSON, Franklin B.	4	Pike	SASSER, Thomas	2	Screven
SANSON, J. B.	3	Randolph	SATAWHITE, Dawson	5	Jasper
SANTINA, Simon	3	Chatham	SATAWHITE, Edward	1	Harris
SAPERETT, William J.	8	Newton	SATAWHITE,		
SAPERRIERE, Ang. D.	12	Jackson	Thomas L.	5	Upson
SAPINGTON, Henry	8	Monroe	SATCHER, Herring	4	Hancock
SAPINGTON, Wm. J.	2	Troup	SATCHER, Maurice	7	Baldwin
SAPP estate	4	Muscogee	SATERWHITE,		
SAPP estate	1	Muscogee	Lawrence	4	Paulding
SAPP, Elizabeth	5	Muscogee	SATERWHITE, James	4	Columbia
SAPP, Estate of	1	Muscogee	SATTERFIELD, Ann	4	Richmond
SAPP, Florney	4	Liberty	SATTERFIELD, John H.	1	Walker
SAPP, Forsyth B.	13	Muscogee	SAUCER, Jacob	2	Houston
SAPP, John	2	Burke	SAUCER, Stephen	8	Baker
SAPP, John	25	Muscogee	SAUDER, T. P.	6	Butts
SAPP, Theopihus	37	Muscogee	SAUDERS, James	8	Stewart
SAPP, Wm.	2	Pulaski	SAUDNERS, William	1	Muscogee
SAPP, Anderson	14	Stewart	SAULS, Mrs. S.	1	Muscogee
SAPP, Augustus	6	Burke	SAULS, Cullen	1	Stewart
SAPP, Dennis	34	Burke	SAULS, Theophus	3	Twiggs
SAPP, Dilson	16	Stewart	SAULSBERRY, Mrs.	12	Muscogee
SAPP, E. estate	39	Burke	SAULTER, Richard R.	6	Clarke
SAPP, Everett estate	24	Burke	SAUNDERS, D. J.	3	Muscogee
SAPP, Hansford	7	Burke	SAUNDERS, Doctor	1	Muscogee
SAPP, Isiah	21	Burke	SAUNDERS, Edward O.	8	Harris
SAPP, John	27	Burke	SAUNDERS, Horn N.	4	Muscogee
SAPP, John G.	1	Baker	SAUNDERS, Peterson	5	Muscogee
SAPP, Madison	11	Stewart	SAUNDERS, Peyton D.	15	Oglethorpe
SAPP, Mrs. A.	17	Decatur	SAUNDERS, Alex.	5	Butts
SAPP, Mrs. Mary T.	5	Burke	SAUNDERS, Nancy	21	Butts
SAPP, P. F.	33	Randolph	SAUNDERS, S. H.	5	Butts
SAPP, Pendleton	9	Burke	SAUNDERS, WilliamC.	23	Thomas
SAPP, William	100	Burke	SAURIE, James T.	2	Floyd
SAPP, Wm. T.	15	Randolph	SAUSELL?, Aug.	5	Pulaski
SAPPINGTON, R. T.	15	Henry	SAUSSY, J. R.	16	Chatham
SARAH STEAM			SAUZER, Lewis		
RICE MILL	11	Chatham	agt for GRAY, B.	37	Houston
SARDESS?, Thomas	16	Morgan	SAVAGE, C. A.	12	Lee

Name	Number	County
SAVAGE, I. W.	1	Marion
SAVAGE, John	6	Chatham
SAVAGE, Susan R.	5	Clarke
SAVAGE, Chas. D.	2	Coweta
SAVAGE, Elizabeth	8	Richmond
SAVAGE, John	3	Columbia
SAVALLY, John	6	McIntosh
SAVANNAH BRICK COMPANY	25	Chatham
SAVANNAH HOSPITAL	1	Chatham
SAVE, William H.	2	Clarke
SAVILL, Wm.	1	Jackson
SAVINGS, richard S.	9	Oglethorpe
SAWRIE, Selic	3	Floyd
SAWYER, Sarah	5	Chatham
SAWYER, W.	2	Crawford
SAWYER, Wm.	1	Randolph
SAWYER, Zadock	18	Randolph
SAWYERS, Francis	3	Newton
SAWYERS, May	27	Newton
SAWYERS, Thomas	3	Newton
SAXON, James	1	Early
SAXON, M.	3	Elbert
SAXON, Robert C.	15	Gordon
SAXON, S. W.	1	Elbert
SAXON, Saml.	4	Wilkes
SAXON, Augustus	1	Burke
SAXON, B. H.	6	Screven
SAXON, Celia	11	Burke
SAXON, Henry	2	Burke
SAXON, J. (?)	3	Coweta
SAXON, Joseph	7	Burke
SAXON, Lewis	3	Cass
SAXON, Mary	2	Burke
SAXON, R. H.	8	Screven
SAY, James	1	Hall
SAY, Millage	10	Newton
SAYE, Richard W.	1	Clarke
SAYER, D.	2	Elbert
SAYERS, David	29	Greene
SAYERS, James M.	8	Greene
SAYRE, N. C.	13	Hancock
SAYRE, R. S.	8	Hancock
SAYRE, Wm. H.	10	Hancock
SCAARBROUGH, Miles	17	Meriwether
SCAILS, G.	5	Elbert
SCAILS, L.	6	Elbert
SCAILS, S. M.	7	Elbert
SCALES, William	17	Gwinnett
SCARBOROUGH, Aden	3	Pulaski
SCARBOROUGH, Ansley?	1	Pulaski
SCARBOROUGH, D. F.	11	Laurens
SCARBOROUGH, Frederick	6	Madison
SCARBOROUGH, Geo. W.	1	Houston
SCARBOROUGH, Henry	10	Laurens
SCARBOROUGH, J. E.	3	Henry
SCARBOROUGH, J. J.	4	Twiggs
SCARBOROUGH, Josey	1	Pulaski
SCARBOROUGH, D.	12	Randolph
SCARBOROUGH, Malta	1	Sumter
SCARBOROUGH, Miles	1	Bullock
SCARBOROUGH, W. B.	1	Decatur
SCARBORRO, Enos H.	6	Screven
SCARBORRO, Jimmima	10	Screven
SCARBOUGH, D.	6	Twiggs
SCARBOUGH, James	3	Baker
SCARBROUGH, H. N.	5	Crawford
SCAREBROOKS, Wm.	10	Putnam
SCARLETT, Francis M.	369	Glynn
SCARLETT, D. C.	118	Camden
SCATTERGONE, Geo.	12	Bibb
SCHACKELFORD, Lloyd W.	3	Clarke
SCHERIFF, Frederick	2	Chatham
SCHEVNELL, R.S.	1	Clarke
SCHLELY, George	4	Chatham
SCHLEY, George	38	Jefferson
SCHLEY, George H.	12	Jefferson
SCHLEY, James M.	3	Chatham
SCHLEY, Philip T.	7	Muscogee
SCHLEY, Phillip	42	Muscogee
SCHLEY, Thomas	8	Muscogee
SCHLEY, Amos estate	24	Richmond
SCHLEY, George	11	Richmond
SCHLEY, George Factory	42	Richmond
SCHLEY, Henry J.	36	Burke
SCHLEY, Mary A.	18	Richmond
SCHLEY, William	24	Richmond
SCHMIDT, Henry	1	Chatham
SCHMIDT, Conrad	1	Chatham
SCHNEIDER & HOGRIFF	3	Richmond
SCHUDDER, John	20	Chatham
SCHUDDER, Amos	1	Chatham
SCHULTZ, John	2	Bibb
SCHUMPRINE, Daniel	2	Effingham
SCHUMPTRINE, John	1	Effingham
SCOFIELD, Ephraim E.	1	Richmond
SCOFIELD, John	3	Bibb
SCOFIELD, P.	1	Crawford
SCOGGIN, James	3	Pike
SCOGGIN, Young	2	Pike
SCOGGINS, F. M.	2	Heard

Name	Number	County	Name	Number	County
SCOGGINS, Thomas	68	Harris	SCOTT, Dennis	1	Screven
SCOGGINS, Thos.	11	Harris	SCOTT, E. B.	11	Crawford
SCOGGINS, W.	2	Chattooga	SCOTT, Eliz. A.	1	Richmond
SCOGIN, Andrew J.	1	Troup	SCOTT, Henry A.	3	Baker
SCOGIN, Gillum	8	Troup	SCOTT, Irby H.	19	Putnam
SCOGIN, Mary H.	8	Troup	SCOTT, Isaac	8	Bibb
SCOGIN, William	1	Troup	SCOTT, J.	16	Decatur
SCONYER, Richard B.	13	Burke	SCOTT, J. W.	8	Stewart
SCOTT, A. T.	6	Greene	SCOTT, James	14	Putnam
SCOTT, Alexander E.	2	Jones	SCOTT, Jane	3	Cass
SCOTT, Archibald	14	Newton	SCOTT, Jas.	1	Stewart
SCOTT, Charles M.	5	Cherokee	SCOTT, John	16	Bibb
SCOTT, Elizabeth	12	Troup	SCOTT, John	6	Burke
SCOTT, G. S.	10	Troup	SCOTT, John	1	Burke
SCOTT, Geo. W.	2	Houston	SCOTT, John	1	Columbia
SCOTT, George	1	Lowndes	SCOTT, John	2	Screven
SCOTT, Henry	4	Warren	SCOTT, John R.	7	Stewart
SCOTT, Henry F.	32	Troup	SCOTT, Joseph	2	DeKalb
SCOTT, Henry M.	9	Harris	SCOTT, Lorenzo	2	Screven
SCOTT, J. O.	5	Chattooga	SCOTT, Margaret	3	Chatham
SCOTT, James	21	Madison	SCOTT, Mrs. C.	2	Muscogee
SCOTT, James	7	Newton	SCOTT, N.	3	Screven
SCOTT, Jas. H.	6	Troup	SCOTT, Nathan	3	Screven
SCOTT, Jeremiah	18	Newton	SCOTT, Perry	6	Baldwin
SCOTT, John	15	Greene	SCOTT, Presilia	1	Taliaferro
SCOTT, John	60	Madison	SCOTT, Sanders	6	Stewart
SCOTT, John	5	Newton	SCOTT, Sarah	6	Columbia
SCOTT, John	1	Pike	SCOTT, T. R.	6	Randolph
SCOTT, John Jr.	9	Madison	SCOTT, Thomas H.	8	Baldwin
SCOTT, John	15	Walton	SCOTT, W. B.	6	Crawford
SCOTT, John P .	3	Greene	SCOTT, William	3	Baker
SCOTT, Joseph	3	Muscogee	SCOTT, William H.	27	Baldwin
SCOTT, Joseph	2	Pike	SCOTT, Wm.	14	Bibb
SCOTT, M.	10	Chattooga	SCOTT?, George S.	3	Cherokee
SCOTT, Margaret	10	Walton	SCOVELL, W. H.	5	Oglethorpe
SCOTT, Mary	1	Hancock	SCRANTON, Alxr.	51	Glynn
SCOTT, Mary L.	47	Glynn	SCRANTON, Daniel T.	5	Chatham
SCOTT, Moses	11	Cass	SCRANTON, Stack		
SCOTT, Nancy	1	Gordon	& Davis	1	Richmond
SCOTT, Patrick	1	Madison	SCRIMSHERE,		
SCOTT, Peter	6	Hancock	William B.	1	Stewart
SCOTT, Robert	4	Cass	SCRIVEN, James O.	26	Troup
SCOTT, Robert	1	Franklin	SCRIVEN, James P.	60	Chatham
SCOTT, Samuel	8	Newton	SCRIVIN, B. S.	19	Liberty
SCOTT, Stephen	1	Fayette	SCRIVIN, William E.	29	Liberty
SCOTT, Thos. C.	1	Laurens	SCROGGENS, James W.	5	Muscogee
SCOTT, W. S.	22	Morgan	SCROGGINS, James F.	3	Cobb
SCOTT, William	14	Monroe	SCROGGINS, David	4	Franklin
SCOTT, William	8	Newton	SCROGGINS, Marshal	1	Harris
SCOTT, William W.	6	Madison	SCROGGINS,		
SCOTT, Young	2	Gordon	Richard M.	5	Jasper
SCOTT, Alexr.	45	Camden	SCROGGINS, Thos. E.	5	Harris
SCOTT, Benjm.	5	Camden	SCROGGINS, B.	2	Coweta
SCOTT, Chas.	33	Columbia	SCROGGINS, Green B.	2	Talbot

Name	Number	County	Name	Number	County
SCROGGINS, William D.	9	Baldwin	SEARS, Timothy	9	Wilkinson
SCRUGGS, Allethea	5	Chatham	SEARS, W. C.	19	Stewart
SCRUGGS, E. V.	5	Jasper	SEAT, Solomon	6	Pike
SCRUGGS, Richard	12	Lowndes	SEATH?, Mary	8	Harris
SCRUGGS, John W.	2	Rabun	SEATS, W. W.	13	Morgan
SCRUGGS, Richard	5	Burke	SEAWELL, James H.	4	Talbot
SCRUGGS, William G.	4	Warren	SEAWRIGHT, Stephen	10	Cherokee
SCRUTCHINS, Thos.	26	Lee	SEAY, James	25	Meriwether
SCRUTCHINS, Sarah	61	Sumter	SEAY, John	30	Jackson
SCUDDER, A. M.	2	Clarke	SEAY, Thomas	59	Murray
SCUDDER, Elizabeth	7	Forsyth	SEAY, William H.	12	Murray
SCUDDER, J. M.	18	Forsyth	SEAY, S. B.	1	Cass
SCUDDER, Saml.	1	Greene	SEBASTIAN, Edward	9	Cherokee
SEA, Cyrus	4	Gilmer	SECKINGER, Benjamin	15	Lowndes
SEA, William	3	Stewart	SECKINGER, Frederick	1	Lowndes
SEABROOK, Martha	21	Jones	SECKINGER, Joshua	1	Effingham
SEAGER, Samuel	15	Burke	SECKINGER, William	1	Effingham
SEAGLE, John	8	Meriwether	SEDDER?, Stephen	2	Franklin
SEAGO, Benj.	1	Cherokee	SEEGAR, Samuel	3	Madison
SEAGO, Abraham	8	Richmond	SEEGAR, Solomon	2	Madison
SEAGO, Middleton	9	Richmond	SEGAR, W. M.	1	Jackson
SEAGO, Nancy	12	Richmond	SEGARS, Francis	1	Jackson
SEAGRAVES, Benjamin	1	Pike	SEGRAVES, Hilsman	3	Pike
SEAGRAVES, Edmund	7	Pike	SEGRAVES, T.	6	Pike
SEAL, John	2	Lincoln	SEGRIST, Laban	1	Houston
SEAL, P. W.	27	Lincoln	SEIG, F. F.	5	Sumter
SEALE, Janus	10	Wilkes	SEIGH ?, Nicholas D.	134	Richmond
SEALES?, Elizabeth	5	Habersham	SEIGLER, Wm.	1	Crawford
SEALEY, John	10	Muscogee	SEIMEN ?, Josiah	1	Ware
SEALEY, John	6	Randolph	SELBY, Nancy	5	Coweta
SEALS, Asberry	1	Harris	SEIRCAS, Edward	2	Thomas
SEALS, Henry M.	1	Hancock	SELEMTE?, John	6	Clarke
SEALS, Archibald	3	Camden	SELF, James	5	Greene
SEALS, William	1	Richmond	SELF, John D.	2	Wilkes
SEALS, William A.	8	Warren	SELFRIDGE, J.	2	Henry
SEAN, Elias	16	Wilkinson	SELIG, Gabriel	4	Talbot
SEANARETT, W. A.	27	Pike	SELLARS, Richard	1	Marion
SEARCEY, B.	3	Bibb	SELLERS, Edwin	1	Chatham
SEARCEY, Benjamin	18	Talbot	SELLERS, Freeman	5	Appling
SEARCEY, Thos. B.	1	Bibb	SELLERS, John M.	12	Appling
SEARCY, Daniel B.	29	Monroe	SELLERS, Judy	10	Hall
SEARCY, John	32	Talbot	SELLERS, Lemuel	8	Appling
SEARCY, John	9	Talbot	SELLERS, Nancy	5	Appling
SEARCY, William	2	Baldwin	SELLERS, Nathan N. H.	2	Houston
SEARCY, William	100	Talbot	SELLERS, William	15	Harris
SEARLES, John	8	Lincoln	SELLERS, A.	5	Bibb
SEARLES, Martha	5	Lincoln	SELLERS, Guard C.	2	Richmond
SEARLES, Thomas	12	Lincoln	SELMAN, Benjamin F.	8	Walton
SEARLES, Thomas	5	Lincoln	SELMAN, J. J.	12	Clarke
SEARLS, H.	5	Harris	SELMAN, Wiley	7	Floyd
SEARS, David C.	9	Marion	SELMAN, Willis	7	Floyd
SEARS, Archibald	7	Stewart	SELPH, Thomas	9	Thomas
SEARS, Henry J.	11	Wilkinson	SELZ, John P.	6	Richmond
SEARS, Martha	7	Talbot	SEMLIC, P. S.	19	Jefferson

Name	Number	County	Name	Number	County
SEMMES, Jno. R.	41	Wilkes	SHACKELFORD, J. C.	1	Meriwether
SEMMES, Paul J.	14	Muscogee	SHACKELFORD, John	23	Jackson
SEMMES, Thos.	30	Wilkes	SHACKELFORD, Lloyd	11	Madison
SEND, Uriah	4	Stewart	SHACKELFORD, Owen	2	Early
SEPIONS ?, Jno.	5	Randolph	SHACKELFORD, Anna	33	Hancock
SEPP, Bartlett W.	4	Appling	SHACKLEFORD, Ele	1	Oglethorpe
SEPPARD, C. H.	10	Washington	SHACKLEFORD,		
SERGANT, Harrison G.	5	Pike	J. A. B.	4	Gordon
SERTON?, James	2	Gwinnett	SHACKLEFORD,		
SERVICE, John H.	2	Richmond	James M.	2	Upson
SESSIONS, Benj.	42	Washington	SHACKLEFORD,		
SESSIONS, Jacob	3	Lee	James P.	2	Franklin
SESSIONS, Joseph	2	Washington	SHACKLEFORD,		
SESSIONS, Winny	5	Pike	Mord. Jr.	2	Heard
SESSIONS, Joseph	28	Stewart	SHACKLEFORD,		
SETTLE, William	2	Richmond	Mordecai	6	Heard
SEVILLE, Benson	13	Lowndes	SHACKLEFORD,		
SEWAL, Joseph	12	Elbert	Thos.	5	Heard
SEWAL, James H.	1	Campbell	SHACKLEFORD,		
SEWARD, Hansel R.	41	Thomas	George W.	3	Richmond
SEWARD, James L.	7	Thomas	SHACKELFORD, James	1	Richmond
SEWEL, M.	1	Coweta	SHACLEFORD, Asa	14	Stewart
SEWEL, Price	3	Coweta	SHAD, Solomon S.	44	Chatham
SEWEL, Wm.	3	Coweta	SHAD, Elias B.	18	Chatham
SEWELL, Charles W.	1	Franklin	SHADIX, Wm.	1	Fayette
SEWELL, Francis	1	Madison	SHADUX, Nancy	6	Fayette
SEWELL, Green B.	7	Franklin	SHAFFER, F.	4	Muscogee
SEWELL, J. L.	5	Meriwether	SHAFFER, Henrietta M.	6	Hancock
SEWELL, James	14	Meriwether	SHAFFER, John A.	1	Chatham
SEWELL, John	11	Franklin	SHAFFER, Dedrick	1	Chatham
SEWELL, John	2	Franklin	SHAFFER, Jacob	17	Chatham
SEWELL, John P.	7	Meriwether	SHAFFER, Margaret	1	Chatham
SEWELL, Levi	1	Franklin	SHAMBLES, John W.	1	Gwinnett
SEWELL, Marion	2	Madison	SHANK, Felix	18	Wilkes
SEWELL, N.	5	Meriwether	SHANK, George	14	Wilkes
SEWELL, R. J.	10	Meriwether	SHANK, John	1	Columbia
SEWELL, Samuel	8	Cobb	SHANK, Savannah	4	Wilkes
SEWELL, Samuel	3	Franklin	SHANKS, John	17	Troup
SEWELL, William	1	Walton	SHANKLAND, Egbert	11	Columbia
SEWELL, Wm. L.	1	Cass	SHANKLE, Eli	8	Jackson
SEWELS, R.	1	Coweta	SHANKLE, Levi H.	1	Jackson
SEXTON, J. G.	3	Chatham	SHANKLIN, J.	6	Bibb
SEY, David	20	Columbia	SHANKS, James D.	34	Lowndes
SEY, Thomas	21	Columbia	SHANNANS, Rual	3	Appling
SEYMORE, Leroy	5	Jasper	SHANNON, C. J.	37	Houston
SEYMORE, Calvin	1	Stewart	SHANNON, David	2	Franklin
SEYMORE, Elijah	2	Stewart	SHANNON, Harriett W.	8	Pike
SEYMORE, G. W.	12	Bibb	SHANNON, James	1	Muscogee
SEYMORE, Mary	2	Bibb	SHANNON, John	37	Monroe
SEYMOUR, H. C.	6	Morgan	SHANNON, Leonard	2	Franklin
SEYMOUR, John R.	2	Jasper	SHANNON, Samuel	2	Franklin
SEYMOUR, H. L.	1	Bibb	SHANNON, Wm.	2	Pulaski
SHACKELFORD, Allen	7	Pike	SHANNON, Peter J.	1	Richmond
SHACKELFORD, H. B.	2	Meriwether	SHARBOR?, George	1	DeKalb

Name	Number	County	Name	Number	County
SHARBUTT, Sarah	1	Troup	SHAW, John W.	1	Richmond
SHARK, Hiram Sen.	3	Carroll	SHAW, Joseph	23	Stewart
SHARK, John A.	2	Meriwether	SHAW, Martin	2	Lowndes
SHARLEY, Thomas	4	Warren	SHAW, Miles M.	3	Greene
SHARMAN, O. C.	12	Upson	SHAWS, Mary	9	Warren
SHARMAN, Thomas S.	26	Upson	SHEALDS, Simpson	4	Floyd
SHARP, A. B.	6	Greene	SHEALEY, Andrew	17	Macon
SHARP, Cyrus	9	Monroe	SHEALY, John	7	Macon
SHARP, H. T.	2	Newton	SHEALY, Wm.	3	Macon
SHARP, J. E.	3	Twiggs	SHEAN, Michel	33	Taliaferro
SHARP, Jane	10	Jackson	SHEARER, Rebecca	1	Chatham
SHARP, Judith	12	Merriwether	SHEARER, Terry	1	Wilkes
SHARP, Lewis J.	2	Jackson	SHEARER, William	1	Chatham
SHARP, Thomas	14	Newton	SHEARHOUS, Elizabeth	4	Effingham
SHARP, William H.	5	Monroe	SHEARHOUSE, Richard	1	Effingham
SHARP, Esley	1	Stewart	SHEARHOUSE, William	1	Effingham
SHARP, Green	18	Screven	SHEATS, Benajah S.	12	Clarke
SHARP, James	37	Chatham	SHEATS, John L.	6	Walton
SHARP, James	1	Taliaferro	SHEATS, M. M.	12	Clarke
SHARP, James L.	4	Taliaferro	SHECK, Elizabeth	4	Chatham
SHARP, Jas. P.	59	Randolph	SHEFFIELD estate	6	Bullock
SHARP, Robert	1	Screven	SHEFFIELD, Arthur	92	Early
SHARP, William	2	Stewart	SHEFFIELD, Elizabeth	6	Early
SHARP, William	1	Stewart	SHEFFIELD, Jacob	10	Morgan
SHARPE, Hamilton W.	17	Lowndes	SHEFFIELD, John	17	Thomas
SHARPE, James T.	8	Harris	SHEFFIELD, Josiah	14	Merriwether
SHARPE, Perma	2	Troup	SHEFFIELD, Pliny	99	Thomas
SHARPE, Richd.	1	Hancock	SHEFFIELD, Robert W.	3	Early
SHARPE, Thos. A.	24	Chattooga	SHEFFIELD, West	4	Early
SHARPE, E. F.	1	Tatnall	SHEFFIELD, Wm. Sen.	21	Hancock
SHARPE, Rebecca	7	Tatnall	SHEFFIELD, Edward O.	9	Dooly
SHARR, Alfred	6	Morgan	SHEFFIELD, John	12	Camden
SHASTIE ?, H. W.	6	Thomas	SHEFFIELD, John B.	1	Richmond
SHATTLES, James	1	Monroe	SHEFFIELD, Nancy	15	Early
SHAW, Alexander	7	Walker	SHEFFIELD, Seabron	5	Early
SHAW, Amos	1	Muscogee	SHEFFIELD, William	9	Bullock
SHAW, Amos	1	Walker	SHEFTALL, Mordecai Jr.	2	Chatham
SHAW, George	1	Walker	SHEFTALL, Mordecai Sen.	7	Chatham
SHAW, H. T.	8	Newton	SHEFTALL, Emanual	6	Chatham
SHAW, James	10	Muscogee	SHEHEE, Sherod B.	16	Pike
SHAW, John	3	Jasper	SHEILS, P. K.	4	Chatham
SHAW, John	8	Liberty	SHELAT, James	3	Gordon
SHAW, Margaret	13	Warren	SHELL, Mary H.	3	Hancock
SHAW, William	10	Jasper	SHELL, J.	2	Coweta
SHAW, William	2	Muscogee	SHELL, Wm. B.	18	Coweta
SHAW, Wm. P.	1	Walker	SHELMAN, C. T.	13	Cass
SHAW, Wm. W.	4	Cass	SHELNUT, Wm.	5	Walton
SHAW, Alexander	2	Randolph	SHELTON, John	1	Franklin
SHAW, Alexander J.C.	51	Chatham	SHELTON, Jourdain	4	Emanual
SHAW, C.	1	Decatur	SHELTON, Lewis	6	Franklin
SHAW, Frederick R.	1	Richmond	SHELTON, Martin	1	Cobb
SHAW, George	2	DeKalb	SHELTON, V. B.	1	Forsyth
SHAW, James	1	Cass			
SHAW, John T.	1	Stewart			

Name	Number	County	Name	Number	County
SHELTON, V. H.	4	Franklin	SHERIFF, Abel	7	Lumpkin
SHELTON, Willis	1	Cobb	SHERLIN, James	1	Washington
SHELTON, David	77	Talbot	SHERLING, R. C.	14	Stewart
SHELTON, David	12	Talbot	SHERMAN, Francis A.	3	Morgan
SHELTON, E. S.	2	Bibb	SHERMAN, John R.	5	Merriwether
SHEPARD, Wm. G.	3	Liberty	SHERMAN, Wm.	22	Cass
SHEPARD, Edwin	12	Coweta	SHERMAN, Edgar	2	Richmond
SHEPARD, Henry	1	Randolph	SHERMAN, Henry	7	DeKalb
SHEPARD, Wm.	18	Randolph	SHERMAN, Jas.	4	Coweta
SHEPERD, E. T.	76	Stewart	SHERMAN, Jas.	19	Randolph
SHEPHERD, A. E.	6	Muscogee	SHERMAN, Jno.	4	Randolph
SHEPHERD, Benjamin	33	Troup	SHERMAN, Nancy	2	Stewart
SHEPHERD, Carter	70	Morgan	SHERMAN, Robert	1	Stewart
SHEPHERD, Henry	4	Houston	SHERMON, Rob J.	4	Stewart
SHEPHERD, J. M.	4	Merriwether	SHEROD, James	2	Jefferson
SHEPHERD, Jacob	1	Wilkinson	SHERRAR, Jno.	2	Henry
SHEPHERD, James M.	4	Merriwether	SHERRAR. Wm.	22	Wilkes
SHEPHERD, Jesse	1	Upson	SHERREER, James B.	1	Washington
SHEPHERD, John	23	Troup	SHERRIL, Mahala	2	Paulding
SHEPHERD, John W.	10	Merriwether	SHERROD, William	3	Emanual
SHEPHERD, John W.	16	Troup	SHERROD, H.	2	Talbot
SHEPHERD, K.	3	Wilkinson	SHERROD, Haywood	4	Talbot
SHEPHERD, Mathew	3	Houston	SHERROD, Robert	2	Talbot
SHEPHERD, N.	3	Morgan	SHERROD, Wright	16	Talbot
SHEPHERD, Nathan	3	Lowndes	SHERROD, Zach	1	Talbot
SHEPHERD, Nathan	9	Merriwether	SHERROD, Zachariah	1	Talbot
SHEPHERD, Robert	15	Houston	SHERROD, Benjamin	1	Emanual
SHEPHERD, Russell	12	Walton	SHERRORD, John	9	Emanual
SHEPHERD, Simion ?	4	Walton	SHERRORD, William G.	7	Emanual
SHEPHERD, Susanah	3	Walton	SHERWOOD, A. C.	9	Bibb
SHEPHERD, Thomas	24	Morgan	SHEWMAKER, Annie	3	Richmond
SHEPHERD, Thomas	21	Newton	SHEWOOD,E. C.	1	Bibb
SHEPHERD, Eliza	2	Screven	SHICK, Peter	2	Chatham
SHEPHERD, Gathara	2	Burke	SHIE, Samuel C.	7	Jasper
SHEPHERD, John M.	15	Stewart	SHIE, Seabron J.	43	Jasper
SHEPHERD, L.D.	1	Screven	SHIELD, John	2	Warren
SHEPHERD, Mourning	1	Screven	SHIELDS, Abraham	5	Warren
SHEPHERD, Richard	10	Butts	SHIELDS, Francis	13	Morgan
SHEPHERD, W. H.	3	Chatham	SHIELDS, J. W.	3	Elbert
SHEPHERD, William	7	DeKalb	SHIELDS, James	12	Jackson
SHEPPARD, Andrew	13	Marion	SHIELDS, John	5	Warren
SHEPPARD,			SHIELDS, John S.	2	Walker
David B. M.	25	Liberty	SHIELDS, Matthew	4	Warren
SHEPPARD, John	1	Washington	SHIELDS, Robert	11	Houston
SHEPPARD, John	7	Washington	SHIELDS, Robert	17	Morgan
SHEPPARD, Jos.	1	Wilkes	SHIELDS, Susannah	7	Madison
SHEPPARD, Samuel	3	Marion	SHIELDS, James	14	Columbia
SHEPPARD, Thomas	15	McIntosh	SHIELDS, James	3	Columbia
SHEPPARD, J. B. agt.	5	Bibb	SHIELDS, James Jun.	1	Columbia
SHEPPEARD, Z. F.	3	Washington	SHIFLETT, P.	8	Elbert
SHERE, Joseph	15	Fayette	SHIFLETT, P.	4	Elbert
SHERFIELD, Wm.	6	Bibb	SHIFLETT, ?	8	Elbert
SHERIDAN, John	9	Talbot	SHIFLETT, ?	7	Elbert
SHERIDEN, Dennis	20	Talbot	SHIFTELL, L.	7	Elbert

Name	Number	County	Name	Number	County
SHIFTELL, L.	1	Elbert	SHOCKLE, Henry	8	Cobb
SHIFTELL, M.	2	Elbert	SHOCKLEY, Cornelius	6	Jackson
SHINE, D. W.	2	Twiggs	SHOCKLEY, K. K.	6	Franklin
SHINE, D. W.	11	Twiggs	SHOCKLEY, Thomas R.	10	Gordon
SHINE, William	4	Houston	SHOCKLY, Thomas	1	Hall
SHINE, Andrew J.	10	Dooly	SHOCKLY, Charles H.	26	Columbia
SHINE, John A.	1	Dooly	SHOEMAKER, C. P.	21	Morgan
SHINE, John M.	6	Dooly	SHOEMATE, B. F.	1	DeKalb
SHINE, Thomas T.	15	Crawford	SHOFNER, Martha	2	Muscogee
SHINHOLSER,			SHOM, Stephen	1	Bullock
William J.	4	Houston	SHOPPEN ?,		
SHINHOLSTER, T. J.	18	Bibb	Lawrence T.	2	Richmond
SHIP, Mark	2	Columbia	SHORT, Anderson F.	4	Pike
SHIP, Richard	8	Walker	SHORT, Archibald	1	Madison
SHIP, W. W.	2	Sumter	SHORT, Branch	7	Columbia
SHIPLEY, J.			SHORT, Ellender	2	Macon
for Ga. R. R. Comp.	5	DeKalb	SHORT, John	3	Wilkes
SHIPP, David	2	Marion	SHORT, Howell	2	Marion
SHIPP, J. L.	1	Fayette	SHORT, Mary	3	Marion
SHIPP, James	8	Pike	SHORT, Robert R.	11	Heard
SHIPP, Lemual	4	Greene	SHORT, Wm. C.	2	Wilkes
SHIPP, Mark	20	Lincoln	SHORT, Adam	8	Chatham
SHIPP, Mark	3	Lincoln	SHORTER,		
SHIPP, Richard	1	Marion	Mrs. Sophia H.	12	Muscogee
SHIPP, William	18	Muscogee	SHORTER, R. C.	4	Muscogee
SHIPP, David J.	5	Stewart	SHOTWELL, Mrs. A.	4	Muscogee
SHIPPE, Wm.	6	Marion	SHRIVAL, Robert G.	13	Burke
SHIPPY, Elizabeth	14	Muscogee	SHROPSHEN, S. J.	2	Fayette
SHIPTRINE, Joshua	2	Pike	SHROPSHIRE,		
SHIRIE, Sarah A.	1	Chatham	James W.	38	Jasper
SHIRLING, Winbern	7	Talbot	SHROPSHIRE, John W.	4	Jones
SHIRRELL, J. D.	4	Pike	SHROPSHIRE, Wesley	21	Chattooga
SHIVER, Bonapart	10	Pulaski	SHROPSHIRE, J. B.	6	Randolph
SHIVER, Burrel	3	Floyd	SHROPSHIRE, Josh. P.	7	Coweta
SHIVER, James	4	Houston	SHROPSHIRE, W. M.	4	Chattooga
SHIVER, Jas. H.	1	Carroll	SHROUND?, Henry	1	Dooly
SHIVER, Jefferson	1	Pulaski	SHUCKLEY, M. L.	4	Monroe
SHIVER, Flemming	2	Baker	SHUFFIELD, Robert	17	Sumter
SHIVER, J. P.	1	Bibb	SHUFORD, E. L.	1	Cherokee
SHIVER, P.	1	Wilkinson	SHUGART, Robert C.	1	Troup
SHIVERS, Barnaby	5	Hancock	SHUMAKER, Joseph A.	33	Burke
SHIVERS, Catherine	1	Hancock	SHUMAKER, Oscar L.	5	Burke
SHIVERS, Eli	6	Houston	SHUMAN, George H.	9	Bryan
SHIVERS, Isaac	14	Pulaski	SHUMAN, Samuel G.	12	Chatham
SHIVERS, Jacob	16	Pulaski	SHUMAN, James	4	Bryan
SHIVERS, James	14	Muscogee	SHUMAN, John M.	9	Bryan
SHIVERS, James A.	14	Warren	SHUMAN, Martin	1	Bryan
SHIVERS, John M.	2	Warren	SHUMAN, Pherebe	10	Bryan
SHIVERS, Jonas	4	Pike	SHUMAN, William	1	Bullock
SHIVERS, Thomas J.			SHUMAN?, Doctor	13	Effingham
agent	6	Muscogee	SHUMANS, Reual	1	Appling
SHIVERS, William	39	Hancock	SHUMATE, Daniel	24	Wilkes
SHIVERS, Sidney	10	Stewart	SHUMATE, Jane	7	Chattooga
SHIVERS, Wm.	3	Bibb	SHUMATE, Benjamin	4	DeKalb

Name	Number	County	Name	Number	County
SHUMATE, Joseph D.	7	Walker	SIMMONS, J. A.	32	Lincoln
SHURLEY, Aaron	2	Crawford	SIMMONS, J. D.	4	Henry
SHURLEY, Charles	7	Warren	SIMMONS, J. M.	1	Muscogee
SHURLEY, J. W.	2	Randolph	SIMMONS, J. R.	3	Floyd
SHURLEY, W. T.	6	Crawford	SIMMONS, James P.	4	Gwinnett
SHURLY, James M.	1	Paulding	SIMMONS, Jas.	4	Pulaski
SHURLY, R.	1	Muscogee	SIMMONS, Jno.	5	Pulaski
SHY, James	9	Hancock	SIMMONS, Joanna	21	Clarke
SHY, James	15	Morgan	SIMMONS, John	2	Lincoln
SIBELEY, A. A.	4	Chatham	SIMMONS, John	1	Monroe
SIBLEY, A. Estate	19	Richmond	SIMMONS, John	7	Pike
SIBLEY, Gabriel	17	Baker	SIMMONS, John B.	13	Hancock
SIBLEY, Jonah	4	Richmond	SIMMONS, John D.	2	Hall
SIBLEY, S. S.	3	Chatham	SIMMONS, John K.	24	Monroe
SIBLEY, William	8	Talbot	SIMMONS, John W.	8	Monroe
SIBLEY, Wm. W.	2	Coweta	SIMMONS, Joseph T.	10	Hancock
SIDDONS, Benj. G.	3	Clarke	SIMMONS, Joshua	19	Hall
SIDWELL, Thomas Y.	1	Warren	SIMMONS, Mary A.	36	Lincoln
SIGLER, George H.	3	Walker	SIMMONS, Mary Ann	2	Marion
SIKES, J. F.	1	Houston	SIMMONS, Nancy	23	Oglethorpe
SIKES, James	5	Houston	SIMMONS, Piety	19	Jones
SIKES, John	1	Pike	SIMMONS, R. S.	7	Floyd
SIKES, Joseph	4	Monroe	SIMMONS, Reuben	1	Floyd
SIKES, Joseph	2	Monroe	SIMMONS, Stern	17	Lincoln
SIKES, Mathew G.	14	Houston	SIMMONS, Wm.	13	Floyd
SIKES, Wiley J.	2	Monroe	SIMMONS, A. G.	15	Crawford
SIKES, Daniel	3	Tatnall	SIMMONS, Asa	1	Putnam
SIKES, Zach.	2	Clarke	SIMMONS, Beverly	2	Carroll
SILBERT, Sarah	3	Richmond	SIMMONS, D. W.	6	Crawford
SILCOX, John	11	Richmond	SIMMONS, Green	7	Putnam
SILVY, J. B.	1	Campbell	SIMMONS, Greenville	2	Richmond
SIM, Isaac	1	Cobb	SIMMONS, J. R.	1	Chattooga
SIMES, John T.	6	Baker	SIMMONS, James	7	Gilmer
SIMINGTON, Moses	4	Pike	SIMMONS, James L.	1	Richmond
SIMINGTON,Theophilus	2	Pike	SIMMONS, John T.	2	Telfair
SIMMONS, -----	60	Chatham	SIMMONS, Martha	7	Baker
SIMMONS, A. Q.	5	Walker	SIMMONS, Mary	3	Telfair
SIMMONS, James W.	32	Hancock	SIMMONS, Samuel	8	Screven
SIMMONS, John	7	Walton	SIMMONS, Sarah	6	Putnam
SIMMONS, Lacy J.	1	Thomas	SIMMONS, W.	4	Crawford
SIMMONS, Richard	12	Floyd	SIMMONS, William	15	Stewart
SIMMONS, Samuel	4	Thomas	SIMMONS, Wm.	16	Coweta
SIMMONS, Thomas	5	Thomas	SIMMONS, Wm.	11	Crawford
SIMMONS, A.	20	Henry	SIMMONS?, William H.	14	Pike
SIMMONS, Benjamin	6	Hancock	SIMMS, Wm.	9	Clarke
SIMMONS, Bennett	1	Madison	SIMMS, A. J.	17	Heard
SIMMONS, C. C.	3	Jefferson	SIMMS, James	2	Clarke
SIMMONS, C. L.	1	Hall	SIMMS, Sanders B.	14	Merriwether
SIMMONS, Caleb	1	Fayette	SIMMS, Wm. G.	15	Meriwether
SIMMONS, Edward	10	Hall	SIMMS, Wm. M.	22	Heard
SIMMONS, Elmore H.	69	Harris	SIMMS, B. Sen.	31	Coweta
SIMMONS, Henry J.	17	Merriwether	SIMMS, J. C.	6	Coweta
SIMMONS, Isaac	12	Madison	SIMMS, John	26	Coweta
SIMMONS, Ivey	25	Lowndes	SIMMS, S. D.	3	Clarke

Name	Number	County	Name	Number	County
SIMMTON?, Thos.	3	Clarke	SIMS, Richard H.	4	Pike
SIMON, ? (Paulson)	6	Richmond	SIMS, Richard T.	64	Newton
SIMONETT, Augustus	3	Richmond	SIMS, Sherman J.	10	Madison
SIMONS, Jesse M.	1	Sumter	SIMS, Sherod	13	Pike
SIMONTON, Joel R.	10	Marion	SIMS, Stephen D.	11	Marion
SIMONTON, John A.	7	Merriwether	SIMS, T. W.	4	Henry
SIMONTON, E.	21	Crawford	SIMS, W.	6	Troup
SIMPKIN, John	1	Oglethorpe	SIMS, Wiley H.	11	Troup
SIMPLER, Elany	4	Merriwether	SIMS, William	17	Lincoln
SIMPSON, A. N.	2	Cobb	SIMS, William	34	Monroe
SIMPSON, Arden	5	Warren	SIMS, William	4	Stewart
SIMPSON, David	6	Pulaski	SIMS, Wm.	6	Henry
SIMPSON, David M.	4	Cobb	SIMS, Anderson	1	Stewart
SIMPSON, Felix	1	Hancock	SIMS, Ann	3	Richmond
SIMPSON, J.	1	Cherokee	SIMS, Benj. T.	14	Coweta
SIMPSON, J. P.	5	Cherokee	SIMS, Caroline	13	Bullock
SIMPSON, John	14	Stewart	SIMS, F. T.	3	Bibb
SIMPSON, Leonard	5	Harris	SIMS, G. R.	14	Coweta
SIMPSON, Matthew	1	Cass	SIMS, Green	7	Stewart
SIMPSON, Milton	12	Pulaski	SIMS, Guz	26	Columbia
SIMPSON, Robert	25	Harris	SIMS, H. H.	4	Decatur
SIMPSON, Samuel	3	Gordon	SIMS, Henry	2	Decatur
SIMPSON, Thomas	1	Fayette	SIMS, J. M.	11	Coweta
SIMPSON, Thomas	7	Jones	SIMS, Jacob	3	Bryan
SIMPSON, Wash.	5	Pulaski	SIMS, Jasper	2	Bullock
SIMPSON, Wm.	4	Pulaski	SIMS, John	10	Sumter
SIMPSON, Charles	9	Stewart	SIMS, John D.	4	Coweta
SIMPSON, Charles	1	Talbot	SIMS, John M.	21	Coweta
SIMPSON, J. A. Agent	55	Randolph	SIMS, Leonard	24	Columbia
SIMPSON, James M.	19	Richmond	SIMS, Littleberry	4	Sumter
SIMPSON, James M.	1	Richmond	SIMS, Lucy	1	Stewart
SIMPSON, John	1	DeKalb	SIMS, R.	4	Decatur
SIMPSON, Joseph	1	Baldwin	SIMS, Robt. W.	8	Coweta
SIMPSON, L. C.	1	DeKalb	SIMS, Samuel	6	Bullock
SIMPSON, S. E.	1	Bibb	SIMS, Susan	9	Bibb
SIMPSON, Samuel	3	Cass	SIMS, William	5	Stewart
SIMPSON, W. R.	1	Bibb	SIMS, William	1	Stewart
SIMPSON, W. W.	50	Wilkes	SIMS?, Barnes	4	Marion
SIMS, Bennett	14	Madison	SIMSON, William	4	Monroe
SIMS, George H.	19	Marion	SINCLAIR, Benj. W.	2	Lowndes
SIMS, George W.	14	Wilkes	SINEATH, Jesse S.	2	Ware
SIMS, H. J.	1	Troup	SINGER, George	4	Stewart
SIMS, Henry L.	2	Walker	SINGER, John	8	Stewart
SIMS, Hope	6	Franklin	SINGLETARY, Brayton	6	Thomas
SIMS, Hull	2	Newton	SINGLETARY, Henry	5	Thomas
SIMS, James	29	Monroe	SINGLETARY, James	2	Thomas
SIMS, James	60	Oglethorpe	SINGLETARY, Joseph	1	Thomas
SIMS, John	49	Oglethorpe	SINGLETARY, Nathan	1	Sumter
SIMS, M.	1	Henry			
SIMS, Mary	10	Oglethorpe	SINGLETERRY, James A.	3	Pike
SIMS, Murdeck	1	Pulaski	SINGLETERRY, Michael	3	Houston
SIMS, Nancy	6	Madison			
SIMS, Rachel	35	Lincoln	SINGLETERRY, Chas.	1	Carroll
SIMS, Redding	4	Wilkes			

Name	Number	County
SINGLETERY, D. E.	2	Randolph
SINGLETERY, Wm.	11	Randolph
SINGLETON, Alexander	2	Monroe
SINGLETON, George W.	2	Houston
SINGLETON, Henry	16	Monroe
SINGLETON, J. J.	7	Lumpkin
SINGLETON, Joseph J.	61	Lumpkin
SINGLETON, Leroy	31	Jones
SINGLETON, Wyatt	8	Pike
SINGLETON, Wyatt R.	8	Marion
SINGLETON, George W. agt ROSS, B.	96	Houston
SINGLETON, J. L.	5	Screven
SINN, James	1	Cass
SINN, Alfred M.	3	Cass
SINQUEFIELD, James M.	13	Jefferson
SINQUEFIELD, Moses	10	Merriwether
SINQUEFIELD, P. G.	12	Merriwether
SINQUEFIELD, William	7	Jefferson
SINTON, John S.	45	Clarke
SIRMONS, Benj.	7	Cllinch
SIRMONS, Josiah	4	Clinch
SISLER, George H.	6	Oglethorpe
SISSON, James	37	Jackson
SISSON, Thomas S.	9	Franklin
SISSON, William B.	8	Franklin
SISTRUNCK, Allen	5	Lincoln
SISTRUNCK, Elizabeth	7	Lincoln
SISTRUNK, Samuel H. J.	13	Houston
SKELTON, ?	2	Elbert
SKELTON, L.	1	Elbert
SKELTON, Noel	2	Franklin
SKELTON, William	3	Newton
SKELTON, A. H.	2	Stewart
SKIDMON, Samuel	35	Morgan
SKINNER, Andrew J.	1	Walton
SKINNER, James	11	Chatham
SKINNER, James	1	Cobb
SKINNER, James R.	1	Gwinnett
SKINNER, John	18	Floyd
SKINNER, John	16	Heard
SKINNER, Jonas H.	2	Burke
SKINNER, Robert	2	Walton
SKINNER, Willis	7	Muscogee
SKINNER, Elizabeth	14	Richmond
SKINNER, James	3	Chatham
SKINNER, Jesse	7	Sumter
SKINNER, John	30	Richmond
SKINNER, Seaborn	17	Richmond
SKINNER, Sutton	1	Chatham
SKINNER, Thomas	22	Richmond

Name	Number	County
SKINNER, William	10	Burke
SKINNER, William	10	Richmond
SKINNER, Wm. J.	1	Coweta
SKITTER(?), N. W.	2	Crawford
SKRINE, E. Benj.	15	Washington
SKRINE, John J.	3	Hancock
SKRINE, Quin	15	Washington
SKRINE, Quintillian	24	Burke
SKYLER, Mrs.	2	Muscogee
SLACK, Joseph B.	49	Morgan
SLACK, Uriah	2	Richmond
SLACK?, John W.	5	Merriwether
SLADE, Elefair	5	Washington
SLADE, John	1	Floyd
SLADE, Joseph H.	6	Jones
SLADE, Samuel	15	Pike
SLADE, Simon	6	Pike
SLADE, Thomas B.	6	Muscogee
SLADE, Thos. B.	2	Muscogee
SLADE, Catherine	6	Dooly
SLADE, Daniel	5	Putnam
SLADE, Harris	2	Talbot
SLADE, Jeremiah	8	Dooly
SLADE, Mrs. F.	1	Decatur
SLADE, William	16	Dooly
SLADE, William	3	Talbot
SLAPPEY, Elizabeth	10	Macon
SLAPPEY, George H.	47	Macon
SLAPPEY, Reubin H.	89	Macon
SLAPPEY, Uriah	34	Macon
SLAPPEY, A. G.	3	Crawford
SLAPPY, R.	68	Twiggs
SLAPPY, William F.	18	Macon
SLAPPY, John G.	16	Baker
SLATEN, L. B.	3	Harris
SLATEN, William	1	Harris
SLATER, John	27	Thomas
SLATER, Horatio	1	Jefferson
SLATIN, Zachariah	2	Heard
SLATON, Henry C.	19	Monroe
SLATON, J. D.	12	Oglethorpe
SLATON, John	1	Cass
SLATON, Mickey	1	Jackson
SLATON, Usavius	1	Fayette
SLATON, Wade	12	Jackson
SLATON, Green	1	Bullock
SLATON, Harriet	1	Bullock
SLATON, John	1	Bryan
SLATON, Joseph	2	Talbot
SLATON, Margaret	1	Bullock
SLATON, Robert	2	Bullock
SLATON, Wm.	60	Wilkes
SLAUGHTER, Beverly	4	Harris
SLAUGHTER, Elizabeth	14	Greene

Name	Number	County	Name	Number	County
SLAUGHTER, H. G.	20	Troup	SMEDLEY, John	1	Troup
SLAUGHTER, Isaac H.	2	Jasper	SMEDLEY, Thos.	23	Troup
SLAUGHTER, Martin G.	4	Cobb	SMILALAR?, A. J.	2	Merriwether
SLAUGHTER, Mrs. R.	2	Merriwether	SMILEY, R.	17	Crawford
SLAUGHTER, R. S.	5	Greene	SMITH, Alexander	1	Floyd
SLAUGHTER, Susannah	1	Greene	SMITH, John C.	1	Franklin
SLAUGHTER, Thomas K.	16	Jasper	SMITH, ?	3	Meriwether
			SMITH, ?	3	Muscogee
SLAUGHTER, Thomas R.	16	Monroe	SMITH, ?	2	Walton
SLAUGHTER, Wm. A.	8	Troup	SMITH, ? A.	3	Morgan
SLAUGHTER, William N.	30	Monroe	SMITH, ? M.	3	Wilkinson
			SMITH, A.	7	Wilkinson
SLAUGHTER, Bradley	27	Putnam	SMITH, A. G.	13	Upson
SLAUGHTER, Henry	5	Telfair	SMITH, A. H.	9	Greene
SLAUGHTER, N. G.	3	Carroll	SMITH, A. L.	1	Newton
SLAUGHTER, Sarah	23	Putnam	SMITH, A. R.	8	Fayette
SLAY, D. R.	10	Troup	SMITH, A. T.	4	Hall
SLAY, John	2	Troup	SMITH, Aaron	1	Madison
SLEDGE, Amos	17	Upson	SMITH, Aaron	8	Pike
SLEDGE, E. H.	14	Troup	SMITH, Aaron S.	7	Cobb
SLEDGE, Wiley	1	Clarke	SMITH, Abraham	15	Jasper
SLEDGE, Jas. A.	8	Troup	SMITH, Absalom	3	Jefferson
SLEDGE, John	15	Troup	SMITH, Acy H.	10	Monroe
SLEDGE, Mins	9	Troup	SMITH, Adaline E.	10	Warren
SLEDGE, Shirley, Jr.	15	Troup	SMITH, Alexander	2	Meriwether
SLEDGE, STERLY	40	Troup	SMITH, Alexander	5	Washington
SLEGE, Alexander	2	Pike	SMITH, Alfred	3	Jackson
SLEIGH, John W.	12	Cobb	SMITH, Alfred B.	2	Warren
SLOAN, A. C.	16	Henry	SMITH, Allen B.	6	Washington
SLOAN, John	8	Chatham	SMITH, Anderson	1	Morgan
SLOCOMB, Wi lliam	5	Jones	SMITH, Andrew	1	Clarke
SLOCOMB, Jesse	5	Baker	SMITH, Andrew D.	4	Macon
SLOCUM, John	3	Newton	SMITH, Ann	5	Jackson
SLOCUM, William	1	Newton	SMITH, Ann Sr.	1	Jackson
SLOCUM, S.	13	Bibb	SMITH, Anthony E.	5	Clarke
SLOCUMB, David	6	Jones	SMITH, Arch	11	Fayette
SLOCUMB, Ezekiel	5	Jones	SMITH, Archibald	19	Cobb
SLOCUMB, Lee R.	2	Jones	SMITH, Asahel B.	5	Gwinnett
SLONE, James	3	Liberty	SMITH, Augustus B.	4	Warren
SLONE, Wm.	2	Irwin	SMITH, Austin	1	Ware
SLUSH?, William	1	Gwinnett	SMITH, B.	1	Elbert
SMALL, D. B.	9	Pulaski	SMITH, B. F.	1	Upson
SMALLEY, James	9	Columbia	SMITH, B. F. Agent	31	Upson
SMALLWOOD, Mark	16	Fayette	SMITH, B. G.	14	Lee
SMALLWOOD, R.	12	Decatur	SMITH, Bailey	6	Franklin
SMALLWOOD, W. J.	21	Decatur	SMITH, Barney	1	Lowndes
SMALLY, Michael	14	Lincoln	SMITH, Benajah	10	Appling
SMARR, Andrew	5	Monroe	SMITH, Benj.	1	Wilkes
SMARR, LaFeyete	3	Monroe	SMITH, Benj. G.	40	Washington
SMARR, Wiliam	9	Monroe	SMITH, Benjamin	1	Lumpkin
SMART, A. D.	15	Decatur	SMITH, Benjamin	1	Paulding
SMART, C.	11	Decatur	SMITH, Benjamin B.	1	Twiggs
SMART, E. B.	2	Campbell	SMITH, Benjamin G.	2	Houston
			SMITH, Benjamin G.	5	Washington

Name	Number	County	Name	Number	County
SMITH, Benjamin R.	12	Washington	SMITH, H. L.	6	Muscogee
SMITH, Bennet	10	Washington	SMITH, Hamilton	10	Laurens
SMITH, Bennett B.	56	Jefferson	SMITH, Hardin J.	16	Pike
SMITH, Briton	6	Walton	SMITH, Hath.	3	Cobb
SMITH, C. H.	17	Oglethorpe	SMITH, Helen A.	2	Harris
SMITH, C. W.	20	Henry	SMITH, Henry	2	Newton
SMITH, Cas. B.	5	Oglethorpe	SMITH, Henry	11	Pike
SMITH, Charles	6	Floyd	SMITH, Henry A.	3	Franklin
SMITH, Charles	20	Harris	SMITH, Henry D.	3	Hancock
SMITH, Charles	1	Jackson	SMITH, Henry P.	9	Madison
SMITH, Charlton	1	Laurens	SMITH, Henry T.	15	Jasper
SMITH, Clarisa	15	Jasper	SMITH, Henry W.	2	Chatham
SMITH, Crawford	2	Muscogee	SMITH, Henry Y.	4	Muscogee
SMITH, Cynthia	12	Greene	SMITH, Horace	6	Newton
SMITH, D. M.	2	Heard	SMITH, Howel H.	2	Macon
SMITH, Daniel N.	16	Jones	SMITH, Hue agent	35	Laurens
SMITH, David	4	Franklin	SMITH, J.	2	Henry
SMITH, David	2	Madison	SMITH, J. A.	24	Henry
SMITH, David O.	12	Houston	SMITH, J. A.	1	Henry
SMITH, David T.	14	Jefferson	SMITH, J. B.	9	Oglethorpe
SMITH, Davis	77	Monroe	SMITH, J. C.	12	Henry
SMITH, Dawson	1	Marion	SMITH, J. G.	5	Henry
SMITH, Duncan	1	Lowndes	SMITH, J. G.	3	Muscogee
SMITH, Edward	1	Monroe	SMITH, J. P.	7	Elbert
SMITH, Elijah	4	Harris	SMITH, Jacob	3	Henry
SMITH, Elijah	16	Jefferson	SMITH, Jacob	2	Lumpkin
SMITH, Elijah J.	5	Jones	SMITH, James	5	Chatham
SMITH, Elisha	3	Jefferson	SMITH, James	7	Cobb
SMITH, Elisha	4	Liberty	SMITH, James	4	Early
SMITH, Elisha	12	Newton	SMITH, James	6	Franklin
SMITH, Elizabeth	4	Hall	SMITH, James	4	Hancock
SMITH, Elizabeth	6	Jackson	SMITH, James	7	Harris
SMITH, Elizabeth	13	Madison	SMITH, James	5	Houston
SMITH, Elizabeth	1	Montgomery	SMITH, James	1	Jackson
SMITH, Elizabeth	10	Morgan	SMITH, James	6	Lumpkin
SMITH, Ely A.	1	Heard	SMITH, James	1	Marion
SMITH, F. C.	2	Oglethorpe	SMITH, James	106	McIntosh
SMITH, Francis	5	Jasper	SMITH, James	3	Monroe
SMITH, Francis M.	1	Jackson	SMITH, James	5	Newton
SMITH, Garret	18	Houston	SMITH, James	1	Newton
SMITH, Garth	3	Morgan	SMITH, James A.	1	Pike
SMITH, Geo. B.	1	Muscogee	SMITH, James B.	1	Chatham
SMITH, Geo. W.	3	Houston	SMITH, James D.	9	Hancock
SMITH, George	1	Gilmer	SMITH, James E.	18	Oglethorpe
SMITH, George L.	3	Marion	SMITH, James G.	6	Harris
SMITH, George W.	2	Hancock	SMITH, James G.	25	Jefferson
SMITH, George W.	10	Morgan	SMITH, James guardian	14	Greene
SMITH, Gideon	2	Macon	SMITH, James L.	9	Cobb
SMITH, Giles G.	1	Pike	SMITH, James M.	4	Clarke
SMITH, Griffin	15	Lee	SMITH, James R.	5	Floyd
SMITH, Guy	42	Morgan	SMITH, James Sen.	26	Greene
SMITH, H.	2	Oglethorpe	SMITH, James Sr.	1	Greene
SMITH, H. J.	6	Morgan	SMITH, Jane	2	Camden
SMITH, H. J.	13	Muscogee	SMITH, Jas.	12	Hancock

Name	Number	County
SMITH, Jas.	17	Henry
SMITH, Jas. M.	110	Camden
SMITH, Jasper S.	8	Cobb
SMITH, Jency E.	11	Fayette
SMITH, Jeremiah G.	6	Jones
SMITH, Jeremiah M.	5	Cass
SMITH, Jesse	1	Harris
SMITH, Jno. M.	1	Henry
SMITH, Job E. M.	4	Lowndes
SMITH, Joel	4	Hancock
SMITH, John	36	Greene
SMITH, John	5	Gwinnett
SMITH, John	1	McIntosh
SMITH, John	3	Muscogee
SMITH, John	11	Newton
SMITH, John M.	3	Muscogee
SMITH, John A.	7	Campbell
SMITH, John A.	44	Fayette
SMITH, John D .	4	Newton
SMITH, John H.	10	Jackson
SMITH, John H.	1	Monroe
SMITH, John J.	5	Jones
SMITH, John M.	3	Macon
SMITH, John N.	3	Fayette
SMITH, John T.	12	Jones
SMITH, John T.	1	Marion
SMITH, John W.	11	Harris
SMITH, John W.	10	Houston
SMITH, John W.	2	Laurens
SMITH, John W. A.	30	Jasper
SMITH, Jos.	1	Cobb
SMITH, Joseph	23	Jones
SMITH, Joseph	6	Liberty
SMITH, Joseph	7	Oglethorpe
SMITH, Joseph R.	1	Pike
SMITH, Joshua	1	Appling
SMITH, Kinzey	11	Chattooga
SMITH, L. E.	7	Laurens
SMITH, L. H.	26	Elbert
SMITH, L. M.	1	McIntosh
SMITH, L. Windsor	3	DeKalb
SMITH, Lawrence	16	Pike
SMITH, Levin	15	Clarke
SMITH, Lindsay	2	Pike
SMITH, Lofton	2	Laurens
SMITH, Loriel	11	Jones
SMITH, Lucy	1	Newton
SMITH, M.	5	Pike
SMITH, M. P.	6	Oglethorpe
SMITH, Margaret	5	Clarke
SMITH, Martha	6	Heard
SMITH, Mary	16	Morgan
SMITH, Mathew	2	Newton
SMITH, Mial	36	Oglethorpe
SMITH, Milor C.	3	Harris
SMITH, Moses	4	Lowndes
SMITH, Mrs. Martha	26	Monroe
SMITH, Mrs. Aug.	2	Muscogee
SMITH, N. G.	1	Muscogee
SMITH, N. H.	31	Oglethorpe
SMITH, Nancy	18	Laurens
SMITH, Nathan Y.	38	Muscogee
SMITH, Nathaniel	15	Hall
SMITH, Needham	39	Houston
SMITH, Noah	1	Fayette
SMITH, Noah	45	Jefferson
SMITH, Noah	31	Jefferson
SMITH, Osbron L.	4	Newton
SMITH, Owen	1	Lowndes
SMITH, Palestine	1	Marion
SMITH, Patience	3	Fayette
SMITH, Patrick	8	Houston
SMITH, Peyton	2	Houston
SMITH, Peyton T. agt for HOLT, S. S.	31	Houston
SMITH, Pinkney P.	24	Oglethorpe
SMITH, R. P.	8	Henry
SMITH, Rachel P.	2	Muscogee
SMITH, Rice	1	Hall
SMITH, Richard	9	Jefferson
SMITH, Richard	1	Monroe
SMITH, Robert	26	Oglethorpe
SMITH, Robert B.	15	Oglethorpe
SMITH, Rolin	24	Jasper
SMITH, Rowena E.	4	Clarke
SMITH, S. B.	2	Jefferson
SMITH, Sam	1	Early
SMITH, Saml.	21	Cass
SMITH, Samuel	9	Jackson
SMITH, Samuel Jun.	1	Jackson
SMITH, Samuel P.	9	Jasper
SMITH, Samuel R.	9	Houston
SMITH, Sarah	3	Jones
SMITH, Sarah	1	Oglethorpe
SMITH, Sarah P.	5	Oglethorpe
SMITH, Seaborn	2	Fayette
SMITH, Seth K.	1	Jefferson
SMITH, Sidney	2	Monroe
SMITH, Simeon	1	Harris
SMITH, Simion	4	Monroe
SMITH, Stephen	10	Merriwether
SMITH, Stephen R.	5	Jones
SMITH, Sterling W.	12	Jones
SMITH, T.	2	Irwin
SMITH, Tenderson	16	Marion
SMITH, Theophilus J.	34	Hancock
SMITH, Thomas G.	22	Heard
SMITH, Thomas J.	33	Cass

Name	Number	County	Name	Number	County
SMITH, Thomas J.	7	Jasper	SMITH, Benjamin D.	4	Campbell
SMITH, Thomas P.	12	Houston	SMITH, Benjamin T. L.	37	Burke
SMITH, Thomas P.	12	Jasper	SMITH, Benjamin	1	Sumter
SMITH, Thomas R.	8	Jasper	SMITH, Britton		
SMITH, Thomas T.	13	Greene	agt for DEAN, James	138	Houston
SMITH, Thos. P.	8	Laurens	SMITH, Burket D.	8	Dooly
SMITH, Thos. T.	8	Muscogee	SMITH, Burwell	10	Stewart
SMITH, Turner	7	Houston	SMITH, C.	4	Bibb
SMITH, W. ?	6	Muscogee	SMITH, C. H.	14	Crawford
SMITH, W. B.	7	Elbert	SMITH, Charles	12	Talbot
SMITH, W. F.	3	Henry	SMITH, Charles	32	Walton
SMITH, W. H.	5	Henry	SMITH, Cicero H.	3	Walton
SMITH, W. H.	2	Oglethorpe	SMITH, Cullen W.	3	Coweta
SMITH, W. P.	1	Oglethorpe	SMITH, Daniel	2	Decatur
SMITH, Wells	11	Marion	SMITH, Daniel	8	Randolph
SMITH, Wesley	15	Monroe	SMITH, Daniel W.	10	Dooly
SMITH, William	2	Effingham	SMITH, David	2	Bibb
SMITH, William	24	Franklin	SMITH, David	2	Butts
SMITH, William	20	Houston	SMITH, David	1	Campbell
SMITH, William	16	Houston	SMITH, David	18	Jasper
SMITH, William	1	Jasper	SMITH, David	3	Walker
SMITH, William	15	Lowndes	SMITH, David	1	Walton
SMITH, William	1	Madison	SMITH, David	7	Walton
SMITH, William	2	Newton	SMITH, David D.	4	DeKalb
SMITH, William A.	3	Hall	SMITH, David T.	2	Dooly
SMITH, William E.	8	Franklin	SMITH, Drewet C.	3	Oglethorpe
SMITH,			SMITH, Drura ?	1	Upson
William G. Senr.	18	Jasper	SMITH, E.	1	Bibb
SMITH, William H.	1	Houston	SMITH, E.	1	Bibb
SMITH, William J.	9	Floyd	SMITH, E. E. C.	2	Bryan
SMITH, William T.	9	Harris	SMITH, Eason	2	Sumter
SMITH, Wilson	4	Houston	SMITH, Edward	1	Cass
SMITH, Winny	25	Harris	SMITH, Eleazer	4	Stewart
SMITH, Wm.	7	Floyd	SMITH, Elbert	24	Wilkes
SMITH, Wm.	17	Liberty	SMITH, Elia A.	3	Walton
SMITH, Wm. C.	18	Hancock	SMITH, Eliza A.	9	Warren
SMITH, Wm. D.	15	Jackson	SMITH, English	30	Washington
SMITH, Wm. H.	2	Henry	SMITH, English	11	Washington
SMITH, Wm. P.	2	Henry	SMITH, Etheldred	4	Washington
SMITH, Wm. P.	1	Jackson	SMITH, Ezekiel B.	38	Talbot
SMITH, Wm. R.	18	Floyd	SMITH, Ezekiel B.	7	Talbot
SMITH, Wyatt R.	19	Jasper	SMITH, F. A.	2	Butts
SMITH, Wyley C.	1	Jackson	SMITH, F. E.	11	Wilkes
SMITH, Zack	1	Laurens	SMITH, Francis D.	2	Warren
SMITH, A. D.	10	Early	SMITH, Freeman R.	4	Walton
SMITH, A. G.	31	Crawford	SMITH, G. E.	23	Coweta
SMITH, Alexander	3	Tatnall	SMITH, Gabriel	16	Randolph
SMITH, Ann S.	9	Carroll	SMITH, Geo.	2	Bibb
SMITH, Archibald	2	Sumter	SMITH, Geo. B.	17	Wilkes
SMITH, Arthur	9	Richmond	SMITH, George	1	Burke
SMITH, B. L. P.	14	Coweta	SMITH, George K.	2	DeKalb
SMITH, Benj.	3	Randolph	SMITH, George L.		
SMITH, Benjamin	19	Talbot	trustee	2	Chatham
SMITH, Benjamin	13	Talbot	SMITH, George T.	3	DeKalb

Name	Number	County	Name	Number	County
SMITH, Gilbert	7	Randolph	SMITH, John	30	Wilkinson
SMITH, Gilla	8	Putnam	SMITH, John A.	9	Troup
SMITH, Green W.	4	Walton	SMITH, John D.	4	Richmond
SMITH, H.	14	Crawford	SMITH, John G.	1	Wilkinson
SMITH, Hardy	3	Coweta	SMITH, John H.	4	Screven
SMITH, Harris	1	Taliaferro	SMITH, John H.	1	Tatnall
SMITH, Henry	6	Richmond	SMITH, John L.	21	Talbot
SMITH, Henry	5	Tatnall	SMITH, John M.	5	DeKalb
SMITH, Henry A.	10	Bryan	SMITH, John P. F.	3	Walton
SMITH, Henry C.	1	Bryan	SMITH, John T.	1	Baldwin
SMITH, Henry C.	1	Randolph	SMITH, John W.	2	Warren
SMITH, Henry J.	79	Columbia	SMITH, John W. G.	32	Talbot
SMITH, Henry J.	1	Richmond	SMITH, Jonathan	9	Randolph
SMITH, Ira E.	54	Coweta	SMITH, Jonathan	2	Walton
SMITH, Isaac	4	Butts	SMITH, Jonathan	29	Wilkes
SMITH, Isaac	7	Washington	SMITH, Jordan R.	41	Washington
SMITH, Isaac L.	3	Washington	SMITH, Jos.	1	Bibb
SMITH, Isham	6	Coweta	SMITH, Joseph	3	Baker
SMITH, Israel	5	Bryan	SMITH, Joseph	3	DeKalb
SMITH, J.	11	Bibb	SMITH, Joseph	6	Walton
SMITH, J. B.	19	Randolph	SMITH, Joseph	2	Warren
SMITH, J. C.	11	Camden	SMITH, Joseph J.	1	Bryan
SMITH, J. C.	2	Decatur	SMITH, Joshua	19	Bryan
SMITH, J. D.	1	Wilkinson	SMITH, Joshua F.	6	Walton
SMITH, J. H.	7	Coweta	SMITH, L.	31	Crawford
SMITH, J. H.	32	Screven	SMITH, L. B.	9	Sumter
SMITH, J. L. agent	16	Crawford	SMITH, L. L.	15	Baldwin
SMITH, J. R.	2	Butts	SMITH, L. M.	9	Coweta
SMITH, J. R.	1	Troup	SMITH, Lawrence	2	Ware
SMITH, J. T.	23	Decatur	SMITH, Levi B.	8	Talbot
SMITH, J.H.	12	Screven	SMITH, Levin	9	Baldwin
SMITH, J.S.	6	Chattooga	SMITH, Lewis	1	Stewart
SMITH, James	3	Bullock	SMITH, Littlebury	1	Walton
SMITH, James	1	DeKalb	SMITH, Lovett B.	27	Sumter
SMITH, James	10	Talbot	SMITH, M. A.	4	Bibb
SMITH, James	1	Ware	SMITH, Martha	3	Baker
SMITH, James B.	2	Talbot	SMITH, Martha	9	Sumter
SMITH, James B.	2	Tatnall	SMITH, Martin H.	1	Carroll
SMITH, James E.	6	Washington	SMITH, Mary	1	Chatham
SMITH, James F.	3	Washington	SMITH, Mary	5	Columbia
SMITH, James H.	2	Decatur	SMITH, Mary	4	Thomas
SMITH, James M.	8	Talbot	SMITH, Mathew	10	Dooly
SMITH, James N.	1	Stewart	SMITH, Matthew	5	Burke
SMITH, James R.	6	Washington	SMITH, Moses	6	Oglethorpe
SMITH, James W.	4	Warren	SMITH, Moses M.	18	Campbell
SMITH, Jas.	22	Wilkes	SMITH, Mrs. Frances	3	Richmond
SMITH, Jefferson	1	Walton	SMITH, Mrs. Susan	16	Burke
SMITH, Jno. R.	2	Wilkes	SMITH, N.	7	Bullock
SMITH, John	4	Butts	SMITH, N.	1	Wilkinson
SMITH, John	5	Cass	SMITH, Nancy	8	Burke
SMITH, John	35	Columbia	SMITH, Nancy	1	Cass
SMITH, John	2	Houston	SMITH, Nathaniel N.	11	Troup
SMITH, John	9	Stewart	SMITH, Neil	2	Randolph
SMITH, John	5	Washington	SMITH, Nicholas	11	Tatnall

Name	Number	County	Name	Number	County
SMITH, Noah	21	Burke	SMITH, W.	15	Decatur
SMITH, Otis	20	Troup	SMITH, W. J.	6	Crawford
SMITH, P. H.	1	Screven	SMITH, W. R.	4	Walton
SMITH, Patsy	20	Baldwin	SMITH, W. S.	5	Butts
SMITH, Peter B.	5	Richmond	SMITH, Walden B.	2	Burke
SMITH, Peter P.	14	Washington	SMITH, Walter	1	Chatham
SMITH, R.	1	Coweta	SMITH, Walton, H.	12	Coweta
SMITH, R.	4	Talbot	SMITH, William	4	Columbia
SMITH, R. M.	6	Butts	SMITH, William	3	Stewart
SMITH, Reuben	4	Talbot	SMITH, William	2	Sumter
SMITH, Reuben	14	Wilkes	SMITH, William	16	Talbot
SMITH, Richard	4	Washington	SMITH, William	7	Talbot
SMITH, Richard	1	Wilkinson	SMITH, William	9	Walker
SMITH, Robert	11	Coweta	SMITH, William	3	Walton
SMITH, Robert	14	DeKalb	SMITH, William	103	Washington
SMITH, Robert	1	Richmond	SMITH, William	2	Thomas
SMITH, Robert C.	5	Baldwin	SMITH, William F.	5	Washington
SMITH, Robert J.	1	Walton	SMITH, William P.	2	Thomas
SMITH, Robert Sen.	16	Butts	SMITH, William R.	3	Dooly
SMITH, Robt. W.	7	Butts	SMITH, Winfield	6	Stewart
SMITH, S. A.	42	Randolph	SMITH, Wm.	1	Butts
SMITH, S. E.	8	Coweta	SMITH, Wm.	19	Crawford
SMITH, S. M.	3	Coweta	SMITH, Wm.	4	Crawford
SMITH, S.E.J.	6	Randolph	SMITH, Wm.	21	Dooly
SMITH, S. S.	4	Thomas	SMITH, Wm. B.	1	DeKalb
SMITH, Saah	5	Stewart	SMITH, Wm. E.	12	Coweta
SMITH, Sam	1	Bullock	SMITH, Wm. E.	6	Wilkes
SMITH, Samuel	3	Baker	SMITH, Wm. J.	5	Troup
SMITH, Samuel	31	Washington	SMITH, Wm. R.	9	Wilkes
SMITH, Samuel	6	Warren	SMITH, Zadock	10	Wilkes
SMITH, Samuel H.	1	Walton	SMITH?, George H.	2	Early
SMITH, Sandford	8	Walton	SMITHSON, D.	1	Floyd
SMITH, Sarah	1	Bibb	SMITHWICK, S. S.	2	Cherokee
SMITH, Sarah	3	Coweta	SMITHWICK, Samuel S.	1	Cherokee
SMITH, Sarah	1	Richmond	SMITHWICK, Tyre	2	Cherokee
SMITH, Sarah	6	Washington	SMITHWICK, Ruebin	5	Randolph
SMITH, Simeon	10	DeKalb	SMITS,		
SMITH, Simeon	2	Upson	Alexander A. Jun.	1	Chatham
SMITH, Simeon A.	58	Thomas	SMITS, Alexander A.	8	Chatham
SMITH, Simon	1	Tatnall	SMITSON, B.B.	2	Crawford
SMITH, Simon P.	5	Tatnall	SMOOT, Robert	1	Pike
SMITH, Solomon	21	Bryan	SMOOT, Robert	2	Upson
SMITH, Stephen	2	Baker	SMOTHO?, Walton M.	1	Gwinnett
SMITH, Stephen	5	Warren	SMYLIE, James	9	Liberty
SMITH, Stephen G.	16	Sumter	SMYLIE, Mrs. Sarah	5	Liberty
SMITH, T. S.	3	Clarke	SMYTH, James M.	9	Richmond
SMITH, T. T.	8	Chatham	SMYTHE,		
SMITH, Thomas	9	Talbot	Dr. George E.	14	Oglethorpe
SMITH, Thomas B.	19	Washington	SNALL, Mathew	8	Walker
SMITH, Thomas H.	1	Dooly	SNEAD, Homer	9	Marion
SMITH, Thos.	2	Columbia	SNEAD, Hamilton	8	Talbot
SMITH, Thos. L .	11	Dooly	SNEAD, John C.	7	Richmond
SMITH, Thos. R .	37	Decatur	SNEAD, Mary	12	Wilkes
SMITH, V. A.	4	Randolph	SNEAD, Tilman	1	Baldwin

Name	Number	County	Name	Number	County
SNEED, Alfred	8	Muscogee	SOLOMON, D.	24	Washington
SNEED, Dudley	14	Lee	SOLOMON, D.	24	Wilkinson
SNEED, Hyram F.	9	Muscogee	SOLOMON,		
SNEED, Jas. R.	11	Wilkes	Francis S. A.	31	Twiggs
SNEED, John	21	Monroe	SOLOMON, H. estate	58	Twiggs
SNEED, Margt.	1	Clarke	SOLOMON, Leonard	12	DeKalb
SNEED, Mrs. Susan	11	Burke	SOLOMON, Lewis	4	Twiggs
SNEED, William	23	Washington	SOLOMON, Peter	7	Bibb
SNEED, Zach P.	1	Muscogee	SOLOMONS, E. W.	3	Chatham
SNEED, Zachariah	32	Upson	SOLOMONS, Lizar	1	Chatham
SNELL, Barnabus L. W.	17	Emanual	SOLOMONS, Samuel	17	Chatham
SNELL, David A.	8	Muscogee	SOLOMONS, William	30	Cass
SNELL, George W. W.	8	Emanual	SONNYTHE ?,		
SNELL, Jackson	3	Pulaski	Charles J.	7	Troup
SNELL, John	23	Emanual	SORELL, Lewis	13	Richmond
SNELL, M.	1	Muscogee	SORESBY, Nancy	5	Burke
SNELL, Mary P.	30	Pulaski	SORRAN?, N.	1	Elbert
SNELL, Seney	9	Emanual	SORRELL, Francis	5	Chatham
SNELL, W. W.	9	Pulaski	SORRELL, Francis		
SNELL, William	39	Macon	trustee	8	Chatham
SNELL, William M.	11	Harris	SORRELLS, Charles	26	Walton
SNELL, Samuel	9	DeKalb	SORRELLS, Charles J.	9	Walton
SNELLGROVE, Harriett	1	Baker	SORRELLS, Charles L.	6	Madison
SNELLGROVE, John	7	Sumter	SORRELLS, Richard W.	12	Madison
SNELLING, P. P.	1	Elbert	SORRELLS, Russell B.	1	Cobb
SNELLING, Virginia	1	Morgan	SORRELS, Bennet W.	1	Walton
SNELLING, Richard	10	Stewart	SORRELS, James N.	2	Walton
SNELLING, Richard J.	104	Stewart	SORRELS, John H.	3	Walton
SNELLINGS, M. B.	8	Morgan	SORRELS, Richard T.	1	Madison
SNELLINGS, R. S.	14	Elbert	SORRELS, Wm. J.	9	Cass
SNELLINGS, S.	49	Elbert	SORRELS, W.	1	Walton
SNELLINGS, Elizabeth	15	Talbot	SORROW, Sarah	2	Oglethorpe
SNELLINGS, Henry	9	Talbot	SORSBY, Battle A.	6	Muscogee
SNELMAN, Joseph M.	3	Chatham	SOULLARD, E. A.	7	Hancock
SNELSON, Joel T.	23	Wilkes	SOUTH, J.	3	Henry
SNELSON, John	16	Merriwether	SOUTH, James J.	1	Meriwether
SNELSON, Nathl.	14	Wilkes	SOUTHALL?, Seabron	5	Pulaski
SNELSON, Wm. D.	7	Wilkes	SOUTHERLAND,		
SNIDER, John	1	Effingham	Amos L.	16	Murray
SNIDER, Benjamin	80	Chatham	SOUTHERLAND, John	4	Greene
SNIDER, Benjamin	8	Chatham	SOUTHERLAND,		
SNIPES, Chesly B.	13	Upson	Thos. Agent	21	Randolph
SNIPES, James	15	Marion	SOUTHERN, John	14	Laurens
SNIPES, John T.	23	Upson	SOUTHWILL,		
SNOIRA?, Lucinda	1	Bibb	George W.	5	Sumter
SNOOK, Rebecca	23	Effingham	SOWELL, Aaron	1	Jackson
SNOW, John P.	23	Walton	SPAIN, John W.	40	Lowndes
SNOW, William	4	Muscogee	SPALDING &		
SNOW, J. W.	1	Bibb	FOREMAN	130	McIntosh
SNOW, M. L.	3	Carroll	SPALDING, Charles	204	McIntosh
SNOW. L.	13	Carroll	SPALDING, Randolph	87	McIntosh
SOHUSTENS?, Samuel	1	Franklin	SPALDING, Thomas	293	McIntosh
SOLMON, Howel	9	Dade	SPALDING, A.	3	DeKalb
SOLOMANS, A. A.	7	Chatham	SPALKING, Isam	5	Camden

Name	Number	County	Name	Number	County
SPANE, Benjamin	9	Monroe	SPEARS, William	4	Talbot
SPANGLER, Rebecca	8	Thomas	SPEED, Terrell	27	Morgan
SPANN, John B.	6	Chatham	SPEER, Hugh L.	2	Heard
SPANN, Seaborn	11	Murray	SPEER, Alexander M.	14	Monroe
SPANN, A.	20	Randolph	SPEER, Amos	1	Heard
SPANN, Henry	5	Stewart	SPEER, George	1	Monroe
SPANN, J. M.	1	DeKalb	SPEER, Thomas	18	Monroe
SPARK, Samuel	3	Muscogee	SPEER, Elizabeth	12	Stewart
SPARK, Wilkerson	22	Harris	SPEERMAN, Edmund	13	Heard
SPARKMAN, Wm.	4	Fayette	SPEIGHT, Andrew	14	Hancock
SPARKS, ? P.	8	Muscogee	SPEIGHT, Jonathan	2	Washington
SPARKS, Carter	23	Floyd	SPEIGHT, Thomas	54	Early
SPARKS, E. W.	2	Pike	SPEIGHT, Thos. L.	7	Lee
SPARKS, Elizabeth	11	Harris	SPEIGHT, Wm. H.	10	Hancock
SPARKS, Judah	6	Franklin	SPEIGHT, John	14	Baldwin
SPARKS, Morgan M.	3	Washington	SPEIGHTS, James	14	Jasper
SPARKS, Thoomas	10	Washington	SPEIR, James	7	Upson
SPARKS, Thomas H.	2	Franklin	SPEIR, John P.	2	Cobb
SPARKS, Thomas H.	47	Paulding	SPEIR, William	11	Effingham
SPARKS, B. H.	15	Randolph	SPELL, John C.	18	Dooly
SPARKS, McCurdy	40	Talbot	SPENCE, Calvin	1	Pulaski
SPARKS, McCurdy	2	Talbot	SPENCE, David W.	40	Gwinnett
SPARKS, Robt.	36	Putnam	SPENCE, James	1	Chatham
SPARKS, W.H.	9	Putnam	SPENCE, Jeremiah	1	Jackson
SPARKS, W. S.	1	Walker	SPENCE, John	4	Meriwether
SPEAD, W.	1	Elbert	SPENCE, Joshua	4	Appling
SPEAR, (?)	8	Columbia	SPENCE, Littleton	1	Emanual
SPEAR, Alexander	15	Muscogee	SPENCE, Mary	2	Emanual
SPEAR, Allison	26	Pike	SPENCE, Mathew	5	Emanual
SPEAR, Ann	1	Jasper	SPENCE, McCauloin	9	Harris
SPEAR, Cimeon F.	14	Pike	SPENCE, Reubin H.	2	Lee
SPEAR, E. A.	42	Jefferson	SPENCE, A. H.	9	Cass
SPEAR, Jefferson	2	Jasper	SPENCE, Elizabeth	5	Stewart
SPEAR, Joshua	1	Jasper	SPENCE, Frances Estate	4	Richmond
SPEAR, Josiah	34	Jasper	SPENCE, Joseph	4	Stewart
SPEAR, Robert H.	5	Jasper	SPENCE, R. H.	7	Randolph
SPEAR, Sarah B.	11	Jasper	SPENCE, Richd.	27	Randolph
SPEAR, Thomas D.	26	Morgan	SPENCE, William	5	Stewart
SPEAR, Thomas J.	2	Jasper	SPENCE, Wm.	4	Lee
SPEAR, Welcom	2	Morgan	SPENCER, B. E.	5	Greene
SPEAR, William A.	14	Troup	SPENCER, J. A.	9	Newton
SPEAR, Caleb	2	Jasper	SPENCER, James W.	1	Pike
SPEAR, J. W.	4	Coweta	SPENCER, Joseph	5	Newton
SPEAR, Jas. F.	3	Coweta	SPENCER, Mrs. Mary	12	Liberty
SPEAR, John	4	Stewart	SPENCER, R. P.	6	Muscogee
SPEAR, Washington	4	Stewart	SPENCER, Samuel B.	8	Liberty
SPEARMAN, Gabriel T.	16	Jasper	SPENCER, John H.	3	Richmond
SPEARS, James	3	Henry	SPERGHTS?, Levi	4	Baldwin
SPEARS, John	3	Jasper	SPERRY, John A.	1	Houston
SPEARS, John B.	1	Jasper	SPHEERS, P. D.	1	Floyd
SPEARS, Joseph C.	3	Pike	SPICER, John F.	58	Baker
SPEARS, William	4	Merriwether	SPICER, Rowan	4	Bibb
SPEARS, William H.	3	Jasper	SPICER, Sarah	6	Baker
SPEARS, Joseph D.	1	Talbot	SPICER, Thomas C.	32	Baker

Name	Number	County	Name	Number	County
SPIKES, John W.	1	Cass	STACY, Ezra	32	Liberty
SPILLER, C. F.	1	Merriwether	STAFFORD, Alvis	6	Pike
SPINKS, John	1	Harris	STAFFORD, Anderson	11	Upson
SPINNYS ?, Joseph	1	Richmond	STAFFORD, Ellis	15	Upson
SPIRES, W. B.	1	Lincoln	STAFFORD, F. N,	1	Henry
SPIRES, William	10	Lincoln	STAFFORD, James	1	Glynn
SPIRES, Zachariah	8	Lincoln	STAFFORD, James H.	11	Upson
SPIVEY, ?	41	Putnam	STAFFORD, Robert	5	Glynn
SPIVEY, E. B. W.	5	Muscogee	STAFFORD, Robt.	6	Wayne
SPIVEY, James A.	26	Houston	STAFFORD, Wm. G.	38	Chatham
SPIVEY, S. G.	13	Jefferson	STAFFORD, Eliza E.	1	Tatnall
SPIVEY, Thos.	4	Harris	STAFFORD, Ezekiel	21	Tatnall
SPIVEY, Caleb	31	Putnam	STAFFORD, Robt.	349	Camden
SPIVEY, M.	4	Putnam	STAILEY, Christian J.	23	Houston
SPIVEY, Wm.	31	Putnam	STAILEY, John	13	Houston
SPIVEY, Wm.	8	Putnam	STALEY, George N.	6	Chatham
SPIVEY, Wm. J.	7	Putnam	STALEY, John A.	8	Chatham
SPIVY, W. M.	1	Wilkinson	STALINGS, W. B.	14	Stewart
SPIVY, William	24	Upson	STALLINGS, James	8	Harris
SPRADLEY, Allen P.	4	Houston	STALLINGS, James	9	Monroe
SPRADLEY, Charles A.	1	Dooly	STALLINGS, Jeremiah	2	Pike
SPRADLEY, D.	2	Twiggs	STALLINGS, Newton	2	Newton
SPRADLEY, Eliza A.	1	Dooly	STALLINGS, Samuel J.	1	Monroe
SPRADLIN, Wm.	3	Coweta	STALLINGS, Wiley	4	Thomas
SPRADLIN, Wm.	1	Coweta	STALLINGS, William	93	Morgan
SPRATLIN, Henry	4	Wilkes	STALLINGS, William	29	Talbot
SPRATLIN, Jas. A.	4	Wilkes	STALLINGS, William	14	Walton
SPRATLIN, Jas. H.	15	Wilkes	STALLINGS, William J.	1	Monroe
SPRATLIN, J. M.	13	Merriwether	STALLINGS, Herbert	1	Richmond
SPRATLIN, Mary	3	Wilkes	STALLINGS, Jesse	5	Stewart
SPRATLING, Martha	34	Madison	STALLINGS, Jesse	6	Talbot
SPRAYBERRY, Mary	3	Chattooga	STALLINGS, Mary	4	Richmond
SPREWELL, Jeptha	4	Talbot	STALLINGS, Moses	5	Carroll
SPRIGHT, Thomas	3	Houston	STALLINGS, Sally	1	Columbia
SPRIGS, A. J.	1	Lumpkin	STALLINGS, Wilson	2	Carroll
SPRIGS, John	26	Lumpkin	STALLINS, John W.	3	Monroe
SPRING, G.	2	Irwin	STALLINS, William	17	Monroe
SPRINGER, John	11	Marion	STALLSWORTH,		
SPRINGER, Dempsey	1	Cherokee	Edmund	13	Henry
SPRUEL, John S.	1	Coweta	STALLWORTH,		
SPUEL?, McCalom	9	Harris	Beauford	9	Jones
SPUR, Rhoda	2	Monroe	STALLWORTH, Joseph	3	Jones
SPURLIN, J. M.	2	Troup	STAMP, Jas.	6	Coweta
SPURLIN, John	1	Macon	STAMP, Moses W.	2	Coweta
SPURLOCK, James	12	Floyd	STAMPER, Sarah	1	Pike
SPURMAN, Robert	16	Heard	STAMPER, Susan	13	Walton
SPYERS ?, John	1	Stewart	STAMPER, James	3	Talbot
SRUETH?, U. E.	1	Campbell	STAMPER, Manning	18	Talbot
ST. GEORGE, Edward	63	Pulaski	STAMPS, John R.	9	Muscogee
ST. JOHN, James	2	Randolph	STAMPS, John	5	Coweta
ST. JOHN, James C.	1	Troup	STANALAND, Booz	1	Thomas
ST. JOHN, Thomas	2	Troup	STANALAND, James O.	1	Thomas
ST. SIMON, Simon	1	Richmond	STANALAND,		
STACY, John W.	7	Liberty	John O. B.	1	Thomas

Name	Number	County
STANALAND, Richard T.	5	Thomas
STANALAND, Thomas C.	6	Thomas
STANDARD, Benjamin	1	Monroe
STANDARD, Daniel H.	17	Wilkes
STANDARD, Danl.	2	Wilkes
STANDARD, George	3	Monroe
STANDFIELD, John	1	Ware
STANDFORD, Dorcus	1	Warren
STANDFORD, James	6	Talbot
STANDFORD, Joseph	9	Talbot
STANDFORD, Monroe	5	Talbot
STANDFORD, Thomas F.	11	Warren
STANDIFER, Archibald	39	Jasper
STANDIFER, Calmit	8	Jasper
STANDLEY, Wm.	1	Randolph
STANDLY, John	13	Randolph
STANDLY, Shadrach	2	Tatnall
STANFELL, Wm.	3	Lowndes
STANFIELD, Eliz.	4	Henry
STANFILL, Beshania	5	Thomas
STANFORD, (?)	15	Columbia
STANFORD, A. W.	13	Monroe
STANFORD, F. A.	3	Muscogee
STANFORD, H. T.	2	Henry
STANFORD, James	5	Monroe
STANFORD, John R.	14	Habersham
STANFORD, S. B.	9	Elbert
STANFORD, Samuel	3	Monroe
STANFORD, W. B.	1	Henry
STANFORD, Wm.	3	Cass
STANFORD, D.	1	Randolph
STANFORD, H.K.	9	Talbot
STANFORD, JohnW. A.	54	Baldwin
STANFORD, Jonathan	7	Sumter
STANFORD, Joseph	3	Putnam
STANFORD, Leven	16	Putnam
STANFORD, Nathan B.	1	Putnam
STANFORD, Neamiah	4	Putnam
STANFORD, Oliver	3	Stewart
STANIFER, William M.	7	Early
STANLEY, J. C.	1	Jackson
STANLEY, Ira	51	Laurens
STANLEY, J.	1	Henry
STANLEY, James	4	Laurens
STANLEY, James J.	8	Laurens
STANLEY, James R.	31	Laurens
STANLEY, Leah C.	16	Laurens
STANLEY, Leary	5	Houston
STANLEY, M.	7	Henry
STANLEY, Martha	5	Hancock
STANLEY, Charles	20	Randolph
STANLEY, Sands	8	Randolph
STANSELL, George	1	Newton
STANSELL, Joel	10	Newton
STANSELL, Levi	7	Newton
STANSELL, Bennett	1	Newton
STANTEN, H. T.	12	Newton
STANTON, Elizabeth B.	18	Newton
STANTON, John	13	Newton
STANTON, John J.	2	Newton
STANTON, Patrick H.	8	Effingham
STANTON, R.	2	Chattooga
STANTON, Robert	4	Newton
STANTON, Wm.	6	Chattooga
STANTON, C. B.	3	Chattooga
STANTON, Wm.	3	Chattooga
STAPLER, Amos	6	Jackson
STAPLER, John R.	40	Lowndes
STAPLER, Thomas	1	Jackson
STAPLER, Thos. L.	8	Jackson
STAPLER, William L.	10	Muscogee
STAPLER, John A.	16	Columbia
STAPLER, John A.	1	Columbia
STAPLES, Jane	4	Wilkes
STAPLES, John	1	Meriwether
STAPLES, Thomas	23	Troup
STAPLES, William J.	7	Troup
STAPLETON, George	9	Jefferson
STAPLETON, James	2	Jefferson
STAPLETON, Jesse W.	4	Jefferson
STAPLETON, Martin	1	Jefferson
STAPLETON, William	1	Jefferson
STAPLETON, John D.	13	Stewart
STAPLETON, Sydney	3	Stewart
STARGEL?, James M.	5	Heard
STARK ?, Thomas M.	9	Walton
STARK, J. W.	35	Morgan
STARK, James H.	40	Pike
STARK, Mrs. Elizabeth	1	Houston
STARK, Wm. T.	1	Clarke
STARK, S. C.	19	Elbert
STARK, W. W.	17	Chatham
STARK, W. W.	177	Screven
STARK, William	12	Walton
STARKS, Benton	3	Jackson
STARLING, David	3	Upson
STARLING, John G.	18	Upson
STARLING, Levi J.	1	Lowndes
STARLING, Wiley J.	77	Troup
STARNES, Ebenezer	7	Richmond
STARR, Benjamin	9	Fayette
STARR, E. F.	1	Floyd
STARR, H. M.	14	Fayette
STARR, J. H.	10	Henry
STARR, John H.	12	Gordon

Name	Number	County	Name	Number	County
STARR, Mary	1	McIntosh	STEDHAM, Simion	1	Paulding
STARR, S. H.	3	Newton	STEED, A. A.	10	Coweta
STARR, Samuel	5	Newton	STEED, A. A.	8	Coweta
STARR, Silas	7	Newton	STEED, Sion P.	7	Coweta
STARR, Silas	5	Newton	STEED, T. L.	1	Campbell
STARR, Charles H.	26	Bryan	STEED, Wiley	1	Campbell
STARR, E. W.	2	Muscogee	STEED, William	4	Talbot
STARR, Henry	8	Stewart	STEED, William	1	Talbot
STARR, William	9	Chatham	STEED, William S.	21	Warren
STARR, Wm.	1	Stewart	STEEDS, Philip	16	Talbot
STARR?, H. W.	2	Bibb	STEEL, A. H.	2	Murray
STARRETT, John	10	Habersham	STEEL, Abraham	5	Murray
STATE OF GA.			STEEL, Alfred	6	Dade
RAILROAD	19	DeKalb	STEEL, Bird	1	Dade
STATEN, Catherine	5	Clinch	STEEL, Isaac	4	DeKalb
STATEN, James W.	3	Clinch	STEELE, A. D.	10	Monroe
STATEN, Quarterman	3	Clinch	STEELE, Andrew	1	Gilmer
STATES?, Mary	15	Bryan	STEELE, John	5	Gwinnett
STATHAM, Charlotte	2	Jackson	STEELE, John A.	2	Jasper
STATHAM, Garland	36	Sumter	STEELE, Lydia	2	Gilmer
STATHAM, R.	23	Stewart	STEELE, John	1	Telfair
STATHOM, Memory W.	7	Greene	STEELY, Bently	6	Stewart
STEADHAM, Jas. H.	3	Carroll	STEGALL, Sarah	1	Henry
STEADHAM, Levi	2	Coweta	STEGALL, Sidney B.	18	Upson
STEAL, C. H.	1	Elbert	STEGALL, Wm.	21	Heard
STEAM BOAT			STEGAR, James C.	2	Pike
WM. GASTON	14	Chatham	STEGAR, Robert M.	15	Pike
STEAM BOAT Co.			STEGER, A. M.	6	Henry
OF Geo.	70	Richmond	STEIGEN, John H.	2	Chatham
STEAM MONMOTH	2	Chatham	STEINBERG, John	1	Chatham
STEAMBOAT C.			STEMBRIDGE, Jas.	1	Crawford
OF GEORGIA	27	Chatham	STEMBRIDGE, Jno.	3	Crawford
STEAMER ELIZA	5	Chatham	STEMBRIDGE, Mary	5	Crawford
STEAMER JOHN			STEMBRIDGE,		
RANDOLPH	14	Chatham	William W.	5	Baldwin
STEAMER LAMAR	11	Chatham	STENSON, M. F.	20	Troup
STEAMER			STEP, Morning?	6	Morgan
METAMONA	13	Chatham	STEPHEN, William W.	2	Monroe
STEAMER OREGON	11	Chatham	STEPHENS, Hiram	1	Gwinnett
STEAMER S. SIBLEY	16	Chatham	STEPHENS, A.	2	Floyd
STEAMER			STEPHENS, Allen R.	14	Bibb
ST. MATHEWS	14	Chatham	STEPHENS, B. G.	4	Thomas
STEAMER			STEPHENS, Benj.	2	Walton
TENNESSEE	17	Chatham	STEPHENS, Cader	1	Lowndes
STEAMER			STEPHENS, Calvin	7	Muscogee
THOS. METCALF	16	Chatham	STEPHENS, Decatur	19	Gordon
STEAMER			STEPHENS, Edmond	4	Twiggs
WILLIAM SEABROOK	13	Chatham	STEPHENS, Greennill	3	Monroe
STEAMER, Isaac Scott	2	Chatham	STEPHENS, Isaac	5	Heard
STEAMER, J. Stone	7	Chatham	STEPHENS, Isaac	1	Wilkinson
STEAMER, Sam Jones	1	Chatham	STEPHENS, Isaac	3	Wilkinson
STEBBINS, Charles	3	Liberty	STEPHENS, J.	4	Wilkinson
STEBBINS, Catherine S.	7	Chatham	STEPHENS, J. W.	1	Henry
STEDHAM, Martin	26	Cass	STEPHENS, James	2	Emanual

Name	Number	County	Name	Number	County
STEPHENS, James	2	Union	STEPHENS, Stephen	17	Taliaferro
STEPHENS, James M.	2	Cherokee	STEPHENS, T. F.	2	Bibb
STEPHENS, Jesse	25	Upson	STEPHENS, Thomas J.	19	DeKalb
STEPHENS, Jno.	4	Henry	STEPHENS, Thos.	1	Crawford
STEPHENS, Jno. C.	7	Wilkes	STEPHENS, West W.	7	Crawford
STEPHENS, John	3	Cass	STEPHENSEN,		
STEPHENS, John	4	Cherokee	Thomas W.	6	Clarke
STEPHENS, John	3	Harris	STEPHENSON, J. L.	6	Merriwether
STEPHENS, John	1	Wilkinson	STEPHENSON, Mary	4	Newton
STEPHENS, Joseph	15	Meriwether	STEPHENSON, Stephen	11	Heard
STEPHENS, Joseph	19	Oglethorpe	STEPHENSON, B. H.	6	Coweta
STEPHENS, Joseph B.	4	Oglethorpe	STEPHENSON, Hardy	1	Stewart
STEPHENS, Luke	2	Pulaski	STEPHENSON, John	4	DeKalb
STEPHENS, M.	1	Henry	STEPHENSON, John	1	Cass
STEPHENS, Margarette	4	Jefferson	STEPHENSON, Sarah	8	Coweta
STEPHENS, Marshal	8	Harris	STEPHENSON, T. J.	13	Coweta
STEPHENS, Minor M.	33	Heard	STEPHENSON, Thomas	40	Talbot
STEPHENS,			STEPHENSON, William	7	Stewart
Mrs. Clementina	12	Houston	STEPHENSON, Wm. J.	4	Coweta
STEPHENS, P. M.	22	Oglethorpe	STEPHENSON, Zach. L.	9	Talbot
STEPHENS, P. M.	6	Oglethorpe	STEPHESON, Wm.	5	Randolph
STEPHENS, Q.	4	Wilkinson	STERK, Samuel	1	Chatham
STEPHENS, Robert J.	5	Jefferson	STERLING, Elizabeth	6	Oglethorpe
STEPHENS, S. W.	1	Jackson	STERLING, Elizabeth	2	Oglethorpe
STEPHENS, Sarah	14	Early	STERLING, Isaac	1	Oglethorpe
STEPHENS, T. B.	5	Oglethorpe	STERLING, Pleasant A.	9	Gwinnett
STEPHENS, Thomas	6	Clarke	STERLING, R. A.	1	Bibb
STEPHENS, Thomas	5	Oglethorpe	STERLING, W.	22	Troup
STEPHENS, Timothy	6	Cobb	STERLING, W. B.	18	Troup
STEPHENS, Whitfield	2	Jefferson	STERNS, Wilson	6	Talbot
STEPHENS, William	11	Emanual	STERNS, Wilson	1	Talbot
STEPHENS, William	1	Meriwether	STETSON, Daniel B.	3	Baldwin
STEPHENS, William	14	Upson	STEVANS, Joseph	1	Newton
STEPHENS, William	27	Upson	STEVANS, S.	2	Elbert
STEPHENS, William B.	4	Monroe	STEVEN, Thos.	24	Oglethorpe
STEPHENS, William J.	10	Monroe	STEVENS, Charles	5	Glynn
STEPHENS, William Jr.	1	Emanual	STEVENS, Hampton	22	Marion
STEPHENS, Willis	1	Madison	STEVENS, Henry	8	Greene
STEPHENS, Wm.	8	Wilkinson	STEVENS, Henry M.	73	Liberty
STEPHENS, Wm. W.	1	Heard	STEVENS, J. D. estate	104	Liberty
STEPHENS,			STEVENS, J. P.	46	Liberty
Alexander H.	13	Taliaferro	STEVENS, Jasper	2	Oglethorpe
STEPHENS, E.	3	Coweta	STEVENS, John	12	Greene
STEPHENS, Elizabeth	21	Stewart	STEVENS, John	9	Liberty
STEPHENS, Geo.	13	Coweta	STEVENS, John W.	2	Oglethorpe
STEPHENS, H. T.	1	Coweta	STEVENS, Joseph L.	29	Liberty
STEPHENS, Henry	5	Stewart	STEVENS, Levi	2	Chatham
STEPHENS, J. F.	2	Stewart	STEVENS, Mrs. A. M.	6	Liberty
STEPHENS, Jackson	1	Talbot	STEVENS, Obediah	15	Oglethorpe
STEPHENS, Jas.	4	Crawford	STEVENS, Oliver	26	Liberty
STEPHENS, John W.	6	Taliaferro	STEVENS, Oliver W.	17	Liberty
STEPHENS, Madison	1	Stewart	STEVENS, R. R.	2	Marion
STEPHENS, Richard	8	Baker	STEVENS, Silas	12	Marion
STEPHENS, S. L.	25	Bibb	STEVENS, Thos.	14	Oglethorpe

Name	Number	County	Name	Number	County
STEVENS, Thos. J.	4	Marion	STEWART, W. A.	3	Henry
STEVENS, William C.	9	Liberty	STEWART, W.N.	5	Twiggs
STEVENS, Wm. B.	3	Marion	STEWART, William	1	Morgan
STEVENS, Andrew	4	Richmond	STEWART, William D.	3	Macon
STEVENS, Hezekial	3	Burke	STEWART, Wm. B.	17	Macon
STEVENS, Isaac	2	Burke	STEWART, . S.	1	Butts
STEVENS, Jesse	2	Greene	STEWART, Amos	8	Taliaferro
STEVENS, John	1	Baldwin	STEWART, Daniel H.	4	Chatham
STEVENS, John S.	2	Baldwin	STEWART, Esther	5	Chatham
STEVENS, Seth E.	14	Baker	STEWART, Hellen	3	Chatham
STEVENSON, J. A.	6	Jefferson	STEWART, J. S.	3	Butts
STEVENSON, Jas. A.	2	Carroll	STEWART, Jas. G.	10	Coweta
STEVENSON, J.	6	Chatham	STEWART, John	3	Camden
STEVENSON, John	12	Union	STEWART, John	14	Stewart
STEWARD, John	1	Newton	STEWART, John	1	Sumter
STEWARD, William	2	Newton	STEWART, John	1	Sumter
STEWARD, John	1	DeKalb	STEWART, Judith	2	Taliaferro
STEWARD, Joseph	1	DeKalb	STEWART, Lawson	4	Taliaferro
STEWARD, L. J.	6	Putnam	STEWART, Martha	11	Taliaferro
STEWART, Andrew M.	1	Cobb	STEWART, Richard	5	Sumter
STEWART, Bennett	1	Marion	STEWART, Richard	1	Sumter
STEWART, Charles	20	Macon	STEWART, Robert	6	Burke
STEWART, Clark	2	Newton	STEWART, Sarah	4	Camden
STEWART, David	5	Walker	STEWART, Thomas H.	1	Sumter
STEWART, Dr.	4	Muscogee	STEWART, Wm. L.	6	Sumter
STEWART, Elias F.	1	Ware	STIBBS, John H.	5	Chatham
STEWART, George	2	Fayette	STIDHAM, Elihu	4	Paulding
STEWART, George	3	Gordon	STIDHAM, John	1	Hancock
STEWART, Henry	9	Marion	STILES, Benjamin	14	Bryan
STEWART, J. S.	3	Henry	STILES, J. estate	43	Chatham
STEWART, James	12	Camden	STILES, Joseph G.	44	Jones
STEWART, James	13	Jasper	STILES, Margaret B.	11	Chatham
STEWART, James	1	Laurens	STILES, B.	56	Houston
STEWART, James	52	Marion	STILES, B. E.	11	Bibb
STEWART, James	3	Newton	STILES, Edward	3	Chatham
STEWART, James	1	Paulding	STILES, Joseph	5	Bibb
STEWART, James N.	1	Murray	STILES, Wm. H .	13	Cass
STEWART, John	2	Chattooga	STILL, Barthalomie	9	Butts
STEWART, John	6	Gwinnett	STILL, C. W.	1	Butts
STEWART, John	6	Heard	STILL, David	4	Walton
STEWART, John D.	6	Muscogee	STILL, Jane	7	Walton
STEWART, Joseph A.	1	Newton	STILL, Jonathan	1	Walton
STEWART, Keneth	5	Marion	STILL, M. P.	2	Butts
STEWART, Lorenzo S.	17	Hancock	STILL, Martin	1	Walton
STEWART, Martha	1	Ware	STILL, Sampson	1	Walton
STEWART, Mary	2	Troup	STILL, William M.	1	Walton
STEWART, Peter	3	Marion	STILLWELL, John E.	3	Chatham
STEWART, Polly	45	Jones	STILLWELL, J.	17	Henry
STEWART, R.	2	Merriwether	STILLWELL, Rich.	9	Butts
STEWART, Richard M.	59	Marion	STILNCHCOMB, L.	2	Elbert
STEWART, Robt. A.	1	Henry	STILWELL, Charles H.	2	Floyd
STEWART, Theophilus	3	Muscogee	STINCHCOMB,		
STEWART, Thomas J.	10	Jones	Nathaniel	14	Fayette
STEWART, Thos.	3	Greene			

Name	Number	County	Name	Number	County
STINCHCOMBE,			STONE, M.	4	Floyd
William A. C.	1	Clarke	STONE, Osborn	6	Harris
STINSON, James W.	58	Merriwether	STONE, Sarah	19	Warren
STINSON, Elyah	1	Stewart	STONE, Sarah	19	Warren
STINSON, John	52	Talbot	STONE, Thomas	32	Walton
STINSON, John	17	Troup	STONE, W. A.	1	Elbert
STINSON, Josep h	1	Talbot	STONE, William	42	Warren
STINSON, Saml.	1	Stewart	STONE, William	13	Wilkes
STIPES, Henry	1	Campbell	STONE, William	42	Warren
STIRK, J. Ellen	7	Chatham	STONE, William B.	1	Jasper
STITH, Ursula	2	Richmond	STONE, William D.	40	Jefferson
STOACKS, A.	9	Elbert	STONE, William V.	10	Walton
STOAGHILL, J.	4	Elbert	STONE, Daniel	20	Stewart
STOCKBERGER, Jacob	1	Murray	STONE, Daniel	19	Sumter
STOCKS, John	2	Paulding	STONE, Daniel agt.	4	DeKalb
STOCKS, Thomas	40	Greene	STONE, Francis M.	24	Chatham
STOCKTON, James M.	4	Jackson	STONE, James G.	23	Burke
STOCKTON, Joseph	3	Columbia	STONE, Jos.	1	Crawford
STODDARD, John	8	Chatham	STONE, Mary	1	Crawford
STODDARD, John	2	Morgan	STONE, Micajah	6	DeKalb
STODGHILL, T. T.	3	Butts	STONE, Wash.	29	Columbia
STODGILL, D.	9	Butts	STONE, Welcome	5	Taliaferro
STODGILL, W. F.	5	Butts	STONE, Wilken	5	Meriwether
STODHILL, W. F.	1	Butts	STONE, William	18	Stewart
STOKES, A. H.	1	Heard	STONECYPHER, John	7	Franklin
STOKES, A. T.	6	Wilkes	STONECYPHER, James	7	Rabun
STOKES, G. M.	2	Lee	STOREY, Andrew J.	7	Warren
STOKES, James S.	6	Monroe	STOREY, Benj. A.	12	Marion
STOKES, John G.	3	Marion	STOREY, Jasper N.	6	Marion
STOKES, M.	2	Henry	STOREY, Stacey	14	Warren
STOKES, Mary	6	Gordon	STOREY, William R.	14	Warren
STOKES, Mary	11	Houston	STORMENT, Henry	15	Henry
STOKES, Miltilda	6	Walton	STORY, Caroon	1	Marion
STOKES, Nathaniel	2	Laurens	STORY, Christiana	5	Jackson
STOKES, Polly	4	Pulaski	STORY, Harry C.	2	Walker
STOKES, W. A.	24	Jefferson	STORY, James	24	Harris
STOKES, W. S.	46	Morgan	STORY, Mitchel	2	Monroe
STOKES, Wm. B.	2	Muscogee	STORY, Wiley	1	Pike
STOKES, Wm. H.	24	Hancock	STORY, B. W. Estate	1	Richmond
STOKES, J. W.	10	Stewart	STORY, E. M.	9	Coweta
STOKES, J. W.	1	Stewart	STORY, Edward	9	Coweta
STOKES, William M.	1	Dooly	STORY, Jesse	1	Talbot
STOKES, Wm. H.	46	Coweta	STORY, Samuel	14	Warren
STOKS, W. W.	105	Lincoln	STORY, Wm. F.	12	Coweta
STONE ?, ?	40	Walton	STORY, Wm. F. Jr.	5	Coweta
STONE, Ann W.	42	Wilkes	STORY, Wm. M.	3	Coweta
STONE, C.	5	Elbert	STOTESBURY, L.	5	Bibb
STONE, Elizabeth	1	Franklin	STOVALL, George H.	6	Franklin
STONE, G. F.	2	Upson	STOVALL, Henry F.	3	Franklin
STONE, G. V.	7	Elbert	STOVALL, James M.	7	Franklin
STONE, James A.	1	Elbert	STOVALL, Jane	17	Lincoln
STONE, John	9	Washington	STOVALL, Jas.	1	Cass
STONE, John T.	1	Greene	STOVALL, John	28	Morgan
STONE, John W. N.	9	Walton	STOVALL, John R.	5	Madison

Name	Number	County	Name	Number	County
STOVALL, M. A.	21	Floyd	STRAWN, David	1	Murray
STOVALL, M. A.	21	Floyd	STRAWN, Hiram	8	Fayette
STOVALL, Mariah	7	Jackson	STRAWN, Absolim	6	Campbell
STOVALL, Marsh	24	Morgan	STRCKLAND, Ephrame	10	Campbell
STOVALL, Ozias	26	Harris	STREET, G. S.	7	Forsyth
STOVALL, P. W.	23	Greene	STREET, Mary	3	Harris
STOVALL, Philip	5	Morgan	STREET, Mrs. P. E.	5	Wayne
STOVALL, Robert	3	Morgan	STREET, Rency A.	3	Harris
STOVALL, S. B.	4	Wilkes	STREET, S. M.	8	McIntosh
STOVALL, Samuel ?	3	Morgan	STREET, Thomas J.	26	Harris
STOVALL, W.	1	Oglethorpe	STREETE, George H.	1	Baker
STOVALL, Bat	11	Crawford	STREETER, Wiley	1	Morgan
STOVALL, Joseph	37	Baldwin	STREETMAN, Elizabeth	1	Jefferson
STOVALL, Joseph	16	Columbia	STREETMAN, Sarepta	1	Jefferson
STOVALL, Masellon P.	6	Richmond	STREETMAN, Amos	2	Stewart
STOVALL, Pleasant	7	Richmond	STREETMAN, Blanton	5	Stewart
STOVALL, S.	1	Campbell	STREETMAN, Isaac	1	Stewart
STOVALL, Thomas	2	Stewart	STRIBLING, Anthony	1	Harris
STOVALL, Thos. P.	5	Cass	STRIBLING, Benj.	9	Harris
STOVE, Mary	6	Hall	STRIBLING, Benj.	6	Harris
STOW, B.	7	Putnam	STRIBLING, F.M.	2	Wilkes
STOW, Elizabeth	17	Thomas	STRIBLING, Robert	3	Franklin
STOW, J. B.	3	Bibb	STRIBLING, Sarah	18	Wilkes
STOWARS, F. G.	13	Elbert	STRIBLING, William	3	Harris
STOWARS, J.	5	Elbert	STRIBLING, Jas.	2	Carroll
STOWARS, L. W.	8	Elbert	STRICKLAND, ?	5	Pike
STOWARS, T.	18	Elbert	STRICKLAND, Aaron	9	Wayne
STOWARS, T. L.	6	Elbert	STRICKLAND, Allen	1	Ware
STOWARS, R.	2	Elbert	STRICKLAND, Alsey	7	Thomas
STOWERS, Jesse	1	Muscogee	STRICKLAND,		
STOWERS, Lewis	4	DeKalb	Bryant E.	2	Gwinnett
STOWERS, Orpha	7	DeKalb	STRICKLAND, Burnet	11	Jackson
STRAH?, Joseph B.	25	Harris	STRICKLAND, Carlos	11	Jackson
STRAHAN, Neill	10	Merriwether	STRICKLAND, Charles	1	Warre
STRAIN, William L.	6	Greene	STRICKLAND,		
STRAND, Orion	66	Walton	Crawford M.	5	Madison
STRAND, S. B.	13	Upson	STRICKLAND, Edmund	1	Jackson
STRANGE ?, Andrew B.	11	Richmond	STRICKLAND, Elijah	5	Henry
STRANGE, Gideon	34	Washington	STRICKLAND, Ellender	12	Ware
STRANGE, J. H.	16	Elbert	STRICKLAND, Ephriam	9	Madison
STRANGE, John A.	20	Washington	STRICKLAND, Hanrdy	1	Forsyth
STRANGE, Richard B.	14	Washington	STRICKLAND, Hardy	22	Forsyth
STRANGE, Ruben G.	13	Washington	STRICKLAND, Hardy	17	Forsyth
STRANGE, Seth Jr.	10	Franklin	STRICKLAND, Hardy	25	Jackson
STRANGE, Seth Sr.	16	Franklin	STRICKLAND, Henry	14	Gwinnett
STRANGE, Thos. C.	11	Washington	STRICKLAND, Henry	13	Gwinnett
STRANGE, Chas. B.	1	Sumter	STRICKLAND, Henry	9	Henry
STRANGE?, William	1	Franklin	STRICKLAND, Henry	9	Lowndes
STRATFORD, Jesse	7	Lee	STRICKLAND, Irany	6	Forsyth
STRATTON, Almond	4	Fayette	STRICKLAND, Isaac	15	Gwinnett
STRATTON, Calvin	2	Muscogee	STRICKLAND, Isaac	19	Madison
STRAUSS, Joseph	1	Burke	STRICKLAND, J.	2	Henry
STRAWHORN, Moses	1	Cass	STRICKLAND, Jacob	14	Forsyth
STRAWN, Amos?	1	Lee	STRICKLAND, James	1	Ware

Name	Number	County	Name	Number	County
STRICKLAND, Joel	10	Forsyth	STRIPLING, Aaron	1	Jones
STRICKLAND, John	3	Heard	STRIPLING, Moses	51	Jones
STRICKLAND, Kinchen	19	Madison	STRIPLING, Robt.	3	Meriwether
STRICKLAND, Lee	5	Henry	STRIPLING, William	6	Jones
STRICKLAND, Madison	15	Jackson	STRIPLING, William	1	Muscogee
STRICKLAND, Matthew	1	Forsyth	STRIPLING,		
STRICKLAND, Milsey	2	Gwinnett	William Sen.	1	Jones
STRICKLAND,			STRIPLING, Alexander	1	Tatnall
Nathaniel	1	Murray	STRIPLING, Benjamin	15	Tatnall
STRICKLAND, Nelson	2	Heard	STRIPLING, Benjamin	1	Tatnall
STRICKLAND, Noah	7	Jackson	STRIPLING, James B.	14	Tatnall
STRICKLAND, Redin	3	Early	STRIPLING, Thos.	7	Crawford
STRICKLAND, Reuben	2	Wayne	STRISS?, J. G.	2	Muscogee
STRICKLAND, Samuel	3	Madison	STROBAST, Francis	1	Chatham
STRICKLAND, Simeon	6	Cobb	STROBELL, P. A.	3	Bibb
STRICKLAND, Simpson	4	Lowndes	STROKER?, E. L.	9	Bibb
STRICKLAND, Sol.	13	Henry	STROND, John T.	4	Walton
STRICKLAND, Sol.	7	Henry	STRONG, Charles	71	Newton
STRICKLAND, Solomon	8	Madison	STRONG, Charles		
STRICKLAND, Tolbat	19	Forsyth	by HOOPER, L. agt	31	Morgan
STRICKLAND,			STRONG,		
Washington	1	Jackson	Christopher B.	3	Houston
STRICKLAND, Willis	9	Madison	STRONG, Creed T.	11	Marion
STRICKLAND, Wilson	4	Heard	STRONG, David	3	Newton
STRICKLAND, Wilson	2	Heard	STRONG, Nathan	2	Heard
STRICKLAND, A. B.	8	Tatnall	STRONG, Noah	4	Forsyth
STRICKLAND, Abraham	3	Tatnall	STRONG, R.	22	Troup
STRICKLAND, E. H.	25	Coweta	STRONG, William	42	Oglethorpe
STRICKLAND, Henry	27	Tatnall	STRONG, William	13	Oglethorpe
STRICKLAND, Jesse	2	Randolph	STRONG, William B.	1	Troup
STRICKLAND, John	2	Bullock	STRONG, L. P.	7	Bibb
STRICKLAND, L. L.	7	Bryan	STRONG, Wm. E	37	Coweta
STRICKLAND,			STROTHER, Mary	22	Hancock
Williamson P.	1	Campbell	STROTHER, J. W.	6	Crawford
STRICKLAND, Wm.	3	Bryan	STROTHER, Thos. H.	13	Wilkes
STRICKLEN, John	9	Meriwether	STROTHERS, C. R.	9	Lincoln
STRICKLEN, Ephraim	4	Cass	STROTHERS, William	26	Lincoln
STRICKLIN, Ephrain	5	Meriwether	STROUD, Benjamin	5	Monroe
STRICKLIN, Henry	14	Cherokee	STROUD, Francis	16	Monroe
STRICKLIN, Joseph	1	Elbert	STROUD, John T.	3	Walton
STRICKLIN, Martha	1	Hall	STROUD, W.	26	Henry
STRICKLIN,			STROUD, Wm.	62	Clarke
Mrs. Elizabeth	9	Meriwether	STROUD, A. B.	4	Sumter
STRICKLING, Cary	6	Pike	STROUP, Moses	9	Cass
STRING, J. H.	8	Wilkinson	STROUS, J. H.	1	Chatham
STRINGER, Daniel	16	Thomas	STROZER, Peter J.	6	Baker
STRINGER, Jefferson	1	Harris	STROZIER,		
STRINGER, John	7	Hall	Mrs. Amanda	17	Meriwether
STRINGER, Williamson	8	Harris	STROZIER, Peter W.	11	Merriwether
STRINGER, Lovett L.	3	Baker	STROZIER, Priscella E.	9	Greene
STRINGFELLOW,			STROZIER, Reuben	52	Meriwether
Wyley	2	Marion	STROZIER, Reuben	7	Merriwether
STRIPLIN, Abel	1	Monroe	STROZIER, Reuben J.	3	Greene
STRIPLIN, James	1	Monroe	STROZIER, Peter	13	Merriwether

Name	Number	County	Name	Number	County
STROZIER, Saml.	1	Bibb	STUMP, Henry	3	Monroe
STROZIER?, Jacob P.	8	Baker	STUMPERT, A mos	8	Muscogee
STRUPPER, John B.	2	Muscogee	STURDEVANT, Gilham	1	Warren
STRUTHERS?, Ensey	5	Newton	STURDIVANT, J.	17	Troup
STUART, Archibald	5	Upson	STURDIVANT, Jas.	9	Chattooga
STUART, Mathew	5	Newton	STURDIVANT, Mary A.	6	Walton
STUART, Samual	1	Floyd	STURDIVANT, S. W.	4	Troup
STUART, Thomas	33	Monroe	STURDIVANT, W.	12	Chattooga
STUART, Thomas	4	Monroe	STURDIVANT, W.	5	Walton
STUART, William	14	Monroe	STURGES, John	3	Morgan
STUART, James	6	Campbell	STURGES, Mary	38	Columbia
STUBB?, P.	7	Bibb	STURGES, William U.	13	Burke
STUBBLEFIELD,			STURKIE, Wesley	4	Muscogee
Calvin	14	Walton	STURTEVANT, John S.	3	Chatham
STUBBLEFIELD,			STURTEVANT, George	1	Chatham
Thomas	5	Muscogee	STURTEVANT, J. C.	2	Chatham
STUBBS, Abner P.	3	Houston	STYLES, Cbourn? M.	7	Campbell
STUBBS, Ann	10	Washington	SUBER, Michael P.	2	Macon
STUBBS, Dennis	6	Fayette	SUDDETH, Elbert	6	Pike
STUBBS, Gabriel W.	10	Washington	SUDDETH, J. L.	7	Lincoln
STUBBS, James	69	Jones	SUDDETH, James	1	Pike
STUBBS, James A.	2	Houston	SUDDETH, Lewis	20	Lincoln
STUBBS, James W.	2	Jones	SUDDETH, Thomas	1	Hall
STUBBS, Sarah	15	Fayette	SUDDETH, William	12	Gwinnett
STUBBS, T.	1	Henry	SUDDETH, S. M.	2	Clarke
STUBBS, Barret	10	Baldwin	SUDETH, J. J.	4	Lee
STUBBS, Edward	12	Bibb	SUGGS, J. T.	1	Early
STUBBS, Everette	1	Tatnall	SUGGS, Amelia	1	Randolph
STUBBS, Frances	5	Bibb	SUGGS, Jas.	15	Randolph
STUBBS, George	2	Bibb	SULEVANT?, G. J.	1	Lee
STUBBS, George W.	4	Cass	SULIVAN, John	1	Houston
STUBBS, H.	16	Randolph	SULIVAN, Lenord	3	Houston
STUBBS, J. J.	3	Putnam	SULIVANT, Jas.	1	Lee
STUBBS, James	7	Randolph	SULIVANT, Saul	3	Lee
STUBBS, James F.	6	DeKalb	SULIVANT, Sol	1	Lee
STUBBS, Leme	2	Randolph	SULLIVAN, George	2	Cherokee
STUBBS, Martha P.	10	Franklin	SULLIVAN, Hilliard	14	Monroe
STUBBS, Peter	12	Bibb	SULLIVAN, Isaac	6	Monroe
STUBBS, Thos.	2	Bibb	SULLIVAN, James J.	4	Upson
STUBBS, Thos. P.	4	Bibb	SULLIVAN, James M.	4	Monroe
STUBBS, Wm. B.	3	Putnam	SULLIVAN, Spencer	33	Monroe
STUBLIN, John	2	Merriwether	SULLIVAN, Thomas A.	1	Cass
STUBS, James W.	22	Baker	SULLIVAN,		
STUCKY, Erasmus	10	Sumter	Zachariah L.	10	Monroe
STUCKY, Mary	4	Wilkinson	SULLIVAN, B.	3	Crawford
STUCKY, Nelson	1	Wilkinson	SULLIVAN, M.	10	Bibb
STUDDARD, ?	1	Morgan	SULLIVAN, Mrs.	1	Bibb
STUDDARD, David	3	Walton	SULLIVAN, Reason	3	Talbot
STUDDARD, James C.	4	Walton	SULLIVAN, Thomas C.	6	Sumter
STUDIVAN, Daniel	2	Putnam	SUMER, Adam	4	Coweta
STUDSTILL, Huster?	5	Lowndes	SUMERFORD, James	1	Houston
STUDSTILL, Jonathan	3	Lowndes	SUMERFORD, William	26	Houston
STUDSTILL, Tibia	2	Telfair	SUMERLIN, Joseph	28	Campbell
STUDSTILL, William	2	Telfair	SUMERLIN?, T.	3	Floyd

Name	Number	County	Name	Number	County
SUMERS, William P.	16	Houston	SUTTON, Frances S.	23	Lincoln
SUMERTON, Robert	3	Walton	SUTTON, J. A.	5	Harris
SUMMER, J. N.	1	Coweta	SUTTON, James E.	3	Merriwether
SUMMER, John Jr.	2	Walton	SUTTON, Jeremiah	9	Harris
SUMMER, Joseph W.	13	Coweta	SUTTON, John	18	Macon
SUMMER, Thos.	2	Bibb	SUTTON, John	31	Merriwether
SUMMER?, Margaret	14	Newton	SUTTON, John C.	2	Muscogee
SUMMERS, Elizabeth	5	Walton	SUTTON, Moses	22	Wilkes
SUMMERALL, William	1	Appling	SUTTON, Thos.	8	Wilkes
SUMMERALL, William	16	Richmond	SUTTON, William	9	Early
SUMMERLIN, C. D.	2	Macon	SUTTON, Wm.	5	Wilkes
SUMMERLIN, Henry	8	Carroll	SUTTON, Booker	16	Columbia
SUMMERLIN, M.	3	Henry	SUTTON, George	3	Dade
SUMMEROUS?,			SUTTON, James	4	Taliaferro
Harrison	30	Forsyth	SUTTON, Leroy	7	Dade
SUMMERS, James A.	8	Heard	SUTTON, Lewis	1	Baker
SUMMERS, Joseph	2	Jones	SUTTON, Lydia	4	Baker
SUMMERS, Sarah	4	Jones	SUTTON, Mary	14	Columbia
SUMMERS, Sebron F.	17	Oglethorpe	SUTTON, Mary	5	Stewart
SUMMERS, Thomas F.	1	Cobb	SWAIN, Jacob	3	Pulaski
SUMMERS, Thomas A.	4	Sumter	SWAIN, James G.	65	Warren
SUMMEUR?, Franklin	11	Lumpkin	SWAIN, Jesse	13	Gordon
SUMMEY, R. A.	15	Clarke	SWAIN, John	1	Thomas
SUMMINS, R. M.	1	Henry	SWAIN, Josiah	2	Marion
SUMMONS, Joseph	10	Laurens	SWAIN, Morgan G.	5	Lowndes
SUMNER, D.	1	Irwin	SWAIN, Elizabeth	2	Telfair
SUMNER, Green	5	Macon	SWAIN, Hiram	3	Telfair
SUMNER, James	2	Jones	SWAIN, Josiah	1	Telfair
SUMNER, Joseph	2	Laurens	SWAIN, Mark	4	Telfair
SUMNER, Mary	3	Jones	SWAIN, Rebecca	2	Telfair
SUMPTER, J.	5	Crawford	SWAIN, Stephen	25	Decatur
SURLES, Durant	1	Stewart	SWAIN, Thomas	3	Telfair
SURRENCY, Robert C.	2	Appling	SWAIN, William W.	4	Warren
SURRENCY, Sameul D.	16	Tatnall	SWAN, John W.	9	Hancock
SUTCLIFFE, Abram	2	Chatham	SWAN, Elijah	4	Newton
SUTHERLAND,			SWAN, Elizabeth	4	Jefferson
James (?)	17	Columbia	SWAN, James	1	Monroe
SUTHERLAND, Jane	15	Columbia	SWAN, James	5	Newton
SUTHERLIN, Edmond	16	Floyd	SWAN, John	10	Greene
SUTRUAK?, Jacob	4	Harris	SWAN, John	6	Newton
SUTTAL, W. M.	2	Elbert	SWAN, S. B.	1	Jefferson
SUTTAN, Johnathan	1	Lumpkin	SWAN, S. D.	3	Newton
SUTTEN, Allen	7	Houston	SWAN, Stephen	3	Monroe
SUTTEN, Frusana	1	Dooly	SWAN, Thomas M.	10	Monroe
SUTTEN, John	1	Dooly	SWAN, William	1	Jefferson
SUTTEN, M.	3	Randolph	SWAN, Richard	2	Stewart
SUTTEN, Stephen	1	Wilkinson	SWANK, Luther M.	2	Baldwin
SUTTEN, Warren	31	Randolph	SWANN, Henry	1	Clarke
SUTTIN, J. A.	1	Irwin	SWANN, B. F.	7	Putnam
SUTTIN, Theophalus	17	Pulaski	SWANN, William	1	Chatham
SUTTLE, John B.	9	Walker	SWANSON, Francis M.	6	Jasper
SUTTLES, Micaja	8	DeKalb	SWANSON, John	12	Chatham
SUTTON, Aaron	10	Monroe	SWANSON, Nancy	38	Troup
SUTTON, Charles M.	6	Monroe	SWANSON, Sam	14	Fayette

Name	Number	County	Name	Number	County
SWANSON, Virgil	3	Fayette	SYKES, M.	4	Bibb
SWANSON, Francis	24	Putnam	SYLE, Charles B.	7	Clarke
SWANTON,			SYLE, David J.	9	Clarke
Benjamin F.	1	Newton	SYMONS, John F.	4	Chatham
SWEARENGEN,			SYMS ?, Mary	1	Walton
Oliver P.	14	Dooly	SYNDER, John A.	2	Richmond
SWEARENSEN, Thomas	11	Dooly	TABB, Edmund	7	Richmond
SWEARINGEN, Thomas	1	Dooly	TABB, Edward	20	Burke
SWEARINGER, William	5	Effingham	TABB, Rebecca	10	Burke
SWEARINGIN, Vann	4	Marion	TABB, William	15	Burke
SWEARINGJEN, John	1	Dooly	TABER, F. A.	7	Franklin
SWEARINGSON,			TABOR, Adissen	7	Madison
Jacob J.	5	Dooly	TABOR, Isaac	1	Franklin
SWEAT, Farley R.	4	Chatham	TABOR, N. L.	2	Habersham
SWEAT, James A.	6	Ware	TABOR, Zach.	13	Crawford
SWEATLAND, T. J.	2	Richmond	TAGGETT, Oliver	11	Stewart
SWEET, R. R. estate	7	Chatham	TAILER, Enoch	1	Heard
SWEET, Jas. L .	21	Randolph	TAILOR, Grant	2	Morgan
SWENNY, E. B.	5	Stewart	TAILOR, Henry	4	Paulding
SWERNGIN, Catherine	3	Monroe	TAILOR, R.		
SWIFT, J. D.	5	Franklin	by agt. HARRIS, R.	42	Morgan
SWIFT, M. A.	12	Morgan	TAILOR, Sarah	2	Morgan
SWIFT, Mrs. Elizabeth	1	Merriwether	TAIT, Mary	3	Madison
SWIFT, George P.	7	Upson	TAIT, Susan	8	Jackson
SWIFT, John	1	Walker	TAITE, E. B.	8	Elbert
SWIFT, Nathaniel	4	Morgan	TAITE, N. O.	130	Elbert
SWIFT, Shelton	12	Muscogee	TAITE, Victor L.	2	Richmond
SWIFT, Thomas	22	Morgan	TAKINTON, A.Whiting	5	Camden
SWIFT, W. A.	3	Elbert	TALBIRD, Charles H.	13	Chatham
SWIFT, William T.	9	Houston	TALBOT, Brabagin	13	Washington
SWIFT, Tyra	35	Franklin	TALBOT, Isiah	4	Wilkes
SWILLEY, Rasen	3	Lowndes	TALBOT, Jno. R.	3	Wilkes
SWILLINGER, Robert Y.	1	Franklin	TALBOT, Joseph	9	Wilkes
SWINDELL, James A.	3	Greene	TALBOT, Mathew	16	Wilkes
SWINDELL, William C.	10	Greene	TALBOT, Sarah A.	26	Wilkes
SWINDLE, Daniel P.	7	Talbot	TALBOT, Thos.	45	Wilkes
SWINDLE, Daniel P.	3	Talbot	TALBOT, Wm.	18	Cass
SWINDLE, Thos.	15	Troup	TALIFERRIO, N.M.	84	Wilkes
SWING, John C.	6	Thomas	TALIFERRO, N. M.	9	Wilkes
SWINNEY, Mark E.	11	Warren	TALIAFERRO		
SWINNEY, Wm. H.	66	Greene	& TORBERT	6	Richmond
SWINT, Barksdale	2	Warren	TALIAFERRO, C. B.	46	Coweta
SWINT, John	7	Washington	TALIAFERRO, C. R.	9	Dooly
SWINT, John	12	Warren	TALIAFERRO,		
SWINT, John	3	Warren	Christopher C.	2	Richmond
SWINT, Mary	12	Washington	TALIAFERRO, Richard	27	DeKalb
SWINT, William	4	Warren	TALIFERRO, Dickinson	2	Murray
SWITZER, Asberry	17	Harris	TALIFERRO, E. M.	8	Henry
SWITZER, Williamson	3	Muscogee	TALLEY, John w.	8	Troup
SWONSON, T. R.	14	Oglethorpe	TALLEY, Robert	4	Walker
SYBERT, J. H.	10	Lincoln	TALLEY, William	1	Murray
SYKES, Daniel	28	Thomas	TALLY, E.	3	Troup
SYKES, J.	2	Henry	TALLY, James B.	1	Heard
SYKES, M.	1	Henry	TALLY, Littleton	17	Heards

Name	Number	County	Name	Number	County
TALLY, Bird	1	Gordon	TARVER, Alfred	1	Upson
TALLY, Elisha	19	Heard	TARVER, Charlotte	11	Jefferson
TALLY, Elizabeth	2	Heard	TARVER, Etheldred	4	Burke
TALLY, George W.	3	Cobb	TARVER, Etheldred	1	Jefferson
TALMADGE, Aaron	11	Monroe	TARVER, F. R.	97	Houston
TALMADGE, William A.	1	Clarke	TARVER, H. H.	113	Twiggs
			TARVER, H. H.	68	Twiggs
TALMADGE, William P.	4	Clarke	TARVER, Hartwell	61	Pulaski
TALMADGE, Samuel K.	4	Baldwin	TARVER, John V.	2	Chatham
TALMAGE, Stephen C.	8	Jasper	TARVER, Nancy	18	Troup
TALMAGE, G. W.	1	Bibb	TARVER, A. H.	53	Stewart
TAMBERLIN, M.	1	Irwin	TARVER, Elizabeth	2	Burke
TAMPLIN, Reuben	2	Warren	TARVER, Elizabeth	39	Richmond
TANER, Archibald	3	Walton	TARVER, Etheldred	7	Richmond
TANKERSLEY, John	2	Lincoln	TARVER, Etheldred J.	21	Richmond
TANKERSLEY, Wiliam	14	Columbia	TARVER, H. H.	18	Baker
TANKERSLEY, Mary	9	Columbia	TARVER, Henry	32	Baker
TANKERSLY, Andrew	2	Lincoln	TARVER, Henry H. H.	55	Baker
TANKERSLY, Catherine	3	Richmond	TARVER, Mark A.	4	Burke
TANKERSLY, Griffin	3	Wilkes	TARVER, Noah	2	Burke
TANKERSLY, J.	3	Bibb	TARVER, Paul E.	84	Baker
TANKESLEY, George W.	3	Harris	TARVER, Samuel	16	Richmond
			TARVER, William H.	36	Baker
TANNER, David	8	Hall	TARVER, Winnefred	3	Burke
TANNER, J. B.	21	Henry	TARWATER, James	3	Greene
TANNER, T. J.	5	Henry	TAST ? Eliza L	1	Richmond
TANNER, Wm. S.	4	Carroll	TAST?, Susan S.	1	Richmond
TANNER, D.	2	Washington	TATAM, Silas	28	Troup
TANNER, F.	8	Washington	TATAM, William	5	Sumter
TANNER, Gideon	13	Butts	TATE, Abram	3	Gordon
TANNER, Jane	3	Crawford	TATE, H. G.	8	Jefferson
TANNER, Mary	5	Baker	TATE, James	24	Heard
TANNER, T.	6	Washington	TATE, L. P. P.	38	Wilkes
TANNER, W.	17	Washington	TATE, M. G.	2	Forsyth
TANNER, W. H.	11	Washington	TATE, N.	6	Hall
TANNER, William H.	11	Washington	TATE, Robert	6	Lumpkin
TANNEY?, Benjamin	7	Bullock	TATE, Thomas M.	6	Harris
TANT, Isaac L.	2	Richmond	TATE, Samuel	22	Cherokee
TANT, Thomas	2	Richmond	TATE, William A.	2	Stewart
TANTERSLY, B.	1	Troup	TATHAM, H.	4	Troup
TAPLEY, Geo. W.	1	Laurens	TATOM, A. T.	8	Troup
TAPLEY, James	9	Emanual	TATOM, John H.	8	Lincoln
TAPPAN, A. B.	1	Greene	TATOM, H.	4	Troup
TAPPER, Berry	6	Pulaski	TATOM, Nancy	17	Lincoln
TARBUTTON, Benjamin	25	Washington	TATOM, Rebecca	9	Lincoln
			TATOM, W. S.	11	Lincoln
TARBUTTON, Joseph	3	Washington	TATON, Thos.	17	Troup
TARPLEY, Archibald	18	Greene	TATUM, John	10	Lumpkin
TARPLEY, Aug. A.	1	Clarke	TATUM, Mins S.	4	Troup
TARPLEY, John L.	2	Greene	TATUM, Nancy E.	30	Troup
TARVER, A. E.	42	Jefferson	TATUM, William	1	Gilmer
TARUIS, Wm.	21	Twiggs	TATUM, Dudley H.	15	Baldwin
TARVER	168	Twiggs	TATUM, Thomas	5	Randolph
			TAUNTON, Henry	1	Macon

Name	Number	County	Name	Number	County
TAUNTON, Penelope	3	Macon	TAYLOR, McKenneth	2	Macon
TAUT?, S. R.	1	Muscogee	TAYLOR, Meridity	1	Houston
TAVIST?, B.	16	Oglethorpe	TAYLOR, Mitchell	1	Houston
TAYLER, Dr. Wm.	8	Wilkinson	TAYLOR, Mona	4	Muscogee
TAYLOR, Drury	3	Washington	TAYLOR, Mrs.Ellendor	11	Houston
TAYLOR, Elbert D.	15	Washington	TAYLOR, Nancy	6	Meriwether
TAYLOR, Jeremiah	11	Monroe	TAYLOR, Nancy	15	Monroe
TAYLOR, (?)	1	Dade	TAYLOR, R. N.	6	Pulaski
TAYLOR, Alferd	1	Newton	TAYLOR, Reuben	2	Merriwether
TAYLOR, Archibald	9	Newton	TAYLOR, Robert	32	Clarke
TAYLOR, B. F.	23	Monroe	TAYLOR, Robert	7	Monroe
TAYLOR, B. R.	3	Elbert	TAYLOR, Robert	3	Troup
TAYLOR, Basil	7	Monroe	TAYLOR, S. S.	2	Pike
TAYLOR, Bryan	3	Pike	TAYLOR, Samuel	5	Twiggs
TAYLOR, Catherine	17	Oglethorpe	TAYLOR, Sarah	2	Monroe
TAYLOR, Chas. E.	49	Pulaski	TAYLOR, Silas W.	3	Glynn
TAYLOR, Chas. E.	4	Pulaski	TAYLOR, Simeon	4	Houston
TAYLOR, Christopher	6	Muscogee	TAYLOR, Simeon	2	Pulaski
TAYLOR, Clark	53	Oglethorpe	TAYLOR, Thomas C.	13	Pike
TAYLOR, Danny W.	3	Houston	TAYLOR, Warren	2	Warren
TAYLOR, Dora	9	Carroll	TAYLOR, Wesley B.	3	Thomas
TAYLOR, E. T.	28	Muscogee	TAYLOR, William	4	Macon
TAYLOR, Ephim	1	Macon	TAYLOR, William	23	Upson
TAYLOR, Frances N.	22	Jasper	TAYLOR, William	6	Washington
TAYLOR, George	20	Monroe	TAYLOR, William B.	6	Cobb
TAYLOR, George N.	3	Cherokee	TAYLOR, William C.	5	Houston
TAYLOR, Grace	1	Chatham	TAYLOR, William F.	1	Jasper
TAYLOR, H. H.	2	Walton	TAYLOR, W. P.	29	Washington
TAYLOR, Henry	8	Appling	TAYLOR, Wm.	4	Bibb
TAYLOR, Henry S..	4	Washington	TAYLOR, Wm. A.	1	Monroe
TAYLOR, J. W.	4	Troup	TAYLOR, Wm. B.	1	Floyd
TAYLOR, James	4	Appling	TAYLOR, Wm. Sen.	3	Bibb
TAYLOR, James	1	Macon	TAYLOR, A. M.	21	Chattooga
TAYLOR, James	1	Troup	TAYLOR, Albert R.	13	Taliaferro
TAYLOR, James J.	8	Clarke	TAYLOR, Alerson	26	Talbot
TAYLOR, James R.	13	Washington	TAYLOR, Benjamin F.	1	Burke
TAYLOR, James W.	33	Macon	TAYLOR, Charlotte	2	Chatham
TAYLOR, Jane F.	15	Chatham	TAYLOR, Clarissa	11	Talbot
TAYLOR, Jesse R.	5	Troup	TAYLOR, Clarissa	4	Talbot
TAYLOR, John	1	Laurens	TAYLOR, Daniel B.	2	Sumter
TAYLOR, John	157	Monroe	TAYLOR, E.	6	Crawford
TAYLOR, John	34	Monroe	TAYLOR, George	6	Talbot
TAYLOR, John	3	Monroe	TAYLOR, H. L.	43	Randolph
TAYLOR, John	5	Washington	TAYLOR, Isaac	2	Randolph
TAYLOR, John C.	11	Troup	TAYLOR, J. H.	3	Bibb
TAYLOR, John H.	3	Greene	TAYLOR, Jashma	2	Carroll
TAYLOR, John M.	14	Monroe	TAYLOR, John	2	Coweta
TAYLOR, John M.	2	Monroe	TAYLOR, John	4	Screven
TAYLOR, John S.	22	Houston	TAYLOR, John H.	5	Dooly
TAYLOR, John S.	3	Warren	TAYLOR, Joseph F.	1	Richmond
TAYLOR, John W.	5	Houston	TAYLOR, Lucy	1	Dade
TAYLOR, Lemuel	2	Twiggs	TAYLOR, P. T.	5	Baldwin
TAYLOR, Littleton	11	Greene	TAYLOR, Rhoda	15	Columbia
TAYLOR, Lorenzo J.	1	Macon	TAYLOR, S.K.	42	Sumter

Name	Number	County	Name	Number	County
TAYLOR, Sir William	5	Burke	TENNISON, Joshua	4	Crawford
TAYLOR, W.	7	Coweta	TENNISON, Linny	11	Crawford
TAYLOR, W.	3	Crawford	TERILL, Thos. H.	37	Randolph
TAYLOR, William	8	Dade	TERREL, Ignatious	2	Pike
TAYLOR, Wm.	1	Bibb	TERREL, Joel H.	13	Paulding
TAYLOR, Wm.	1	Bibb	TERREL, John B.	19	Jefferson
TAYLOR, Wm.	68	Randolph	TERREL, Margaret	3	Merriwether
TAYLOR?, Abraham	6	Lee	TERREL, Mrs. Sarah	16	Gwinnett
TEAL, Calvin	3	Harris	TERREL, Thomas W.	17	Thomas
TEAL, Erasmus	6	Harris	TERREL, David M.	7	Troup
TEARRY, Joseph	6	Elbert	TERREL, Joel L.	18	Jasper
TEASDALE, Mrs. M. M.	4	Muscogee	TERRELL, Alexander H.	3	Franklin
TEASLEY, Alfred	5	Cherokee	TERRELL, B. D.	1	Habersham
TEASLEY, B. A.	15	Elbert	TERRELL, Catherine W.	3	Franklin
TEASLEY, E.	8	Elbert	TERRELL, David S.	64	Greene
TEASLEY, Isham	18	Cherokee	TERRELL, Henry	4	Walton
TEASLEY, J. A.	21	Elbert	TERRELL, Henry	44	Wilkes
TEASLEY, O. G.	7	Elbert	TERRELL, James	8	Cass
TEASLEY, T. H.	11	Elbert	TERRELL, Jas. P.	10	Gordon
TEASLEY, T. J.	16	Elbert	TERRELL, John T.	2	Gordon
TEASLEY, W. H.	4	Elbert	TERRELL, Joseph	4	Cass
TEASLY, J. A.	6	Elbert	TERRELL, Kenion	7	Gwinnett
TEASLY, J. R.	6	Elbert	TERRELL, Richmond	18	Newton
TEASLY, W. A.	1	Elbert	TERRELL, Thomas	9	Newton
TEBEAU, John R.	3	Chatham	TERRELL, William	23	Greene
TEBEAU, F. E.	26	Chatham	TERRELL, William	163	Hancock
TEDFORD, Charles	12	Harris	TERRELL, William	68	Washington
TEDFORD, Charles	1	Harris	TERRELL, Joel. W.	20	Coweta
TEEL, John	16	Sumter	TERRELL, John A.	6	Cass
TEFT, Israel K.	11	Chatham	TERRELL, P. B .	39	Coweta
TALFAIR, Mrs.	60	Washington	TERRIL, Catherine	43	Putnam
TELFAIR, Mary	66	Chatham	TERRILL, D. M.	16	Merriwether
TELLER?, Mason	27	Randolph	TERRY, Frederic J.	29	Harris
TEMPLE, Frederick	3	Early	TERRY, Frederic J.	17	Harris
TEMPLES, Thomas	1	Wilkinson	TERRY, G. B.	15	Muscogee
TEMPLES, Tom	2	Wilkinson	TERRY, James	1	Hancock
TEMPLETON, Martha	4	Macon	TERRY, Jeremiah	2	Muscogee
TEMPLETON, Alexr.	12	Richmond	TERRY, John	2	Campbell
TEMPLETON, James	5	Stewart	TERRY, John	2	Forsyth
TENCKS, Ebenezar	42	Chatham	TERRY, John	24	Marion
TENDERSON, James D.	14	Marion	TERRY, J.	11	Troup
TENDERSON, Jesse	7	Marion	TERRY, Lewis	5	Murray
TENISON, Elizabeth	1	Emanual	TERRY, Samuel C.	1	Pike
TENISON, James H.	2	Richmond	TERRY, Stephen	2	Forsyth
TENISON, John	3	Burke	TERRY, Stephen	23	Harris
TENISON, L.	5	Troup	TERRY, Thomas	37	Muscogee
TENLEY, Mut	1	Talbot	TERRY, William	2	Muscogee
TENNEL?, W.	1	Elbert	TERRY, Wm.	3	Forsyth
TENNENT, John	3	Franklin	TERRY, Daniel	3	Stewart
TENNENT?, Churchwell	1	Harris	TERRY, Ebenezer T.	4	Richmond
TENNILLE, A. S.	15	Randolph	TERRY, John	24	Talbot
TENNILLE, Robert	11	Washington	TERRY, R.	3	Stewart
TENNILLE, Wm. A.	36	Randolph	TERRY, Stephen	1	DeKalb
TENNISON ?, John	2	Richmond	TERRY, Wm.	2	DeKalb

Name	Number	County	Name	Number	County
TETLER, Daniel	5	Chatham	THOMAS, Geo. W.	69	Camden
TEYNAC, Andrew	6	Chatham	THOMAS, George w.	5	Walton
TEYNAC, John	6	Chatham	THOMAS, Grigsby	18	Muscogee
THAMES, Joseph G.	1	Paulding	THOMAS, Harrison	4	Muscogee
THARP, Benj.	6	Twiggs	THOMAS, Henry L.	1	Merriwether
THARP, Benjamin F.	28	Houston	THOMAS, Hiram	2	Harris
THARP, John	20	Twiggs	THOMAS, Howard	1	Walton
THARP, Mrs. Martha	65	Houston	THOMAS, Isaac	1	Laurens
THARP, C.	5	Bibb	THOMAS, Isham B.	5	Lowndes
THARP, R. A.	1	Crawford	THOMAS, J.	34	Elbert
THARPE, C. S.	25	Twiggs	THOMAS, James	42	Hancock
THARPE, Robert D.	16	Troup	THOMAS, James	5	Walton
THAXTON, Th os.	1	Henry	THOMAS, James S.	15	Hancock
THAXTON, Yelverton	6	Butts	THOMAS, Jas. L.	4	Hancock
THAXTON, Wm.	2	Butts	THOMAS, Jas. O. B.	12	Hancock
THAYER & BUTT	1	Richmond	THOMAS, Jesse S.	13	Hancock
THEATT, James	86	Monroe	THOMAS, Jethro	12	Burke
THERKELD, Jon	9	Stewart	THOMAS, Job	6	Union
THERKILD, William	4	Monroe	THOMAS, Joel	1	Franklin
THEUS, Simeon	29	Thomas	THOMAS, John	2	Chatham
THEUS, Thomas H.	9	Chatham	THOMAS, John	18	Jones
THEUS, B. T.	4	Chatham	THOMAS, John	1	Laurens
THIERS, John	1	Dooly	THOMAS, John.	7	Lincoln
THIESS, Jacob	3	Liberty	THOMAS, John	2	Morgan
THIGPEN, G. B.	1	Washington	THOMAS, John	3	Murray
THIGPEN, Henry F.	17	Early	THOMAS, John A.	104	McIntosh
THIGPEN, Joshua	1	Houston	THOMAS, John H.	93	Monroe
THIGPEN, Melaneton	3	Emanual	THOMAS, John S.	92	Dooly
THIGPEN, Travis	1	Emanual	THOMAS, John T.	6	Chatham
THIGPEN, William	7	Emanual	THOMAS, Joseph	1	Chatham
THILFORD, William	4	Walker	THOMAS, Leonard C.	1	Gwinnett
THODE, John H.	1	Chatham	THOMAS, Lewis	2	Cobb
THOMAS ?, John Estate	23	Richmond	THOMAS, Lewis	1	Ware
THOMAS, (?)	8	Columbia	THOMAS, Lovick P.	19	Clarke
THOMAS, Alexander	3	Chatham	THOMAS, M. H.	7	Franklin
THOMAS, Andrew	12	Appling	THOMAS, Mary	2	Cobb
THOMAS, Archibald	5	Merriwether	THOMAS, Mary A.	116	McIntosh
THOMAS, Barbary	27	Thomas	THOMAS, Maryaland	4	Houston
THOMAS, Benjamin	1	Gwinnett	THOMAS, Merrill	6	Clarke
THOMAS, Charnick	2	Houston	THOMAS, Micajah	32	Lumpkin
THOMAS,			THOMAS, Milton H.	1	Gwinnett
Christopher C.	4	Cobb	THOMAS, Mrs. Martha	34	Burke
THOMAS, Col. Henry	5	Gwinnett	THOMAS, N. G.	3	Hall
THOMAS, D. B.	1	Irwin	THOMAS, Nancy	3	Clarke
THOMAS, David	1	Gwinnett	THOMAS, Owen	29	Muscogee
THOMAS, David A.	2	Pike	THOMAS, Owen	4	Muscogee
THOMAS, Dicey	12	Warren	THOMAS, Owen	3	Muscogee
THOMAS, E. W.	7	Monroe	THOMAS, Owen?	19	Muscogee
THOMAS, Edward L.	4	Newton	THOMAS, P. W.	22	Clarke
THOMAS, Eldridge B.	2	Heard	THOMAS, Penina	51	Monroe
THOMAS, Eliz.	31	Pulaski	THOMAS, Richard	9	Thomas
THOMAS, Euphema	10	Washington	THOMAS, Richard	4	Harris
THOMAS, F.	4	Laurens	THOMAS, Robert	36	Oglethorpe
THOMAS, G. W.	3	Floyd	THOMAS, Robt.	12	Camden

Name	Number	County	Name	Number	County
THOMAS, Samuel W.	2	Walker	THOMAS, Spencer	10	Randolph
THOMAS, Stephen	2	Merriwether	THOMAS, William	3	Burke
THOMAS, Steven	28	Jackson	THOMAS, William B.	2	Baker
THOMAS, Stevens	15	Clarke	THOMAS, William B.	4	Chatham
THOMAS, W.	1	Walton	THOMAS, William M.	14	Columbia
THOMAS, W. B.	23	McIntosh	THOMAS, Wm.	2	Decatur
THOMAS, W. L.	18	Laurens	THOMAS, Wm. H.	1	Coweta
THOMAS, Washington	1	Clarke	THOMAS, Stephen	2	Randolph
THOMAS, William	7	Clarke	THOMASON, Bartlett	5	Walker
THOMAS, William	3	Fayette	THOMASON, John	3	Campbell
THOMAS, William	1	Franklin	THOMASON, Thomas	32	Jasper
THOMAS, William	4	Harris	THOMASON, J. S.	2	Chattooga
THOMAS, William J.	21	Monroe	THOMASON, Wm. B.	2	Coweta
THOMAS, William R.	4	Morgan	THOMASSON, Nancy	7	Henry
THOMAS, Wm. S.	2	Troup	THOMASSON, P. R.	13	Morgan
THOMAS, A. S.	7	Randolph	THOMASSON, William	8	Cobb
THOMAS, Alexander	4	Chatham	THOMASSON, Wm. B.	2	Heard
THOMAS, Ann	1	Randolph	THOMASSON, Eugenia	3	Chatham
THOMAS, D.	3	Decatur	THOMASTON, J. C.	9	Troup
THOMAS, Daniel	4	Cass	THOMASTON, John B.	6	Harris
THOMAS, David	1	DeKalb	THOMASTON, J.	10	Crawford
THOMAS, Davis	3	Richmond	THOMASTON, J. C.	2	Butts
THOMAS, Davis H.	5	Talbot	THOMASTON, R. F.	4	Troup
THOMAS, Drucilla	9	Camden	THOMASTON, T. S.	8	Carroll
THOMAS, Edward	15	Richmond	THOMASTON, V.	4	Troup
THOMAS, Emeline	2	Richmond	THOMERSON, Leonard	1	Butts
THOMAS, Floyd	3	Richmond	THOMPKIN, O. P.	9	Oglethorpe
THOMAS, Francis	7	Talbot	THOMPKINS, estate	9	Camden
THOMAS, G. R.	10	Putnam	THOMPKINS, Pardon	12	Jefferson
THOMAS, H.	9	Decatur	THOMPKINS, John	8	Camden
THOMAS, J. B.	15	Sumter	THOMPKINS, John	1	Stewart
THOMAS, J. M.	10	Decatur	THOMPKINS, Robt.	6	Camden
THOMAS, Jesse	1	Franklin	THOMPSON, ?	7	Elbert
THOMAS, Jno.	4	Randolph	THOMPSON, Andrew	19	Hall
THOMAS, Jno. W.	12	Randolph	THOMPSON,		
THOMAS, John	7	Columbia	Anthony M.	10	Houston
THOMAS, John M.	22	Coweta	THOMPSON, Asa E.	34	Houston
THOMAS, John S.	12	Baldwin	THOMPSON, Asberry	4	Harris
THOMAS, Jos.	29	Camden	THOMPSON, Bell	4	Warren
THOMAS, Joseph	10	Richmond	THOMPSON, Benj. M.	2	Madison
THOMAS, Joseph D.	41	Burke	THOMPSON, C. A.	1	Walton
THOMAS, Joseph D.	10	Burke	THOMPSON, C. A.	1	Walton
THOMAS, Joseph D.	29	Richmond	THOMPSON, Charles J.	21	Lumpkin
THOMAS, Mary	11	Baldwin	THOMPSON,		
THOMAS, Mrs.	20	Decatur	Charles W.	1	Morgan
THOMAS, Mrs. H.	1	Decatur	THOMPSON, D.	2	Walton
THOMAS, Nancy	9	Columbia	THOMPSON, Daniel	2	Thomas
THOMAS, Owen J.	3	Randolph	THOMPSON, Daniel	3	Houston
THOMAS, P. W.	9	Clarke	THOMPSON, David	8	Newton
THOMAS, Peter G.	2	Chatham	THOMPSON, David	6	Walton
THOMAS, Phebe	2	Randolph	THOMPSON, Dawson	1	Merriwether
THOMAS, Richard	5	DeKalb	THOMPSON, Duery?	4	Bibb
THOMAS, Sarah	3	Richmond	THOMPSON, Edmund	2	Jefferson
THOMAS, Seaborn	9	Randolph	THOMPSON, Elijah	2	Upson

Name	Number	County	Name	Number	County
THOMPSON, Elzy	3	Thomas	THOMPSON, Mary	7	Warren
THOMPSON, Ephraim	7	Paulding	THOMPSON, Mary A.	1	Butts
THOMPSON, G. G.	8	Hall	THOMPSON, Matthew	2	Hancock
THOMPSON, G. W.	2	Greene	THOMPSON, Matthew	7	Murray
THOMPSON, George W.	5	Murray	THOMPSON, Melvin	8	Jefferson
THOMPSON, Green L.	5	Jackson	THOMPSON, Middleton	13	Clarke
THOMPSON, H. G.	2	Henry	THOMPSON, Nancy	1	Newton
THOMPSON, H. J.	11	Morgan	THOMPSON, Nancy	1	Walker
THOMPSON, Hannah	2	Richmond	THOMPSON, Nathaniel	5	Muscogee
THOMPSON, Henry	6	Hancock	THOMPSON, Nathaniel	3	Warren
THOMPSON, J.	6	Henry	THOMPSON,		
THOMPSON, J. C.	41	Wilkinson	Nichdemus	12	Houston
THOMPSON, J. E.	4	Marion	THOMPSON, Norman B.	4	Houston
THOMPSON, J.W.	1	Forsyth	THOMPSON, Obediah	1	Hall
THOMPSON, Jabez	4	Jefferson	THOMPSON, Obediah	20	Madison
THOMPSON, James	1	Jefferson	THOMPSON, Peter	3	Merriwether
THOMPSON, James	1	Walton	THOMPSON, Portlock	6	Dooly
THOMPSON, James G.	3	Harris	THOMPSON, Robert	11	Clarke
THOMPSON, James Jr.	4	Madison	THOMPSON, Robt.	31	Lee
THOMPSON, James Sr.	17	Madison	THOMPSON, S. C.	4	Henry
THOMPSON, James R.	5	Wilkinson	THOMPSON, Sampson	3	Newton
THOMPSON, James S.	7	Walton	THOMPSON, Samuel	6	Clarke
THOMPSON, James Y.	7	Newton	THOMPSON, Samuel	1	Cobb
THOMPSON, Jane	6	Jefferson	THOMPSON, Samuel	2	Fayette
THOMPSON, Jas.	4	Camden	THOMPSON, Samuel	7	Jefferson
THOMPSON, Jeffry E.	15	Muscogee	THOMPSON, Saml.	7	Troup
THOMPSON, Jeremiah	4	Fayette	THOMPSON, Samuel W.	1	Cherokee
THOMPSON, Jeremiah	2	Warren	THOMPSON, Shadrick	2	Jefferson
THOMPSON,			THOMPSON, Seborn J.	8	Troup
Jeremiah B.	1	Hancock	THOMPSON, Smith	3	Fayette
THOMPSON, Jesse	2	Murray	THOMPSON,		
THOMPSON, John	12	Burke	Stephen D.	2	Houston
THOMPSON, John	22	Early	THOMPSON, T. J.	1	Greene
THOMPSON, John	7	Newton	THOMPSON, Thomas	52	Greene
THOMPSON, John	1	Upson	THOMPSON, Thomas M.	3	Harris
THOMPSON, John B.	2	Newton	THOMPSON, Thos.	1	Pulaski
THOMPSON, John F.	1	Jasper	THOMPSON, Thos. S.	4	Greene
THOMPSON, John P.	10	Meriwether	THOMPSON, U. A.	7	Henry
THOMPSON, John P.	1	Newton	THOMPSON,		
THOMPSON, John W.	27	Muscogee	Verdenburgh	2	Walker
THOMPSON, John W.	6	Walton	THOMPSON, William	4	Jefferson
THOMPSON, Jno. D.	18	Wilkes	THOMPSON, William	3	Jefferson
THOMPSON, Jos.	4	Chattooga	THOMPSON, William	19	Madison
THOMPSON, Jos.	2	Chattooga	THOMPSON, William	1	Newton
THOMPSON, Jos. R.	3	Forsyth	THOMPSON, William	2	Warren
THOMPSON, Joseph	2	Hall	THOMPSON,		
THOMPSON, Joseph H.	12	Houston	William D.	26	Merriwether
THOMPSON, Joseph R.	6	Chatham			
THOMPSON, L. Q. C.	3	Paulding	THOMPSON,		
THOMPSON, Lewis T.	2	Fayette	William H.	1	Harris
THOMPSON, M.	1	Hancock	THOMPSON,		
THOMPSON, M.	7	Wilkinson	William H.	11	Jasper
THOMPSON, Mary	2	Chatham	THOMPSON, William S.	9	Jackson
THOMPSON, Mary	3	Jefferson	THOMPSON, Wm.	2	Bibb

Name	Number	County	Name	Number	County
THOMPSON, A. F.	6	Stewart	THORANTON,		
THOMPSON, Americus			Thomas J.	39	Troup
agt for NAPPIER	26	Houston	THORANTON,		
THOMPSON, Ann	1	Chatham	Thomas J.	14	Troup
THOMPSON, Charles	55	Houston	THORANTON, Willis	5	Troup
THOMPSON, Chas.	12	Bibb	THORNBROUGH,		
THOMPSON, Danl. B.	2	Richmond	John R.	1	Cass
THOMPSON, David	8	Butts	THORNEBURY,		
THOMPSON, Eli C.	4	Dooly	James W.	4	Baker
THOMPSON, Elizabeth	4	Chatham	THORNHILL, H.	2	Lee
THOMPSON, G. L.	4	Butts	THORNHILL, Newil	1	Macon
THOMPSON, George A.	1	Campbell	THORNIGTON, Mary	3	Harris
THOMPSON, Guy	1	Sumter	THORNTON, B.	3	Elbert
THOMPSON, H.	4	Bibb	THORNTON, Benjamin	28	Elbert
THOMPSON, J.	17	Chattooga	THORNTON, Beverly A.	1	Muscogee
THOMPSON, J. N.	2	Butts	THORNTON, Cullen	11	Monroe
THOMPSON, James	2	Sumter	THORNTON, D.	7	Elbert
THOMPSON, James P.	6	Screven	THORNTON, Dozier	55	Muscogee
THOMPSON, Jas.	2	Coweta	THORNTON, E. G.	1	Muscogee
THOMPSON, John	1	Stewart	THORNTON, E. W.	2	Elbert
THOMPSON, John F.	3	Stewart	THORNTON, F	7	Elbert
THOMPSON, Joseph	23	DeKalb	THORNTON, F. W.	7	Forsyth
THOMPSON, M. S.	10	Bibb	THORNTON, Green	17	Muscogee
THOMPSON, P.F.	2	Sumter	THORNTON, H.	1	Troup
THOMPSON, Pricelia	9	Taliaferro	THORNTON, Isaac	9	Forsyth
THOMPSON, R. M.	7	Clarke	THORNTON, Isaac	4	Muscogee
THOMPSON, Rhody	1	Screven	THORNTON, J. M.	3	Elbert
THOMPSON, Robt.	8	Screven	THORNTON, J. S.	15	Hancock
THOMPSON, Saml. M.	3	Richmond	THORNTON, J.T.B.	29	Early
THOMPSON, S. T.	2	Chatham	THORNTON, Jesse	2	Gwinnett
THOMPSON, Thomas	9	Clarke	THORNTON, Johnson	8	Pike
THOMPSON, William	9	Dooly	THORNTON, M.	3	Elbert
THOMPSON, William	1	Stewart	THORNTON, M. L.	1	Walton
THOMPSON?,			THORNTON, Marion C.	1	Walton
James A. L.	1	Campbell	THORNTON, Mark	4	Merriwether
THOMPSOON, Isham	3	Richmond	THORNTON, Mark	6	Murray
THOMSON, John	2	Pike	THORNTON,		
THOMSON, John S.	2	Jasper	Micajah C.	3	Jackson
THOMSON, Nancy	2	Jasper	THORNTON, Nat. M.	39	Muscogee
THOMSON, William	32	Liberty	THORNTON, Newman	6	Merriwether
THOMSON, William	22	Walton	THORNTON, Phillip	8	Wilkes
THOMSON, Arthur	4	Coweta	THORNTON, Pinkney	3	Forsyth
THOMSON, E. P.	1	Randolph	THORNTON, R.	29	Elbert
THOMSON, Jno.	8	Randolph	THORNTON, Reubin	3	Hall
THOMSON, Wm. H.	4	Coweta	THORNTON, T. S.	1	Elbert
THOMSTON, James A.	16	Greene	THORNTON, Thos.	17	Forsyth
THOMTON, Nancy	20	Talbot	THORNTON, V. R.	48	Greene
THORN, Elizabeth	9	Washington	THORNTON, W. E.	1	Elbert
THORN, Middleton	14	Burke	THORNTON, W. T.	1	Elbert
THORN, Joseph	5	Baker	THORNTON, Wiley	19	Pike
THORN, William	1	Burke	THORNTON, Wiley A.	4	Clarke
THORANTON,			THORNTON, D.	1	Screven
Hannah P.	2	Troup	THORNTON, J. A.	1	Stewart
THORANTON, Sarah	3	Troup	THORNTON, Midleton	1	Campbell

Name	Number	County	Name	Number	County
THORNTON, R. C.	26	Stewart	THURINGTON, John T.	13	Harris
THORNTON, Reddick	2	Camden	THURKILL, Mrs.	6	Muscogee
THORNTON, Reuben	17	Talbot	THURLKILL, (none)	1	Muscogee
THORNTON, Richard	17	Randolph	THURMAN, Benj.	2	Wilkes
THORNTON, Rolin	1	Butts	THURMAN, Felix	12	Wilkes
THORNTON, S. A.	3	Stewart	THURMAN, George	6	Lowndes
THORNTON, W. R.	1	Stewart	THURMAN, J. B.	5	Butts
THORP, John	4	Washington	THURMAN, J. M.	8	Butts
THORPE, Charles C.	6	McIntosh	THURMON, John W.	1	Franklin
THORPE, James R. J.	15	Liberty	THURMON, Y.	2	Elbert
THORTON, Dred	2	Oglethorpe	THURMOND, Jas. W.	2	Jackson
THORTON, Isaac	23	Oglethorpe	THURMOND, James	1	Jackson
THORTON, John	2	Oglethorpe	THURMOND, Jefferson	11	Jackson
THORTON, Margert	5	Oglethorpe	THURMOND, John	1	Jackson
THORTON, William B.	3	Pike	THURMOND, John	118	Jasper
THORTON, R. C.	11	Stewart	THURMOND, Nancy	1	Muscogee
THOSTON?, John	27	Oglethorpe	THURMOND, Philip	3	Walton
THRALKILL, E. H.	1	Harris	THURMOND, Richard O.	9	Fayette
THRASH, David	55	Monroe	THURMOND, Thos. J.	3	Jackson
THRASH, Elizabeth	14	Troup	THURMOND, Wm. A.	2	Jackson
THRASH, George	22	Troup	THURMOND, Wm. Sr.	5	Jackson
THRASH, Isaac	11	Merriwether	THURMOND, J. D.	7	Coweta
THRASH, John	3	Troup	THURMOND, M.	11	Coweta
THRASH, M.	6	Merriwether	THURMOND, Wm. T.	26	Coweta
THRASH, Mary	19	Merriwether	THWEATT, James	40	Upson
THRASH, William	5	Merriwether	THWEATT, Kinchen P.	11	Upson
THRASH, William	5	Monroe	TICER, Robert	1	Warren
THRASH, Willis	2	Merriwether	TICKNER, Frances H.	2	Jones
THRASHER, Albert	3	Monroe	TIDWELL, B.	1	Merriwether
THRASHER, Barton C.	7	Clarke	TIDWELL, Celia	1	Forsyth
THRASHER, David	17	Newton	TIDWELL, J. J.	7	Merriwether
THRASHER, Earley W.	22	Morgan	TIDWELL, L. B.	4	Merriwether
THRASHER, James	5	Newton	TIDWELL, Mark	3	Merriwether
THRASHER, Susan	5	Clarke	TIDWELL, Mary	6	Merriwether
THRASHER, Thomas	6	Newton	TIDWELL, Mathew	9	Harris
THRASHER, Wm. H.	3	Clarke	TIDWELL, Milan M.	7	Fayette
THRASHER, Bartin	42	Clarke	TIDWELL, Simeon J.	5	Meriwether
THRASHER, Isaac	42	Clarke	TIDWELL, William	1	Merriwether
THRASHER, J. J.	15	DeKalb	TIDWELL, William U.	2	Harris
THREAT, James	26	Houston	TIDWELL, B. F.	17	Putnam
THREEWITTS,			TIDWELL, Wm. D.	2	Coweta
Thomas P. F.	11	Warren	TIERNEY, Patrick	2	Chatham
THRELAHA, J. J.	5	Pike	TIFFANY, Hampton	1	Jefferson
THROGILL?, John	5	Habersham	TIFFANY, Levi	1	Jefferson
THRONTON, Jno. B.	18	Wilkes	TIFT & MERSER	12	Baker
THROPE (THORPE?),			TIFT, Nelson	8	Baker
C. J. W.	7	McIntosh	TIGNOR, Urban	11	Talbot
THROUGH?, George P.	26	Pike	TILBEAN, Frederick	2	Effingham
THROWER, Margaret	10	Pike	TILER, Asa	3	Talbot
THROWER, Thomas	23	Pike	TILER, Mary	2	Talbot
THROWER, Lewis	9	Stewart	TILGHMAN, A. H.	1	Fayette
THROWER, Lewis	5	Stewart	TILKEY, John	1	Richmond
THROWER, Lewis	3	Stewart	TILKEY, Newse ?	4	Richmond
THUART, S. P.	3	Pike	TILLER, B.	4	Oglethorpe

Name	Number	County	Name	Number	County
TILLER, E.	2	Oglethorpe	TINER, John	1	Sumter
TILLER, Ephraim E.	7	Jasper	TINGLE, John	1	Monroe
TILLER, Martin	9	Greene	TINGLE, Purifoy	10	Monroe
TILLER, Mitchel D.	6	Oglethorpe	TINLEY, Jas.	12	Bibb
TILLER, Payton	4	Gwinnett	TINLEY, Jesse	1	Richmond
TILLER, William	11	Oglethorpe	TINLEY, John	1	Richmond
TILLER?, Randall	2	Oglethorpe	TINLEY, John L.	16	Richmond
TILLERY, Samuel F.	10	Lincoln	TINLEY, Lucy	1	Richmond
TILLERY, Sidney	11	Columbia	TINLEY, Phillip	1	Richmond
TILLEY, Mrs.	2	Muscogee	TINLEY, Thomas	2	Richmond
TILLEY, Nancy	2	Habersham	TINSLEY, D. R.	16	Monroe
TILLEY, Robt. A.	3	Floyd	TINSLEY, Elizabeth	11	Monroe
TILLINGHART, E. H.	3	Bibb	TINSLEY, James W.	31	Monroe
TILLINGHURST,			TINSLEY, Jas.	19	Wilkes
Parris J.	19	Muscogee	TINSLEY, Jeffersn	1	Newton
TILLINHAST, Parris R.	4	Muscogee	TINSLEY, Wiley F.	10	Monroe
TILLIS, William	5	Burke	TINSLEY, William	7	Muscogee
TILLMAN, David	1	Marion	TINSLEY, Wm. Jun.	5	Muscogee
TILLMAN, Gassanan?	19	Thomas	TINSLEY, E.	3	Richmond
TILLMAN, Henry	65	Montgomery	TINSLEY, Green	12	Baker
TILLMAN, Henry	5	Pulaski	TINSLEY, William	17	Sumter
TILLMAN, James	22	Appling	TINSLEY, William B.	11	Baldwin
TILLMAN, James	1	Appling	TIPPINGS, William W.	2	Tatnall
TILLMAN, Jeremiah	3	Lowndes	TIPPINS, George W.	3	Cherokee
TILLMAN, John	2	Appling	TIPPINS, James	5	Cherokee
TILLMAN, John	2	Thomas	TIPPINS, John J.	7	Cherokee
TILLMAN, Joseph	1	Appling	TISHER, Louis	2	Monroe
TILLMAN, Lazarus	10	Merriwether	TISON, Abner	26	Dooly
TILLMAN, Elza	3	Telfair	TISON, John M.	24	Glynn
TILLMAN, Henry	13	Bullock	TISON, Kathaarine	1	Emanual
TILLMAN, James	14	Tatnall	TISON, Moses B.	14	Lee
TILLMAN, Richard N.	1	Baker	TISON, Noah B.	15	Cobb
TILLMAN, Stephen	5	Richmond	TISON, M. E.	3	Randolph
TILLMAN?, John	4	Merriwether	TISON, W. W.	22	Dooly
TILLMON, John	12	Jasper	TISON, William O.	4	Warren
TILLY, Ebenezer	2	DeKalb	TISSANEW, B.	1	Bibb
TILLY, Sarah	1	Paulding	TITCOMB, George H.	1	Chatham
TILLY, John W.	1	DeKalb	TOBE?, James	5	Harris
TILLY, Josiah	11	Taliaferro	TOBERT, James P.	46	Jefferson
TILLY, Stephen	8	DeKalb	TOBEY, Henry	1	DeKalb
TILMAN, Hezekiah	3	Walton	TOBEY, Solomon	1	Richmond
TILMAN, William J.	2	Macon	TODD, Benjamin	20	Jones
TIMMONS, Mary A.	1	Cobb	TODD, Elkhanah	3	Warren
TIMMONS, Stephen	14	Glynn	TODD, George W.	2	Monroe
TIMMONS, Zachariah	4	Glynn	TODD, H. B.	22	Jefferson
TIMMONS, Susan	2	Chatham	TODD, Henry	2	Wayne
TIMMONS, Thos. T.	1	DeKalb	TODD, Isaac	8	Lumpkin
TINDALL, Elizabeth	14	Clarke	TODD, J. W.	2	Wilkinson
TINDALL, Everett	4	Burke	TODD, James	6	Lumpkin
TINDALL, Henry	2	Bibb	TODD, James	16	Warren
TINDALL, Sampson J.	6	Burke	TODD, John B.	1	Jones
TINDALL, William B.	18	Columbia	TODD, Joseph W.	16	Monroe
TINDLY, M.	7	Gordon	TODD, Chas.	4	Cass
TINER, Jackson	4	Sumter	TODD, Elizabeth	5	Putnam

Name	Number	County	Name	Number	County
TODD, Mary	5	Wilkinson	TOMPSON, Hardy B.	1	Washington
TODD, Richard E.	3	Wilkinson	TOMPSON, James	2	Heard
TODD, Washington	1	Tatnall	TOMPSON, John	12	Heard
TODD, William	9	McIntosh	TOMPSON, John E.	3	Washington
TODD, William	3	Tatnall	TONEY, Charles	1	Franklin
TODD, Wm.	27	Wilkinson	TONEY, Charles	2	Marion
TOGUN?, Francis	24	Habersham	TONEY, Nancy	5	Franklin
TOKIN, Thomas	2	Richmond	TONEY, Wm.	45	Randolph
TOLAND, T. J.	5	Monroe	TONEY, Wm. Jr.	11	Randolph
TOLBERT, John	16	Coweta	TONNER ?, Walter	1	Warren
TOLBOT, John	37	Stewart	TONY, Jasper	1	Monroe
TOLER ?, Thomas T.	3	Richmond	TOOK, Allen Esq.	36	Houston
TOLER, William J.	1	Harris	TOOK, J.	34	Houston
TOLEY, John	1	Bibb	TOOK, Joseph	104	Houston
TOLIN, Michael	30	Jasper	TOOK, Sterling	26	Houston
TOLIN, Asa	5	Dooly	TOOKE, Joseph E.	6	Houston
TOLLER, William	14	Paulding	TOOKE, James P.	10	Talbot
TOLLESON, Birdsong	2	Cobb	TOOL, George	16	Columbia
TOMBERLIN, Harris	8	Clinch	TOOL, William T.	2	Sumter
TOMBERLIN, Thomas	15	Telfair	TOOLEY, Mary S.	2	Jones
TOMBERLIN?, D.	23	Irwin	TOOMBS, Gabriel	6	Wilkes
TOMBLIN, Robert G.	12	Burke	TOOMBS, H.	11	Houston
TOMBS, Robert	17	Wilkes	TOOMBS, J. S.	28	Houston
TOMKINS, (?)	22	Columbia	TOOMER, Henry	70	Houston
TOMLIN, Mary J.	15	Marion	TOOTLE, Rebecca	1	Washington
TOMLIN, Miss Zelpha	15	Burke	TOOTLE, Willilam	9	Tatnall
TOMLIN, Pleasant	1	Muscogee	TOOTLEN, Edward	5	Appling
TOMLIN, John	4	Burke	TOPKINS, John	5	Monroe
TOMLIN, West W.	2	Burke	TORBAT, Huh	3	Monroe
TOMLINSON, H.	22	Henry	TORBERT, George T.	2	Sumter
TOMLINSON, R. L.	1	Pike	TORBUT, Samuel C.	6	Upson
TOMLINSON, Sarah	2	Carroll	TORLAY, A. F.	4	Chatham
TOMLINSON, William	5	Houston	TORLEY, Alfred F.	1	Chatham
TOMLINSON, H. W.	3	Chattooga	TORLICH, David R.	4	Richmond
TOMLINSON, J. F.	11	Carroll	TORRANCE,		
TOMLINSON, Jared	59	Sumter	Miss Harriett	8	Muscogee
TOMLINSON, Jared Sr.	1	Sumter	TORRENCE, Albert	2	Newton
TOMLINSON, John	20	Ware	TORRENCE, John E.	1	Warren
TOMLINSON, Moses	10	Ware	TORRENCE, Paulus E.	17	Baldwin
TOMLINSON, Susan	22	DeKalb	TOUCHSTONE, W. A.	9	Pike
TOMLINSON, Wm. L.	16	Crawford	TOUCHTONE, James	1	Lowndes
TOMMEY, John W.	2	Harris	TOUCHTONE, Henry W.	6	Lowndes
TOMMEY, John W.	16	Sumter	TOUTTE, Robert	1	Effingham
TOMMY, V. R.	1	Muscogee	TOUTTE, Robert	1	Effingham
TOMPKINS, Elizabeth	8	Washington	TOW, Sophia	3	Chatham
TOMPKINS, Martha	1	Marion	TOWERS, John R.	2	Cass
TOMPKINS, Nicholas	30	Heard	TOWERS, Isiah	8	DeKalb
			TOWERS, Larkin	8	Cass
TOMPKINS, John			TOWERS, Lewis	2	DeKalb
estate of	59	Baker	TOWLER, A. R.	9	Walton
TOMPKINS, Sarah	15	Putnam	TOWLER, Benj.	1	Walton
TOMPKINS, Samuel	1	Warren	TOWLES, John	109	Jones
TOMPKINS, Wiley J.	7	Baldwin	TOWNS, Benj.	7	Clarke
TOMPSEN, Frances M.	1	Baker	TOWNS, C.	1	Wilkes

Name	Number	County	Name	Number	County
TOWNS, Capel	1	Franklin	TRAYLER, George H.	22	Troup
TOWNS, James H.	4	Troup	TRAYLOR, Dunston	7	Troup
TOWNS, Jarrel O.	36	Jasper	TRAYLOR, Edward	23	Upson
TOWNS, John	23	Murray	TRAYLOR, Elizabeth K.	8	Troup
TOWNS, Matilda	5	Pike	TRAYLOR, John M.	14	Harris
TOWNS, Elizabeth	12	Taliaferro	TRAYLOR, Thomas G.	8	Jasper
TOWNS, George W.	7	Baldwin	TRAYLOR, William	10	Upson
TOWNS, George W.	6	Talbot	TRAYWICK, James W.	2	Washington
TOWNSAND, James W.	17	Upson	TREADWELL, David	12	Lowndes
TOWNSEN, Malinda	9	Cass	TREADWELL, Hardy	9	Walton
TOWNSEND, Edward	7	Cherokee	TREADWELL, J.	1	Henry
TOWNSEND, J. C.	4	McIntosh	TREADWELL, Jno. Jun.	8	Henry
TOWNSEND, John	1	Cobb	TREADWELL, Martha	7	Clarke
TOWNSEND, Richard P. H.	7	Paulding	TREADWELL, Smith	2	Murray
			TREADWELL, T.	2	Elbert
TOWNSEND, Sarah	19	Jones	TREADWICK, Harvy ?	4	Walton
TOWNSEND, William R.	5	McIntosh	TREDWELL, Lenerd Jun.	5	Newton
TOWNSLEY, Sarah	1	Houston	TREMBER, W. C.	1	Henry
TOWNSLEY, V. S.	3	Muscogee	TREMBLE, A.C.	45	Cass
TOWNSON, John	14	Floyd	TREMBLE, James	1	Newton
TOWSON, Thos.	28	Randolph	TREMBLE, S.	1	Henry
TRABLEY, W.	11	Elbert	TRIBBLE, R. T.	1	Clarke
TRACEY, Caroline	13	Bibb	TRIBBLE, Sarah	3	Walton
TRACY, Green B.	5	Gordon	TRIBLE, Spillsby	2	Madison
TRACY, G. R.	2	Cass	TRIBLE, William	1	Cobb
TRAMEL, Elizabeth	7	Oglethorpe	TRICE, D. L.	5	Randolph
TRAMEL, Frances M.	15	Harris	TRICE, Ezekiel	1	Baldwin
TRAMEL, Pulasky	4	Harris	TRICE, James	14	Upson
TRAMELL, Jasper S.	1	Murray	TRICE, John P.	1	Upson
TRAMELL, Thomas J.	6	Walton	TRICE, William	17	Upson
TRAMMEL, J. N.	2	Floyd	TRICE, William R.	7	Upson
TRAMMEL, J.	1	Coweta	TRICE, Zach.	28	Talbot
TRAMMEL, John	4	Coweta	TRICE, Zach.	1	Talbot
TRAMMELL, C. B.	4	Clarke	TRICKLING, S.	2	Pike
TRAMMELL, Eliz.	7	Clarke	TRIGGS, John J.	6	Burke
TRAMMELL, James J.	5	DeKalb	TRILLEY?, Lewis W.	2	Harris
TRAMMELL, Noreden	2	Stewart	TRIMBLE, Elisha	4	Murray
TRAPE, Lewis	1	Taliaferro	TRIMBLE, Eliza	15	Monroe
TRAPP, B.	5	Bibb	TRIMBLE, Joseph	8	Meriwether
TRAPP, Malichi	1	Baldwin	TRIMBLE, Moses	14	Fayette
TRAPP, Martha	1	Baldwin	TRIMBLE, Moses	10	Meriwether
TRAPP, Rachael	16	Baldwin	TRIMBLE, Nancy	11	Morgan
TRAPP, Robert W.	8	Baldwin	TRIMBLE, James C.	8	Burke
TRASH, William B.	3	Tatnall	TRIMMER, Marcus T.	8	Habersham
TRAVICK, Singleton L.	17	Troup	TRIMYER, C. W.	2	Walker
TRAVIS, Harbard	6	Fayette	TRIMYER, O. W.	1	Walker
TRAVIS, Hiram	8	Fayette	TRIPLETT, James M.	7	Taliaferro
TRAVIS, Martin T.	2	Fayette	TRIPP, Henry M.	11	Greene
TRAVIS, Nancy	2	Henry	TRIPP, John	17	Monroe
TRAWICK, Fred.	12	Hancock	TRIPP, H. M.	8	Putnam
TRAWICK, Moses W.	4	Washington	TRIPP, Jno. B.	8	Putnam
TRAWICK, Seaton F.	12	Hancock	TRIPP, John	20	Putnam
TRAWICK, Shadrach	14	Hancock	TRIPP, Reubin J.	8	Troup
			TRIPP, W. W.	15	Crawford

Name	Number	County	Name	Number	County
TRIPPE, H. P.	4	Hancock	TUCKER, William E.	2	Fayette
TRIPPE, Patience	3	Hancock	TUCKER, ?	1	Elbert
TRIPPE, R. B.	6	Monroe	TUCKER, Charles A.	1	Warren
TRIPPE, Robert	13	Monroe	TUCKER, D.	52	Wilkinson
TRIPPE, Henry	22	Putnam	TUCKER, Daniel R.	1	Wilkinson
TRIPPE, Nancy	10	Taliaferro	TUCKER, Dean	4	Oglethorpe
TRIPPE, Turner H.	31	Cass	TUCKER, E.	4	Lee
TRIPPE, Wm.	14	Putnam	TUCKER, E. G.	2	Merriwether
TRITTAU, George H.	5	Chatham	TUCKER, Francis	4	Hancock
TROLIE, Lawrence J.	13	Richmond	TUCKER, G. C.	6	Lee
TROOP, James estate	59	McIntosh	TUCKER, G. C.	1	Lee
TROTMAN, Susan	8	Stewart	TUCKER, H.	25	Wilkinson
TROTMAN, Susan	4	Stewart	TUCKER, H. L.	18	Merriwether
TROTMAN, Thomas	12	Stewart	TUCKER, J.	4	Troup
TROTTER, Hezekiah	12	Dooly	TUCKER, James D.	7	Oglethorpe
TROTTER, Robt.	3	Habersham	TUCKER, Jesse	4	Lee
TROTTER, Wm.	1	Habersham	TUCKER, John F.	31	Chatham
TROUP, Col. G. M.	143	Laurens	TUCKER, John R.	19	Washington
TROUP, Col. Geo. M.	135	Laurens	TUCKER, John R.	40	Washington
TROUP, D. B. H.	298	Glynn	TUCKER, M.A.	5	Troup
TROUP, George M.	65	Montgomery	TUCKER, M. B.	11	Meriwether
TROUT, Gideon	1	Cobb	TUCKER, Mary W.	5	Hancock
TROUT, J.	19	Floyd	TUCKER, McKendre	5	Newton
TROUT, Jas. W.	1	Jackson	TUCKER, Mrs.	2	Irwin
TROUT, Robt. W.	1	Cherokee	TUCKER, Nathan	63	Laurens
TROUTMAN, H. B.	66	Crawford	TUCKER, Omir D.	10	Houston
TROWBRIDGE, John	3	Floyd	TUCKER, Pointon	2	Jasper
TROWBRIDGE,			TUCKER, R.	2	Irwin
Nelson C.	30	Richmond	TUCKER, Robert	18	Meriwether
TROWEL, John	16	Screven	TUCKER, Tarpley	4	Oglethorpe
TRUCKELUT?, E. J.	1	Chatham	TUCKER, Warren J.	10	Jasper
TRUIT, John E.	2	Harris	TUCKER, William	3	Jasper
TRUIT, John H.	2	Harris	TUCKER, William H.	2	Cobb
TRUIT, Saml.	6	Harris	TUCKER, William T.	1	Oglethorpe
TRUIT, Saml.	3	Harris	TUCKER, Daniel R.	13	Baldwin
TRUIT, William P.	18	Harris	TUCKER, Eli	16	Sumter
TRUITT, Jas.	13	Troup	TUCKER, Harper	69	Baldwin
TRUITT, Purnal	18	Wilkes	TUCKER, Isaac	3	Camden
TRUITTE, Nathan	99	Merriwether	TUCKER, Joel	67	Baldwin
TRULOCK, A.	2	Decatur	TUCKER, John A.	9	Stewart
TRULOCK, George	2	Decatur	TUCKER, Jordan	4	Baker
TRULOCK, Joseph	16	Decatur	TUCKER, Nathan	6	Bibb
TRUNDLE, L. L.	4	Walker	TUCKER, R. B.	3	Randolph
TRUMAN, R. S.	1	Bibb	TUCKER, Reuben	12	Sumter
TRUMPLER, Conrad	2	Chatham	TUCKER, W. D.	7	Crawford
TRUSLOW, Jno. W.	1	Wilkes	TUCKER, William	5	Richmond
TRUSSEL, Mary A.	3	Jasper	TUCKER, Wm.	3	Bibb
TRUSSEL, William H.	2	Jasper	TUCKER, Wm.	10	Randolph
TUBMAN, Emily	27	Columbia	TUCKSTOM?, Dennis	6	Pike
TUBMAN, Emily H.	4	Richmond	TUDOR, Thomas	8	Columbia
TUCK, Burel	3	Lumpkin	TUFTS, J. B.	4	Chatham
TUCK, B. W.	2	Wilkes	TUFTS, Johnston B.	2	Chatham
TUCK, Eli B.	1	Clarke	TUFTS, Mary P.	53	Jones
TUCK, Thomas A.	1	Clarke	TUFTS, Sanford M.	9	Jones

Name	Number	County	Name	Number	County
TUGGLE, A. L.	9	Greene	TURNER, A. W.	21	Henry
TUGGLE, Capt. Jas.	2	Gwinnett	TURNER, Absalom	3	Emanual
TUGGLE, Edward	2	Thomas	TURNER, Alexander R.	6	DeKalb
TUGGLE, Elizabeth	8	Jasper	TURNER, Alfred M.	8	Murray
TUGGLE, George	2	Floyd	TURNER, Allen	4	Newton
TUGGLE, P. J.	12	Greene	TURNER, Anderson S.	14	Newton
TUGGLE, W. J. L.	9	Jasper	TURNER, Annie	5	Fayette
TUGGLE, William Senr.	33	Greene	TURNER, Archibald	15	Greene
TUGGLE, Wm. Jr.	31	Greene	TURNER, Charles G.	12	Pike
TUGGLE, Ludowick	5	DeKalb	TURNER, David B.	3	Troup
TUGGLE, Nancy	3	Stewart	TURNER, Geo. J.	3	Laurens
TUKES, William A.	14	Dooly	TURNER, Green B.	3	Cobb
TULL, Bennett	2	Twiggs	TURNER, Green B.	43	Newton
TULLEY, Willis	2	Wilkes	TURNER, Green M.	3	Jefferson
TULLIS, Gibson	7	Muscogee	TURNER, Gregory J.	47	Macon
TULLIS, James M.	1	Marion	TURNER, Henry E.	10	Chatham
TULLIS, Moses	4	Muscogee	TURNER, Henry P.	4	Jefferson
TULLOS, Henry J.	9	Effingham	TURNER, Isaac	5	Lincoln
TULLY, Allen	1	Columbia	TURNER, J. A.	2	Henry
TUMBLE, Mary	7	Troup	TURNER, J. B.	12	Henry
TUMBLIN, G.	6	Floyd	TURNER, J. H.	5	Lincoln
TUMLIN, George W.	11	Cass	TURNER, J. H.	11	Newton
TUMLIN, John	1	Cass	TURNER, J. M.	2	Heard
TUMLIN, Lewis	51	Cass	TURNER, J. P.	14	Henry
TUMLIN, Lewis	2	Cass	TURNER, J. W.	1	Henry
TUMLIN, Wm.	6	Cass	TURNER, James A.	2	Heard
TUNDEE, Charles R.	14	Sumter	TURNER, James A.	6	Newton
TUNISON, Tunis	12	Putnam	TURNER, James M.	4	Troup
TUNNEL, George S.	3	Greene	TURNER, James R.	2	Monroe
TUPPER, Frederick A.	17	Chatham	TURNER, Jane	9	Pike
TURENTINE, Samuel	21	Merriwether	TURNER, Jarret	2	Union
TURHUNE, C. D.	11	Cass	TURNER, Jesse	8	Macon
TURK, Henry	4	Merriwether	TURNER, Jesse M.	1	Newton
TURK, T. F.	14	Monroe	TURNER, John B.	3	Monroe
TURK, Thomas	49	Baldwin	TURNER, John G.	2	Harris
TURK, William	16	Franklin	TURNER, John H.	1	Walker
TURK, William H.	4	Franklin	TURNER, Johnson	6	Morgan
TURK, John	8	Putnam	TURNER, Joseph M.	6	Chatham
TURK, John M.	18	Baldwin	TURNER, Kimbro	15	Wilkes
TURK, Theodosins	1	Baldwin	TURNER, L. H.	15	Henry
TURKETT, George A.	45	Richmond	TURNER, Lassiter	7	Marion
TURKETT,			TURNER, Leuan	10	Pike
George A. Jr.	3	Richmond	TURNER, Levi	13	Macon
TURLINGTON, Thomas	7	Washington	TURNER, Lewis	49	Chatham
TURMAN, James	7	Franklin	TURNER, Luke	31	Wilkes
TURMON, A. T.	5	Elbert	TURNER, M. C.	16	Henry
TURMON, J. B.	1	Elbert	TURNER, M. D.	3	Lincoln
TURMON, T. Y.	33	Elbert	TURNER, Mary	19	Merriwether
TURMON, Thomas	7	Elbert	TURNER, Miles G.	6	Monroe
TURMON, Thomas M.	1	Elbert	TURNER, Moses	1	Fayette
TURNELL, George	1	Clarke	TURNER, Nancy	2	Monroe
TURNER ?, James	2	Stewart	TURNER, P. B.	5	Henry
TURNER, A.	15	Henry	TURNER, R.	14	Henry
TURNER, A.	7	Merriwether	TURNER, Radford J.	17	Jones

Name	Number	County	Name	Number	County
TURNER, Richard	1	Meriwether	TUTLE, Rachel	5	Screven
TURNER, Richard	15	Newton	TUTOR, Thomas P.	2	Wayne
TURNER, Riley	3	Merriwether	TUTT, B. M.	15	Lincoln
TURNER, Roberson H.	12	Jasper	TUTT, Benjamin	38	Lincoln
TURNER, Ruebin	1	Meriwether	TUTT, E. E.	10	Pike
TURNER, S.	1	Irwin	TUTT, H.W.	12	Lincoln
TURNER, S. T.	2	Troup	TUTTLE, Isaac L.	16	Richmond
TURNER, Sarah	12	Troup	TUTTON, Joshua	1	Habersham
TURNER, Shadrick	8	Pike	TWEDLE, Wm. S.	9	Cobb
TURNER, Susan	14	Harris	TWEED, William	2	Muscogee
TURNER, Thomas	1	Newton	TWIGGS, George S.	97	Richmond
TURNER, Thomas H.	6	Pike	TWIGGS, George W. S.		
TURNER, Thomas M.	42	Hancock	for Jr.	20	Richmond
TURNER, Tobias	3	Chatham	TWILLEY, James	3	Muscogee
TURNER, W. H.	36	Henry	TYE, Lurena	6	Jones
TURNER, W. K.	7	Lincoln	TYE, Rueben	1	Randolph
TURNER, W. M.	3	Henry	TYLER, Job	5	Jasper
TURNER, William	12	Lincoln	TYLER, John A.	12	Murray
TURNER, William	11	Morgan	TYLER, S. S.	9	McIntosh
TURNER, Wm.	4	Wilkes	TYLER, William P.	19	Pike
TURNER, Zechariah	1	Cass	TYLER, Benj. F.	13	Richmond
TURNER, A. W.	2	Stewart	TYLER, James W.	8	Stewart
TURNER, Delia	22	Lincoln	TYLER, William H.	3	Richmond
TURNER, Edmond	11	Dooly	TYLOR, Thomas	13	Monroe
TURNER, Edwin A.	3	DeKalb	TYNER, James	12	Muscogee
TURNER, Elizabeth	1	Putnam	TYNER, R.	10	Bibb
TURNER, F. R.	1	Crawford	TYNS, Wm. G.	8	Hancock
TURNER, Isey	2	Burke	TYRES, James	3	Monroe
TURNER, John	8	Coweta	TYRES, John L.	2	Monroe
TURNER, John	38	Stewart	TYSON, Hiram	28	Marion
TURNER, John	1	Talbot	TYSON, Josiah	1	Carroll
TURNER, John C.	11	DeKalb	TYSON, Moses	2	Sumter
TURNER, John M.	9	Richmond	TYSON, Penelope	21	Thomas
TURNER, Joseph	3	Stewart	TYSON, Winson C.	2	Richmond
TURNER, Joseph A. S.	48	Sumter	UBELE, Christian	1	Chatham
TURNER, Lewis T.	3	Bryan	ULMER, John	8	Chatham
TURNER, Memory H.	9	Campbell	ULMER, John P.	2	Effingham
TURNER, N.	1	Crawford	ULMER, Philip	54	Chatham
TURNER, Nathan	7	DeKalb	ULMON, J.	1	Decatur
TURNER, Richaard T.	3	Chatham	ULMON, J.	1	Decatur
TURNER, Samuel J.	1	Chatham	UMPHRA, Noel	2	Taliaferro
TURNER, Thomas B.	32	Talbot	UMPHREYS, John	4	Dooly
TURNER, Thomas M.	14	Chatham	UNDERWOOD, A. A.	28	Putnam
TURNER, Thomas Sr.	3	Putnam	UNDERWOOD, C.	22	Wilkinson
TURNER, Thos. Jun.	7	Putnam	UNDERWOOD,		
TURNER, William	4	Stewart	Elizabeth	1	Laurens
TURNER,			UNDERWOOD,		
William ? Jun.	10	Putnam	Gaston M.	20	Merriwether
TURNER, Wm.	25	Putnam	UNDERWOOD, George	5	Warren
TURNER, Wm. B.	1	Coweta	UNDERWOOD, Isaac	14	Carroll
TURNIPSEED, Matthew	3	Fayette	UNDERWOOD, J. W. D.	3	Habersham
TURRENTINE, James	17	Houston	UNDERWOOD, James	5	Washington
TURRINTINE, Mrs. H.	5	Muscogee	UNDERWOOD, John	1	Wilkinson
TURRINTINE, William	3	Merriwether	UNDERWOOD, Joseph	2	Habersham

Name	Number	County
UNDERWOOD, Josiah	7	Henry
UNDERWOOD, L. B.	2	Franklin
UNDERWOOD, Robert	10	Gwinnett
UNDERWOOD, T.	2	Wilkinson
UNDERWOOD, W.	4	Henry
UNDERWOOD, William J.	5	Murray
UNDERWOOD, Wm. H.	1	Floyd
UNDERWOOD, Jas. B.	23	Cass
UNDERWOOD, John	9	Coweta
UNDERWOOD, Reuben	3	Cass
UNION STEAM BOAT Co.	21	Richmond
UNITED STATES ARSENAL	1	Richmond
Unnamed	21	Floyd
Unnamed	13	Franklin
Unnamed	7	Franklin
unreadable	3	Early
unreadable	1	Early
Unreadable	5	Elbert
Unreadable	2	Elbert
Unreadable	1	Elbert
Unreadable	1	Elbert
Unreadable	1	Habesham
Unreadable	3	Lee
Unreadable	1	Lee
Unreadable	4	Lumpkin
Unreadable	2	Muscogee
Unreadable	1	Muscogee
Unreadable	1	Muscogee
Unreadable	1	Muscogee
UNREADABLE	10	Richmond
UNREADABLE	8	Richmond
UNREADABLE	4	Richmond
UNREADABLE	4	Richmond
UNREADABLE	3	Richmond
UNREADABLE	2	Richmond
UNREADABLE	2	Richmond
UNREADABLE	1	Richmond
UNREADABLE	1	Richmond
UNREADABLE	1	Richmond
UNREADABLE, Hilary B.	18	Richmond
UNREADABLE, Joseph B.	4	Richmond
unreadable,	4	Early
Unreadable,	2	Richmond
Unreadable,	5	Habersham
UNREADABLE, Ann	2	Richmond
UNREADABLE, Joseph	6	Richmond
Unreadable, Seaabron	6	Pulaski
Unreadable, Alexander C.	4	Muscogee

Name	Number	County
Unreadable, Arthur	2	Pulaski
unreadable, Benjamin	12	Early
Unreadable, C.	3	Muscogee
UNREADABLE, Charles	12	Richmond
Unreadable, Christopher	4	Habersham
Unreadable, D. C.	2	Pulaski
UNREADABLE, David S.	4	Richmond
Unreadable, E. S.	1	Pike
Unreadable, Elijah	6	Gwinnett
Unreadable, Eliza U.	6	McIntosh
Unreadable, Elizabeth	1	Habersham
UNREADABLE, Estate Augustus	5	Richmond
Unreadable, F.	5	Muscogee
UNREADABLE, Francis A.	5	Richmond
Unreadable, Francis C.	2	Muscogee
Unreadable, G. M.	1	Pike
Unreadable, G. H.	1	Pike
unreadable, George	3	Effingham
Unreadable, H.	1	Pike
Unreadable, H. J.	1	Muscogee
Unreadable, Henry	1	Pulaski
UNREADABLE, Hilary	3	Richmond
Unreadable, Isaac A.	1	Muscogee
Unreadable, Isaac A.	1	Muscogee
UNREADABLE, Isiah	3	Richmond
Unreadable, J. J. M.	1	Lee
Unreadable, J. J. W.	1	Oglethorpe
unreadable, J. W.	2	Early
Unreadable, James	11	Lowndes
Unreadable, James	1	Muscogee
UNREADABLE, James	1	Richmond
Unreadable, Jasper	1	Newton
Unreadable, Jeremiah	2	Muscogee
Unreadable, John	3	Floyd
Unreadable, John	1	Muscogee
Unreadable, John	8	Pulaski
Unreadable, Joseph	2	Muscogee
Unreadable, Josiah M.	6	Harris
Unreadable, L. J.	1	Muscogee
Unreadable, Malender	2	Habersham
Unreadable, Martha C.	4	Pike
Unreadable, Mary	1	Habersham
Unreadable, Micajah	1	Harris
Unreadable, Mrs. Ann B. M.	5	Houston
Unreadable, Ned	4	Muscogee
Unreadable, Nicholas	1	Newton
Unreadable, Peny	1	Muscogee
Unreadable, Perry	4	Muscogee
Unreadable, Perry	2	Muscogee
Unreadable, R. M.	3	Heard

Name	Number	County	Name	Number	County
Unreadable, Reddick	6	Pike	UNREADABLE,		
Unreadable, Richard	1	Muscogee	George H.	5	Richmond
Unreadable, Robert	2	Muscogee	UNREADABLE, H. & L.	3	Richmond
Unreadable, Samuel	2	Lumpkin	UNREADABLE, Hays	13	Richmond
Unreadable, Samuel	4	Muscogee	UNREADABLE, Henry	2	Richmond
Unreadable, Sarah A.	10	Gwinnett	UNREADABLE,		
Unreadable, Sarah B.	5	Oglethorpe	Hudson R.	2	Richmond
Unreadable, Selvester	1	Pulaski	UNREADABLE, Isaac	3	Richmond
Unreadable, Susannah	1	Habersham	UNREADABLE,		
Unreadable, T. C.	6	Pike	Jackson T.	3	Richmond
Unreadable, Thomas	2	Lumpkin	UNREADABLE, Jacob	9	Richmond
Unreadable, Thomas	3	Muscogee	UNREADABLE,		
Unreadable, Thomas C.	2	Harris	Jacob A.	2	Richmond
Unreadable, Thomas W.	16	Paulding	UNREADABLE, James	1	Richmond
Unreadable, W. B.	1	Pulaski	UNREADABLE,		
Unreadable, W. G.	7	Pike	James P.	1	Richmond
Unreadable, W. H.	5	Pike	UNREADABLE, John	1	Richmond
Unreadable, W. R.	6	Pike	UNREADABLE, John B.	1	Richmond
Unreadable, Wesley	3	Pike	UNREADABLE, John L.	5	Richmond
Unreadable, William	3	Newton	UNREADABLE, John T.	2	Richmond
Unreadable, William R.	2	Madison	UNREADABLE, Joseph	6	Richmond
Unreadable, Wilson	2	Lumpkin	UNREADABLE,		
Unreadable, Wm.	1	Habersham	Lindsay C.	10	Richmond
Unreadable, Wm.	1	Pulaski	Unreadable, Mahulda	1	Habersham
Unreadable, Wm. M.	2	Gordon	UNREADABLE,		
UNREADABLE, Adelaid	1	Richmond	Mary E.	2	Richmond
UNREADABLE, Alex J.	5	Richmond	UNREADABLE, Mary L.	2	Richmond
UNREADABLE, Alfred	4	Richmond	UNREADABLE,		
UNREADABLE,			Michael J.	16	Richmond
Allen C.	2	Richmond	UNREADABLE, Nancy	2	Richmond
UNREADABLE, Ann	30	Richmond	UNREADABLE,		
UNREADABLE, Ann	5	Richmond	Oliver J.	2	Richmond
UNREADABLE, Ann M.	3	Richmond	UNREADABLE, Patrick	1	Richmond
UNREADABLE, Artema	9	Richmond	UNREADABLE, Peter	2	Richmond
UNREADABLE,			UNREADABLE, Peter	2	Richmond
Benjamin	2	Richmond	UNREADABLE,		
UNREADABLE,			Peter T. C.	1	Richmond
Blaze L.	1	Richmond	UNREADABLE,		
UNREADABLE,			Sarah G.	6	Richmond
Christopher	8	Richmond	UNREADABLE,		
UNREADABLE, David	1	Richmond	Solomon L.	11	Richmond
UNREADABLE, Dawson	3	Richmond	UNREADABLE,		
UNREADABLE, Edw.	3	Richmond	Tabitha Estate	1	Richmond
UNREADABLE, Edward	1	Richmond	UNREADABLE, Thomas	4	Richmond
UNREADABLE,			UNREADABLE, William	5	Richmond
Elizabeth	3	Richmond	UNREADABLE, William	1	Richmond
UNREADABLE,			UNREADABLE,		
Elizabeth	8	Richmond	William V.	1	Richmond
UNREADABLE,			UNREADABLE, Wm. G.	6	Richmond
Frederick C.	4	Richmond	UNREADABLE, Wm. P.	13	Richmond
Unreadable, G. S.	1	Pike	unreadablel, Lewis	4	Early
UNREADABLE, George	1	Richmond	UNREADABLLE	1	Richmond
UNREADABLE,			Unreadalbe, A.A.	4	Pike
George M.	3	Richmond	UPCHURCH, E.	1	Henry

316

Name	Number	County	Name	Number	County
UPCHURCH, H.	2	Henry	VANDERSHINE, D.	5	Chatham
UPPER STEAM			VANDIFORD, John	6	Murray
RICE MILL	67	Chatham	VANDIFORD, Thos.	2	Randolph
UPSHAW, James	1	Meriwether	VANDIGRIFF, John	11	Henry
UPSHAW, John	2	Walton	VANDIVER, Alphonse S.	1	Murray
UPSHAW, John J.	4	Chattooga	VANDIVER, Mary	5	Gordon
UPSHAW, Lucinda	31	Cass	VANDIVER, Martha	7	Sumter
UPSHAW, Lucinda	1	Gordon	VANDUSER, Jas.	1	Bibb
UPSHAW, Tinsly	1	Walton	VANHORN, Hubbard	4	Muscogee
UPSHAW, William	12	Meriwether	VANHORUS, Charles	5	Chatham
UPSHAW, Adkin	7	Coweta	VANLANDINGHAM,		
UPSHAW, John A.	4	Cass	Ann	6	Morgan
UPSON, F. L.	10	Oglethorpe	VANLANDINGHAM, T.	19	Newton
UPSON, J. C.	1	Bibb	VANN, David	3	Floyd
UPTON, Asa	5	Jefferson	VANN, Mary	1	Twiggs
UPTON, David W.	2	Talbot	VANN, Thomas	2	Wilkinson
UPTON, John	6	Stewart	VANN, Washington	11	Floyd
UPTON, William	9	Columbia	VANN, W. W.	2	Washington
URQUART, Samuel J.	10	Burke	VANOVER, J. B.	9	Lee
URQUHART, John	7	Muscogee	VANT, Isaac	12	Stewart
URSHER, Sarah	11	Bibb	VARDEL, D. B.	44	Elbert
USERY, John	10	Jones	VARDEL, Sarah E.	1	Fayette
USHEN?, Robert O.	26	Newton	VARDEMAN,		
USHER, Henry	34	Richmond	Thomas D.	1	Harris
USHER, Robt.	15	Bibb	VARNADORE, John	14	Dooly
USINA, E. B.	2	Washington	VARNER, David N.	3	Pike
USRY, Frances M.	4	Warren	VARNER, Early	12	Jasper
USRY, John	29	Warren	VARNER, Edwd.	3	Butts
USRY, Peter	11	Warren	VARNER, H.	22	Henry
USSERY, William	15	Jones	VARNER, J. F.	8	Henry
UTLEY, William	11	Burke	VARNER, John J.	2	Cobb
UTTER, William R.	4	Union	VARNER, Joseph	28	Greene
VACHLISON, Robert	14	Chatham	VARNER, M.	27	Oglethorpe
VAIL, A. L.	4	Elbert	VARNER, Robert	1	Franklin
VALENTINE, James D.	1	Houston	VARNER, Samuel D.	5	Jasper
VALENTINE, Hannah	1	Chatham	VARNER, William	52	Monroe
VALENTINE, Lewis	5	Bibb	VARNER, Edward	9	Butts
VALGAN, Gustane	2	Richmond	VARNER, James	5	Sumter
VALLELAU, Ann	1	Chatham	VARNER, Mary	20	Campbell
VAMER?, Hendly	5	Pike	VARNUM, Asa	20	Jackson
VAMON, T.	2	Chattooga	VASEN, Nancy	3	Newton
VAN HOOK, David	3	Union	VASON, Rebecca	15	Morgan
VAN HUNTER, D.	5	Clarke	VASON, David A.	48	Baker
VAN BUREN, Jarvis	5	Habersham	VATRY, Aramenta	11	DeKalb
VAN HORN, Charles	24	Chatham	VAUGHAN, Asa	2	Forsyth
VAN NESS, S. J.	3	Chatham	VAUGHAN, John	40	Monroe
VAN VALKENBERG, J.	12	Bibb	VAUGHAN, John	2	Montgomery
VAN ZANT, John	1	Muscogee	VAUGHAN, G.W.	5	Coweta
VANBRACKEL,			VAUGHN, A.	6	Elbert
Wm. H.	25	Bryan	VAUGHN, Albert	18	Jasper
VANCE, John	22	Clarke	VAUGHN, Daniel	10	Twiggs
VANCE, Thos.	1	Camden	VAUGHN, Frederic	11	Newton
VANDANIER, A. F. N.	2	Oglethorpe	VAUGHN, Howel	1	Fayette
VANDERFORD, William	1	Walton	VAUGHN, J. A.	3	Oglethorpe

Name	Number	County	Name	Number	County
VAUGHN, J. D.	11	Elbert	VERNADO, Samuel M.	24	Liberty
VAUGHN, James	2	Houston	VERNAN, Nehemiah	3	Forsyth
VAUGHN, James	2	Pike	VERNON, John G.	1	Cherokee
VAUGHN, James W.	18	Pike	VERNON, S.	7	Elbert
VAUGHN, Jno.	10	Henry	VERNON, E. P.	4	Cass
VAUGHN, Lucinda	3	Pike	VERNON, E. W.	4	Cass
VAUGHN, Nelson	5	Wilkes	VERNOY, James	1	Muscogee
VAUGHN, Thos.	41	Heard	VERTHOSE, Sarah	2	Chatham
VAUGHN, William H.	16	Pike	VESDERY, Ben	22	Columbia
VAUGHN, Wm. T.	1	Twiggs	VESEY, Benj. F.	11	Early
VAUGHN, Cara	2	Cass	VESTIL, William	2	Campbell
VAUGHN, John	11	Bibb	VEUL, Anderson C.	1	Newton
VAUGHN, Willis	3	Baldwin	VEZIE, John	5	Troup
VAUGHTERS, Hiram	1	Franklin	VICKERS, Ann	2	Butts
VAUTOR, L.	2	Elbert	VICKERS, Ashley E.	41	Laurens
VAWTER, R.	7	Elbert	VICKERS, Berrien	2	Troup
VEAL, Jas. H.	4	Hancock	VICKERS, C. D.	3	Troup
VEAL, Allen J.	3	Gwinnett	VICKERS, Drew	8	Lowndes
VEAL, Burwell	5	Twiggs	VICKERS, Henry	1	Lowndes
VEAL, Edward	3	Washington	VICKERS, J.	15	Irwin
VEAL, George	3	Washington	VICKERS, James	12	Laurens
VEAL, George W.	19	Clarke	VICKERS, John	3	Irwin
VEAL, Irvin F.	4	Hancock	VICKERS, Lewis	7	Lowndes
VEAL, John T.	3	Washington	VICKERS, Matthew	2	Lowndes
VEAL, Joseph	2	Putnam	VICKERS, Mrs.	8	Irwin
VEAL, J. J. for			VICKERS, Robt. H.	9	Wilkes
Ga. R. R. Co.	3	DeKalb	VICKERS, Sarah	7	Troup
VEAL, Jas.	3	Putnam	VICKERS, Y.	6	Irwin
VEAL, Nathan	2	Washington	VICKERS, Marmaduke	2	Walker
VEAL, William	12	DeKalb	VICKORY, Thos.	2	Camden
VEAL, Wm.	3	Wilkinson	VICTORY, William	3	Harris
VEASEY, Jane	20	Taliaferro	VIGAL, Henry	1	Muscogee
VEASEY, Jesse	23	Taliaferro	VIGAL, Geo.	10	Bibb
VEASY, A. E.	6	Heard	VILLALONGA, J. L.	10	Camden
VEASY, John P	6	Paulding	VINCENT, Elisha	3	Harris
VEASY, Wm. C.	2	Taliaferro	VINCENT, F. A.	1	Walker
VEAZEY, Albert A.	4	Green	VINCENT, George	1	Harris
VEAZEY, John	29	Warren	VINCENT, Henry	1	Jasper
VEELE, Simeon	18	Talbot	VINCENT, Isaac S.	29	Clarke
VEMES ?, John	1	Walton	VINCENT, James	8	Muscogee
VENABLE, Isabella	9	Forsyth	VINCENT, John	2	Jones
VENABLE, John	4	Jackson	VINCENT, John A.	1	Baldwin
VENABLE, John Sen.	3	Jackson	VINCENT, Nancy	2	Harris
VENABLE, Lucus	1	Cherokee	VINCENT, P. P.	7	Putnam
VENABLE, Samuel	1	Forsyth	VINCENT, Thomas	54	Jasper
VENABLE, Sarah	8	Jackson	VINCENT, Thos. M.	2	Harris
VENT, Peter F. L.	2	Warren	VINCENT, Wiley	1	Harris
VERDEN, John	5	Warren	VINCENT, Ailsey	3	Cass
VERDERY?, Aug. N.	27	Floyd	VINCENT, Amos	2	DeKalb
VERDEY, Martha	7	Richmond	VINCENT, Nat	9	Putnam
VEREDEY ?, Eugene	37	Richmond	VINCENT, Wm.	17	Putnam
VERGIN, J.	2	Bibb	VINES, William H.	1	Dooly
VERGIN, S. S.	3	Bibb	VINES, William P.	1	Dooly
VERNADO, Nathaniel	105	Liberty	VINEYARD, Wm.	5	Coweta

Name	Number	County	Name	Number	County
VINEYARD, Jas.	12	Coweta	WADE, Wm. H. Sr.	72	Early
VINING, Simeon	3	Troup	WADE, Ann	5	Chatham
VINSANT, Lewis	2	Union	WADE, Elijah	4	Dooly
VINSON, Anna	1	Hancock	WADE, Eliza	1	Baldwin
VINSON, Benjamin	1	Houston	WADE, Ellen	22	Burke
VINSON, Debby	1	Houston	WADE, P.L.	241	Screven
VINSON, Ebenezer C.	11	Hancock	WADE, R. C.	2	Coweta
VINSON, James	21	Houston	WADE, Thomas	5	Dooly
VINSON, John	18	Twiggs	WADE, W. B.	2	Chattooga
VINSON, Josiah	5	Early	WADE, William	1	Talbot
VINSON, Josiah	12	Houston	WADFORD, Hardy?	3	Newton
VINSON, Josiah	11	Houston	WADKINS, Benjamin	28	Monroe
VINSON, Tully	21	Morgan	WADKINS, Irvin	3	Muscogee
VINSON, David	1	Columbia	WADKINS, W.	7	Henry
VINSON, E.	2	Crawford	WADKINS, William	4	Muscogee
VINSON, Elender	2	Dooly	WADKINS, A.	6	Bibb
VINSON, George W.	2	Houston	WADKINS, C.	2	Crawford
VINSON, Henry	6	Crawford	WADLEY, Moses	9	Jefferson
VINYARD, Nicuses	7	Gwinnett	WADLEY, William M.	17	Washington
VINZANT, Harriet	1	Walker	WADSWORTH,		
VISHER, D. W.	15	Houston	Archibald	1	Pike
VOCILLE, J.	5	Camden	WADSWORTH, Elbert	12	Macon
VOLOTAN, Frances	9	Burke	WAGNER, William		
VON GLANN, Henry	1	Chatham	(overseer)	13	Paulding
VORDIN, Samuel	1	Pike	WAGNER, Henry	1	Muscogee
WADDALL, Henry	11	Marion	WAGNER, William	1	Paulding
WADDEL, James P.	11	Clarke	WAGNON, Harriet	20	Greene
WADDEY, Jas. E.	8	Wilkes	WAGNON, John P.	7	Greene
WADDLE, Nicholas	1	Cherokee	WAGNON, Wm.	5	Bibb
WADDLE, Sarah	8	Cobb	WAID, Harris	1	Cobb
WADDLE, Mathew?	5	Rabun	WAILES, S.A.	13	Putnam
WADDY, William	5	Troup	WAIT, Levi	1	Jasper
WADE, (?)	11	Columbia	WAIT, Susan	2	Chatham
WADE, (?)	1	Columbia	WAITS, Alexander	1	Jasper
WADE, Asa	3	Gwinnett	WAITS, George M.	3	Jasper
WADE, Asa	2	Gwinnett	WAITS, John C.	2	Cass
WADE, Daniel F.	21	Macon	WAITS, Leroy	9	Jasper
WADE, Elijah	1	Dooly	WAITYFELDER, E.	2	Baldwin
WADE, Elizabeth	7	Jasper	WAKEFIELD, J. B.	5	Floyd
WADE, James A.	25	Morgan	WAKEFIELD, Charles	14	Butts
WADE, James H.	12	Early	WALACE?, Jacob	8	Meriwether
WADE, Jesse	19	Murray	WALBERGER, Jack		
WADE, Jesse L.	1	Coweta	see WILIAMS	7	Habersham
WADE, John	1	Clarke	WALDBURG,		
WADE, John	3	Twiggs	George W.	99	Liberty
WADE, John D.	10	Baker	WALDBURG, Jacob	119	Liberty
WADE, John W.	10	Morgan	WALDEN, Amos	1	Warren
WADE, Mary	91	Morgan	WALDEN, Chas.	3	Laurens
WADE, Nathaniel	2	Dooly	WALDEN, David	6	Morgan
WADE, Robert	1	Warren	WALDEN, Elias D.	1	Ware
WADE, Solomon	1	Warren	WALDEN, Green	15	Houston
WADE, Thomas	7	Clarke	WALDEN, Henry	9	Jefferson
WADE, William	6	Muscogee	WALDEN, John	1	Washington
WADE, Wm. H. Jr.	1	Early	WALDEN, John M.	5	Washington

Name	Number	County	Name	Number	County
WALDEN, Kinion	1	Jefferson	WALKER, David	3	Houston
WALDEN, Marenda	4	Jefferson	WALKER, David	36	Pulaski
WALDEN, Mitchell	4	Jefferson	WALKER, Druscilla	3	Cherokee
WALDEN, Morris	9	Jefferson	WALKER, E.	23	Henry
WALDEN, Pleasant	5	Jefferson	WALKER, E.	6	Henry
WALDEN, Seaborn J.	1	Lee	WALKER, E. H.	26	Monroe
WALDEN, Thomas	4	Macon	WALKER, Edmond	51	Morgan
WALDEN, M.	14	Decatur	WALKER, Fleming	4	Lowndes
WALDEN, William G.	4	Warren	WALKER, G. W.	1	Floyd
WALDEN, Wm.	3	Wilkinson	WALKER, George	25	Houston
WALDEN, Wm. J.	3	Dooly	WALKER, George	8	Houston
WALDEN, Wm. L.	9	Wilkinson	WALKER, Hackey	10	Jasper
WALDERMAN, Mildred	8	Cobb	WALKER, Henry	22	Greene
WALDING, Jesse G.	1	Heard	WALKER, Henry	31	Jasper
WALDING, John	35	Thomas	WALKER, Isaac	47	Morgan
WALDROP, Milton	4	Newton	WALKER, J.	1	Clarke
WALDROP, Daviston	4	DeKalb	WALKER, I. G.	2	Lincoln
WALDROUP, Aaron	1	Jasper	WALKER, J. K.	1	Lumpkin
WALDROUP, Hiram	11	Coweta	WALKER, I. S.	3	Morgan
WALDRUP, Jefferson	4	Butts	WALKER, James	2	McIntosh
WALDRUP, Simion	1	Monroe	WALKER, James T.	11	Harris
WALDRUP, Mary	1	Butts	WALKER, James W.	10	Morgan
WALDRUP, Mary A.	1	Coweta	WALKER, Jer.	5	Henry
WALE, Robert	11	Burke	WALKER, Jeremiah G.	15	Muscogee
WALEA, Eliza	1	Emanual	WALKER, Jeremiah G.	9	Muscogee
WALEA, Severn	3	Emanual	WALKER, Joel	56	Houston
WALKER & BRYSON	6	Richmond	WALKER, John A.	1	Franklin
WALKER, Allen A.	3	Washington	WALKER, John A.	7	Muscogee
WALKER, Benjamin	20	Upson	WALKER, John B.	135	Morgan
WALKER, David	10	Washington	WALKER, John D.	11	Houston
WALKER, Elizabeth	1	Washington	WALKER, John E.	8	Greene
WALKER, George	85	Pulaski	WALKER, John H.	9	Pike
WALKER, J. F.	15	Upson	WALKER, John S.	14	Jones
WALKER, James	8	Upson	WALKER, John T.	17	Muscogee
WALKER, James	39	Ware	WALKER, John W.	7	Marion
WALKER, James R.	33	Troup	WALKER, Jonathan	7	Morgan
WALKER, Jane	1	Ware	WALKER, Lee	7	Early
WALKER, John	2	Troup	WALKER, Martha	14	Pulaski
WALKER, Lott	6	Washington	WALKER, Mary	1	Pulaski
WALKER, Maria	20	Walton	WALKER, Mary C.	29	Harris
WALKER, Mason	1	Troup	WALKER, Matilda	7	Lincoln
WALKER, Miss	25	Harris	WALKER, Miss	6	Harris
WALKER, Nathaniel H.	79	Upson	WALKER, Pheby	18	Putnam
WALKER, Persons	6	Warren	WALKER, R. H.	2	Wilkes
WALKER, A. M.	3	Muscogee	WALKER, R. M.	2	Henry
WALKER, A. W.	24	Henry	WALKER, R. S.	10	Morgan
WALKER, Arthur B.	28	Jefferson	WALKER, Robert	20	Pike
WALKER, B. B.	12	Oglethorpe	WALKER, Robt. W.	12	Hancock
WALKER, Benjamin	3	Franklin	WALKER, Saml. R.	21	Greene
WALKER, C.	8	Henry	WALKER, Samuel	11	Muscogee
WALKER, Charles	2	Merriwether	WALKER, Sanders K.	3	Upson
WALKER, Chas.	89	Pulaski	WALKER, Sanders K.	3	Upson
WALKER, Cornelia	34	Muscogee	WALKER, Solomon	8	Lowndes
WALKER, D. H.	16	Monroe	WALKER, Sylvanus	21	Hancock

Name	Number	County
WALKER, T. W.	1	Franklin
WALKER, Thacker V.	54	Harris
WALKER, Thacker V.	5	Harris
WALKER, Thomas	1	Merriwether
WALKER, Thomas	16	Monroe
WALKER, Thomas	2	Newton
WALKER, William H.	4	Monroe
WALKER, William L.	3	Pike
WALKER, William W.	7	Jasper
WALKER, Wm. R.	33	Greene
WALKER, W.L.	9	Walton
WALKER, William D.	1	Washington
WALKER, William H.	2	Washington
WALKER, Alexr. C.	57	Richmond
WALKER, B.	1	Bibb
WALKER, C.	1	Talbot
WALKER, C. H.	34	Crawford
WALKER, C. J.	5	Stewart
WALKER, Calvin	2	Stewart
WALKER, Edward	7	DeKalb
WALKER, Francis J.	23	Burke
WALKER, Freeman	10	Stewart
WALKER, G.W.	25	Putnam
WALKER, George	29	Baker
WALKER, George A. B.	15	Richmond
WALKER, George M.	5	Richmond
WALKER, Henry J.	24	Sumter
WALKER, Henry Sr.	33	Sumter
WALKER, James	6	Talbot
WALKER, James B.	5	Richmond
WALKER, James E.	1	Baker
WALKER, James E.	1	Baker
WALKER, James F.	1	DeKalb
WALKER, Jeremiah	3	Sumter
WALKER, Joel	37	Putnam
WALKER, Joel	36	Sumter
WALKER, John	3	Columbia
WALKER, John	4	Sumter
WALKER, John	10	Talbot
WALKER, John F.	5	Talbot
WALKER, John M.	5	DeKalb
WALKER, Jonathan	8	Richmond
WALKER, M.	6	Talbot
WALKER, M. T.	2	DeKalb
WALKER, M.E. by guard. B.A. Allen	26	Richmond
WALKER, Martha	3	Richmond
WALKER, Mary	20	Putnam
WALKER, Mary	7	Randolph
WALKER, Mary G.	10	Richmond
WALKER, Moses	32	Burke
WALKER, Persons	27	Talbot
WALKER, Pheby	1	Putman
WALKER, Rebecca	14	Richmond
WALKER, Robert D.	7	Chatham
WALKER, Saml.	6	Coweta
WALKER, Samuel	11	DeKalb
WALKER, Thomas	1	Baker
WALKER, Valentine	75	Richmond
WALKER, W.	1	Coweta
WALKER, Watson ?	1	Screven
WALKER, William	3	Screven
WALKER, William E.	18	Burke
WALKER, Wm. L.	6	Talbot
WALL, B. C.	60	Elbert
WALL, Cain	2	Lee
WALL, Jesse	5	Lee
WALL, Jesse	2	Marion
WALL, Luellen W.	3	Marion
WALL, Marilla	4	Marion
WALL, Shadrach	13	Marion
WALL, Solomon	4	Marion
WALL, Thomas O.	2	Marion
WALL, W.	6	Elbert
WALL, William	7	Jasper
WALL, William D.	2	Montgomery
WALL, Ann	1	Chatham
WALL, Benjamin H.	4	Chatham
WALL, Cader	5	Richmond
WALL, James	7	Washington
WALL, James G.	22	Twiggs
WALL, William	2	Warren
WALL, Thomas	9	Taliaferro
WALLACE, Abel B.	2	Burke
WALLACE, Benj.	25	Wilkes
WALLACE, Bland	6	Marion
WALLACE, Cargel	1	Marion
WALLACE, Harabard	5	Cobb
WALLACE, J. C.	4	Meriwether
WALLACE, James E.	12	Lincoln
WALLACE, Jesse	2	Lincoln
WALLACE, Jno.	3	Pulaski
WALLACE, Josiah	5	Newton
WALLACE, Martha D.	8	McIntosh
WALLACE, Mary	30	Chatham
WALLACE, Norman	11	Chatham
WALLACE, Sarah	5	Newton
WALLACE, William	1	Lumpkin
WALLACE, William J.	4	McIntosh
WALLACE, William T.	1	Cobb
WALLACE, Woodford	11	Greene
WALLACE, Adam	5	Burke
WALLACE, Ambrose	6	Talbot
WALLACE, Ambrose	3	Talbot
WALLACE, Herbert	19	Sumter
WALLACE, James	5	Talbot
WALLACE, James	8	Taliaferro
WALLACE, John H.	34	Talbot

Name	Number	County	Name	Number	County
WALLACE, John H.	13	Talbot	WALTERS, Jesse	14	Dooly
WALLACE, Joseph	2	Taliaferro	WALTERS, R.	1	Wilkinson
WALLACE, Nathan	1	DeKalb	WALTERS, William	31	Twiggs
WALLACE, Simeon	11	Burke	WALTHALL, Edward	1	Merriwether
WALLACE, Stiring	1	Burke	WALTHAUER, Israel F.	12	Lowndes
WALLACE,			WALTHOUR,		
William Senr.	6	Burke	George W.	204	Liberty
WALLAR, Smith	3	Monroe	WALTHOUR, Wm. L.	16	Liberty
WALLAR?, Wm. B.	1	Muscogee	WALTON, B. F.	7	Monroe
WALLER, David S.	1	Jasper	WALTON, Dorothy	19	Lincoln
WALLER, Ed.	3	Wilkes	WALTON, Geo. H.	12	Wilkes
WALLER, Irwin	14	Hancock	WALTON, Henry	26	Monroe
WALLER, John	1	Hancock	WALTON, Henry	10	Morgan
WALLER, John T.	15	Hancock	WALTON, Henry B.	28	Jasper
WALLER, Luther	2	Early	WALTON, Isaac L.	97	Jasper
WALLER, Minerva	1	Pike	WALTON, J. J.	1	Muscogee
WALLER, William	1	Muscogee	WALTON, J. W.	16	Morgan
WALLER, Anderson W.	6	Richmond	WALTON, Jesse	2	Paulding
WALLER, B. R.	11	Putnam	WALTON, Mary A.	26	Morgan
WALLER, H.	5	Putnam	WALTON, Mary F.	40	Morgan
WALLER, J. N.	28	Putnam	WALTON, P. W.	101	Morgan
WALLER, John	2	Putnam	WALTON, P. W. estate	66	Morgan
WALLER, John R.	1	Putnam	WALTON, R. T.	35	Wilkes
WALLER, Levi	1	Putnam	WALTON, Thomas	13	Merriwether
WALLER, Mary	1	Crawford	WALTON, Washington	48	Morgan
WALLER, Newbal	3	Talbot	WALTON, Wm.	18	Wilkes
WALLER, Nimrod	5	Wilkes	WALTON, Isiah	1	Crawford
WALLER?, John G.	1	Dooly	WALTON, Jesse	96	Columbia
WALLIS, A.J.	8	Troup	WALTON, John H.	73	Talbot
WALLIS, Reuben	7	Fayette	WALTON, Keziah	2	Columbia
WALLIS, Reubin	2	Fayette	WALTON, Overton	12	Columbia
WALLIS, Madison	1	Campbell	WALTON, Robert	12	Richmond
WALLIS, W. F.	1	Bibb	WALTON, S. B.	11	Stewart
WALLIS, William	4	Baker	WALTON, Simpsoon	4	Stewart
WALLIS, William G.	20	Dooly	WALTON, W. N.	37	Lincoln
WALLS, Deloza	2	Gordon	WALTON, William A.	1	Richmond
WALLS, Jacob	1	Chatham	WALTON?, A. R.	1	Carroll
WALLS, Maddox	3	Muscogee	WAMACH, Jesse	4	Monroe
WALLS, Oliver	1	Upson	WAMACH, Lucy	6	Monroe
WALLS, Sarah	4	Habersham	WAMACK, Sanford	1	Muscogee
WALPOLE, Thos.	4	Crawford	WAMBLE, Ann	35	Talbot
WALSH, Edmund	4	Chatham	WAMBLE, D. W.	6	Talbot
WALSH, Catherine	1	McIntosh	WAMBLE, Mrs. J.	3	Stewart
WALSH, Thomas J.	11	Chatham	WAMMACK, Jacob	6	Muscogee
WALSH, Thomas J.	1	Chatham	WAMMACK, A. T.	3	Sumter
WALSTON, Sarah	2	Troup	WAMMACK,		
WALTERS, Anna	1	Franklin	William G.	5	Sumter
WALTERS, Elijah	8	Franklin	WAMMOCK, Elener	1	Bullock
WALTERS, Jackson M.	3	Franklin	WAMMOCK, Lewis P.	2	Walton
WALTERS, Jeremiah	2	Dooly	WANSLOW, A. M.	13	Elbert
WALTERS, Jesse	20	Macon	WARBINGTON, A.	7	DeKalb
WALTERS, Joseph	28	Floyd	WARD, Andrew J.	26	Harris
WALTERS, Thos. G.	1	Floyd	WARD, Ann	16	Chatham
WALTERS, Jas. A.	2	Coweta	WARD, Ann E.	18	Chatham

Name	Number	County	Name	Number	County
WARD, B. D.	8	Jefferson	WARD, Martha A.	1	Burke
WARD, Bethany	5	Greene	WARD, Mary	26	Putnam
WARD, Daniel	12	Troup	WARD, Payton	24	Baldwin
WARD, Davis W.	2	Heard	WARD, Thomas A.	7	Burke
WARD, E. H.	1	Lee	WARD, Thos.	9	Randolph
WARD, E. W.	22	Troup	WARD, Uriah	28	Putnam
WARD, Edward K.	11	Clarke	WARD, William G.	2	Stewart
WARD, G. M.	6	Elbert	WARDEN, Isaac	1	Dooly
WARD, Hugh	8	Warren	WARDLAW, G. B.	1	Early
WARD, J.	9	Henry	WARDLAW, George	14	Houston
WARD, James	8	Wilkinson	WARDLAW, J. C.	5	Walker
WARD, James W.			WARDLAW, Micajah	7	Muscogee
agt for BRYAN, Wm.	33	Houston	WARDLAW, John B.	2	Sumter
WARD, Jesse	4	Fayette	WARDLOW, Cyntha	9	Jones
WARD, John B.	1	Morgan	WARDLOW, Jas.	2	Pulaski
WARD, John E.	5	Chatham	WARE, A. G.	5	Washington
WARD, John L. D.	3	Clarke	WARE, A. H.	19	Greene
WARD, John W.	3	Heard	WARE, Albert	1	Cass
WARD, Joshua	11	Franklin	WARE, Alexander	12	Paulding
WARD, Lorena	14	Troup	WARE, Asa J.	6	Madison
WARD, Lucy	20	Heard	WARE, Augustus G.	15	Floyd
WARD, Malthus A.	7	Clarke	WARE, Benj. F. L.	13	Floyd
WARD, Martha	15	Newton	WARE, Britian S.	17	Madison
WARD, Nancy	9	Monroe	WARE, David	6	Twiggs
WARD, Nathan	4	Murray	WARE, David	4	Twiggs
WARD, Obadiah	4	Merriwether	WARE, David R.	1	Hancock
WARD, P. Z.	22	Henry	WARE, E.	1	Floyd
WARD, R. H.	40	Greene	WARE, Edward	73	Floyd
WARD, R. N.	7	Elbert	WARE, Elizabeth R.	10	Madison
WARD, Seth	11	Henry	WARE, H. C.	2	Greene
WARD, Thadeus	7	Wilkinson	WARE, J. M.	14	Wilkinson
WARD, William	16	Harris	WARE, J. R.	3	Lincoln
WARD, Wm.	1	Clarke	WARE, James	38	Twiggs
WARD, Zackery	5	Harris	WARE, James	11	Twiggs
WARD, A. E.	32	Putnam	WARE, James M.	16	Paulding
WARD, Abram	40	Stewart	WARE, James W. P.	16	Floyd
WARD, Abram	40	Stewart	WARE, John	2	Newton
WARD, B. F.	59	Butts	WARE, Josiah	1	Newton
WARD, Bartholomew	1	Richmond	WARE, L.	9	Floyd
WARD, Calvin	2	Burke	WARE, N. C.	?	Wilkes
WARD, Charles	9	Burke	WARE, Robert A.	10	Muscogee
WARD, D.	4	Randolph	WARE, Shedrick	45	Twiggs
WARD, Elsy	1	Chatham	WARE, Susan	2	Lincoln
WARD, Francis	3	Burke	WARE, Swansey	2	Pike
WARD, George W.	7	Baldwin	WARE, William	9	Hancock
WARD, Gilbert A.	13	Burke	WARE, Wm.	9	Floyd
WARD, James	16	Burke	WARE, Wm.	1	Marion
WARD, James	8	Talbot	WARE, (?)	2	Columbia
WARD, James H.	5	Burke	WARE, A. G.	1	DeKalb
WARD, John	6	Stewart	WARE, J. S.	2	Stewart
WARD, John	5	Taliaferro	WARE, John	6	Stewart
WARD, John W.	11	Putnam	WARE, Joseph	23	Richmond
WARD, Louisa	2	Burke	WARING, Wm. R. estate	3	Chatham
WARD, Martha	3	Burke	WARING, Wm.R. estate	121	Chatham

Name	Number	County
WARNELL, Asa	1	Liberty
WARNELL, Wm. E.	1	Liberty
WARNER & HOOKER	5	Chatham
WARNER, B.	2	Muscogee
WARNER, R. A.	2	Muscogee
WARNER, William	10	Chatham
WARNER, Hiram	74	Meriwether
WARNOCK, John	18	Early
WARNOCK, Mary	4	Burke
WARNOCK, Mrs.	1	Laurens
WARNOCK, Nancy	16	Burke
WARNOCK, Simeon	18	Burke
WARRAN, J. S.	20	Elbert
WARRELL, Josiah	1	Stewart
WARREN, ?	7	Muscogee
WARREN, Benj. H.	5	Richmond
WARREN, Bray	2	Macon
WARREN, Dred	5	Macon
WARREN, E. W.	5	Lee
WARREN, Eli	16	Houston
WARREN, Eppes	2	Hancock
WARREN, Francis	2	Macon
WARREN, Frederick	7	Houston
WARREN, George W.	1	Greene
WARREN, James	2	Newton
WARREN, John	4	Heard
WARREN, John	8	Muscogee
WARREN, John M.	3	Putnam
WARREN, L. C	36	Jefferson
WARREN, L. E .	39	Jefferson
WARREN, M. E.	1	Fayette
WARREN, Ment W.	39	Morgan
WARREN, Moses	8	Early
WARREN, Sherod	2	Heard
WARREN, Thomas	40	Jasper
WARREN, Thos.	2	Heard
WARREN, Washington	1	Pike
WARREN, William	59	Hancock
WARREN, William	4	Newton
WARREN, A.	3	Randolph
WARREN, Benjamin H.	97	Richmond
WARREN, Charles	6	Stewart
WARREN, James	4	Dooly
WARREN, James R.	4	Baker
WARREN, Lott	20	Baker
WARREN, Samuel	11	Burke
WARTERS, James	1	Wilkinson
WARTHAN, James M.	22	Washington
WARTHAN, William	23	Washington
WARTHEN, Richard	83	Washington
WARTHEN, W. B.	2	Washington
WARTHIN, Thos. J.	59	Washington
WARWICK, Allen	3	Cass
WASDEN, Politha	4	Warren
WASDON, B. J.	2	Jefferson
WASH, H. J.	16	Randolph
WASH, Wm. W.	35	Chatham
WASHBURN, David	6	Habersham
WASHBURN, Joseph	3	Chatham
WASHBURN, Dorcus	2	Chatham
WASHINGTON, A.	11	Floyd
WASHINGTON, John W.	1	Merriwether
WASHINGTON, Elizabeth	7	Baldwin
WASHINGTON, Elizabeth	2	Richmond
WASHINGTON, Jas. H.	14	Bibb
WASHINGTON, M. Gibson	29	Columbia
WASHINGTON, R. B.	8	Bibb
WASSON, John A.	10	Greene
WATER, Clement	1	Franklin
WATERER, Wm.	8	Lee
WATERHOUSE, Euclid	2	Murray
WATERMAN, Joseph	3	Jones
WATERS, Abner	3	Gilmer
WATERS, Alexander	4	Bullock
WATERS, Daniel S.	3	Cobb
WATERS, Elizabeth	9	Twiggs
WATERS, Geo.	20	Bryan
WATERS, James	15	Newton
WATERS, John	5	Hall
WATERS, John C.	51	Jasper
WATERS, Major George	57	Gwinnett
WATERS, Mayr. G.	4	Gwinnett
WATERS, R. H .	8	Hall
WATERS, Richard	31	Washington
WATERS, Thomas J.	36	Gwinnett
WATERS, William	1	Hall
WATERS, Amos	7	Bullock
WATERS, C.	1	Randolph
WATERS, E. D.	4	Decatur
WATERS, Eliza	4	Chatham
WATERS, Henry	4	Screven
WATERS, Isaac	1	Bullock
WATERS, James	1	Bullock
WATERS, Jeremiah	31	Baker
WATERS, Michele	1	Bullock
WATERS, Michial	5	Screven
WATERS, Robert	1	Bullock
WATERS, S. M.	27	Decatur
WATERS, Seaborn	1	Sumter
WATERS, Simon	2	Sumter
WATERS, Thomas	3	Bullock
WATERS, Thomas Sen.	8	Bullock
WATERS, Washington	1	Bullock
WATERS, William	9	Burke

Name	Number	County	Name	Number	County
WATERS, William	7	Chaham	WATSON, James	4	Harris
WATERS, William	76	Screven	WATSON, James M.	10	Cobb
WATERSON, Kesiah	6	Fayette	WATSON, Jesse H.	12	Lee
WATHALL, Ann	1	Jackson	WATSON, Nathan M.	1	Marion
WATHRALL, John H.	10	Meriwether	WATSON, Paris	5	Cobb
WATKIN, Philip Sen.	25	Oglethorpe	WATSON, Richard	15	Monroe
WATKINS, E. P.	4	Henry	WATSON, Robert	12	Meriwether
WATKINS, Elisha	14	Burke	WATSON, Rufus H.	9	Monroe
WATKINS, Frank	1	Twiggs	WATSON, Samuel	14	Franklin
WATKINS, Gasta ?	2	Wilkes	WATSON, Samuel	12	Jackson
WATKINS, H. P.	5	Jefferson	WATSON, Sandel	17	Monroe
WATKINS, Henry	1	Lumpkin	WATSON, Solomon	21	Hancock
WATKINS, J. D.	57	Elbert	WATSON, T. E.	4	Franklin
WATKINS, John C.	2	Dooly	WATSON, Thomas	2	Harris
WATKINS, Mitchel	1	Washington	WATSON, Thomas	4	Houston
WATKINS, P. H.	7	Laurens	WATSON, William	2	Chatham
WATKINS, Redden	3	Washington	WATSON, William	56	Greene
WATKINS, Reese	28	Oglethorpe	WATSON, William	1	Jackson
WATKINS, Samuel	6	Muscogee	WATSON, William	10	Meriwether
WATKINS, William	8	Morgan	WATSON, William	21	Monroe
WATKINS, William	5	Washington	WATSON, William	2	Walton
WATKINS, Willis	3	Jackson	WATSON, William	3	Warren
WATKINS, Wm. P.	19	Oglethorpe	WATSON, William L.	3	Harris
WATKINS, A. A.	4	Butts	WATSON, Winchester	1	Monroe
WATKINS, A. M.	5	Butts	WATSON, Z.	1	Henry
WATKINS, Benjamin	11	Campbell	WATSON, Ben	6	Columbia
WATKINS, James	1	Richmond	WATSON, F.	9	Dooly
WATKINS, Jas.	13	Coweta	WATSON, Jas.	1	Coweta
WATKINS, Jason	1	Richmond	WATSON, Jesse	1	Columbia
WATKINS, Reese	1	Campbell	WATSON, John	2	Stewart
WATKINS, Robert H.	5	Richmond	WATSON, John	3	Fayette
WATKINS, Tom	3	Columbia	WATSON, John P.	1	Campbell
WATLEY, Hampton	10	Floyd	WATSON, Malcom	1	Telfair
WATLEY, James M.	2	Pike	WATSON, Nero	1	Harris
WATS, Edward	3	DeKalb	WATSON, S. W.	1	Campbell
WATSON, A.	1	Houston	WATSON, Thos.	34	Columbia
WATSON, A. J.	12	Greene	WATSON, Tyron	4	Carroll
WATSON, Abner	8	Marion	WATSON, William	3	Columbia
WATSON, Arthur	6	Merriwether	WATSON, William	3	Columbia
WATSON, Bryant	3	Greene	WATSON, William	1	Dooly
WATSON, Calvin	2	Franklin	WATSON, William Sen.	4	Columbia
WATSON, Dorothy	1	Harris	WATSON, Wm.	4	Crawford
WATSON, Douglas	58	Monroe	WATT, Alexander	3	Effingham
WATSON, Douglass C.	27	Greene	WATT, Charles	4	Muscogee
WATSON, Elisha	6	Walton	WATT, Mrs.	14	Muscogee
WATSON, George F.	1	Harris	WATT, Thomas		
WATSON, Gideon	10	Macon	& Franklin	7	Muscogee
WATSON, Green	7	Burke	WATT, William J.	7	Harris
WATSON, Hiram	2	Harris	WATT, Robt.	3	Stewart
WATSON, Hiram B.	5	Harris	WATTERS, Michael	1	Marion
WATSON, J. R.	3	Pulaski	WATTERS, Allen	12	Dooly
WATSON, Jacob	5	Harris	WATTS, Blanford G.	1	Jones
WATSON, Jacob	1	Harris	WATTS, Amanda	1	Sumter
WATSON, Jacob	8	Houston	WATTS, Harrison	14	Greene

Name	Number	County	Name	Number	County
WATTS, Hope H.	4	Floyd	WEAVER, Andrew B.	13	Campbell
WATTS, Mark	11	Gwinnett	WEAVER, Benjamin	2	Gwinnett
WATTS, Mary	4	Greene	WEAVER, Francis	5	Newton
WATTS, Mary A.	10	Troup	WEAVER, Graves H.	4	Walton
WATTS, Mrs. M. K.	2	Heard	WEAVER, Henry	3	Marion
WATTS, Paschal	20	Monroe	WEAVER, Isham	37	Newton
WATTS, Samuel	1	Hancock	WEAVER, Jarrett	1	Butts
WATTS, Thomaas	5	Heard	WEAVER, Jesse M.	1	Newton
WATTS, Thomas	3	Heard	WEAVER, John	1	DeKalb
WATTS, W. T	8	Greene	WEAVER, John	8	Newton
WATTS, William	84	Hancock	WEAVER, Travis A.D.	11	Upson
WATTS, Wm. B.	2	Bibb	WEAVER, William W.	56	Greene
WATTS, J.	2	Chattooga	WEAVER, ? M.	10	Putnam
WATTS, L. B.	22	Campbell	WEAVER, Anthony G.	7	Baker
WATTS, P.	7	Gordon	WEAVER, D. A.	9	Putnam
WATTS, S. B.	3	Campbell	WEAVER, Frances	13	Putnam
WAUGH, Cynthia	2	Henry	WEAVER, James	8	Sumter
WAUGH, J. W.	1	Henry	WEAVER, John	1	Sumter
WAVER, John J.	1	Chatham	WEAVER, Saml.	24	Coweta
WAY, Addison	2	Thomas	WEAVER, Thos. J.	11	Putnam
WAY, E. B.	33	Liberty	WEAVER, William	10	Newton
WAY, Edward	9	Liberty	WEBB, A. M.	1	Meriwether
WAY, E. F.	11	Twiggs	WEBB, Alfred	12	Lumpkin
WAY, Henry	19	Liberty	WEBB, Augustus	7	Newton
WAY, John	22	Jefferson	WEBB, Austin	3	Walton
WAY, Miss Sarah W.	29	Liberty	WEBB, B. G.	5	Oglethorpe
WAY, Moses W.	3	Liberty	WEBB, C.	5	Elbert
WAY, Rev. R. Q.	7	Liberty	WEBB, C.	10	Meriwether
WAY, Samuel	27	Liberty	WEBB, Charles	4	Monroe
WAY, Thos. G.	2	Liberty	WEBB, Clinton	8	Forsyth
WAY, William J.	8	Chatham	WEBB, Davis?	5	Pulaski
WAY, Wm. N.	39	Liberty	WEBB, Edmond J.	10	Monroe
WAY, A. S.	3	Stewart	WEBB, Elijah W.	1	Madison
WAY, Moses W.	1	Bryan	WEBB, Etheldrd	3	Wilkinson
WAY, Wm. J.	72	Bryan	WEBB, Giles B.	2	Macon
WAYNE, Eliza C.	6	Chatham	WEBB, G. G.	1	Washington
WAYNE, Richaard	13	Chatham	WEBB, Isaac	11	Muscogee
WAYNE, Thomas S.			WEBB, Isham	1	Marion
trustee	1	Chatham	WEBB, J.T.	3	Lee
WAYNESBORO			WEBB, James	1	Dooly
R. R. COMPANY	22	Burke	WEBB, James W.	2	Walton
WEAKS, Poleman S.	8	Harris	WEBB, Jesse B.	3	Early
WEAME?, J.	13	Early	WEBB, John	6	Muscogee
WEATHERBY,			WEBB, John	35	Newton
William S.	3	Clarke	WEBB, John	18	Washington
WEATHERLY, Isaac	1	Telfair	WEBB, John	1	Washington
WEATHER, James	3	Upson	WEBB, John N.	1	Upson
WEATHERS, Allen	7	Morgan	WEBB, Mary	1	Jasper
WEATHERS, Valentine	6	Lincoln	WEBB, Mary E.	45	Chatham
WEATHERS, Daniel	13	Talbot	WEBB, Phoeba A.	9	Muscogee
WEATHERS, Seaborn	2	Talbot	WEBB, Richard T.	3	Muscogee
WEATHERSBEE,			WEBB, Robert	1	Cobb
John F.	10	Jones	WEBB, Wiley	2	Macon
WEATHERSBY, Mary	3	Burke	WEBB, William	4	Washington

Name	Number	County	Name	Number	County
WEBB, Willis	9	Jackson	WELBORN, Carllin	34	Houston
WEBB, Benjamin	9	Dooly	WELBORN, Curtis	4	Morgan
WEBB, Cullen	1	Dooly	WELBORN, Lucinda	12	Wilkes
WEBB, E.	45	Crawford	WELBORN, Martha	24	Wilkes
WEBB, Eli D.	3	Dooly	WELBORN, Oliver H.	6	Houston
WEBB, John	4	Dooly	WELBORN, William E.	2	Murray
WEBB, John	12	Stewart	WELBORN, William R.	13	Franklin
WEBB, Joseph T.	2	Dooly	WELBORN, Mary	26	Columbia
WEBB, Mary	3	Randolph	WELBORN, P. S.	21	Randolph
WEBB, P.T.	2	Putnam	WELBORNE, Margaret	15	Morgan
WEBB, Robert	2	Burke	WELCH, ?	1	Union
WEBB, Samuel	19	Dooly	WELCH, Daniel	1	Cass
WEBB, Samuel B.	1	Baker	WELCH, Elizabeth	1	Clarke
WEBB, William	5	Stewart	WELCH, Ellizabeth	6	Washington
WEBB, William B.	1	Talbot	WELCH, G. W.	5	Henry
WEBBER, Richard	1	McIntosh	WELCH, Jacob P.	50	Washington
WEBSTER, John	3	Upson	WELCH, Margaret	17	Walker
WEBSTER, Mrs. Elizabeth	5	Muscogee	WELCH, Washington	3	Washington
WEBSTER, Richard	1	Washington	WELCH, Wesley C.	12	Henry
WEBSTER, Ruben	5	Floyd	WELCH, Franklin O.	2	Baker
WEBSTER, T. R.	3	Hall	WELCH, George B.	5	Chatham
WEBSTER, Walter R.	7	Floyd	WELCH, Jas. A.	5	Coweta
WEBSTER, William	11	Harris	WELCH, John	10	Putnam
WEBSTER, William	2	Muscogee	WELDEN, Milton	17	Twiggs
WEBSTER, William	1	Washington	WELDER, Calvin S.	2	Franklin
WEBSTER, Malinda	5	Talbot	WELDON, John	5	Jasper
WEBSTER, Swift	4	Chatham	WELDON, Moses	1	Harris
WEDDINGTON, Zeno	6	Muscogee	WELDON, Robert	24	Harris
WEEDE, E. B.	9	Bibb	WELDON, Wm.	5	Henry
WEEGLE ? , George A.	1	Richmond	WELLBORN, Alfred	130	Merriwether
WEEKLY, Thomas	3	Talbot	WELLBORN, Amos	3	Walker
WEEKS, A. E.	5	Pulaski	WELLBORN, C. B.	3	Forsyth
WEEKS, Caleb	1	Washington	WELLBORN, Elijah	1	Forsyth
WEEKS, Joseph C.	2	Heard	WELLBORN, James M.	52	Warren
WEEKS, Rufus G.	5	Jefferson	WELLBORN, Marshall H.	36	Warren
WEEKS, Henry S.	4	Stewart	WELLBORN, William W.	3	Harris
WEEKS, John H.	8	Talbot	WELLBORN, C. T.	1	Coweta
WEEKS, Thomas	3	Richmond	WELLBORN, S. T.	3	Coweta
WEEKS, William	1	Richmond	WELLEFORCE, Saml.	1	Stewart
WEEMS, Asa	1	Franklin	WELLMAKER, Felix	5	Wilkes
WEEMS, B. J.	17	Henry	WELLMAN, Margaret	4	Chatham
WEEMS, Johnson	1	Franklin	WELLONS, J.	2	Crawford
WEEMS, Lock	93	Muscogee	WELLONS, Wm.	10	Crawford
WEEMS, S. R.	11	Henry	WELLS, B.	2	Muscogee
WEEMS, Saml.	12	Henry	WELLS, Berry	23	Lowndes
WEEMS, T. D.	23	Henry	WELLS, David	5	Jefferson
WEEVER, S.	7	Randolph	WELLS, David	23	Macon
WEGINGS ?, Wm. W.	15	Twiggs	WELLS, Eliah	3	Pike
WEIGLE, George	5	Richmond	WELLS, G.	1	Troup
WEIR, James A.	5	Jackson	WELLS, Henry M.	4	Gwinnett
WEIR, Nancy	27	Clarke	WELLS, J. T.	1	Pike
WEITMAN, Lewis	9	Effingham	WELLS, Jesse	1	Lincoln
WELBORN, Burket	16	Morgan			

Name	Number	County	Name	Number	County
WELLS, John	2	Pike	WEST, John C.	10	Houston
WELLS, John A.	7	Camden	WEST, Levin	13	Harris
WELLS, John R.	5	Jefferson	WEST, Mary	18	Stewart
WELLS, John W.	5	Merriwether	WEST, Moses	4	Dooly
WELLS, Levi	3	Floyd	WEST, Phillip	13	Lee
WELLS, Mary E.	2	Chatham	WEST, Reuben S.	1	Greene
WELLS, Michael	1	Marion	WEST, Robert	3	Jackson
WELLS, Robert	1	Merriwether	WEST, Susan	5	Fayette
WELLS, S. G.	4	Floyd	WEST, Tillman D.	11	Muscogee
WELLS, Thomas F.	27	Jefferson	WEST, W. D.	15	Morgan
WELLS, William	20	Marion	WEST, William	14	Houston
WELLS, William	2	Merriwether	WEST, William E.	40	Paulding
WELLS, William H.	1	Pike	WEST, Charles	29	Stewart
WELLS, Wm.	6	Marion	WEST, Charles W.	44	Burke
WELLS, Wyley W.	24	Gwinnett	WEST, Dr. Charles	1	Burke
WELLS, Andrew	1	DeKalb	WEST, Hamberton	6	Sumter
WELLS, Delila	1	Sumter	WEST, Henry	48	Troup
WELLS, Elijah	19	Talbot	WEST, J. S.	3	Randolph
WELLS, Elijah	5	Telfair	WEST, Jas.	2	Putnam
WELLS, Elizabeth	1	DeKalb	WEST, John	24	Columbia
WELLS, George T.	9	Sumter	WEST, John	4	Dooly
WELLS, Henry L.	12	Telfair	WEST, John	3	Early
WELLS, J. E.	2	Bibb	WEST, John	61	Stewart
WELLS, Jacob H.	1	Screven	WEST, Jno. Q.	65	Wilkes
WELLS, John M.	5	Screven	WEST, Jno. Q.	1	Wilkes
WELLS, John V.	8	Bryan	WEST, Margaret	1	Dooly
WELLS, Jos.	2	Coweta	WEST, Moses T.	7	Baldwin
WELLS, Thos.	9	Carroll	WEST, Pemberton	23	Sumter
WELLS, William	3	Bryan	WEST, Sarah	6	Baldwin
WELSH, Joshua	3	Cobb	WEST, Thomas D.	27	Baldwin
WELTHALL, Turman	15	Butts	WEST, Wm.	62	Stewart
WEMBERLY, Ezekiel	13	Houston	WESTBERRY,		
WENDERWILLE, Wm.	2	Irwin	Jefferson R.	14	Dooly
WENFREY, R.	38	Oglethorpe	WESTBROOK, Alferd	1	Newton
WENFREY, R. R.	10	Oglethorpe	WESTBROOK, Jas.	9	Carroll
WENTWORTH, Walter	1	DeKalb	WESTBROOK, M. H.	1	Fayette
WESBROOK, Daniel J.	4	Sumter	WESTBROOK,		
WESCOT, Henry	1	Bibb	Stephen B.	10	Franklin
WEST, Allen	1	Fayette	WESTBROOK, Thomas	6	Franklin
WEST, Andrew	30	Monroe	WESTBROOK,		
WEST, Charles	85	Houston	Wesley J.	2	Franklin
WEST, Charles	7	Houston	WESTBROOK, R. W.	40	Houston
WEST, Charles	24	Muscogee	WESTBROOK, Thomas	11	Sumter
WEST, Ephriam	10	Heard	WESTBROOKS, T.S.	5	Henry
WEST, Francis	5	Pike	WESTERN, Sarah	11	Stewart
WEST, George	3	Gilmer	WESTFALL, Thomas G.	2	Baker
WEST, George G.	18	Pike	WESTFIELD, David	18	Murray
WEST, George W.	33	Paulding	WESTMORELAND, C.	15	Henry
WEST, Isaac C.	34	Houston	WESTMORELAND,		
WEST, Isaac W.	2	Houston	Mark	5	Muscogee
WEST, James	10	Habersham	WESTMORELAND,		
WEST, Jane	10	Paulding	Mark W.	3	Fayette
WEST, Jeremiah	4	Harris	WESTMORELAND,		
WEST, John	10	Pike	Robt.	24	Fayette

Name	Number	County
WESTMORELAND, Harrison	5	DeKalb
WESTMORELAND, R. C.	12	Coweta
WESTMORELAND, W. W.	6	Coweta
WESTMORLAND, M.	6	Pike
WESTON, Jos.	12	Stewart
WESTWOOD, John	6	Harris
WETHERALL, Joseph	13	Marion
WETHERINGTON, John R.	1	Richmond
WETHERS, Rachel	3	Lincoln
WETHERS, Daniel	8	Talbot
WETHERSBY, Elizabeth	9	Randolph
WHALEY, B. B.	2	Murray
WHALEY, J. H.	29	Thomas
WHALEY, J. R.	8	Hancock
WHALEY, Jno.	5	Henry
WHALEY, Jno. K.	1	Pulaski
WHALEY, Thos.	49	Hancock
WHALEY, Ebenezer	12	Talbot
WHALEY, Eligah	4	Stewart
WHALEY, J. B.	4	Randolph
WHALEY, J. T.	4	Randolph
WHALEY, Josiah	1	Putnam
WHALEY, Mrs. C.	3	Decatur
WHALY, George	8	Upson
WHALY, W. D.	6	Randolph
WHATEY, Wilson W.	5	Fayette
WHATLEY, A.	5	Troup
WHATLEY, V. D.	3	Troup
WHATLEY, W. J.	9	Troup
WHATLEY, Floyd	1	Monroe
WHATLEY, James	48	Pike
WHATLEY, John R.	8	Floyd
WHATLEY, Johnson	5	Fayette
WHATLEY, Robert	1	Monroe
WHATLEY, S. J.	9	Harris
WHATLEY, Walton	8	Monroe
WHATLEY, William	3	Fayette
WHATLEY, William	13	Jones
WHATLEY, Wilson O. B.	22	Paulding
WHATLEY, L. A.	9	Coweta
WHATLEY, Wm. M.	9	Coweta
WHATLY, Daniel	1	Marion
WHATLY, Wilson	17	Paulding
WHEALLER, G. W.	5	Randolph
WHEAT, Harvey	14	Lincoln
WHEAT, Jonathan	5	Greene
WHEAT, Augustus	1	DeKalb
WHEATLEY, B. O.	33	Newton
WHEATLEY, Joseph	1	Wilkes

Name	Number	County
WHEATLEY, William	7	Jones
WHEATLY, W. H.	1	Randolph
WHEELEES, Hardy	4	Talbot
WHEELER, (?)	6	Columbia
WHEELER, Charles A.	11	Floyd
WHEELER, Elbert	4	Newton
WHEELER, Freeman	11	Franklin
WHEELER, Hardy	1	Dooly
WHEELER, Henry C.	15	Hancock
WHEELER, J.	3	Cherokee
WHEELER, James	1	Gwinnett
WHEELER, John	2	Marion
WHEELER, Lawrence L. F.	10	Greene
WHEELER, Lewis	1	Pike
WHEELER, Pinkney	1	Thomas
WHEELER, Richard	13	Franklin
WHEELER, Robert T.	4	Liberty
WHEELER, S.	1	Wilkinson
WHEELER, Thomas J.	26	Warren
WHEELER, William	3	Effingham
WHEELER, Wm.	1	Monroe
WHEELER, Avery	4	Sumter
WHEELER, Green M.	3	Sumter
WHEELER, Jacob	11	Screven
WHEELER, Joseph	7	Richmond
WHEELER, Levi	1	Talbot
WHEELER, William J.	2	Richmond
WHEELES, Lion	8	Meriwether
WHEELES, Thomas	1	Merriwether
WHEELUS, Isham	6	Randolph
WHELCHEL, Davis	20	Hall
WHELCHEL, Davis	11	Hall
WHELCHEL, Francis	2	Hall
WHELCHEL, Francis	21	Lumpkin
WHELCHEL, John	8	Hall
WHELCHEL, Moses	4	Hall
WHELCHEL, T.	8	Hall
WHELCHEL, T. D.	2	Hall
WHELCHEL, Valentine	1	Hall
WHELER, John	1	Troup
WHELESS, Martha D.	4	Merriwether
WHELIS, Joseph	1	Houston
WHELLER, Richard J.	1	Dooly
WHIDBY, John	5	Jones
WHIDBY, Sarah A.	18	Jones
WHIGHAM, John G.	15	Jefferson
WHIGHAM, John W.	18	Jefferson
WHIGHAM, Saml.	5	Harris
WHIGHAM, William J.	10	Jefferson
WHIGHAM, Wm. P.	8	Jefferson
WHILDEN, J. B.	3	Screven
WHIPPLE, Benj. F.	1	Lowndes
WHITAKER, Benjamin	5	Early

Name	Number	County	Name	Number	County
WHITAKER, Daniel	8	Heard	WHITE, Joseph C.	83	Jones
WHITAKER, John J.	6	Fayette	WHITE, Luke	2	Madison
WHITAKER, Pleasant H.	75	Heard	WHITE, Mary S.	2	Merriwether
WHITAKER, Saml. T.	10	Harris	WHITE, Mathis	1	Jones
WHITAKER, Simon T.	5	Fayette	WHITE, Melton	8	Monroe
WHITAKER, James C.	39	Baldwin	WHITE, Miller H.	1	Troup
WHITAKER, John	1	Decatur	WHITE, Moses	2	Cobb
WHITAKER, Margaret	11	Baldwin	WHITE, Nathaniel H.	8	Franklin
WHITAKER, N.	1	Wilkinson	WHITE, Newton	10	Walker
WHITAKER, Thomas R.	4	Wilkinson	WHITE, R.	1	Elbert
WHITAKER, Samuel	41	Baldwin	WHITE, Reuben	13	Upson
WHITCHER, William	1	Newton	WHITE, Richard	14	Pike
WHITE, A. A.	2	Troup	WHITE, Robert	1	Hall
WHITE, B.	1	Merriwether	WHITE, Robert	3	Jackson
WHITE, B. B.	16	Upson	WHITE, Robert	2	Newton
WHITE, Bailey	5	Hancock	WHITE, S.	9	Elbert
WHITE, Benj. P.	1	Heard	WHITE, Samuel	5	Effingham
WHITE, Benjm.	6	Walton	WHITE, Samuel	1	Macon
WHITE, Berry	3	Walker	WHITE, Stephen	24	Madison
WHITE, Benjamin A.	44	Jones	WHITE, Sterling	1	Jackson
WHITE, Blumer H.	24	Pike	WHITE, T. C.	13	Elbert
WHITE, David	1	Newton	WHITE, Tabitha E.	20	Jones
WHITE, Edw. A.	2	Muscogee	WHITE, Thomas C.	14	Jones
WHITE, Edward	23	Liberty	WHITE, Timothy	2	Morgan
WHITE, Edward	15	Monroe	WHITE, W.	7	Elbert
WHITE, Elizabeth	26	Upson	WHITE, W.	2	Pike
WHITE, Elizabeth H.	41	Jones	WHITE, W. H. H.	4	Clarke
WHITE, Eppy	21	Elbert	WHITE, William	1	Jackson
WHITE, G. M.	3	Troup	WHITE, William	1	Marion
WHITE, George	1	Cobb	WHITE, William	1	Walker
WHITE, George	5	Floyd	WHITE, William A.	6	Madison
WHITE, George	27	Hancock	WHITE, William C.	9	Pike
WHITE, George O. K.	37	Jefferson	WHITE, William W.	17	Harris
WHITE, Henry	3	Madison	WHITE, William Z.	2	Monroe
WHITE, Henry P.	3	Madison	WHITE, Wm.	11	Floyd
WHITE, Hugh	6	Newton	WHITE, Wm. B.	34	Elbert
WHITE, Isiah M.	6	Madison	WHITE, Wm. M.	7	Troup
WHITE, J. H.	2	Henry	WHITE, Wm. S.	3	Troup
WHITE, J. M.	39	Laurens	WHITE, ?	1	Elbert
WHITE, James	1	Chatham	WHITE, ?	10	Putnam
WHITE, James	13	Monroe	WHITE, Amelia	14	Burke
WHITE, James	8	Newton	WHITE, Anderson	2	Stewart
WHITE, James D.	2	Newton	WHITE, Ann M.	10	Chatham
WHITE, James R.	10	Madison	WHITE, Benj. B.	2	Sumter
WHITE, John	26	Clarke	WHITE, Benjamin A.	9	Baldwin
WHITE, John	5	Clarke	WHITE, C. G.	19	Screven
WHITE, John	1	Clarke	WHITE, Carter	1	Carroll
WHITE, John	50	Harris	WHITE, David	1	Richmond
WHITE, John	2	Newton	WHITE, E.	13	Chattooga
WHITE, John Jun.	1	Jackson	WHITE, E. E.	3	Decatur
WHITE, John Sen.	31	Jackson	WHITE, Edd	1	Stewart
WHITE, John A.	3	Chattooga	WHITE, Gabriel	3	Clarke
WHITE, John H.	20	Pike	WHITE, Henry	7	Burke
WHITE, John T.	6	Upson	WHITE, J. C.	20	Coweta

Name	Number	County
WHITE, J. T.	9	Bibb
WHITE, James	1	DeKalb
WHITE, James	38	Sumter
WHITE, Jas. A.	2	Randolph
WHITE, John	23	Decatur
WHITE, John	10	Talbot
WHITE, Joseph	10	Stewart
WHITE, Joseph	15	Sumter
WHITE, Mary	4	DeKalb
WHITE, Mary	14	Richmond
WHITE, Peter	2	Chatham
WHITE, Peter G.	2	Sumter
WHITE, Robt.	20	Coweta
WHITE, Rolley	1	Campbell
WHITE, Samuel G.	3	Baldwin
WHITE, Thomas S.	36	Coweta
WHITE, Thos. H.	12	Columbia
WHITE, W. B.	8	Crawford
WHITE, W. W.	1	DeKalb
WHITE, Waid	16	Campbell
WHITE, William	2	Chatham
WHITE, William P	19	Chatham
WHITE, Wm.	11	Chattooga
WHITE, Wm. agt for MATHEWS, J. G.	11	Habersham
WHITE, Zachariah	1	Talbot
WHITECOTTON, G. W.	3	Murray
WHITEFIELD, Briant	15	Harris
WHITEFIELD, N. B.	1	Washington
WHITEFIELD, Ruben	9	Washington
WHITEHEAD, A. B.	2	Walton
WHITEHEAD, B. C.	5	Houston
WHITEHEAD, Bennet	41	Laurens
WHITEHEAD, C. C.	5	Twiggs
WHITEHEAD, Dr. James estate	56	Burke
WHITEHEAD, Dr. James estate	9	Burke
WHITEHEAD, Eld.	1	Jackson
WHITEHEAD, Hillery	17	Harris
WHITEHEAD, J. P.	17	Hancock
WHITEHEAD, James	32	Harris
WHITEHEAD, Joel	1	Oglethorpe
WHITEHEAD, John	33	Burke
WHITEHEAD, John B.	38	Burke
WHITEHEAD, John P. C.	90	Burke
WHITEHEAD, John T.	40	Harris
WHITEHEAD, Samuel	4	Newton
WHITEHEAD, Sanford	9	Clarke
WHITEHEAD, Thos.	37	Harris
WHITEHEAD, W. R.	5	Clarke
WHITEHEAD, W. W.	58	Laurens

Name	Number	County
WHITEHEAD, William	71	Harris
WHITEHEAD, William	26	Harris
WHITEHEAD, Amos C.	82	Burke
WHITEHEAD, Charles	14	Burke
WHITEHEAD, Dr. Jas. estate	3	Burke
WHITEHEAD, James	2	Macon
WHITEHEAD, James S.	9	Burke
WHITEHEAD, Jas.Troup	53	Burke
WHITEHEAD, John	53	Burke
WHITEHEAD, William	5	Dooly
WHITEHEAD, Z.	2	Bibb
WHITEHEAD, Z.	12	Chatham
WHITEHORN, L. B.	2	Carroll
WHITEHURST, Charles	7	Houston
WHITEHURST, J.	31	Wilkinson
WHITEHURST, Morgan	12	Twiggs
WHITEHURST, S.F.	1	Twiggs
WHITELELY, Elizabeth	1	Decatur
WHITENER, David	5	Murray
WHITES, Elizabeth	9	Baldwin
WHITESIDES, A. J.	2	Greene
WHITESIDES, John	4	Muscogee
WHITESIDES, Noah	3	Cass
WHITESIDES, Wm. H.	3	Greene
WHITESIDES, Jonathan	8	Cass
WHITFIELD, Ann T.	42	Troup
WHITFIELD, Benj.	1	Cobb
WHITFIELD, Benj. F.	10	Morgan
WHITFIELD, J. V.	1	Oglethorpe
WHITFIELD, James H.	5	Burke
WHITFIELD, M. A.	2	Pulaski
WHITFIELD, Mathew	90	Jasper
WHITFIELD, Mrs.	4	Dooly
WHITFIELD, Robert	29	Washington
WHITFIELD, Thomas	2	Cobb
WHITFIELD, Thomas	1	Thomas
WHITFIELD, William H.	17	Jasper
WHITFIELD, George	10	Burke
WHITFIELD, George	16	Columbia
WHITFIELD, Louis	13	Burke
WHITFIELD, Wm.	25	Putnam
WHITHURST, William	6	Talbot
WHITIKER, W.	2	Troup
WHITING, Charles	4	Morgan
WHITLEY, Thos. H.	4	Carroll
WHITLEY, W.	1	Irwin
WHITLEY, E. R.	8	Campbell
WHITLOCK, Isaac	7	Morgan
WHITLOCK, J. M.	8	Franklin
WHITLOCK, Charles	4	DeKalb
WHITLOCK, Isaac W.	6	Richmond
WHITLOCK?, Eliza	10	Morgan
WHITLOW, Mile W.	2	Walker

Name	Number	County	Name	Number	County
WHITLOW, Nathaniel	13	Greene	WIGGENS, Allen	24	Houston
WHITLOW, John J.	3	DeKalb	WIGGERS, Christr.	21	Henry
WHITLOW, Wm. D.	8	DeKalb	WIGGINS, Alfred	6	Pike
WHITMAN, Cullen	1	Upson	WIGGINS, Benj.	1	Clarke
WHITMAN, R. L.	2	Greene	WIGGINS, Benjamin	5	Macon
WHITMAN, William	9	Harris	WIGGINS, Eli	1	Clarke
WHITMAN, William	1	Harris	WIGGINS, Emily	4	Washington
WHITMIRE, C.	2	Forsyth	WIGGINS, John Jr.	7	Emanual
WHITMIRE, Henry	1	Jackson	WIGGINS, John M.	1	Emanual
WHITSETT, James	10	Lee	WIGGINS, John Sr.	11	Emanual
WHITSETT, John	39	Lee	WIGGINS, Joseph	9	Glynn
WHITSIT, Thomas	23	Dooly	WIGGINS, Joseph	20	Wayne
WHITT, William	1	Newton	WIGGINS, Lemual G.	5	Muscogee
WHITTAKER, John	2	Stewart	WIGGINS, Michael	3	Emanual
WHITTED, N. C.	8	Hancock	WIGGINS, Michael	3	Jefferson
WHITTEN, G. S.	2	Walton	WIGGINS, Mrs.	5	Muscogee
WHITTEN, George	12	Monroe	WIGGINS, Osbon	10	Macon
WHITTEN, J. S.	68	Hancock	WIGGINS, Penelope	3	Jefferson
WHITTEN, James	3	Harris	WIGGINS, Pleasant	1	Emanual
WHITTEN, Nelson	1	Hancock	WIGGINS, Ric.	1	Washington
WHITTEN, Wliam	1	Murray	WIGGINS, Richard A.	8	Marion
WHITTENBURG,			WIGGINS, Wiley G.	18	Macon
James	1	Murray	WIGGINS, Amos. W.	66	Burke
WHITTINGTON, Allen	1	Macon	WIGGINS, Green	3	Putnam
WHITTINGTON, John	2	Muscogee	WIGGINS, James A.	18	Baldwin
WHITTINGTON, J.	20	Crawford	WIGGINS, Jesse	1	Bibb
WHITTLE, George W.	2	Murray	WIGGINS, Jonathan	3	Stewart
WHITTLE, James	3	Marion	WIGGINS, Robert	1	Richmond
WHITTLE, L. N.	14	Bibb	WIGGINS, Whit	7	Stewart
WHITTLE, L. W.	20	Bibb	WIGHAM, N. K.	5	Jefferson
WHITTLESEY, J. H.	7	Muscogee	WIGHAM, William	12	Jefferson
WHITTY, Sarah	2	Walton	WIGHT, Samuel B.	1	Baker
WHITWORTH, John C.	3	Gwinnett	WIGHTMAN ?, John M.	2	Richmond
WHITWORTH, Richard	4	Gwinnett	WIGLY, William	1	Cobb
WHITWORTH, Wm. B.	33	Cass	WILBANKS, Solomon	12	Jackson
WHITWORTH, Wm. K.	1	Forsyth	WILBANKS, Wm. F.	3	Jackson
WHORTON, Jeptha	3	Marion	WILBORN, W. R.	17	Lincoln
WHORTON, James M.	1	Stewart	WILBOURN, Samuel J.	16	Jasper
WHTE, James	1	DeKalb	WILBURN, Wm. F.	9	Greene
WHTEHURST, H. L.	12	Bibb	WILCHAR, Jordan	17	Marion
WIAT, William	10	Merriwether	WILCHAR, William	5	Warren
WICH?, Jno. B.	6	Carroll	WILCHER, Jeremiah	2	Marion
WICHAN, J.	4	Crawford	WILCOX, Baker	3	Richmond
WICKER, A & T	14	Washington	WILCOX, Jonathan	1	Richmond
WICKER, J. R.	7	Washington	WILCOX, Mary	2	Richmond
WICKER, John	7	Walker	WILCOXEN, John	15	Hancock
WICKER, Margaret S.	13	Washington	WILCOXON, Levi	11	Coweta
WICKER, Nathaniel	8	Washington	WILCOXON, Wiley	6	Coweta
WICKER, P. R.	1	Washington	WILCOXTON, Reason	12	Jones
WICKER, R. H.	7	Washington	WILD, John M.	8	Richmond
WICKER, T. E.	7	Washington	WILDE, Mary Ann	2	Richmond
WIDDINGTON,			WILDEN, John C.	3	Talbot
William	3	Cobb	WILDER,	3	Pike
WIER, John	5	Clarke	WILDER, Charles	32	Warren

Name	Number	County	Name	Number	County
WILDER, Frances	2	Jones	WILKERSON, J.	1	Meriwether
WILDER, James	7	Pike	WILKERSON, James	4	Jones
WILDER, Jas.	1	Crawford	WILKERSON, James P.	5	Walton
WILDER, Levi	4	Madison	WILKERSON, John	2	Murray
WILDER, Luke	7	Jones	WILKERSON, John E.	44	Troup
WILDER, M. C.	9	Troup	WILKERSON, John E.	8	Troup
WILDER, Matilda	6	Jones	WILKERSON, Peter J.	2	Merriwether
WILDER, Peter L. B.	1	Madison	WILKERSON, Samuel	17	Butts
WILDER, William	4	Jones	WILKERSON,		
WILDER, William	2	Lowndes	William G.	13	Muscogee
WILDER, Wm.	7	Monroe	WILKERSON, Calvin	3	Campbell
WILDER, C.	1	Bibb	WILKERSON, James	14	Bullock
WILDER, E.	8	Crawford	WILKERSON, John S.	43	Baker
WILDER, Green?	7	Bibb	WILKERSON, R.	12	Troup
WILDER, John R.	5	Chatham	WILKERSON, Robert	7	Campbell
WILDER, Jonathan	1	Bibb	WILKERSON, Wm. H.	19	Walton
WILDER, Rabun M.	2	Warren	WILKES, A.	20	Troup
WILDER, Sampson B,	20	Taliaferro	WILKES, Benjamin M.	7	Troup
WILDER, W.	23	Screven	WILKES, J. W.	4	Troup
WILDER, Wm. H.	5	Taliaferro	WILKES, John	46	Troup
WILDMAN, Philo	10	Muscogee	WILKES, S.	1	Oglethorpe
WILDMAN, Elijah	1	Carroll	WILKES, Saml.	1	Clarke
WILDON, Isaac	2	Merriwether	WILKES, Sarah	8	Troup
WILEFORD, John	7	Stewart	WILKES, F. N.	13	Putnam
WILEY, David by			WILKES, W. M.	3	Troup
HENDERSON, agt	81	Houston	WILKES?, Thomas E.	1	Gwinnett
WILEY, Edwin	40	Hancock	WILKIN, Samuel	8	Pike
WILEY, George W.	2	Gwinnett	WILKINS, A. B.	43	Jefferson
WILEY, Jacob	1	Early	WILKINS, Allen	7	Heard
WILEY, Nancy	19	Columbia	WILKINS, Archibald	7	Hancock
WILEY, S. H.	9	Hancock	WILKINS, F. G.	16	Muscogee
WILEY, Wesley	5	Jackson	WILKINS, James L.	31	Chatham
WILEY, William	12	Franklin	WILKINS, John	9	Effingham
WILEY, William J.	2	Franklin	WILKINS, Joseph C.	53	Liberty
WILEY, Ben	14	Columbia	WILKINS, Matthew	7	Lee
WILEY, J. B.	4	Bibb	WILKINS, Samuel	2	Fayette
WILEY, John H.	32	Columbia	WILKINS, Samuel Sr.	9	Fayette
WILEY, Witham	5	DeKalb	WILKINS, William	51	Early
WILHITE, Manford	1	Merriwether	WILKINS, Andrew F.	1	Stewart
WILHITE, P. A .	2	Franklin	WILKINS, C.	35	Elbert
WILHITE, Penelope	19	Merriwether	WILKINS, James	15	Bryan
WILHITE, Thomas M.	3	Madison	WILKINS, Jno. H.	12	Randolph
WILHITE, Wm. M.	3	Jackson	WILKINS, Sarah	10	Columbia
WILIAMS, Hamilton	21	Bullock	WILKINSON, B. B.	1	Lee
WILIFORD, M. C.	2	Stewart	WILKINSON, H. J.	22	Wilkes
WILIFORD, Wm. S.	3	Bibb	WILKINSON, Irwin	6	Troup
WILKENS, Micajah	5	Pulaski	WILKINSON, Jane	9	Chatham
WILKERSON, A.	21	Harris	WILKINSON, Joel J.	3	Heard
WILKERSON, Calvin R.	2	Muscogee	WILKINSON, John	2	Twiggs
WILKERSON, Daniel	2	Wayne	WILKINSON, Jos. W.	14	Wilkes
WILKERSON, Elizabeth	5	Merriwether	WILKINSON, N.K.	6	Troup
WILKERSON, Francis	12	Troup	WILKINSON, S. G.	9	Twiggs
WILKERSON, Francis	2	Troup	WILKINSON, Thomas B.	11	Franklin
WILKERSON, Isaac	4	Clarke	WILKINSON, Thos. B.	16	Heard

Name	Number	County
WILKINSON, W. B.	4	Merriwether
WILKINSON, Zachry	2	Pike
WILKINSON, Burton	10	Columbia
WILKINSON, Charles	39	Columbia
WILKINSON, James Jr.	1	Bullock
WILKINSON, Mary C.	5	Baker
WILKINSON, Matilda	27	Talbot
WILKISON, Thomas D.	1	Pike
WILKS, Benjamin M.	2	Troup
WILKS, Elisha	12	Emanual
WILKS, Henry J.	2	Twiggs
WILKS, James J.	2	Twiggs
WILKS, Wiley T.	5	Macon
WILKS, John B.	10	Dooly
WILKS, Wm. C.	5	Putnam
WILLARD, R.	7	Henry
WILLBANKS, R.	9	Chattooga
WILLCHER, Jordan	7	Marion
WILLCOX, Geo.	39	Irwin
WILLCOX, George	4	Appling
WILLCOX, J. L.	38	Irwin
WILLCOX, J. W.	3	Irwin
WILLCOX, T.	25	Irwin
WILLCOX, James	1	Telfair
WILLCOX, John	8	Telfair
WILLCOX, John Jr.	21	Telfair
WILLCOX, Mark	58	Telfair
WILLCOX, Mitchell G.	8	Telfair
WILLCOX, Sarah	21	Telfair
WILLCOX, Woodson	33	Telfair
WILLERFORD, H.	7	Crawford
WILLES, Benjamin T.	1	Pike
WILLETT, Slaughter	2	Muscogee
WILLETT, A. H.	7	Sumter
WILLETT, George M.	27	Chatham
WILLETT, George W.	3	Chatham
WILLEY, William E.	10	Thomas
WILLHELM, F.	3	Muscogee
WILLHITE, C. F.	5	Elbert
WILLHITE, R. A.	2	Elbert
WILLHITE, T.	13	Elbert
WILLIAM, Margaret	17	Chatham
WILLIAM, Robt.	3	Cobb
WILLIAM, Martha M.	2	DeKalb
WILLIAMS ?, Robert	1	Sumter
WILLIAMS, (?)	29	Columbia
WILLIAMS, (none)	1	Muscogee
WILLIAMS, ?	1	Muscogee
WILLIAMS, A.	4	Merriwether
WILLIAMS, A. J.	1	Habersham
WILLIAMS, A. M.	4	Hancock
WILLIAMS, Abbott	2	Newton
WILLIAMS, Abner A.	42	Early
WILLIAMS, Abraham	23	Hancock

Name	Number	County
WILLIAMS, Albert	6	Chatham
WILLIAMS, Alford	20	Gwinnett
WILLIAMS, Allen	8	Houston
WILLIAMS, Allen A.	16	Cass
WILLIAMS, Amanda	2	Muscogee
WILLIAMS, Ambrose A.	5	Jones
WILLIAMS, Anabina?	6	Muscogee
WILLIAMS, Anderson	2	Effingham
WILLIAMS, Ann M.	1	Chatham
WILLIAMS, Augustus	1	Lumpkin
WILLIAMS, Augustus	2	Murray
WILLIAMS, Augustus J.	5	Meriwether
WILLIAMS, B.	1	Henry
WILLIAMS, B.	11	Oglethorpe
WILLIAMS, B.	7	Oglethorpe
WILLIAMS, Benj.	28	Harris
WILLIAMS, Benjamin	13	Harris
WILLIAMS, Birdy	2	Madison
WILLIAMS, Birdy O.	2	Madison
WILLIAMS, Britain	39	Harris
WILLIAMS, Char. J.	5	Muscogee
WILLIAMS, Charles D.	34	Montgomery
WILLIAMS, Chas. A.	1	Richmond
WILLIAMS, Clark L.	10	Merriwether
WILLIAMS, Daniel J.	11	Walker
WILLIAMS, David	2	Floyd
WILLIAMS, David	26	Merriwether
WILLIAMS, Dawson	21	Jackson
WILLIAMS, Doctor	4	Upson
WILLIAMS, Dr. W. F.	1	Oglethorpe
WILLIAMS, Duke	6	Greene
WILLIAMS, Duke	21	Upson
WILLIAMS, E. P.	16	Habersham
WILLIAMS, Edward	5	Habersham
WILLIAMS, Edward	2	Harris
WILLIAMS, Elijah	5	Macon
WILLIAMS, Elijah	18	Madison
WILLIAMS, Elizabeth	1	Gwinnett
WILLIAMS, Elizabeth A.	7	Lowndes
WILLIAMS, Enoch	7	Marion
WILLIAMS, Francis B.	8	McIntosh
WILLIAMS, Frederick	1	Lowndes
WILLIAMS, Frully?	20	Pulaski
WILLIAMS, G. W.	1	Lee
WILLIAMS, Geo.	1	Irwin
WILLIAMS, George	5	Clarke
WILLIAMS, George	23	Macon
WILLIAMS, Griffin	3	Gilmer
WILLIAMS, Griffin	2	Lowndes
WILLIAMS, H. J.	1	Walton
WILLIAMS, Hampton	3	Walton
WILLIAMS, Harrison L.	1	Walton
WILLIAMS, Henry	5	Cass

334

Name	Number	County	Name	Number	County
WILLIAMS, Henry	1	Jackson	WILLIAMS, L. A.	13	Hancock
WILLIAMS, Hiram	9	Harris	WILLIAMS, Lawson	1	Jefferson
WILLIAMS, Hiram R.	14	Gwinnett	WILLIAMS, Lina	1	Washington
WILLIAMS, Isaac	8	Greene	WILLIAMS, Lott	6	Marion
WILLIAMS, Isaac	2	Houston	WILLIAMS, Luke	13	Jasper
WILLIAMS, Isham	7	Gwinnett	WILLIAMS, Malinda	5	Troup
WILLIAMS, J.	3	Henry	WILLIAMS, Marcus	4	Warren
WILLIAMS, J.	22	Pike	WILLIAMS, Martha	3	Wilkes
WILLIAMS, J. D.	13	Harris	WILLIAMS, Margaret	9	Chatham
WILLIAMS, J. M.	16	Merriwether	WILLIAMS, Maria	3	Camden
WILLIAMS, J. T.	3	Hancock	WILLIAMS, Marian	2	Lee
WILLIAMS, Jacob	1	Merriwether	WILLIAMS, Mary	58	Chatham
WILLIAMS, Jacob	2	Muscogee	WILLIAMS, Mary	3	Jones
WILLIAMS, James	1	Clarke	WILLIAMS, Mary	2	Muscogee
WILLIAMS, James	3	Effingham	WILLIAMS, Mary	13	Warren
WILLIAMS, James	1	Emanual	WILLIAMS, Mary W.	1	Warren
WILLIAMS, James	14	Jefferson	WILLIAMS, Maryan	1	Gwinnett
WILLIAMS, James	5	Merriwether	WILLIAMS, Membrance	4	Jones
WILLIAMS, James D.	5	Jones	WILLIAMS, Moses	1	Fayette
WILLIAMS, James P.	6	Walker	WILLIAMS, Moses	3	Washington
WILLIAMS, James M.	15	Jasper	WILLIAMS, Mrs. C.	5	Muscogee
WILLIAMS, James M.	10	Jefferson	WILLIAMS, Nancy	2	Hancock
WILLIAMS, James P.	8	Henry	WILLIAMS, Nancy	6	Walton
WILLIAMS, James S.	6	Muscogee	WILLIAMS, Nathan	3	Meriwether
WILLIAMS, James T.	1	Heard	WILLIAMS, Newborn	1	Gordon
WILLIAMS, James W.	5	Hancock	WILLIAMS, Newton	3	Macon
WILLIAMS, Jas. D.	29	Greene	WILLIAMS, Orren	2	Merriwether
WILLIAMS, Jeptha	7	Marion	WILLIAMS, Parthena	1	Gwinnett
WILLIAMS, Jesse	20	Early	WILLIAMS, Penulope	4	Pike
WILLIAMS, Jesse	1	Harris	WILLIAMS, Philip	17	Harris
WILLIAMS, Jesse	19	Wilkes	WILLIAMS, Rebecca	9	Clarke
WILLIAMS, Jesse A.	6	Pike	WILLIAMS, Reuben G.	32	Lee
WILLIAMS, John	1	Chatham	WILLIAMS, Reubin K.	1	Lee
WILLIAMS, John	47	Clarke	WILLIAMS, Rev. Jas.	2	Gwinnett
WILLIAMS, John	33	Jones	WILLIAMS, Richard	8	Effingham
WILLIAMS, John	11	Merriwether	WILLIAMS, Richard	5	Macon
WILLIAMS, John	5	Wilkinson	WILLIAMS, Richrd	9	Macon
WILLIAMS, John	11	Walker	WILLIAMS, Robert	1	Forsyth
WILLIAMS, John	4	Ware	WILLIAMS, Robert	6	Madison
WILLIAMS, John	14	Washington	WILLIAMS, Robert	4	Newton
WILLIAMS, John F.	2	Merriwether	WILLIAMS, Rufus	5	Warren
WILLIAMS, John E.	1	Harris	WILLIAMS, S.	8	Troup
WILLIAMS, John J.	2	Houston	WILLIAMS, Samuel	1	Macon
WILLIAMS, John W. S.	27	Troup	WILLIAMS, Samuel L.	19	Jones
WILLIAMS, John Y.	1	Madison	WILLIAMS, Sarah	4	Jefferson
WILLIAMS, Jonathan	1	Gordon	WILLIAMS, Sarah	10	Lowndes
WILLIAMS, Jonathan	17	Monroe	WILLIAMS, Sery?	5	Muscogee
WILLIAMS, Joseph	12	Fayette	WILLIAMS, Simeon	2	Jefferson
WILLIAMS, Joseph	2	Madison	WILLIAMS, Simeon	9	Twiggs
WILLIAMS, Joseph	3	Oglethorpe	WILLIAMS, Stephen	6	Pike
WILLIAMS, Joseph	5	Pike	WILLIAMS, Tabitha	11	Warren
WILLIAMS, Joshua	1	Warren	WILLIAMS, Theophois	4	Pike
WILLIAMS, Josiah	3	Fayette	WILLIAMS, Thomas	3	Gwinnett
WILLIAMS, L. A.	3	Greene	WILLIAMS, Thomas	5	Thomas

Name	Number	County	Name	Number	County
WILLIAMS, Thomas J.	26	Jones	WILLIAMS, Hand	2	Richmond
WILLIAMS, Thomas P.	11	Monroe	WILLIAMS, Henry O.	3	Columbia
WILLIAMS, Thos. A.	8	Harris	WILLIAMS, Hezekiah	11	Richmond
WILLIAMS, Thos. A.	3	Walker	WILLIAMS, Hiram	6	Sumter
WILLIAMS, Thos. E.	1	Forsyth	WILLIAMS, Hubbard	19	Butts
WILLIAMS, Tickner? S.	5	Lee	WILLIAMS, J.	8	Bibb
WILLIAMS, Tilman	3	Macon	WILLIAMS, J.	1	Coweta
WILLIAMS, W.	1	Cherokee	WILLIAMS, Jefferson G.	1	Tatnall
WILLIAMS, W. H.	1	Henry	WILLIAMS, Jesse	1	DeKalb
WILLIAMS, W. L.	12	Merriwether	WILLIAMS, John	1	Baker
WILLIAMS, Wiley	4	Muscogee	WILLIAMS, John	2	Coweta
WILLIAMS, William	3	Early	WILLIAMS, John	3	Richmond
WILLIAMS, William H.	13	Pike	WILLIAMS, John	1	Talbot
WILLIAMS, William L.	3	Merriwether	WILLIAMS, John B.	8	Stewart
WILLIAMS, Willis	2	Early	WILLIAMS, John C.	1	Bullock
WILLIAMS, Willis	1	Greene	WILLIAMS, John G.	3	Bullock
WILLIAMS, Willis	13	Merriwether	WILLIAMS, Joseph B.	12	Telfair
WILLIAMS, Wilson	17	Merriwether	WILLIAMS, Josiah	20	Talbot
WILLIAMS, Wm.	13	Marion	WILLIAMS, Levi	2	DeKalb
WILLIAMS, Wm. T.	4	Forsyth	WILLIAMS, Lewis	5	Richmond
WILLIAMS,			WILLIAMS, Lowry	24	Cass
William W.	3	Walton	WILLIAMS, M. B.	1	Carroll
WILLIAMS, Wm.	3	Wilkes	WILLIAMS, Matthew	3	Putnam
WILLIAMS, Wright	7	Lumpkin	WILLIAMS, Mrs. Edney	2	Stewart
WILLIAMS, Zach.	14	Marion	WILLIAMS, Mrs. L.A.	14	Stewart
WILLIAMS, (?)	10	Columbia	WILLIAMS, Mrs. Lucy	35	Stewart
WILLIAMS, A.	8	Decatur	WILLIAMS, Mrs. Lucy	12	Stewart
WILLIAMS, A. J.	4	Sumter	WILLIAMS, Mrs. R.	1	Decatur
WILLIAMS, Ammi	7	DeKalb	WILLIAMS, Nancy	11	Putnam
WILLIAMS, Ann	6	Richmond	WILLIAMS, Peter I.	14	Baldwin
WILLIAMS, B.	6	Bibb	WILLIAMS, R.	4	Decatur
WILLIAMS, Berrian	10	Carroll	WILLIAMS, Robert	27	Bullock
WILLIAMS, Betsey	2	Tatnall	WILLIAMS, Robert	11	Screven
WILLIAMS, Brownan	1	Campbell	WILLIAMS, Roxy	16	Bullock
WILLIAMS, Bryant	5	Telfair	WILLIAMS, Rubun?	12	Bibb
WILLIAMS, C.A.			WILLIAMS, S. R.	7	Carroll
& M. H.	1	Richmond	WILLIAMS, Samuel	1	Dooly
WILLIAMS, Catherine	2	Richmond	WILLIAMS, Savannah	1	Bullock
WILLIAMS, D. R.	3	Chattooga	WILLIAMS, Sherod	2	Cass
WILLIAMS, Daniel A.	3	Taliaferro	WILLIAMS, Stephen	20	Bullock
WILLIAMS, David	3	Bullock	WILLIAMS, Stephen	3	Chatham
WILLIAMS, David	4	Screven	WILLIAMS, Susannah	14	Bullock
WILLIAMS, David J.	11	Telfair	WILLIAMS, Thomas	7	Stewart
WILLIAMS, Duke	4	Stewart	WILLIAMS, Thos.	8	Dade
WILLIAMS, E.	6	Screven	WILLIAMS, Uriah	1	Bibb
WILLIAMS, Earley	2	Randolph	WILLIAMS, W. P.	6	Hancock
WILLIAMS, Elisha			WILLIAMS, W. Thorne	5	Chatham
for WALBERGER	7	Habersham	WILLIAMS, Wiley	1	Bullock
WILLIAMS, Elizabeth	3	Sumter	WILLIAMS, William	8	Bullock
WILLIAMS, Elihu	2	Walker	WILLIAMS, William H.	1	Chatham
WILLIAMS, Ezekiel	58	Burke	WILLIAMS, William K.	1	Sumter
WILLIAMS, Francis H.	1	Chatham	WILLIAMS,		
WILLIAMS, Garrett	12	Bullock	William Thad.	25	Chatham
WILLIAMS, George W.	7	Richmond	WILLIAMS, William W.	9	Richmond

Name	Number	County	Name	Number	County
WILLIAMS, Wm.	22	Bullock	WILLIAMSON, N. C.	10	Butts
WILLIAMS, Wm.	3	Camden	WILLIAMSON, R. J.	8	Crawford
WILLIAMS, Wm.	2	Camden	WILLIAMSON, R. M.	103	Screven
WILLIAMS, Wm.	94	Decatur	WILLIAMSON, Rich.	2	Screven
WILLIAMS, Wm. A.	7	Dade	WILLIAMSON,		
WILLIAMS, Wm. B.	25	Bibb	Richard M.	6	Screven
WILLIAMS, Wm. H.	6	Telfair	WILLIAMSON, Richd.	5	Screven
WILLIAMS, Wm. N.	24	Greene	WILLIAMSON, Rob.	3	Screven
WILLIAMS, Wm. P.	2	Decatur	WILLIAMSON, T. E.	84	Clarke
WILLIAMS, Wm. R.	5	Bibb	WILLIAMSON,		
WILLIAMS. N. J.	2	Stewart	William T.	10	Baldwin
WILLIAMS?, W.	14	Harris	WILLIFORD, Charles	2	Fayette
WILLIAMS?, W. R.	1	Putnam	WILLIFORD, Henry	6	Madison
WILLIAMSON, A. P.	3	Jackson	WILLIFORD, J. D.	3	Muscogee
WILLIAMSON, Adam	10	Jackson	WILLIFORD,		
WILLIAMSON,			William W.	5	Madison
Benjamin	12	Heard	WILLIFORD, Benjamin	1	DeKalb
WILLIAMSON, C. B.	3	Jackson	WILLIFORD, G. W.	58	Stewart
WILLIAMSON, E. C.	61	Washington	WILLIFORD, M. C.	2	Stewart
WILLIAMSON,			WILLILAMSON,		
George W.	4	Pike	Zachariah	2	Stewart
WILLIAMSON, Isaac B.	51	Pike	WILLINGHAM, Avell	3	Newton
WILLIAMSON, J. L.	20	Jackson	WILLINGHAM, B. V.	33	Oglethorpe
WILLIAMSON, J. M.	2	Jackson	WILLINGHAM, B. V.	4	Oglethorpe
WILLIAMSON, James	1	Cherokee	WILLINGHAM, D. S.	2	Henry
WILLIAMSON, Jane	4	Cass	WILLINGHAM,		
WILLIAMSON, John	70	Chatham	Dr. Willis	72	Oglethorpe
WILLIAMSON, John	1	DeKalb	WILLINGHAM, Elijah	4	Newton
WILLIAMSON, John	1	Troup	WILLINGHAM,		
WILLIAMSON, Jno. C.	9	Wilkes	Elizabeth	12	Jasper
WILLIAMSON, John N.	70	Newton	WILLINGHAM, Isaac	10	Jasper
WILLIAMSON,			WILLINGHAM, Jackson	1	Forsyth
Josh. C.	6	Wilkes	WILLINGHAM, James	7	Upson
WILLIAMSON, Littleton	11	Heard	WILLINGHAM, Joseph	4	Cass
WILLIAMSON,			WILLINGHAM, Lucretia	3	Forsyth
McAlister	4	Jones	WILLINGHAM, Peter?	3	Muscogee
WILLIAMSON, M. C.	18	Washington	WILLINGHAM,		
WILLIAMSON, Mary	10	Wilkes	Rolly S.	2	Walton
WILLIAMSON, Sarah	6	Jones	WILLINGHAM, Sarah	9	Lincoln
WILLIAMSON, T. J.	10	Henry	WILLINGHAM, Wilkins	4	Newton
WILLIAMSON, Thos. C.	3	Greene	WILLINGHAM, Isaac	10	Lincoln
WILLIAMSON,			WILLINGHAM, Joseph	8	Columbia
William J.	1	Pike	WILLINGHAM, R. S.	3	Lincoln
WILLIAMSON, Winney	40	Jackson	WILLINK, Henry F.	19	Chatham
WILLIAMSON, Wm.	1	Muscogee	WILLIS, Aaron	11	Upson
WILLIAMSON, ? E.	3	Richmond	WILLIS, Andrew L.	7	Harris
WILLIAMSON, B.	8	Screven	WILLIS, Cary	20	Muscogee
WILLIAMSON, C.	27	Screven	WILLIS, D. C.	6	Elbert
WILLIAMSON, Guarry	1	Talbot	WILLIS, Daniel	7	Monroe
WILLIAMSON, Henry	3	Talbot	WILLIS, E.	2	Elbert
WILLIAMSON, James	12	Talbot	WILLIS, George	12	Walker
WILLIAMSON, John	6	Chatham	WILLIS, George A.	24	Monroe
WILLIAMSON, John	1	Dade	WILLIS, George A.	2	Monroe
WILLIAMSON, Madeline	11	Chatham	WILLIS, J.	2	Irwin

Name	Number	County	Name	Number	County
WILLIS, J. B.	7	Washington	WILLSON, Fennel H.	4	Jackson
WILLIS, J. M.	4	Pike	WILLSON, Henry	16	Muscogee
WILLIS, James M.	41	Elbert	WILLSON, Jesse	2	Muscogee
WILLIS, Jas. D.	58	Wilkes	WILLSON, Nancy	8	Muscogee
WILLIS, Jas. H.	36	Wilkes	WILLSON, Sarah	3	Muscogee
WILLIS, John	32	Monroe	WILLSON, William	7	Jackson
WILLIS, John T.	12	Greene	WILLY, James H.	3	Morgan
WILLIS, Lowden	22	Greene	WILMOT, Eli T.	14	Franklin
WILLIS, N. F.	5	Irwin	WILOMAN, Elijah Jun.	1	Carroll
WILLIS, Owen J.	47	Monroe	WILSON, -----	1	Burke
WILLIS, R. J.	88	Greene	WILSON, -----	10	Early
WILLIS, Redin	5	Wilkinson	WILSON, (?)	6	Columbia
WILLIS, S. H.	17	Meriwether	WILSON, ?	5	Morgan
WILLIS, S. H.	4	Wilkes	WILSON, Alexander	2	Marion
WILLIS, T. F.	10	Elbert	WILSON, Alfred	7	Jasper
WILLIS, Thomas N.	5	Upson	WILSON, Allen	15	Thomas
WILLIS, Wiley F.	2	Effingham	WILSON, Ancel	6	Jackson
WILLIS, William	12	Pike	WILSON, Andrew	2	Bibb
WILLIS, A.	6	Camden	WILSON, Andrew	7	Bullock
WILLIS, Antony G.	2	Richmond	WILSON, Andrew	9	Jackson
WILLIS, C. C.	4	Randolph	WILSON, Andrew J.	15	Jasper
WILLIS, Dempsey	13	Talbot	WILSON, Arkellis	16	Jasper
WILLIS, Dempsey J.	1	Talbot	WILSON, B. J.	1	Walton
WILLIS, Furney	1	Bibb	WILSON, Barnet	3	Clarke
WILLIS, James	22	Talbot	WILSON, Benj.	21	Hancock
WILLIS, James	13	Talbot	WILSON, Benj.	2	Troup
WILLIS, James	1	Talbot	WILSON, Charles	1	Monroe
WILLIS, Joab	3	Crawford	WILSON, Charles T.	6	Jones
WILLIS, John	5	Talbot	WILSON, Cyrus W.	6	Pike
WILLIS, Joseph	1	Bibb	WILSON, Danl. S.	2	Chatham
WILLIS, Kessiah	6	Baldwin	WILSON, E. N.	5	Monroe
WILLIS, Mary E.	3	Richmond	WILSON, Edward G.	1	Chatham
WILLIS, Robert	10	Baldwin	WILSON, Elias	70	Warren
WILLIS, Thomas	2	Baldwin	WILSON, Elihu	26	Effingham
WILLIS, William	4	DeKalb	WILSON, Elijah	9	Henry
WILLIS, William	2	Talbot	WILSON, Elizabeth	9	Jasper
WILLIS, William	8	Upson	WILSON, G. F.	5	Monroe
WILLIS, William	24	Upson	WILSON, George	1	Walker
WILLIS, William H.	2	Pike	WILSON, H. M.	6	Troup
WILLIS, Wm. M.	1	Dooly	WILSON, Henry	3	Effingham
WILLKINSON, J.	4	Richmond	WILSON, Hugh	3	Walker
WILLLIAMS, Jesse	5	Marion	WILSON, J. J.	22	Jasper
WILLLIAMS, William	3	Muscogee	WILSON, James	25	Effingham
WILLLIAMS, Clayton	5	DeKalb	WILSON, James	2	Gwinnett
WILLLIAMS, Redolphus	14	Stewart	WILSON, James	16	Troup
WILLMAKER, John	11	Pike	WILSON, James	6	Warren
WILLOBY, James	12	Clarke	WILSON, James C.	1	Clarke
WILLOBY, J. M.	9	Clarke	WILSON, Jane	1	Paulding
WILLS, Abner	11	Jackson	WILSON, Jas. S.	1	Jackson
WILLS, Edward S.	5	Jackson	WILSON, Jeremiah	1	Effingham
WILLS, L. W.	2	Muscogee	WILSON, Jeremiah Jr.	2	Lowndes
WILLS, Randolph	4	Jackson	WILSON, Jeremiah Sen.	10	Lowndes
WILLS, William	14	Macon	WILSON, Jesse M.	31	Newton
WILLS, Thomas	17	Jackson	WILSON, Jno. B.	1	Columbia

Name	Number	County	Name	Number	County
WILSON, John	1	Campbell	WILSON, Francis	2	Screven
WILSON, John	12	Effingham	WILSON, G.	15	Decatur
WILSON, John	8	Greene	WILSON, J.	6	Crawford
WILSON, John	2	Walker	WILSON, J. B.	2	DeKalb
WILSON, John B.	2	Upson	WILSON, J. R.	4	Butts
WILSON, John C.	23	Campbell	WILSON, J. W.	2	Baker
WILSON, John K. M.	8	Warren	WILSON, James	35	Putnam
WILSON, John T.	1	Heard	WILSON, James	2	Screven
WILSON, Joseph	27	Gordon	WILSON, James	1	Stewart
WILSON, Joshua	5	Merriwether	WILSON, James D.	16	Talbot
WILSON, L.C.	43	Walker	WILSON, James H.	20	Campbell
WILSON, Lemuel	4	Upson	WILSON, Jane	1	Bullock
WILSON, Lucy	7	Henry	WILSON, Jasper	10	Bullock
WILSON, Mary	16	Monroe	WILSON, John	10	Columbia
WILSON, Morris	4	DeKalb	WILSON, John	10	Coweta
WILSON, N. M.	3	Oglethorpe	WILSON, John	4	Coweta
WILSON, Payton F.	4	Walton	WILSON, John S.	3	DeKalb
WILSON, Pleasant	5	Monroe	WILSON, Joseph	2	Bullock
WILSON, R. L.	10	Hancock	WILSON, Joseph	8	Talbot
WILSON, Robert	10	Meriwether	WILSON, Joshua	7	Talbot
WILSON, Robert	1	Newton	WILSON, Judy	6	Bibb
WILSON, Robert C.	7	Clarke	WILSON, Margaret	12	Richmond
WILSON, S. A.	3	Oglethorpe	WILSON, McG. R.	1	Sumter
WILSON, Saml. W.	319	Glynn	WILSON, Mrs. Mary	7	Decatur
WILSON, Samuel	3	Jefferson	WILSON, N.	1	Decatur
WILSON, Samuel	8	Upson	WILSON, Overton	1	Bullock
WILSON, Samuel D.	10	Paulding	WILSON, R.	7	Decatur
WILSON, Samuel R.	7	Warren	WILSON, Richd.	2	Clarke
WILSON, Seth	1	Warren	WILSON, Samuel C.	2	Richmond
WILSON, Stephen	1	Jackson	WILSON, Thomas A.	1	Chatham
WILSON, Stephen	10	Muscogee	WILSON, W. H.	8	Butts
WILSON, Stephen L.	2	Monroe	WILSON, Wimberly	5	Burke
WILSON, Terrel	9	Upson	WILSON, Wm.	1	Carroll
WILSON, Thomas	1	Heard	WILSON, Wm.	7	DeKalb
WILSON, Thomas	7	Monroe	WILSON, Wm. E.	12	Putnam
WILSON, Thos.	1	Wilkes	WILSON, Wm. W.	5	Hancock
WILSON, Thos. B.	16	Greene	WILTBERGER, Peter	62	Chatham
WILSON, W. W.	7	Effingham	WIMBERLEY, Robert H.	3	Baldwin
WILSON, Wiley	14	Troup	WIMBERLY, Abraham	1	Twiggs
WILSON, William	4	Chatham	WIMBERLY, C. H.	27	Twiggs
WILSON, William	1	Jefferson	WIMBERLY, E.	25	Twiggs
WILSON, William	4	Newton	WIMBERLY, Ezekiel	23	Houston
WILSON, William S.	16	Hancock	WIMBERLY, H. P.	29	Lee
WILSON, Wm. J.	2	Fayette	WIMBERLY, H. S.	60	Twiggs
WILSON, Wm. J.	2	Fayette	WIMBERLY, Henry	27	Houston
WILSON, Wm. J.	4	Monroe	WIMBERLY, James	16	Muscogee
WILSON, Zachariah	2	Monroe	WIMBERLY, John J.	28	Houston
WILSON, Alfred	20	Richmond	WIMBERLY, Mary	8	Twiggs
WILSON, Andrew J.	13	Bullock	WIMBERLY, N.	22	Twiggs
WILSON, C.	3	Cass	WIMBERLY, O. H.	16	Houston
WILSON, C. A.	7	DeKalb	WIMBERLY, Perry	13	Muscogee
WILSON, C. C.	1	Burke	WIMBERLY, William	1	Marion
WILSON, E. B., trustee	3	Chatham	WIMBERLY,		
WILSON, Elizabeth	17	Taliaferro	William G.	7	Muscogee

Name	Number	County
WIMBERLY, Zachariah	15	Burke
WIMBERLY, Frances	3	Burke
WIMBERLY, John	1	Burke
WIMBERLY, Leasten	16	Burke
WIMBERLY, Lewis	6	Richmond
WIMBERLY, Mack	1	Talbot
WIMBERLY, Mark	13	Talbot
WIMBERLY, Mc	1	Talbot
WIMBERLY, Randle	1	Burke
WIMBERLY, Richard	2	Richmond
WIMBERLY, Sarah	6	Stewart
WIMBERLY, William	3	Stewart
WIMBERLY?, Joseph W.	17	Houston
WIMBISH, H. S.	56	Merriwether
WIMBRAY, John A.	2	Pike
WIMBUSH, Amy	8	Jones
WIMBUSH, Elizabeth	7	Jones
WIMBUSH, Mary	6	Jasper
WIMBUSH, J. C.	25	Bibb
WIMBUSH, Thomas	2	Sumter
WIMBUSH, William	22	Sumter
WIN ?, Peter O.	7	Thomas
WIN, Thos.	3	Troup
WINCHER, Albert	18	Putnam
WINCHESTER, Jesse	18	Heard
WINCHESTER, Tubal C.	1	Heard
WINCHESTER, Zella	2	Heard
WINCHILL, B.	6	Bibb
WIND, John	2	Thomas
WINDER, Elizabeth	1	Walton
WINDHAM, James	1	Coweta
WINDOM, Peter	2	Meriwether
WINDOM, William	3	Meriwether
WINDOM, William	3	Meriwether
WINDSOR, A. H. agt.	24	Bibb
WINFIELD, Matthew	14	Greene
WINFIELD, William	3	Newton
WINFREY, A. T.	22	Lumpkin
WINFREY, B.	3	Oglethorpe
WINFREY, Giles T.	2	Clarke
WINFREY, John B.	4	Floyd
WINFREY, Martha	1	Floyd
WINFREY, Peter B.	7	Madison
WINFREY, R.	1	Oglethorpe
WINFREY, Reuben	7	Newton
WINFREY, Reubin	27	Columbia
WINFRY, Matilda	8	Monroe
WING, George F.	2	McIntosh
WINGARD, Daniel	1	Baker
WINGFIELD, ?	15	Wilkes
WINGFIELD, A. S.	55	Wilkes
WINGFIELD, Caroline S.	12	Wilkes
WINGFIELD, Chas. E.	24	Wilkes
WINGFIELD, F. G.	38	Wilkes
WINGFIELD, F. G.	4	Wilkes
WINGFIELD, G.	44	Wilkes
WINGFIELD, J. N.	7	Wilkes
WINGFIELD, Mrs. J.	5	Wilkes
WINGFIELD, James L.	11	Pike
WINGFIELD, John	14	Morgan
WINGFIELD, O.	12	Wilkes
WINGFIELD, O.	2	Wilkes
WINGFIELD, William S.	1	DeKalb
WINGO, Zachariah	2	Forsyth
WINKFIELD, J.	3	Putnam
WINKLER, Jane	25	Chatham
WINKLER, Jane	48	Effingham
WINKLER, Zachaariah M.	93	Chatham
WINN, A. B.	2	Forsyth
WINN, Asel	1	Troup
WINN, Charles J.	2	Clarke
WINN, David	9	Floyd
WINN, David H.	3	Oglethorpe
WINN, E. M.	6	Habersham
WINN, Elisha M.	10	Gwinnett
WINN, G.	10	Floyd
WINN, James W.	71	Liberty
WINN, John A.	7	Jackson
WINN, John D.	9	Houston
WINN, Joseph	21	Walton
WINN, Joseph J.	1	Ware
WINN, L. D.	4	Cobb
WINN, Mary P.	13	Gwinnett
WINN, Mrs. E.	4	Liberty
WINN, Mrs. E. estate	25	Liberty
WINN, R. W.P.	9	Hall
WINN, Thos.	8	Columbia
WINN, Thos. S.	12	Liberty
WINN, Washington	23	Liberty
WINN, Wiliard W.	1	Cobb
WINN, Wm. W.	6	Liberty
WINN, Abial	33	Liberty
WINN, James J.	5	DeKalb
WINN, John	11	Bryan
WINN, Sioman	10	Carroll
WINN, Terrell	4	Sumter
WINNING, Louisa	3	Marion
WINPEY, Wm.	7	Floyd
WINSER, Alexander	4	Stewart
WINSHIP, Joseph	23	Jones
WINSHIP, Isaac	8	Bibb
WINSOR, Wm.	4	Early
WINSOR, Elijah	1	Stewart
WINSTEAD, Sarah	6	Clarke
WINSTON, G. H.	9	Troup

Name	Number	County	Name	Number	County
WINSTON, Thos.	19	Harris	WITCHER, Daniel	1	Paulding
WINSTON, Thos.	45	Troup	WITCHER, Ephriam	11	Heard
WINSTON, Thos. J.	3	Coweta	WITCHER, James	3	Paulding
WINTER, Charles	5	Harris	WITCHER, Nancy Ann	4	Paulding
WINTER, Geo. W.	21	Muscogee	WITCHER, D. H.	6	Carroll
WINTER, John G.	60	Muscogee	WITHERSPOON,		
WINTER, John Z.	23	Muscogee	Elizabeth	4	Clarke
WINTER, Frederick	5	Richmond	WITHINGTON,		
WINTER, Jeremiah	19	Richmond	James E.	1	Chatham
WINTERS, C.	6	Oglethorpe	WITHROW, Susan	1	Gilmer
WINTERS, John	1	Cobb	WITT, Charles	7	Jackson
WINTERS, John	6	Greene	WITT, Middleton	24	Jackson
WINZER, ?	16	Stewart	WITTICK, Eliza	5	Morgan
WIRK, Caroline	1	Chatham	WOFFALL, Rebecca	8	Merriwether
WIRTHINGTON, H.	1	Bibb	WOFFORD, James	1	Cass
WISDOM, Wm. C.	11	Troup	WOFFORD, Thos. J.	14	Cass
WISE, ?	2	Morgan	WOFFORD, W. H.	3	Cass
WISE, ?	5	Oglethorpe	WOFFORD, Wm. B.	48	Habersham
WISE, Catherine	10	Pike	WOFFORD, Wm. T.	3	Cass
WISE, Charles	2	Muscogee	WOFFORD, Thos. D.	2	Cass
WISE, Cynthia	19	Oglethorpe	WOLF, Andrew	1	Wilkes
WISE, George	1	Gilmer	WOLF, Benj. L.	24	Early
WISE, Jacob	1	Gilmer	WOLF, David	7	Thomas
WISE, Jacob E.	1	Marion	WOLF, Elizabeth	4	Macon
WISE, John W.	8	Jefferson	WOLF, Jacob	1	Wilkes
WISE, Wayne	3	Clarke	WOLFE, Calvin	1	Effingham
WISE, Augustus	1	Butts	WOLFE, Daniel	1	Richmond
WISE, Bridges J.	4	Bullock	WOLFE, Daniel M.	1	Richmond
WISE, Burrel	8	Bibb	WOMACK, Charles	18	Marion
WISE, C. T.	10	Butts	WOMACK, Sherwood R.	6	Troup
WISE, D.	5	Wilkinson	WOMACK, W.	20	Crawford
WISE, F. M.	3	Butts	WOMBLE, James Agent	3	Upson
WISE, J. A.	1	Troup	WOMBLE, Nathan N.	18	Houston
WISE, J. I.	1	Washington	WOMBLE, Edward	2	Stewart
WISE, John	9	Washington	WOMBLE, Willliam F.	6	Washington
WISE, Mrs. Nancy	7	Burke	WOMMACK, Josiah	1	Hancock
WISE, Prudence	1	Troup	WOOD, A. M.	3	Heard
WISE, Rachael	3	Chatham	WOOD, Allen	12	Monroe
WISE, W. C.	10	Butts	WOOD, Allen J.	3	Jackson
WISE, W. W.	3	Bibb	WOOD, Benj.	6	Washington
WISE, William	1	Cherokee	WOOD, Caleb	1	Jackson
WISEMAN, Wm.	2	Randolph	WOOD, Cary	60	Newton
WISENBAKER,			WOOD, Coleman	5	Lumpkin
Christian	12	Effingham	WOOD, Constantine	8	Walker
WISENBAKER,			WOOD, David	2	Pike
Christian	8	Effingham	WOOD, Dempsey	5	Lowndes
WISENBAKER, James	7	Lowndes	WOOD, E.	9	Hall
WISENBAKER, John	10	Lowndes	WOOD, George B.	3	Jackson
WISENBAKER,			WOOD, Green	6	Washington
Richard H.	12	Lowndes	WOOD, Henry	1	Harris
WISENBAKER, Wm.	3	Lowndes	WOOD, Henry	1	Monroe
WITCHER, ? , K.	10	Paulding	WOOD, Henry	9	Washington
WITCHER, Amfroson	12	Oglethorpe	WOOD, Henry agent	2	Habersham
WITCHER, Charles T.	2	Heard	WOOD, Isaac	8	Twiggs

Name	Number	County	Name	Number	County
WOOD, James	1	Baldwin	WOOD, William	7	Baldwin
WOOD, James	15	Jackson	WOODALL William	14	Columbia
WOOD, James	1	Newton	WOODALL, Leah	9	Jones
WOOD, James F.	2	Jackson	WOODALL, Charles W.	7	Gwinnett
WOOD, James H.	2	Houston	WOODALL, Jefferson P.	6	Jones
WOOD, James M.	8	Floyd	WOODALL, Robert	17	Jones
WOOD, James N.	5	Washington	WOODALL, Robert	1	Oglethorpe
WOOD, Jesse M.	1	Paulding	WOODALL, Thomas	16	Walton
WOOD, John C.	45	Morgan	WOODALL, William T.	3	Jones
WOOD, John H.	1	Cherokee	WOODALL, James	4	Baldwin
WOOD, John T.	6	Troup	WOODALL, James	2	Bibb
WOOD, Jonathan	4	Pulaski	WOODALL, Johnson	13	Taliaferro
WOOD, Joseph	9	Thomas	WOODALL, Martin	31	Taliaferro
WOOD, Joshua	4	Jackson	WOODALL, Pleasant	1	Marion
WOOD, Mary	2	Muscogee	WOODALL, Robert	5	Talbot
WOOD, Milton B.	2	Jackson	WOODALL, Sarah	5	Talbot
WOOD, Miss E. C.	1	Muscogee	WOODALL, Sarah	2	Talbot
WOOD, Mrs. A.	1	Muscogee	WOODARD, Aaron	4	Henry
WOOD, P. H.	13	Heard	WOODARD, Asa	5	Houston
WOOD, P. H.	6	Heard	WOODARD, Green	1	Laurens
WOOD, Philip	12	Twiggs	WOODARD, Irwin	30	Monroe
WOOD, Robert	4	Hancock	WOODARD, Isaac	30	Houston
WOOD, S. D.	4	Gordon	WOODARD, James	9	Houston
WOOD, Samuel	5	Newton	WOODARD, John	7	Laurens
WOOD, Stephen	27	Merriwether	WOODARD, John L.	58	Monroe
WOOD, Tabitha	7	Heard	WOODARD, Jonathan	8	Greene
WOOD, Thomas	2	Cobb	WOODARD,		
WOOD, Thos. C.	22	Morgan	Mrs. Emiline	11	Houston
WOOD, Thos. G.	3	Walton	WOODARD, Oren C.	28	Monroe
WOOD, W. G.	14	Early	WOODARD, Thomas	13	Houston
WOOD, William	1	Early	WOODARD, W. J.	5	Henry
WOOD, William	11	Jones	WOODARD, Elisha	9	Stewart
WOOD, William	4	Washington	WOODARD, Stephen	28	Bibb
WOOD, William P.	11	Paulding	WOODBERRY, J. T.	2	Harris
WOOD, Winston	18	Heard	WOODBERRY, William	1	Richmond
WOOD, Wm. B	9	Clarke	WOODBRIDGE,		
WOOD, Wm. M.	2	Jackson	Grafton D.	17	Cass
WOOD, Young	4	Heard	WOODBRIDGE, Wylly	10	Chatham
WOOD, Charles H.	9	DeKalb	WOODBRIGDE, Grafton	2	Cass
WOOD, Elias	1	DeKalb	WOODGARD, James	7	Morgan
WOOD, Emma	1	Chatham	WOODHAM, Peggy	2	Greene
WOOD, Henry	9	Bibb	WOODHOUSE, Mary	1	Chatham
WOOD, I. J.	6	DeKalb	WOODING, John W.	7	Marion
WOOD, J. G.	3	Bibb	WOODING, Joyce	5	Warren
WOOD, Jesse	1	DeKalb	WOODING, Alford	6	DeKalb
WOOD, Joseph	1	Decatur	WOODING, Benjamin L.	9	Burke
WOOD, Joseph	20	Stewart	WOODING, Robert A.	10	Columbia
WOOD, Martha	8	Coweta	WOODLAW, Joseph M.	5	Walker
WOOD, Mrs. C.	5	Bibb	WOODLEY, J. B.	5	Henry
WOOD, Orlando A.	5	Chatham	WOODLEY, Vardy	21	Glynn
WOOD, Robert	1	Stewart	WOODLEY, Billy	3	Bibb
WOOD, Robinson	2	Cherokee	WOODLIFF, Isibelle	6	Forsyth
WOOD, Thos.	6	Bibb	WOODLIFF, J. H.	3	Forsyth
WOOD, Wiley E.	11	Chattooga	WOODLY, Andrew	2	Pike

Name	Number	County
WOODROOF, Clifford	14	Meriwether
WOODROOF, J. W.	5	Meriwether
WOODROOF, David	2	Meriwether
WOODROUGH, James	1	Newton
WOODROUGH, Reuben	5	Newton
WOODRUF, Jas. W.	1	Meriwether
WOODRUFF, Joseph	1	Walton
WOODRUFF, M.	10	Muscogee
WOODRUFF, Samuel	12	Floyd
WOODRUFF, W. W.	3	Pike
WOODRUFF, Samuel	7	Floyd
WOODRUM, Betty	6	Bullock
WOODS, Allen S.	1	Cherokee
WOODS, Archibald	3	Walker
WOODS, J. M.	1	Pulaski
WOODS, Jas. S.	3	Pike
WOODS, John	14	Oglethorpe
WOODS, John	10	Pulaski
WOODS, John	8	Walker
WOODS, John A.	2	Macon
WOODS, John L.	3	Emanual
WOODS, William	2	Lincoln
WOODS, William	3	Macon
WOODS, William	2	Morgan
WOODS, Wm.	5	Marion
WOODS, Granville	4	Bibb
WOODS, John	18	Sumter
WOODS, Jonathan	24	Columbia
WOODS, Wm.	2	Coweta
WOODSARD?, Littleberry	2	Harris
WOODSON, Creed T.	26	Houston
WOODSON, Benj.	3	DeKalb
WOODSON, ?D.	1	Upson
WOODSON, J. C.	10	Bibb
WOODSTOCK, Wm. T.	1	Richmond
WOODWARD, Aaron	36	Butts
WOODWARD, D. B.	11	Lee
WOODWARD, Robt.	8	Butts
WOODWARD, Henry W.	1	Baker
WOODWARD, J. S.	20	Crawford
WOODWARD, N.	11	Butts
WOODY, David	1	Burke
WOOLBRIGHT, Barney	1	Walker
WOOLBRIGHT, D.	22	Lee
WOOLBRIGHT, John	16	Lee
WOOLBRIGHT, W.	11	Lee
WOOLDRIDGE, Thomas F.	21	Muscogee
WOOLF, Michael	11	Chatham
WOOLF, Peter	1	Henry
WOOLF, Elizabeth	8	Chatham
WOOLF, Thomas	3	Chatham

Name	Number	County
WOOLFALK, Thos.	30	Bibb
WOOLFOLK, John	152	Muscogee
WOOLFOLK, John W.	10	Houston
WOOLFOLK, Joseph	26	Muscogee
WOOLFOLK, Thomas	44	Jones
WOOLFOLK, William G.	21	Muscogee
WOOLFOLK, J. W.	32	Houston
WOOLHANKS?, Gilliam	1	Habersham
WOOLHOPTER, Sarah	12	Chatham
WOOLLY, Jno. Sen.	7	Carroll
WOOLLY, Elias	1	DeKalb
WOOLLY, John	1	Stewart
WOOLRIDGE, William G.	29	Muscogee
WOOLRIDGE, J. W.	3	Clarke
WOOLSEY, A. R.	43	Dooly
WOOLSY, John M.	3	Monroe
WOOLY, David	3	Lincoln
WOOLY, Andrew	26	Cass
WOOTEN, A. A.	9	Pike
WOOTEN, Henry	4	Montgomery
WOOTEN, James	2	Muscogee
WOOTEN, John	20	Monroe
WOOTEN, John	5	Monroe
WOOTEN, Richard	10	Monroe
WOOTEN, Simion	2	Monroe
WOOTEN, William (overseer)	28	Paulding
WOOTEN, Bryant	6	Telfair
WOOTEN, C. L.	1	Decatur
WOOTEN, H. P.	42	Chattooga
WOOTEN, J. T.	2	Bibb
WOOTEN, James D.	2	Thomas
WOOTEN, Joel B.	9	Thomas
WOOTEN, John D.	1	Walker
WOOTEN, Joseph	7	DeKalb
WOOTEN, M. P.	10	Chattooga
WOOTEN, Paschal H.	12	Sumter
WOOTEN, R.	12	Decatur
WOOTEN, Reddin	33	Thomas
WOOTEN, Richard	6	Telfair
WOOTEN, Richard A.	1	Walker
WOOTEN, Simon	8	Randolph
WOOTEN, Simon	5	Telfair
WOOTON, W. H.	11	Oglethorpe
WOOTTEN, Jno. B.	32	Wilkes
WOOTTEN, Jno. L.	8	Wilkes
WOOTTEN, Redden	8	Lowndes
WOOTTEN, R. W.	20	Wilkes
WOOTTEN, Wm. L.	8	Wilkes
WORBELL, Dlilah	11	Newton
WORCHESTER, Mnna	1	Troup
WORD, Abnor	2	Oglethorpe

Name	Number	County	Name	Number	County
WORD, J. M.	3	Pike	WRAGG, John A.	5	Chatham
WORD, Jno. B.	3	Carroll	WRAY, Thomas	9	Clarke
WORD, Joice	8	Cass	WRAY, Thomas	75	Greene
WORD, Bill	1	Coweta	WRAY, William	40	Oglethorpe
WORD, Robert C.	1	Cass	WRAY, Jane	1	Richmond
WORD, Wm.	1	Campbell	WREN, James J.	1	Jefferson
WORD, Wm. B.	9	Coweta	WREN, John	1	Jefferson
WORDS, Ely	3	Coweta	WREN, John B.	1	Jefferson
WORLD, Sarah	14	Jefferson	WREN, G. W.	9	Putnam
WORMUCK, Francis	1	Newton	WRENN, M.	2	Baker
WORNUCK, John	5	Emanual	WRIGHT, A. R.	10	Jefferson
WORRELL, Martha	13	Newton	WRIGHT, A. S.	6	Meriwether
WORRELL, John	2	Sumter	WRIGHT, A. T.	3	Franklin
WORRELL, T. C.	6	Elbert	WRIGHT, A. W.	4	Walton
WORRILL, Edmond H.	7	Talbot	WRIGHT, Abram	9	Merriwether
WORSHAM, David	4	Marion	WRIGHT, Agnes	8	Lincoln
WORSHAM, John H.	3	Jackson	WRIGHT, Allen R.	28	Chatham
WORSHAM, Nancy	7	Jackson	WRIGHT, Ann	9	Glynn
WORSHAM, Wynn A.	3	Jackson	WRIGHT, Asa B.	1	Gwinnett
WORSHAM, D. G.	18	Crawford	WRIGHT, B. H.	7	Heard
WORSHAM, J. G.	2	Crawford	WRIGHT, Benjamin	18	Lincoln
WORSHAM, L. B.	4	Crawford	WRIGHT, Blackton	13	Newton
WORSHAM, R.	7	Crawford	WRIGHT, C. A.	5	Jefferson
WORTH ?, Berry G.	4	Richmond	WRIGHT, C. C.	4	Pike
WORTH?, Marcus D.	15	Cobb	WRIGHT, Columbus	10	Newton
WORTHALL,			WRIGHT, David	5	Muscogee
Leonard H.	6	Paulding	WRIGHT, Dr. E. H.	23	Liberty
WORTHAM, Columbus	2	Meriwether	WRIGHT, Edwin	10	Floyd
WORTHAM, John	1	Wilkes	WRIGHT, F. K.	1	Laurens
WORTHAM, Mrs. S.	20	Meriwether	WRIGHT, Frances	3	Murray
WORTHAM, S.	4	Meriwether	WRIGHT, Frances T.	6	Warren
WORTHAM, Wm. C.	7	Coweta	WRIGHT, Franklin	18	Lee
WORTHAN, Elijah	21	Talbot	WRIGHT, Franklin	7	Newton
WORTHINGER,			WRIGHT, George K.	13	Effingham
William	3	Houston	WRIGHT, George R.	5	Effingham
WORTHINGTON,			WRIGHT, George W.	1	Merriwether
Dennis	1	Lowndes	WRIGHT, Gillis	7	Jones
WORTHINGTON,			WRIGHT, Henry	35	Jefferson
Richard	3	Cass	WRIGHT, Hugh G.	3	Pike
WORTHY, Anderson	37	Upson	WRIGHT, Isaac	3	Harris
WORTHY, Kinchen	18	Upson	WRIGHT, J. M.	7	Murray
WORTHY, Z. P.	1	Oglethorpe	WRIGHT, James	33	Laurens
WORTHY, Ellison	4	Hancock	WRIGHT, James	10	Wilkinson
WORTHY, Leonard	16	Pike	WRIGHT, James R.	9	Greene
WORTHY, William	5	Murray	WRIGHT, James T.	1	Heard
WORTHY, William	33	Upson	WRIGHT, Jane A.	3	Cobb
WORTHY, William H.	1	Stewart	WRIGHT, Jas. C.	16	Wilkes
WOST, Jane E.	2	Chatham	WRIGHT, Jefferson J.	9	Greene
WOTEN, Joel	9	Meriwether	WRIGHT, John	19	Wilkes
WOTTEN, W. H.	7	Oglethorpe	WRIGHT, John B.	3	Muscogee
WOZENCRAFT,			WRIGHT, John B.	65	Washington
James T.	3	Clarke	WRIGHT, John G.	13	Oglethorpe
WOZENCRAFT,			WRIGHT, John M.	23	Washington
Thomas	4	Clarke	WRIGHT, John S.	2	Clarke

Name	Number	County	Name	Number	County
WRIGHT, John T.	46	Wilkinson	WRIGHT, Amey G.	2	Baldwin
WRIGHT, John W.	3	Greene	WRIGHT, B. B.	23	Decatur
WRIGHT, Johnson	10	Jackson	WRIGHT, Henry	2	Dooly
WRIGHT, Joseph	21	Early	WRIGHT, J.	1	Henry
WRIGHT, Joseph M.	5	Harris	WRIGHT, J. C.	1	Coweta
WRIGHT, L. D.	4	Wilkes	WRIGHT, Jas.	8	Putnam
WRIGHT, L. S.	2	Muscogee	WRIGHT, Jas. W.	4	Putnam
WRIGHT, N.	3	Troup	WRIGHT, John	1	Richmond
WRIGHT, M. C. B.	4	Glynn	WRIGHT, John W.	8	Taliaferro
WRIGHT, Margaret	1	Cobb	WRIGHT, Lorenzo	5	Bibb
WRIGHT, Mark	2	Lee	WRIGHT, M. F.	1	Coweta
WRIGHT, Mary	7	Newton	WRIGHT, M. L.	2	DeKalb
WRIGHT, Mary A.	2	Greene	WRIGHT, Margt.	2	Camden
WRIGHT, Mary F.	5	Lincoln	WRIGHT, Mary	2	Bibb
WRIGHT, Mastin A.	1	Heard	WRIGHT, Mathew	10	Stewart
WRIGHT, Milton	9	Floyd	WRIGHT, N.	3	Crawford
WRIGHT, Moses	8	Floyd	WRIGHT, Peter	11	Columbia
WRIGHT, Moses	27	Oglethorpe	WRIGHT, Richard W.	10	Putnam
WRIGHT, Mrs. Elizabeth	3	Houston	WRIGHT, S. S.	16	Crawford
WRIGHT, Nathan	8	Lincoln	WRIGHT, Sarah	2	Bibb
WRIGHT,			WRIGHT, Spencer P.	4	DeKalb
Nichodemus K.	3	Jackson	WRIGHT, T. W.	8	Putnam
WRIGHT, R.	13	Troup	WRIGHT, Warren	1	Bibb
WRIGHT, Roberson	2	Monroe	WRIGHT, William	22	Chatham
WRIGHT, Robert	1	Franklin	WRIGHT, William F.	3	Baldwin
WRIGHT, Robert	5	Jasper	WRIGHT, Wm.	7	Coweta
WRIGHT, Robert	46	Newton	WRIGHT, Wm.	7	Coweta
WRIGHT, Robt. T.	5	Greene	WRIGHT, Wm. C.	1	Campbell
WRIGHT, Rubin	54	Monroe	WRIGHT, Wm. C.	12	Taliaferro
WRIGHT, Samuel	9	Greene	WRIGHT, Wm. G.	7	Laurens
WRIGHT, Sarah	6	Jefferson	WRIGHTMAN,		
WRIGHT, Sharlotty	4	Lincoln	Catherine	15	Richmond
WRIGHT, Stephen L.	3	Warren	WTERS, Allen	3	Bullock
WRIGHT, Thomas	22	Washington	WTERS, Amus	1	Bryan
WRIGHT, Timothy	7	Harris	WYATT, Jno. G.	9	Henry
WRIGHT, W.	2	Henry	WYATT, John	4	Chattooga
WRIGHT, W. D.	34	Lee	WYATT, John W.	30	Jasper
WRIGHT, Whitten D.	2	Paulding	WYATT, S.	5	Henry
WRIGHT, William M.	1	Warren	WYATT, S. A.	5	Henry
WRIGHT, Wiley	10	Greene	WYATT, Thomas	114	Jasper
WRIGHT, William	8	Newton	WYATT, Thos.	3	Troup
WRIGHT, William	8	Newton	WYATT, Thos.	11	Morgan
WRIGHT, William A.	2	Jasper	WYATT, William H.	22	Jasper
WRIGHT, William A.	1	Pike	WYATT, E.	19	Chattooga
WRIGHT, William B.	15	Monroe	WYCH, G. C.	3	Elbert
WRIGHT, William B.	30	Paulding	WYCH, J. M.	6	Elbert
WRIGHT, William J.	9	Newton	WYCHE, Elizabeth	29	Lowndes
WRIGHT, Willis	6	Greene	WYCHE, Henry	48	Thomas
WRIGHT, Winfield	29	Laurens	WYCHE, Henry	4	Thomas
WRIGHT, Wingfield	17	Warren	WYCHE, Jeremiah	16	Marion
WRIGHT, A. H.	6	Camden	WYCHE, Samuel C.	7	Lee
WRIGHT, A. R.	25	Cass	WYCHE, Thomas C.	37	Thomas
WRIGHT, Alexa nder	3	Putnam	WYCHE, A. H.	4	Bibb
WRIGHT, Ambrose R.	13	Baker	WYCHE, Alfred	5	Baldwin

Name	Number	County	Name	Number	County
WYCHE, T. T.	4	Bibb	WYNN, Robert J.	16	Putnam
WYER, Henry O.	8	Chatham	WYNN, S. N.	2	Butts
WYGLAND, Anna E.	4	Habersham	WYNNE, A.	1	Wilkinson
WYLDS, Thomas	10	Richmond	WYNNE, Elizabeth	24	Warren
WYLEY, Alexander W.	102	McIntosh	WYNNE, James	45	Warren
WYLEY, O. C.	18	Gordon	WYNNE, Thomas	27	Warren
WYLEY, Wm. C.	27	Cass	YAARBOROUG H,	16	Cass
WYLIE, H. L.	17	Wilkes	YANCY, James	1	Fayette
WYLIE, N.	18	Wilkes	YANCY, Lewis D.	9	Jasper
WYLLY, Leonidas	9	Effingham	YANCY, Sarah	1	Jasper
WYLLY, Margaret	52	Glynn	YANCY, Benjamin C.	50	Taliaferro
WYLLY, Elisha	10	Chatham	YANCY, Jas.	2	Putnam
WYLLY, George W.	7	Chatham	YANCY, Louis P.	4	Putnam
WYLY, J. R.	16	Union	YANCY, Robert	1	DeKalb
WYLY, John H.	7	Habersham	YARBER, Grove	1	Franklin
WYLY, Leonidas	5	Effingham	YARBER, Thomas L.	10	Warren
WYNENS, Elisha S.	5	Jasper	YARBORO, Nancy	3	Columbia
WYNN, B. J. decd.	89	Hancock	YARBOROUGH, Wade	1	Lumpkin
WYNN, Daniel	1	Madison	YARBOROUGH, Wiley	6	Oglethorpe
WYNN, F. H.	2	Chattooga	YARBOROUGH, Willis	5	Pulaski
WYNN, Gabril	7	Monroe	YARBOROUGH, John	23	Stewart
WYNN, George	39	Monroe	YARBOROUGH, Lewis	2	Randolph
WYNN, Hezekiah	6	Madison	YARBOROUGH, Henry P.	13	Pike
WYNN, James M.	6	Monroe	YARBROUGH, John	1	Floyd
WYNN, Jno. A.	13	Pulaski	YARBROUGH, John W.	2	Merriwether
WYNN, John	2	Gwinnett	YARBROUGH, Nathan	5	Floyd
WYNN, John	4	Houston	YARBROUGH, Robt.	3	Marion
WYNN, John	45	Oglethorpe	YARBROUGH, Wm. D.	6	Marion
WYNN, John	19	Oglethorpe	YARBROUGH, Richard	20	Crawford
WYNN, Jno. L.	57	Wilkes	YATES, Frances	1	Heard
WYNN, Martha	18	Monroe	YATES, George W.	3	Monroe
WYNN, Richard D.	11	Gwinnett	YATES, Joel G.	1	Campbell
WYNN, Robert	11	Monroe	YATES, Joseph.	7	Thomas
WYNN, Robert	1	Monroe	YATES, Matthew	6	Fayette
WYNN, Saml.	47	Wilkes	YATES, Mrs. Clarisa	2	Houston
WYNN, Thomas	7	Monroe	YATES, William	6	Campbell
WYNN, Thomas B.	66	Thomas	YATES, William	11	Thomas
WYNN, Thomas H.	16	Muscogee	YATES, William F.	2	Washington
WYNN, Thos.	10	Oglethorpe	YAWNS, Chesley A.	1	Dooly
WYNN, Wiley	4	Harris	YEARBY, Robert	6	Madison
WYNN, William	9	Oglethorpe	YELDING, Robert	32	Early
WYNN, William	10	Wilkinson	YELLOWLY, Eliza	1	Camden
WYNN, William D.	39	Hancock	YELVERTON, Gidion	8	Marion
WYNN, William S.	6	Gwinnett	YELVERTON, Goodman	1	Lowndes
WYNN, William			YELVINGTON, Nancy	1	Camden
see WYNN, B. J.		Hancock	YEOMANS, John	2	Emanual
WYNN, William T.	5	Harris	YERBY, Bronell	30	Clarke
WYNN, WilliamT.	11	Cobb	YERBY, Everett	7	Clarke
WYNN, Willis	8	Monroe	YERBY, Sarah H.	14	Clarke
WYNN, Anderson	8	Talbot	YETEROWERS, estate	3	Bullock
WYNN, C.	5	Talbot	YEWBANK, Kesiah	11	Dooly
WYNN, G. O.	21	Coweta	YOAKUM, W. C.	12	Clarke
WYNN, G. W.	4	Coweta	YOBER, George W.	3	Cobb
WYNN, Mahaley	3	Campbell	YONG, L. H.	12	Troup

Name	Number	County	Name	Number	County
YONGE, George	9	McIntosh	YOUNG, John R.	4	Greene
YONGE, Moses	10	McIntosh	YOUNG, L. E. R.	1	Murray
YONGE, P. R.	18	McIntosh	YOUNG, M. H.	3	Oglethorpe
YONGE, W. P.	3	Chatham	YOUNG, M. K.	8	Henry
YOPP, J. H.	44	Laurens	YOUNG, Matthew	16	Lowndes
YOPP, J. H.	19	Laurens	YOUNG, Milus	10	Houston
YOPP, J. H.	11	Laurens	YOUNG, Robert	23	Hall
YOPP, Samuel	25	Laurens	YOUNG, Robert	16	Hall
YOPP, Thos. M.	8	Laurens	YOUNG, S. A. T.	3	Hall
YORK, Cyrus B.	1	Cobb	YOUNG, Samuel	16	Cobb
YORK, Josiah C.	1	Paulding	YOUNG, W. H. see		
YORK, J. T.	2	Troup	HUTCHENS, Nath.	7	Gwinnett
YORK, J. T.	2	Troup	YOUNG, W. P.	3	Cobb
YORK, Lewis	1	Randolph	YOUNG, Wiley	1	Oglethorpe
YORK, Scamore	6	Rabun	YOUNG, William	1	Washington
YORK, Wm	11	Randolph	YOUNG, William W.	9	Jefferson
YOUBANK, Jane	5	Dooly	YOUNG, Wm. J.	1	Carroll
YOUBANKS, Zenimon	2	Dooly	YOUNG, Wm. M.	5	Floyd
YOUG, Jane K.	12	McIntosh	YOUNG, A.	2	Coweta
YOULES, Walter	1	Wayne	YOUNG, Betsy	8	Columbia
YOUNG, A.	2	Union	YOUNG, David	5	Stewart
YOUNG, Chesley W.	3	Thomas	YOUNG, David	3	Talbot
YOUNG, E. M.	5	Thomas	YOUNG, Elijah	5	Baldwin
YOUNG, Elijah R.	108	Thomas	YOUNG, Enos	5	Dooly
YOUNG, Elizabeth	1	Jefferson	YOUNG, Francis M.	2	Sumter
YOUNG, Emanuel	10	Thomas	YOUNG, Henry	20	Oglethorpe
YOUNG, Hamilton	3	Walker	YOUNG, Hose	1	Macon
YOUNG, J. L.	5	Walker	YOUNG, James	40	Bullock
YOUNG, J. T.	1	Troup	YOUNG, James	14	Screven
YOUNG, James	13	Walker	YOUNG, James	8	Screven
YOUNG, James E.	20	Thomas	YOUNG, Jas.	3	Coweta
YOUNG, Michael	92	Thomas	YOUNG, John	11	Columbia
YOUNG, Robert M.	2	Walker	YOUNG, John	3	Sumter
YOUNG, Thomas estate	10	Chatham	YOUNG, Jos.	7	Coweta
YOUNG, Alexander	1	Pulaski	YOUNG, Laura	1	Chatham
YOUNG, Augustin	24	Paulding	YOUNG, P.	19	Chatham
YOUNG, Catharine	1	Jefferson	YOUNG, Robert	15	Putnam
YOUNG, D. C.	6	Irwin	YOUNG, Robert M	28	Cass
YOUNG, E. W.	13	Macon	YOUNG, Thomas	23	Clarke
YOUNG, Edward	2	Oglethorpe	YOUNG, W. S.	6	Henry
YOUNG, Elam	8	Jefferson	YOUNG, William B.	2	Talbot
YOUNG, Giles	13	Oglethorpe	YOUNG, Willis	64	Screven
YOUNG, Henry	1	Murray	YOUNGBLOOD,		
YOUNG, J.	3	Irwin	Abraham	11	Burke
YOUNG, J. J.	3	Jefferson	YOUNGBLOOD, Arthur	1	Early
YOUNG, James	10	Paulding	YOUNGBLOOD,		
YOUNG, James Jr.	3	Jefferson	Benjamin H.	5	Upson
YOUNG, James Jr.	1	Jefferson	YOUNGBLOOD,		
YOUNG, James M.	6	Oglethorpe	Frances	14	Hancock
YOUNG, John	1	Gwinnett	YOUNGBLOOD, Isaac	3	Jefferson
YOUNG, John	3	Jasper	YOUNGBLOOD,		
YOUNG, John	22	Macon	Thomas	1	Hancock
YOUNG, John A.	4	Cobb	YOUNGBLOOD,		
YOUNG, John Jr.	15	Macon	Thornton	2	Pike

Name	Number	County	Name	Number	County
YOUNGBLOOD, W.	3	Meriwether	ZORN, James	3	Upson
YOUNGBLOOD, B. L.	1	Bibb	ZORN, William	2	Upson
YOUNGBLOOD, Cornelius	1	Baldwin	ZOUCKS, David	2	Liberty
			ZUBER, Wm. M.	4	Greene
YOUNGBLOOD, E.	1	Wilkinson	ZUBER, Charles	10	Merriwether
YOUNGBLOOD, Nathan	4	Dooly	ZUBER, Daniel	9	Floyd
ZACHARY, Burtrand	3	Murray	ZUBER, Daniel H.	2	Merriwether
ZACHARY, William	33	Columbia	ZUBER, John F.	5	Oglethorpe
ZACHERY, Lee	16	Columbia	ZUBER, Joshua	3	Greene
ZACHERY, W. T.	2	Twiggs	ZUBER, L. P.	1	Harris
ZACHRY, A. J.	17	Morgan	ZUBER, Thomas E.	3	Floyd
ZACHRY, Abner S.	15	Jones	ZUBER, Williamson	1	Floyd
ZACHRY, Benj.	1	Heard	ZURR, Paul	11	Hall
ZACHRY, David	11	Heard	ZURR, StephenG.	3	Hall
ZACHRY, James B.	39	Newton	ZURR, T. S.	1	Hall
ZACHRY, John J.	11	Greene	ZUTTON, John	1	Muscogee
ZACHRY, Lewis	16	Newton	ZUTTON, Joseph	11	Muscogee
ZACHRY, Wm.	5	Carroll			
ZACHRY, Z.	14	Newton			
ZACKERY, Daniel	2	Harris			
ZACKRY, Amanda	5	Morgan			
ZACKRY, Asa C.	31	Morgan			
ZACKRY, Benjamin	17	Heard			
ZACKRY, C. R. estate	28	Morgan			
ZANT, Sol	15	Cass			
ZEIGHLER, Solomon	8	Chatham			
ZEIGLER, Davis	1	Effingham			
ZEIGLER, Joshua	4	Effingham			
ZEIGLER, William	22	Lowndes			
ZEIGLER, Jacob J.	18	Lowndes			
ZEIGLER, Wm.	90	Crawford			
ZELLARS, Jacob	17	Lincoln			
ZELLARS, John	35	Lincoln			
ZELLARS, Solomon	11	Campbell			
ZELLERS, Peter	18	Troup			
ZELLNER, Andrew	16	Monroe			
ZELLNER, Benjamin H.	4	Monroe			
ZELLNER, Berton	5	Monroe			
ZELLNER, Francis	4	Monroe			
ZELLNER, George	2	Monroe			
ZIGLER, Isreal	3	Screven			
ZIGLER, Solomon	1	Screven			
ZILLINOR, John	13	Harris			
ZIM, Jane D.	1	Richmond			
ZIM, JOHN W.	4	Richmond			
ZIM, John W.	1	Richmond			
ZIMMERMAN, John F.	10	Greene			
ZIPPERER, Emanual	1	Effingham			
ZIPPERRER, Zachariah	7	Chatham			
ZIPPERRER, George J.	10	Chatham			
ZITROWER, Johanna	7	Chatham			
ZITROWER, E. S.	18	Chatham			
ZOGBAUM, Charles	2	Clarke			
ZOPP, Jno. W.	15	Laurens			

www.ingramcontent.com/pod-product-compliance
Lightning Source LLC
Chambersburg PA
CBHW060140280326
41932CB00012B/1577